TWELFTH EDITION

Exceptional Learners

AN INTRODUCTION TO SPECIAL EDUCATION

DANIEL P. HALLAHAN
University of Virginia

JAMES M. KAUFFMAN
University of Virginia

PAIGE C. PULLEN
University of Virginia

Boston Columbus Indianapolis New York San Francisco Upper Saddle River
Amsterdam Cape Town Dubai London Madrid Milan Munich Paris Montreal Toronto
Delhi Mexico City Sao Paulo Sydney Hong Kong Seoul Singapore Taipei Tokyo

Vice President and Editor in Chief: Jeffery W. Johnston
Executive Editor: Ann Castel Davis
Editorial Assistant: Penny Burleson
Senior Development Editor: Alicia Reilly
Vice President, Director of Marketing: Margaret Waples
Marketing Manager: Joanna Sabella
Marketing Coordinator: Brian Mounts
Senior Managing Editor: Pamela D. Bennett
Senior Project Manager: Sheryl Glicker Langner
Senior Operations Supervisor: Matthew Ottenweller
Senior Art Director: Diane C. Lorenzo

Text and Cover Designer: Candace Rowley
Photo Coordinator: Lori Whitley
Permissions: Elizabeth Tuckwiller
Cover Image: Fotosearch
Media Producer: Autumn Benson
Media Project Manager: Rebecca Norsic
Composition: S4Carlisle Publishing Services
Printer/Binder: Courier-Kendallville
Cover Printer: Lehigh-Phoenix
Text Font: Garamond

Credits and acknowledgments borrowed from other sources and reproduced, with permission, in this textbook appear on appropriate page within text.

Every effort has been made to provide accurate and current Internet information in this book. However, the Internet and information posted on it are constantly changing, so it is inevitable that some of the Internet addresses listed in this textbook will change.

Photo Credits are on page xxvii.

Library of Congress Cataloging-in-Publication Data

Hallahan, Daniel P.,
 Exceptional learners: an introduction to special education / Daniel P. Hallahan, James M. Kauffman, Paige C. Pullen. — Twelfth ed.
  p. cm.
 ISBN-13: 978-0-13-703370-6
 ISBN-10: 0-13-703370-2
 1. Special education—United States. I. Kauffman, James M. II. Pullen, Paige C. III. Title.
 LC3981.H34 2012
 371.90973–dc22

                                                        2010038138

10 9 8 7 6 5 4 3 2 1

www.pearsonhighered.com

ISBN 10:   0-13-703370-2
ISBN 13:   978-0-13-703370-6

Daniel P. Hallahan is the Charles S. Robb Professor of Education and Director of Doctoral Studies for the Curry School of Education at the University of Virginia. He was the inaugural occupant of the Virgil S. Ward Professor of Education Endowed Chair from 1996 to 1998 and was appointed to the university's Cavaliers' Distinguished Teaching Professorship from 2002 to 2004. He received the University of Virginia Outstanding Teaching Award in 1998. In 2003, he was one of ten recipients of the State Council of Higher Education for Virginia's Outstanding Faculty Award. He has served on numerous editorial boards and was the inaugural editor of *Exceptionality*. He is a past president of the Division for Learning Disabilities of the Council for Exceptional Children (CEC), and in 2000 he received the CEC Career Research Award. He has contributed over 100 journal articles and co-authored or co-edited 17 books. In addition to *Exceptional Learners*, his most recent Pearson books are Hallahan, Lloyd, Kauffman, Weiss, & Martinez (2005), *Learning Disabilities: Foundations, Characteristics, and Effective Teaching* (3rd ed.) and Kauffman, J. M., & Hallahan, D. P. (2005), *Special Education: What It Is and Why We Need It.*

James M. Kauffman is Professor Emeritus of Education at the University of Virginia, where he held both the William Clay Parrish chair (1992–1994) and the Charles S. Robb chair (1999 until retirement in 2003) in education. In 2007, his former students edited a book in his honor, Crockett, J. B., Gerber, M. M., & Landrum, T. J. (Eds.), *Achieving the Radical Reform of Special Education: Essays in Honor of James M. Kauffman.* Among his other honors and awards are the 2006 Award for Effective Presentation of Behavior Analysis in the Mass Media from the Society for Applied Behavior Analysis, the 2002 Outstanding Leadership Award from the Council for Children with Behavioral Disorders, the 1997 Outstanding Faculty Award from the Curry School of Education Foundation, and the 1994 Research Award from the Council for Exceptional Children. He is a past president of the Council for Children with Behavioral Disorders (CCBD) and a former teacher in both general elementary and special education for students with emotional or behavioral disorders. He is author or co-author of more than 100 journal publications in special education and author or co-author or co-editor of numerous books, including the following: Kauffman, J. M., & Hallahan, D. P. (Eds.), *Handbook of Special Education*; Kauffman, J. M., & Landrum, T. J., *Characteristics of Emotional and Behavioral Disorders of Children and Youth* (9th ed.); Kauffman, J. M., & Brigham, F. J. *Working with Troubled Children*; and Kauffman, J. M. *The Tragicomedy of Public Education: Laughing and Crying, Thinking and Fixing.*

Paige C. Pullen is an associate professor of special education at the University of Virginia. Dr. Pullen teaches courses in reading methods for students with reading disabilities and reading diagnosis and remediation. She has served as an investigator on several large-scale projects funded by the NICHD and OSEP. Her primary area of interest and research is early literacy development and the prevention of reading disabilities. Paige has also worked extensively with schools and serves as a consultant for the Eastern Regional Reading First Technical Assistance Center (ERRFTAC). She is the co-author of *Phonological Awareness Assessment and Instruction,* with Dr. Holly Lane, and *Students with Learning Disabilities*, with Dr. Cecil Mercer.

PREFACE

Exceptional Learners: An Introduction to Special Education, Twelfth Edition, is a general introduction to the characteristics of exceptional learners and their education. (*Exceptional* is the term that traditionally has been used to refer to people with disabilities as well as to those who are gifted.) This book emphasizes classroom practices as well as the psychological, sociological, and medical aspects of disabilities and giftedness.

We've written this text with two primary audiences in mind: those who are preparing to be special educators and those who are preparing to be general educators. Given the federal legislative mandates for including students with disabilities in general education classrooms whenever possible, general educators must be prepared to understand exceptional learners and be ready to work with special educators to provide appropriate educational programming for these students. This book also is appropriate for professionals in other fields who work with exceptional learners (e.g., speech-language pathologists, audiologists, physical therapists, occupational therapists, adapted physical educators, counselors, and school psychologists).

We believe we've written a text that reaches the heart as well as the mind. Our conviction is that professionals working with exceptional learners need to develop not only a solid base of knowledge, but also a healthy attitude toward their work and the people whom they serve. Professionals must constantly challenge themselves to acquire a solid understanding of current theory, research, and practice in special education and to develop an ever more sensitive understanding of exceptional learners and their families.

WHAT'S NEW IN THIS EDITION?

As with all of our previous revisions, we've approached this one with an eye toward providing the reader with the latest, cutting-edge information on research and best practices in special education. We've renamed and reorganized Chapter 2 to highlight teachers' responsibilities as well as the current focus on student outcomes. We also provide current information in several chapters on response-to-intervention (RTI), more internet resources (see margin notes throughout the chapters), and a multitude of new references with digital object identifiers (DOIs) for references that have them. A sampling of specific additions to each chapter includes:

Chapter 1

- Expanded coverage of the nature-nurture controversy
- New coverage highlighting Eunice Kennedy and the Special Olympics
- Elimination of details of IDEA, IEPs, and responsibilities of teachers, which are better included in Chapter 2

Chapter 2

- Extensive coverage of the Response-to-Intervention
- Reorganized structure to focus on current practices to address the needs of exceptional learners
- New focus on the roles and responsibilities of teachers
- Updated discussion on assessment practices in the age of accountability

Chapter 3

- New coverage on the effects of RTI on multicultural and bilingual special education
- Research on disproportionate representation of ethnic minorities in special education

Chapter 4

- Research on the positive influences parents can have on their children with disabilities
- Information on the impact of a child with a disability on *extended* family members
- Information on the impact of a child with a disability on siblings
- Research on a family-centered approach to children with disabilities
- Information on the importance of transition from preschool to kindergarten for children with disabilities and their families

Chapter 5

- Research on the international prevalence of low-birthweight babies
- Information on erroneous convictions of persons with intellectual disabilities
- Updated information on early childhood programs for the prevention of intellectual disabilities
- Updated information on transition to adulthood of persons with intellectual disabilities
- Updated discussion of self-determination skills
- Discussion of the controversial issue of persons with intellectual disabilities as parents
- Information on school-sponsored work experiences for students with intellectual disabilities
- Information on customized employment and self-employment for persons with intellectual disabilities

Chapter 6

- Research on RTI
- Updated research on neuroimaging techniques
- Extensive reorganization and updating of information on educational considerations
- Updated information on secondary students' outcomes
- Discussion of the role of summary of performance (SOP) in transition planning

Chapter 7

- New information linking recognition of ADHD to work in the 18th Century
- Discussion of the American Psychiatric Association's impending revision to its criteria for diagnosis of ADHD
- Updated research on role of executive functions
- Updated research on medication treatments
- Updated research on early intervention programming
- Updated research on adult symptoms and outcomes

Chapter 8

- Clarification of the ecological approach to emotional and behavioral disorders
- Expanded information on zero tolerance, functional behavioral analysis, and positive behavioral supports
- More information on interim alternative educational settings
- Added clarifications on bias in identification and successful multicultural education

Chapter 9

- Discussion of the American Psychiatric Association's impending revision to its criteria for diagnosis of ASD
- Extensive update on prevalence
- Updated research on the debate about vaccinations as cause of ASD
- Updated research on genetics and ASD
- Updated information on diagnostic tests for identification of ASD

- Updated information on social behavior of persons with ASD
- More discussion of functional behavioral assessment (FBA) and positive behavioral and intervention
- More information on pivotal response training/teaching as an effective educational approach
- Discussion of the Early Intensive Behavioral Interventions (EIBI) program
- Updated research on adult outcomes

Chapter 10

- New research on reading difficulties of students with language disorders
- New research on the social interaction of students with communication disorders

Chapter 11

- Updated information on screening of infants, as well as tests for young and hard-to-test children
- Updated information on otitis media and congenital cytomegalovirus
- Updated research on effects of hearing loss on academic achievement
- Updated information on the Gallaudet Movement
- Updated research on efficacy of the bicultural-bilingual approach

Chapter 12

- Updated information on functional vision assessments
- Updated information on cortical visual impairment and retinopathy of prematurity and added information on optic nerve hypoplasia
- More information on the use of guide dogs
- Updated information on visual prostheses

Chapter 13

- Coverage of traumatic brain injury (TBI) of soldiers returning from Iraq and Afghanistan
- Updated research on causes of the CHARGE syndrome and Usher syndrome and the prevalence of the latter

Chapter 14

- Updated information on various physical disabilities and health impairments, including first aid for seizures

Chapter 15

- New information on high schools emphasizing science, technology, engineering, and mathematics (STEM high schools) that cater to students with special gifts and talents
- Additional coverage of disabilities and giftedness

PEOPLE CONNECTIONS

PEER CONNECTIONS

We believe that students reading this book will have a better understanding of exceptionality if they read about the lives of exceptional learners who are young adults. The new peer connections features, based on interviews conducted by Mira Cole, highlight individuals with a disability between the ages of 18–25. Students reading the textbook will get to know individuals with disabilities through their personal stories and realize that their peers with disabilities are very much like themselves.

PEER CONNECTIONS: ERIC BREEDEN

ERIC BREEDEN was born in Charlottesville, Virginia. He is currently a high school senior at Albemarle High School. Eric was diagnosed with a learning disability in fifth grade. His mother initially had concerns about disruptive behavior that his teachers were noticing in the classroom. Once Eric was diagnosed, changes were made in the classroom, and this behavior disappeared. Since fifth grade, Eric has had optional services that include sitting in the front of the classroom and having notes taken for him, more time for tests, and a resource class and teacher. Eric has found some of these adaptations more beneficial than others and has gone on to have a successful high school career. Eric is an avid athlete and is looking forward to going to college, where he hopes to play football and pursue a degree in criminal justice.

What do you do for fun? I hang out with friends and play football.

classes like my peers. Because of the resource class, I couldn't fit an arts class or a foreign language into my schedule. This was difficult, but in tenth grade I decided that I wanted to try school without having a resource class. It worked out well, and now I still receive guidance from a resource teacher but I rarely notice my learning disability because I'm not singled out as much. I feel that I can do all of my work without a lot of trouble.

Do you see your disability as affecting your ability to achieve what you want in your life? No, I think that I will still be able to graduate high school. When I had my resource class I wasn't going to be able to graduate with an advance diploma because I couldn't take a foreign language. But when they let me stop resource class, I took Spanish, and now I will graduate with an advance diploma. I also plan to go to college, and even hopefully play football in college.

SUCCESS STORIES: SPECIAL EDUCATORS AT WORK

Special educators work in a variety of settings, ranging from general education classrooms to residential institutions. Although their main function involves teaching, these professionals also engage in a variety of activities, such as counseling, collaborating, and consulting. To illustrate this variety, each of the eleven categorical chapters (Chapters 5–15) includes an example of a special educator at work. Written by Dr. Jean B. Crockett of the University of Florida, an experienced special education administrator and teacher educator, each story focuses on a special educator's work with an individual student and shows readers the wide range of challenges faced by special educators, the dynamic nature of their positions, and the competent, hopeful practice of special education. This feature emphasizes the importance of education for students with special needs that is intensive, relentless, and specific, and includes questions for students that relate to CEC Standards.

Success Stories

HARD WORK AT HOME AND SCHOOL HELPS RANDY READ ON GRADE LEVEL

Special Educator Celia Gottesman: "Unless you work harder, faster, and more intensively, they won't catch up."

Ten-year-old Randy Daniels is reading on grade level as he starts fifth grade at Lake Forest Elementary School in Florida.

These are the keys to his success:

★ Intensive instruction in reading and math
★ Relentless progress monitoring
★ Specific incentives and parental support

RANDY DANIELS ended third grade reading at a second-grade level, 1 year behind many of his classmates. This year he has caught up, and he is proud of it. "I did it! I did it! I did it!" he said when he heard the good news. "Randy moved 2 years ahead in reading in 1 year with two intensive summer school experiences, and that's a tremendous

year their high-poverty school met its goals for adequate yearly progress (AYP). Celia Gottesman teaches reading and math to exceptional learners at Lake Forest Elementary school. Waltraud Schmid also taught special education at the school before she retired. As a school volunteer, she now helps Celia plan and deliver systematic instruction 5 days

PERSONAL PERSPECTIVES

These features present the human side of having a disability, within a variety of real-world contexts, expanding on text topics to show how they relate to the personal lives of students, teachers, parents, and all people.

Personal PERSPECTIVES

No Overalls for Sophie!

The other day, my friend Kim gave me a pair of hot pink velvet overalls her daughters have outgrown. I stared at them, and pictured my own daughters. . . . Probably the perfect size for Sophie, who will be two next month. But I can't put Sophie in overalls. It's one of the things I promised myself I'd never do. Sophie has Down syndrome. She's retarded. We don't know how retarded at this point. I personally think she's pretty darn smart. . . .

Still, the fact remains. Sophie's retarded. And I have a strong belief that retarded people should not wear overalls. It's not a good look. I know what you're thinking. That woman is going straight to hell. Probably. But I'll go with a strong sense of style. And so will my children. Particularly Sophie. . . .

I'm still not 100 percent sure why I feel the way I do about retarded people and overalls. . . . I told my husband.

pushed Sophie's stroller through the crowd, Sophie waved her hands furiously at everyone in sight, laughing hysterically, having a great time. No one was waving back, no one even really looking at her. I suddenly flashed forward a decade to Sophie the 12-year-old doing the same thing in a crowd, goofily retarded. For a minute, I was not OK with that. Tears burned my eyes.

And then I realized that I have to be OK with that. I don't have any other choice. But I can choose what Sophie wears, so I put the overalls away and dressed my daughter in a beautiful pink-striped onesie, and we went out, . . . where she giggled and blew kisses and waved. Lots of people smiled and waved back.

By Amy Silverman

RESPONSIVE *INSTRUCTION*
MEETING THE NEEDS OF STUDENTS WITH INTELLECTUAL DISABILITIES

Classwide Peer Tutoring

WHAT THE RESEARCH SAYS

In an effort to meet the instructional needs of students with mild intellectual disabilities within inclusive settings, researchers have explored instructional methods that provide the necessary structure, individualization, and level of corrective feedback critical for success for this population. One such method is classwide peer tutoring (CWPT) (Delquadri, Greenwood, Stretton, & Hall, 1983). CWPT involves the use of peers to provide instruction and feedback in a reciprocal format. Paired students have the opportunity to serve as a tutor and as a tutee during each session. CWPT procedures were designed to address the need for higher levels of active academic engagement for all students, but particularly for students with the greatest academic deficits (Greenwood, 1991).

RESEARCH STUDY

A team of researchers conducted a study to examine the effectiveness of CWPT on the spelling performance of eight students

the tutor awarded the tutee 2 points; if the word was spelled incorrectly, the tutor spelled the word correctly and the tutee wrote the word three times while naming each letter. The tutee could receive 1 point for correctly spelling the practice word. After 10 minutes, the roles were reversed.

7. The teacher assigned bonus points for pairs that were working cooperatively and following the instructional protocol.

8. When the 20-minute session was over, the teacher calculated team points on the basis of partner points. The winning team received privileges such as lining up first for recess.

9. Modifications made for the students with mild intellectual disabilities included shortened word lists, enlarged practice sheets, and tutee reading of words when the student with mild intellectual disabilities was the tutor and was unable to read the word.

RESPONSIVE INSTRUCTION: MEETING THE NEEDS OF STUDENTS

It's our firm belief that most students with disabilities require intensive instruction in order to maximize their potential. Located throughout the text are boxed features, authored by Dr. Kristin Sayeski of the University of Nevada, Las Vegas, that feature a variety of sound, research-based strategies (e.g., mnemonics, self-monitoring and group contingency, classwide peer tutoring, computer-based video instruction, functional behavioral assessment, testing accommodations) for teaching students with disabilities. Although these strategies can't possibly take the place of a full-blown course and text in teaching methods, we think they offer practical suggestions for meeting the needs of exceptional learners through intensive instruction. In keeping with this era of accountability, these boxes stress teaching practices that have a sound research base.

MAKING IT WORK
COLLABORATION AND CO-TEACHING FOR STUDENTS WITH LEARNING DISABILITIES

"How can she help me if she doesn't know algebra like I do?"

How can co-teaching with a special educator to meet the needs of students with learning disabilities work if the special educator is not as much of a content area specialist as the general educator? Though you might think that would mean an end to equal collaboration in, say, a biology or advanced literature course, teachers of students with learning disabilities have knowledge about learning that can help make them an active part of any co-teaching team.

WHAT DOES IT MEAN TO BE A TEACHER OF STUDENTS WITH LEARNING DISABILITIES?

Most programs for teachers of students with learning disabilities focus on the learning process and effective strategies for learning across the content areas. Specifically, the Council for Exceptional Children (2003) states that teachers of students with learning disabilities should be able to:

1. Use methods for teaching individuals to independently use cognitive processing to solve problems.

to read the textbook I was using, and I became interested in learning disabilities.

After earning a Masters in Special Education, one of my first positions required co-teaching in an 8th-grade pre-algebra classroom. I knew the material, but wasn't as confident that I knew the best way to teach it. My co-teacher and I ended up with a class of 18 students, 11 of whom were identified with disabilities (nine with learning disabilities) and the rest had done poorly in their previous math courses. The textbook prescribed a rigid plan for the classroom: review homework, teach the next lesson, do some practice problems. The pacing guide provided by the district (and part of my co-teacher's evaluation criteria) did not leave many opportunities for creativity in instruction. Though we were both on the same 8th-grade team, we could use very little of the team meeting time to plan together. So, after many philosophical discussions, we plunged into the course. After a few weeks, we found a rhythm that seemed to work with the students.

First, my co-teacher taught the lesson as I took notes on the overhead for the students. I would often create a circle on the overhead with the example problem in the middle.

MAKING IT WORK: COLLABORATION AND CO-TEACHING

Each of the categorical chapters (Chapter 5–15) includes a feature, authored by Dr. Margaret Weiss, devoted to co-teaching and collaboration among special and general education teachers, families, and other professionals. Because we believe that it's important for all teachers to understand the expertise special educators can contribute to collaborative, general education classrooms, the first section of each box includes information about knowledge and skills special educators should possess as they enter the field, as identified by the Council for Exceptional Children (CEC) in its Performance-Based Professional Standards (2008)*. The second section contains examples of research-based instructional practices that teachers can use when collaborating or descriptions of successful collaborations in real classrooms. Each box contains specifics about how to get more information about the strategy or classroom described.

*Council for Exceptional Children. (2008). *What every special educator must know: Ethics, standards, and guidelines for special educators* (6th ed.). Arlington, VA: Author.

FIELD CONNECTIONS

FOCUS ON CONCEPTS

These features stimulate critical thinking about current research and special topics that are of interest to all educators.

MISCONCEPTIONS ABOUT EXCEPTIONAL LEARNERS: MYTHS AND FACTS BOXES

We start each chapter with a feature that juxtaposes several myths and facts about the subject of the chapter. This popular feature, familiar to longtime users of previous editions, serves as an excellent advance organizer for the material to be covered.

CHAPTER-OPENING QUOTES

Going back to our first edition is the practice of opening each chapter with an excerpt from literature or song. Students continue to tell us that they find these quotes to be effective at grabbing their attention and leading them into some of the issues contained in the text.

INTERNET RESOURCES

Websites that provide useful and interesting information relevant to text discussions are identified.

Artiles, A. J., Trent, S. C., Hoffman-Kipp, P., & Lopez-Torres, L. (2000). From individual acquisition to cultural-historical practices in multicultural teacher education. *Remedial and Special Education, 21*, 79–89, 120. doi:10.1177/074193250002100203

DIGITAL OBJECT IDENTIFIERS

We've included electronic addresses at which users of the text may find digital copies of articles we have cited, if such addresses are available.

SUPPLEMENTS

This edition boasts the most comprehensive and integrated collection of supplements to date to assist students and professors alike in maximizing learning and instruction. All instructor supplements are available at the Pearson Instructor's Resource Center. Go to www.pearsonhighered.com and click on the "Educators" link. Here you will be able to login or complete a one-time registration for a user name and password to gain access to the following supplements.

Online Instructor's Manual and Test Bank

The Online Instructor's Manual and Test Bank synchronizes all of the resources available for each chapter and can be used for traditional courses as well as online, or online-supported, courses. The Instructor's Manual is fully integrated with the MyEducationLab that accompanies this text and includes many ideas and activities to help instructors teach the course. The Test Bank provides hundreds of multiple-choice, short-answer, and essay questions, all with answer keys.

Pearson MyTest

Pearson MyTest is a powerful assessment generation program that helps instructors easily create and print quizzes and exams. Questions and tests are authored online, allowing ultimate flexibility and the ability to efficiently create and print assessments anytime, anywhere! Instructors can access Pearson MyTest and their test bank files by going to www.pearsonmytest.com to log in, register, or request access. Features of Pearson MyTest include:

Premium assessment content

- Draw from a rich library of assessments that complement your Pearson textbook and your course's learning objectives.
- Edit questions or tests to fit your specific teaching needs.

Instructor-friendly resources

- Easily create and store your own questions, including images, diagrams, and charts using simple drag-and-drop and Word-like controls.
- Use additional information provided by Pearson, such as the question's difficulty level or learning objective, to help you quickly build your test.

Time-saving enhancements

- Add headers or footers and easily scramble questions and answer choices—all from one simple toolbar.
- Quickly create multiple versions of your test or answer key, and when ready, simply save to MS-Word or PDF format and print!
- Export your exams for import to Blackboard 6.0, CE (WebCT), or Vista (WebCT)!

Online PowerPoint slides/Transparency Masters

These visual aids display, summarize, and help explain core information presented in each module. All PowerPoint slides have been updated for consistency and to reflect content in the new edition.

MYEDUCATIONLAB

myeducationlab *The power of classroom practice*

In *Preparing Teachers for a Changing World*, Linda Darling-Hammond and her colleagues point out that grounding teacher education in real classrooms—among real teachers and students and among actual examples of students' and teachers' work—is an important, and perhaps even an essential, part of training teachers for the complexities of teaching in today's classrooms. MyEducationLab is an online learning solution that provides contextualized interactive exercises, simulations, and other resources designed to help develop the knowledge and skills teachers need. All of the activities and exercises in MyEducationLab are built around essential learning outcomes for teachers and are mapped to professional teaching standards. Utilizing classroom video, authentic student and teacher artifacts, case studies, and other resources and assessments, the scaffolded learning experiences in MyEducationLab offer preservice teachers and those who teach them a unique and valuable education tool.

For each topic covered in the course you will find most or all of the following features and resources:

CONNECTION TO NATIONAL STANDARDS Now it is easier than ever to see how coursework is connected to national standards. Each topic on MyEducationLab lists intended learning outcomes connected to the appropriate national standards. And all of the activities and exercises in MyEducationLab are mapped to the appropriate national standards and learning outcomes as well.

ASSIGNMENTS AND ACTIVITIES Designed to enhance student understanding of concepts covered in class and save instructors preparation and grading time, these assignable exercises show concepts in action (through video, cases, and/or student and teacher artifacts). They help students deepen content knowledge and synthesize and apply concepts and strategies they read about in the book. (Correct answers for these assignments are available to the instructor only under the Instructor Resource tab.)

BUILDING TEACHING SKILLS AND DISPOSITIONS These learning units help students practice and strengthen skills that are essential to quality teaching. After presenting the steps involved in a core teaching process, students are given an opportunity to practice applying this skill via videos, student and teacher artifacts, and/or case studies of authentic classrooms. Providing multiple opportunities to practice a single teaching concept, each activity encourages a deeper understanding and application of concepts, as well as the use of critical thinking skills.

IRIS CENTER RESOURCES The IRIS Center at Vanderbilt University (http://iris.peabody .vanderbilt.edu—funded by the U.S. Department of Education's Office of Special Education Programs (OSEP) develops training enhancement materials for pre-service and in-service teachers. The Center works with experts from across the country to create challenge-based interactive modules, case study units, and podcasts that provide research-validated information about working with students in inclusive settings. In your MyEducationLab course we have integrated this content where appropriate.

TEACHER TALK This feature emphasizes the power of teaching through videos of master teachers, each speaker telling their own compelling stories of why they teach. These videos help teacher candidates see the bigger picture and consider why what they are learning is important to their career as a teacher. Each of these featured teachers has been awarded the Council of Chief State School Officers Teachers of the Year award, the oldest and most prestigious award for teachers.

STUDY PLAN SPECIFIC TO YOUR TEXT A MyEducationLab Study Plan is a multiple choice assessment tied to chapter objectives, supported by study material. A well-designed Study Plan offers multiple opportunities to fully master required course content as identified by the objectives in each chapter:

- *Chapter Objectives* identify the learning outcomes for the chapter and give students targets to shoot for as you read and study.

- *Multiple Choice Assessments* assess mastery of the content. These assessments are mapped to chapter objectives, and students can take the multiple choice quiz as many times as they want. Not only do these quizzes provide overall scores for each objective, but they also explain why responses to particular items are correct or incorrect.
- *Study Material: Review, Practice and Enrichment* give students a deeper understanding of what they do and do not know related to chapter content. This material includes text excerpts, activities that include hints and feedback, and interactive multi-media exercises built around videos, simulations, cases, or classroom artifacts.
- *Flashcards* help students study the definitions of the key terms within each chapter.

COURSE RESOURCES The Course Resources section on MyEducationLab is designed to help students, put together an effective lesson plan, prepare for and begin their career, navigate their first year of teaching, and understand key educational standards, policies, and laws.

The Course Resources Tab includes the following:

- The **Lesson Plan Builder** is an effective and easy-to-use tool that students can use to create, update, and share quality lesson plans. The software also makes it easy to integrate state content standards into any lesson plan.
- The **IEP Tutorial** shows how to develop appropriate IEPs and how to conduct effective IEP conferences.
- The **Preparing a Portfolio** module provides guidelines for creating a high-quality teaching portfolio.
- **Beginning Your Career** offers tips, advice, and other valuable information on:
  - *Resume Writing and Interviewing*: Includes expert advice on how to write impressive resumes and prepare for job interviews.
  - *Your First Year of Teaching*: Provides practical tips to set up a first classroom, manage student behavior, and more easily organize for instruction and assessment.
  - *Law and Public Policies*: Details specific directives and requirements teachers need to understand under the No Child Left Behind Act and the Individuals with Disabilities Education Improvement Act of 2004.
- **Special Education Interactive Timeline**. Use this tool to build your own detailed timelines based on different facets of the history and evolution of special education.
- **Introduction to Teaching and Foundations of Teaching Interactive Timeline** (OPTIONAL). Use this tool to build detailed timelines based on different facets of the history and evolution of education and the teaching profession.

CERTIFICATION AND LICENSURE The Certification and Licensure section is designed to help students pass their licensure exam by giving them access to state test requirements, overviews of what tests cover, and sample test items.

The Certification and Licensure tab includes the following:

- **State Certification Test Requirements:** Here students can click on a state and will then be taken to a list of state certification tests.
- Students can click on the **Licensure Exams** they need to take to find:
  - Basic information about each test
  - Descriptions of what is covered on each test
  - Sample test questions with explanations of correct answers
- **National Evaluation Series**™ by Pearson: Here students can see the tests in the NES, learn what is covered on each exam, and access sample test items with descriptions and rationales of correct answers. They can also purchase interactive online tutorials developed by Pearson Evaluation Systems and the Pearson Teacher Education and Development group.
- **ETS Online Praxis Tutorials:** Here students can purchase interactive online tutorials developed by ETS and by the Pearson Teacher Education and Development group. Tutorials are available for the Praxis I exams and for select Praxis II exams.

Visit *www.myeducationlab.com* for a demonstration of this exciting new online teaching resource.

ACKNOWLEDGMENTS

We are grateful to those individuals who provided valuable comments on the eleventh edition and drafts of our twelfth edition chapters: Thomas Bierdz, Governors State University; Betty Davidson, University of Missouri-St. Louis; Vicki Nicholson, Eastern Kentucky University; William Thomas Southern, Miami University; and Marcee M. Steele, University of North Carolina, Wilmington.

We thank Elizabeth Tuckwiller, currently an assistant professor at the Florida State College in Jacksonville, who oversaw the tedious task of securing permissions for quoted material. We are once again thankful for the wonderful support and assistance we received from the folks at Pearson. Alicia Reilly, our Developmental Editor, continues to amaze us with her ability to balance family responsibilities while attending to all the details of our book. We simply can't thank her enough for all she does for us. She is a gem. Sheryl Langner, a new Production Editor for this edition, brought all the complex pieces of the project to completion flawlessly. Editorial Assistant Penny Burleson's responsiveness to our e-mails and phone calls was critical to meeting deadlines. Our copy editor, Luanne Dreyer Elliott, did a terrific job of keeping us stylistically and grammatically correct. We thank Lori Whitley, Photo Researcher, for such a splendid job of finding just the right photos. We're sure readers will agree that the extra attention you gave to the project has paid off—the photos are terrific. We are also grateful to Ann Davis, Executive Editor, for her continued support of this project. We appreciate her professionalism, efficiency, sense of humor, and her extensive knowledge of fine restaurants.

SOME FINAL THOUGHTS

Given that this is the twelfth edition, some readers might legitimately be wondering whether we have lost any enthusiasm for the sometimes tedious task required to produce a thorough, up-to-date revision. We assure you that we didn't approach this edition any differently than we did the first. For those loyal users of previous editions, we assure you that we weighed carefully each change or update. We hope you agree that our revisions reflect the myriad changes in the field of special education over the past few years as well as the information explosion brought about by ever more accessible computer databases and the Internet. We also hope you'll agree that we haven't failed in our continuing commitment to bring you the best that research has to offer with regard to educating exceptional learners.

DPH
JMK
PCP

BRIEF CONTENTS

CONTENTS

13 LEARNERS WITH LOW-INCIDENCE, MULTIPLE, AND SEVERE DISABILITIES 366

14 LEARNERS WITH PHYSICAL DISABILITIES AND OTHER HEALTH IMPAIRMENTS 396

15 LEARNERS WITH SPECIAL GIFTS AND TALENTS 426

SPECIAL FEATURES

PHOTO CREDITS

Lori Whitley/Merrill, pp. 2, 22, 236; © Robin Nelson/PhotoEdit, p. 6; By the courtesy of the Association of Mouth and Foot Painting Artists Worldwide, p. 7 (left & right); Courtesy of AbleNet, Inc., pp. 9, 118; Spencer Grant/PhotoEdit Inc., pp. 11, 58; Richard Hutchings/PhotoEdit Inc., p. 17; George Dodson/PH College, p. 25; Pearson Scott Foresman, pp. 26, 250; © Bob Daemmrich/PhotoEdit, p. 33; Laura Bolesta/Merrill, pp. 37, 178, 210; Creatas, p. 39; iStockphoto, pp. 40, 54, 56, 79, 80, 83, 85, 120, 200, 205, 214, 281; © Mark Richards/PhotoEdit, p. 43; Courtesy of Livescribe, p. 44; Jack Hollingsworth/Thinkstock, p. 46; Getty Images, Inc—Comstock Images RF, p. 50; David Mager/Pearson Learning Photo Studio, pp. 62, 175; Katelyn Metzger/Merrill, pp. 63, 186, 328, 350, 411; © Bob Daemmrich/The Image Works, pp. 66, 309; © John Birdsall/The Image Works, p. 69; © Barbara Laws/John Birdsall Archive/The Image Works, p. 74; © David Young-Wolff/PhotoEdit, pp. 77, 407; Robin Nelson/PhotoEdit Inc., pp. 89, 302; Photodisc/Getty Images, pp. 91, 161, 372; Jeff Greenberg/PhotoEdit Inc., pp. 92, 270; © Richard Hutchings/CORBIS All Rights Reserved, p. 100; © Mika/Corbis, p. 104; © Grabowsky U./SV-Bilderdienst/The Image Works, p. 108; Streissguth, A.P., Clarren, S.K., & Jones, K.L. (1985, July). Natural history of the Fetal Alcohol Syndrome: A ten-year follow-up of eleven patients. *Lancet, 2*, 85–91., p. 111; © Steve Skjold/Alamy, p. 113; © Bettmann/Corbis, p. 114; Courtesy of the Williams Syndrome Foundation, p. 115; Valerie Schultz/Merrill, p. 117; Ellen B. Senisi/The Image Works, p. 134; Hope Madden/Merrill, p. 137; © Jacksonville Journal Courier/The Image Works, p. 139; Patrick White/Merrill, pp. 152, 237; Courtesy of the authors, p. 154; Annie Pickert/AB Merrill, pp. 159, 286; GeoStock/Gerry Images, Inc.—Photodisc/Royalty Free, p. 168; © Doug Menuez/Getty Images, p. 183; © Annie Griffiths Belt/Corbis, p. 184; Corbis RF, p. 190; David Graham/PH College, p. 206; © Mitch Wojnarowicz/The Image Works, p. 207; © Gabe Palmer/Corbis, p. 209; SW Productions/Getty Images, Inc.—Photodisc/Royalty Free, pp. 211, 239; Mary Kate Denny/PhotoEdit Inc., p. 215; AP Photo/The Plain Dealer, Chuk Crow, p. 232; Shutterstock, pp. 246 (four photos), 390, 426, 432, 443; © Bob Mahoney/The Image Works, p. 258; Courtesy of the subject, p. 260; © Christina Kennedy/PhotoEdit, pp. 264, 276; © Mary Kate Denny/PhotoEdit, p. 273 (top); Scott Cunningham/Merrill, pp. 273 (bottom), 314, 318, 401; Photo provided courtesy of Prentke Romich Company (PRC). www.prentrom.com, p. 280; Ruth Jenkinson © Dorling Kindersley, p. 288; © Michael Newman/PhotoEdit, pp. 294, 409; AP Images/Don Ryan, p. 299; © OSWALDO RIVAS/Reuters/Corbis, p. 306; AP Photo/Patricia McDonnell, p. 317; Gallaudet University, p. 322; National Eye Institute, p. 337 (five photos); © Bubbles Photolibrary/Alamy, p. 338; Marion Ettlinger, p. 341; © Dion Ogust/The Image Works, p. 347 (left); © Tony Savino/The Image Works, p. 347 (right); © Robin Sachs/PhotoEdit, p. 351; © Spencer Grant/PhotoEdit, p. 352 (top); Courtesy of NASA, ESA, B. Wentworth III (CSDB) and STScI, p. 352 (bottom); Courtesy of Michael May, www.CrashingThrough.com, p. 356 (both); © Jamie Bloomquist.com, p. 362; © Elizabeth Crews/The Image Works, p. 366; AP Images, p. 370; AP Images/Bucks County Courier Times, Donna Lere, p. 375; Courtesy of Perkins School for the Blind, Watertown, MA, p. 381; Andrew Shurtleff, p. 385 (three photos); BoldStock/Fotosearch/© Unlisted Images, Inc. All Rights Reserved, p. 396; © George Steinmetz, p. 406; AP Images/Andrew Medichini, p. 412; © Blend Images/Alamy, p. 430; Robert Houser/Jupiter Images Royalty Free, p. 434; © Katherine Frey, p. 437; © Tony Freeman/PhotoEdit, p. 439; Anthony Magnacca/Merrill, p. 441; All Peer Connections photos and Success Stories photos are courtesy of the subjects.

Exceptionality and Special Education

Only the brave dare look
upon the gray—
upon the things which
cannot be explained easily,
upon the things which often
engender mistakes,
upon the things whose cause
cannot be understood,
upon the things we must
accept and live with.
And therefore only the brave
dare look upon difference
without flinching.

Richard H. Hungerford • *"On Locusts"*

QUESTIONS **to guide your reading of this chapter . . .**

- How can we get oriented to exceptionality and special education?
- What is the educational definition of *exceptional learners*?
- What is the prevalence of exceptional learners?
- What is the definition of *special education*?
- What are the history and origins of special education?
- What legislation and litigation have affected special education?
- What is our perspective on the progress of special education?

MISCONCEPTIONS ABOUT
Exceptional Learners

MYTH • Public schools may choose not to provide education for some students with disabilities.

FACT • Federal legislation specifies that to receive federal funds, every school system must provide a free appropriate public education (FAPE) for every student, regardless of any disabling condition.

MYTH • The causes of most disabilities are known, but little is known about how to help individuals overcome or compensate for their disabilities.

FACT • In most cases, the causes of disabilities are not known, although progress is being made in pinpointing why many disabilities occur. More is known about the treatment of most disabilities than about their causes.

MYTH • People with disabilities are just like everyone else.

FACT • First, no two people are exactly alike. People with disabilities are unique individuals, just like everyone else. In most cases, most of their abilities are much like those of the average person who is not considered to have a disability. Nevertheless, a disability is a characteristic that is not shared by most people. It is important that disabilities be recognized for what they are, but individuals with disabilities must be seen as having many abilities—other characteristics that they share with the majority of people.

MYTH • A disability is a handicap.

FACT • A disability is an inability to do something, the lack of a specific capacity. A handicap, on the other hand, is a disadvantage that is imposed on an individual. A disability might or might not be a handicap, depending on the circumstances. For example, the inability to walk is not a handicap in learning to read, but it can be a handicap in getting into the stands at a ball game. Sometimes handicaps are needlessly imposed on people with disabilities. For example, a student who cannot write with a pen but can use a typewriter or word processor would be needlessly handicapped without such equipment.

PEARSON
myeducationlab

To check your comprehension on the content covered in Chapter 1, go to the Book-Specific Resources in the MyEducationLab (www.myeducationlab.com) for your course, select your text, and complete the Study Plan. Here you will be able to take a chapter quiz, receive feedback on your answers, and then access review, practice, and enrichment activities to enhance your understanding of chapter content. ■

The study of exceptional learners is the study of differences. The exceptional learner differs in some way from the average. In very simple terms, such a person might have problems or special talents in thinking, seeing, hearing, speaking, socializing, or moving. More often than not, he has a combination of special abilities or disabilities. Today, more than 6 million learners with these differences have been identified in public schools throughout the United States. More than 1 of every 10 school-age students in the United States is considered exceptional. The fact that even many so-called normal students have school-related problems makes the study of exceptionality very demanding.

The study of exceptional learners is also the study of similarities. Exceptional individuals are not different from the average in every way. In fact, most exceptional learners are average in more ways than they are not. Until recently, professionals—and laypeople as well—tended to focus on the differences between exceptional and nonexceptional learners, almost to the exclusion of the ways in which all individuals are alike. Today, we give more attention to what exceptional and nonexceptional learners have in common—to similarities in their characteristics, needs, and ways of learning. As a result, the study of exceptional learners has become more complex, and many so-called facts about children and youths with disabilities and those who have special gifts or talents have been challenged.

GETTING ORIENTED TO EXCEPTIONAL LEARNERS AND SPECIAL EDUCATION

Students of one of the hard sciences might boast about the difficulty of the subject matter because of the many facts they must remember and piece together. Students of special education face quite different problems. To be sure, they study facts, but the facts they must master are relatively few compared to the unanswered questions or ambiguities with which they must deal. Any study of human beings must take into account inherent ambiguities, inconsistencies, and unknowns. In the case of the individual who deviates from the norm, we must multiply all the mysteries of normal human behavior and development by those pertaining to the person's exceptionalities. Because no single theory of normal development is universally accepted, it is not at all surprising that relatively few definite statements can be made about exceptional learners and many controversies remain (Kauffman, 2008; Kauffman & Hallahan, 2005a, 2011).

Reasons for Optimism

Patches of sunlight now shine in the bleak gray painted by Hungerford (1950) in his classic but still highly relevant poem quoted in this chapter's opening page. In the vast majority of cases, professionals are unable to identify the exact reason *why* a person is exceptional but are making progress in determining the causes of some disabilities. In Chapter 5, for example, we discuss the detection of causal factors in **Down syndrome**, a condition that results in the largest number of children classified as having moderate intellectual and developmental disabilities (mental retardation, which is now called either intellectual disability, ID, or intellectual and developmental disability, IDD). Likewise, the incidence of **retinopathy of prematurity**, at one time a leading cause of blindness, has been greatly reduced since the discovery of its cause. The metabolic disorder **phenylketonuria (PKU)** was discovered decades ago, and now infants are routinely tested for PKU soon after birth, so that this type of intellectual disability can be prevented. More recently, the gene responsible for **cystic fibrosis**—an inherited condition characterized by chronic respiratory and digestive problems—has been identified. Advances in drug treatments appear to hold the potential for a cure for **muscular dystrophy**, another inherited disorder characterized by progressive degeneration of muscles (Welch et al., 2007). In the future, the specific genes governing many other diseases and disorders will also likely be found. Scientific advances raise the possibility of medications or gene therapies to prevent or correct many disabling conditions. Physicians can now perform surgery to correct some identifiable defects on a fetus before birth (in utero), completely avoiding some conditions, such as **hydrocephalus** (an accumulation of fluid around the brain that can cause mental or physical disabilities if not corrected). And before long, research might lead to the ability to grow new organs from tissues taken from a person or from stem cells, perhaps allowing replacement of a poorly functioning lung, pancreas, or other internal organ and avoidance of the associated physical disabilities. Advances in reproductive technology also hold promise for preventing many disabilities (Kauffman & Hallahan, 2009).

Besides these and other medical breakthroughs, research is enhancing understanding of the ways in which the individual's psychological, social, and educational environments are related to learning. For example, special educators, psychologists, and pediatricians are increasingly able to identify environmental conditions that increase the likelihood that a child will have learning or behavior problems (see Bolger & Patterson, 2001; Hallahan, Lloyd, Kauffman, Weiss, & Martinez, 2005; Hart & Risley, 1995; Kauffman & Landrum, 2009; Walker & Sprague, 2007).

Educational methodology has also made strides. In fact, compared to current knowledge about causes, the knowledge about how exceptional learners can be taught and managed effectively in the classroom is much more complete. Although special educators lament that not all the questions have been answered, considerably more is known today about how to educate exceptional learners than was the case years ago (e.g., Hallahan et al., 2005; Heward, 2003; Kauffman & Hallahan, 2011; Lloyd, Forness, & Kavale, 1998; Stichter, Conroy, & Kauffman, 2008).

INTERNETRESOURCES

You might Google "advances in treatment of disability" to see what you turn up. Or, you might go to http://www .childrensdisabilities.info/ parenting/batshaw.html for an interview with a prominent physician who has written widely about disabilities.

We must not allow people's disabilities to keep us from recognizing their abilities or to become so much the focus of our concern that we overlook their capabilities.

INTERNETRESOURCES

You can visit the site of the World Congress on Disabilities at http://www.thewcd.org (or simply Google "World Congress on Disabilities"). For news about special education, you might go to http://www.specialeducationews.com

Before moving to the specific subject of exceptional learners, we must point out that we vehemently disagree with Hungerford on an important point: We all must certainly learn to live with disabling exceptionalities, but we must never accept them. We prefer to think there is hope for the eventual eradication of many of the disabling forms of exceptionality. In addition, we believe that it is of paramount importance to realize that even individuals whose exceptionalities are extreme can be helped to lead fuller lives than they would without appropriate education.

The Importance of Abilities

Many people with disabilities have abilities that go unrecognized because their disabilities become the focus of concern and distract attention from what the individual can do. We must study the disabilities of exceptional children and youths if we are to learn how to help them make maximum use of their abilities in school. Some students with disabilities that are not obvious to the casual observer need special programs of education and related services to help them live full, happy, productive lives. However, we must not lose sight of the fact that the most important characteristics of exceptional learners are their abilities, not their disabilities.

Disability Versus Handicap

We recognize an important distinction between disability and handicap: A disability is an inability to do something, a diminished capacity to perform in a specific way (an impairment); a handicap, however, is a disadvantage imposed on an individual. Thus, a disability might or might not be a handicap, depending on the circumstances. Likewise, a handicap might or might not be caused by a disability. For example, blindness is a disability that can be anything but a handicap in the dark. In fact, in the dark, the person who has sight is the one who is handicapped. Needing to use a wheelchair might be a handicap in certain circumstances, but the disadvantage may be caused by architectural barriers or other people's reactions, not the inability to walk. Other people can handicap those who differ from themselves (in color, size, appearance, language, and so on) by stereotyping them or not giving them opportunities to do the things they are able to do. When working and living with exceptional individuals who have disabilities, we must constantly strive to separate their disabilities from the handicaps. That is, our goal should be to confine the handicaps to those characteristics and circumstances that can't be changed and to make sure that we impose no further handicaps by our attitudes or our unwillingness to accommodate their disabilities.

Disability Versus Inability

Another important distinction is that between inability and disability. All disabilities are an inability to do something. However, not every inability to do something is a disability. That is, disability is a subset of inability: "A disability is an inability to do something that most people, with typical maturation, opportunity, or instruction, can do" (Kauffman & Hallahan, 2005a, p. 30; see also Stichter et al., 2008). Consider age and ability. Most

6-month-old infants cannot walk or talk, but they are not thought of as having a disability because their inability is age appropriate. However, if that inability extends well past the time when most children learn to walk and talk, then we consider their inability a disability. Consider the role of instruction. An adult's inability to read is not a reading disability if she or he has not had reading instruction. Weigh the factor of typical adult human abilities. A typical adult male might not be able to lift 400 pounds, but this isn't considered a disability, because most men simply can't lift 400 pounds. Judging inability in the context of old age, the average 70-year-old can't run 10 miles, but most 70-year-olds can walk a considerable distance. Not being able to run 10 miles is not considered a disability for a 70-year-old, but being unable to walk at all is. The point is, simply, that disability is a significant difference from what we expect most people to be able to do, given their age, opportunities, and instruction.

INTERNETRESOURCES

Many interesting films are made about and by people with disabilities. You may want to see some of these films and preview them at http://www.gosprout.org/touring. To find out more about Sprout as an organization, go to http://www.gosprout.org

EDUCATIONAL DEFINITION OF *EXCEPTIONAL LEARNERS*

For purposes of education, exceptional learners are those who require special education and related services if they are to realize their full human potential (Kauffman & Hallahan, 2005a). They require special education because they differ markedly from most students in one or more of the following ways: They may have intellectual disabilities, learning or attention disabilities, emotional or behavioral disorders, physical disabilities, disorders of communication, autism, traumatic brain injury, impaired hearing, impaired sight, or special gifts or talents. The chapters that follow define as exactly as possible what it means to have an exceptionality.

Two concepts are important to this educational definition of exceptional learners: (1) diversity of characteristics and (2) need for special education. The concept of diversity is inherent in the definition of exceptionality; the need for special education is inherent in an educational definition. Exceptional learners differ from most (typical or average) individuals in a particular way that is relevant to their education. Their particular educationally relevant difference demands instruction that differs from what most (typical or average) learners require (Kauffman & Hallahan, 2005a; Kauffman & Konold, 2007; Stichter et al., 2008).

Consider the case described in the accompanying Personal Perspectives feature. Doug Landis's exquisite drawings and paintings of wildlife illustrate how the focus on persons with disabilities must be on what they can do rather than on how they are limited.

Personal PERSPECTIVES

Doug Landis

Doug Landis became quadriplegic (paralyzed from the neck down) in high school as a result of a wrestling accident. His brother thought he was watching too much television and challenged him to start drawing by putting a pencil in his mouth. Using a pencil attached to a mouth stick, Doug has become a major artist whose detailed line drawings of wildlife are highlighted, but he is gifted at drawing many things. He has also made short animated films. You may want to visit his Website at http://www.mouthart.com/mouthart/ or explore www.vdmfk.com

By the courtesy of the Association of Mouth and Foot Painting Artists Worldwide.

By the courtesy of the Association of Mouth and Foot Painting Artists Worldwide.

Sometimes seemingly obvious disabilities are never identified, and the consequences for the person and her family, as well as for the larger society, are tragic (Kauffman & Brigham, 2009). Sometimes disabilities are identified but special education is not provided, and opportunities for the child's development are thus squandered. Although early identification and intervention hold the promise of preventing many disabilities from becoming worse, preventive action often is not taken (Kauffman, 1999b, 2005; Kauffman & Brigham, 2009; Stichter et al., 2008).

Consider the case of author Martha Randolph Carr (Carr, 2004). She describes her son's learning disability (related to his attention deficit hyperactivity disorder) and her own inability, until he was in high school, to see the disability. Her unwillingness to see his disability was motivated by the typical objections: labels and self-image.

> When Louie was in first grade it became obvious to me that he was having difficulty reading. To avoid labels being placed on my young son, I did what I thought was best: I started reading to Louie. . . . Through elementary and middle school, Louie grew into a thoughtful, intelligent, articulate boy who earned mostly Bs, but who had trouble comprehending the little he could read. No one else knew, and Louie and I rarely talked about it.
>
> His reading difficulty was the only problem I saw, and I accepted that everything else was fine. I told myself that I was doing the right thing because Louie might feel badly about himself if he thought there was something wrong and because mainstream colleges wouldn't accept a kid with learning disabilities. Fortunately, time and high school caught up with both of us.

Finally, in high school, Ms. Carr and Louie could no longer cover up his disability. But his response to recognizing his disability—to its finally being diagnosed—was very different from what she had anticipated.

> When I told Louie about the diagnosis, he didn't look hurt or confused. Instead, his face relaxed and he shouted, "You mean I'm not stupid?!" I was so taken aback that I started to cry. Louie said, still very relieved, "Were you worried, too?" I cried harder.
>
> By denying the truth to myself and thus keeping it from Louie, I had left him with the only other plausible answer that he could come up with as to why he always worked so much harder than his friends and didn't get the same grades.

Special education does not always work as it should, but when it does, educators identify a student's disability early and provide effective special education in the least restrictive environment. The student's parents are involved in the decision about how to address the student's needs, and the outcome of special education is the student's improved achievement and behavior.

Students with exceptionalities are an extraordinarily diverse group in comparison to the general population, and relatively few generalizations apply to all exceptional individuals. Their exceptionalities can involve sensory, physical, cognitive, emotional, or communication abilities or any combination of these. Furthermore, exceptionalities may vary greatly in cause, degree, and effect on educational progress, and the effects may vary greatly depending on the individual's age, sex, and life circumstances. Any individual presented as an example of an "exceptional learner" is likely to be representative of exceptional learners in some respects but unrepresentative in others.

The typical student who receives special education has no immediately obvious disability. He (more than half of the students served by special education are males) is in elementary or middle school and has persistent problems in learning and behaving appropriately in school. His problems are primarily academic and social or behavioral and may not be apparent to many teachers until they have worked with him for a period of weeks or months. His problems persist despite teachers' efforts to meet his needs in the regular school program in which most students succeed. He is most likely to be described as having a learning disability or to be designated by an even broader label indicating that his academic and social progress in school is unsatisfactory owing to a disability.

By federal law, schools should not identify these exceptional students as eligible for special education until careful assessment indicates that they are unable to make satisfactory progress in the regular school program without special services designed to meet their extraordinary needs (Huefner, 2006). Federal special education laws and regulations include definitions of several conditions (categories such as learning disability, autism, and hearing impairment) that might create a need for special education. These laws and regulations require that schools provide special services to meet whatever special needs are created by a disabling condition that can't be met in the regular educational program. The law doesn't require provision of special education simply because a student has a disability.

PREVALENCE OF EXCEPTIONAL LEARNERS

Prevalence refers to the percentage of a population or number of individuals having a particular exceptionality. The prevalence of intellectual disability, for example, might be estimated at 2.3%, which means that 2.3% of the population, or 23 people in every 1,000, are assumed to have intellectual disabilities. If the prevalence of giftedness is assumed to be between 3% and 5%, then somewhere between 30 and 50 people in a sample of 1,000 would have special gifts of some kind. Obviously, accurate estimates of prevalence depend on the ability to count the number of people in a given population who have a certain exceptionality.

The task of determining the number of students with exceptionalities might appear simple enough, yet the prevalence of most exceptionalities is uncertain and a matter of considerable controversy. Multiple factors make it hard to state the number of exceptional individuals with great accuracy and confidence. These factors include vagueness in definitions, frequent changes in definitions, and the role of schools in determining exceptionality— matters that we discuss in later chapters (see also Kauffman & Hallahan, 2005a, 2011).

Government figures show that about 10 of every 100 students were receiving special education in the early 21st century (U.S. Department of Education, 2008). Beginning in the mid-1970s, the number of students served by special education grew steadily, from about 3.75 million in 1976 to more than 6 million in the early 21st century. Most of the children and youths who are served by special education are between the ages of 6 and 17. Although preschoolers and youths ages 18 to 21 are being identified with increasing frequency as having disabilities, school-age children and youths in their early teens make up the bulk of the identified population.

The percentage of the special education population identified as having certain disabilities has changed considerably over several decades. For example, the number of students identified as having learning disabilities has more than doubled since the mid-1970s; these students now make up about half of the number of students receiving special education. In contrast, the percentage of students whose primary disability is speech or language impairments declined substantially (but is growing again), and the percentage identified as having intellectual disabilities is now about half of what it was in 1976. No one has an entirely satisfactory explanation of these changes. However, they might in part reflect alterations in definitions and diagnostic criteria for certain disabilities and the social acceptability of the "learning disability" label. In subsequent chapters, we discuss the prevalence of specific categories of exceptionality.

INTERNET RESOURCES

For annual reports to Congress on implementation of federal special education law, go to http://www2.ed .gov/about/reports/annual/ osep/index.html

High-Incidence and Low-Incidence Categories

Some disabilities occur with a relatively high frequency and are called *high-incidence disabilities* because they are among the most common. Learning disabilities, communication (speech and

The identification of **autism** or **autistic spectrum disorder** has increased dramatically, probably representing improved identification procedures and identification of milder cases of autism, not an epidemic.

language) disorders, emotional disturbance, and mild intellectual disabilities are among those usually considered high incidence (Stichter et al., 2008). Other disabilities (such as low vision and blindness, deafness, deaf-blindness, and severe intellectual disabilities) occur relatively rarely and are considered low-incidence disabilities.

Although the rates of occurrence of most of the high-incidence disabilities have remained relatively stable in the early 21st century, some of the low-incidence categories have increased dramatically. For example, the identification of **autism** or **autistic spectrum disorder** has increased dramatically since about 1995 (discussed further in Chapter 9; see also Stichter et al., 2008). Other low-incidence categories showing a substantial increase in numbers include **traumatic brain injury (TBI)** and orthopedic impairments; much of this is due to increases in spinal cord injury and in survival of severe physical trauma owing to better medical care.

Much of the increase in diagnosis of autism probably represents improved identification procedures and identification of milder cases of autism, not an epidemic (National Research Council, 2001). Although some of the increase in TBI might represent better diagnosis, it might also reflect actual increases in brain injuries, as we will discuss in Chapter 13. Increases in orthopedic impairments might reflect the increasing survival rates of infants born with significant physical anomalies and of children involved in accidents. Increases in hearing and vision impairments might represent better diagnosis of these disabilities, too.

DEFINITION OF *SPECIAL EDUCATION*

Special education means specially designed instruction that meets the unusual needs of an exceptional student (see Huefner, 2006) and that might require special materials, teaching techniques, or equipment and/or facilities. Students with visual impairments might require reading materials in large print or braille; students with hearing impairments might require hearing aids and/or instruction in sign language; those with physical disabilities might need special equipment; those with emotional or behavioral disorders might need smaller and more highly structured classes; and students with special gifts or talents might require access to working professionals. Related services—special transportation, psychological assessment, physical and occupational therapy, medical treatment, and counseling—might be necessary if special education is to be effective. The single most important goal of special education is finding and capitalizing on exceptional students' abilities.

The best general education cannot replace special education; special education is more precisely controlled in pace or rate, intensity, relentlessness, structure, reinforcement, teacher pupil ratio, curriculum, and monitoring or assessment (Kauffman & Hallahan, 2005a; Kauffman & Landrum, 2007). We think it's a good idea to improve the education of all children, an objective of the federal education laws of the early 21st century. However, good or reformed general education does not and cannot replace special education for those students at the extremes of the range of disabilities (Kauffman & Hallahan, 2005a; Kauffman & Konold, 2007; Kauffman & Wiley, 2004; Zigmond, 2007; Zigmond & Kloo, 2011; Zigmond, Kloo, & Volonino, 2009).

HISTORY AND ORIGINS OF SPECIAL EDUCATION

There have always been exceptional learners, but there haven't always been special educational services to address their needs (see Holmes, 2004; Metzler, 2006). During the closing years of the 18th century, following the American and French Revolutions, effective procedures were devised for teaching children with sensory impairments (i.e., those who were blind or deaf; Winzer, 1993). Early in the 19th century, the first systematic attempts were made to educate "idiotic" and "insane" children—those who today are said to have **intellectual disabilities** and **emotional or behavioral disorders** (or **emotional disturbance**; Kauffman & Landrum, 2006; Stichter et al., 2008).

In the prerevolutionary era, the best that society offered most children with disabilities was protection—asylum from a cruel world into which they didn't fit and in which they couldn't survive with dignity, if they could survive at all. But as the ideas of democracy, in-

INTERNETRESOURCES

You may want to learn more about the history of special education by going to http://www.disabilityhistory.org or npr.org/programs/disability Another good site is http://www.museumofdisability.org

dividual freedom, and egalitarianism swept across America and France, a change in attitude occurred. Political reformers and leaders in medicine and education began to champion the cause of children and adults with disabilities, urging that these "imperfect" or "incomplete" individuals be taught skills that would allow them to become independent, productive citizens. These humanitarian sentiments surpassed a desire to protect and defend people with disabilities. The early leaders sought to normalize exceptional people to the greatest extent possible and confer on them the human dignity they presumably lacked.

Contemporary educational methods for exceptional children can be traced directly to techniques pioneered during the early 1800s. Many (perhaps most) of today's vital, controversial issues have been issues ever since the dawn of special education. Some contemporary writers believe that the history of special education is critically important to understanding today's issues and should receive more attention because of the lessons we can learn from our past (e.g., Gerber, 2011; Kauffman, 1999a; Kauffman & Landrum, 2006). In our discussion of some of the major historical events and trends since 1800, we comment briefly on the history of people and ideas, the growth of the discipline, professional and parent organizations, and legislation.

People and Ideas

Most of the originators of special education were European physicians. They were primarily young, ambitious people who challenged the wisdom of the established authorities, including their own friends and mentors (Kanner, 1964; see also Kauffman & Landrum, 2006; Stichter et al., 2008).

Most historians trace the beginning of special education as we know it today to Jean-Marc-Gaspard Itard (1775–1838), a French physician who was an authority on diseases of the ear and on the education of deaf students. In the early years of the 19th century, this young doctor began to educate a boy of about 12 years of age who had been found roaming naked and wild in the forests of France (sometimes referred to as the "wild child" or the "wild boy of Avyron"). Itard's mentor, Philippe Pinel (1745–1826), a prominent French physician who was an early advocate of humane treatment of "insane" people, advised Itard that his efforts would be unsuccessful because the boy, Victor, was a "hopeless idiot." But Itard persevered. He did not eliminate Victor's disabilities, but he did dramatically improve the wild child's behavior through patient, systematic educative procedures (Itard, 1962).

One of Itard's students, Édouard Séguin (1812–1880), immigrated to the United States in 1848. Séguin had become famous as an educator of so-called idiotic children, even though most thinkers of the day were convinced that such children could not be taught anything of significance.

The ideas of the first special educators were truly revolutionary for their times. These are a few of the revolutionary ideas of Itard, Séguin, and their successors that form the foundation for present-day special education:

- *Individualized instruction*, in which the child's characteristics, rather than prescribed academic content, provide the basis for teaching techniques
- *A carefully sequenced series of educational tasks*, beginning with tasks the child can perform and gradually leading to more complex learning
- *Emphasis on stimulation and awakening of the child's senses*, to make the child more aware of and responsive to educational stimuli

Special educators have the responsibility to offer not just good instruction, but also instruction that is highly individualized, intensive, relentless, urgent, and goal directed.

- *Meticulous arrangement of the child's environment*, so that the structure of the environment and the child's experience of it lead naturally to learning
- *Immediate reward for correct performance*, providing reinforcement for desirable behavior
- *Tutoring in functional skills*, to make the child as self-sufficient and productive as possible in everyday life
- *Belief that every child should be educated to the greatest extent possible*, because every child can improve to some degree

So far, we've mentioned only European physicians who figured prominently in the rise of special education. Although much of the initial work occurred in Europe, many U.S. researchers contributed greatly during those early years. They kept informed of European developments as best they could, some of them traveling to Europe for the specific purpose of obtaining firsthand information about the education of children with disabilities.

Among the young U.S. thinkers who were concerned with the education of students with disabilities was Samuel Gridley Howe (1801–1876), an 1824 graduate of Harvard Medical School. Besides being a physician and an educator, Howe was a political and social reformer, a champion of humanitarian causes and emancipation. He was instrumental in founding the Perkins School for the Blind in Watertown, Massachusetts, and also taught students who were deaf and blind. His success in teaching Laura Bridgman, who was deaf and blind, greatly influenced the education of Helen Keller. In the 1840s, Howe was also a force behind the organization of an experimental school for children with intellectual disabilities [mental retardation] and was personally acquainted with Séguin.

When Thomas Hopkins Gallaudet (1787–1851), a minister, was a student at Andover Theological Seminary, he tried to teach a girl who was deaf. He visited Europe to learn about educating the deaf and in 1817 established the first American residential school, in Hartford, Connecticut, for students who were deaf (now known as the American School of the Deaf). Gallaudet University in Washington, D.C., the only liberal-arts college for students who are deaf, was named in his honor.

The early years of special education were vibrant with the pulse of new ideas. It isn't possible to read the words of Itard, Séguin, Howe, and their contemporaries without being captivated by the romance, idealism, and excitement of their exploits. The results they achieved were truly remarkable for their era. Today, special education remains a vibrant field in which innovations, excitement, idealism, and controversies are the norm. Teachers of exceptional children—and that includes all teachers—must understand how and why special education emerged as a discipline (see Gerber, 2011).

One of the great controversies involving the education of exceptional learners is the extent to which nature and nurture contribute to what a child becomes. What is attributable to biological factors such as genetics and other aspects of physical endowment, and what is attributable to environmental factors such as opportunity, encouragement, and teaching? This is a very old but still controversial idea. It was part of Itard's work in the early 19th century, and it's still being debated by psychologists (e.g., Pinker, 2002) and popular writers (e.g., Gladwell, 2008) of the early 21st century. (See the accompanying Focus on Concepts feature.)

Normalization, Deinstitutionalization, and Inclusion

Among the major 20th-century ideas in special education is **normalization**, the philosophy that we should use "means which are as culturally normative as possible, in order to establish and/or maintain personal behaviors and characteristics which are as culturally normative as possible" (Wolfensberger, 1972, p. 28). With normalization, society breaks down the barriers to participation of people with disabilities in normal life. The concept of normalization was in itself important and led to related ideas, such as closing institutions and including exceptional learners in general education classrooms and schools.

Normalization continues to be a goal in special education and all other aspects of responding to disability. Consider the case of Kathy Koons, described in the Personal Perspectives feature on page 14. She's a young woman with a physical disability and relatively

FOCUS ON Concepts

THE NATURE–NURTURE CONTROVERSY

For many years, theoreticians tended to view the nature–nurture issue from an either/or perspective: Either you believed that heredity held the key to determining intellectual development or you believed that the environment was the all-important factor. Today, however, most authorities believe that both heredity and the environment are critical determinants of intelligence. Some scientists have tried to discover how much of intelligence is determined by heredity and how much by the environment, but many view this quest as futile. They assert that heredity and environment do not combine in an additive fashion to produce intelligence. Instead, the interaction between genes and environment results in intelligence.

The following exchange between a professor of biopsychology and his student points out the importance of viewing intelligence in this way—that is, as the result of an interaction between genetics and experience and not a simple addition of the two:

One of my students told me that she had read that intelligence was one-third genetic and two-thirds experience, and she wondered whether this was true. She must have been puzzled when I began my response by describing an alpine experience. "I was lazily wandering up a summit ridge when I heard an unexpected sound. Ahead, with his back to me, was a young man sitting on the edge of a precipice, blowing into a peculiar musical instrument. I sat down behind him on a large sun-soaked rock, and shared his experience with him. Then, I got up and wandered back down the ridge, leaving him undisturbed.

I put the following question to my student: "If I wanted to get a better understanding of the music, would it be reasonable for me to begin by asking how much of it came from the musician and how much of it came from the instrument?"

"That would be dumb," she said, "The music comes from both; it makes no sense to ask how much comes from the musician and how much comes from the instrument. Somehow the music results from the interaction of the two, and you would have to ask about the interaction."

"That's exactly right," I said. "Now, do you see why. . . ."

"Don't say any more," she interrupted. "I see what you're getting at. Intelligence is the product of the interaction of genes and experience, and it is dumb to try to find how much comes from genes and how much comes from experience." (Pinel, 2006, p. 23)

low tested intelligence who is anticipating making the transition to independent living in the community. For her, normalization of personal relationships, employment, and community living are important goals.

Breaking down barriers to participation of people with disabilities in activities with non-handicapped individuals was one of the ideas leading to the **deinstitutionalization** movement of the late 20th century. At one time, it was common to place nearly all children and adults with intellectual disability (mental retardation) and/or mental illness in residential institutions. In the 1960s and 1970s, systematic efforts were made to move people out of institutions and back into closer contact with the community. This led to more children with disabilities being raised by their families and resulted in the closure of many institutions regardless of the nature of the problems of the people involved. Today, smaller facilities within local neighborhoods are common. Halfway houses exist for individuals with emotional difficulties, who no longer are thought to need the more isolated environment of a large institution. However, much still needs to be done to improve the quality of life for some people with disabilities who have been released from institutions. In fact, many people who were or formerly would have been in institutions are now homeless or in jail (see Earley, 2006; Goin, 2007; Lamb & Weinberger, 2001; Nomani, 2007; Torrey & Zdandowic, 1999).

Perhaps the most controversial issue growing out of the idea of normalization is **inclusion**. Actually inclusion, or integration, has long been an issue with all exceptional students, including those with special gifts or talents. Although historically, educators built educational programming for students with disabilities on the assumption that a variety of service delivery options need to be available (Crockett & Kauffman, 1999, 2001; Kauffman et al., 2008), inclusion of exceptional learners in ordinary classrooms with their nonexceptional peers has become the single most important issue for some advocates. The issue of inclusion became controversial among parents and others in the late 20th century and continues to be a topic of heated opinion and discussion.

 **Personal PERSPECTIVES**

Kathy Koons

Kathy is a 19-year-old young woman with spina bifida. She has an electric wheelchair that she can control in a very limited way. An instructional assistant works with Kathy to ensure that she is able to get around the school and to assist her with classroom activities. She requires assistance in writing and getting her supplies ready for class, getting her lunch and feeding herself, and controlling her wheelchair.

Kathy is a middle child; she has an older, married sister and a brother who is age 14. Her father is an electrician and her mother does not work outside of the home. The family lives in a very nice house, which has had some modifications made for the wheelchair.

Her school attendance has been very poor. Mrs. Koons has kept Kathy at home for extended periods of time throughout the years, stating that Kathy was not well enough to attend school. The family was told that Kathy would not live to be 5 years old and they have taken care of her every need. The mother does many things that Kathy could do on her own, but would take her a long time to get done. When Kathy is at home, she spends the majority of the time in her wheelchair in front of the TV or stretched out on a blanket on the floor. There is nothing that Kathy does at home for herself or the family.

Kathy is in four resource classes (math, language arts, social studies, and vocational exploration), is in two regular education classes (computers and home economics), and

spends one hour a day with an instructional assistant working on daily living and functional living skills. Kathy is working on grooming skills, kitchen skills, making change, telling time, and mobility. She has good verbal skills, but has very limited written language skills because of her limited mobility. She is learning to use a computer so that she can increase her written expressive skills. Kathy has indicated an interest in doing a job that would utilize telephone skills, which is something she feels she could learn to do. She has several friends at school. She says that she would like to have a boyfriend and talks about relationships quite often. She is very concerned about not having someone to marry, being able to leave home, and living on her own.

Kathy's Verbal Scale IQ is 84, Performance Scale IQ is 64, and Full Scale IQ is 75. Curriculum-based assessment results indicate skills functioning at the 7.5 grade level in reading and at the 6.8 grade level in math. She is aware of her academic limitations, but wants to do something with her life. Kathy indicates that she wants to learn to live more independently and to develop job skills. She is older than most of the students in the high school and plans are being made for her to go to a residential independent living center for young adults with physical disabilities, where she will have the opportunity to learn many of the things needed to allow her to live in a group home and have a job. Kathy is very excited about these plans, but her parents are somewhat hesitant.

Source: Sitlington, P. L., & Clark, G. M. (2006). *Transition education and services for students with disabilities* (4th ed., p. 83). Boston: Allyn & Bacon/Pearson. Reprinted with permission.

At the unfolding of the 21st century, the inclusion controversy was sharpened, especially by the higher standards expected of all students. The direction the controversy will take is anyone's guess (see Bateman, 2011; Kauffman & Hung, 2009; Kauffman & Landrum, 2009; Kauffman et al., 2008; Kauffman & Hallahan, 2005b; Kauffman & Konold, 2007; Warnock, 2005; Zigmond & Kloo, 2011; Zigmond, et al., 2009). We can't overemphasize the importance of intensive instruction in meeting the needs of exceptional learners. In our opinion, exceptional children should be placed where such instruction is most likely to be provided.

Council for Exceptional Children and Development of the Profession

Special education didn't suddenly spring up as a new discipline or develop in isolation from other disciplines. The emergence of psychology and sociology and especially of the widespread use of mental tests in the early years of the 20th century had enormous implications for the growth of special education. Psychologists' study of learning and their prediction of school failure or success by means of tests helped to focus attention on children with special needs. Sociologists, social workers, and anthropologists drew attention to the ways in which exceptional children's families and communities responded to them and affected their learning and adjustment. Anecdotal accounts of intellectual disabilities or mental disorders can be found in the 19th-century literature, but they are not presented within the conceptual frameworks that we recognize today as psychology, sociology, and special education (see, e.g., Hallahan & Kauffman, 1977; Kauffman & Landrum, 2006). Even in the early 20th century, the concepts of disability seem crude by today's standards.

As the education profession itself matured and as compulsory school attendance laws became a reality, there was a growing realization among teachers and school administrators that a large number of students must be given something beyond the ordinary classroom experience. Elizabeth Farrell, a teacher in New York City in the early 20th century, was highly instrumental in the development of special education as a profession. She and the New York City superintendent of schools attempted to use information about child development, social work, mental testing, and instruction to address the needs of children and youths who were being ill served in or excluded from general eduaction classes and schools. Farrell was a great advocate for services for students with special needs. Her motives and those of the teachers and administrators who worked with her were to see that every student—including every exceptional child or youth—had an appropriate education and received the related health and social services necessary for optimum learning in school (Gerber, 2011; Hendrick & MacMillan, 1989). In 1922, Farrell and a group of other special educators from across the United States and Canada founded the Council for Exceptional Children (CEC), which is still the primary professional organization of special educators.

Contemporary special education is a professional field with roots in several academic disciplines—especially medicine, psychology, sociology, and social work—in addition to professional education. It's a discipline that is sufficiently different from the mainstream of professional education to require special training programs but sufficiently like the mainstream to maintain a primary concern for schools and teaching.

Individuals, Parents, and Organizations

Individuals and ideas have played crucial roles in the history of special education, but it's accurate to say that much of the progress that has been made over the years has been achieved primarily by the collective efforts of parents and professionals. Professional groups were organized first, beginning in the 19th century. Effective national parent organizations have existed in the United States only since about 1950. (See the accompanying Personal Perspectives feature, "Parent's Thoughts on Inclusion of Their Children with Severe Disabilities.")

Many people who were or are influential in the development of special education or other opportunities for individuals with disabilities could be named. Among them is the late Eunice Kennedy Schriver, whose sister had an intellectual disability and who originated the Special Olympics. Having sports competitions in which individuals with disabilities could compete no doubt enriched the lives of many. Even though the Special Olympics has generated criticism, it stands as an example of advocacy for caring and fair treatment of individuals with disabilities, and Ms. Schriver undeniably changed the self-perception of many people with disabilities and the perceptions of disabilities by the general public—changed these perceptions for the better and improved the quality of life for many.

Parent organizations, though offering membership to individuals who may not have exceptional children, primarily comprise parents who do have such children and concentrate on issues that are of special concern to them. Parent organizations have typically served three essential functions: (1) provide an informal group for parents who understand one another's problems and needs and help one another deal with anxieties and frustrations, (2) provide information regarding services and potential resources, and (3) provide the structure for obtaining needed services for their children. Some of the organizations that came about primarily as the result of parents' efforts include the ARC (formerly the Association for Retarded Citizens), the National Association for Gifted Children, the Learning Disabilities Association, the Autism Society of America, and the Federation of Families for Children's Mental Health.

INTERNETRESOURCES

For information about the Council for Exceptional Children, explore http://www.cec.sped.org You may learn more about the ARC by going to http://www.thearc.org, the Special Olympics by going to http://www.specialolympics.org, the Learning Disabilities Association by going to http://www.ldanatl.org, or any of the other professional or parent organization by Googling its name.

 **Personal PERSPECTIVES**

Parents' Thoughts on Inclusion of Their Children with Severe Disabilities

Parents of children with severe disabilities cite the following reasons for supporting inclusion:

1. The child acquires more academic or functional skills because of the higher expectations and greater stimulation in the general education classroom.
2. Nondisabled students benefit by learning to know children with disabilities; they become more sensitive to people with disabilities.
3. Being around "normal" kids helps students with disabilities acquire social skills.
4. Siblings with and without disabilities go to the same school.
5. Segregation of any kind is morally wrong; inclusion is morally right.

Parents of children with severe disabilities have mentioned the following reasons for not supporting inclusion:

1. The type or severity of the child's disability precludes benefits from inclusion.
2. Inclusion would overburden or negatively affect regular classroom teachers and students.

3. The curriculum of the general education classroom doesn't match the needs of the child.
4. The child does not get the needed teacher attention or services in general education.
5. The child is unlikely to be treated well by nondisabled children in the regular classroom.
6. The child is not likely to benefit but is likely to be overwhelmed by the surroundings in the regular classroom.
7. The child is too young (and needs more supervision or structure) or too old (having become used to a special class) to benefit from inclusion.
8. The child needs to be around other children with similar disabilities; he or she fits in better, feels less stigmatized or different, and has more real friends in a special setting.
9. The child is too disruptive or aggressive or has too many behavior problems for a regular class.
10. Teachers and others in general education don't have the appropriate training for dealing with the child's needs.

Source: From "Taking Sides: Parent's Views on Inclusion for their Children with Severe Disabilities," by D. S. Palmer, K. Fuller, T. Arora, & M. Nelson, 2001, *Exceptional Children, 67,* 467–484. Copyright © 2001 by the Council for Exceptional Children. Reprinted with permission.

Legislation and Litigation

Much of the progress in meeting the educational needs of children and youths with disabilities is attributable to laws requiring states and localities to include students with special needs in the public education system (Bateman, 2007, 2011; Bateman & Linden, 2006; Huefner, 2006). We focus here on recent legislation that represents a culmination of decades of legislative history. However, litigation (lawsuits or court decisions) has also played a major role in special education (see Rozalski, Miller, & Stewart, 2011; Yell, Katsiyannis, & Bradley, 2011).

A landmark federal law was passed in 1975: the **Education for All Handicapped Children Act**, commonly known as PL 94-142.* In 1990, this law was amended to become the **Individuals with Disabilities Education Act (IDEA)**. In 1997, the law was amended again, but its name was not changed (see Bateman & Linden, 2006, and Yell, 2006, for details). The law was reauthorized again in 2004, as the Individuals with Disabilities Education Improvement Act (IDEIA; see Huefner, 2006, for details). The 2004 reauthorization is sometimes referred to as IDEA 2004 (Stichter et al., 2008), but for the sake of simplicity we refer to it more simply as IDEA, as the basic requirements of the law have not changed. The federal law known as IDEA ensures that all children and youths with disabilities have the right to a free, appropriate public education.

---

*Legislation is often designated PL (for public law), followed by a hyphenated numeral; the first set of digits represents the number of the Congress that passed the bill, and the second set represents the number of that bill. Thus, PL 94-142 was the 142nd public law passed by the 94th Congress.

FOCUS ON Concepts

MAJOR PROVISIONS OF IDEA

Each state and locality must have a plan to ensure*:

Identification	Extensive efforts to screen and identify all children and youths with disabilities.
Free Appropriate Public Education (FAPE)	Every student with a disability has an appropriate public education at no cost to the parents or guardian.
Due Process	The student's and parents' rights to information and informed consent before the student is evaluated, labeled, or placed, and the right to an impartial due process hearing if they disagree with the school's decisions.
Parent/Guardian Surrogate Consultation	The student's parents or guardian are consulted about the student's evaluation and placement and the educational plan; if the parents or guardian are unknown or unavailable, a surrogate parent must be found to act for the student.
Least Restrictive Environment (LRE)	The student is educated in the least restrictive environment consistent with his or her educational needs and, insofar as possible, with students without disabilities.
Individualized Education Program (IEP)	A written individualized education program is prepared for each student with a disability, including levels of functioning, long-term goals, extent to which the student will *not* participate in the general education classroom and curriculum, services to be provided, plans for initiating and evaluating the services, and needed transition services (from school to work or continued education).
Nondiscriminatory Evaluation	The student is evaluated in all areas of suspected disability and in a way that is not biased by his language or cultural characteristics or disabilities. Evaluation must be by a multidisciplinary team, and no single evaluation procedure may be used as the sole criterion for placement or planning.
Confidentiality	The results of evaluation and placement are kept confidential, though the student's parents or guardian may have access to the records.
Personnel Development, In-service	Training for teachers and other professional personnel, including in-service training for general education teachers, in meeting the needs of students with disabilities.

*Detailed federal rules and regulations govern the implementation of each of these major provisions.

Another landmark federal law, enacted in 1990, is the **Americans with Disabilities Act (ADA)**. ADA ensures the right of individuals with disabilities to nondiscriminatory treatment in other aspects of their lives; it provides protections of civil rights in the specific areas of employment, transportation, public accommodations, state and local government, and telecommunications.

IDEA and another federal law focusing on intervention in early childhood (PL 99-457) mandate a free appropriate public education for every child or youth between the ages of 3 and 21, regardless of the nature or severity of the disability. PL 99-457 also provides incentives for states to develop early intervention programs for infants with known disabilities and those who are considered to be at risk. Together, these laws require public school systems to identify all children and youths with disabilities and to provide the special education and related services to these students.

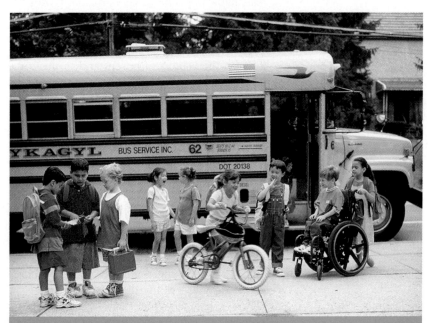

The Individuals with Disabilities Education Act (IDEA), passed in 1990 and renewed in 1997 and 2004, requires public schools to provide equal educational opportunities for all students with disabilities.

The federal law we now know as IDEA was revolutionary because it was the first federal law mandating free appropriate public education for all children with disabilities. Its basic provisions are described in the Focus on Concepts on page 17.

Historically, legislation has been increasingly specific and mandatory. Beginning in the 1980s, however, a renewed emphasis on states' rights and local autonomy plus a political strategy of federal deregulation led to attempts to repeal some of the provisions of IDEA (then still known as PL 94-142) and loosen federal rules and regulations. Federal disinvestment in education and deregulation of special education programs remain popular ideas. It's not surprising that federal mandates for special education have come under fire. Dissatisfaction with federal mandates is due in part to the fact that the federal government contributes relatively little to the funding of special education. Although the demands of IDEA are detailed, state and local governments pay most of the cost of special education programs. Some have characterized the legal history of special education as a "long, strange trip" (Yell, Rogers, & Rogers, 1998, p. 219). Special education law is highly controversial, and battles over IDEA are ongoing. The amendment and continuation of IDEA in 1997 and 2004 represented a sustained commitment to require schools, employers, and government agencies to recognize the abilities of people with disabilities, but the extent to which the 2004 revision of the law represents actual improvement is debatable (Turnbull, 2007; Vitello, 2007). IDEA and ADA require reasonable accommodations that will allow those who have disabilities to participate to the fullest extent possible in all the activities of daily living that individuals without disabilities take for granted. The requirements of ADA are intended to grant equal opportunities to people with disabilities in employment, transportation, public accommodations, state and local government, and telecommunications.

In the early 21st century, under the administration of President George W. Bush, the federal No Child Left Behind Act (NCLB) became a major factor in the focus of public schooling, including special education (see Huefner, 2006; Yell & Drasgow, 2005). NCLB was an attempt to improve the academic performance of all students, including those with disabilities. In fact, under NCLB and IDEA, most students with disabilities are expected to take standard tests of academic achievement and to achieve at a level equal to that of students without disabilities. Moreover, NCLB included the requirement that eventually all teachers be "highly qualified," a designation that leaves much to interpretation (Gelman, Pullen, & Kauffman, 2004). Some have noted that core requirements of NCLB are neither reasonable nor achievable, particularly with reference to special education (Kauffman, 2004, 2005, 2010; Kauffman & Konold, 2007; Rothstein, Jacobsen, & Wilder, 2006).

Laws often have little or no effect on the lives of individuals with disabilities until courts interpret exactly what the laws require in practice. Exceptional children, primarily through the actions of parent and professional organizations, have been getting their day in court more frequently since IDEA and related federal and state laws were passed. Therefore, we must examine litigation to complete the picture of how the U.S. legal system may safeguard or undermine appropriate education for exceptional children.

Zelder (1953) noted that in the early days of public education, school attendance was seen as a privilege that could be awarded to or withheld from an individual child at the discretion of local school officials. During the late 19th and early 20th centuries, the courts typically found that disruptive children or those with mental retardation (intellectual disabilities) could be excluded from school for the sake of preserving order, protecting the teacher's time from excessive demands, and sparing children the discomfort of seeing others who are disabled. In the first half of the 20th century, the courts tended to defend the majority of schoolchildren from a disabled minority. But now the old excuses for excluding students with disabilities from school are no longer thought to be valid.

Today, the courts must interpret laws that define school attendance as the right of every child, regardless of her disability. Litigation is now focused on ensuring that every child receives an education that is appropriate for her individual needs. As some legal scholars have pointed out, this doesn't mean that laws or litigation support full inclusion of all children with disabilities in general education (Bateman, 2007, 2011; Dupre, 1997; Huefner, 1994, 2006).

Litigation may involve legal suits filed for either of two reasons: (1) because special education services aren't being provided for students whose parents want them or (2) because students are being assigned to special education when their parents believe that they shouldn't be. Suits for special education have been brought primarily by parents whose children are unquestionably disabled and are being denied any education at all or are being given very meager special services. The parents who file these suits believe that the advantages of their children's identification for special education services clearly outweigh the disadvantages. Suits against special education have been brought primarily by parents of students who have mild or questionable disabilities and who are already attending school. These parents believe that their children are being stigmatized and discriminated against rather than helped by special education. Thus, the courts today are asked to make decisions in which individual students' characteristics are weighed against specific educational programs.

Parents want their children with disabilities to have a free public education that meets their needs but doesn't stigmatize them unnecessarily and that permits them to be taught in the general education classroom as much as possible. The laws governing education recognize parents' and students' rights to such an education. In the courts today, the burden of proof is ultimately on local and state education specialists, who must show in every instance that the student's abilities and disabilities have been completely and accurately assessed and that appropriate educational procedures are being employed. Much of the special education litigation has involved controversy over the use of intelligence (IQ) and other standardized testing to determine students' eligibility for special education. Although the debate about IQ tests has been acrimonious, some scholars have found that IQ scores themselves haven't been the primary means of classifying children as eligible for special education (MacMillan & Forness, 1998).

One historic court case of the 1980s deserves particular consideration. In 1982, the U.S. Supreme Court made its first interpretation of PL 94-142 (now IDEA) in *Hudson v. Rowley*, a case involving Amy Rowley, a child who was deaf (*Board of Education of Hendrick Hudson v. Rowley*, 1982). The Court's decision was that appropriate education for a deaf child with a disability does not necessarily mean education that will produce the maximum possible achievement. Amy's parents had contended that she might be able to learn more in school if she were provided with a sign language interpreter. But the Court decided that because the school had designed an individualized program of special services for Amy and she was achieving at or above the level of her nondisabled classmates, the school system had met its obligation under the law to provide an appropriate education.

Future cases will undoubtedly help to clarify what the law means by "appropriate education" and "least restrictive environment" (Bateman, 2007; Crockett & Kauffman, 1999; Huefner, 1994, 2006; Yell, 2006). In Chapter 2, we go into more detail about the law and what it requires. We pay particular attention to writing individualized education programs (IEPs) and to the meaning of *least restrictive environment (LRE)*.

COMMENT ON PROGRESS IN SPECIAL EDUCATION

Special education has come a long way since it was introduced into U.S. public education over a century ago. It has become an expected part of the public education system, a given rather than an exception or an experiment. Much progress has been made since IDEA was enacted more than a quarter century ago. Now parents and their children have legal rights to a free appropriate education; they aren't powerless in the face of school administrators who don't want to provide appropriate education and related services. The enactment of IDEA was one of very few events in the 20th century that altered the power relationship between schools and parents (Gerber, 2011; Sarason, 1990).

Although IDEA and related laws and court cases have not resulted in flawless programs for exceptional children, they have done much to move U.S. public schools toward providing better educational opportunities for those with disabilities (Bateman, 2007). Laws enacted in the 20th and 21st centuries help to ensure that all infants and toddlers with disabilities receive early intervention. Laws such as ADA help to ensure that children and adults with disabilities won't be discriminated against in U.S. society. Laws and court cases can't eliminate all problems in our society, but they can certainly be of enormous help in our efforts to equalize opportunities and minimize handicaps for people with disabilities. But more than law is required to give exceptional learners the education they need. Special education also depends on guidance from other concepts and perspectives, specifically, the

INTERNETRESOURCES

For updated information about special education law, you may want to Google special education law or go to the Wrightslaw web site at http://www.wrightslaw.com

chapter

2

Current Practices for Meeting the Needs of Exceptional Learners

Come writers and critics
Who prophesize with your pen
And keep your eyes wide,
The chance won't come again.
And don't speak too soon
For the wheel's still in spin
And there's no tellin' who
That it's namin'
For the loser now
Will be later to win
For the times they are a-changin'.

QUESTIONS **to guide your reading of this chapter . . .**

- How are students with exceptionalities evaluated and identified for special education services in school settings?
- How is the intent of special education law implemented in individualized education for students with disabilities?
- What are the various placement options for exceptional learners?
- What are the main arguments for and against full inclusion?
- What are the current practices in schools regarding collaboration and response to intervention?
- What are the roles of general and special educators in providing exceptional learners an individualized education program?
- What are the trends and issues in integrating students with exceptionalities into schools?
- What impact does standards-based reform have on special education?
- What are our concluding thoughts about providing services to exceptional learners?

MISCONCEPTIONS ABOUT
Learners with Disabilities

MYTH • All professionals agree that technology should be used to its fullest to aid people with disabilities.

FACT • Some believe that technology should be used cautiously because it can lead people with disabilities to become too dependent on it. Some professionals believe that people with disabilities can be tempted to rely on technology instead of developing their own abilities.

MYTH • All students with disabilities must now be included in standardized testing, just like students without disabilities.

FACT • Most students with disabilities will be included in standardized testing procedures, but for some, a given test is deemed inappropriate. Some students will require adaptations of the testing procedure to accommodate their specific disabilities. However, students with disabilities can no longer be automatically excluded from participating in standardized assessment procedures.

MYTH • Research has established beyond a doubt that special classes are ineffective and that inclusion is effective.

FACT • Research comparing special versus general education placement is inconclusive because most of these studies have been methodologically flawed. Researchers are now focusing on finding ways to make inclusion work more effectively.

MYTH • Everyone agrees that teachers in early intervention programs need to assess parents as well as their children.

FACT • Some authorities now believe that although families are an important part of intervention programming and should be involved in some way, special educators should center their assessment efforts primarily on the child, not the parents.

MYTH • Everyone agrees that good early childhood programming for students with or without disabilities should be the same.

FACT • Considerable disagreement exists among professionals about whether early intervention programming for children with disabilities should be child directed, as is typical of regular preschool programs, or more teacher directed.

MYTH • Professionals agree that all students with disabilities in secondary school should be given a curriculum focused on vocational preparation.

FACT • Professionals are in conflict over how much vocational versus academic instruction students with mild disabilities should receive.

ob Dylan could have written "The Times They Are A-Changin'" (see excerpt on p. 23) for special education, which has a rich history of controversy and change. Controversy and change make teaching and studying disabilities challenging and exciting. The history of special education, described briefly in Chapter 1, is replete with unexpected twists and turns. Many developments in the past have had unanticipated consequences, and many of today's events and conditions will have consequences that we don't foresee.

Dramatic changes have occurred in the first decade of the 21st century, and more changes will undoubtedly follow. One critically important issue in special education today is the identification of students for special education services, particularly in the area of learning disabilities. The long-term debate over methods of identification has resulted in response to intervention, an approach to identifying students with learning disabilities, which has captured the attention of researchers and practitioners alike. The movement toward multicultural special education—the subject of Chapter 3—has also been in the forefront of the special education field. In this chapter we explore the major trends in providing services to exceptional learners as well as the significant issues in responding to the needs of individuals with disabilities.

EVALUATION AND IDENTIFICATION OF EXCEPTIONAL LEARNERS

Although the landscape of special education has changed dramatically since the passage of PL 94-142: The Education for All Handicapped Children Act, one issue has remained constant. In 1975 the intent of the original law was the same as the intent today, to ensure that all children with disabilities receive a free appropriate public education (FAPE) (Yell & Crockett, 2011). To provide students with disabilities appropriate educational services in the setting that maximizes their potential (the least restrictive environment), schools must employ effective practices in identifying exceptional learners. A longstanding debate continues on how to best identify students who are exceptional learners. In the following sections, we discuss two primary methods for identifying students for special education services.

PEARSON
myeducationlab

To check your comprehension on the content covered in Chapter 2, go to the Book-Specific Resources in the MyEducationLab (www .myeducationlab.com) for your course, select your text, and complete the Study Plan. Here you will be able to take a chapter quiz, receive feedback on your answers, and then access review, practice, and enrichment activities to enhance your understanding of chapter content. ■

Prereferral Teams

Traditionally, when a teacher observed that a child was struggling in school, a group of professionals (e.g., special education teachers, counselors, administrators, psychologists), called a **prereferral team (PRT)**, was convened to work with the general education teacher to help identify alternative educational strategies for the student before making a referral for special education evaluation. A teacher typically asked for help after exhausting her own strategies for helping a student who was difficult to teach. The team reviewed the information about a student that the teacher brought to the group. The colleagues then offered suggestions about what the teacher might try to do to help the student. If the student continued to struggle, he was then referred to special education, and a full evaluation was conducted.

Groups of professionals sometimes work with general education teachers to help identify strategies for students who are struggling.

Although PRTs have been very popular and are still in practice today, little research has been conducted on their effectiveness (see Hallahan, Lloyd, Kauffman, Weiss, & Martinez, 2005).

Response to Intervention

In the most recent reauthorization of the Individuals with Disabilities Education Act (IDEA), Congress included an additional option for determining eligibility for special education in the case of suspected learning disabilities that forces varying levels of support in general education before referral to special education. The regulations state: "in determining whether a child has a specific learning disability, states may rely on a process that determines whether the child responds to scientific, research-based intervention as a part of the evaluation." In practice, this concept has been termed **response to intervention (RTI)**.

INTERNETRESOURCES

For more information about the effective implementation of Response to Intervention, visit the website of the RTI Action Network at http://www.rtinetwork.org/ And you can find a collection of papers describing the roles of professionals in the RTI process at http://www.asha.org/uploadedFiles/slp/schools/prof-consult/rtiroledefinitions.pdf

WHAT IS RTI?   Response to intervention refers to a student's change (or lack of change) in academic performance or behavior as a result of instruction (Duhon, Messmer, Atkins, Greguson, & Olinger, 2009; Fuchs, Mock, Morgan, & Young, 2003; O'Connor & Sanchez, 2011). In an RTI identification model, a student must first receive quality instruction in the general education classroom before a formal evaluation for special education services. Teachers gather data to determine whether the student is benefiting from that instruction. Only after educators determine that a student is nonresponsive to quality, research-based instruction by a general educator would a formal evaluation to special education occur.

RTI is usually associated with learning disabilities and academic learning. However, it has implications for students with any disability and is not confined to academic learning but can be applied to social behavior as well (Cheney, Flower, & Templeton, 2008; Fairbanks, Sugai, Guardino, & Lathrop, 2007). Practitioners have applied various RTI approaches for students with various disabilities, including emotional and behavioral disorders, intellectual disabilities, autism, and giftedness.

MULTITIERED MODEL FOR IDENTIFICATION   The RTI approach is based on a multitiered model of prevention. No model is universally accepted; however, RTI typically provides for three progressively more intensive tiers of instruction for students who are experiencing difficulties (Mercer, Mercer, & Pullen, 2011; O'Connor & Sanchez, 2011). Generally, the first tier includes screening of students who may be at risk of academic failure; implementation of quality, research-based instruction; and weekly monitoring of student progress (Fuchs, Fuchs, & Stecker, 2010). The teacher monitors the student's progress in the curriculum and in relation to peers and provides differentiated instruction. If the student's achievement improves, no other action is taken. If the student's performance doesn't improve, the student moves to Tier 2. In Tier 2, the student usually receives small-group instruction by a teacher or highly-trained assistant three to four times per week with a research-validated program in the areas of difficulty (e.g., reading or writing). If the student's performance doesn't improve at this level, a multidisciplinary team is convened to determine whether a student has a disability and therefore qualifies for Tier 3, which is special education. Tier 3 includes more intensive intervention provided by a special educator in an appropriate placement. Figure 2.1 illustrates how instruction and possible placement in special education is facilitated in an RTI framework.

ASSESSMENT PRACTICES IN AN RTI MODEL   The basic purposes of assessment in an RTI model are to identify students who may be at increased risk of school failure and to collect data to determine the effectiveness of instruction so that appropriate instructional decisions can be made (Mercer et al., 2011). The two most common forms of assessment in an RTI process are screening and progress monitoring.

Teachers or school psychologists use **screening instruments** to identify those students who may be at increased risk of school failure. Screening instruments are typically administered to an entire group of students and may be given to a large number of students in a short period of time. School personnel use results of the screening administrations to identify students for whom additional progress monitoring and Tier-2 instruction are required.

Progress monitoring assessments are frequent, quick-and-easy measures that teachers administer at regular intervals and that provide information on whether a student is learning as expected. The purpose of administering progress-monitoring instruments is to de-

Federal law requires that the inclusion of students with disabilities in assessments of progress in the general education curriculum must be addressed in every individualized education program (IEP).

FIGURE 2.1 Three-tiered response-to-intervention model

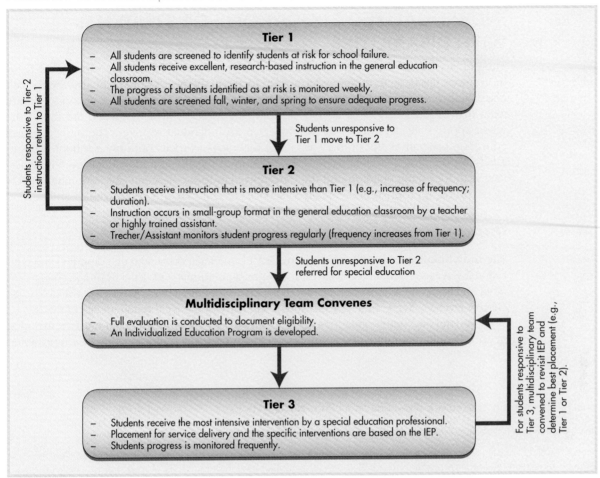

termine whether current instructional practices are appropriate for individual students and to identify instructional needs. One common form of progress monitoring is **curriculum-based measurement (CBM)**. CBM involves students' responses to their usual instructional materials; it entails direct and frequent samples of performance from the students' curriculum. CBM measures are commonly used as a way to determine students' responsiveness to RTI (L. S. Fuchs et al., 2007). We discuss CBM in more detail throughout the text as it relates to the assessment and instruction of students with various exceptionalities.

SUPPORT FOR RTI IDENTIFICATION MODELS   Advocates of an RTI identification model claim that it will reduce the number of students referred to special education. The argument is that as a result of high-quality instruction provided at every level, RTI helps to determine whether a student is truly a student with a disability and not a student who has been subjected to poor or missing instruction (see Boardman & Vaughn, 2007). Unfortunately, little research evidence is available to determine whether RTI is effective. Only a few school districts in the country have used it on a wide scale (Fuchs et al., 2003). Nevertheless, IDEA gives schools the option of using RTI for identification of learning disabilities, as well as a means of improving instruction for all students. Recently, some have argued that although RTI is defensible as a way of improving early intervention and instruction for struggling learners, its use as a means of identifying disabilities is questionable (Boardman & Vaughn, 2007; Kavale, Kauffman, & Bachmeier, 2007). We discuss these issues further in Chapter 6, on learning disabilities.

THE INTENT OF SPECIAL EDUCATION LAW: INDIVIDUALIZED EDUCATION FOR STUDENTS WITH DISABILITIES

The primary intent of the special education law passed in 1975 and the subsequent reauthorizations has been to require educators to focus on the needs of individual students with disabilities to ensure that they receive appropriate educational services. A multidisciplinary team that includes school or agency personnel as well as the parents and the individual when appropriate determines the services that an individual receives. The individualized education program is the primary aspect of this focus; it spells out how a school plans to meet an exceptional student's needs. In addition to the IEP, the individualized family service plan for young children and the transition plan for adolescents are important aspects of providing appropriate individualized services to children and youth with disabilities.

Individualized Education Programs

The **individualized education program (IEP)** is the legal document that describes the educational services a student receives. IEPs vary greatly in format and detail from one child to another and from one school district to another. Guides for help in writing IEPs are available (e.g., Gibb & Dyches, 2007). Table 2.1 provides a summary of the legal requirements of the IEP.

Federal and state regulations don't specify exactly how much detail must be included in an IEP, only that it must be a written statement developed in a meeting of a representa-

TABLE 2.1 Legal requirements of the Individualized Education Program (IEP)

According to the Individuals with Disabilities Education Act (IDEA) 2004, the required contents of an IEP include the following:

1. A statement of the child's present levels of academic achievement and functional performance. On many IEP forms, this is called the PLOP (present level of performance). In some cases the PLOP is now listed as the PLAAFP (present level of academic achievement and functional performance).
2. A statement of measurable annual goals, including academic and functional goals. The law states clearly that the goals should enable the child to access the general education curriculum.
3. A description of how the child's progress toward meeting the annual goals will be measured and when periodic reports on the progress the child is making toward meeting the annual goals will be provided.
4. A statement of the special education and related services and supplementary aids and services the child will receive. The services must be based on peer-reviewed research.
5. A statement of any individual appropriate accommodations that are necessary to measure the academic achievement and functional performance of the child on standardized achievement assessments. If the child is to take an alternate assessment instead of a particular regular state or districtwide assessment, a statement of why the child cannot participate in the regular assessment and why the particular alternate assessment selected is appropriate for the child.

The IEP also requires the following related-to-transition services for students at age 16:

1. Appropriate measurable postsecondary goals based on age-appropriate transition assessments related to training, education, employment, and independent living skills (if appropriate).
2. The transition services (including courses of study) needed to assist the child in reaching those goals.

The law also stipulates the make-up of the IEP team. The following individuals must be a part of the IEP team:

1. The parents of a child with a disability.
2. A minimum of one regular education teacher.
3. A minimum of one special education teacher or special education provider of the child.
4. A representative of the local educational agency. This individual should be qualified to provide, or supervise the provision of, specially designed instruction to meet the unique needs of children with disabilities, knowledgeable about the general education curriculum, and knowledgeable about the availability of resources.
5. An individual who can interpret the instructional implications of evaluation results.
6. Other individuals who have knowledge or special expertise regarding the child, including related services personnel as appropriate. The parents or the local education agency (LEA, i.e., school) may appoint these individuals as they see appropriate.
7. The child with a disability, whenever appropriate.

Source: Individuals with Disabilities Education Act, U. S. Department of Education.

tive of the local school district, the teacher, the parents or guardian, and (whenever appropriate) the child, and that it must include certain elements. The IEP that is written in most schools contains much information related to the technical requirements of IDEA in addition to the heart of the plan: its instructional components. Figure 2.2 shows what an IEP might look like. Curt "is a ninth-grade low achiever who was considered by the district to be a poorly motivated disciplinary problem student with a 'bad attitude.' His parents recognized him as a very discouraged, frustrated student who had learning disabilities, especially in language arts" (Bateman, 2011; Bateman & Linden, 2006, p. 150).

FIGURE 2.2 Sample IEP for Curt

Individualized Education Program

Student: Curt   Age: 15   Grade: 9   Date: 2010

Unique educational needs, characteristics, and measured present levels of academic achievement and functional performance (PLOPs) *(including how the disability affects the student's ability to participate & progress in the general curriculum)*	Special education, related services and supplemental aids and services, (based on peer-reviewed research to the extent practicable); assistive technology and modifications or personnel support *(including anticipated starting date, frequency, duration, and location for each)*	Measurable annual goals and short-term objectives (progress markers),[1] including academic and functional goals to enable students to be involved in and make progress in the general curriculum and to meet other needs resulting from the disability *(including progress measurement method for each goal)*
Present Level of Social Skills: Curt lashes out violently when not able to complete work, uses profanity, and refuses to follow further directions from adults.[2] **Social Needs:** • To learn anger management skills, especially regarding swearing • To learn to comply with requests	1. Teacher and/or counselor consult with behavior specialist regarding techniques and programs for teaching skills, especially anger management. 2. Provide anger management for Curt. Services 3 times/week, 30 minutes. 3. Establish a peer group which involves role playing, etc., so Curt can see positive role models and practice newly learned anger management skills. Services 2 times/week, 30 minutes. 4. Develop a behavioral plan for Curt which gives him responsibility for charting his own behavior. 5. Provide a teacher or some other adult mentor to spend time with Curt (talking, game playing, physical activity, etc.). Services 2 times/week, 30 minutes. 6. Provide training for the mentor regarding Curt's needs/goals.	*Goal:* During the last quarter of the academic year, Curt will have 2 or fewer detentions for any reason. Obj. 1: At the end of the 1st quarter, Curt will have had 10 or fewer detentions. Obj. 2: At the end of the 2nd quarter, Curt will have had 7 or fewer detentions. Obj. 3: At the end of the 3rd quarter, Curt will have had 4 or fewer detentions. *Goal:* Curt will manage his behavior and language in an acceptable manner as reported by all of his teachers. Obj. 1: At 2 weeks, asked at the end of class if Curt's behavior and language were acceptable or unacceptable, 3 out of 6 teachers will say "acceptable." Obj. 2: At 6 weeks, asked the same question, 4 out of 6 teachers will say "acceptable." Obj. 3: At 12 weeks, asked the same question, 6 out of 6 teachers will say "acceptable."

[1]For students who take an alternative assessment and are assessed against other than grade-level standards, the IEP **must** include short-term objectives (progress markers). For other students, the IEP **may** include short-term objectives. The IEP **must** for all students clearly articulate how the student's progress will be measured, and that progress must be reported to parents at designated intervals.
[2]This PLOP would be more useful if it were qualified, e.g., more than 4 times daily.

(continued)

FIGURE 2.2 Continued

Unique educational needs, characteristics, and measured present levels of academic achievement and functional performance (PLOPs)	Special education, related services and supplemental aids and services, (based on peer-reviewed research to the extent practicable); assistive technology and modifications or personnel support	Measurable annual goals and short-term objectives (progress markers),[1] including academic and functional goals to enable students to be involved in and make progress in the general curriculum and to meet other needs resulting from the disability
(including how the disability affects the student's ability to participate & progress in the general curriculum)	*(including anticipated starting date, frequency, duration, and location for each)*	*(including progress measurement method for each goal)*
Study Skills/ Organizational Needs: • How to read text • Note taking • How to study notes • Memory work • Be prepared for class, with materials • Lengthen and improve attention span and on-task behavior Present Level: Curt currently lacks skill in all these areas.	1. Speech/lang. therapist, resource room teacher, and content area teachers will provide Curt with direct and specific teaching of study skills, i.e. • Note taking from lectures • Note taking while reading text • How to study notes for a test • Memorization hints • Strategies for reading text to retain information 2. Assign a "study buddy" for Curt in each content area class. 3. Prepare a motivation system for Curt to be prepared for class with all necessary materials. 4. Develop a motivational plan to encourage Curt to lengthen his attention span and time on task. 5. Provide aide to monitor on-task behaviors in first month or so of plan and teach Curt self-monitoring techniques. 6. Provide motivational system and self-recording form for completion of academic tasks in each class.	*Goal:* At the end of academic year, Curt will have better grades and, by his own report, will have learned new study skills. Obj. 1: Given a 20–30 min. lecture/oral lesson, Curt will take appropriate notes as judged by that teacher. Obj. 2: Given 10–15 pgs. of text to read, Curt will employ an appropriate strategy for retaining info.—i.e., mapping, webbing, outlining, notes, etc.—as judged by the teacher. Obj. 3: Given notes to study for a test, Curt will do so successfully as evidenced by his test score.

[1]For students who take an alternative assessment and are assessed against other than grade-level standards, the IEP **must** include short-term objectives (progress markers). For other students, the IEP **may** include short-term objectives. The IEP **must** for all students clearly articulate how the student's progress will be measured, and that progress must be reported to parents at designated intervals.

When writing an IEP, the team should develop a document that is clear, useful, and legally defensible. The relationships among IEP components must be clear and explicit in order to maintain the focus of the individualized program—special, individually tailored instruction to meet unique needs. In Curt's IEP (Figure 2.2), the relationships among the components are maintained by the alignment of information across columns. Reading across the form, we find first a description of the unique characteristic or need and present level of performance, then the special services and modifications that will address that need, and then the annual goals and objectives or benchmarks related to the need.

FIGURE 2.2 Continued

Unique educational needs, characteristics, and measured present levels of academic achievement and functional performance (PLOPs)	Special education, related services and supplemental aids and services, (based on peer-reviewed research to the extent practicable); assistive technology and modifications or personnel support	Measurable annual goals and short-term objectives (progress markers),[1] including academic and functional goals to enable students to be involved in and make progress in the general curriculum and to meet other needs resulting from the disability
(including how the disability affects the student's ability to participate & progress in the general curriculum)	*(including anticipated starting date, frequency, duration, and location for each)*	*(including progress measurement method for each goal)*
Academic Needs/ Written Language: Curt needs strong remedial help in spelling, punctuation, capitalization, and usage. **Present Level:** Curt is approximately 2 grade levels behind his peers in these skills.	1. Provide direct instruction in written language skills (punctuation, capitalization, usage, spelling) by using a highly structured, well-sequenced program. Services provided in small group of no more than four students in the resource room, 50 minutes/day. 2. Build in continuous and cumulative review to help with short-term rote memory difficulty. 3. Develop a list of commonly used words in student writing (or use one of many published lists) for Curt's spelling program.	*Goal :* Within one academic year, Curt will improve his written language skills by 1.5 or 2 full grade levels to a 6.0 grade level as measured by a standardized test. Obj. 1: Given 10 sentences of dictation at his current level of instruction, Curt will punctuate and capitalize with 90% accuracy (checked at the end of each unit taught). Obj. 2: Given 30 sentences with choices of usage, at his current instructional level, Curt will make the correct choice in 28 or more sentences. Obj. 3: Given a list of 150 commonly used words in 6th grade writing, Curt will spell 95% of the words correctly.
Adaptations to Regular Program: • In all classes, Curt should sit near the front of the class. • Curt should be called on often to keep him involved and on task. • All teachers should help Curt with study skills as trained by spelling/language specialist and resource room teacher. • Teachers should monitor Curt's work closely in the beginning weeks/months of his program.		

[1]For students who take an alternative assessment and are assessed against other than grade-level standards, the IEP **must** include short-term objectives (progress markers). For other students, the IEP **may** include short-term objectives. The IEP **must** for all students clearly articulate how the student's progress will be measured, and that progress must be reported to parents at designated intervals.

Source: Reprinted with permission from Bateman, B. D., & Linden, M. A. (2006). *Better IEPs: How to develop legally correct and educationally useful programs* (4th ed.). Verona, WI: Attainment.

The process of writing an IEP and the document itself are perhaps the most important features of compliance with the spirit and letter of IDEA. Bateman and Linden (2006) summarize this compliance; when the IEP is prepared as intended by the law:

- The student's needs have been carefully assessed.
- A team of professionals and the parents have worked together to design a program of education to best meet the student's needs.
- Goals and objectives are stated clearly so that progress in reaching them can be evaluated.

A major problem is that the IEP is often written at the wrong time and for the wrong reason (Bateman & Linden, 2006). As Figure 2.3 illustrates, the legal IEP is written after evaluation and identification of the student's disabilities and before a placement decision is made: Educators first determine what the student needs and then make a decision about placement in the least restrictive environment in which the needed services can be provided. Too often, we see the educationally wrong (and illegal) practice of basing the IEP

INTERNET RESOURCES

A helpful resource for developing IEPs is available from Wrightslaw at http://www.wrightslaw.com/info/iep.index.htm

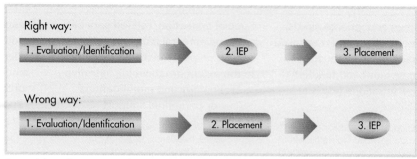

Source: Adapted by permission from Bateman, B. D., & Linden, M. A. (2006). *Better IEPs: How to develop legally correct and educationally useful programs* (4th ed.). Verona, WI: Attainment.

on an available placement; that is, a student's IEP is written after available placements and services have been considered.

Another common error in writing the IEP is a reliance on state standards. A "standards-based" IEP is one that focuses on outcomes based on state standards rather than on individual student needs (Bateman, 2011). Clearly, state standards and access to the general education curriculum are important; however, a student's *individualized* education program should be based on outcomes appropriate for the child and not on dictated state standards.

Individualized Family Service Plan

Federal laws now require that a variety of early intervention services be available to all infants and toddlers who are identified as having disabilities. Such services include special education instruction, physical therapy, speech and language therapy, and medical diagnostic services. As with school-age children with disabilities, a legal document, **individualized family service plan (IFSP)** describes the services that the child will receive. An IFSP is similar to an IEP for older children, but it broadens the focus to include the family as well as the child. In fact, federal regulations stipulate that the family be involved in the development of the IFSP. Table 2.2 describes the legal requirements of an IFSP. As Noonan and McCormick (2006) note, an IFSP may be written for children up to 6 years of age, but usually an IFSP is written for infants and children up to 3 years of age, with the IEP being more common for children three and older.

Transition Plans for Adolescents with Disabilities

Most students complete high school and find jobs, enter a vocational training program, or go to college without experiencing major adjustment difficulties. We know that dropout and

TABLE 2.2 Individuals with Disabilities Education Act (IDEA) requirements for the Individualized Family Services Plan (IFSP)

An IFSP must include

1. A statement of the child's present level of development in these areas: physical (including vision, hearing, and health status), cognitive, communication, psychosocial, and adaptive behavior.
2. A statement of family strengths, resources, concerns, and priorities related to the child's development.
3. A statement of the major outcomes expected to be achieved for the child and family.
4. A statement of the frequency, intensity, and method of delivering the early intervention services necessary to produce desired outcomes for the child and family.
5. A statement of the natural environments where services will be provided or a statement explaining why services will not be provided in natural environments.
6. Projected dates for the initiation of services and anticipated duration of services.
7. The name of a service coordinator responsible for implementation of the IFSP and coordination with other agencies/professionals.
8. Steps to be implemented to ensure successful transition (a transition plan) to preschool services provided by the public schools.
9. Written consent from the parents or legal guardian.

unemployment rates are far too high for all youths, especially in economically depressed communities, but the outlook for students with disabilities is perhaps even worse. We must view published figures on dropout rates with caution because there are many different ways of defining the term and computing the statistics. Studies strongly suggest, however, that a higher percentage of students with disabilities, compared to students without disabilities, have difficulty in making the transition from adolescence to adulthood and from school to work. As a result, many individuals with disabilities do not achieve postsecondary degrees, are unemployed or underemployed, and have lower quality of life outcomes (Everson & Trowbridge, 2011; Moon, 2011; & Scanlon, 2011). Thus, transition to adulthood—which includes employment, postsecondary education, independent living, and community engagement—is an ongoing issue of great importance.

Federal laws, including IDEA, require attention to **transition plans** for older students, and these must be incorporated in students' IEPs. Transition services include a coordinated set of outcome-oriented activities that promote movement from school to postsecondary education, vocational training, integrated employment (including **supported employment**), continuing adult education, adult services, independent living, or community participation.

IDEA requires that each student's IEP contain a statement of needed transition services, when the student is 16 years of age and annually thereafter. (For students for whom it is appropriate or who are deemed at risk of failure, the transition statement must be included in the IEP at a younger age.) In addition, the IEP must include a statement of the linkages and/or responsibilities of each participating agency before the student leaves the school setting.

PROVIDING SPECIAL EDUCATION: PLACEMENT ISSUES FOR EXCEPTIONAL LEARNERS

Several administrative plans are available for the education of exceptional learners, ranging from a few special provisions made by the student's general education teacher to 24-hour residential care in a special facility. Who educates exceptional students and where they receive their education depend on two factors: (1) how and how much the student differs from typical students and (2) what resources are available in the school and community. Administrative plans for education vary according to the degree of physical integration—the extent to which exceptional and nonexceptional students are taught in the same place by the same teachers.

Beginning with the least specialized environment, the general education teacher who is aware of the individual needs of students and is skilled at meeting them may be able to acquire appropriate materials, equipment, and/or instructional methods. This level might not require the direct services of specialists; the expertise of the general education teacher might meet the student's needs. Some students with disabilities can be accommodated without special education.

Alternatively, the general education teacher might need to *consult* with a special educator or other professional (e.g., the school psychologist) in addition to acquiring the special materials, equipment, or methods. The special educator might instruct the general education teacher, refer the teacher to other resources, or demonstrate the use of

INTERNET RESOURCES

Two helpful resources for Early Childhood Special Education include The National Early Childhood Technical Assistance Center at http://www.nectac.org/default.asp and the National Dissemination Center for Children with Disabilities, which provides resources for both individualized family service plans and transition plans for individuals with disabilities at http://www.nichcy.org/

General education teachers often consult with a special education or other professional who can provide resources and advice about specialized methods of instruction for students in inclusive classrooms.

materials, equipment, or methods. Alternatively, the general and special educators might *co-teach*, with each providing instruction and the special educator emphasizing instruction of the exceptional student(s).

A *resource teacher* provides services for students and teachers in a single school. The students served are enrolled in the general education classroom and work with the specially trained teacher for a length of time and at a frequency determined by the nature and severity of their particular problems. The resource teacher continually assesses the needs of the students and their teachers and usually works with students individually or in small groups in a special *resource room*, where special materials and equipment are available. Typically, the resource teacher also serves as a consultant to the classroom teacher, advising on how to instruct and manage the student in the classroom and perhaps demonstrating instructional techniques. The flexibility of the plan and the fact that the student remains with nondisabled peers most of the time have traditionally made this a particularly attractive and popular alternative.

One of the most visible—and, in recent years, controversial—service alternatives is the special *self-contained class*. Such a class typically enrolls 15 or fewer exceptional students with particular characteristics or needs. The teacher ordinarily has been trained as a special educator and provides all or most of the instruction, assisted by a paraeducator. The students assigned to such classes usually spend most or all of the school day separated from their nondisabled peers. Often, students with disabilities are included with nondisabled students during part of the day (perhaps for physical education, music, or some other activity in which they can participate well).

Special *day schools* provide an all-day special placement for exceptional learners who need this level of specialization or dedication to their needs. The day school usually is organized for a specific category of exceptional students and may contain special equipment necessary for their care and education. These students return to their homes during non-school hours.

Hospital or homebound instruction is most often required by students who have physical disabilities, although it's sometimes an option for those with emotional or behavioral disorders or other disabilities when no alternative is readily available. Typically, the youngster is confined to the hospital or the home for a relatively short time, and the hospital or homebound teacher maintains contact with the general classroom teacher.

In a *residential school*, exceptional students receive 24-hour care away from home, often at a distance from their communities. This is the highest level of specialization or dedication on the continuum of alternative placements required by IDEA. These students might make periodic visits home or return each weekend, but during the week, they are residents of the institution, where they receive academic instruction in addition to management of their daily living environment.

Figure 2.4 illustrates the idea of variation in the separation of children from their general education classrooms and peers. It also illustrates the increasing specialization of envi-

FIGURE 2.4 Continuum of placement options showing hypothetical relationship between degree of separateness from general education classroom peers and degree of specialness of education

ronments. The degree to which education is "special" is a continuum. That is, education can be "sort of" special or very, very specialized.

In the process of trying to find effective and economical ways of serving exceptional students, many school systems combine or modify these alternatives and the roles special educators and other professionals play in service delivery. School systems vary widely in the kinds of placements made for particular kinds of students.

Least Restrictive Environment

As we noted in Chapter 1, special education law requires placement of the student in the **least restrictive environment (LRE)**, which usually means that the student should be separated from nondisabled classmates and from home, family, and community as little as possible (see Rozalski & Miller, 2011). That is, the student's life should be as normal as possible, and the intervention should be consistent with individual needs and not interfere with individual freedom any more than is absolutely necessary. For example, students should not be placed in special classes if they can be served adequately by resource teachers, and they should not be placed in a residential school if a special class will serve their needs just as well.

Although placement of exceptional students in the LRE is laudable, the definition of *least restrictive* is not as simple as it seems. Years ago, Cruickshank (1977) pointed out that greater restriction of the physical environment does not necessarily mean greater restriction of psychological freedom or human potential (see also Bateman, 2007; Crockett & Kauffman, 1999, 2001). In fact, it is conceivable that some students could be more restricted in the long run in a general education class where they are rejected by others and fail to learn necessary skills than in a special class or day school where they learn happily and well (Gliona, Gonzales, & Jacobson, 2005; Kauffman, Bantz, & McCullough, 2002; Warnock, 2005).

It is important to keep our ultimate goals for the students in mind and to avoid letting the term *least restrictive* become a hollow slogan that results in shortchanging them in their education (Crockett & Kauffman, 1999, 2001; Huefner, 2006; Kauffman, 1995; Kauffman, McGee, & Brigham, 2004). Mercer and colleagues suggest that the *least restrictive environment* may be better termed the *most enabling environment* (Mercer et al., 2011).

Gliona and colleagues (2005) have suggested a "direct access model" for conceptualizing LRE. As depicted in Figure 2.5, the student is at the center and can access any of the placement options that meet her needs. Figure 2.5 shows LRE choices for two different students. In the first case (a), the IEP team has determined that the student's LRE is a special school. In the second case (b), the IEP team has determined that the student's LRE is a combination of resource room services and regular class placement with consultation.

FIGURE 2.5 Direct access model of placement in the least restrictive environment (LRE). (a) A student whose LRE is a special school. (b) A student whose LRE is a combination of programs.

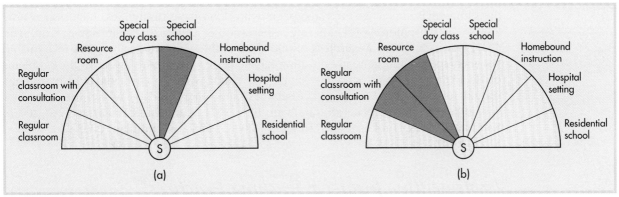

Source: Gliona, M. F., Gonzales, A. K., & Jacobson, E. S. (2005). *Dedicated, not segregated: Suggested changes in thinking about instructional environments and in the language of special education.* In J. M. Kauffman & D. P. Hallahan (Eds.), *The illusion of full inclusion: A comprehensive critique of a current special education bandwagon* (2nd ed., p. 144). Austin, TX: Pro-Ed.

FIGURE 2.6 Approximate percentages of students with disabilities in various placement options in the early 21st century

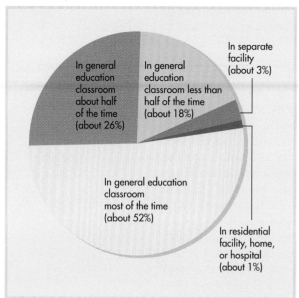

In separate facility (about 3%)

In general education classroom about half of the time (about 26%)

In general education classroom less than half of the time (about 18%)

In general education classroom most of the time (about 52%)

In residential facility, home, or hospital (about 1%)

Source: Data from the annual reports of the U.S. Department of Education (2009) to Congress on the Implementation of the Individuals with Disabilities Education Act.

Since the late 1980s, data have shown a steady trend toward placing more students with disabilities in general education classes and a corresponding trend toward placing fewer students with disabilities in resource rooms, separate classes, and separate facilities (U.S. Department of Education, 1995, 2005, 2009). Considerable variation exists in the placement of students with disabilities from state to state and among school systems within a given state. However, most exceptional students are now educated in general education classes. Nationwide, more than 50% of exceptional children and youths are now served primarily in general education classes. Relatively few students with disabilities are placed outside of regular schools. Figure 2.6 shows the approximate percentage of students served in each type of placement in the early 21st century.

Children under the age of 6 less often receive education in general education classes and more often attend separate schools than do school-age children. Older teenagers and young adults more often attend special classes, separate schools, and other environments such as homebound instruction than do students in elementary and high schools. We can explain these differences with several facts:

- Preschoolers and young adults who are identified for special education tend to have more severe disabilities than do students in kindergarten through grade 12.

- Some school systems do not have general education classes for preschoolers and young adults; therefore, placements in other than general education classes are typically more available and more appropriate.

- Curriculum and work-related educational programs for older teens and young adults with disabilities are frequently offered off the campuses of general education high schools.

LRE depends in part on the individual's exceptionality. For example, students whose primary disability is a speech impairment almost never need placement in a separate class or separate school. Likewise, most students with learning disabilities can be appropriately educated primarily in general education classes. On the other hand, the resources needed to teach students with severe hearing and vision impairments might require that these students attend separate schools or classes for at least part of their school careers.

Inclusion in Schools

Educators often use the term *inclusion* to describe teaching students with disabilities in the same environment as their age peers who don't have disabilities. Inclusion is now an issue in education worldwide (e.g., Anastasiou & Keller, 2011; Simpson & Kauffman, 2007; Warnock, 2005). Regardless of one's views, the controversy about the relationship between special and general education has made teachers more aware of the problems of deciding just which students should be taught specific curricula, which students should receive special attention or services, and where and by whom these services should be provided (Crockett & Kauffman, 1999, 2001; Kauffman & Hallahan, 1997, 2005b; Kauffman, Mock, Tankersley, & Landrum, 2008; Mock & Kauffman, 2005; Zigmond & Kloo, 2011).

Implementing Inclusive Teaching Practices

Whether or not one supports the concept of full inclusion, the fact is that most educators favor some degree of integration of students with disabilities with nondisabled students.

Schools generally use five methods to help students with disabilities participate in the general education classroom:

1. Collaborative consultation
2. Cooperative teaching and other team arrangements
3. Curricula and instructional strategies
4. Accommodations and adaptations
5. Training general education teachers to accommodate diversity

The current trend is toward a variety of collaborative arrangements. All are intended to increase the cooperation between general and special education for the benefit of students with disabilities.

COLLABORATIVE CONSULTATION   Once the IEP team has determined that a student is in fact a student with a disability, the student may receive special education services within the general education classroom through **collaborative consultation**. In collaborative consultation, the special education teacher or psychologist acts as an expert who provides advice to the general education teacher. The special educator might suggest changes to instruction or additional supports, such as behavior plans or school–home notes.

CO-TEACHING   Sometimes referred to as *collaborative teaching* or **cooperative teaching**, co-teaching takes mutuality and reciprocity in collaborative consultation one step further (see Cook, McDuffie, Oshita, & Cook, 2011; Scruggs, Mastropieri, & McDuffie, 2007; Walsh & Jones, 2004). **Co-teaching** between general and special educators means "two or more professionals delivering substantive instruction to a diverse, or blended, group of students in a single physical space" (Cook & Friend, 1998, p. 454).

Effective collaboration among general educators, special educators, and other professionals is a key ingredient in the successful participation of students with disabilities in general education classrooms.

Schools use many forms of co-teaching, but the most common appears to be for one teacher to instruct and the other to assist in some way (Scruggs et al., 2007). Sometimes, teachers find it very effective and workable. Other times, co-teaching can present incredible challenges to teachers and to students. Unfortunately, research on how to ensure that cooperative teaching works is scarce (Zigmond, 2007).

Although there are no pat answers to the questions about how special and general education should work together to ensure that every student receives an appropriate education, it's clear that the relationship must be one of cooperation and collaboration. Despite their differing roles, general and special educators should not function on independent or mutually exclusive educational tracks. In Chapters 5 through 15, a special feature called Making It Work addresses specific issues of inclusion for each disability area.

CURRICULA AND INSTRUCTIONAL STRATEGIES   In addition to teacher cooperation, specific curricula and instructional strategies can help students with disabilities succeed in the general education classroom. **Cooperative learning** is an instructional strategy that many proponents of inclusion believe is an effective way to integrate students with disabilities into groups of nondisabled peers. In cooperative learning, students work together in heterogeneous small groups to solve problems or practice responses.

Another research-based instructional strategy to enhance the integration of students with disabilities is **peer-mediated instruction** (Fuchs et al., 2001; Gardner et al., 2001; Maheady, Harper, & Mallette, 2001; see also Fulk & King, 2001, and the Websites they list).

INTERNETRESOURCES

Vanderbilt University has developed and researched a peer-tutoring model. Resources for this model are provided on their website at http://kc.vanderbilt.edu/kennedy/pals/

Peer-mediated instruction may refer to **peer tutoring**, the use of **peer confederates** in managing behavior problems, or any other arrangement in which teachers deliberately recruit and train peers to help teach an academic or social skill to a classmate (Falk & Wehby, 2001).

When the whole class is involved, the strategy is referred to as **classwide peer tutoring (CWPT)**; all students in the general education classroom routinely engage in peer tutoring for particular subject matter, such as reading or math (Greenwood, Arrega-Mayer, Utley, Gavin, & Terry, 2001; Kourea, Cartledge, & Musti-Rao, 2007). CWPT doesn't mean that the teacher provides no instruction. On the contrary, teachers must provide instruction in how to do peer tutoring and in the content of the tutoring sessions. Peers tutor each other to provide drill and practice of skills they already have.

Partial participation, another instructional strategy, means having students with disabilities participate, on a reduced basis, in virtually all activities experienced by all students in the general education classroom. It questions the assumption that including students with severe intellectual or physical limitations is a waste of time because they cannot benefit from the activities in the same way that nondisabled students can. Whether partial participation actually achieves these goals to the benefit of students is an open question.

INSTRUCTIONAL ACCOMMODATIONS AND ADAPTATIONS Instruction may be modified for learners with disabilities. **Modifications** usually take the form of amended materials or assignments and differ from changes in curricula or instructional strategies. **Accommodations** include changes in instruction that don't significantly change the content or conceptual difficulty level of the curriculum. Alternatively, **adaptations** generally involve more significant modifications of instruction than accommodations (Miller, 2002).

Tiered assignments (Tomlinson, 2001) are an example of adaptations, wherein teachers provide choices for assignments on a single topic that vary in difficulty. For example, when studying a novel, some students might write paragraphs that identify and describe the characters; others might write paragraphs or papers that analyze the traits of each character, using examples from the book. In this case, both the assignment and the subsequent grading differ.

TRAINING GENERAL EDUCATION TEACHERS   One point of view is that both general education and special education teachers are necessary, and that they should work together, but that they have distinct roles to play. Zigmond (2007) describes teaching students with disabilities as a two-person job, meaning that truly effective special education requires both a general education teacher and a special education teacher trained to do different things, not merely to work together with a common purpose. In the press for inclusion and collaboration, Zigmond suggests, perhaps the primary role and function of the special education teacher has gotten lost:

> I propose that a "special education coach" be assigned to each school building to provide consultation and job-embedded staff development that helps build capacity among general education teachers for meeting the needs of diverse learners in their content classes. (p. 130)

Zigmond (2007) argues that the popular co-teaching model of collaboration can't provide the kind of intensive instruction that students with learning disabilities and behavior disorders (and, presumably, many students with other disabilities as well) require if they are to make adequate progress. Moreover, she argues that special education teachers need special expertise in teaching specialized and individualized curricula. General education teachers are content specialists and should be trained by the "special education coach" to address a wider range of instructional needs than they otherwise would have, but they can't take the place of special education teachers (Zigmond & Kloo, 2011).

TEACHERS' ROLES IN PROVIDING SPECIAL EDUCATION

We have noted that most students in public schools who have been identified as exceptional are placed in general education classrooms for at least part of the school day. Furthermore, there is good reason to believe that a large number of public school students who have not been identified as disabled or gifted share many of the characteristics of those who are exceptional. Thus, all teachers must be prepared to deal with exceptional students, although it's unreasonable to expect all teachers to teach all exceptional students (Kauffman & Hallahan, 2005a; Mock & Kauffman, 2002; Zigmond, 2007; Zigmond & Kloo, 2011).

The roles of general and special education teachers are not always clear in a given case. Sometimes, uncertainty about the division of responsibility can be extremely stressful; teachers may feel uneasy because it's not clear whose job it is to make special adaptations for a pupil or just what they are expected to do in cooperating with other teachers.

Relationship Between General and Special Education

During the 1980s, radical reformers began recommending that special education be eliminated as a separate, identifiable part of education, calling for a single, unified educational system in which all students are viewed as unique, special, and entitled to the same quality of education. Although many of the suggested reforms have great appeal and some could produce benefits for exceptional students, the basis for integration of special and general education and the ultimate consequences this might bring have been questioned (e.g., Bateman, 2007; Crockett & Kauffman, 1999, 2001; Fuchs & Fuchs, 1994; Hockenbury, Kauffman, & Hallahan, 1999–2000; Kauffman, 1995, 1999–2000; Kauffman & Hallahan, 2005a, 2005b; Martin, 1995; Mock & Kauffman, 2002, 2005; Warnock, 2005; Zigmond, 2007; Zigmond & Kloo, 2011).

Special Education and Students at Risk

The term *at risk* is often not clearly defined, but it generally refers to students who perform or behave poorly in school and appear likely to fail or fall far short of their potential. Some advocates of reform suggest that at-risk students cannot be or should not be distinguished from those with mild disabilities. Others argue that the problems of at-risk students tend to be ignored because special education siphons resources from general education. Should special education and general education merge for the purpose of making general education better able to respond to students who are at risk? Or should special education maintain its separate identity and be expanded to include these students?

The term *at risk* is often not clearly defined, but generally refers to students who perform or behave poorly and appear likely to fail or fall short of their potential. Should special education be expanded to include these students?

These questions have no ready answers. Regardless of where one draws the line separating students who are considered to be at risk from students with disabilities, the line is arbitrary and leads to doubts about some students. In other words, no entirely clear distinction exists between *at risk* and *disability* because educational achievement and social competence can vary from a little to a lot, and no sudden, dramatic break exists in students' level of attainment (Boardman & Vaughn, 2007; Kauffman & Hallahan, 2005a; Kauffman & Konold, 2007).

Expectations for All Educators

One limitation of all teachers is that they cannot accomplish the miracles portrayed in the popular media, even if they are very good at what they do (Moore, 2007). Real teachers can't be as perky, self-sacrificing, idealistic, and influential as those shown in films, and most teachers can't achieve the same results as those who win awards for exceptional performance. However, competent teachers can make a significant difference in the lives of the children with whom they work, but the expectations set up by media portrayals—and too often by government or the general public—are unrealistic. Teachers, like those employed in other lines of work, must do the best they can with the resources at their disposal. Striving for excellence is admirable, but recognizing one's real-world limitations, keeping one's duties and accomplishments in perspective, and being happy with the best one can do, even if it's less than perfection, is as important for teachers as it is for students.

General and special education teachers share responsibility for determining and implementing effective strategies to meet the special needs of their students.

Regardless of whether teachers are specifically trained in special education, they may be expected to participate in educating exceptional students in any one of the following ways:

1. *Make maximum effort to accommodate individual students' needs.* Teaching in public schools requires dealing with diverse students in every class. All teachers must participate in the RTI process, making an effort to meet the needs of individuals who might differ in some way from the average or typical student. RTI requires the implementation of evidence-based instruction that increases in intensity as necessary. Flexibility, adaptation, accommodation, and special attention are expected of every teacher. Special education should be considered necessary only when a teacher's best efforts to meet a student's individual needs aren't successful.

2. *Evaluate academic abilities and disabilities.* Although a psychologist or other special school personnel might administer a student formal standardized tests in academic areas, adequate evaluation requires the teacher's assessment of the student's performance in the classroom. Teachers must be able to report specifically and precisely how students can and cannot perform in all academic areas for which they are responsible as part of the RTI process.

3. *Refer for evaluation.* By law, all public school systems must make extensive efforts to screen and identify all children and youths of school age who have disabilities. A student shouldn't be referred for special education unless teachers have made extensive and unsuccessful efforts to accommodate the student's needs in general education classes. Before referral, school personnel must document the strategies that have been used to teach and manage the student in general education. Referral is justified only if these strategies have failed. This is typically facilitated through the RTI process.

4. *Participate in eligibility conferences.* Before a student is provided special education, an interdisciplinary team must determine the student's eligibility. Therefore, teachers must be ready to work with other teachers and with professionals from other disciplines (e.g., psychology, medicine, or social work) in determining a student's eligibility for special education.

5. *Participate in writing individualized education programs.* Every student identified with a disability and receiving special education must have a written IEP. Teachers must be ready to participate in a meeting (possibly including the student and/or parents as well as other professionals) to develop the program.

6. *Communicate with parents or guardians.* Educators must consult parents (sometimes surrogate parents) or guardians during the evaluation of the child's eligibility for special education, formulation of the IEP, and reassessment of any special program that may be designed. Teachers must contribute to the school's communication with parents about the child's problems, placement, and progress.

7. *Participate in due process hearings and negotiations.* Parents, guardians, or students with disabilities themselves who are dissatisfied with the school's response to educational needs may request a due process hearing or negotiations regarding appropriate services. Teachers might be called on to offer observations, opinions, or suggestions in such hearings or negotiations.

8. *Collaborate with other professionals in identifying and making maximum use of exceptional students' abilities.* General and special education teachers are expected to share responsibility for educating students with special needs. In addition, teachers

might need to collaborate with other professionals, depending on the given student's exceptionality (e.g., psychologists, counselors, physicians, physical therapists).

A high level of professional competence and ethical judgment is required to conform to these expectations. Teaching demands a thorough knowledge of child development and expertise in instruction. Furthermore, teachers are sometimes faced with serious professional and ethical dilemmas in trying to serve the needs of students and their parents, on the one hand, and in attempting to conform to legal or administrative pressures, on the other (Crockett & Kauffman, 1999; Kauffman & Hallahan, 2007). For example, when a teacher observes indications that a student might have a disability, should the teacher refer the student for evaluation and possible placement in special education, knowing that her school offers only inadequate or inappropriate services? Should a teacher who believes strongly that teenage students with mild intellectual disabilities need sex education refrain from giving students any information because sex education isn't part of the prescribed curriculum and is frowned on by the school board?

Expectations for Special Educators

In addition to being competent enough to meet the expectations for all teachers, special education teachers must attain special expertise in the following areas of skill and knowledge:

1. *Instructing students with learning problems.* The majority of students with disabilities have more difficulty learning academic skills than do those without disabilities. This is true for all categories of disabling conditions because sensory impairments, physical disabilities, and intellectual or emotional disabilities all tend to make academic learning more difficult. Often, the difficulty is slight; sometimes it is extreme. Special education teachers must have more than patience and hope, though they do need these qualities; they must also have the technical skill to present academic tasks so that students with disabilities will understand and respond appropriately. Exceptional instruction is the key to improving special education (Kauffman & Hallahan, 2005a; Kauffman & Landrum, 2007). Table 2.3 lists eight dimensions of instruction that make special education special, although these dimensions are not unique to special education. That is, they are not dimensions of instruction that *only* special educators know about or use. They are modifications or alterations of instructional processes that all teachers use in some way. What makes special education special is not the instruction alone but instruction that is altered to meet the needs of exceptional learners. Kauffman and Hallahan (2005a) point out that general education may be sort of special; Zigmond (2007) concludes it often takes special education teachers to make it as special as it should be.

TABLE 2.3 Dimensions of special education that can make it truly special

Dimension of Instruction	Definition	Alteration of Instruction
1. Pace (Rate)	Speed of lesson; speed of introducing new concepts	Made slower or faster to meet student characteristics
2. Intensity	Demandingness; difficulty; complexity	Size of steps in learning, number of trials, frequency of reviews adjusted to fit learner
3. Relentlessness or Persistence	Insistence; tenacity; stick-to-it-iveness	Repeated attempts, using different methods as required
4. Structure	Explicitness, predictability, teacher direction, tolerance, immediacy of consequences	Adjusted (tightened or loosened) to fit individual student
5. Reinforcement	Reward for desired behavior	Increased, made more frequent, immediate, and explicit or tangible as necessary
6. Pupil/Teacher Ratio (Class Size)	Number of students per teacher	Smaller, more individual
7. Curriculum	Content of instruction, purpose of activity	Determined by individual need
8. Monitoring (Assessment)	Keeping track of progress	Daily or near daily checking (testing) of achievement of specific tasks and goals

2. *Managing serious behavior problems.* Many students with disabilities have behavior problems in addition to their other exceptionalities. Some, in fact, require special education primarily because of their inappropriate or disruptive behavior. Special education teachers must be able to deal effectively with more than the usual troublesome behavior of students. Besides having understanding and empathy, special education teachers must master techniques to draw out particularly withdrawn students, control those who are hyperaggressive and persistently disruptive, and teach critical social skills. Positive, proactive behavior intervention plans are essential for all students who receive special education and exhibit serious behavior problems, regardless of their diagnostic label or classification (Kauffman, Mostert, Trent, & Pullen, 2006; Landrum & Kauffman, 2006).

3. *Evaluating technological advances.* Technology is increasingly applied to the problems of teaching exceptional students and improving their daily lives. Special education teachers must be able to evaluate its advantages and disadvantages for teaching the exceptional children and youths with whom they work.

4. *Knowing special education law.* For good or ill, special education today involves many details of law. The rights of students with disabilities are spelled out in considerable detail in federal and state legislation. These laws, as well as the rules and regulations that accompany them, are constantly being interpreted by new court decisions. Special education teachers don't need to be lawyers, but they do need to be aware of legal requirements and prohibitions if they are to be adequate advocates for students with disabilities (Bateman, 2007; Huefner, 2006; Yell, 2006).

The knowledge and skills that every special education teacher is expected to master have been detailed by the primary professional organization of special educators, the Council for Exceptional Children (1998). These are general expectations and areas of competence with which every special educator will necessarily be concerned; however, special educators have a responsibility to offer not just good instruction but instruction that is highly individualized, intensive, relentless, urgent, and goal directed (Hallahan, 2007; Kauffman & Hallahan, 2005a; Kauffman & Landrum, 2007; Zigmond, 2003, 2007). To this end, the special feature "Responsive Instruction: Meeting the Needs of Students," in Chapters 3 to 15, provides information about research-based practices to help make instruction intensive, relentless, and goal directed.

INTEGRATION OF PEOPLE WITH DISABILITIES INTO THE LARGER SOCIETY

The trend of integrating people with disabilities into the larger society began many decades ago and is stronger than ever today. Champions of integration are proud that they've reduced the number of people who live in institutions and the number of students who attend special schools and special classes. Schools are a part of society, but they aren't miniature reproductions of the larger society (Warnock, 2005). This is why in addition to having discussed inclusion in schools, we next discuss integration into the larger society.

We also note that many of the issues we discuss overlap. For example, universal design for learning, differentiated instruction, and inclusion are not completely separate or distinct issues. Self-determination is often seen as part of transition planning for adolescents and young adults with disabilities. The integration and inclusion of individuals with disabilities into society and school are multifaceted issues, and our discussion is organized around major themes in these processes.

Self-Determination

Deinstitutionalization has fostered increasing recognition that people with and without disabilities have a right to exercise **self-determination**—the right to make one's own decisions about important aspects of one's life, including where to work and live, with whom to become friends, and what education to pursue. "*Self-determination* might be defined by students as 'making our own decisions'" (Sitlington & Clark, 2006, p. 238). Schwartz, Jacobson, and Holburn (2000) suggest that the primary hallmark of **person-centered planning** is that "the person's activities, services and supports are based upon his or her dreams, interests, preferences, strengths, and capacities" (p. 238). The main idea is that people with disabilities should exercise personal control of their lives (Brolin & Loyd, 2004; Chambers et al., 2007; Greene & Kochhar-Bryant, 2003; Powers et al., 2007); other people—such as psychologists, counselors, physicians, parents, teachers, and administrators—should not make decisions for people with disabilities.

Making schools places where all children have a significant voice or say in important decisions is critical. Researchers increasingly recognize that self-determination is learned and should be taught in schools, even in the elementary grades (Browder, Wood, Test, Karvonen, & Algozzine, 2001; Hughes, Wood, Konrad, & Test, 2006; Jones, 2006; Palmer & Wehmeyer, 2003).

TAKING CHARGE OF ONE'S LIFE   In general, self-determination means taking charge of one's life. Teachers can play an important role in promoting the abilities and attitudes students will need to take charge of their lives, through providing instruction in self-determination skills and creating environments where these skills can be practiced. Some professional organizations have policy statements regarding self-determination. We discuss self-determination further in Chapter 5.

DOES SELF-DETERMINATION FIX DISABILITIES?   For some disabilities, such as severe mental illness, making decisions about one's own treatment may be perpetuating human degradation (Earley, 2006). Thus, what may seem to be a universally accepted idea may, in fact, apply only within narrow cultural traditions or environmental circumstances or may depend on the nature of the disability.

A key goal for individuals with disabilities is learning skills that promote self-determination, which is the ability to make choices, control their own lives, and be self-advocates.

Also at issue is whether person-centered planning, as part of self-determination, represents a false hope rather than a tested and proven strategy for integrating people with developmental disabilities into the larger society. Osborne (2005), for example, states:

> I have argued that PCAs [person-centered approaches] . . . are the latest in a long line of *faux fixes*, all purportedly techniques to deal with persons who have developmental disabilities. A *faux fixe* is literally a false fix of a problem. Usually it is politically correct (for the moment at least) procedure or movement in the social sciences, of which there is uncritical adoption . . . in the face of difficult-to-solve problems. (p. 318)

Universal Design and Universal Design for Learning

Based on the architectural principles of **universal design**, **universal design for learning (UDL)** serves the general purpose of making learning accessible to more students in inclusionary programs. The idea is that with modifications of *representation* (materials), *expression* (methods of communication), and *engagement* (how students respond to curriculum), teachers can include a much wider range of students in typical classroom instruction (Spooner, Baker, Harris, Ahlgrim-Delzell, & Browder, 2007).

MAKING THINGS USABLE BY MORE PEOPLE   Access to the World Wide Web by people with disabilities is a current trend with significant implications for design. Section 508 of the Rehabilitation Act requires that federal agencies must ensure equal access by those with and without disabilities to new electronic and information technology as well as information and services. Furthermore, IDEA urges educators to consider the use of assistive technology in servicing students with disabilities, to allow a greater diversity of students to be accommodated in typical classrooms (Spooner et al., 2007).

INTERNETRESOURCES

The Office of Special Education Programs (OSEP) has a useful toolkit of UDL resources at http://www .osepideasthatwork.org/UDL/ letter.asp

DOES UNIVERSAL DESIGN ELIMINATE THE NEED FOR CUSTOM DESIGN?   One continuing issue is when to assume that the limits of universal design have been reached and go ahead with production. Inventors and designers may do their best to be "smart from the start" (Pisha & Coyne, 2001), but perhaps no one can be certain that no potential user's needs have been overlooked. At some point, someone decides to put a gadget or technology into production under the assumption that the design is as universal as it can be made at that time.

Modifications of instruction used in UDL can make lessons appropriate for a wider range of students than has typically been the case. Thus, teachers must not overlook the possibility that they could be designing lesson plans that are appropriate for a greater variety of students.

Perhaps the term *universal*, like the term *all*, should not be taken too literally, or it becomes self-defeating. Very likely, the need to "customize" for individuals will always exist. Even in instruction, some special education researchers note that students with disabilities need individualized instruction that is not most appropriate for students without disabilities (e.g., Zigmond, 2007).

Technological advances of all types can have implications for people with disabilities.

Use of New Technologies

As technology becomes ever more sophisticated, the issue of independence will become ever more important. One general guideline might be that if the technology allows people with disabilities to do something they couldn't do without it, then the technology is in their best interest. However, if it allows them to do something new or better but at the same time imposes new limitations, then one might need to rethink the technology's benefits.

Technological advances of all types can have implications for people with disabilities. Advances in three technologies stand out as particularly important: (a) medical treatment, (b) human reproduction, and (c) communication. Some of these advances, particularly those in medical treatment and human reproduction, are very controversial. The controversy is typically about whether something that *can* be done *should* be done, and it may involve two or three of the technologies we discuss. For example, should **cochlear implantations**, artificial inner ears, (discussed further in Chapter 11), be used to allow deaf children to hear whenever possible? This issue involves both medical treatment and communication, and it could involve human reproduction as well. Should disabilities be corrected surgically before birth (in utero), if that is possible? Should the findings of fetal stem cell research be applied to cure or correct physical disabilities if possible? What characteristics of their children should parents be allowed to choose? These are some of the controversial ethical issues that we discuss in later chapters.

THE UPSIDE AND THE DOWNSIDE OF TECHNOLOGY   As the pace of technology quickens, so do applications of these technologies to the daily lives of people with disabilities. In many ways, technologies expand the abilities of people with or without disabilities to access information, communicate, travel, and accomplish many other everyday tasks. Technological applications can also allow some people with disabilities to function like those without disabilities.

Some downsides are dependence on technology and the problem of reliability. People tend to rely on whatever technology they use rather than learn how to do things in alternative ways, so they have no idea how to do things the "old-fashioned" way when a gadget malfunctions.

SHOULD WE DO SOMETHING BECAUSE WE CAN?   An issue that is likely to become more controversial is whether we *should* do all the things that we *can* with new technologies. The moral and ethical dilemmas created by the availability of means to eliminate limitations such as being unable to hear, see, walk, or communicate—whether they are considered disabilities or not—will increase in years to come. Particularly troubling will be

INTERNETRESOURCES

For more information about technology and special education, visit the Website of the Center for Applied Science Technology at http://www.cast.org

the issue of whether we *should* allow parents to create "designer babies" to any extent that we *can*. For example, should we allow parents to create children with or without what most people consider disabilities? The ability to select embryos (or create them) with or without certain characteristics (e.g., deafness, dwarfism, diabetes, tendency toward schizophrenia or depression), in addition to presenting ethical dilemmas, raises difficult issues about the definition and meaning of disability (Kauffman & Hallahan, 2007).

SPECIAL EDUCATION IN THE CONTEXT OF STANDARDS-BASED REFORM

The standards-based reform movement of the 1990s and early 2000s has been based on the fact that state and federal policy makers became concerned about what they perceived as a general decline in students' educational achievement. As a result, they emphasized "standards-based" reforms. These reforms involve setting standards of learning that are measured by standardized tests. The reformers believed that teachers' expectations have been too low and that all students should be held to higher standards (see Finn, Rotherham, & Hokanson, 2001; Hoover & Patton, 2004; Pugach & Warger, 2001; Thurlow, 2000; Thurlow, Nelson, Teelucksingh, & Draper, 2001).

The standards-based reform movement has brought with it a heavy emphasis on access to the general education curriculum for students with disabilities (Hoover & Patton, 2004; Pierangelo & Giuliani, 2006; Thurlow & Quenemoen, 2011; Zigmond, 2007). The curriculum for students with disabilities often has differed from the curriculum in general education. Failure to teach students with disabilities the same things that are taught in general education has been interpreted to mean that the expectations for these students are lower, resulting in their low achievement and failure to make a successful transition to adult life.

Understandably, the standards-based reform movement has generated much controversy: What should be the curriculum? What should the standards be? Who should set the standards? How should achievement of or progress toward the standards be measured? What should be the consequences for students—and for schools or states—if standards aren't met? What should be given up in music, art, poetry, physical education, and other areas to ensure progress on standardized tests in core curriculum areas of reading and math?

For students with disabilities, additional questions arise: Should all standards apply to all students, regardless of disability? Under what circumstances are alternative standards appropriate? Under what circumstances should special accommodations be made in assessing progress toward a standard? Answering questions like these requires professional judgment in the individual case, and such judgment is required by law (see Bateman, 2007, 2011; Huefner, 2006; Johns, 2003; Kauffman & Hallahan, 2005a; Yell, 2006). Moreover, expecting students with disabilities to score the same, on average, as students without disabilities is expecting the impossible (Kauffman, 2004; Kauffman & Konold, 2007; Kauffman & Wiley, 2004).

Currently, the Elementary and Secondary Education Act (ESEA) is undergoing reauthorization. It will likely have a new name; No Child Left Behind (NCLB) will be a name of the past. Subsequent to the reauthorization of ESEA will be a reauthorization of IDEA. Both laws will undoubtedly focus on standards-based assessment, accountability, and access to the general education curriculum for students with disabilities.

Assessment Issues in the Age of Accountability

The intent of the laws discussed previously (NCLB and IDEA 1997, 2004) was to improve the instruction of students with disabilities to ensure that these students are included in the assessments of educational progress demanded of all students. Although assessment has always been an important factor in special education, it has taken the spotlight in the era of standards-based reform. NCLB required that the average scores of various subgroups of students be reported and that all groups, including students with disabilities, show progress.

The intent of special education law has been to improve the instruction of students with disabilities to ensure that these students are included in the assessments of educational progress demanded of all students.

The assessments in which students with disabilities are expected to participate in order for these comparisons to be made are considered outcome measures.

OUTCOME MEASURES   Outcome measures differ from the screening and progress monitoring measures described earlier in the context of RTI. Educators use screening and progress measures to identify students who may be at risk for disability and to provide ongoing data to assist in program planning and typically administer these measures in group settings. Outcome measures compare a student's performance with other students, or compare a state's or district's performance with other states or districts.

TESTING ACCOMMODATIONS   Some students with disabilities who are included in standardized measures of achievement are entitled to receive testing accommodations. Testing accommodations are procedures that ensure equitable assessment access for students with disabilities (Thurlow, 2010). Although testing accommodation may involve altering the administration procedure or format of a test, the construct that is being measured does not change (Lazurus, Thurlow, Lail, & Christensen, 2009).

Accommodations for evaluation procedures might involve altering setting, the presentation format, or the response format. The nature of the accommodation is based on the specific need of the student. Setting or scheduling accommodations alter the setting or time of the assessment, such as small-group administration and extended time. Presentation accommodations alter the way the assessment is presented to the student, such as having problems and directions read aloud. Response accommodations alter the way in which the student answers questions on the assessment, such as oral or typed responses.

Can We Solve the Dilemma of Standards and Disability?

Some consider it cruel to both students and teachers to require all students with disabilities, and those for whom the tests are inappropriate for other reasons, to take state exams (Kauffman, 2002, 2004; Kauffman & Konold, 2007; Kauffman & Wiley, 2004). However, testing to determine outcomes is necessary if we want to know whether programs for students with disabilities are "working" (Kauffman & Konold, 2007). Standardized tests have a legitimate place in assessing outcomes, and demonizing the tests themselves is not helpful. However, it's important to understand that "testing is useful only if you make the right comparisons for the right reasons" (Kauffman, 2002, p. 240). When it comes to special education, it's wrong to compare outcomes for students with disabilities to outcomes for students without disabilities. The right comparisons are contrasting students with disabilities who receive special education (or any given treatment) to those who don't receive it, or comparing students with disabilities before and after they receive special education (Kauffman, 2004; Kauffman & Hallahan, 2005a).

CONCLUDING THOUGHTS REGARDING SPECIAL EDUCATION

It is understandable to feel overwhelmed by the controversial nature of special education; a number of unanswered questions face our field. It seems that just as we find what we think are the right answers to a certain set of questions about how to educate students with disabilities, more challenging questions emerge.

It would be easy to view this inability to reach definitive conclusions as indicative of a field in chaos. We disagree. This constant state of questioning is a sign of health and vigor, an indication that special education is based on scientific understanding, not on philosophy or mere speculation. Far from seeking and providing final answers, science thrives on the unknown and on controversy. True, there are rules for inquiry: science is all about examining the most reliable information (see Kauffman & Sasso, 2006a, 2006b; Mostert, Kavale, & Kauffman, 2008; Sasso, 2001, 2007).

The controversial nature of special education makes it exciting and challenging. We would be worried (and we believe people with disabilities and their families would be worried, too) if professionals in special education were suddenly in complete agreement on all important issues in the field. We should constantly strive to find better ways to provide education and related services for people with disabilities based on the best evidence we can obtain (Lloyd & Hallahan, 2007). In this endeavor, differences of opinion are inevitable.

SUMMARY

How are exceptional learners evaluated and identified to receive special education services?

- Pre-referral teams have a long history in the special education identification process.
- *Response to intervention* refers to students' response to scientific, research-based instruction.
- Although response to intervention has been suggested as a means of identifying students with learning disabilities, some question its usefulness as an identification tool.

How is the intent of special education law implemented in individualized education for students with disabilities?

- The primary concern of the law (IDEA) is that every child with a disability be given a free appropriate public education (FAPE).
- The IEP is an attempt to make certain a program has been written for each child with a disability and that:
  - The student's needs have been carefully assessed.
  - A team of professionals and the parents have worked together to design a program of education to best meet the student's needs.
  - Goals and objectives are stated clearly so that progress in reaching them can be evaluated.
- The IEPs of students with disabilities must, by law, incorporate transition plans at a minimum by age 16.
- Early intervention is mandated by law; a cornerstone of early intervention is the individualized family service plan (IFSP).

How is special education provided?

- Special education may range from a few special provisions made by the student's regular teacher to 24-hour residential care in a special facility. The plan that is chosen depends on two factors:
  - How and how much the student differs from average students
  - What resources are available in the school and community
- Different placement options include the following, including combinations:
  - General education placement with the teacher making accommodations
  - General education with consultation with a special education teacher
  - Itinerant services from a specialist
  - Resource room services
  - Special self-contained class
  - Special day school
  - Hospital or homebound instruction
  - Residential school
- Federal law (IDEA) calls for placement in the least restrictive environment (LRE) that is compatible with the student's needs

What are the current practices for integrating students with exceptionalities into schools?

- The major issues involve full inclusion, collaboration with general education, response to intervention, participation in assessments of educational progress, early intervention, transition, and discipline.

What are the controversies related to full inclusion?

- Full inclusion is very controversial; it is based on four assumptions:
  - Labeling of people is harmful.
  - Special education pullout programs have been ineffective.
  - People with disabilities should be viewed as a minority group.
  - Ethics should take precedence over empiricism.
- Opponents of full inclusion put forth the following arguments:
  - Professionals and parents are largely satisfied with the current level of integration.
  - General educators are unwilling and/or unable to cope with all students with disabilities.
  - Although equating disabilities with minority group status is in many ways legitimate, there are limitations in translating it into educational programming recommendations.
  - An unwillingness to consider empirical evidence is professionally irresponsible.
  - Available empirical evidence does not support full inclusion.
  - In the absence of data to support one service-delivery model, special educators must preserve the continuum of placements.

What are the current practices in collaboration with general education?

- *Collaboration* with general education means that special educators and general educators work together in arrangements such as prereferral teams, consultation, and co-teaching.
- Some educators question the effectiveness of popular forms of collaboration such as co-teaching and recommend that special education teachers be involved either in training general education teachers to accommodate a wider range of students or in actually teaching students with disabilities.

What are the strategies for integrating people with disabilities into the larger society?

- The major trends and issues involve normalization, deinstitutionalization, self-determination, universal design, and the use of new technologies.

What are the trends and issues in universal design?

- *Universal design* refers to the principle that a device or program should be workable for as many potential users as possible.
- Although devices and programs may be designed for a wide variety of users, few can be made usable by literally all, and custom designs will probably always be necessary for some users.

What are the current strategies in the use of technologies?

- The major technologies that are controversial for people with disabilities involve medical advances, human reproduction, and communications.
- There is controversy about whether we *should* do something just because we *can*.

What are the issues related to special education in the context of standards-based reform?

- Both IDEA and NCLB require the participation of most students with disabilities in general assessments of educational progress.
- Proponents of participation suggest that special education has not been held accountable for students' progress.
- Some educators point out that even with good instruction the average achievement of students with disabilities will always be lower than the average for students without disabilities.

What are our concluding thoughts about current practices in special education?

- We believe controversy indicates that the field of special education is alive and well.
- We should constantly strive to make special education better.

COUNCIL FOR EXCEPTIONAL CHILDREN

Addressing the Professional Standards

Council for Exceptional Children (CEC) Common Core Knowledge and Skills addressed in this chapter: ICC1K4, ICC1K6, ICC7K5, ICC7S1, ICC7S2, ICC7S7, ICC7S9, ICC8K3, ICC8K4, ICC8S1, ICC8S4, ICC9S12, ICC10S5, ICC10S6, ICC8S6, ICC10K1, ICC10K3, ICC10S2, ICC10S4

Appendix: Provides a full listing of the CEC Common Core Standards and associated Knowledge and Skill Statements listed here.

MYEDUCATIONLAB

Now go to Topic 1: Law, LRE, & IEPs in the MyEducationLab (www.myeducationlab.com) for your course, where you can:

- Find learning outcomes for the broad concepts covered in this chapter along with the national standards that connect to these outcomes.
- Complete Assignments and Activities that can help you more deeply understand the chapter content.
- Examine challenging situations presented in the IRIS Center Resources.
- Apply and practice your understanding of the core concepts and skills identified in the chapter with the Building Teaching Skills and Dispositions learning units.
- Check your comprehension on the content covered in the chapter by going to the Study Plan in the Book-Specific Resources for your text. Here you will be able to take a chapter quiz, receive feedback on your answers, and then access Review, Practice, and Enrichment activities to enhance your understanding of chapter content.
- Watch video clips of CCSSO Teacher of the Year award winners responding to the question: "Why I teach?" in the Teacher Talk section.

chapter

3

Multicultural and Bilingual Aspects of Special Education

I think schools are a crucial—probably the most crucial—site for inviting us to view ourselves in a different mirror. I think schools have the responsibility to teach Americans about who we are and who we have been. This is where it's important for schools to offer a more accurate, a more inclusive multicultural curriculum. The classroom is the place where students who come from different ethnic or cultural communities can learn not only about themselves but about one another in an informed, systematic and non-intimidating way. I think the schools offer us our best hope for working it out. I would be very reluctant to depend upon the news media or the entertainment media, which do not have a responsibility to educate.

Ronald Takaki • *"Reflections from a Different Mirror"*

QUESTIONS to guide your reading of this chapter . . .

- In what ways do we see universality of cultural pride and shame?
- What is American about multiculturalism?
- What are the important concepts about cultural diversity for education?
- What are the most important aspects of multicultural and bilingual special education?

MISCONCEPTIONS ABOUT
Multicultural and Bilingual Aspects of Special Education

MYTH • Multicultural education addresses the concerns of ethnic minorities who want their children to learn more about their history and the intellectual, social, and artistic contributions of their ancestors.

FACT • This is a partial truth. In fact, multicultural education seeks to help the children of all ethnic groups appreciate their own and others' cultural heritages—plus our common American culture that sustains multiculturalism.

MYTH • Everyone agrees that multicultural education is critical to our nation's future.

FACT • Some people, including some who are members of ethnic minorities, believe that multicultural education is misguided and diverts attention from our integration into a distinctive, cohesive American culture.

MYTH • Implementing multicultural education is a relatively simple matter of including information about all cultures in the curriculum and teaching respect for them.

FACT • Educators and others are struggling with how to construct a satisfactory multicultural curriculum and multicultural instructional methods. Nearly every aspect of the task is controversial: which cultures to include, how much attention to give to each, and what and how to teach about them.

MYTH • Multiculturalism includes only the special features and contributions of clearly defined ethnic groups.

FACT • Ethnicity is typically the focal point of discussions of multiculturalism, but ethnicity is sometimes a point of controversy if it is defined too broadly (for example, by lumping all Asians, all Africans, or all Europeans together). Besides ethnic groups, other groups and individuals—such as people identified by gender, sexual orientation, religion, and disability—need consideration in a multicultural curriculum.

MYTH • Disproportionate representation of ethnic minorities in special education is no longer a problem.

FACT • Some ethnic minorities are still underrepresented or overrepresented in certain special education categories. For example, African American students, especially males, are overrepresented in programs for students with emotional disturbance and underrepresented in programs for gifted and talented students.

MYTH • Disability is never related to ethnicity.

FACT • Some disabilities are genetically linked and therefore more prevalent in some ethnic groups. For example, sickle-cell disease (a severe, chronic, hereditary blood disease) occurs disproportionately in children with ancestry from Africa, Mediterranean and Caribbean regions, Saudi Arabia, and India.

MYTH • If students speak English, their teachers do not need to be concerned about bilingual education.

FACT • Conversational English is not the same as the more formal and sometimes technical language used in academic curriculum and classroom instruction. Educators must make sure that students understand the language that is used in teaching, not just informal conversation.

Many nations and regions are splintered into factions, clans, tribes, and gangs. In some cases, this splintering has been accompanied by extreme cruelty of individuals or groups toward others. Differences—especially those of national origin, religion, ethnic origin, color, custom, sexual orientation, social class, and disability—are too often the basis for viciousness.

No personal characteristic of skin color, ethnic identity, sexual identity, nationality, religion, disability—or any other cultural marker—immunizes one against the mistreatment of others. This remains a central problem of humankind. In the early 21st century, slavery is still practiced in some nations of the world, and "civilized" people mistreat prisoners who might or might not differ from their guards in nationality, ethnicity, religion, or other cultural features. Suicide bombers kill and maim others. Terrorists kill, maim, and threaten, and acts of war do the same. Not so long ago, systematic efforts were made in a highly "civilized" society to exterminate people with disabilities, and we would be wise to learn the lessons history can teach us about our personal and collective capacity for brutality (Mostert, 2002).

Despite the ongoing mistreatment of others based on cultural difference, few of us would want to live in a world without diversity. Cultural diversity should be a valued component in the human experience; it is one that has sparked periods of advancement and change throughout history. The adventures of Marco Polo in China brought about changes in Italian culture and eventually the entire European continent. Similarly, when African slaves in America encountered European music, they blended it with their African music to create the spirituals, and out of the spirituals grew other musical genres such as blues, jazz, and gospel (Gardner, Ohio State University). History provides countless examples of cultures learning from each other, as well as, unfortunately, countless examples of people of one culture devaluing individuals from another.

All cultures and ethnic groups of the world can take pride in much of their heritage, but all also bear a burden of indignity because at some time they have engaged in the ruthless treatment or literal enslavement of others. Sometimes this treatment has extended to minority members of their own larger group whose differences have been viewed as undesirable or intolerable. Not only is religion the basis for conflict (in places such as Northern Ireland and Iraq), but just the appearance of being different or assumptions about appearances have been sufficient to trigger discrimination. For example, in his memoir *Angela's Ashes*, Frank McCourt (1996) describes how in the mid-20th century, some Catholics in Ireland looked askance at what they called "Protestant hair":

> Come here till I comb your hair, said Grandma. Look at that mop, it won't lie down. You didn't get that hair from my side of the family. That's that North of Ireland hair you got from your father. That's the kind of hair you see on Presbyterians. If your mother had married a proper decent Limerickman you wouldn't have this standing up, North of Ireland, Presbyterian hair. (p. 128)

In virtually every nation, society, religion, ethnic group, tribe, or clan, discrimination exists against those who are different. It's therefore critically important that we learn to accept the principle that those who differ from us are equals as human beings. Furthermore, all educators need to understand the purpose of **multicultural education**, which aims for educational institutions and curricula that provide equal educational opportunities to students regardless of their gender, social class, ethnicity, race, disability, or other cultural identity. It also seeks to socialize students to a multicultural norm: acceptance of and respect for those whose culture differs from one's own and knowledge of our shared history. Schools play a central role in multicultural education, as Takaki notes in his comments in the chapter's opening quotation.

Multiculturalism also involves the specter of collective versus individual pride and guilt in behavior. Is the entire group of people that compose a culture justified in taking pride in the fact that one of their group has accomplished something notable? Is an entire group of people—perhaps a nation—guilty for the acts of some of its members? Clearly, the assignment of collective guilt is a convenient, time-honored way of perpetuating discrimination, ethnic cleansing, genocide, and other acts of violence. Collective pride can blind people to the faults of members of a group and create a false sense of worthiness.

myeducationlab

To check your comprehension on the content covered in Chapter 3, go to the Book-Specific Resources in the MyEducationLab (www.myeducationlab.com) for your course, select your text, and complete the Study Plan. Here you will be able to take a chapter quiz, receive feedback on your answers, and then access review, practice, and enrichment activities to enhance your understanding of chapter content. ∎

INTERNETRESOURCES

The Kennedy Center's ArtsEdge provides arts-integrated resources for the K–12 classroom. America, A Home for Every Culture includes lesson plans related to multicultural education (http://artsedge.kennedy-center.org/content/2316/). The Yale-New Haven Teacher's Institute also provides resources for the classroom (http://www.yale.edu/ynhti/curriculum/units/1994/4/94.04.04.x.html).

AMERICA AND MULTICULTURALISM

Nothing in this world reflects diversity more than nature. The landscape of Earth is an intricate mix of shapes, forms, and colors each with its own identity and spirit, separate, and yet a piece of a whole. The land we live in probably best reflects this notion. The landscape of the United States, a quilt woven of dramatically different terrains, is populated by people equally as unique and diverse. Glancing over the entire country from the Pacific to the Atlantic, you see many different environments coexisting: warm deserts, snowcapped mountains, golden plains, green valleys, lush marshlands, sandy beaches, and bustling cities. All are different, yet one: the United States. No less than its geography, the people who inhabit the United States also exemplify nature's diversity (de Melendez & Beck, 2010, p. 5).

America is an increasingly diverse country, as de Melendez and Beck (2010) eloquently describe. Our desire as Americans should be to build a diverse but just society in which the personal freedom and pride of all cultural groups and respect for others' cultural heritage are the norm, a society in which fear, hate, and abuse are eliminated and in which guilt or accomplishment is not determined by association. Working toward this ideal demands a multicultural perspective, one from which we can simultaneously accomplish two tasks. First, we must renew our efforts to achieve social justice and take specific steps to understand and appreciate one another's cultures. Second, in doing so, we must pledge our first loyalty to common cultural values that make diversity a strength rather than a fatal flaw. We seek a commitment to our common humanity and to democratic ideals that bind people together for the common good and give all of them freedom for the rightful honoring of their heritage.

Multicultural education has its critics, some of whom see it as eroding the moral foundations of society and undermining the central purpose of schooling: ensuring the academic competence of students. Multiculturalism is sometimes distorted into indefensible ideology (Ravitch, 2003); we don't understand how the multicultural education that we advocate can be anything but helpful in students' academic learning and socialization to American ideals.

Since the civil rights movement of the 1960s, educators have become increasingly aware of the extent to which differences among cultural and ethnic groups affect children's schooling. Gradually, educators and others are coming to understand that the cultural diversity of the United States and the world demands multicultural education. Progress in constructing multicultural education has been slow, however, in part because of the way in which all cultural groups tend to view themselves as the standard against which others should be judged.

Education that takes full advantage of the cultural diversity in our schools and the larger world requires much critical analysis and planning. It can be very difficult for all cultural or ethnic groups to find common satisfaction in any specific curriculum, even if they are all seeking what they consider the multicultural ideal. Moreover, some argue that the more important goal is finding the common American culture and ensuring that our children have a common cultural literacy (Ravitch, 2003). Even the metaphors that we use for dealing with cultural diversity and cultural unity are points of controversy. The United States has often been called a "cultural melting pot," but some now reject the notion of total melding or amalgamation; they reject the metaphor of an alloy in which metals are dissolved in each other and fused into a new substance. Those who reject the alloy or melting pot metaphor want each identifiable group to be recognized as separate, distinct, and legitimate in its own right.

It's common to dwell on the problems associated with cultural differences. However, a world void of diversity would be dull and uneventful. Multiculturalism is an intricate component to the human experience and the advancement of societies.

Personal PERSPECTIVES
Desegregation and Degeneration

With a shortage of smart teachers (and any teachers in some areas), it is not surprising that the least experienced and lowest-scoring teachers are teaching the neediest students. Districts want to keep middle-class parents and good teachers happy, so they rarely challenge union seniority policies that allow the best teachers to clump together in less needy schools. When resources are scarce, the least powerful get the least.

Choice is the new euphemism for white flight. Now that those who desire schools that enroll "our kind" have pushed suburban sprawl to its limit, they have turned to parental choice, including vouchers, as a way to use public funds for private purposes. The parental choice provisions of the No Child Left Behind (NCLB) act were almost an afterthought in many urban school districts, which already catered to primarily middle-class parents through extensive choice programs. Charters are another form of separation, as a recent study found in Boston: no English-language learner was enrolled in a charter school, only half of the charter school students were low-income compared to three-fourths in the traditional Boston schools, and only one in 10 had a disability. Charter schools now seem to offer a new haven for the advantaged.

Source: Lewis, A. C. (2004). Desegregation and degeneration. *Phi Delta Kappan, 85,* 643–644. Reprinted by permission.

That racism and discrimination remain serious problems in the United States and most other nations and societies of the world is obvious. People of every cultural description struggle with the meaning of differences that might seem trivial or superficial to some but elicit powerful emotional responses and discrimination from others. As Anne Lewis points out in the accompanying Personal Perspectives feature, the problems of desegregating schools have remained in the face of the May 1954 *Brown vs. Board of Education* Supreme Court decision that ended legal racial segregation (Lewis, 2004). The No Child Left Behind Act of 2002 (NCLB) can be seen as another law making "white flight" and segregation of school possible (see Kauffman & Konold, 2007).

Misunderstanding and suffering are still often associated with differences in color as well as gender, religion, sexual orientation, family affiliation, abilities and disabilities, and political beliefs. Antisemitism and other racist attitudes still exist in all regions of America as well as in all nations of the world, and no cultural group is entirely free of prejudice and other racist sentiments. Consider the experience of Susie Kay, a Jewish teacher in a Washington, DC, high school where all the students are African American:

> Kay's students say they know about white culture mainly from television shows; hardly any interact regularly with whites—"Caucasians," as they call them. Most have never met a Jewish person, except for Miss Kay, who wears her Star of David necklace every day. Prompting students to ask, "Isn't that the star of the Devil?"
>
> "And what's the difference between a white person and a Jew anyway?" asks another. "Both are rich, right?" (Horwitz, 1998, p. F1)

The solution is not as simple as becoming sensitized to differences. Too often, Eurocentrism is met with Europhobia, Afrocentrism with Afrophobia, homocentrism with homophobia, sensitivity to difference with hypersensitivity about being different. Nor is the solution to become "blind" to difference (see Hicks, 2005). The simple reality is that we cannot accept or accommodate what we do not see and label (Kauffman, 2001, 2003; Kauffman & Hallahan, 2005). Perhaps the solution includes both engendering sensitivity to differences and building confidence that one's own differences won't be threatened by others. The solution might also require helping students learn how to view themselves and others from different perspectives.

We're optimistic about multicultural education because it's an opportunity to face our nation's shared problems squarely and to extract the best human qualities from each cultural heritage. It provides the opportunity to develop an appreciation of our individual and shared cultural treasures and to engender acceptance, if not love, of all differences that are not destructive of the human spirit. The best antidote for cultural insularity is inclusiveness. Insularity will be overcome by adherence to truly American values of multiculturalism.

Multiculturalism is now a specialized field of study and research in education, and its full exploration is far beyond the scope of this chapter. Of particular concern to special educators is how exceptionalities are related to cultural diversity and the way in which special education fits within the broader general education context in a multicultural society. Cultural diversity presents particular challenges for special educators in three areas: assessment of abilities and disabilities, instruction, and socialization. Before discussing each of these challenges, we summarize some of the major concepts about education and cultural diversity that set the context for multicultural and bilingual special education.

EDUCATION AND CULTURAL DIVERSITY

Culture has many definitions. However, most definitions include the following elements:

1. Values and typical behavior
2. Languages or dialects
3. Nonverbal communication
4. Awareness of one's cultural identity
5. World views or general perspectives

These elements can together make up a national or shared culture. Within the larger culture are many **subcultures** that share the common characteristics of the larger culture. The term *subculture* shouldn't be interpreted to mean anything other than a part (not the total) of the larger or general culture. Subculture doesn't mean lesser in importance, nor does it indicate that one group is dominated by another. We prefer the term *subculture* to *microculture* simply because *sub* can mean associated with or part of whereas *micro* means small. Some subcultures aren't small and may, in fact, be the majority group in a given region, state, organization, or other group. European Americans are a subculture in the United States of America, although they have to date been the majority of Americans. But, of course, European Americans can be considered as subcultures described by their region or nation of origin, as well as by other categories.

Subcultures include all of the various subcategories of citizens that one might name, including various political parties, ethnic identities, gender, sexual orientation, age, and disability (and subcultures include the largest subgroup in any given area, which, although perhaps the largest in its region, is not all of the larger culture). Subcultures may have unique values, behavior, languages or dialect, nonverbal communication, awareness, identity, and views. Some subcultures are voluntary (e.g., religion, political party), and some are involuntary (e.g., skin color, gender). Figure 3.1 illustrates that an individual might identify with the larger, general culture and also belong to many different subcultures. The variety of subcultures to which a person belongs affects his or her behavior. The larger, general culture in the United States consists of certain overarching values, symbols, and ideas, such as justice, equality, and human dignity. Within the United States, subcultures might share these common values but differ in many other ways.

The number of subcultures represented in U.S. schools has increased in recent decades because of the variety of immigrants from other countries, particularly Southeast Asia. The number has also increased, however, because of greater recognition of and sensitivity to subcultures, such

Effective multicultural education promotes pride in their own cultures and understanding and appreciation of different cultures among all students, and it ensures equal educational opportunities for all students, regardless of cultural background.

as those represented by disability, age, sexual orientation, religion, and so on.

Many American children live in poverty. Poverty clearly places children at higher risk of disability compared to children who are reared in conditions of economic advantage (Fujiura & Yamaki, 2000). Poor living conditions and lack of quality health care may result in both physical and psychological distress leading to chronic health concerns and disability (Lustig & Strauser; 2007). Many urban children spend a great deal of time on the streets or are homeless (Walker, 2000). Thus, the United States in the 21st century is more diverse than ever in the subcultures it includes—diverse in ethnic groups, economic status, lifestyles, and disabilities.

Students from some subcultures in U.S. society do extremely well in school, but others don't. The factors accounting for the school performance of subcultures are complex, and social scientists are still searching for the attitudes, beliefs, traditions, and opportunities that foster the success of specific cultural groups. Although considerable evidence indicates that various ethnic minority communities have a strong influence on students' achievement and school behavior, we offer three cautions. First, we need to guard against stereotypes—assumptions that one's cultural identity is sufficient to explain academic achievement or economic success. Second, the fact that some minority communities may have a strong influence on school success doesn't relieve schools of the obligation to provide a multicultural education. All students need to feel that they and their cultural heritage are included in the mainstream of American culture and schooling. Third, unless teachers and other school personnel value minority students—see value and promise in them and act accordingly by setting challenging but not unreachable expectations—the support of families and the minority community may be insufficient to improve the academic success of minority students. Too often, minority students are devalued in school, regardless of their achievements and behaviors.

The general purposes of multicultural education are to promote pride in the positive aspects of one's own cultural heritage and understanding of cultures that differ from one's own, foster positive attitudes toward cultural diversity, and ensure equal educational opportunities for all students. These purposes cannot be accomplished unless students develop an understanding and appreciation of their own cultural heritage, as well as an awareness and acceptance of cultures different from their own. Understanding and appreciation are not likely to develop automatically through unplanned contact with members of other cultures. Rather, teachers must plan experiences that teach about culture and provide models of cultural awareness and acceptance and the appreciation of cultural diversity.

On the surface, teaching about cultures and engendering an acceptance and appreciation of cultural diversity appear to be simple. However, two questions immediately complicate things: Which cultures shall we include? What and how shall we teach about them? The first question demands that we consider all the cultures that might be represented in the school and the difficulties inherent in including them all. In some urban school districts with large numbers of immigrant children, more than 20 different languages may be spoken in students' homes. If any subgroup is not represented in any given class or school activity or if the proportion of students in any given class or school activity isn't the same as the proportion of that group in the student body, then some people will consider it to be segregated. Answering the second question is also problematic because it's often difficult to know what to teach and how. Some cultural groups find the traditions, ceremonies, values, holidays, and other characteristics of other cultures unacceptable or even offensive. That is, when it comes to what and how to teach about other cultures, the stage may be set

FIGURE 3.1 Individuals belong to many different subculture groups

Source: Reprinted with permission from James A. Banks (2006), *Cultural Diversity and Education: Foundations, Curriculum and Teaching, Fifth Edition.* Boston: Allyn & Bacon/Pearson, p. 77.

for conflict. Treating all cultures with equal attention and respect can present substantial or seemingly insurmountable logistical and interpersonal problems.

Ethnic or national origin is only one dimension of cultural diversity, one branch of many in the multicultural program. Ethnicity isn't the only representation of culture, and much variation of culture occurs within any ethnic group (Anastasiou, Gardner, & Michail, 2011). In fact, assuming that all individuals of a particular racial, ethnic, disability, or other cultural group have the same values and perspectives is a form of stereotyping (see Kauffman, Conroy, Gardner, & Oswald, 2008).

One of the most controversial aspects of multicultural education is the use of language. For instance, is it appropriate to refer to a *minority* or *minorities* when the group to which we refer constitutes half or more of the population in a given school, district, region, or state? What labels and terms are acceptable for designating various groups? What languages or dialects should teachers use for instruction? With the arrival of many immigrants to the United States, the issue of bilingual education and its relationship to multiculturalism has become increasingly important. As we discuss later, bilingual education is of even greater concern when considering children with disabilities (Gersten & Baker, 2000).

Given the multiplicity of subcultures, each wanting—if not demanding—its precise and fair inclusion in the curriculum, it isn't surprising that educators sometimes feel caught in a spiral of factionalism and feuding. Additional questions about cultural values inevitably must be addressed: Which cultural values and characteristics should we embrace? Which, if any, should we shun? Would we, if we could, fully sustain some cultures, alter some significantly, and eliminate others? Consider, for example, cultures in which women are treated as chattel, as well as the drug culture, the culture of street gangs, and a culture that tolerates slavery. To what extent does every culture have a right to perpetuate itself? How should we respond to some members of the Deaf culture, for example, who reject the prevention of deafness or procedures and devices that enable deaf children to hear, preferring deafness to hearing and wishing to sustain the Deaf culture deliberately (see Kauffman & Hallahan, 2005; Mundy, 2002)? How should educators view and react to subcultures that reject studying and school achievement (see Welsh, 2004)?

Depending on how we define culture, the values of our own cultural heritage, and our role in multicultural education, we might find ourselves embroiled in serious cultural conflicts. No wonder that some describe the late 20th and early 21st centuries as an era of "culture wars." To deal effectively with the multicultural challenge, we must focus on the challenges that are most pertinent to special education.

MULTICULTURAL AND BILINGUAL SPECIAL EDUCATION

The subcultures that are of particular importance for special education are ethnic groups and exceptionality groups. Banks and Banks (2010) note that an *ethnic group* has a common historic origin and a shared identity, heritage, and tradition. It has value orientations, behavioral patterns, and often political and economic interests that differ from those of other groups in the larger society. An ethnic group may be a majority or a minority of people in a given country or region. We define an *exceptionality group* as a group sharing a set of specific abilities or disabilities that are especially valued or that require special accommodation within a given subculture. Thus, a person may be

One of the most controversial aspects of multicultural education is the use of language. With the arrival of many immigrants to the United States, the issue of bilingual education has become increasingly important.

identified as exceptional in one ethnic group (or other subculture defined by gender, social class, religion, etc.) but not in another. The inability to read or speak standard English, for example, may identify a student as having a disability in an English-speaking culture, but the same student would not be considered disabled in a culture in which English-language skills are unimportant.

What is the best way to train teachers to be aware of their own cultural histories and biases? Because of the relatively poor performance of many students of color in schools, many parents and policy makers, as well as teacher educators, see better teacher education as critically important. Making certain that every classroom is staffed by a "highly qualified" teacher is one of the objectives of NCLB, but "highly qualified" is a concept that is open to question (Gelman, Pullen, & Kauffman, 2005). In fact, in the reauthorization of that law, the language of a "highly qualified" teacher is likely to be replaced with the term "highly effective" teacher.

Part of the better training of teachers is helping them to be more knowledgeable about and responsive to both their own and their students' cultures. Some teacher educators suggest that this can be accomplished only if teachers understand their own culture's history of community, rules, ways of handling tasks, language, and values related to people and outcomes (Artiles, Trent, Hoffman-Kipp, & Lopez-Torres, 2000; Osher et al., 2004).

Ethnicity and exceptionality are distinctly different concepts. In fact, multicultural special education must focus on two primary objectives that exceed the general purposes of multicultural education:

1. Ensure that ethnicity is not mistaken for educational exceptionality.
2. Increase understanding of the subculture of exceptionality and its relationship to other cultures.

Ethnicity can be mistaken for exceptionality when one's own ethnic group is viewed as setting the standard for all others. For example, patterns of eye contact, physical contact, use of language, and ways of responding to people in positions of authority vary greatly among ethnic groups. Members of each ethnic group must realize that what they see as deviant or unacceptable in their own group might be normal and adaptive in another ethnic group. That is, we must not mistakenly conclude that students have a disability or are gifted just because they are different.

Students may be particularly likely to be identified or not identified as having certain disabilities depending on their gender and ethnicity. Data suggest that students who are Native American or African American are at an increased risk for placement in special education particularly in the categories of learning disabilities, intellectual disabilities, and emotional disturbance (Anastasiou et al., 2011; U. S. Department of Education, 2009). Likewise, males, African Americans, and Hispanics who receive early intervention are less likely to be declassified as having a disability at school age than are girls or European American students (Daley & Carlson, 2009).

This disproportional representation of males and ethnic minority students in special education is a problem of long standing. Boys make up considerably more than half of the students with certain disabilities. Approximately 75% of students with severe emotional disturbance are male (Coutinho & Oswald, 2011; George & Vannest, 2009). Likewise, the percentage of students with certain disabilities who are ethnic minorities is disproportionately high—or, in some cases, disproportionately low.

Table 3.1 shows the discrepancies between the percentages of all public school students who are white, black, Asian/Pacific Islander, Hispanic, and American Indian and the percentages of these minorities who are identified as having certain disabilities and are receiving special education. Notice that white and Asian/Pacific Islander students receive special education at percentages somewhat below their representation in the general population, whereas black and American Indian students are overrepresented in special education. One has to be careful not to misinterpret these figures. For example, a common misinterpretation is that 20% of black students are receiving special education (Reschly, 2001). Such misinterpretations demean the image of minority students and may undermine the seriousness of the problem of overrepresentation. The actual meaning of the figures shown in Table 3.1 is that about 20% of the students receiving special education are black, a far different matter than the common misinterpretation.

INTERNETRESOURCES

The National Association for Bilingual Education provides resources and research regarding bilingual education at http://www.nabe.org

TABLE 3.1 Percentage of students of various ethnic groups in the total school population and the percentage of those receiving special education

	White	Black	Asian/Pacific Islander	Hispanic	American Indian
Percentage of total school population	62.1	15.1	4.1	17.2	0.98
Percentage of those receiving special education	58.7	20.5	2.1	17.7	1.5

Source: U.S. Department of Education (2009). *Twenty-eighth annual report to Congress on the implementation of the Individuals with Disabilities Education Act.* Washington, DC: Author.

It's also important to recognize that disproportionality is not an equal problem in all special education categories, schools, localities, or states for any given ethnic group. The problem of overrepresentation varies with ethnic group and the proportion of the school population that is minority (see Anastasiou et al., 2011; Coutinho & Oswald, 2000; Osher et al., 2004; Oswald & Coutinho, 2001).

Important civil rights are involved in the issue of disproportional representation in special education. On the one hand, children with disabilities have a right to appropriate education regardless of their ethnicity, even if their ethnic group is statistically overrepresented in special education. On the other hand, children also have a right to freedom from discrimination and segregation. The disproportional placement of ethnic minority students in special education strongly suggests that, in some cases, students are misidentified and wrongly placed (and stigmatized and segregated) in special education, whereas in other cases, ethnic minority students' disabilities are ignored (and the students are therefore denied appropriate education) (Kauffman & Landrum, 2009).

The reasons for the disproportional representation of certain groups in special education might involve assessment of students' abilities, but other factors such as community standards and resources might be implicated as well. There is little argument that children of color disproportionately experience poverty or that poverty is a risk factor for disability. Moreover, data suggest that low academic achievement is a significant predictor of identification for special education, and it is well recognized that disproportionate numbers of children of color receive substandard schooling and score relatively low on tests of academic achievement (Hosp & Reschly, 2004). However, the problem of disproportionality is very complex, and no simple solutions exist (Anastasiou et al., 2011; Oswald & Coutinho, 2001). The Individuals with Disabilities Education Improvement Act (IDEA) directs schools to address the problem but does not say precisely how.

The complexity of this issue requires an integrated and multifaceted effort to promote greater educational access and excellence for ethnic minority students that involves policy makers, educators, researchers, parents, advocates, students, and community representatives. The disproportionate representation of ethnic minority students in special education programs and classes indicates the need to do the following:

1. Have available strong academic programs that foster success for all students in general and special education.
2. Implement effective, appropriate special education policies and procedures for early intervention, referral, assessment, eligibility, classification, placement, and reevaluation.
3. Increase the level of home, school, and community involvement in education.
4. Use diverse community resources to enhance and implement educational programs for all students.

Disproportionality isn't the only multicultural issue in special education. People with certain exceptionalities can develop their own subcultures (Gollnick & Chinn, 2006). Those with severe hearing impairments, for example, are described by some as belonging to a Deaf culture that is not well understood by most normally hearing people and that results in feelings of isolation or separation from people with normal hearing. An important aspect of multicultural special education is developing an increased awareness, understanding, and appreciation of cultural differences involving disabilities. Multicultural special education is not merely a matter of overcoming students' prejudice and stereotyping. We must also educate ourselves as teachers to improve methods of assessment, provide effective instruction, and foster appropriate socialization.

IDENTIFICATION AND CLASSIFICATION OF DISABILITIES

Assessment is a process of collecting information about individuals or groups for the purpose of making decisions. In education, assessment ordinarily refers to testing, interviewing, and observing students. Assessment serves various purposes, including screening (quick measurement to determine who may need further assessment and possible intervention), diagnosis (measurement to identify specific problems), progress monitoring (frequent measurement to help guide instruction), and evaluating outcomes (measurement to determine the effectiveness of educational programming). Clearly, assessment often results in important decisions about people's lives; therefore, great concern for accuracy, justice, and fairness in educational assessments is widespread in the United States.

Unfortunately, the accuracy, justice, and fairness of many educational assessments, especially those involving special education, are open to question (McDonnell, McLaughlin, & Morison, 1997; Utley & Obiakor, 2001a). Particularly when ethnic subcultures are involved, traditional assessment practices have frequently violated the U.S. ideals of fairness and equal opportunity regardless of ethnic origin, gender, or disability. That is, the assessment practices of educators and psychologists have frequently come under attack as being biased, resulting in misrepresentation of the abilities and disabilities of ethnic minorities and exceptional students, which then results in classification and overrepresentation in special education rather than improved educational programming (Artiles, Rueda, Salazar, & Higareda, 2005; Macswan & Rolstad, 2006). Even prereferral practices, in which the objective is to find solutions to educational problems before referral for evaluation, are subject to bias.

The problems in assessing students are numerous and complex, and no simple solutions exist (Thurlow, Nelson, Teelucksingh, & Draper, 2001; Utley & Obiakor, 2001a). Many of the problems are centered on traditional standardized testing approaches to assessment that have serious limitations: (1) They don't take cultural diversity into account, (2) they focus on deficits in the individual alone, and (3) they don't provide information useful in teaching. Although these problems haven't been entirely overcome, awareness of these limitations and the use of more appropriate assessment procedures for diverse learners are increasing. Assessment must not result in the misidentification of children whose language or other characteristics are merely different, but it must identify those whose differences represent disabilities.

Response to Intervention in Multicultural and Bilingual Special Education

Schools are using response to intervention (RTI), which we introduced in Chapter 2, more widely to identify students with disabilities. RTI practices may have distinct advantages for students who are culturally and linguistically diverse; however, the research that supports its use as an effective method of identification is based on monolingual students. Furthermore, the effective interventions on which RTI is based, particularly for identifying students with reading disability, have been validated only with monolingual, English-speaking students (Linan-Thompson, Vaughn, Prater, & Cirino, 2006). While educators have concerns about the current evidence base for culturally and linguistically diverse learners, RTI models, which rely on quality instruction before identification, may prevent students from falling behind and thus being identified for special education (Klingner & Edwards, 2006). In addition, RTI relies more heavily on curriculum-based measurement and less on standardized tests, which may contain cultural bias. Like other areas of assessment and instruction, more research is needed to determine whether RTI methods are appropriate for use with English language learners and other minority populations.

Traditional assessment practices have frequently been viewed to be in violation of the U.S. ideals of fairness and equal opportunity regardless of culture, ethnicity, gender, or disability.

Issues in the Identification of Special Gifts and Talents

Finally, we note that fair and accurate assessment is an issue in identifying special gifts and talents as well as disabilities. Too often, the extraordinary abilities of students of color or other ethnic difference and students with disabilities are overlooked because of bias or ignorance on the part of those responsible for assessment. Currently, alternative methods for identifying students for gifted and talented programs are being investigated. In one study (Pierce et al., 2007), an alternative identification procedure resulted in an increased representation of Hispanic and English language learners in a gifted program. In Chapter 1, we emphasized the importance of identifying the abilities as well as the disabilities of students. To that, we add the importance of being aware of culturally relevant gifts and talents and recognizing and valuing the abilities of minority students.

ASSESSMENT ISSUES IN MULTICULTURAL AND BILINGUAL SPECIAL EDUCATION

Educators should be aware of the potential cultural biases in assessment procedures as they evaluate their students' progress toward annual goals and short-term objectives. As we discussed in Chapter 2, assessment practices have increased in the age of standards-based accountability. More students with disabilities are being included in state- and district-wide achievement tests. However, informal assessments of students' progress have also increased.

Fortunately, methods to monitor students' response to interventions have become more common as a result of current legislation (i.e., NCLB and IDEA). The increase in informal measures to assess student progress is particularly beneficial to students from diverse populations—progress monitoring assessments are typically less biased than traditional standardized tests. For example, **curriculum-based measurement (CBM)**, which entails direct and frequent samples of performance from the curriculum in which students are being instructed, is more useful for teachers than traditional testing and decreases the likelihood of cultural bias.

Standardized tests are often implemented to document students' achievement as it relates to annual goals, as well as for issues of accountability. These tests may be biased because most of the test items draw on specific experiences that students from different subcultures may not have had. For example, tests may be biased in favor of the likely experiences of European American, middle-class students or may be couched in language that is unfamiliar to members of a certain subculture (Singh, Baker, Winton, & Lewis, 2000). Tests may be administered in ways that penalize students with impaired vision, hearing, or ability to answer in a standard way.

Testing accommodations are provided to students with disabilities and students with limited English proficiency for the purpose of assessing student knowledge on an equal basis with students without disabilities and for whom English is a first language. Accommodations should not give an advantage to students but should provide students an equal opportunity to demonstrate knowledge and skills. In the chapters that follow, we describe specific accommodations for individuals with various disabilities. Here we discuss accommodations appropriate for students who are culturally or linguistically diverse.

Testing accommodations for English language learners should reduce the language barriers that may interfere with assessment results (Albus, Thurlow, Liu, & Bielinski, 2005). The most common accommodations include administration modifications (e.g., extended time and small-group and individual administration) and the use of a bilingual dictionary. Other accommodations include translation of tests to the student's **native language** and bilingual versions of tests, but these are not as common (Abedi, Hofstetter, & Lord, 2004). Unfortunately, empirical evidence isn't available on the efficacy of these accommodations. A study on the efficacy of using an English dictionary during testing did not demonstrate an advantage for students using this accommodation (Albus et al., 2005).

Multicultural education must balance goals that might on the surface appear to be at odds: Equalizing opportunity and achievement for all learners while differentiating instruction to accommodate learner differences.

INSTRUCTION IN MULTICULTURAL AND BILINGUAL SPECIAL EDUCATION

A major objective of multicultural education is ensuring that all students are instructed in ways that do not penalize them because of their cultural differences and that, in fact, capitalize on their cultural heritage (see Council for Exceptional Children, 2000). The methods that are used to achieve this objective are among the most controversial topics in education today. All advocates of multicultural education are concerned with the problem of finding instructional methods that help to equalize educational opportunity and achievement for all cultural groups—that is, methods that break down the inequities and discrimination that have been part of the U.S. public education system and that IDEA seeks to eliminate. Yet considerable debate continues over the question of what instructional methods are most effective in achieving this goal.

If students' differences are ignored, then students will probably receive instruction not suited to their needs. They will likely fail to learn many skills, which will in turn deny them power and opportunity in the larger culture. For example, if we ignore non-English-speaking students' language and cultural heritage and force them to speak English, they may have great difficulty in school.

However, the answer to this problem is not necessarily recognition of students' differences, because instruction that is geared to individual students' subculture might teach only skills that are valued by the subculture. Because the larger or more general culture does not value these skills, the students' difference will be perpetuated. For example, if non-English-speaking students are taught in their native language and are not required to learn English, then their progress in the English-speaking society will be slowed.

Should students who speak no English be forced to give up their native language in school and learn to use only English (ignoring the cultural-linguistic difference)? Or should teachers use the students' native languages as the primary vehicle of instruction, and teach English as a second language (acknowledging the cultural-linguistic difference)? We could pose similar questions for students with severe hearing impairments: Should we teach them by using primarily sign language or spoken language? The same dilemma appears in providing instruction for students with other disabilities: To what extent should they be treated as different and provided with special accommodations, and to what extent should they be treated just like everyone else (Kauffman, McGee, & Brigham, 2004)?

Clearly, the problem of instruction in multicultural education isn't easily resolved, especially for bilingual students in special education (Gersten & Baker, 2000). Most authorities now agree, however, that accepting and fostering cultural diversity must not be used as an excuse for not teaching students the skills they need to survive and prosper in the larger context of American culture.

Many educators call for instructional practices that are culturally sensitive or culturally responsive, meaning attuned to the particular cultural characteristics of learners (e.g., McIntyre, 2007; Shealey & Callins, 2007; Villegas & Lucas, 2007). The assumption underlying many assertions about culturally sensitive or culturally responsive instruction is that students with different cultural backgrounds need to be taught differently, that certain aspects of cultural heritage determine to a significant extent how students learn best. Perhaps it's understandable that schools that emphasize differences in the ways in which students learn also emphasize devising special programs and schools that cater to these differences. Furthermore, the greater the diversity of cultural backgrounds of students in one class, the greater the difficulty in teaching all students effectively—if we assume that cultural background determines how students are best taught.

If children from a particular culture learn better when taught in a certain way, then it may be extremely difficult to teach multicultural groups of students. Which is the lesser evil: grouping students for instruction based on their cultural affiliation, or shortchanging some by using a particular instructional method? Can either evil be avoided entirely? Do students learn best when they are taught by someone who shares their cultural heritage? If so, what does that mean for recruiting and assigning teachers, and what does it mean for grouping students for instruction? How do we best address the problem of increasing the cultural and linguistic diversity of special education teachers (see Kauffman et al., 2008; Tyler, Yzquierdo, Lopez-Reyna, & Flippin, 2004)? Which is more important in a teacher: instructional competence or cultural affiliation? If neither is more important than the other, how should teachers be recruited and trained?

Of course, we might hypothesize that certain methods of instruction are equally effective for all students in a culturally diverse group (see Council for Exceptional Children, 2000; Kauffman et al., 2008). That is, some instructional approaches (e.g., direct instruction, cooperative learning, peer tutoring, and cross-age grouping) allow teachers to provide culturally sensitive instruction to all members of a diverse group at once. **Classwide peer tutoring** may, in fact, be particularly useful in helping children at the elementary school level who are not proficient in English to learn English more efficiently (Fulk & King, 2001; Greenwood, Arrega-Mayer, Utley, Gavin, & Terry, 2001). Evidence also suggests that peer tutoring is effective for improving important reading skills (i.e., DIBELS Nonsense Word Fluency and Phonemic Segmentation Fluency; Good & Kaminski, 2002) of Hispanic students (Calhoon, Al Otaiba, Greenberg, King, & Avalos, 2006; Calhoon, Al Otaiba, Cihak, King, & Avalos, 2007) and social interactions (Xu, Gelfer, Sileo, Filler, & Perkins, 2008). One group of researchers concluded that "Specific teacher behaviors (e.g., positive reinforcement, questioning techniques) have been shown to lead to better student outcomes, and we assume that the absence of these behaviors has a deleterious effect on student learning" (Tyler et al., 2004, pp. 27–28). Sensitivity to individuals, regardless of their culture, and effective instruction are essential elements of multicultural education worthy of the name. Kauffman et al. (2008) concluded:

> All things considered, we believe that we can be passionately committed to education as a science while maintaining sensitivity to the cultural differences of individual children and their families. However, first and foremost we must recognize that the most culturally responsive practices are empirically validated instructional strategies (Heward, 2003). At this point the data seem to suggest that this applies to all children, regardless of their ethnicity. . . .
>
> In short, we believe that cultural sensitivity in education is based on scientifically grounded regard for the individual student. In our opinion, it's impossible for educators to be sensitive to the needs of a student while being insensitive to that student's culture. Ultimately, ineffective [instructional] procedures are insensitive to both the needs of the student and to his or her culture in spite of any attempts to cast them as "culturally responsive." In all cases, cultural sensitivity requires using the most effective acceptable means to help students achieve socially validated objectives.

Both special and general education must adopt instructional programs that value all students and help all to be as successful as possible in American society, regardless of their specific cultural heritage. This is supported by both research and by our common commitment to the American values of equality of opportunity and fairness for all, and is contained in five instructional goals:

1. Teach tolerance and appreciation of difference.
2. Work cooperatively with families.
3. Improve instruction for language-minority students.
4. Adopt effective teaching practices.
5. Identify and implement effective reading instruction for English language learners.

The responsive instruction box on page 72 provides an example of one teaching practice that is appropriate for students who are culturally and linguistically diverse.

Teaching Tolerance and Appreciation

By *tolerance*, we don't mean merely toleration of others who are seen as undesirable, nor does the publication *Teaching Tolerance* mean such toleration. Our definition of *tolerance* is an appreciation and valuing—the opposite of rejection, denigration, or toleration of a necessary evil. It means working for equity and fair treatment, seeing those who are different in culture as equal. Still, mere toleration would be a step away from the hostile rejection, ridicule, and subjugation that intolerance breeds.

Noted historian Ronald Takaki (1994), interviewed for an article in *Teaching Tolerance*, recalls that his grandparents were Japanese immigrant plantation laborers in Hawaii. Nobel laureate and author Elie Wiesel (2004), writing in the Sunday magazine *Parade*, recalls his rescue from a concentration camp. Both suggest that the American promise of equality and fairness can become a reality only if we free ourselves from a legacy of racism and prejudice. We can do so by acknowledging the reality of our past and learning more about ourselves and our heritage.

Overcoming prejudice and teaching students to appreciate those who are different from themselves is by no means easy. Moreover, this is not an area in which research can provide definitive guidelines. Yet proposed methods for how teachers can help students learn both self-esteem and tolerance of difference seem promising (Banks & Banks, 2010; Utley & Obiakor, 2001c). Some schools focus on incorporating diversity by design or organizing anti-bias clubs that encourage understanding and tolerance of others (e.g., Bennett, 2000; Collins, 2000; McAfee, 2000).

Teaching tolerance and appreciation of difference is not, of course, limited to ethnic, regional, sexual orientation, or language differences but includes differences of all types, including disabilities.

INTERNETRESOURCES

Teaching Tolerance magazine and teaching ideas can be found at http://www .tolerance.org/teach

Working with Families

Schools have always depended, in part, on family involvement and support for their success. Because working with families is so important, we have devoted Chapter 4 to the topic.

Different cultural traditions mean that parents have different views of exceptionality and disability and different ways of accommodating these differences in their children (Cho, Singer, & Brenner, 2000; Pullen, 2004). An understanding of the cultural basis for parents' attitudes and wishes, particularly for families that have recently come to the United States, is therefore critical. When combined with other differences, difficulties for students with disabilities are increased.

Improving Instruction for Language-Minority Students

Students for whom English is a second language face the simultaneous demands of learning a new language and mastering traditional subject matter. Those who also have disabilities encounter a third demand of coping with the additional hurdles imposed by their exceptionalities. Bilingual special education is therefore particularly controversial, presenting difficult dilemmas and paradoxes. Moreover, NCLB's demand that students who aren't fluent in English score, on average, the same as those who are fluent in English has created extraordinary controversy about language learning.

Educational programming must challenge all learners to stretch their abilities and not lower expectations for minority students.

One approach to teaching language-minority students is to emphasize use of their native languages. In this approach, teachers initially provide all academic instruction in each student's native language and teach English as a separate subject. Later, when the students demonstrate adequate fluency in English, they make the transition to instruction in English in all academic subjects.

Another approach is to offer content-area instruction in English from the beginning of the student's schooling but at a level that is "sheltered," or constantly modified to make sure the student understands it. The goal of this approach is to help the student learn English while learning academic subjects as well.

In the first approach—native-language emphasis—students are taught for most of the day in their native languages and later make a transition to English. In the **sheltered-English approach**, students receive instruction in English for most of the school day from the beginning of their schooling. The question as to which approach is better for students with disabilities has not been answered, although it's clear that changing from one approach to the other when students change schools creates particular difficulties (Gersten & Baker, 2000).

Another issue for language-minority instruction is whether an emphasis on the natural uses of language or, alternatively, on skills such as vocabulary and pronunciation is most effective. However, this controversy might be based on a false dichotomy. What students need is an effective balance between skill building and language that is meaningful and relevant to their lives and interests (Gersten & Baker, 2000). Moreover, instruction of language-minority students needs to be consistent with effective teaching.

Adopting Effective Teaching Practices

In a sense, effective multicultural education requires only that we implement what we know about effective instruction. Effective teaching practices are sensitive to each individual student's cultural heritage, sense of self, view of the world, and acquired knowledge and skills. Teaching about various cultures, individual differences, and the construction of knowledge should permeate and transform the curriculum (Banks & Banks, 2010). Nonetheless, for language-minority students—indeed, for all students—we can articulate more specific components of effective teaching (see Kauffman et al., 2008). Gersten, Brengelman and Jimenez (1994) outlined six components of effective teaching:

INTERNETRESOURCES

The Division for Learning Disabilities (DLD) offers a plethora of resources for teachers. The Practice Alerts series provides up-to-date information on teaching strategies, including mnemonic instruction. To learn more about mnemonic instruction, visit their website at http://www.teachingld.org/ld_resources/alerts/5.htm

1. *Scaffolding and strategies.* Students learn more efficiently when teachers provide a scaffold, or structure, for ideas and strategies for problem solving. In **scaffolded instruction**, the teacher assists the student in learning a task and then phases out the help as the student learns to use the strategy independently. Means of helping students learn more easily include stories, visual organizers (e.g., pictures, diagrams, outlines), **mnemonics** (tactics that aid memory, such as rhymes or images), and **reciprocal teaching** (in which the student sees the teacher use a learning strategy and then tries it out).

2. *Challenge.* Even in special education, students are too often not appropriately challenged. All students—including those who are from cultural minorities, who are at high risk for failure, and who have disabilities—need to be given challenging tasks. Appropriately challenging tasks are those that a given student finds just manageable. These are the tasks that are not impossible, but do require serious effort and stretch the student's capabilities. Too often, teachers underestimate the capabilities of minority and exceptional students and underteach them.

3. *Involvement.* Students must be engaged in extended conversations, in which they use complex linguistic structures. Verbal exchanges between teachers and pupils must not always be short, simple, and direct (although such exchanges have their place). Rather, teachers must probe with questions, share experiences, and elicit from pupils the kind of language that demonstrates their active involvement in learning.

4. *Success.* Students who are at the highest risk of failure and dropping out are those who have low rates of success in daily school activities. All students need to experience frequent success, and teachers must present challenging tasks at which each student can succeed. Failure should not be perpetuated.

5. *Mediation and feedback.* Too often, students work for long periods without receiving feedback, or they receive incomprehensible feedback, or their teachers ask for rote responses to which students attach little or no meaning. Providing frequent, comprehensible feedback on performance is vital to effective teaching, as is focusing on the meanings of responses. Teachers need to be aware of the use of evidence and logic, both in how they construct questions and in their students' answers.

6. *Responsiveness to cultural and individual diversity.* Teachers must ensure that the content of instruction relates to students' experiences, including those as individuals and as members of various cultural groups. The issues of cultural and individual diversity cannot be adequately considered in a few special lessons; rather, they must be included routinely in all curriculum areas. (p. 9)

Implementing Effective Reading Instruction

Of all academic skills, reading is critically important. It's a skill that is necessary for school and life success, and reading instruction should be based on the best scientific evidence possible (Reyna, 2004). However, students who are English language learners often have difficulty learning to read (McCardle, McCarthy, & Leos, 2005; Pollard-Durodola, Mathes, Vaughn, Cardenas-Hagan, & Linan-Thompson, 2006; Vaughn, Mathes, Linan-Thompson, & Francis, 2005). Fortunately, federal funding has provided extensive research on teaching reading skills to English language learners (McCardle & Leung, 2006). Researchers are currently examining whether methods that are effective with monolingual students at risk for reading disability are also effective for non-English speakers. One early finding of this research program is that comprehensive interventions (i.e., including explicit instruction in phonemic awareness, alphabetic principle, fluency, vocabulary, comprehension) produced significant improvements for these students (Linan-Thompson et al., 2006; Vaughn, Cirino, et al., 2006; Vaughn, Linan-Thompson, et al., 2006; Vaughn, Mathes, et al., 2006). Less comprehensive interventions did not produce significant results (Denton, Anthony, Parker, & Hasbrouck, 2004). With this increased emphasis on reading intervention research for non-English speakers, educators may soon have empirically validated methods for teaching effectively. For example, the accompanying Responsive Instruction feature provides an empirically validated strategy.

INTERNETRESOURCES

The Launching Young Readers: Reading Rockets Website provides resources and research on reading strategies for English Language Learners. Visit this site at http://www.readingrockets.org/article/c61/

RESPONSIVE *INSTRUCTION*
MEETING THE NEEDS OF ENGLISH LANGUAGE LEARNERS WITH SPECIAL NEEDS

Concept Mapping to Improve Achievement

WHAT THE RESEARCH SAYS

To create educational environments conducive to academic success for English language learners, it is important to understand the range of challenges schools can pose to such students. Cloud (2002) identifies five areas through which teachers can address the needs of English language learners and create culturally responsive environments: (1) curriculum and materials, (2) classroom interactions, (3) teaching approaches, (4) resource management, and (5) counseling and parent outreach. By selecting material that is relevant to the students' experience, establishing classroom interactions that are comfortable to the student (e.g., some students may prefer more peer-to-peer interactions, whereas others prefer more teacher-directed instruction), and engaging in effective instructional strategies that promote vocabulary and language development, teachers create classroom environments that support academic success.

Concept mapping is a particular teaching approach demonstrated in the research to be effective for both English language learners and students with special needs (Chularut & DeBacker, 2003; Gersten & Baker, 2000). Concept mapping applications can be created using culturally relevant materials and designed to enhance vocabulary and concept development.

RESEARCH STUDY

Chularut and DeBacker (2003) investigated the influence of concept mapping on the academic achievement of English language learners. Concept maps are instructional tools that promote learning through the use of visual representation of related topics. Concept maps allow students to see how concepts are related within a network of relationships (see Figure A for an example).

For their study, the researchers randomly assigned two groups of English language learners (*n* = 79) to either concept map instruction or individual study plus discussion. The 4-week research study consisted of pretesting, five study sessions on five different reading passages that included work with concept maps or individual study plus discussion, and posttesting. The concept map group received instruction and daily practice in creating concept maps. Instructors monitored the development of the maps and provided instructional feedback. The instructors did not, however, read or interpret the content.

The individual study plus discussion group received the same reading materials as the concept map group. The individual study group, however, also received supplemental vocabulary pages that contained definitions of challenging words or con-

FIGURE A A concept map: Honeybees

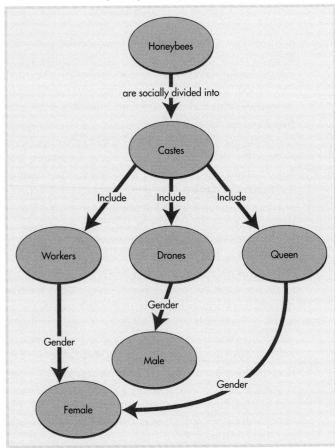

Source: Sutphin, M. (2007, January). *Mapping concepts from the classroom to the computer: Instructors hope to combine concept maps and the Internet to test agriculture students.* Blacksburg, VA: Virginia Technical University College of Agriculture and Life Sciences. Reprinted with permission.

cepts. After studying the passages independently (asking for assistance when needed), the students participated in an instructor-led, whole-group discussion on the meaning and implications of the passage. Both groups were aware that they would be tested on the material.

RESEARCH FINDINGS

The results of the posttest showed that students in the concept map group scored higher than students in the individual study plus discussion group. In addition, within the concept map group, students who had higher English proficiency made greater gains than students in the lower English-proficiency group. The results demonstrated that although both groups benefited from the opportunity to study the passages individually, students derived greater benefit from working with the concept maps. Therefore, the construction of the concept maps led to greater retention of the material and increased understanding of the content. These findings support the use of concept maps with English language learners at a range of proficiency and skill levels.

APPLYING THE RESEARCH TO TEACHING

Teachers implement concept mapping in their classrooms either by providing teacher-created maps or by having students generate their own maps. Research has shown that both uses have educational benefit, but greater gains result when students generate the maps themselves (Ruzic & O'Connell, 2001). Teachers can use concept maps to help students brainstorm ideas for writing, communicate or represent complex ideas, link prior knowledge with new information, or assess understanding or misunderstanding.

Steps for creating concept maps include:

1. Gather research and drawing materials. If students are creating their own maps, identify and collect the relevant possible resources (i.e., textbooks, reference materials, teacher-selected Websites, photos, graphs). Drawing materials may include colored pencils and shape stencils.

2. Select one of the concept map formats. The variety of different types of concept maps include spider maps, hierarchy maps, and flowchart maps, to name a few. The topic selected will influence the type of map needed.

3. In the standard concept map (Novak & Gowin, 1984), concepts are circled and links drawn to connect these concepts. The links are then labeled to explain the relationship between or among the concepts. Each concept should be listed only once on the map (Ahlberg, 2004).

4. Generate the map by brainstorming concepts related to the overall question or theme of the map. Connect the concepts, and label the relationships.

5. Revise and refine the maps. Typically, final maps should be the result of several drafts.

■ ■ ■ ■ ■ ■ ■ ■ ■ ■

For young children in particular, research increasingly points to the importance of an environment in which children have the opportunity to listen to reading, examine books, engage in activities such as saying nursery rhymes, writing, and seeing and talking about printed materials (Hammill, 2004; Peck & Scarpati, 2004). This means encouraging such literacy-related activities in the home, which cannot occur unless the teacher is competent in addressing cultural differences among families. It also means teaching with a sense of urgency, as described in the accompanying Focus on Concepts feature, and understanding that effective instruction is special education's bottom line (Kauffman & Hallahan, 2005; Kauffman et al., 2008).

A viable multicultural curriculum cannot be created and simply handed out to teachers (Banks & Banks, 2010). Teachers must be invested in the endeavor, because their values, perspectives, and teaching styles will affect what is taught and how. The effective implementation of a multicultural curriculum requires teaching strategies that are involvement oriented, interactive, personalized, and cooperative.

This perspective applies to our own teaching and writing as well. In any textbook, the adequate treatment of multicultural issues cannot be confined to a single chapter. A chapter like this one—devoted specifically to multicultural education—may be necessary to ensure that the topic is given sufficient focused attention. Our intention in this book, however, is to prompt consideration of multicultural issues in every chapter.

Reading may be the most important skill for academic and life success. Federally funded research on teaching reading skills to English language learners indicates that intensive intervention produces significant improvements (McCardle & Leung, 2006).

Socialization

Academic instruction is one of two primary purposes of education. The other, socialization, involves helping students develop appropriate social perceptions and interactions with others and learn how to work for desirable social change. Socializing the student does not mean that any kind of behavior or attitude is acceptable in school; nor does it mean ignoring the student's cultural heritage. Commonalities among children are greater than their differences

FOCUS ON Concepts

A COMMON SENSE OF URGENCY

We need to exercise caution with well-intended but general concepts, for much very poor instruction has occurred as a result of misguided interpretations. To illustrate, we often stress that good teachers should care about and demonstrate concern for their students. One teacher who was brought to my attention would display very caring behaviors by taking time on her weekends to expose some of her poor urban students to community cultural events such as art shows, museums, and libraries. On the other hand, extensive observations in her general education elementary classroom revealed constant chaos and little meaningful instruction. Although she wanted to be effective, she was incapacitated by her lack of skill, and her students suffered accordingly. To be specific, I would propose that a school with a sense of community is one that is united in the urgency of helping each child master the grade-level curriculum. Classroom time is not wasted, teachers are well trained in teaching strategies that work, children's progress is monitored constantly, remedial actions are taken when needed, and there is the clear expectation that all children can and will meet mastery.

Schools with underachieving culturally diverse students clearly need this common sense of urgency. Most educators will say that they care about their students and have no racial or cultural animus, but relatively few teachers are aware that one of the best examples of the absence of bias is to teach with this sense of urgency, fully expecting children to learn. Schools that fail to be alarmed when two thirds to three quarters of their students are two to three grades behind academically are consciously or unconsciously subscribing to this bias.

Source: Cartledge, G. (2004). Another look at the impact of changing demographics on public education for culturally diverse learners with behavior problems: Implications for teacher preparation. In L. M. Bullock & R. A. Gable (Eds.), Quality personnel preparation in emotional/behavioral disorders: Current perspectives and future directions (pp. 64–69). Denton, TX: Institute for Behavioral and Learning Differences at the University of North Texas. Reprinted with permission.

(Cushner, McClelland, & Safford, 2006), but cultural and linguistic differences nonetheless pose significant challenges for teachers, who must make the classroom an affirming place for students (Cartledge & Loe, 2001; see also Osher et al., 2004).

In some cases, helping children learn appropriate social skills might require helping parents learn how to teach their children (Elksnin & Elksnin, 2000). This requires understanding the cultural and linguistic diversity of families. Destructive and stereotypic social perceptions and interactions among differing subcultural groups are long-standing problems in schools and communities in the United States, particularly when students have cultural differences in language and social behavior (Osher et al., 2004). Part of the process of multicultural socialization is giving students experiences that make them question the way we think about other cultures.

The most obvious examples involve racial discrimination, although sex discrimination and discrimination against people of differing religions and disabilities are also common in our society. For example, Adelaide Ruffner, a woman with cerebral palsy, was considered not acceptable as a teacher in the 1960s but went on to earn a master's degree and to be recognized for her extraordinary work with children with disabilities and their families. In a report of Ruffner's award-winning work, Dadurka (2004) related:

> Though her family was supportive, others were not always so accepting. When Ruffner began her student-teaching term at Johnson Elementary in the 1960s, she was let go after six weeks.
>
> "The parents complained. Back then you were judged by your exterior. . . . People were scared," she said. "It was like segregation." (p. A2)

There is no guarantee that discrimination such as that experienced by Adelaide Ruffner will not be encountered today. Teachers and teacher educators must become keenly aware of their own cultural heritages, identities, and biases before they can help their students deal with cultural diversity in ways that enhance democratic ideals, such as human dignity, justice, and equality (Banks & Banks, 2007). Becoming comfortable with one's own identity as a member of subcultural groups is an important objective for both teachers and students. Depending on the cultural context, accepting and valuing one's identity can be quite difficult.

Teaching about different cultures and their value may be important in reducing racial and ethnic conflict and promoting respect for human differences. Equally important, however, is structuring classroom interactions to promote the understanding and appreciation of others. One of the most effective ways of breaking down prejudice and encouraging appropriate interaction among students with different characteristics is **cooperative learning**. When engaged in cooperative learning, students of different abilities and cultural characteristics work together as a team, fostering interdependence.

Teachers of exceptional children and youths must be aware of the potential variety of subcultural identities of their students. Review the multiple aspects of cultural identity suggested by Figure 3.1 (page 57), and reflect on the combinations of these and other subcultures that a given student might adopt. One of the cultural identities that is not included in Figure 3.1 is sexual orientation, yet many children and adolescents, including many with educational exceptionalities, experience serious difficulties with what some have called the "invisible" culture of gay and lesbian youth. Students who are "straight" might struggle with their own prejudices against homosexuals, prejudices that are all too often fostered by both their peers and adults and sometimes given justification by identification with a religious or political subculture. Gay and lesbian students are often harassed and abused verbally and physically in school and may suffer from serious depression or other psychological disorders as a result; even the appearance or assumption of being gay can lead to abuse (see Associated Press, 2004; Bell, 2004). Gay students need to be able to be themselves without fear of harassment or discrimination (Elliot, 2000). Consider also that a student might be both gay or lesbian and gifted, physically disabled, intellectually disabled, or have another educational exceptionality.

Our point is that the task of socialization in a multicultural society demands attention to the multitude of identities that students may assume. It also demands an awareness that any of these identities may carry the consequence of social rejection, isolation, and alienation. Many children with disabilities are lonely and need to develop friendships (Pavri, 2001). Our task as educators is to promote understanding of cultural differences and acceptance of individuals whose identities differ from one's own. Building pride in one's cultural identity is a particular concern in teaching exceptional students. As we have noted elsewhere, many people in the Deaf community prefer to be called *the Deaf*, which runs contrary to the current use of terms such as *hearing impaired*. Deaf people and blind people have begun to express pride in their identities and cultures and, at the same time, foster multicultural experiences involving other languages and customs (Gallucci, 2000). In fact, for increasing numbers of people with disabilities, labels are to be embraced, not hidden.

People from many segments of society—such as parents of children with disabilities, senior citizens, religious groups, and recovering alcoholics—find that congregating for mutual support and understanding enhances their feelings of self-worth. Educators need to consider the possible value of having students with disabilities congregate for specific purposes.

By trying to avoid labels and insisting that students with disabilities always be placed with those who do not have disabilities, perhaps we risk giving the message that those who have disabilities are less desirable or even not fit to associate with as peers. Bateman (1994) suggests that "something is terribly and not very subtly insulting about saying a bright learning disabled student ought not attend a special school with other students who have learning disabilities because he needs to be with non-disabled students" (p. 516). In striving for true multicultural awareness, we might learn that it's more productive in the long run to embrace identities associated with exceptionalities, while working to increase tolerance and understanding of differences, than it is to avoid labels or refrain from congregating students with specific characteristics.

One of the most difficult tasks of teaching is socializing students through classroom discipline—that is, through the management of classroom behavior. Managing classroom behavior presents a serious challenge for nearly all teachers and a particularly difficult challenge for most special education teachers (see Evertson & Weinstein, 2006; Kauffman, Mostert, Trent, & Pullen, 2006). Two considerations are critical: the relationship between the teacher's approach to classroom discipline and the parents' child-rearing practices and the teacher's sensitivity to cultural differences in responses to discipline.

Teachers might have an approach to classroom discipline that they consider effective and humane but that differs radically from some cultures' accepted child-rearing practices. Educators, like everyone else, are often ethnocentric, believing that their views are right and those of others are wrong based on cultural values. In a given case, they might be right, in that their view is more humane or effective, but they might also be insensitive to the values of students and their families. Teachers must be sensitive to individuals and families, but that sensitivity does not allow ignoring what reliable research tells us about human behavior (Kauffman et al., 2008).

In the case of discipline involving students of culturally diverse backgrounds, the teacher might face difficult ethical decisions about child abuse or neglect. When do one's own beliefs about the treatment of children demand that a culturally condoned disciplinary practice be confronted as abuse or neglect? Answering this question is not easy.

Finally, we note that education should not merely socialize students to fit into the existing social order. The goals of multicultural education include teaching students to work for social change, which entails helping students who are members of oppressed minorities become advocates for themselves and other members of their subcultures (Banks & Banks, 2010; Utley & Obiakor, 2001b).

RESPONSIVE *INSTRUCTION*
MEETING THE NEEDS OF STUDENTS WHO ARE
CULTURALLY OR LINGUISTICALLY DIVERSE

Response Cards for Increased Participation and Reduced Behavioral Disruptions

WHAT THE RESEARCH SAYS

Research on students who are culturally and linguistically diverse (CLD) reveals the importance of active student participation to facilitate academic success (Cartledge & Kourea, 2008). Significant gaps in achievement persist for students who are CLD, in part, due to fewer opportunities to respond during class (Greenwood, Hart, Walker, & Risley, 1994). CLD students who are also low-income spend significantly less time in class actively engaged when compared to their peers from higher-income families (Good & Nichols, 2001). Research on the use of response cards, signs or cards held up by students to indicate their answer or response, to increase response rates has demonstrated social validity (students will use them) and power (learning does occur) witht their use (Christle & Schustesr, 2003; Lampert, Cartledge, Heward, & Lo, 2006).

RESEARCH STUDY

Lampert and colleagues (2006) conducted a study on the use of response cards on the social and academic behaviors of forth grade students in an urban classroom. Participants were low-performing, minority students who qualified for free or reduced priced lunch, and who exhibited frequent behavioral disruptions in the classroom.

Data were collected on disruptive behaviors, hand raising, academic responses, correct responses, and satisfaction with the use of response cards. Throughout instruction the teachers would prompt students to respond to a question using one of two formats—raising a hand or using the response card. Under the response card condition, students recorded their answers on a white board and held it up. Under the hand raising condition, students raised their hands to respond. Teachers alternated conditions within an instructional period. Following the study, researchers conducted interviews/surveys with students and teachers on their preferred response method.

RESEARCH FINDINGS

All of the target students in the study exhibited fewer behavioral disruptions when teachers employed the response cards. In addition, the study was able to demonstrate a clear connection between the use of response cards and a decrease in disruptive behaviors. Students also responded more frequently during the response card condition.

APPLYING THE RESEARCH TO TEACHING

Teachers can easily integrate the use of response cards into their teaching. White boards provide a flexible response tool for students as students can respond in a variety of ways (e.g., writing a term or terms, drawing a picture, writing an answer to a math problem, indicating a letter for a multiple-choice prompt). Guidelines for implementing response cards during instruction include: (1) create a streamlined procedure for distributing the response cards, (2) maintain a brisk but reasonable presentation rate, (3) allow students time to get comfortable with the tool prior to intensive use, and (4) encourage students to keep their responses private until the teacher prompts for the response (Randolf, 2007).

SUMMARY

In what ways do we see universality of cultural pride and shame?

- People of every identity take justifiable pride in aspects of their heritage.
- People of every identity have conducted themselves in ways that bring shame to their group.
- Collective guilt and collective pride are problems for every group.

What is American about multiculturalism?

- The United States is a very diverse society that seeks justice for all.
- Ideally, American culture is one that celebrates diversity within a framework of clearly defined common values.

What are the important concepts about cultural diversity for education?

- American society is made of many subcultures (cultures that are a part, not all, of the larger society), each of which is characterized by:

- Values and typical behavior
- Language or dialects
- Nonverbal communication
- Awareness of one's cultural identity
- World views or general perspectives
- Special education must foster achievement in the context of cultural diversity.

What are the most important aspects of multicultural and bilingual special education?

- Identification and classification procedures that result in accurate placement and services for students
- Assessment that honors the student's cultural heritage and does not penalize the student
- Instruction that uses the student's cultural strengths and that involves teaching tolerance and appreciation of culture, working with families, improving language instruction for language-minority students, improving literacy instruction for language-minority students, and adopting effective teaching practices
- Socialization to multicultural norms

COUNCIL FOR EXCEPTIONAL CHILDREN

Addressing the Professional Standards

Council for Exceptional Children

Council for Exceptional Children (CEC) Common Core Knowledge and Skills addressed in this chapter: ICC1K5, ICC1K8, ICC2K3, ICC3K3, ICC3K4, ICC3K5, ICC4S3, ICC5K8, ICC5K9, ICC5S1, ICC5S13, ICC6K2, ICC6S1, ICC7S2, ICC7S8, ICC8S2, ICC8S4, ICC10K3, ICC10K4, ICC10S3, ICC10S4

Appendix: Provides a full listing of the CEC Common Core Standards and associated Knowledge and Skill Statements listed here.

MYEDUCATIONLAB

PEARSON myeducationlab

Now go to Topic 4: Cultural/Linguistic Diversity in the MyEducationLab (www.myeducationlab.com) for your course, where you can:

- Find learning outcomes for the broad concepts covered in this chapter along with the national standards that connect to these outcomes.
- Complete Assignments and Activities that can help you more deeply understand the chapter content.
- Examine challenging situations presented in the IRIS Center Resources.
- Apply and practice your understanding of the core concepts and skills identified in the chapter with the Building Teaching Skills and Dispositions learning units.
- Check your comprehension on the content covered in the chapter by going to the Study Plan in the Book-Specific Resources for your text. Here you will be able to take a chapter quiz, receive feedback on your answers, and then access Review, Practice, and Enrichment activities to enhance your understanding of chapter content.
- Watch video clips of CCSSO Teacher of the Year award winners responding to the question: "Why I teach?" in the Teacher Talk section.

Parents and Families

I am often asked to describe the experience of raising a child with a disability—to try to help people who have not shared that unique experience to understand it, to imagine how it would feel. It's like this. . . .

When you're going to have a baby, it's like planning a fabulous vacation trip—to Italy. You buy a bunch of guide books and make your wonderful plans. The Coliseum. The Michelangelo David. The gondolas in Venice. You may learn some handy phrases in Italian. It's all very exciting.

After months of eager anticipation, the day finally arrives. You pack your bags and off you go. Several hours later, the plane lands. The stewardess comes in and says, "Welcome to Holland."

"Holland?!?" you say. "What do you mean Holland?? I signed up for Italy! I'm supposed to be in Italy. All my life I've dreamed of going to Italy."

But there's been a change in the flight plan. They've landed in Holland and there you must stay.

The important thing is that they haven't taken you to a horrible, disgusting, filthy place, full of pestilence, famine and disease. It's just a different place.

So you must go out and buy new guide books. And you must learn a whole new language. And you will meet a whole new group of people you would never have met.

It's just a different place. It's slower-paced than Italy, less flashy than Italy. But after you've been there for a while and you catch your breath, you look around . . . and you begin to notice that Holland has windmills . . . and Holland has tulips. Holland even has Rembrandts.

But everyone you know is busy coming and going from Italy . . . and they're all bragging about what a wonderful time they had there. And for the rest of your life, you will say "Yes, that's where I was supposed to go. That's what I had planned."

And the pain of that will never, ever, ever, ever go away . . . because the loss of that dream is a very very significant loss.

But . . . if you spend your life mourning the fact that you didn't get to Italy, you may never be free to enjoy the very special, the very lovely things . . . about Holland.

—Emily Perl Kingsley • *"Welcome to Holland"*

QUESTIONS **to guide your reading of this chapter . . .**

- How have professionals' views of parents changed?
- What are the effects of a child with a disability on the family?
- What are the best ways for families to be involved in treatment and education?

MISCONCEPTIONS ABOUT
Parents and Families of Persons with Disabilities

MYTH • Professionals need to focus their intervention efforts only on the parents, especially the mother, of children with disabilities.

FACT • Professionals now believe that the family (including extended family) as well as friends should be included in intervention programming for children with disabilities.

MYTH • Parents are to blame for many of the problems of their children with disabilities.

FACT • Parents can influence their children's behavior, but so, too, can children affect how their parents behave. Research shows that some children with disabilities are born with difficult temperaments, which can affect parental behavior.

MYTH • Parents must experience a series of reactions—shock and disruption, denial, sadness, anxiety and fear, and anger—before adapting to the birth of a child with a disability.

FACT • Parents don't go through emotional reactions in lockstep fashion. They may experience some, or all, of these emotions but not necessarily in any particular order.

MYTH • Many parents of infants with disabilities go from physician to physician, "shopping" for an optimistic diagnosis.

FACT • Just the opposite is often true. Parents frequently suspect that something is wrong with their baby but are told by professionals not to worry—that the child will outgrow the problem. Then they seek another opinion.

MYTH • The father is unimportant in the development of the child with a disability.

FACT • Although they are frequently ignored by researchers and generally do experience less stress than mothers, fathers can play a critical role in the dynamics of the family.

MYTH • Parents of children with disabilities are destined for a life of stress and misery.

FACT • Some parents experience high degrees of disruption and stress, but over time many come to learn to cope. And some actually gain unanticipated positive benefits from having a child with a disability.

MYTH • Siblings are usually unaffected by the addition of a child with a disability to the family.

FACT • Siblings often experience the same emotional reactions as parents do, and their lack of maturity can make coping with these emotions more difficult.

MYTH • The primary role of the early intervention professional should be to provide expertise for the family.

FACT • Many authorities now agree that professionals should help parents become more involved in making decisions for the family.

MYTH • The typical family in the United States has two parents, is middle class, and has only the father working outside the home.

FACT • Demographics are changing rapidly. In many more families, both parents now work outside the home, and the numbers of single-parent families and families living in poverty have increased.

MYTH • Parents who elect not to be actively involved in their child's education and treatment are neglectful.

FACT • Although it's desirable for parents to be involved, it is sometimes very difficult for them to do so because of their commitments to other family functions (e.g., work and child care).

MYTH • Professionals are always in the best position to help families of people with disabilities.

FACT • Informal sources of support, such as extended family and friends, are often more effective than formal sources of support, such as professionals and agencies, in helping families adapt to a family member with a disability.

MYTH • Teachers should respect the privacy of parents and communicate with them only when absolutely necessary—for example, when their child has exhibited serious behavior problems.

FACT • Teachers should initiate some kind of contact with parents as soon as possible, so that if a problem such as a serious behavior infraction does occur, some rapport with the parents will already have been established.

A s Emily Perl Kingsley—the mother of a child with Down syndrome—points out in this chapter's opening quotation (see p. 75), the birth of a child with a disability can have a profound effect on the family. But the exact nature of the effect is not always certain. Reactions of family members to the individual with a disability can run the gamut from absolute rejection to complete acceptance, from intense anger to intense love, from total neglect to overprotection. But most important, a child with disabilities does not always threaten the family's well-being. In fact, some parents and siblings testify that having a family member with a disability has strengthened the family bonds.

In this chapter, we explore the dynamics of families with children with disabilities and discuss parental involvement in treatment and education. First, however, we present a historical perspective of the role of parents and families of children who are disabled.

myeducationlab

To check your comprehension on the content covered in Chapter 4, go to the Book-Specific Resources in the MyEducationLab (www.myeducationlab.com) for your course, select your text, and complete the Study Plan. Here you will be able to take a chapter quiz, receive feedback on your answers, and then access review, practice, and enrichment activities to enhance your understanding of chapter content. ■

The prevailing philosophy now dictates that whenever possible, professionals should seek the special insights that parents can offer by virtue of living with their children.

PROFESSIONALS' CHANGING VIEWS OF PARENTS AND FAMILIES

Today, knowledgeable professionals who work with exceptional learners are aware of the importance of the family; importantly, most recognize that families and not just parents are crucial for successful outcomes for persons with disabilities. As one influential team of family intervention advocates has put it:

> Until early intervention developed a family-centered approach, almost all emphasis was on parents and not on families. . . . Policy makers and professionals now recognize that partnerships should not be limited to parents only (especially to mothers only). Partnerships can and should involve relationships between professionals and other family members, such as fathers, grandparents, brothers and sisters, and even close family friends. Each of these people can support and enhance the educational outcomes for students with exceptionalities. (Turnbull, Turnbull, Erwin, & Soodak, 2006)

Although educators now recognize the crucial importance of considering the concerns of parents and families in treatment and educational programs for individuals who are disabled, this wasn't always the case. Professionals' views of the role of parents have changed dramatically. In the not too distant past, some professionals labeled parents as the primary cause of the child's problems or blamed parents when practitioners' interventions were ineffective. For at least two reasons, educators now know that automatically holding parents responsible for their children's problems is inappropriate.

First, research has shown that the direction of causation between child and adult behavior is a two-way street (Bell & Harper, 1977; Bellefontaine, Hastings, Parker, & Forman, 2006; Mangelsdorf & Schoppe-Sullivan, 2007). Sometimes the parent changes the behavior of the child or infant. However, sometimes the reverse is true. Research over several years has confirmed that the behaviors of individuals with a wide variety of disabilities ranging in age from infancy through adolescence can affect the behavior of their parents toward them (Brooks-Gunn & Lewis, 1984; Mahoney & Robenalt, 1986; Orsmond, Seltzer, Greenberg, & Krauss, 2006; Slonims & McConachie, 2006; Smith, Greenberg, Seltzer, & Hong, 2008). For example, some infants who are disabled are relatively unresponsive to stimulation from caregivers, making it more difficult to interact with these children. With an understanding of the reciprocal nature of parent–child interaction, we're more likely to sympathize with a mother's frustration in trying to cuddle an infant with severe developmental disabilities or a father's anger in attempting to deal with his teenager who has an emotional or behavioral disorder.

Second, researchers have found that many parents of children with a disability are very adept at adjusting their interactions with their children to maximize positive development (Guralnick, Neville, Hammond, & Connor, 2008; L. E. Smith et al., 2008). Maternal and paternal instincts often help foster positive outcomes for children with disabilities. Although many researchers used to think that parents needed training to achieve a positive effect on their children, the prevailing philosophy now dictates that whenever possible, professionals should seek the special insights that parents can offer. Furthermore, authorities today are less likely to view the purpose of early intervention to be training parents to assume the role of quasi-therapist or quasi-teacher (Berry & Hardman, 1998). Instead, many professionals now believe that the goal of early intervention should be to develop and preserve the natural parent–child relationship as much as possible. In sum, a healthy parent–child relationship is inherently beneficial.

Recognizing the importance of the family, Congress has passed several federal laws stipulating that schools make a concerted effort to involve parents and families in the education of their children with disabilities. Current law mandates that schools attempt to include parents in crafting their children's individualized education programs (IEPs; see Chapter 1). In the case of infants and toddlers from birth through age 2 years, schools must involve parents in developing **individualized family service plans (IFSPs)**. The focus of the IFSP is family centered; it not only addresses the needs of the individual child who has a disability, but also focuses on the child's family by specifying what services the family needs to enhance the child's development.

INTERNETRESOURCES

The U.S. Department of Education's *My Child's Special Needs* Website offers several resources for parents of children with disabilities: http://www2.ed.gov/ parents/needs/speced/ edpicks.jhtml

TABLE 4.1 Importance of families to teachers and teachers to families

Families . . .
- Provide teachers with personal information that can explain why certain students' behaviors are occurring in the classroom.
- Provide background information and medical histories to teachers and to the school that can help teachers understand why a student behaves or learns in certain ways.
- Reinforce directives that teachers give their students, especially on homework assignments.
- Support teachers by serving as chaperones or volunteers in the classroom.
- Help teachers determine students' interests so that teachers and parents can establish long-term education or vocation goals.
- Tell teachers about which types of discipline and learning strategies work best with their children.
- Help teachers determine each student's strengths and needs so that teachers can create appropriate instructional goals.

Teachers . . .
- Provide families with documented evidence of their children's progress and successes.
- Help families become more actively involved in their children's education.
- Help families determine where a student's interests lie so that parents can establish appropriate long-term goals.
- Teach and reinforce social skills that students need in order to be successful, contributing members of the communities in which families live.
- Tell families when their children exhibit inappropriate behaviors or academic needs in the classroom.
- Provide important educational and community data to help families stay current and knowledgeable about opportunities available for children.
- Lend a helping hand, a supportive ear, and a friendly face to all families served.

Source: Adapted from O'Shea, D. J., & O'Shea, L. J. (2001). Why learn about students' families? In D. J. O'Shea, L. J. O'Shea, R. Algozzine, D. J. Hammitte (Eds.), *Families and teachers of individuals with disabilities: Collaborative orientations and responsive practices* (pp. 5–24). Austin: Pro-Ed, Inc. Copyright © 2001. Adapted by permission of Pro-Ed, Inc.

The fact is that parents and teachers have a symbiotic relationship. Each group can benefit enormously from the other (see Table 4.1).

The Effects of a Child with a Disability on the Family

The birth of any child can have a significant effect on the dynamics of the family. The parents and other children must undergo a variety of changes to adapt to the presence of a new member. The effects on the family of the birth of a child with a disability can be even more profound.

For families who have a child with a disability, the everyday routines that most families take for granted are frequently disrupted (Keogh, Garnier, Bernheimer, & Gallimore, 2000; Stoneman & Gavidia-Payne, 2006). For example, the child with a disability might require alterations in housing (e.g., the family might decide to move closer to therapists), household maintenance schedules (e.g., chores might not be done as quickly because of lack of time), and even parents' career goals might change. For example, one survey of families with children with disabilities found that over half reported that one or more family members altered their work hours, worked fewer hours, changed jobs, or quit working altogether because of having a child with a disability (Anderson, Larson, Lakin, & Kwak, 2002).

It's important to note that the child with a disability can have an impact on both parents and siblings, and in different ways.

The birth of any child has a profound effect on his or her family, and when the child is born with a disability, the effect is even more so.

Parents' Reactions

A STAGE THEORY APPROACH   Traditionally, researchers and clinicians have suggested that parents go through a series of stages after learning they have a child with a disability. Some of these stages parallel the proposed sequence of responses that accompany a person's reactions to the death of a loved one. Based on interviews of parents of infants with serious physical disabilities, a representative set of stages includes shock and disruption, denial, sadness, anxiety and fear, anger, and finally adaptation (Drotar, Baskiewicz, Irvin, Kennell, & Klaus, 1975).

Several authorities have questioned the wisdom of this stage approach in understanding parental reactions. One argument against a strict stage model comes from the fact that many parents report that they don't engage in denial. In fact, they're often the first to suspect a problem. It's largely a myth that parents of children who are disabled go from physician to physician, "shopping" for a more favorable diagnosis. In fact, all too frequently, they have to convince the doctor that there is something wrong with their child.

Although parents might not go through these reactions in a rigid fashion, some do experience some or all these emotions at one time or another. A commonly reported reaction is guilt.

THE ROLE OF GUILT   The parents of a child with a disability frequently wrestle with the feeling that they are in some way responsible for their child's condition. Even though absolutely no basis for such thoughts exists in the vast majority of cases, guilt is one of the most commonly reported feelings of parents of exceptional children.

The high prevalence of guilt is probably due to the fact that the primary cause of so many disabilities is unknown. Uncertainty about the cause of the child's disability creates an atmosphere conducive to speculation by the parents that they themselves are to blame. Mothers are particularly vulnerable. As Featherstone (1980), the mother of a boy who was blind and had hydrocephaly, severe intellectual disability, cerebral palsy, and seizures, described it:

> Our children are wondrous achievements. Their bodies grow inside ours. If their defects originated in utero, we blame our inadequate bodies or inadequate caution. If . . . we accept credit for our children's physical beauty (and most of us do, in our hearts), then inevitably we assume responsibility for their physical defects.
>
> The world makes much of the pregnant woman. People open doors for her, carry her heavy parcels, offer footstools and unsolicited advice. All this attention seems somehow posited on the idea that she is creating something miraculously fine. When the baby arrives imperfect, the mother feels she has failed not only herself and her husband, but the rest of the world as well.
>
> Soon this diffuse sense of inadequacy sharpens. Nearly every mother fastens on some aspect of her own behavior and blames the tragedy on that. (pp. 73–74)

People with disabilities are inevitably faced with inappropriate reactions from those around them, and parents often must help their children respond to such behavior.

DEALING WITH THE PUBLIC   In addition to ambivalence about the cause of the child's disability, parents can feel vulnerable to criticism from others about how they deal with their child's problems. Parents of children with disabilities sometimes sense, correctly or not, that others are scrutinizing their decisions about their child's treatment, educational placement, and so forth. See the accompanying Personal Perspectives feature for an example of one mother's determination not to succumb to such feelings of scrutiny.

The public can sometimes be cruel in their reactions to people with disabilities. People with disabilities—especially those with disabilities that are readily observable—are inevitably faced with inappropriate reactions from those around them. And understandably, parents often assume the burden of responding to inappropriate or even cruel reactions from the public. The following experience of the mother of a child with autism is illustrative:

> Worn out, I toss my purse under the seat and look absently out the window onto the dark tarmac. Last to

Personal PERSPECTIVES
No Overalls for Sophie!

The other day, my friend Kim gave me a pair of hot pink velvet overalls her daughters have outgrown. I stared at them, and pictured my own daughters. . . . Probably the perfect size for Sophie, who will be two next month. But I can't put Sophie in overalls. It's one of the things I promised myself I'd never do. Sophie has Down syndrome. She's retarded. We don't know how retarded at this point. I personally think she's pretty darn smart. . . .

Still, the fact remains. Sophie's retarded. And I have a strong belief that retarded people should not wear overalls. It's not a good look. I know what you're thinking. That woman is going straight to hell. Probably. But I'll go with a strong sense of style. And so will my children. Particularly Sophie. . . .

I'm still not 100 percent sure why I feel the way I do about retarded people and overalls. . . . I told my husband. He looked at me funny for a while, then he finally said, "I think it's John Malcovich in 'Of Mice and Men.' You know, he was retarded and wore overalls.". . .

For the past two years, Sophie has been just a baby. She's smaller than other kids her age, which masks her developmental delays. But lately, I've noticed people looking at her. They can tell. We were at a carnival recently, and as I pushed Sophie's stroller through the crowd, Sophie waved her hands furiously at everyone in sight, laughing hysterically, having a great time. No one was waving back, no one was even really looking at her. I suddenly flashed forward a decade to Sophie the 12-year-old doing the same thing in a crowd, goofily retarded. For a minute, I was not OK with that. Tears burned my eyes.

And then I realized that I have to be OK with that. I don't have any other choice. But I can choose what Sophie wears, so I put the overalls away and dressed my daughter in a beautiful pink-striped onesie, and we went out, . . . where she giggled and blew kisses and waved. Lots of people smiled and waved back.

By Amy Silverman

Amy Silverman is a writer, editor and teacher. She is Managing Editor at Phoenix New Times, the local alternative newsweekly paper where she's worked for 16 years. Amy's work has also appeared on the radio show This American Life and in publications including the New York Times, Travel + Leisure, salon.com, George, Playboy, and Fit Pregnancy. She is also the author of the blog, "Girl in a Party Hat" (http://www.girlinapartyhat.com/), whose main focus is on parenting a child with Down syndrome.

Source: Silverman, A. (2005). A version of this first appeared on KJZZ, the National Public Radio Affiliate in Phoenix, AZ.

board, a woman and a girl of about ten struggle to get into the small, crowded plane. The girl flaps her hand frantically near her face. The pair move in a sort of lunging, shuffling duet. The mother's eyes are firmly fixed toward the rear of the plane and her hand is vise-gripped to the girl's wrist. I know this scenario: mother and child with autism traveling. Small world.

Loud guttural sounds, almost a moan, almost a scream, come from the girl. Her first utterance causes the people near me to shift around in their seats and nervously clear their throats. . . .

The girl's sounds begin to escalate as the plane hits some turbulence. Fellow passengers murmur. To me, of course, this feels like home. . . .

More NOISE. The child is obviously upset and uncomfortable. At least that's obvious to me. The pressure in her ears is probably giving her excruciating pain. I am jarred from my internal reflection by a man's cold remark.

"Why can't she make her be quiet?" the passenger behind me complains loudly.

"Why the hell did she bring her on a plane," hisses the other. Passengers in the seats next to them chuckle.

It's all I can do not to turn around and shout, "Be glad that you aren't that uncomfortable. Be glad that you aren't that child's caretaker, having to dread taking a short, forty-minute flight because of cutting remarks from jerks like you. Aren't you glad she isn't your child because if she was you couldn't just get off a plane and walk away from her!" But I stew in silence.

The plane is descending. We will touch ground soon. The people behind me will get off the plane and glide down to their baggage and their cars. Perhaps they will stop for a martini before they go home, with only themselves to worry about.

The mother in the rear of the plane will wait until everyone else is off, struggle down the rickety steps, carrying too many bags and trying to keep her grip on the tired, crotchety girl. A week from now the others will not even remember this flight or the girl who was making so much noise. I will not be able to forget her. (Gerlach, 1999, pp. 108–110)

DEALING WITH THE CHILD'S FEELINGS   In addition to dealing with the public's reactions to their child's disability, parents face the delicate task of talking with the child about his disability. This can be a difficult responsibility because parents need to address the topic without making the disability seem more important than it actually is. In other words, parents don't want to alarm the child or make the child more concerned about the disability than is necessary.

Nevertheless, the child with a disability usually has questions about it: How did I get it? Will it go away? Will it get worse? Will I be able to live independently as an adult? If possible, parents should wait for the child to ask specific questions to which they can respond, rather than lecture about generalities. However, it is a good idea for parents to talk honestly with the child at as early an age as possible, especially before the teenage years, when so many parents and children have problems communicating.

DEALING WITH EXTENDED FAMILY MEMBERS' FEELINGS   Often overlooked is the impact that the child with a disability will have on extended family members (e.g., parents, grandparents, brothers, sisters). And their reactions are important because extended family members can often play a critical role in providing comfort and support to the immediate family, as the following excerpt illustrates:

I think of all the phone calls I've ever had to make to my parents over the years. The missed curfews. A car accident. The time I decided I wanted to take a year off from college. Moving west with Tom. The two of us deciding to build a life here, thousands of miles away. And still, they are nothing at all, compared to this. It will be the hardest phone call of my life.

I dial the numbers. I say the words over and over again: "Avery has Down syndrome, Avery has Down syndrome, Avery has Down syndrome," to my mom, to my dad and his wife, Pam, to my only sibling, Glynnis.

Dad says, "He'll be one of the better ones," and Pam says, "He's healthy, right? That's all that matters. He'll do great."

Mom says, "Oh, my," then, "Honey, is there anything I can do for you?"

Glynnis says, "I'm proud you are my sister."

It's a blur of tears and words "*I love you*" and "*It will be okay*" and "*Keep in touch*" and it's done.

I have to concentrate to keep my hands from shaking.

I breath. Inhale, exhale. There will be more people to call, but it will have to wait. For now I am done. (Groneberg, 2008, p. 43)

INTERNETRESOURCES

The Fathers Network is a Website devoted to information for fathers of children with disabilities and special health needs: www .fathersnetwork.org ■ ■ ■

Parents' Adjustment

Abundant evidence shows that parents of children with disabilities undergo more than the average amount of stress (Fiedler, Simpson, & Clark, 2007). The stress is usually not the result of major catastrophic events but rather the accumulation of daily responsibilities related to child care. A single event, such as a family member coming down with a serious illness, can precipitate a family crisis, but its effects are even more devastating if the family was already under stress because of a multitude of daily hassles.

PARENTAL REACTION TO STRESS   Contrary to what one might think, stress isn't always linked to the severity of the child's disability. For example, parents of children with more severe disabilities might have greater child-care burdens, but parents of children with milder disabilities might be more likely to experience additional stress related to that felt by parents of children without disabilities (e.g., stress pertaining to school achievement, dating, driving a car). Stress, however, does appear to be more prevalent in parents of children who exhibit poor social skills and behavior problems (Davis & Carter, 2008; Plant & Sanders, 2007), especially if the problems involve socially offensive and disruptive behaviors (Hastings, Daley, Burns, & Beck, 2006; Orsmond et al., 2006).

The factors that appear to be most predictive of how parents will cope with the stress are their prior psychological makeup and marital happiness and the quality and degree of informal support they receive from others. Although there are exceptions, it's fair to say that parents who were well adjusted and happily married before the birth of the child have a better chance of coping than do those who were having psychological or marital problems.

Social support that parents receive from each other, extended family members, friends, and others can be critical in helping parents cope with the stress of raising a child with a disability (Plant & Sanders, 2007; Singer, 2002). The support can be physical, such as offering child care, or it can be psychological. Just having someone to talk to about problems can be helpful.

CHANGING VIEWS OF PARENTAL ADJUSTMENT   At one time, most professionals assumed that parents of children with disabilities were destined for a life of stress and misery. Although professionals now know this assumption to be largely invalid, research does show that parents, especially mothers, of children with disabilities have an undeniably greater likelihood of depression. Across several studies, researchers have found that mothers of children with developmental disabilities are at an increased risk of experiencing depression (Singer, 2006). Twenty-nine percent of these mothers experienced depression.

The figure of 29% certainly signals that mothers of children with disabilities are vulnerable to depression, but it's important to keep in mind that it also means that 71% did not become depressed. Furthermore, strong evidence indicates that this depression tends to diminish as the child grows older (Glidden & Jobe, 2006; Singer, 2006).

Given the research available, professionals should have a heightened sensitivity to the possibility that parents of children with disabilities may experience varying levels of depression. At the same time, many parents cope very well, with numerous anecdotal accounts of parents who report that adding a child with a disability to the family actually has resulted in unanticipated positive benefits (Ferguson, 2002; Scorgie & Sobsey, 2000; Skinner, Bailey, Correa, & Rodriguez, 1999). They report undergoing life-changing experiences, which include becoming:

- More tolerant of differences in other people
- More concerned about social issues
- Better parents
- A closer-knit family
- More philosophical or spiritual about life

Interestingly, evidence suggests that Latino families are more likely than Anglo families to view having a child with a disability as a positive rather than a negative experience. One team of researchers (Blacher & Baker, 2007) attributes this to a philosophical attitude toward adversity as exemplified by the expression, "No hay mal que por bien no venga [there is nothing bad out of which good cannot come]" (Zuniga, 1992, p. 115). It may also be due to the importance of the family in the Latino culture and the social supports that strong family ties can provide.

Some parents report that having a child with a disability in the family has unanticipated positive results, including greater tolerance of differences in other people, being better parents, and having a closer-knit family.

Elizabeth King Gerlach's (1999) philosophical outlook on society's obsession with normalcy was undoubtedly shaped by her having a child with a disability:

> Society views disability as a "tragedy." In fact, the greater tragedy is society's larger and erroneous view that there is such a state as "normal." . . .
>
> "Normal" does exist, but you have to look for it. It is a place that is somewhere between the middle of two extremes. For instance, [a] good example of normal can be found on my clothes dryer, between "fluff," and "shrink it." This area is marked "normal." I use this setting because it is the closest to normal that my life usually gets.
>
> The truth is, "normal" is not a word that should apply to the human condition. People are different, and they constantly change. A close approximation to "normal" might be "balanced." . . . And some of us endeavor to maintain a balanced state within ourselves, our families, and our communities. We have to discover what this means for ourselves, and this too changes over time.
>
> I used to think there was such a thing as a "normal, happy family" and that it was something attainable. I hadn't experienced that as a child, so I set out to create it as an adult. Autism bombed that notion. Just as well. I'm not pretending that autism, in its varying degrees of severity, isn't painful in many ways for everyone involved. It is. I'm simply saying that some of that pain is relieved with understanding and acceptance. Having a child with a disability has shown me how precious life really is and that being human means learning to love. The simplicity and complexity of this understanding never cease to amaze me. (pp. 4–6)

Our intent is not to minimize the fact that the added stress a child with a disability often brings can have a devastating impact on the stability of the family. It's dangerous to assume, though, that the birth of a child with a disability automatically spells doom for the psychological well-being of the parents or for the stability of their marriage.

INTERNETRESOURCES

Author Brady Udall has narrated a short story that poignantly explores the feelings of a sibling toward his brother with a disability. It's available for purchase as download at National Public Radio's *This American Life:* http://www.thisamericanlife .org/radio-archives/episode/ 154/In-Dog-We-Trust?bypass =true ■ ■ ■

Siblings' Reactions

Although a relatively large body of literature pertains to parental reactions, much less information is available about siblings of people with disabilities. What is available, however, indicates that siblings can and frequently do experience the same emotions—fear, anger, guilt, and so forth—that parents do. In fact, in some ways, siblings might initially have an even more difficult time than their parents in coping with some of these feelings, especially when they are younger. Being less mature, they might have trouble putting some of their negative thoughts into proper perspective. And they might be uncomfortable asking their parents the questions that bother them. Table 4.2 provides examples of sibling concerns.

Although some feelings about their siblings' disabilities might not appear for many years, a substantial number of accounts indicate that nondisabled siblings are aware at an early age that their brothers or sisters are different in some way. The following excerpt from a blog kept by Amy Silverman, the mother of Sophie, the girl with Down syndrome in the preceding Personal Perspectives feature (see p. 81), illustrates how parents can struggle for the right words when explaining a child's disability to her sibling. It also points out that young children can sometimes be surprisingly insightful about the nature of disabilities:

> Last night after Sophie had gone to bed, Annabelle and I settled down on the couch. As the older sister, she gets to stay up a little later.
>
> "Sophie's turning 5 tomorrow," Annabelle said.
>
> "Yes."
>
> "Is she really going to kindergarten? She doesn't talk very well."
>
> "You know why that is, right?"
>
> "No."
>
> (I think she does, but who knows. I've been known to play dumb a time or two, myself, in this life.)
>
> "Well, Sophie has Down syndrome. That makes her a little different from us, from other kids her age."

TABLE 4.2 Sibling concerns about . . .

Their sibling with a disability	• What caused the disability? • Why does my brother behave so strangely? • Will my sister ever live on her own?
Their parents	• Why do they let my brother get away with so much? • Why must all their time be given to my sister? • Why do they always ask me to babysit?
Themselves	• Why do I have such mixed feelings about my sister? • Will I catch the disability? • Will we have a normal brother–sister relationship?
Their friends	• How can I tell my best friend about my brother? • Will my friends tell everyone at school? • What should I do when other kids make fun of people with disabilities?
Their school and community	• What happens in special education classes? • Will I be compared with my sister? • What should I tell strangers?
Adulthood	• Will I be responsible for my brother when my parents die? • Do I need genetic counseling? • Should I join a parents' and/or siblings' group?

Source: Adapted from *Brothers & sisters—A special part of exceptional families* (3rd ed.), by P. A. Gallagher, T. H. Powell, & C. A. Rhodes, 2006, Baltimore, MD: Paul H. Brookes. Reprinted by permission.

"Yeah."

Luckily, Ray had just come in from a bike ride. He was summoned to the couch, where he explained that every person starts with one cell, and that in Sophie's case, that cell was different (we'll have to come up with a different word, whoops, for different; he also learned that the phrase "genetic material" doesn't work on an almost 7 year old) and therefore, every bit of Sophie's just a little bit different. (Sometimes more than a little bit.)

"Does that make you sad, that she's different?" I asked.

"No," Annabelle replied matter of factly. "If that's her, that's her." (Silverman, 2005)

As nondisabled siblings grow older, their concerns often become focused on how society views them and their siblings who are disabled. Adolescence can be a particularly difficult period. Teens, fearing rejection by peers, often don't want to appear different, and having a sibling with a disability can single a person out.

Siblings' Adjustment

Children, like parents, can adapt well or poorly to having family members with disabilities. Not much research exists on this topic. The little solid research evidence that does exist is in the area of intellectual disabilities and suggests that, although siblings are at a slightly elevated risk, they are at lower risk than parents of experiencing depression and anxiety (Rossiter & Sharpe, 2001). As is the case with parents, however, some people report having benefited from having a sibling with a disability; see the accompanying Personal Perspectives: Lessons from My Brother.

Why some siblings respond negatively whereas others do not isn't completely understood. Although not definitive, some evidence suggests

Siblings of children with disabilities often recount being aware at a very early age that something was different about their brothers or sisters. Siblings' attitudes change at different stages of their lives; for example, adolescents become more concerned about public perception of themselves and their siblings with disabilities.

Personal PERSPECTIVES
Lessons from My Brother

I never actually thought about how much or if my younger brother's Down syndrome affected my decision to become a doctor until the question was posed recently. After much introspection, I finally decided that my experience with my brother did not influence the decision to practice, but the way I practice medicine. The skills learned while participating in his care have served me well in my dual roles as physician and mother.

His short sixteen years of life had a lasting effect on my life and my view of others. Carlton taught me patience, attentive listening, never to underestimate or allow myself to be underestimated, it's never too late to learn, and the enjoyment of simple pleasures of life. All aspects of my life were changed by the brief time he spent with us, and I am just realizing all he taught. . . .

At the age of sixteen he appeared to be a three-and-a-half foot, thin baby. Carlton remained a "baby" for the rest of his life; wearing diapers, crawling everywhere only able to walk if supported and was carted about with long legs dangling from my petite mother's hips like extra appendages.

He would periodically press his protruding eyes further out of their sockets with his thumbs for some optical pleasure known only to him. As a little girl, in trying to understand why he performed the only activity that could even be considered self-inflicted harm, I tried this maneuver myself, although not as aggressively. Seeing only a few scattered bursts of light, I gave up and chalked it up to different wiring in our brains. Even then, Carlton was teaching me to at least try to see things from another's perspective. The lesson learned in the literal was later easily expanded to the figurative and empathy was the result.

After watching someone with a toddler's mentality for over a decade bask happily in the sun or laugh ecstatically in a mass of squirming puppies, a newfound recognition and appreciation of all things simple cannot help but develop. . . .

Watching my mother care for an exceptional child with limited resources and my brother thrive despite all that was lacking sowed the seeds of fortitude that I would need to succeed in my medical career. I now recognize that the odds were stacked against this poor African American girl from rural Alabama ever becoming a physician. I never even saw the long line of hurdles as a whole and simply took them one at a time; failure was not an option. Because of Carlton I never learned to underestimate others or myself.

By Valencia Clay

Dr. Valencia Clay is a graduate of the University of Alabama School of Medicine. She is board certified in Internal Medicine and works as a medical director for a disability insurance company and as a hospice medical consultant.

Source: Clay, V. (2006). Lessons from my brother. *Exceptional Parent, 36*(12), 24–25. Reprinted by permission.

INTERNETRESOURCES

The Sibling Support Project (http://www.siblingsupport .org) provides extensive resources about sibshops.

that birth order, gender, and age differences between siblings have some bearing on adjustment. Although girls who are older than their sibling with a disability may experience more stress because their parents often rely on them to help with child care, research is mixed on whether they harbor more negative feelings than boys toward their siblings (Fiedler et al., 2007; Floyd, Purcell, Richardson, & Kupersmidt, 2009). At older ages, however, when siblings are adults, evidence shows that women experience more favorable attachments than men do to their sibling with a disability, and adults who are of the same gender as their sibling with a disability experience more favorable emotional responses (Orsmond & Seltzer, 2000).

Access to information is one key to adjustment for siblings of children with disabilities. As noted in Table 4.2, siblings have myriad questions pertaining to their sibling's disability. Straightforward answers to these questions can help them cope with their fears. Teachers, as well as parents, can provide answers to some of these questions. An excellent resource for providing information and support to siblings are **sibshops**, workshops (Meyer & Vadasy, 2008) specifically designed to help siblings of children with disabilities.

A FAMILY-CENTERED APPROACH TO TREATMENT AND EDUCATION

As noted earlier, today educators are more likely to recognize the positive influence parents can have on their exceptional children's development. This more positive attitude toward parents is reflected in educators' changed approach to involving parents in the treatment and education of their children.

At one time, most early intervention programs for families of children with disabilities operated according to the philosophy that the professionals had the expertise and the families needed that expertise to function. Most authorities today, however, advocate a **family-centered model** (Bailey, Raspa, Humphreys, & Sam, 2011; Mangelsdorf & Schoppe-Sullivan, 2007). Under a family-centered model, professionals encourage the families to make their own decisions with respect to services while mobilizing resources and formal and informal supports for the family's goals. The family-centered approach is a model in which the professionals work *for* the family. Research indicates that a family-centered approach leads to positive outcomes for families (Bailey et al., 2011).

In addition to bringing about positive outcomes for families, a family-centered approach

exemplifies the values we hold as a society for respect for individuals, personal dignity, and freedom of choice. By engaging in family-centered practices, we affirm the premise that . . . intervention is a consumer-oriented enterprise that ought to be responsive to the needs and desires of families and respectful of their preferences for goals and services. Research in both early intervention and medical contexts consistently shows that, when professionals adopt a family-centered approach, . . . [a] number of tangible benefits are evident, ranging from increased satisfaction to improvements in parenting practices. (Bailey et al., 2011)

Family-centered models reflect a change from viewing parents as passive recipients of professional advice to viewing them as equal partners in the development of treatment and educational programs for their children. The notion is that when professionals don't just provide direct services but also encourage the family to help themselves and their children, the family assumes control over their own lives and avoids the dependency that is sometimes associated with typical professional–family relationships.

Achieving the right balance between offering assistance and allowing families to make independent decisions can be challenging. For example, interviews with parents have resulted in the following recommendations:

- Be direct—but don't tell us what to do.
- Tell the truth and be honest—but also be hopeful and encouraging.
- Be knowledgeable—but admit when you don't know the answer.
- Don't overwhelm—but don't hold back information. (Meadow-Orlans, Mertens, & Sass-Lehrer, 2003)

Family-centered models are consistent with another current trend in services for families with disabilities—wraparound service systems. **Wraparound service systems** involve using not only educational services but available community services (e.g., mental health, social welfare, juvenile justice, and so forth) to meet the individualized needs of children and their families (Fiedler et al., 2007). These various services are "wrapped around" the family so that service providers give attention to as many of the family's needs as possible.

Family Systems Theory

The emphasis on understanding the individual's behavior in the context of the family and understanding the family's behavior in the context of other social systems is the basic principle underlying **family systems theory** (Lambie, 2000). Researchers have developed several family systems theories, all of which assume that treatment and educational programs will be more likely to succeed if they take into account the relationships and interactions among family members. One model developed specifically with people with disabilities in mind includes four interrelated components: family characteristics, family interaction, family functions, and family life cycle (Turnbull et al., 2006).

FAMILY CHARACTERISTICS   **Family characteristics** include basic information about the family, such as the type and severity of the disability, the family's size, cultural background, socioeconomic status, coping styles, and special conditions (e.g., spousal abuse,

INTERNETRESOURCES

Fiesta Educativa is a project focused on providing information for Spanish-speaking families that have a child with a disability: www .fiestaeducativa.org

maternal depression). Family characteristics help to determine how family members interact with each other and with others outside the family. These characteristics can include, for example, whether the child is learning disabled or deaf, is an only child or has five siblings, is of the upper middle class or lives in poverty, and so forth.

Recent trends in U.S. society make it even more important for educators to take into account family characteristics. In particular, teachers should be attentive to the expanding ethnic diversity in the United States, which has resulted in a wider mismatch between the ethnicities of teachers and students, especially students in special education. One of the difficulties facing many special education teachers, who are often white, is knowing how to involve families from a different culture. Perhaps the most important thing to remember is that parents from diverse backgrounds do not have any one particular way of interacting with teachers or other professionals. For example, some researchers have found that family members from culturally and/or linguistically diverse backgrounds have a tendency to defer to professionals as the "experts," but others have pointed out that they can sometimes mistrust school personnel (Parette & Petch-Hogan, 2000). In other words, professionals need to be alert to such possible differences and be ready to try to accommodate them. In the case of families being suspicious of schools, for example, teachers might try contacting people in the community (e.g., a minister, physician, retired teacher of the same ethnicity) who are trusted by the families to serve as bridges between the family and the school.

In addition to wider ethnic diversity, other changes in families include increases in the number of families in which both parents work outside the home, single-parent families, same-sex unions, and families living in poverty. Families particularly vulnerable to the stresses of raising a child with disabilities are those facing additional struggles arising from poverty or single-parent status. Unfortunately, a higher prevalence of disabilities exists in single-parent families and families in poverty (Parish, Rose, Grinstein-Weiss, Richman, & Andrews, 2009).

Another group on the rise in numbers and facing considerable challenges raising children with disabilities are military families. The changing demographics of those in the military have contributed to these problems. An increasing number of low-income women are looking to the military for career opportunities; more than 80% of the military are married with children, and the military is the largest employer of single parents in the United States (Taylor et al., 2005). Perhaps the biggest change in recent years has been the additional stresses associated with the separation of soldiers from their families due to deployment overseas. This stress not only has been difficult for the spouse of a soldier, but also has been especially difficult for the family when the mother, herself, is a soldier. As one team of researchers concluded after in-depth interviews with low-income mothers in the military who were attempting to raise a child or children with disabilities:

> Although the women in our study entered the military as a career and felt very positively about the opportunities it could offer them when they enlisted, once they became mothers of a child with disabilities, the economic hardship and inflexibility in the workplace proved incompatible with successfully parenting a child with a disability. (Taylor et al., 2005, p. 96)

Coupled with these demographic changes—and to a certain extent influenced by them—families today live under a great deal of stress. Adding to this stress is the threat of terrorism subsequent to the attacks on the World Trade Center and the Pentagon on September 11, 2001, as well as uncertainties accompanying the economic crises of the past few years. On the one hand, children need attention and reassurance more than ever; but on the other hand, because of pressures to earn a living, parents have fewer resources to draw on to provide comfort to their children.

These dramatic societal changes present formidable challenges in working with families of children with disabilities. As family configurations change, professionals need to alter their approaches. For example, approaches that are successful with two-parent families might not be suitable for single mothers. Also, professionals need to understand that today's parents are living under increasing stress and might find it correspondingly difficult to devote time and energy to working on behalf of their children.

FAMILY INTERACTION   In the Turnbulls' model, **family inter-actions** reflect family cohesion and adaptability, important determinants of the "health" of a family (Turnbull et al., 2006). In general, families are healthier if they have moderate degrees of cohesion and adaptability.

Cohesion   *Cohesion* refers to the degree to which an individual family member is free to act independently of other family members. An appropriate amount of family cohesion permits the individual to be her own person while at the same time drawing on other family members for support as needed. Families with low cohesion might not offer the child with a disability the necessary support, whereas the overly cohesive family might be overprotective. Research suggests that good cohesion has positive benefits for the child as well as other family members (Howell, Hauser-Cram, & Kersh, 2007; Magana, Schwartz, Rubert, & Szapocznik, 2006).

Otherwise healthy families often have difficulty finding the right balance of cohesion. They sometimes go overboard in wanting to help their children and, in so doing, limit their children's independence. Adolescence can be a particularly stressful time, when it's normal for teenagers to loosen their familial bonds. Adolescence is difficult for many families of children with disabilities; because of the disability, the family by necessity has often been more protective of the child. Cohesion can also be an issue for adults with disabilities. Current thinking dictates that people with disabilities should live in the community, but many will need support from their families to succeed. Living in the community demands a number of daily living skills—such as managing personal finances, keeping to a work schedule, and planning and preparing meals—that don't always come easily even to nondisabled young adults. Finding the right degree of independence from the family for young adults with disabilities can be a significant challenge. As one mother explained about future living arrangements for her daughter with severe intellectual disabilities:

Adults with intellectual disabilities, especially those who live at home, often have special problems finding the right degree of independence from their families. When they do live away from home, parents are often concerned about providing enough support so their children don't become socially isolated.

> I would like to see her live fairly close. . . . She's going to have to have some support, I know that. . . . And I would like to see her close enough so that we always have the constant, not constant, [sic] but we will always be there if she needs us. And both Tim and I agree that that's something we will always do. We will be here. But, on the other hand, if we want to go away for a month, we'll know there are other people that can be called upon to give her the support she needs. (Lehmann & Baker, 1995, p. 30)

Adaptability   *Adaptability* refers to the degree to which families are able to change their modes of interaction when they encounter unusual or stressful situations. Some families are so chaotic that it's difficult to predict what any one member will do in a given situation. In such an unstable environment, the needs of the family member who is disabled might be overlooked or neglected. At the other end of the continuum are families characterized by extreme rigidity. Each family member has his prescribed family role. Such rigidity makes it difficult to adjust to the addition of a new family member, especially one with a disability. For example, the mother's involvement in transporting the child with a disability to therapy sessions might necessitate that the father be more involved taking care of the other children.

Family Functions   **Family functions** are the numerous routines in which families engage to meet their many and diverse needs—economic, daily care, social, medical, and educational.

An important point for teachers and other professionals to consider is that education is only one of several functions in which families are immersed. For some students, especially those with multiple disabilities, several professionals might be vying for the parents' time. It's natural, of course, for teachers to want to involve parents as much as possible.

Positive benefits can occur when parents are part of the treatment program. At the same time, however, teachers need to respect the fact that education is just one of the many functions to which families must attend.

Several authorities have reported that some families of students with disabilities prefer a passive, rather than an active, degree of involvement in their children's education (Turnbull & Turnbull, 2006). Families often have legitimate reasons for playing a more passive role. For example, in some cultures it's customary for parents to refrain from interfering with the roles of school personnel in educational matters. Furthermore, some parents might simply be so busy attending to other family functions that they are forced to delegate most of the educational decisions to teachers. Teachers should respect the parents' desire to play a relatively passive role in their child's education.

FAMILY LIFE CYCLE   Several family theorists have noted that the impact of a child with a disability on the family changes over time (Berry & Hardman, 1998; O'Shea, O'Shea, Algozzine, & Hammitte, 2001) and have noted the value in looking at families of children with disabilities from a **family life cycle** perspective. Most family theorists consider four stages in the lives of families based on the ages of the children: early childhood, childhood, adolescence, and adulthood.

Transitions between life cycle stages are often stressful for families, especially families with children who are disabled. We've already mentioned the difficulties facing families at the transition point when their child, as an adult, moves into more independent work and living settings. A particularly difficult issue for some parents of children with disabilities who are entering adulthood is that of mental competence and guardianship. Parents who decide that their children are not competent to make rational choices without endangering themselves can go through legal channels to obtain guardianship of their children. **Guardianship** means that one person has the authority, granted by the courts, to make decisions for another person. Guardianship can range in degree from total to more limited or temporary authority to make decisions.

Another particularly troublesome transition can be from the relatively intimate confines of an infant or preschool program to the larger context of a kindergarten setting, which requires more independence on the part of the child. As Amy Silverman observed, as her daughter with Down syndrome went off to her last day of preschool:

> This morning, I put Sophie on the bus for her last ride. She handed thank you gifts to the driver Dorothy and Tina . . . and I wished Dorothy well. She's retiring. She looked at me and smiled and said, "I have a feeling that kindergarten's going to be a lot harder for you than it is for Sophie."
>
> She read my mind. That's not hard these days, since I can feel my thoughts sticking out my ears. I have to remind myself that I felt the same way the first day I dropped Sophie off at day care, the first day she moved to the pre-school room, the first time I put her on the bus. It doesn't help that I've developed an attachment bordering on co-dependence with Janice, Sophie's pre-school teacher. (Silverman, 2005)

Transitions between stages are difficult because of the uncertainty that each new phase presents to the family. One of the reasons for the uncertainty pertains to replacements of the professionals who work with the child who is disabled. In particular, parents of a child with multiple disabilities, who requires services from multiple professionals, can be anxious about the switches in therapists and teachers that occur many times throughout the child's life, especially at transition points.

Social Support for Families

Families can derive tremendous benefit from social support provided by others (Lenhard et al., 2007; Singer, 2002). **Social support** refers to emotional, informational, or material aid that is provided to persons in need. In contrast to assistance that comes from professionals and agencies, social support is informal, coming from such sources as extended family, friends, church groups, neighbors, and social clubs.

INTERNETRESOURCES

The Gillian Film is an excellent documentary about a mother's struggles with coming to terms with the transition into independent living of her daughter who is intellectually disabled: http://www.thegillianfilm.com/index.html

INTERNETRESOURCES

Several projects, many of which are funded by the federal government, focus on providing information and support to families of children with disabilities. Following are some examples:
PACER Center: www.pacer.org
Beach Center: www.beachcenter.org
Federation for Children with Special Needs: www.fcsn.org
Family Village of the Waisman Center, University of Wisconsin: www.familyvillage.wisc.edu/index.htmlx
Parents Helping Parents: http://www.php.com/
Through the Looking Glass: www.lookingglass.org
National Center for Infants, Toddlers and Families:
Zero to Three: www.zerotothree.org
Exceptional Parent is a magazine focused on families with children with disabilities. It also provides useful information on its Website: www.eparent.com

ETHNICITY AND SOCIAL SUPPORT   Research shows evidence of familial and religious support in ethnic minority families (Harry, 2002; Magana et al., 2006). The values of some minority groups place heavy emphasis on caring for one's own family members, disabled or not. The family's church plays a major social support role for many minorities, again regardless of whether they are disabled or not.

PARENTAL SUPPORT GROUPS   One common type of social support, especially for parents of recently diagnosed children, is parental support groups that consist of parents of children with the same or similar disabilities. Such groups can be relatively unstructured, meeting infrequently with unspecified agendas, or they can be more structured. They serve as a means for parents to share their experiences, thus providing educational and emotional support. Parental support groups, however, are not of benefit to everyone. Some parents actually experience more stress from sharing problems and listening to the problems of others (Berry & Hardman, 1998).

INTERNET RESOURCES FOR PARENTS   The Internet is an excellent resource for parents of children with disabilities. Dozens of electronic mailing lists, newsgroups, blogs, and Websites are now devoted to disability-related topics. Through these means, parents of children with disabilities can communicate with each other, with people who have disabilities, and with professionals concerning practical as well as theoretical issues. There are sites for specific disabilities (e.g., Down syndrome, attention deficit hyperactivity disorder, cerebral palsy, cystic fibrosis) as well as more general ones.

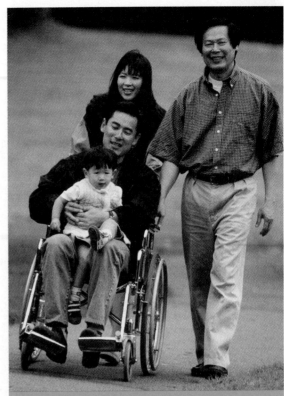

Research shows evidence of familial and religious support of members with disabilities in ethnic minority families (Harry, 2002; Magana et al., 2006).

PARENT CENTERS   The U.S. Department of Education has established more than 100 Parent Training and Information Centers and Community Parent Resource Centers; each state has at least one of these centers. (The January, 2009, issue of *Exceptional Parent Magazine* lists all of the centers in each of the states.) The Technical Assistance Alliance for Parent Centers (http://www.taalliance.org/about/index.asp) assists and coordinates the work of these centers. The general purpose of the centers is to "provide training and information to parents of infants, toddlers, children, and youth with disabilities and to professionals who work with them. This assistance helps parents to participate more effectively with professionals in meeting their children's educational needs" (Technical Assistance Alliance for Parent Centers, 2009).

Positive Behavioral Intervention and Support for Challenging Behaviors

Some children with disabilities engage in behaviors that are particularly challenging for professionals and family members alike. Children with emotional or behavioral disorders and those with autism, for example, sometimes exhibit outbursts of aggressive or self-injurious behavior. As one team of researchers documented, such behaviors can have a profound impact on the family:

> The families we interviewed described a family life that was deeply and pervasively affected. . . . The entire family system was engaged in multiple accommodations in response to the child's problem behavior. . . . These families were changed as a result of the persistent and overwhelming demands of physically intervening with their child or worrying about their child's problem behavior. As researchers, we found it difficult to construct the prose that would adequately

convey the emotional, physical, and structural impact of problem behavior on family life. Problem behavior relentlessly affected family relationships, physical circumstances, social networks, and daily activities. (Fox, Vaughn, Wyatte, & Dunlap, 2002, p. 448)

Positive behavioral intervention and support (PBIS) for families might include mealtimes, seasonal celebrations, visits to relatives, etc. as opportunities for reinforcing positive or appropriate behavior.

Such extreme behaviors often require more than just social support from friends and the community. In such cases, professionals may need to help families apply behavioral principles in interacting with their child. Two effective approaches for dealing with behavioral problems are **functional behavioral assessment (FBA)** and **positive behavioral intervention and support (PBIS)**. (We discuss these more fully in Chapter 8.) Briefly, FBA is the evaluation of the antecedents, consequences, and contextual factors that maintain inappropriate behaviors, and PBIS is the systematic use of scientific principles emphasizing supporting or reinforcing appropriate behavior instead of punishing inappropriate behavior. Table 4.3 lists examples of questions parents can ask themselves as part of participating in an FBA.

In applying PBIS with families, the focus is on **family activity settings**, routines that families engage in, such as mealtimes, seasonal celebrations, visits to relatives, shopping, going on vacations, and eating in restaurants (Lucyshyn, Horner, Dunlap, Albin, & Ben, 2002; Singer, Goldberg-Hamblin, Peckham-Hardin, Barry, & Santarelli, 2002). Under the guidance of professionals, families typically begin by concentrating on just one or two settings before expanding to more. The key to reducing challenging behaviors in the home through FBA and PBIS is close communication between parents, who know their children best, and professionals, who have the expertise to help parents apply behavioral principles effectively.

Communication Between Parents and Professionals

Virtually all family theorists and practitioners agree that no matter which particular approach one uses to work with parents, the key to the success of a program is how well parents and professionals work together. Even the most creative, well-conceived model is doomed to fail if professionals and parents cannot communicate effectively.

TABLE 4.3 Examples of questions parents can ask themselves when participating in a functional behavior analysis

- What are my child's biggest strengths?
- What activities, objects, or other items are most reinforcing to my child?
- What behavior is of most concern to me?
- How often does this behavior occur?
- When/where does it happen most/least frequently?
- What do I and other family members usually do in response to the behavior?
- Can I think of anything that seems to increase/decrease the behavior?
- Do I have any hypotheses about why my child engages in this behavior?

Source: Adapted from Fiedler, C. R., Simpson, R. L., & Clark, D. M. (2007). *Parents and families of children with disabilities: Effective school-based support services* (p. 238). Upper Saddle River, NJ: Pearson.

Unfortunately, such communication doesn't come easily—not too surprising, considering the ingredients of the situation. On the one hand are the parents, who are trying to cope with the stresses of raising a child with a disability in a complex and changing society. On the other hand are the professionals—teachers, speech therapists, physicians, psychologists, physical therapists, and so forth—who might be frustrated because they don't have all the answers to the child's problems.

One of the keys to avoiding professional–parent misunderstandings is communication (Kauffman, Mostert, Trent, & Pullen, 2011). It's critical that teachers receive information *from* parents as well as provide information *to* them. The parents have spent considerably more time with the child and have more invested in the child emotionally; they can be an invaluable source of information about the child's characteristics and interests. By keeping parents informed of activity in class, teachers can foster a relationship in which they can call on parents for support should the need arise.

Homework is one area in particular that's often a source of misunderstanding and conflict and that requires parental cooperation. The accompanying Focus on Concepts: Homework offers some strategies for enhancing the homework experience for students with disabilities.

FOCUS ON Concepts

HOMEWORK

Tips for Teachers and Administrators

A considerable amount of research has addressed how best to deal with homework assignments. Warger (2003–2004) reviewed much of this research and developed several pointers for teachers and administrators to consider. Here are some of the tips:

Give Clear and Appropriate Assignments

If the homework is too hard, is perceived as busy work, or takes too long to complete, students might tune out and resist doing it. Never send home any assignment that students cannot do. Homework should be an extension of what students have learned in class.

- Make sure students and parents have information regarding the policy on missed and late assignments, extra credit, and available adaptations.
- Remind the students of due dates periodically.
- Coordinate with other teachers to prevent homework overload.
- Establish a routine at the beginning of the year for how homework will be assigned.
- Assign homework at the beginning of class.
- Explain how to do the homework, provide examples, and write directions on the chalkboard.
- Have students begin the homework in class, check that they understand, and provide assistance as necessary.

Make Homework Accommodations

- Provide additional one-on-one assistance to students.

- Allow alternative response formats (e.g., allow the student to audiotape an assignment).
- Adjust the length of the assignment.
- Provide a peer tutor or assign the student to a study group.
- Provide learning tools (e.g., calculators).
- Adjust evaluation standards.
- Give fewer assignments.

Ensure Clear Home–School Communication

Recommended ways in which teachers can improve communications with parents include

- Provide a list of suggestions on how parents might assist with homework. For example, ask parents to check with their children about homework daily.
- Provide parents with frequent written communication about homework.

Ways in which administrators can support teachers in improving communication include

- Supply teachers with the technology needed to aid communication (e.g., telephone answering systems, e-mail, homework hotlines).
- Provide incentives for teachers to participate in face-to-face meetings with parents (e.g., release time, compensation).
- Suggest that the school district offer after-school and/or peer tutoring sessions to give students extra help with homework.

Most authorities agree that communication between the teacher and parents should start as soon as possible and that it should not be initiated only by negative student behavior. Parents, especially those of students with behavior disorders, often complain that the only time they hear from school personnel is when their child has misbehaved. To establish a degree of rapport with parents, some teachers make a practice of sending an e-mail or a brief form letter at the beginning of the school year, outlining the goals for the year. Others send periodic e-mails or newsletters or make occasional phone calls to parents. By establishing a line of communication with parents early in the year, the teacher is in a better position to initiate more intensive and focused discussions should the need arise. Three such methods of communication are parent–teacher conferences, home-note programs, and traveling notebooks.

PARENT–TEACHER CONFERENCES   Parent–teacher conferences can be an effective way for teachers to share information with parents. Likewise, they're an opportunity for teachers to learn more about the students from the parents' perspective. In addition to regularly scheduled meetings open to all parents, teachers might want to hold individual conferences with the parents of particular students. Planning is key to conducting successful parent–teacher conferences. How the teacher initiates the meeting, for example, can be crucial. Table 4.4 presents questions teachers should ask themselves in order to facilitate their parent–teacher conferences.

No matter the purpose of the meeting, research has shown that a key to communicating with parents is for professionals to talk about the child in such a way that it's obvious that they consider the child an individual, with unique strengths, weaknesses, and interests (Esquivel, Ryan, & Bonner, 2008). Nothing turns parents off more than getting the impression that their child is being defined by a diagnostic or special education category (e.g., learning disabled, behavior disordered).

If the focus of the meeting is the student's poor work or misbehavior, the teacher will need to be as diplomatic as possible. Most authorities recommend that the teacher find

TABLE 4.4 Questions teachers should ask themselves about parent–teacher conferences

Have you done your homework?
- Reviewed the student's cumulative records.
- Consulted with other professionals.
- Documented the student's academic and behavioral progress.
- Established rapport with the parents before the conference.
- Familiarized yourself with the student and family's culture.

Have you involved the parents *before* the conference?
- Discussed the goals of the meeting with the parents and solicited their input.
- Involved the student, as appropriate.
- Scheduled a mutually convenient day and time for the meeting.
- Provided written notice prior to the meeting.

How do you involve the parents *during* the meeting?
- Welcome the parents and speak informally with them before the beginning.
- Reiterate the goals of the meeting.
- Begin with a discussion of the child's strengths.
- Support your points with specific examples and documentation.
- Encourage parents to share insights.
- Ask open-ended questions.
- Avoid jargon.
- Practice active listening. Remember, one of your big jobs is to listen to parents.
- Review the main points of the meeting and determine a course of action.
- Provide additional resources (e.g., support groups, family resource centers, Websites).

What do you do *after* the meeting?
- Document the results of the meeting.
- Share results with colleagues who work with the student.
- Follow up with the parents as needed to discuss changes.

Source: Adapted from Kauffman, J. M., Pullen, P. L., Mostert, M. P., & Trent, S. C. (2011). *Managing classroom behaviors: A reflective case-based approach* (5th ed.). Upper Saddle River, NJ: Pearson.

something positive to say about the student while still providing an objective account of what the student is doing that is troubling. The teacher needs to achieve a delicate balance of providing an objective account of the student's transgressions or poor work while demonstrating advocacy for the student. If parents detect that the teacher is angry, this can make them apprehensive about the treatment the child might be receiving. Conveying only good news can also lose the parents' sense of trust. If the parents hear only good news, then they will be taken by surprise if a serious incident does occur.

HOME-NOTE PROGRAMS Sometimes referred to as home-contingency programs, home-note programs are a way of communicating with parents and having them reinforce behavior that occurs at school (Jurbergs, Palcic, & Kelley, 2007; Kelley, 1990). By having parents dispense the reinforcement, the teacher takes advantage of the fact that parents usually have a greater number of reinforcers at their disposal than do teachers.

Teachers can choose from several types of home notes. (They can also elect to implement an electronic version of home notes via e-mail or a Website.) A typical home-note program consists of a simple form on which the teacher records "yes," "no," or "not applicable" to certain categories of behavior (e.g., social behavior, homework completed, homework accurate, in-class academic work completed, in-class academic work accurate). The form also may contain space for the teacher and the parents to write a few brief comments. The student takes the form home, has her parents sign it, and returns it the next day. The parents deliver reinforcement for the student's performance. The teacher often starts out sending a note home each day and gradually decreases the frequency until the notes are being sent once a week.

For home notes to work, it's important that both teachers and parents agree philosophically with a behavioral approach to managing student behavior. If either is opposed to using reinforcement as a means of shaping behavior, the home-note program is unlikely to succeed.

TRAVELING NOTEBOOKS **Traveling notebooks**, which go back and forth between school and home, are less formal than home notes and are particularly appropriate for students who see multiple professionals. The teacher and other professionals, such as speech and physical therapists, can write brief messages to the parents and vice versa. In addition, a traveling notebook allows the different professionals to keep track of what each is doing with the student. Figure 4.1 provides excerpts from a traveling notebook of a 2-year-old with cerebral palsy.

Parent Advocacy

As we noted in Chapter 1, the Individuals with Disabilities Education Act (IDEA) provides parents with a number of safeguards regarding their children. For example, they're entitled to a **due process hearing**, a noncourt proceeding held before an impartial hearing officer. Unfortunately, due process hearings don't always satisfy both sides, which can result in costly, drawn-out court proceedings. Each year, school districts across the United States spend well over $100 million resolving disputes between families of children with disabilities and school districts (Mueller, Singer, & Draper, 2008).

Although sometimes associated with the notion of confrontations between parents and professionals, ideally, parent advocacy can be a way to help prevent such disputes. Parents and professionals should work together in their advocacy efforts. Advocacy can foster needed or improved services for children while helping parents gain a sense of control over outcomes for their children.

Parents can focus their advocacy on helping their own children as well as other people with disabilities. The latter might involve volunteering for advisory posts with schools and agencies as well as political activism—for example, campaigning for school board members who are sympathetic to educational issues pertinent to students with disabilities.

As important as advocacy is, not all parents have the personalities or the time to engage in such activities. Also, advocacy may be more or less suitable to some parents at various stages in their child's development. For example, some parents might be heavily involved in such efforts when their children are young but become exhausted over the years and reduce their involvement. On the other hand, some parents might not see the need for

INTERNETRESOURCES

The National Dissemination Center for Children with Disabilities has information on the IEP process, as well as a wealth of information on other topics that parents should find valuable: http://www.nichcy.org/Pages/Home.aspx
The Disability Rights Education Defense Fund's mission is to advance the civil and human rights of people with disabilities through legal advocacy, training, education, and public policy and legislative development: http://www.dredf.org/about/index.shtml

INTERNETRESOURCES

To see the complete address
of Sharon Davis, a
representative from the Arc,
regarding the Human
Genome Project, visit www
.ornl.gov/hgmis/resource/
arc.html

Prenatal Causes

We can group prenatal causes into (1) **chromosomal disorders**, (2) inborn errors of metabolism, (3) developmental disorders affecting brain formation, and (4) environmental influences.

CHROMOSOMAL DISORDERS   As noted previously, scientists are making great strides in identifying genetic causes of intellectual disabilities. At least 1,000 genetic syndromes have been identified as causes of intellectual disabilities (Hodapp & Dykens, 2007). A few of the most common of these genetic syndromes are Down syndrome, Fragile X syndrome, Prader-Willi syndrome, and Williams syndrome.

By far the most common genetic syndrome, Down syndrome is usually not an inherited condition, but, rather, an anomaly at the 21st pair of chromosomes. Also referred to as trisomy 21, Down syndrome is the most common form of intellectual disability that can be identified at birth.

Down Syndrome   Many, but not all, genetic syndromes are transmitted hereditarily. However, by far the most common of these syndromes, **Down syndrome**, is usually *not* an inherited condition. Down syndrome involves an anomaly at the 21st pair of **chromosomes**. In the vast majority of cases of Down syndrome, the 21st set of chromosomes (the normal human cell contains 23 pairs of chromosomes) is a triplet rather than a pair; hence, the most common form of Down syndrome is also referred to as **trisomy 21**. Down syndrome is the most common form of intellectual disability that is present at birth (Beirne-Smith, Patton, & Kim, 2006).

Down syndrome is associated with a range of distinctive physical characteristics that vary considerably in number from one individual to another. People with Down syndrome may have thick epicanthal folds in the corners of the eyes, making the eyes appear to slant upward slightly at the outside corners. Other common characteristics include small stature, decreased muscle tone (hypotonia), hyperflexibility of the joints, a small oral cavity that can result in a protruding tongue, short and broad hands with a single palmar crease, heart defects, and susceptibility to upper respiratory infections (R. L. Taylor, Richards, & Brady, 2005). Evidence also indicates a link between Down syndrome and Alzheimer's disease (see the accompanying Focus on Concepts).

The degree of intellectual disability among people with Down syndrome varies widely, but most individuals fall in the moderate range. In recent years, more children with Down syndrome have achieved IQ scores in the mildly intellectually disabled range than previously, presumably because of intensive special education programming. The likelihood of having a child with Down syndrome increases with the age of the mother (Beirne-Smith et al., 2006). In addition to the age of the mother, researchers point to other variables as possible causes, such as the age of the father, exposure to radiation, and exposure to some viruses. Research on these factors is still preliminary, however.

Methods are available for screening for Down syndrome and some other birth defects. These methods include the following:

- **Maternal serum screening (MSS)**: A blood sample is taken from the mother and screened for the presence of certain elements that indicate the possibility of **spina bifida** (a condition in which the spinal column fails to close properly) or Down syndrome. If the results are positive, the physician can recommend a more accurate test, such as amniocentesis or chorionic villus sampling.

FOCUS ON Concepts

DOWN SYNDROME AND ALZHEIMER'S DISEASE

Researchers first noted a high prevalence of senility in persons with Down syndrome well over a century ago (Fraser & Mitchell, 1876, cited in Evenhuis, 1990). In the early 20th century, postmortem studies of the brains of people with Down syndrome revealed neuropathological signs similar to those of people with Alzheimer's disease (Carr, 1994). It was not until the 1980s and 1990s, however, that scientists started to address this correlation seriously.

Postmortem studies of the brains of people with Down syndrome indicate that virtually all who reach the age of 35 have brain abnormalities very similar to those of persons with Alzheimer's disease (Alvarez, 2008; Hof et al., 1995). And behavioral signs of dementia, or mental deterioration, occur in well over half of people with Down syndrome older than 60 years of age. Unfortunately, maladaptive behaviors, such as aggression, fearfulness, and sadness, often increase as the dementia advances (Urv, Zigman, & Silverman, 2008).

Findings that link Down syndrome to Alzheimer's disease have made researchers optimistic about uncovering the genetic underpinnings of both conditions. For example, researchers have found that some types of Alzheimer's disease are related to mutations of the 21st pair of chromosomes (Bush & Beail, 2004). And evidence suggests that a particular protein may be the key to the rapid onset of Alzheimer's in people with Down syndrome (Tansley et al., 2007). Interestingly, no evidence shows that Alzheimer's occurs more frequently in adults whose intellectual disabilities are due to other causes (Alvarez, 2008).

- **Amniocentesis**: The physician takes a sample of amniotic fluid from the sac around the fetus and analyzes the fetal cells for chromosomal abnormalities. In addition, the amniotic fluid can be tested for the presence of proteins that may have leaked out of the fetus's spinal column, indicating the presence of spina bifida.
- **Chorionic villus sampling (CVS)**: The physician takes a sample of villi (structures that later become the placenta) and tests them for chromosomal abnormalities. One advantage of CVS is that it can be done earlier than amniocentesis.
- **Nuchal translucency sonogram**: Fluid from behind the fetus's neck is analyzed; this can also be done earlier than amniocentesis. A greater than normal amount of fluid indicates the possibility of Down syndrome.

Fragile X Syndrome   **Fragile X syndrome** is the most common known hereditary cause of intellectual disabilities. And it's the second most common syndrome, after Down syndrome, that causes intellectual disabilities (Polloway et al., 2011). In association with intellectual disabilities, it occurs in 1 in 4,000 males and 1 in 6,000 females (Meyer & Batshaw, 2002). In association with milder cognitive deficits, such as learning disabilities, the prevalence may be as high as 1 in 2,000 (Hagerman, 2001). It is associated with the X chromosome in the 23rd pair of chromosomes. In males, the 23rd pair consists of an X and a Y chromosome; in females, it consists of two X chromosomes. This disorder is called Fragile X syndrome because in affected individuals, the bottom of the X chromosome is pinched off in some of the blood cells. Fragile X occurs less often in females because they have an extra X chromosome, giving them better protection if one of their X chromosomes is damaged. People with Fragile X syndrome may have a number of physical features, such as a large head; large, flat ears; a long, narrow face; a prominent forehead; a broad nose; a prominent, square chin; large testicles; and large hands with nontapering fingers. Although this condition usually results in moderate rather than severe intellectual disabilities, the effects are highly variable; some people have less severe cognitive deficiencies and some, especially females, score in the normal range of intelligence (Dykens, Hodapp, & Finucane, 2000).

Prader-Willi Syndrome   Most people with **Prader-Willi syndrome** have inherited a chromosomal abnormality from their father, with a minority having inherited the condition from their mother (Percy, Lewkis, & Brown, 2007). Prader-Willi syndrome has two distinct phases. Infants are lethargic and have difficulty eating. Starting at about 1 year of age, however, they become obsessed with food. In fact, Prader-Willi is the leading genetic cause of obesity. Although a vulnerability to obesity is usually their most serious medical problem, people with Prader-Willi are also at risk for a variety of other health problems, including short stature due to growth hormone deficiencies; heart defects; sleep disturbances, such as excessive daytime drowsiness and **sleep apnea** (cessation of breathing while sleeping); and **scoliosis** (curvature of the spine). The degree of intellectual disability varies, but the majority fall within the mildly intellectually disabled range, and some have IQs in the normal range (R. L. Taylor et al., 2005).

Williams Syndrome   **Williams syndrome** is caused by the absence of material on the seventh pair of chromosomes. People with Williams syndrome have intellectual disabilities in the mild to moderate range (Mervis & Becerra, 2007). In addition, they often have heart defects, an unusual sensitivity to sounds, and "elfin" facial features. Williams syndrome typically occurs without any prior family history of the condition. In other words, it's not typically inherited; however, people who have Williams syndrome can pass it on to each of their children (Haldeman-Englert, 2008).

INBORN ERRORS OF METABOLISM   **Inborn errors of metabolism** result from inherited deficiencies in enzymes used to metabolize basic substances in the body, such as amino acids, carbohydrates, vitamins, or trace elements (Medline Plus, 2007). One of the most common of these is **phenylketonuria (PKU)**. PKU involves the inability of the body to convert a common dietary substance—phenylalanine—to tyrosine; the consequent accumulation of phenylalanine results in abnormal brain development. All states routinely screen babies for PKU before they leave the hospital. Babies with PKU are immediately put on a special diet, which prevents the occurrence of intellectual disabilities. For example, milk, eggs, and the artificial sweetener aspartame are restricted because they contain significant amounts of phenylalanine. At one time, physicians thought that the diet could be discontinued in middle childhood. However, authorities now recommend continuing the diet indefinitely, for two important reasons: Those who stop the diet are at risk for developing learning disabilities or other behavioral problems, and women with PKU who go off the diet are at very high risk of giving birth to children with PKU.

DEVELOPMENTAL DISORDERS OF BRAIN FORMATION   A number of conditions can affect the structural development of the brain and cause intellectual disabilities. Some of these are hereditary and accompany genetic syndromes, and some are caused by other conditions such as infections. Two examples of structural development affecting the brain are microcephalus and hydrocephalus. In **microcephalus**, the head is abnormally small and conical in shape. The intellectual disability that results usually ranges from severe to profound. No specific treatment is available for microcephaly, and life expectancy is short (National Institute of Neurological Disorders and Stroke, 2008).

Hydrocephalus results from an accumulation of cerebrospinal fluid inside or outside the brain. The blockage of the circulation of the fluid results in a buildup of excessive pressure on the brain and enlargement of the skull. The degree of intellectual disability depends on how early the condition is diagnosed and treated. Two types of treatment are available: surgical placement of a shunt (tube) that drains the excess fluid away from the brain to abdomen or insertion of a device that causes the fluid to bypass the obstructed area of the brain.

ENVIRONMENTAL INFLUENCES   A variety of environmental factors can affect a woman who is pregnant and thereby affect the development of the fetus she is carrying. One example is maternal malnutrition. If the mother-to-be doesn't maintain a healthy diet, fetal brain development might be compromised.

We're also now much more aware of the harmful effects of a variety of substances, from obvious toxic agents, such as cocaine and heroin, to more subtle potential poisons, such as tobacco and alcohol. In particular, **fetal alcohol spectrum disorders (FASD)** include a range of disorders in children born to women who have consumed excessive

INTERNETRESOURCES

The National Organization on Fetal Alcohol Syndrome provides a variety of information for professionals and parents at http://www .nofas.org/

amounts of alcohol while pregnant. One of the most severe of those disorders is **fetal alcohol syndrome (FAS)**. Children with FAS are characterized by a variety of abnormal facial features and growth retardation, as well as intellectual disabilities.

The hazards of radiation to an unborn fetus have been recognized for some time. For example, physicians are cautious not to expose pregnant women to X-rays unless absolutely necessary, and the public has become concerned over the potential dangers of radiation from improperly designed or supervised nuclear power plants.

Infections in the mother-to-be can also affect the developing fetus and result in intellectual disabilities. **Rubella (German measles)**, in addition to being a potential cause of blindness, can also result in intellectual disabilities. Rubella is most dangerous during the first trimester (3 months) of pregnancy.

Perinatal Causes

A variety of problems occurring while giving birth can result in brain injury and intellectual disabilities. For example, if the child is not positioned properly in the uterus, brain injury can result during delivery. One problem that sometimes occurs because of difficulty during delivery is **anoxia** (complete deprivation of oxygen).

Low birthweight (LBW) can result in a variety of behavioral and medical problems, including intellectual disabilities (H. G. Taylor, Klein, Minich, & Hack, 2000). Because most babies with LBW are premature, the two terms—*LBW* and *premature*—are often used synonymously. LBW is usually defined as 5.5 pounds or lower, and it is associated with a number of factors: poor nutrition, teenage pregnancy, drug abuse, and excessive cigarette smoking. LBW is more common in mothers living in poverty. And surprisingly, worldwide, only Africa has a higher rate of premature births than North America (United States and Canada combined), with Asia and Latin America having a lower rate than the United States (Beck et al., 2010).

Infections such as **syphilis** and **herpes simplex** can be passed from mother to child during childbirth. These venereal diseases can potentially result in intellectual disabilities. (Herpes simplex, which shows as cold sores or fever blisters, is not usually classified as a venereal disease unless it affects the genitals.)

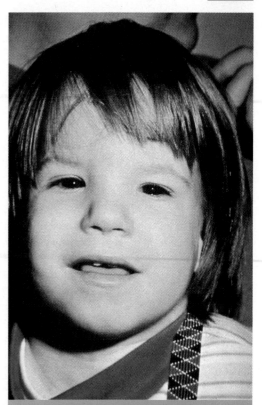

We're well aware of the harmful effects of toxic agents such as cocaine and heroin and more subtle potential poisons such as tobacco and alcohol. Fetal alcohol spectrum disorders (FASD) include a range of disorders in children born to women who have consumed excessive amounts of alcohol while pregnant.

Postnatal Causes

We can group causes of intellectual disabilities occurring after birth into two very broad categories: those that are biological in nature and those that are psychosocial in nature.

BIOLOGICAL POSTNATAL CAUSES   Examples of biological postnatal causes are infections, malnutrition, and toxins. **Meningitis** and **encephalitis** are two examples of infections that can cause intellectual disabilities. Meningitis is an infection of the covering of the brain that may be caused by a variety of bacterial or viral agents. Encephalitis, an inflammation of the brain, results more often in intellectual disabilities and usually affects intelligence more severely. One of the toxins, or poisons, that's been linked to intellectual disabilities is lead. Although lead in paint is now prohibited, infants still become poisoned by eating lead-based paint chips, particularly in impoverished areas. The effect of lead poisoning on children varies; high lead levels can result in death.

PSYCHOSOCIAL POSTNATAL CAUSES   Children who are raised in poor environmental circumstances are at risk for intellectual disabilities. It should be obvious that extreme cases of abuse, neglect, or understimulation can result in intellectual disabilities. However, most authorities believe that less severe environmental factors, such as inadequate exposure to stimulating adult–child interactions, poor teaching, and lack of reading materials, also can

INTERNETRESOURCES

The March of Dimes Website has a section devoted to information pertaining to the low birthweight and its prevention: http://www .marchofdimes.com/ professionals/14332_ 1153.asp

result in intellectual disabilities, especially mild intellectual disability. For example, in one large-scale study of 267,277 children, those who were born to teenage mothers who had fewer than 12 years of education were at increased risk for mild and moderate intellectual disabilities (Chapman, Scott, & Mason, 2002).

Although environmental causes of mild intellectual disabilities are undeniable, heredity can also play a role. For example, in a major study of heredity and mild intellectual disabilities, researchers looked at the degree of similarity in intellectual performance of monozygotic twins versus similarity in performance of dizygotic twins (Spinath, Harlaar, Ronald, & Plomin, 2004). Monozygotic, or identical, twins come from the same egg and have the same genetic makeup. Dizygotic, or fraternal, twins come from separate eggs. In those who scored in the mildly intellectual disability range, the degree of similarity was much higher in monozygotic twins than in dizygotic twins, thus indicating high heritability.

For many years, it's been assumed that psychosocial factors are the cause of the vast majority of cases of mild intellectual disabilities, whereas organic, or biological, factors are the cause of more severe intellectual disabilities. In recent years, however, authorities are beginning to suspect that many cases of mild intellectual disabilities might be caused by specific genetic syndromes (Dykens et al., 2000; Hodapp & Dykens, 2007; Polloway, Smith, & Antoine, 2010). They point to the many cases of people with Prader-Willi syndrome and Williams syndrome, as well as females with Fragile X syndrome, who have mild intellectual disabilities, and they speculate that in the near future, new genetic syndromes will be discovered as causes of mild intellectual disabilities.

IDENTIFICATION

Assessment to determine whether a person is intellectually disabled addresses two major areas: intelligence and adaptive behavior.

Intelligence Tests

Many types of IQ tests are available. Because of the accuracy and predictive capabilities of IQ tests, school psychologists use individually administered tests rather than group tests when identifying students for special education. One of the most commonly used IQ tests for children is the WISC-IV (Wechsler, 2003). The WISC-IV consists of a Full-Scale IQ, as well as four composite scores: Verbal Comprehension, Perceptual Reasoning, Working Memory, and Processing Speed.

Although not all IQ tests call for this method of calculation, dividing **mental age** (the age level at which a person is functioning) by **chronological age** and multiplying by 100 provides a rough approximation of a person's IQ. For example, a 10-year-old student who performs on an IQ test as well as the average 8-year-old (and thus has a mental age of 8 years) would have an IQ of 80.

Compared to many psychological tests, IQ tests such as the WISC-IV are among the most valid: the instrument measures what it is supposed to measure. A good indicator of the validity of an IQ test is the fact that it is generally considered the best single index of how well a student will do in school. It's wise to be wary, however, of placing too much faith in a single score from any IQ test. There are at least four reasons for caution:

1. An individual's IQ can change from one testing to another, and although not common, sometimes the change can be dramatic (Whitaker, 2008).
2. All IQ tests are culturally biased to a certain extent. Largely because of differences in language and experience, people from minority groups are sometimes at a disadvantage in taking such tests.
3. The younger the child, the less validity the test has. Infant intelligence tests are particularly questionable.
4. IQ tests are not the absolute determinant when it comes to assessing a person's ability to function in society. A superior IQ does not guarantee a successful and happy life, and a low IQ does not doom a person to a miserable existence. Other variables

are also important determinants of a person's coping skills in society. That is why, for example, professionals also assess adaptive behavior.

Adaptive Behavior

The basic format of instruments used to measure adaptive behavior requires that a parent, teacher, or other professional answer questions related to the person's ability to perform adaptive skills. We discuss some of these measures later in the section entitled, "Assessment of Adaptive Behavior."

PSYCHOLOGICAL AND BEHAVIORAL CHARACTERISTICS

Some of the major areas in which people with intellectual disabilities are likely to experience deficits are attention, memory, language, self-regulation, motivation, and social development. In considering psychological and behavioral characteristics, remember that a given individual with intellectual disabilities may not display all of these characteristics.

The importance of attention for learning is critical. A person must be able to attend to the task at hand before he can learn it. Often attending to the wrong things, persons with intellectual disabilities have difficulty allocating their attention properly.

People with intellectual disabilities have widespread memory difficulties, but they often have particular problems with working memory (Conners, 2003; Van der Molen, Van

Children with intellectual disabilities may have problems making and keeping friends, but positive social interactions are certainly achievable and should be nurtured and encouraged.

Luit, Jongmans, & Van der Molen, 2007). **Working memory** involves the ability to keep information in mind while simultaneously doing another cognitive task. Trying to remember an address while listening to instructions on how to get there is an example of working memory.

Virtually all persons with intellectual disabilities have limitations in language comprehension and production. The exact types of problems depend largely on the cause of their intellectual disabilities (Abbeduto, Keller-Bell, Richmond, & Murphy, 2006).

Self-regulation is a broad term referring to the ability to regulate one's own behavior. People who are intellectually disabled also have difficulties with metacognition, which is closely connected to the ability to self-regulate (Bebko & Luhaorg, 1998). **Metacognition** refers to a person's awareness of what strategies are needed to perform a task, the ability to plan how to use the strategies, and the evaluation of how well the strategies are working. Self-regulation is thus a component of metacognition. (We discuss metacognition again in Chapter 6.)

A key to understanding the behavior of persons with intellectual disabilities is to appreciate their problems with motivation (Switsky, 2006). Having usually experienced a long history of failure, they are likely to believe that they have little control over what happens to them. Therefore, they tend to look for external rather than internal sources of motivation.

People with intellectual disabilities are prime candidates for a variety of social problems. In addition to having difficulties making friends due to inappropriate behavior, they often lack awareness of how to respond in social situations (Snell et al., 2009). One particular problem of responding in social situations that has received a great deal of research, especially in individuals with intellectual disabilities who have higher IQs, is gullibility. **Gullibility** can be defined as the "tendency to believe something, usually a highly questionable statement or claim, despite scanty evidence" (Greenspan, Loughlin, & Black, 2001, p. 102). See the accompanying Focus on Concepts.

FOCUS ON Concepts

GULLIBILITY: FROM PUPPETS TO THE U. S. SUPREME COURT

Stephen Greenspan, a prominent researcher in the field of intellectual disabilities, has made a strong case for social intelligence, gullibility in particular, as being the hallmark of intellectual disability, especially in those who are mildly intellectually disabled (Greenspan, 2004, 2006a, 2006b, 2009; Greenspan et al., 2001). Greenspan holds that gullibility likely results from a combination of cognitive and personality factors. The cognitive limitation is the inability to determine when something is a deceptive claim, and the personality factors relate to an overreliance on external motivational sources. Greenspan points to the character Pinocchio, from the classic 19th-century Italian children's novel of the same name, as the perfect example of someone who is mildly intellectually disabled by virtue of his gullibility:

Source: Collodi. (1883). *Pinocchio: The adventures of a puppet.* (1930, Translated by M. A. Murray), New York: A. L. Burt Co.

> Pinocchio was a marionette made of wood who yearned to be a real boy, and who engaged in a long series of adventures seeking to reunite with his "father/creator," the lonely old man Gepetto. As a result of a series of encounters with manipulators and deceivers, Pinocchio is repeatedly duped and sidetracked from attaining his goal. Finally, with the help and forgiveness of the "Fairy with Blue Hair," Pinocchio develops both the social intelligence and moral backbone to survive and prevail in a world of swindlers and con artists, and becomes reunited with Gepetto and turned into a real boy. (Greenspan, 2004, p. 123)

The implications of gullibility beyond just marionettes from a children's fable are demonstrated by its role in how people with intellectual disabilities are dealt with by the legal system. Gullibility has figured into the wrongful conviction of numerous persons with intellectual disabilities. For example, false confessions are documented in at least 53 instances.

Robert Perske (2008) has collected dozens of these cases. Here are just two examples:

Saved by DNA: Michael Gayles (2001, Michigan)

Gayles, 18, with "an IQ of 71," underwent 36 hours of interrogation before finally confessing to the rape and murder of a 12-year-old girl. He signed a typed confession that he could not read. Two weeks after his arrest, DNA evidence exonerated Gayles, and he was released (Kresnak, 2001). (Perske, 2008, p. 470)

Saved by DNA: Lourdes Torres (2007, New York)

"Illiterate, mentally retarded," and an illegal immigrant from Mexico, this 31-year-old woman sat in prison for 4 years before confessing to the murder of her former 49-year-old boyfriend. The confession was received after 14 hours of interrogation. Torres claimed that the police promised to let her go if she confessed. Later, it was clear that elements in the confession did not coincide with the facts of the murder. Then came DNA evidence showing that two men were the killers (Dienst, 2007). (Perske, 2008, p. 475)

The issue of gullibility of persons with intellectual disabilities has also been the topic of a landmark U.S. Supreme Court decision. After several years of debate in the courts, in 2002 the U.S. Supreme Court in *Atkins v. Virginia* ruled against the use of the death penalty for persons who are intellectually disabled. Many of the arguments in favor of this decision focused on gullibility. Experts argued that, among other things, gullibility made such individuals vulnerable to being tricked into committing crimes without realizing their ramifications or to confessing to crimes that they had not actually committed (Patton & Keyes, 2006). The *Atkins* decision has also reinforced the claims of Greenspan and others that adaptive behavior, gullibility in particular, should figure more prominently in any future changes to the definition of intellectual disabilities (Greenspan & Switsky, 2006).

Linking Genetic Syndromes to Particular Behavioral Phenotypes

Until recently, most authorities paid little attention to the type of intellectual disability when considering behavioral characteristics. However, researchers have begun to find general patterns of behavioral characteristics, or **behavioral phenotypes**, associated with some of the genetic syndromes.

Researchers have identified the four genetic syndromes that we discussed under prenatal causes of intellectual disabilities—Down syndrome, Williams syndrome, Fragile X syn-

Personal PERSPECTIVES

Williams Syndrome: An Inspiration for Some Pixie Legends?

Folktales from many cultures feature magical "little people"—pixies, elves, trolls, and fairies. A number of physical and behavioral similarities suggest that at least some of the fairies in the early tales might have been modeled on people who had Williams syndrome. Such a view is in keeping with the contention of historians that a good deal of folklore and mythology is based on real life.

The facial traits of persons with Williams syndrome are often described as pixielike. In common with pixies in folklore and art, many people with Williams syndrome have small, upturned noses, a depressed nasal bridge, "puffy" eyes, oval ears, and broad mouths with full lips accented by a small chin. Indeed, those features are so common that children with Williams syndrome tend to look more like one another than their relatives, especially as children. The syndrome

The children in the photograph, who are unrelated, display elfin facial features that clinicians associate with Williams syndrome.

also is accompanied by slow growth and development, which leads most individuals with Williams syndrome to be relatively short.

The "wee, magical people" of assorted folktales often are musicians and storytellers. Fairies are said to "repeat the songs they have heard" and can "enchant" humans with their melodies. Much the same can be said of people with Williams syndrome, who in spite of typically having subnormal IQs, usually display vivid narrative skills and often show talent for music. (The large pointed ears that are so often associated with fairies might symbolically represent the sensitivity of those mythical individuals—and of people with Williams syndrome—to music and to sound in general.)

As a group, individuals with Williams syndrome are loving, trusting, caring, and extremely sensitive to the feelings of others. Similarly, elves are frequently referred to as the "good people" or as kind and gentle-hearted souls. Finally, individuals with Williams syndrome, much like the fairies of legend, require order and predictability. In people with Williams syndrome, this need shows up as rigid adherence to daily routines and a constant need to keep abreast of future plans.

In the past, storytellers created folktales about imaginary beings to help explain phenomena that they did not understand—perhaps including the distinguishing physical and behavioral traits of Williams syndrome. Today researchers turn to people with Williams syndrome in a quest to understand the unknown, hoping to decipher some of the secrets of how the brain functions.

Source: Adapted from article. Williams syndrome and the brain by Howard M. Lenhoff, Paul P. Wang, Frank Greenberg, & Ursula Bellugi (1997, December) p. 73. Copyright © 1997 by *Scientific American, Inc.* All rights reserved. Adapted with permission.

drome, and Prader-Willi syndrome—as having relatively distinctive behavioral phenotypes (Abbeduto, Murphy, et al., 2003, 2006, 2007; Dykens, 2001; Dykens et al., 2000; Fidler, Hepburn, Most, Philofsky, & Rogers, 2007; Hatton et al., 2003; Hodapp & Fidler, 1999; Mervis & Becerra, 2007; Moldavsky, Lev, & Lerman-Sagie, 2001; Roberts, Price, & Malkin, 2007). For example, people with Down syndrome often have significant impairments in language and grammar compared to visual-spatial skills; for individuals with Williams syndrome, the reverse is often true. In fact, the storytelling ability of the latter, including their ability to modulate the pitch and volume of their voices to interject emotional tone in their stories, together with their sociability and elflike faces, have led to some speculation that the pixies, elves, or fairies depicted in folktales were people with Williams syndrome. (See the accompanying Personal Perspectives.)

INTERNETRESOURCES

The propensity for those with Prader-Willi to crave food has raised ethical issues pertaining to allowing them to eat and the concept of least restrictive environment. The Prader-Willi Association (USA) has issued a policy statement on the subject. See www.pwsausa.org/postion/ps002.htm ■ ■ ■

TABLE 5.1 Links between genetic syndromes and behavioral phenotypes

Genetic Syndrome	Behavioral Phenotype	
	Relative Weaknesses	Relative Strengths
Down syndrome	Receptive and expressive language, especially grammar Problems interpreting facial emotions Cognitive skills tend to worsen over time Early onset of Alzheimer's disease	Visual-spatial skills Visual short-term memory
Williams syndrome	Visual-spatial skills Fine-motor control Anxieties, fears, phobias Overly friendly Social relationships	Expressive language, vocabulary Verbal short-term memory Imitation of emotional responses Facial recognition and memory Musical interests and skills
Fragile X syndrome	Short-term memory Sequential processing Repetitive speech patterns Reading Social anxiety and withdrawal	Receptive and expressive vocabulary Long-term memory Adaptive behavior
Prader-Willi syndrome	Auditory processing Feeding problems in infancy Overeating, obesity in childhood and adulthood Sleep disturbances Obsessive-compulsive behaviors	Relatively high IQ (average about 70) Visual processing Facility with jigsaw puzzles

Sources: Abbeduto et al., 2003, 2007; Abbeduto, Murphy, et al., 2006; Bailey, Raspa, Holiday, Bishop, & Olmsted, 2009; Belser & Sudhalter, 2001; Dimitropoulos, Feurer, Butler, & Thompson, 2001; Dykens et al., 2000; Fidler et al., 2007; Fidler, Hodapp, & Dykens, 2002; Hodapp & Dykens, 2007; Hatton et al., 2003; John, Rowe, & Mervis, 2009; Kasari, Freeman, & Hughes, 2001; Mervis & Becerra, 2007; Mervis, Klein-Tasman, & Mastin, 2001; Moldavsky et al., 2001; Roberts et al., 2007.

Table 5.1 lists some of the major behavioral characteristics associated with Down syndrome, Williams syndrome, Fragile X syndrome, and Prader-Willi syndrome. It's important to keep in mind that no one-to-one correspondence exists between the diagnosis and the characteristics. Not all individuals with each of these conditions will have all of the symptoms.

EDUCATIONAL CONSIDERATIONS

In general, the focus of educational programs varies according to the degree of the student's intellectual disability or how much support the student requires. For example, the lesser the degree of intellectual disability, the more the teacher emphasizes academic skills; the greater the degree of intellectual disability, the more the teacher stresses self-help, community living, and vocational skills. In practice, however, all students who are intellectually disabled, no matter the severity level, need some instruction in academic, self-help, community living, and vocational skills. We focus on the elementary school level here; we discuss preschool and secondary programming in later sections.

A major issue facing special educators is how to ensure that students with intellectual disabilities have access to the general education curriculum, as dictated by the Individuals with Disabilities Education Act (IDEA; see Chapter 1), while still being taught functional skills. The more severe the level of intellectual disability, the more complex the issue of access. Authorities recommend a merger of functional and academic curricular standards. This notion of blending academics and functional skills is embodied in **functional academics**, teaching academics in the context of daily living skills. Whereas children who do not have disabilities are taught academics (e.g., reading) to learn other academic content (e.g., history), the child with intellectual disabilities is often taught reading to learn to function independently. In functional reading, the child learns academics to do such things as read a newspaper, read the telephone book, read labels on goods at the store, and fill out job applications.

Educational programming for students with intellectual disabilities, especially those with more severe intellectual disabilities, often includes two features: systematic instruction and instruction in real-life settings with real materials.

Systematic Instruction

Effective teaching of students with intellectual disabilities involves **systematic instruction**: the use of instructional prompts, consequences for performance, and strategies for the transfer of stimulus control (Davis & Cuvo, 1997). Students who are intellectually disabled often need to be prompted or cued to respond in the appropriate manner. These prompts can be verbal, gestural, or physical, or teachers may use modeling (Davis & Cuvo, 1997). A verbal prompt can be a question such as "What do you need to do next?" or a command such as "Put your socks in the top dresser drawer." A gestural prompt might involve pointing to the socks and/or the dresser drawer while stating the question or the command. Taking the student's hand and placing it on the socks and/or drawer is an example of a physical prompt. The adult might also model putting the socks in the drawer before then asking the student to do it.

With respect to consequences, research has consistently shown that students who are positively reinforced for correct responses learn faster. Positive reinforcers range from verbal praise to tokens that can be traded for prizes or other rewards. For students with severe intellectual disabilities in particular, the more immediate the reinforcement, the more effective it is. Once the student demonstrates the desired behavior consistently, the goal is to wean the student from reliance on external reinforcers as soon as possible. The goal is to reach a point when the student doesn't have to rely on prompts and can be more independent. To transfer the control away from the prompts to more naturally occurring stimuli, teachers use several techniques, including delaying the time between a request and the prompt (Kaiser & Grim, 2006). For example, with **constant time delay**, the teacher starts by making a request ("Please put your clothes away") and giving a prompt simultaneously ("Put your clothes in the top dresser drawer"). On subsequent occasions, the adult might wait a set period of time (e.g., 5 seconds) between the request and the prompt. With **progressive time delay**, the teacher also starts with a simultaneous prompt and request, but then gradually increases the latency period between the two.

Research shows that students who are positively reinforced for correct responses learn faster. For students with severe intellectual disabilities in particular, the more immediate the reinforcement, the more effective it is (Kaiser & Grim, 2006).

Instruction in Real-Life Settings with Real Materials

Instruction can take place in the classroom, under simulated conditions, or in real-life settings. Research indicates that instruction of daily living skills for students with intellectual disabilities is generally more effective when conducted in the actual settings where students will use these skills (McDonnell, 2011). Because it's easier to hold instruction in classrooms than in real-life settings, the teacher might start out with instruction in the classroom and then supplement it with instruction in real-life situations. For example, the teacher might use worksheets and photos of various shopping activities in class or set up a simulated store with shelves of products and a cash register (Morse & Schuster, 2000). The teacher could then supplement these classroom activities with periodic visits to real grocery stores. Likewise, the use of real cans of food and real money is preferable in teaching students to read product labels and to make change.

Service Delivery Models

Placements for school-age students with intellectual disabilities range from general education classes to residential facilities. Although special classes for these students tend to be the norm, more and more students with intellectual disabilities are being placed in more integrated settings. The degree of integration tends to be determined by the level of severity; students who are less severely intellectually disabled are the most integrated.

When students with intellectual disabilities are included in general education classes, special and general educators must plan ways to make the experience successful. Without this planning, students are likely to be inattentive and socially isolated. Designating general education peers as "buddies" has been found to be a promising way to increase social interactions (Carter et al., 2005).

Even students with severe disabilities, however, are sometimes placed in general education classrooms, with schools providing extra support services (e.g., a special aide or special education teacher) in the class. Researchers have found class-wide peer tutoring to be an effective technique for helping to integrate students with intellectual disabilities into general education classrooms (Delquadri et al., 1983; Greenwood, 1991). (See the accompanying Responsive Instruction feature.)

Although not all authorities agree on how much inclusion should be practiced, virtually all agree that placement in a self-contained class with no opportunity for interaction with nondisabled students is inappropriate. And still fewer believe large residential institutions are the best placement. At one time, such institutions were a relatively common placement. However, since the deinstitutionalization movement, which began in the 1960s, the number of persons with intellectual disabilities living in institutions has declined steadily. The number of residents in state institutions for persons with intellectual disabilities is less than 20% what it was in 1970 (Scott, Lakin, & Larson, 2008).

INTERNETRESOURCES

For more information on Best Buddies, see www .bestbuddies.org

When students with intellectual disabilities are included in general education classes, it's important that special and general educators work together to plan for students to succeed. Without this planning the students are likely to be inattentive and to be socially isolated (Carter, Hughes, Guth, & Copeland, 2005; Kemp & Carter, 2006). Designating general education peers as "buddies" can be a promising way to increase social interactions (Carter et al., 2005); similarly, the Best Buddies College Program (through Best Buddies International, a nonprofit organization) has been found beneficial for both the students with intellectual disabilities and the college students who serve as "Buddies" (Hardman & Clark, 2006).

ASSESSMENT OF PROGRESS

Assessment of students with intellectual disabilities focuses on a variety of domains, including academic skills, adaptive behavior, and quality of life. The academic skills of students with intellectual disabilities may be assessed using methods that are common across disability categories, such as curriculum-based measurement (CBM). Some students with intellectual disabilities participate in standardized academic assessments. Many students with intellectual disabilities, however, require accommodations to participate in standardized assessments or receive an alternative assessment method if they cannot participate in traditional assessments with accommodations.

Assessment of Adaptive Behavior

Assessments of adaptive behavior may be integrated with interventions so that services are provided in a data-based decision framework. Interviews, observations, and self-report techniques can be helpful in monitoring students' progress in adaptive skills (Harrison & Boney, 2002). Standardized assessments of adaptive behavior are available to provide outcome data as to an individual's success following intervention. Typically, special educators or other professionals measure adaptive behavior indirectly, in that an "informant" provides information on a rating scale or interview (Venn, 2007). The informant should be intimately familiar with the student and is usually a parent, grandparent, teacher, or other primary caregiver. The Vineland Adaptive Behavior Scale—Second Edition (Vineland-II; Sparrow, Chicchetti, & Balla, 2005) is a popular measure of adaptive behavior for individuals from birth to 18 years. It includes several domains: communication, daily living skills, socialization, motor skills, and maladaptive behavior.

RESPONSIVE *INSTRUCTION*
MEETING THE NEEDS OF STUDENTS WITH INTELLECTUAL DISABILITIES

Classwide Peer Tutoring

WHAT THE RESEARCH SAYS

In an effort to meet the instructional needs of students with mild intellectual disabilities within inclusive settings, researchers have explored instructional methods that provide the necessary structure, individualization, and level of corrective feedback critical for success for this population. One such method is classwide peer tutoring (CWPT) (Delquadri, Greenwood, Stretton, & Hall, 1983). CWPT involves the use of peers to provide instruction and feedback in a reciprocal format. Paired students have the opportunity to serve as a tutor and as a tutee during each session. CWPT procedures were designed to address the need for higher levels of active academic engagement for all students, but particularly for students with the greatest academic deficits (Greenwood, 1991).

RESEARCH STUDY

A team of researchers conducted a study to examine the effectiveness of CWPT on the spelling performance of eight students (four students with mild intellectual disabilities and four students with no disabilities) participating in a general education class (Mortweet et al., 1999). The students with mild intellectual disabilities were included in general education classrooms for spelling, a social activity period, and lunch. The CWPT model was compared to traditional teacher-led instruction during the spelling period. The investigators used the following structure for the CWPT sessions:

1. Each student with mild intellectual disabilities was paired with a peer without disabilities.
2. Tutoring sessions occurred four times a week for 20 minutes per day.
3. Tutoring materials included the list of spelling words, point sheets, and practice sheets.
4. The teacher assigned each pair to one of two competing classroom teams. (Points earned by the pairs contributed to daily team point totals.) Partners and teams were reassigned on a weekly basis.
5. During each session, students served as the tutor for 10 minutes and as the tutee for the other 10 minutes.
6. Instruction consisted of the tutor reading the spelling word to the tutee. The tutee wrote the spelling word while saying each letter aloud. If the word was spelled correctly, the tutor awarded the tutee 2 points; if the word was spelled incorrectly, the tutor spelled the word correctly and the tutee wrote the word three times while naming each letter. The tutee could receive 1 point for correctly spelling the practice word. After 10 minutes, the roles were reversed.
7. The teacher assigned bonus points for pairs that were working cooperatively and following the instructional protocol.
8. When the 20-minute session was over, the teacher calculated team points on the basis of partner points. The winning team received privileges such as lining up first for recess.
9. Modifications made for the students with mild intellectual disabilities included shortened word lists, enlarged practice sheets, and tutee reading of words when the student with mild intellectual disabilities was the tutor and was unable to read the word.

RESEARCH FINDINGS

When compared to the teacher-led condition, the CWPT resulted in improved academic performance for all students, increased amount of engaged academic time (approximately 5 to 10 minutes more per student per session), and positive acceptance from the teachers and students. Thus, CWPT provides teachers with a flexible instructional strategy to meet the varying needs of an inclusive classroom.

APPLYING THE RESEARCH TO TEACHING

Given the effectiveness of CWPT, teachers can establish similar procedures in their classes. Tasks such as math facts, spelling, letter sounds, and word identification make great CWPT topics. Following the model established in the study, teachers can create their own tutoring materials. Key features of CWPT include partnering of a higher and lower skilled student, explicit instruction in the tutoring activities (i.e., ample training before independent partner work), structured tasks for the tutor to guide the tutee in completing, reciprocal roles so the tutee has the opportunity to be a tutor, and use of points to reward desired behavior.

• By Kristin L. Sayeski

Assessment of Quality of Life

With the current emphasis on self-determination (which we discuss later in this chapter), more and more professionals are concerned with measuring the quality of life of persons with intellectual disabilities. However, measuring quality of life presents a challenge because a particular individual's perceived quality of life may differ from that of larger society (Brown & Brown, 2005; Cummins, 2005a). Consequently, outcome measures should include both objective and subjective measures that consider society's view of quality of life along with an individual's perceived level of satisfaction.

One measure commonly used to assess adolescents and adults with intellectual disabilities is the Quality of Life Questionnaire (QOL-Q; Schalock & Keith, 1993), which can be used with both English- and Spanish-speaking populations (Caballo, Crespo, Jenaro, Verdugo, & Martinez, 2005). It addresses five factors: satisfaction, well-being, social belonging, dignity, and empowerment/control (Schalock et al., 2002). A more objective scale is the Life Experiences Checklist (LEC; Ager, 1990), which measures the extent to which an individual has ordinary life experiences. It comprises five areas including home, relationships, freedom, leisure, and opportunities for self-enhancement (Cummins, 2005b).

Testing Accommodations and Alternate Assessment

Accommodations for students with intellectual disabilities on standardized tests can include modifications in scheduling, presentation format, and response format. Common scheduling accommodations include extended or unlimited time, or breaking the assessment into smaller, more manageable portions over several days. A typical presentation accommodation involves reading directions and problems to the student. Some students with intellectual disabilities may have physical difficulties and require response accommodations. For example, a student may dictate responses or use a word processor.

Alternate assessments are for students who can't be tested using traditional methods, even if accommodations are provided. Students with intellectual disabilities who participate in an alternate curriculum (e.g., life skills, vocational skills) instead of the general (more academic) curriculum may participate in alternate assessments. Alternate assessments should measure authentic skills, cover a variety of domains, and include multiple measures across time (Ysseldyke & Olsen, 1999). They can include direct observations of specific behaviors, checklists, rating scales, and curriculum-based measures. Several domains should be covered, for example, functional literacy, communication, leisure-recreation skills, domestic skills, and vocational skills (Spinelli, 2006).

EARLY INTERVENTION

We can categorize preschool programs for children with intellectual disabilities as those intended to prevent intellectual disabilities or those designed to further the development of children who have already been identified as intellectually disabled. In general, the former address children who are at risk for mild intellectual disabilities, and the latter are for children with more severe intellectual disabilities.

Early Childhood Programs Designed for Prevention

Toward the end of the 20th century, the federal government provided funding for several infant and preschool programs for at-risk children and their families, with the goal being to research their ef-

Successful early intervention programs are designed to further the development of children with intellectual disabilities.

fects. Most such programs have focused on families in poverty. Two of the most well known, the Perry Preschool Project and the Abecedarian Project, resulted in positive benefits. The first focused on preschool children, and the second was implemented with infants and their families. The Perry Preschool Project researchers (Schweinhart et al., 2005), conducted follow-up studies of students who had received preschool intervention. At ages 27 and 40, the participants demonstrated a number of differences favoring them over individuals who had not received the intervention:

- They had scored higher on achievement and intelligence tests while in school.
- Fewer were classified as intellectually disabled while in school.
- More had graduated from a regular high school.
- Fewer had been arrested.
- More owned their own homes.
- Fewer had become pregnant in their teens.
- They earned a higher income.

Furthermore, a cost–benefit analysis that took into account such things as costs of welfare and the criminal justice system and benefits of taxes on earnings showed a return of $12.90 for every dollar invested in the Perry Preschool Project.

For the Abecedarian Project (Ramey & Campbell, 1984, 1987), participants were identified before birth by targeting pregnant women living in poverty. After birth, the infants were randomly assigned to one of two groups: half to a day-care group that received special services and half to a control group that received no such services. The day-care group participated in a program that provided experiences to promote perceptual-motor, intellectual, language, and social development. The families of these children also received a number of social and medical services. Results of the Abecedarian Project, reported through the age of 20, indicated that the infants from the day-care group attained better scores on intellectual and academic measures and were more likely to have attended a 4-year college (Campbell, Ramey, Pungello, Sparling, & Miller-Johnson, 2002).

Early Childhood Programs Designed to Further Development

Early childhood programs designed to enhance the development of children already identified with intellectual disabilities place a great deal of emphasis on language and conceptual development. Because these children often have multiple disabilities, other professionals—for example, speech therapists and physical therapists—are frequently involved in their education. Also, many of the better programs include opportunities for parent involvement. Note in the accompanying Success Stories feature, for example, how much Nolan Smith's parents have collaborated with his teachers and therapists. Through practice with their children, parents can reinforce some of the skills that teachers work on. For example, parents of infants with physical disabilities, such as cerebral palsy, can learn from physical therapists the appropriate ways of handling their children to further their physical development. Similarly, parents can learn appropriate feeding techniques from speech therapists.

TRANSITION TO ADULTHOOD

In secondary school, the vast majority of students with intellectual disabilities take at least one vocational course and a life skills/social skills course. And when they do take general education courses, the majority receive a modified general education curriculum (Institute of Education Sciences, National Center for Special Education Research, 2009).

Although most authorities agree that the degree of emphasis on transition programming should be greater for older than for younger students, they also believe that such programming should begin in the elementary years. Table 5.2 (p. 124) depicts some examples of curriculum activities pertaining to domestic, community living, leisure, and vocational skills.

INTERNET RESOURCES

The Teachings of Jon is a documentary that chronicles the life of a man with Down Syndrome from birth to adulthood. To find out more about his life visit http://www.teachingsofjon.com/ ■ ■ ■

Success Stories

NOLAN'S TEAM OF PARENTS AND PROFESSIONALS HELPS HIM GAIN ACCESS TO THE GENERAL EDUCATION CURRICULUM

Special Educator Sheryl Simmons: "Members of Nolan's team, including his parents, tailor materials to meet his needs in learning the general curriculum."

Nine-year-old Nolan Patrick Smith attends Sunflower Elementary School in Kansas.
These are the keys to his success:

★ Intensive and strategic instruction
★ Relentless collaboration among team members
★ Specific goals and social supports

NOLAN SMITH, who has Down syndrome, is the second oldest of Kris Kohnke's and Sean Smith's four children. Within 3 weeks of his birth, Nolan started speech and language early intervention services. Intensive language and literacy instruction is still important to his success. Since he was an infant, Nolan has thrived on intensive, relentless, and specific special education.

★ **Intensive and Strategic Instruction.** Nolan is now an outgoing 9-year-old boy with a broad range of cognitive abilities not easily summarized by a single score. He enjoys participating with children his age, but he struggles with reading, writing, and mathematics. Nolan reads at a first-grade level, and helping him move beyond sight words is a challenge. He's eager to decode text, and he has some strategies, but cognitive problems impede his progress. Handwriting is also challenging for Nolan, and he uses an adaptive keyboard for written assignments. "Nolan loves the computer," says Sean Smith. "Now the question is, how is he going to use it?"

Nolan is easily distracted. Frequent prompts help keep him on task. "He can be silly, and the structure of the school day can be difficult for him," says Kris Kohnke. Nolan spends half the school day in third grade with 20 of his classmates. This year the focus of his inclusion is on ac-

ademics (science and social studies) and social development. Nolan is learning that reading has a purpose, and he's eager to demonstrate what he knows. With the help of a paraprofessional, Nolan starts the morning with his classmates and goes to a quiet room for 60 minutes of intensive instruction in reading and mathematics with special educator Sheryl Simmons. He also gets strategic instruction in the resource room before joining his classmates for science, health, or social studies. "A visual approach works well for Nolan," says Mrs. Simmons, who adapts materials in visually stimulating formats to ensure he comprehends and can apply what he learns. According to his individualized education program (IEP), another successful strategy for Nolan is practicing answers to content-based questions with an adult before sharing them with the class. This strategy reinforces his recall and reduces his tendency to stutter when he speaks.

★ **Relentless Collaboration.** Much of Nolan's success depends on coordinated support from his parents, teachers, and therapists. "A real strength for Nolan is that he can understand concepts if we present them in multiple ways and in formats other than print," says Sean Smith. Nolan learned about rain forests through the efforts of relentless collaboration between home and school. His teachers

Self-Determination

A major goal of transition programming is to help persons with intellectual disabilities to achieve as much self-determination as possible. **Self-determination** is the ability to act autonomously, be self-regulated, act in a psychologically empowered manner, and act in a self-realized manner (Wehmeyer & Mithaug, 2006). *Acting autonomously* means behaving according to your own preferences without dependency on others. Being *self-regulated* means evaluating and revising your own behavior. Being *psychologically empowered* is believing that you have control over events to the extent that you'll be able to influence desired outcomes. Being *self-realized* connotes knowing and accepting your own strengths and weaknesses and using that knowledge to attain goals.

modified a science study guide so Nolan's parents and his speech therapist could help him practice rain forest vocabulary. "By the time he took the pretest, he already knew the concepts of camouflage, endangered species, and global warming," says Sheryl Simmons. "He was so proud of his accomplishment."

Collaboration with school personnel is a high priority. Nolan's parents meet every 3 weeks with Mrs. Simmons and Nolan's general education teacher to stay on top of communication and expectations for his progress. Nolan's annual goals are addressed but in the context of the third-grade classroom and curriculum. "With inclusion too many meetings happen 'on the fly,' and most IEP meetings are formal and nerve wracking" says Sean Smith. "By scheduling regular, informal meetings, we can talk more easily about Nolan and better target what he needs at school, and how we can support his learning at home."

★ Specific Goals and Social Supports. Kris Kohnke and Sean Smith are strong advocates who want Nolan's goals to be practical and meaningful for him. This year's annual goals target sight-word vocabulary, reading fluency and comprehension, and building numeracy skills with money and time so Nolan can solve real-world math problems. Every other week he has a Lunch Bunch social skills group with the school counselor to strengthen his peer relationships. Nolan's goals for adapted physical education, and occupational and speech therapies help improve his physical coordination, self-care, and communication.

Strengthening academic, functional, and social skills helps Nolan in his busy life outside of school. The four Smith children are active in their community, and Nolan is no exception. Lawrence Parks and Recreation's All-Star Sports and Special Olympics are a big part of his life, as are play-dates with teammate and best buddy, George. Nolan's parents also make sure he participates in typical activities with his brother and sisters. "Sometimes it's hard on siblings when one child needs so much attention. Celebrations like the Down Syndrome Association's 'Buddy Walk' let Nolan's siblings see him in a positive way as part of a larger community," says Sean Smith. "This year 7000 people participated in Kansas City's celebration, and Nolan's sister said, 'look at all those other people with Down syndrome and their families and friends!'"

CEC'S STANDARDS: PAVING THE WAY TO SUCCESS

Assess your steps to success in meeting the CEC Knowledge and Skill Base for All Beginning Special Education Teachers of Students with Mental Retardation/Developmental Disabilities. Use the following questions to reflect on the growth of your own professional knowledge, skills, and dispositions.

REFLECTING ON YOUR OWN PROFESSIONAL DEVELOPMENT:

If you were Nolan's teacher . . .

- What are some areas about educating students with mental retardation/developmental disabilities that you would need to know more about?
- What are some specific skills that would help you address his academic and behavioral challenges?
- What personal dispositions do you think are most important for you to develop in teaching students with limited cognitive abilities?

Using the CEC Standards . . .

- What are some behavioral problems associated with individuals with mental retardation or developmental delays? MR1K6
- What approaches could you utilize to create positive learning environments for individuals with mental retardation and developmental disabilities? MR5K1
- What are some ways to foster respectful and beneficial relationships between families and professionals? CC10S3

• By Jean B. Crockett

Although most professionals recommend emphasizing self-determination as early as possible in elementary school, the focus becomes even greater in adolescence and adulthood. Because people with intellectual disabilities have reduced cognitive ability, professionals and parents alike have traditionally considered them incapable of making their own decisions. In a sense, this paternalistic attitude often resulted in a self-fulfilling prophecy by not providing persons with intellectual disabilities an opportunity to take more control over their lives. Today, however, many professionals and parents champion the notion of promoting self-determination in persons who are intellectually disabled. In fact, the major parent organization in the field, The Arc, and the major professional organization, AAIDD, have adopted position statements supporting the idea of self-determination.

RESPONSIVE *INSTRUCTION*
MEETING THE NEEDS OF STUDENTS WITH INTELLECTUAL DISABILITIES

Using Technology to Support Cooking

WHAT THE RESEARCH SAYS

Independence is an important goal for many students with intellectual disabilities. Transition planning for students with intellectual disabilities typically includes strategies for promoting self-reliance through self-management and self-monitoring techniques (Sands & Wehmeyer, 2005). The process of food preparation, a valuable and economical aspect of independent living, has been studied by researchers for decades (Agran, Fodor-Davis, Moore, & Deer, 1989; Lancioni, O'Reilly, Seedhouse, Furniss, & Cunha, 2000; Martin, Rusch, James, Decker, & Trtol, 1982). The ability to prepare food creates the opportunity for both self-sufficiency and job employment. Researchers have used a variety of approaches, ranging from the use of static pictures to video modeling to video prompting to promote the development of independent cooking skills. Recent research has also looked to more portable, student-directed tools such as handheld computers or portable DVDs to promote multi-step skills such as cooking (Lancioni et al., 2000; Mechling, Gast, & Fields, 2008; Sigafoos et al., 2005). These technologies provide new avenues for support and independence.

RESEARCH STUDY

Mechling and co-workers (2008) had participants use portable DVD players as a support for completing cooking tasks. Three adults, ages 19 to 22, with moderate intellectual disabilities participated in the study. Each had the goal of preparing a simple meal as a part of his or her transition plan.

For the study, video segments of each step in the cooking process were created. Students could control the video by using the "Play," "Pause," and "Skip (Previous)" buttons on the portable DVD player. The modeling was provided from a subjective point of view (i.e., from the viewpoint of the student performing the task). To prepare the video, researchers conducted a step-by-step task analysis of the various cooking tasks (e.g., making grilled cheese, preparing a ham salad, cooking Hamburger Helper). The intervention included three phases: (1) teaching the students to use the DVD player—particularly, the play and repeat sequence process—to mastery, (2) following the cooking steps without the DVD player, and (3) cooking following the DVD self-prompting procedure. For each step in the video-prompting phase, students were evaluated as to whether they (a) successfully completed the step, (b) failed to complete the step, or (c) did not respond to the prompt. If a student failed to complete the step, three levels of prompting could occur. For the first prompt, a self-prompt, the student could replay the step using the skip/repeat function of the DVD player. For the second level of prompt, the instructor gave a verbal prompt. In the final level of prompt, the instructor completed the step.

RESEARCH FINDINGS

All participants benefited from the intervention, as evidenced by an overall increase in the percentage of correctly completed steps. The steps that presented the greatest challenges were setting the digital timer, operating the stove dial, and waiting for the timer—all tasks involved in preparing of the grilled cheese sandwich. Students did experience success in their ability to use the skip/repeat function of the DVD but in many instances required instructor prompting to do so.

APPLYING THE RESEARCH TO TEACHING

Teachers of students with intellectual disabilities can make use of the portable DVD player to support independent living tasks such as cooking. The dual advantages of relatively low-cost technology and student control through the play, pause, and repeat functions make portable DVD players a useful tool for teaching, which can transition with students as they move out of their educational settings. Teachers can create their own video models with prompts by following the steps established in the study by Mechling and co-workers (2008). After conducting a task analysis of skill, record simple video segments of each step. At the conclusion of each step, provide an auditory cue, "PAUSE," to prompt students to pause the video and conduct the step. Mechling and colleagues recommend identifying foods students like or activities students want to learn to increase student motivation and success with the tool.

• By Kristin L. Sayeski

TABLE 5.3 Suggested instructional activities, methods, and self-determination skills for promoting community living outcomes

Suggested Instructional Activity and Methods	Self-Determination Skill
Ask students to set a housing goal. "Where would you like to live 3 years after leaving high school?" Use maps, newspapers, telephone directories, and the Internet to explore social studies activities.	Self-knowledge Decision-making skills Goal-setting skills
Hold a discussion about roommates. Have students discuss what they would like and dislike about a roommate. "Would you prefer someone who is quiet or someone who likes to talk?" "Would you mind sharing a bathroom?" Help students to write an ad to place in a newspaper advertising for a roommate. Role play interviewing someone as a roommate.	Self-knowledge Choice-making skills Decision-making skills Goal-setting skills Self-advocacy skills
Ask students to discuss the skills they think someone needs to learn before moving away from home. "Do you help with any of these chores at home?" "What do you need to learn before you move away from home?" "What do you need help with?" "Who helps you now?" "How would you find help if you lived on your own?"	Self-knowledge Self-evaluation skills Goal-setting skills Self-instruction skills Self-advocacy skills
Have students volunteer with a housing initiative such as Habitat for Humanity or Neighborhood Watch.	Self-advocacy
Visit local community living programs such as group homes, supported apartments, or homeownership initiatives. Hold a discussion about what they liked and disliked about each. "Which option did you like best? Least? Why?"	Choice-making skills Decision-making skills Goal-setting skills Self-advocacy
Invite speakers with disabilities to speak to the class about their housing experiences.	Decision-making skills

Source: Adapted from Everson, J. M., & Trowbridge, M. H. (2011). Preparing students with low-incidence disabilities for community living opportunities. In J. M. Kauffman & D. P. Hallahan (Eds.), *The handbook of special education.* New York: Routledge.

such as their own home, mobile home, condominium, or apartment. The idea is to enable them to choose to live in places that are available to typical residents in the community (Everson & Trowbridge, 2011). Some evidence shows that supported living arrangements lead to a higher level of self-determination in people with intellectual disabilities than do CRFs (Stancliffe, Abery, & Smith, 2000).

More and more authorities point to the family as a critical factor in determining whether persons with intellectual disabilities will succeed in community adjustment and employment. Even though many professionals hold supported living as an ideal, the fact is that the vast majority of adults with intellectual disabilities live with their families (MR/DD Data Brief, 2001). Even for individuals who live away from home, the family can still be a significant source of support for living in the community and finding and holding jobs.

Employment

Overwhelming evidence shows that adults with intellectual disabilities have high rates of unemployment (Rusch, 2008; Sitlington, Neubert, & Clark, 2010). Although employment statistics for workers who are intellectually disabled have been discouraging, most professionals working in this area are optimistic about the potential for providing training programs that will lead to meaningful employment for these adults. Research indicates that with appropriate training, individuals with intellectual disabilities can hold down jobs with a good deal of success, based on measures of attendance, employer satisfaction, and length of employment (McDonnell, Hardman, & McDonnell, 2003).

Schools often address preparing students with intellectual disabilities for employment by providing opportunities for them to gain experiences in the world of work. Some immediately place students in work settings, while others introduce work experiences first in the

TABLE 5.4 Common types of school-sponsored work experience

Type	Example
Less intensive	
Field trip or tour	Math class visits environmental engineering firm to see practical uses of math in the world of work
Informational interview	English class assigned to interview an employee and write about her career
Job shadowing	Students matched with an employee in a field of interest to spend two half-days observing
In-school job	Student works 1 hour per day replacing books on shelves in school library
School-based enterprise	School science department contracts with engineering firm for students to conduct monthly tests of local river water quality
Internship in a community business	Half of senior class spends 3 days per week at work sites in fall semester; second half does the same in spring semester
More Intensive	
School-supported job	School develops and supports community jobs for students during a "postsenior" year, based on their interests and skills

Source: Adapted from Rusch, F. R. (2008). *Beyond high school: Preparing adolescents for tomorrow's challenges.* Upper Saddle River, NJ: Pearson.

school setting itself and then gradually provide opportunities for working in real work settings (Drew & Hardman, 2007). Table 5.4 lists some of the most common work experiences offered by schools.

Once students with intellectual disabilities leave school, most of their employment options are subsumed under two very different kinds of arrangements: the sheltered workshop and supported competitive employment. Closely related to supported employment are customized employment and self-employment.

SHELTERED WORKSHOPS   A **sheltered workshop** is a structured environment in which a person receives training and works with other workers with disabilities on jobs requiring relatively low skills. This can be either a permanent placement or a transitional placement before a person obtains a job in the competitive job market. At one time, sheltered workshops were virtually the only type of employment available for persons with intellectual disabilities. Although sheltered workshops are still the most common work setting for individuals with disabilities (Winsor & Butterworth, 2008), more and more authorities are voicing dissatisfaction with these workshops. Among the criticisms are the following:

1. Workers make very low wages because sheltered workshops rarely turn a profit. Usually managed by personnel with limited business management expertise, they rely heavily on charitable contributions.

2. Sheltered workshops have no integration of workers who are disabled with those who are nondisabled. This restricted setting makes it difficult to prepare workers who are intellectually disabled for working side by side with nondisabled workers in the competitive workforce.

3. Sheltered workshops offer only limited job-training experiences. A good workshop should provide opportunities for trainees to learn a variety of new skills. All too often, however, the work is repetitive and doesn't make use of current industrial technology.

SUPPORTED COMPETITIVE EMPLOYMENT In contrast to sheltered employment, **competitive employment** provides jobs for at least the minimum wage in integrated work settings where most of the workers are not disabled. In **supported competitive employment**, the person with intellectual disabilities has a competitive employment position but receives on-going assistance, often from a **job coach**. In addition to on-the-job training, the job coach might provide assistance in related areas, such as finding an appropriate job, interacting with employers and other employees, using transportation, and involvement with other agencies.

More research is needed; however, research now indicates that supported competitive employment leads to better employment outcomes (McDonnell et al., 2003). Although the ultimate goal for some adults with intellectual disabilities might be competitive employment, many will need supported employment for some period of time or even permanently.

In comparison to sheltered workshops, supported competitive employment is more in keeping with the philosophy of self-determination. However, to achieve the goal of self-determination, clients should not become too dependent on their job coach. The role of the job coach therefore has changed in recent years. Many professionals now advocate that the job coach involve co-workers of persons with intellectual disabilities as trainers and/or mentors (Mank, Cioffi, & Yovanoff, 2003). After a period of time, the worker can be weaned from relying on the job coach and can learn to use more natural supports. Recall the quotation at the beginning of the chapter (p. 101), in which Sandra Kaufman talks about the change in philosophy toward the use of natural supports in the form of relatives, neighbors, friends, and co-workers rather than social agency personnel.

In addition to competitive employment, two other closely related employment models designed to foster self-determination are gaining in popularity: customized employment and self-employment.

CUSTOMIZED EMPLOYMENT AND SELF-EMPLOYMENT **Customized employment** is based on an assessment of the individual's strengths, weaknesses, and interests (Inge & Moon, 2011). Employers are targeted who have jobs that match the person's profile of interests and skills. Customized employment is similar to supported employment, but the latter has a stronger emphasis on individualizing and negotiating a job match (Inge & Moon, 2011). Depending on supports available, some persons with intellectual disabilities can have a customized, self-employed job. At first glance, it would seem that self-employment wouldn't be possible because it's assumed that owning a business means running the business entirely; however, business owners often rely on other professionals (e.g., accountants, sales staff, and so forth). So, with enough support, from family members, for example, owning a business is not out of the question for some individuals with intellectual disabilities. For example, a person with intellectual disabilities with an interest in animals, with help from family members, a job coach, and others, might establish a pet-sitting business.

Prospects for the Future

Current employment figures and living arrangements for adults with intellectual disabilities might look bleak, but there is reason to be optimistic about the future. Outcomes for adults with intellectual disabilities are improving, albeit slowly, with respect to employment and living arrangements. As Kaufman noted at the beginning of the chapter, with the development of innovative transition programs, many people with intellectual disabilities are achieving levels of independence in community living and employment that were never thought possible. Most of this success requires the collaboration of parents, students, and many professionals. The accompanying Making It Work feature describes a successful program from a parent's perspective.

MAKING IT WORK
COLLABORATION AND CO-TEACHING WITH TEACHERS OF STUDENTS WITH INTELLECTUAL AND DEVELOPMENTAL DISABILITIES

"Why should this student be in my classroom?"

WHAT DOES IT MEAN TO BE A TEACHER OF STUDENTS WITH INTELLECTUAL DISABILITIES?

Collaboration for students with intellectual disabilities can include general and special educators and, often, other related service personnel and parents. Coordinating all of these participants is the responsibility of the special educator and requires both management and interpersonal skills. Teachers of students with intellectual disabilities are expected to:

1. Develop and implement comprehensive, longitudinal individualized programs in collaboration with team members.
2. Incorporate and implement instructional and assistive technology into the educational program.
3. Select, adapt, and use instructional strategies and materials according to characteristics of the individual with exceptional learning needs.
4. Use performance data and information from all stakeholders to make or suggest modifications in learning environments.
5. Design, implement, and evaluate instructional programs that enhance social participation across environments (Council for Exceptional Children, 2003).

SUCCESSFUL STRATEGIES FOR COLLABORATION

Pat Daniels is the mother of Will, a high school student with Down syndrome. Will's high school education required collaboration between parents, general educators, special educators, and coaches. In the end, Will received his special education diploma and was awarded one of the school's 10 Faculty Awards. Pat describes their experiences:

> Open lines of communication between the teachers and the parent were extremely important. I made a point to meet each teacher before the school year began. French was one of the more successful classes. The teacher was unaware of what she was getting with Will, but she was willing and eager to learn. She began by getting to know him, not his weaknesses. She let him try activities, putting him in situations where he was successful and challenged. He had a textbook and did homework with the class, taking tests aimed at what

> he had learned. She helped find a volunteer "study-buddy." This teacher understood that he was working at his own level but she, like others, was often surprised and delighted by his contributions to the class.

> The general education teachers and I communicated most frequently about tests and special projects. For example, one history teacher would call me before a test, and we would generate specific review questions. Another teacher would send the class's study sheets home with specific items highlighted. Phone calls by teachers describing class projects helped establish exactly what Will was expected to accomplish (Will was not always accurate about the specific instructions given orally in class). When the special education teachers knew of a project, they incorporated time to work on that project into Will's special classes.

> Will's drama class was also successful. The teacher let him participate as he was able, even performing at a teachers' meeting. Students' positive attitudes were important to both the French and drama classes. These teachers set the example. Will sat among other students, teachers called upon him, and they assigned him to teams to participate in activities. Will's participation was valued, as was every other student's.

> Will was also the manager for two girls' varsity teams and was a member of the track team. The special education teacher was the assistant coach of the volleyball team, so she was able to work with the coach to teach Will the duties of a manager. The basketball coach saw Will in action and asked for his help. The coaches expected Will to do what any manager would do, including filling in at practice for missing players and riding the bus to away games. The coaches communicated with me and I discussed any of Will's frustrations with them. The coaches made decisions based on Will's abilities, resulting in two "good finishes" each meet. At many track meets, the encouragement to "RUN" came from teammates and from participants and spectators from the opposing team. Our collaboration with coaches encouraged a student with a hearing impairment and his interpreter to join the team!

• By Margaret P. Weiss

SUMMARY

Why are many professionals now using the term intellectual disabilities?

- *Intellectual disabilities* is now used by many to refer to persons who, in the past, would have been designated as mentally retarded.
- The switch from *mental retardation* to *intellectual disabilities* is primarily due to the fact that the former, especially its shortened form, *"retard,"* has become a slur.

How do professionals define intellectual disabilities?

- The American Association on Intellectual and Developmental Disabilities (AAIDD) defines intellectual disability as "a disability characterized by significant limitations both in intellectual functioning and in adaptive behavior as expressed in conceptual, social, and practical adaptive skills. This disability originates before age 18."
- The definition reflects two principles: (1) Intellectual disability involves problems in adaptive behavior, not just intellectual functioning, and (2) persons with intellectual disability can improve.
- Most schools and several professional organizations use the following classifications: mild (IQ of about 50 to 70), moderate (IQ of about 35 to 50), severe (IQ of about 20 to 35), and profound (IQ below about 20).

What is the prevalence of intellectual disabilities?

- From a purely statistical-theoretical perspective and relying only on scores on IQ tests, 2.27% of the population would be intellectually disabled; however, only about 1% of the school-age population is identified as intellectually disabled.
- The reason for the lower prevalence in the schools is probably due to (1) schools using low adaptive behavior as well as low IQ as criteria and (2) a preference by some to identify students as learning disabled rather than intellectually disabled because they perceive a learning disability to be less stigmatizing.

What causes intellectual disabilities?

- Prenatal causes include (1) chromosomal disorders, (2) inborn errors of metabolism, (3) developmental disorders affecting brain formation, and (4) environmental influences.
  - Chromosomal disorders include Down syndrome, Fragile X syndrome, Prader-Willi syndrome, and Williams syndrome. Down syndrome and Williams syndrome typically result from chromosomal

abnormalities; Fragile X syndrome and Prader-Willi syndrome are inherited.
  - Phenylketonuria (PKU) is an example of a cause of intellectual disabilities due to an inborn error of metabolism.
  - Microcephalus and hydrocephalus are examples of disorders of brain formation.
  - Prenatal environmental influences include maternal malnutrition, fetal alcohol syndrome, and rubella (German measles).
  - Prenatal screening for Down syndrome and other conditions is available.
- Perinatal causes include anoxia (lack of oxygen), low birth weight, and infections such as syphilis and herpes simplex.
- Postnatal causes include those that are biologically or psychologically based.
  - Biological causes include traumatic brain injury and infections such as meningitis and encephalitis.
  - Psychosocial causes (e.g., unstimulating adult–child interactions) can also cause mild intellectual disabilities.
  - Although environmental causes of mild intellectual disabilities are undeniable, heredity can also play a role. Most authorities now believe that heredity and environment interact to determine intelligence.
  - Recent research suggests that many cases of mild intellectual disabilities are caused by specific genetic syndromes.

What methods of assessment are used to identify individuals with intellectual disabilities?

- Individual IQ tests are used to assess intelligence. The following cautions are important: (1) An individual's IQ score can change; (2) all IQ tests are culturally biased to some extent; (3) the younger the child, the less valid are the results; and (4) the ability to live a successful and fulfilling life does not depend solely on IQ.
- Adaptive behavior measures usually involve a parent, teacher, or other professional answering questions related to the person's independence and daily living skills and maladaptive behavior.

What are some of the psychological and behavioral characteristics of learners with intellectual disabilities?

- Major areas of problems for people with intellectual disabilities are attention, memory (especially working memory), language, self-regulation, motivation, and social development.

- Some professionals have described gullibility as an area of social development that is particularly limited in persons with intellectual disabilities, especially mild intellectual disabilities.
- Researchers are beginning to link genetic syndromes to particular behavioral patterns, or phenotypes.
  - Down syndrome is linked to relatively low expressive language, relatively high visual-spatial skills.
  - Williams syndrome is linked to relatively low visual spatial skills, relatively high expressive language skills.
  - Fragile X syndrome is linked to relatively low short-term memory, relatively high adaptive behavior.
  - Prader-Willi syndrome is linked to relatively low auditory processing, compulsive eating, and relatively high visual processing.

What are some educational considerations for learners with intellectual disabilities?

- The lesser the degree of intellectual disability, the more the teacher emphasizes academic skills; and the greater the degree of intellectual disability, the more stress there is on self-help, community living, and vocational skills.
- Authorities recommend a merger of functional and academic curricular standards, which can be accomplished by teaching functional academics.
- Effective teaching of students with intellectual disabilities involves *systematic instruction*: instructional prompts, consequences for performance, and strategies for the transfer of stimulus control.
- Although special classes for these students tend to be the norm, more and more students with intellectual disabilities are being placed in more integrated settings.

How do professionals assess the progress of students with intellectual disabilities?

- Curriculum-based measurement can be used to monitor *academic progress*.
- Interviews, observations, and self-reports, some of which are standardized, can be helpful in assessing *adaptive behavior*.
- Standardized questionnaires are available to assess *quality of life*.
- Accommodations for students with intellectual disabilities include modifications in
  - Scheduling (e.g., extended time)
  - Presentation format (e.g., reading directions to the student)
  - Response format (e.g., allowing the student to dictate responses)

- Alternate assessments for those who can't be tested using traditional methods, even with accommodations, may include direct observation of specific behaviors, checklists, and curriculum-based measures of functional literacy and leisure-recreation, domestic, and vocational skills.

What should educators consider with respect to early intervention for learners with intellectual disabilities?

- Preschool programs differ in their goals according to whether they are aimed at preventing intellectual disabilities or furthering the development of children who have already been identified as intellectually disabled.
- In general, prevention programs are aimed at children who are at risk of developing mild intellectual disabilities, whereas programs for children who have been identified as intellectually disabled focus on children with more severe intellectual disabilities.
- Research supports the clear link between such interventions and success later in life.

What are some important considerations with respect to transition to adulthood for learners with intellectual disabilities?

- Promoting self-determination has become a major guiding principle in educating persons with intellectual disabilities.
- Transition programming involves two related areas: community adjustment and employment.
  - Community survival skills include managing money, using public transportation, and maintaining living environments. Large residential institutions are fast disappearing in favor of smaller community residential facilities (CRFs). Some people favor supported living, whereby people with intellectual disabilities live in their own apartment or home, over CRFs.
  - Two very different types of employment models are the sheltered workshop and supported competitive employment. Sheltered workshops offer structured training with other workers with disabilities on jobs requiring relatively low skills. Supported competitive employment involves receiving at least minimum wage in settings where most of the workers are not disabled, accompanied by ongoing assistance from a job coach. Two other models—customized employment and self-employment—share supported employment's goal of fostering self-determination.

COUNCIL FOR EXCEPTIONAL CHILDREN
Addressing the Professional Standards

Council for Exceptional Children (CEC) Common Core Knowledge and Skills addressed in this chapter: ICC1K5, ICC1K6, ICC1K8, ICC2K1, ICC2K5, ICC2K6, ICC3K3, ICC4S4, ICC4S5, ICC4S6, ICC5S3, ICC7K2, ICC7S1, ICC7S5, ICC7S7, ICC8K2, ICC8S6, ICC10K1, ICC10K3, ICC10S4

Appendix: Provides a full listing of the CEC Common Core Standards and associated Knowledge and Skill Statements listed here.

MYEDUCATIONLAB

Now go to Topic 9: Intellectual Disabilities, in the MyEducationLab (www .myeducationlab.com) for your course, where you can:

- Find learning outcomes for the broad concepts covered in this chapter along with the national standards that connect to these outcomes.
- Complete Assignments and Activities that can help you more deeply understand the chapter content.
- Examine challenging situations presented in the IRIS Center Resources.
- Apply and practice your understanding of the core concepts and skills identified in the chapter with the Building Teaching Skills and Dispositions learning units.
- Check your comprehension on the content covered in the chapter by going to the Study Plan in the Book-Specific Resources for your text. Here you will be able to take a chapter quiz, receive feedback on your answers, and then access Review, Practice, and Enrichment activities to enhance your understanding of chapter content.
- Watch video clips of CCSSO Teacher of the Year award winners responding to the question: "Why I teach?" in the Teacher Talk section.

chapter

6

Learners with Learning Disabilities

As much as I want to find the perfect words to express what it is like to be dyslexic, I cannot. I can no more make you understand what it is like to be dyslexic than you can make me understand what it is like not to be. I can only guess and imagine. For years, I have looked out, wanting to be normal, to shed the skin that limits me, that holds me back. All the while, others have looked upon me, as well. There were those who have pitied me and those who have just given up on me, those who stood by, supporting me and believing in me, and those who looked at me as if I were an exhibit in a zoo. But, in general, people have shown a desire to understand what dyslexia is and how to teach those afflicted with it. Each side, it seems, longs to understand the other.

Lynn Pelkey • "In the LD Bubble" (2001)

QUESTIONS **to guide your reading of this chapter . . .**

- How do professionals define learning disabilities?
- How do professionals identify students with learning disabilities?
- What is the prevalence of learning disabilities?
- What causes learning disabilities?
- What are some of the psychological and behavioral characteristics of learners with learning disabilities?
- What are some educational considerations for learners with learning disabilities?
- How do professionals assess the academic progress of students with learning disabilities?
- What are some important considerations with respect to early intervention for learners with learning disabilities?
- What are some important considerations with respect to transition to adulthood for learners with learning disabilities?

MISCONCEPTIONS ABOUT
Learners with Learning Disabilities

MYTH • IQ–achievement discrepancy is a straightforward, error-free way of determining whether a student has a learning disability.

FACT • Numerous conceptual problems arise when using an IQ–achievement discrepancy.

MYTH • Response to intervention (RTI) has been documented to be an error-free way of determining whether a student has a learning disability.

FACT • Little research exists on RTI, especially when implemented on a large scale; therefore, many questions remain regarding how best to implement it.

MYTH • All students with learning disabilities are brain damaged.

FACT • Many authorities now refer to students with learning disabilities as having central nervous system (CNS) dysfunction, which suggests a malfunctioning of the brain rather than actual tissue damage.

MYTH • The fact that so many definitions of learning disabilities have been proposed is an indicator that the field is in chaos.

FACT • Although at least 11 definitions have been proposed at one time or another, professionals have settled on two: the federal definition and the National Joint Committee on Learning Disabilities definition. And although they differ in some ways, these two definitions have a lot in common.

MYTH • The rapid increase in the prevalence of learning disabilities is due solely to sloppy diagnostic practices.

FACT • Although poor diagnostic practices may account for some of the increase, there are plausible social/cultural reasons for the increase. In addition, evidence indicates that school personnel may "bend" the rules to identify students as learning disabled instead of the more stigmatizing identification of "intellectually disabled."

MYTH • We know very little about what causes learning disabilities.

FACT • Although no simple clinical test exists for determining the cause of learning disabilities in individual cases, recent research strongly suggests causes related to neurological dysfunction possibly resulting from genetic factors, toxins, or medical factors.

MYTH • Math disabilities are relatively rare.

FACT • Math disabilities may be just as prevalent (or close to it) as reading disabilities.

MYTH • We needn't be concerned about the social-emotional well-being of students with learning disabilities because their problems are in academics.

FACT • Many students with learning disabilities also develop problems in the social-emotional area.

MYTH • Most children with learning disabilities outgrow their disabilities as adults.

FACT • Learning disabilities tend to endure into adulthood. Most individuals with learning disabilities who are successful must learn to cope with their problems and make extraordinary efforts to gain control of their lives.

MYTH • For persons with learning disabilities, IQ and achievement are the best predictors of success in adulthood.

FACT • The best predictors of success for adults with learning disabilities are perseverance, goal setting, realistic acceptance of weaknesses and ability to build on strengths, exposure to intensive and long-term educational intervention, and especially the ability to take control of their lives.

Lynn Pelkey's (2001) comment in this chapter's opening quote about having dyslexia, or reading disability, should provide some degree of solace to researchers, teachers, parents, and policymakers who have struggled to define learning disabilities since its formal recognition by the federal government in the 1960s. Pelkey has one specific (albeit the most common) form of learning disabilities: a reading disability. Yet even after having lived with the condition for 35 years, she was still unable to articulate its essence.

The inability of Pelkey and the best of theoreticians and practitioners to define learning disabilities in precise language, however, doesn't mean that her disability isn't real. If you were to go on to read the rest of her story, you would find that like millions of others who have learning disabilities, she faced tremendous challenges not only academically but also socially. You would also find that Pelkey was able eventually to overcome her feelings of rejection, successfully hold a job, and receive an associate's degree with honors from a community college. Her success, however, came not only from hard work and the support of others (as she notes in the opening quote), but also from coming to terms with her learning disability: "Not long ago, it became very clear to me that I would have to come face-to-face with my feelings about being stupid if I was going to find peace within myself" (Pelkey, 2001, p. 27). As we discuss later in this chapter, being able to take control of one's life is often what separates people with learning disabilities who function successfully as adults from those who do not.

The struggle to elucidate the nature of learning disabilities has often led to professional turmoil over the best ways to educate these students. As the field has matured, however, greater consensus has developed about key issues, such as how to define and identify learning disabilities, what causes learning disabilities, and the best educational treatment approaches. But even though consensus has been reached, there is by no means unanimity on some of these issues. For example, healthy disagreements still exist with respect to the related issues of definition and identification.

DEFINITION

At a parents' meeting in the early 1960s, Samuel Kirk (1963) proposed the term *learning disabilities* as a compromise because of the confusing variety of labels in use to describe the child with relatively normal intelligence who was having learning problems. Such a child was likely to be referred to as *minimally brain injured*, a *slow learner*, *dyslexic*, or *perceptually disabled*.

Many parents as well as teachers believed the label "minimal brain injury" to be problematic. **Minimal brain injury** refers to individuals who show behavioral but not neurological signs of brain injury. They exhibit behaviors (e.g., distractibility, hyperactivity, and perceptual disturbances) similar to those of people with real brain injury, but their neurological examinations are indistinguishable from those of nondisabled individuals. Historically, the diagnosis of minimal brain injury was sometimes dubious because it was based on questionable behavioral evidence rather than on more solid neurological data. Moreover, minimal brain injury was not an educationally meaningful term, because such a diagnosis offered little real help in planning and implementing treatment. The term *slow learner* described the child's performance in some areas but not in others; and intelligence testing indicated that the ability to learn existed. *Dyslexic*, too, fell short as a definitive term because it described only reading disabilities, and many of these children also had problems in other academic areas, such as math. To describe a child as *perceptually disabled* just confused the issue

To check your comprehension on the content covered in Chapter 6, go to the Book-Specific Resources in the MyEducationLab (www.myeducationlab.com) for your course, select your text, and complete the Study Plan. Here you will be able to take a chapter quiz, receive feedback on your answers, and then access review, practice, and enrichment activities to enhance your understanding of chapter content. ■

INTERNETRESOURCES

For first-person accounts of having a learning disability, visit LD OnLine, a national educational service of WETA-TV, the PBS station in Washington, D.C., WETA, at http://www.ldonline.org/firstperson ■■■

Educators have struggled to formulate a clear and comprehensive definition of the term *learning disability*, which generally describes children of seemingly normal intelligence who, nevertheless, have learning problems.

further, for perceptual problems might be only part of a puzzling inability to learn. So the parents' group finally agreed on the educationally oriented term *learning disabilities*. Accordingly, they founded the Association for Children with Learning Disabilities, now known as the Learning Disabilities Association of America. A few years later, following the lead of the parents, professionals and the federal government officially recognized the term.

The interest in learning disabilities evolved as a result of a growing awareness that a large number of children were not receiving needed educational services. Because they tested within the normal range of intelligence, these children didn't qualify for placement in classes for children with intellectual disabilities. And although many of them exhibited inappropriate behavior disturbances, some of them did not. Placement in classes for students with emotional disturbance therefore was thought to be inappropriate. Parents of children who weren't achieving at their expected potential—children with learning disabilities—wanted their children's academic achievement problems corrected.

Eleven different definitions of learning disabilities have enjoyed some degree of acceptance since the field's inception in the early 1960s (Hammill, 1990). Created by individual professionals and committees of professionals and lawmakers, each definition provides a slightly different slant. The two most influential definitions have been the federal definition and the definition of the National Joint Committee on Learning Disabilities (NJCLD).

The Federal Definition

The majority of states use a definition based on the federal government's definition. This definition, first signed into law in 1975, was (with a few minor wording changes) adopted again in 1997 by the federal government and reauthorized in 2004. As we discuss in the next section, changes have occurred in identification procedures. However, the 2004 reauthorization of the Individuals with Disabilities Education Act (IDEA) did not change the definition contained in the 1997 reauthorization:

> GENERAL—The term "specific learning disability" means a disorder in one or more of the basic psychological processes involved in understanding or in using language, spoken or written, which disorder may manifest itself in an imperfect ability to listen, think, speak, read, write, spell, or do mathematical calculations.
>
> DISORDERS INCLUDED—Such term includes such conditions as perceptual disabilities, brain injury, minimal brain dysfunction, dyslexia, and developmental aphasia.
>
> DISORDERS NOT INCLUDED—Such term does not include a learning problem that is primarily the result of visual, hearing, or motor disabilities, of mental retardation, of emotional disturbance, or of environmental, cultural, or economic disadvantage. (IDEA, Amendments of 1997, Sec. 602(26), p. 13)

The National Joint Committee on Learning Disabilities Definition

The NJCLD, composed of representatives of the major professional organizations involved with students with learning disabilities, came up with an alternative definition. They deemed it necessary to present their own definition because of dissatisfaction with the following factors in the federal definition:

1. *Reference to psychological processes.* Many of the early pioneers in the learning disabilities field believed that the processing of visual and auditory information, or the making sense of this information (as distinct from visual and auditory acuity problems of those identified as blind or deaf), was the underlying cause of academic problems, such as reading disabilities. Furthermore, they believed that training students in visual- and auditory-processing skills in isolation from academic material would help them conquer their reading problems (Frostig & Horne, 1964; Kephart, 1971; Kirk & Kirk, 1971). Researchers ultimately determined that these perceptual and perceptual-motor

The fact that students with learning disabilities have apparently normal intelligence but still experience learning problems can be frustrating for them, as well as teachers and parents.

exercises did not result in benefits for students' reading achievement (see Hallahan, 1975, and Hallahan & Cruickshank, 1973, for reviews). In reaction to the widespread adoption of unproven perceptual training programs, the NJCLD objected to the "basic psychological processes" phrase.

2. *Omission of the intrinsic nature of learning disabilities.* The federal definition makes no mention of causal factors, but the NJCLD considered learning disabilities to be due to central nervous system (CNS) dysfunction within the individual.

3. *Omission of adults.* The NJCLD responded to the growing awareness that learning disabilities is not just a disability of childhood. It's a lifelong condition.

4. *Omission of self-regulation and social interaction problems.* The NJCLD responded to the growing awareness that students with learning disabilities often experience difficulties in self-regulation and social interaction.

5. *Inclusion of terms difficult to define.* The NJCLD believed that the federal definition was confusing because of its inclusion of terms such as *perceptual handicaps, dyslexia*, and *minimal brain dysfunction*, which have been so difficult to define (Hammill, Leigh, McNutt, & Larsen, 1981).

6. *Confusion about the exclusion clause.* The federal definition excludes a learning problem that is primarily due to other disabling conditions, such as mental retardation (intellectual disabilities), but it's vague with respect to whether one could have both a learning disability and another disability. The NJCLD preferred to be explicit about the possibility that someone with another disabling condition, such as intellectual disability, could also have a learning disability.

7. *Inclusion of spelling.* The NJCLD believed that there was no need to mention spelling because it thought spelling was included in writing.

On the basis of these seven purported weaknesses of the federal definition, the NJCLD proposed the following definition:

> Learning disabilities is a general term that refers to a heterogeneous group of disorders manifested by significant difficulties in the acquisition and use of listening, speaking, reading, writing, reasoning, or mathematical abilities. These disorders

are intrinsic to the individual, presumed to be due to central nervous system dysfunction, and may occur across the life span. Problems in self-regulatory behaviors, social perception and social interaction may exist with learning disabilities but do not by themselves constitute a learning disability.

Although learning disabilities may occur concomitantly with other handicapping conditions (for example, sensory impairment, mental retardation, serious emotional disturbance) or with extrinsic influences (such as cultural differences, insufficient or inappropriate instruction), they are not the result of those conditions or influences. (National Joint Committee on Learning Disabilities, 1989, p. 1)

IDENTIFICATION

Identification procedures for learning disabilities are currently in a state of transition. As we noted in Chapter 1, the federal government reauthorized the IDEA in 2004. With this reauthorization, the way in which students may be found eligible for special education services as learning disabled has changed dramatically. In this chapter, we discuss achievement–ability discrepancy, which is the traditional approach to identifying learning disabilities. Then we discuss response to intervention (RTI), which is the federally preferred way of identifying learning disabilities contained in the reauthorization. We say "federally preferred" because, even though the law allows for either one of these methods to be used, the wording of the law, as well as the research priorities of the federal government, definitely favor the use of RTI. For example, the law insists that states **must not require** the use of a severe discrepancy between intellectual ability and achievement. And it specifically requires that states **must permit** the use of RTI.

Achievement–Ability Discrepancy

INTERNETRESOURCES

In 2001, the U. S. Department of Education held a Learning Disabilities Summit that focused on identification practices for students with learning disabilities. The Summit's Website contains links to the papers: http://ldsummit.air.org/ Presenters' and respondents' papers were also published: Danielson, L., Bradley, R., & Hallahan, D. P. (Eds.). (2002). *Identification of learning disabilities: Research to practice.* Mahwah, NJ: Erlbaum.

Shortly after presenting its definition in 1977, the federal government published regulations on how to identify students with learning disabilities. The key element in these regulations was that to be identified as learning disabled, the student needed to exhibit a "severe discrepancy between achievement and intellectual ability." In other words, a child who was achieving well below his potential would be identified as learning disabled.

The federal government left it up to individual states to decide precisely how they determined whether a student had a severe discrepancy. Most states relied on an **IQ–achievement discrepancy**, which is a comparison between scores on standardized intelligence and achievement tests. Many states adopted different statistical formulas for identifying IQ–achievement discrepancies. However, some of the formulas are statistically flawed and lead to inaccurate judgments, and those that are statistically adequate are difficult and expensive to implement. Furthermore, they give a false sense of precision. That is, they tempt school personnel to reduce to a single score the complex and important decision of identifying a learning disability.

In addition to the problem of using formulas, some authorities have objected to using an IQ–achievement discrepancy on other conceptual grounds. For example, some authorities have pointed out that IQ scores of students with learning disabilities are subject to underestimation because performance on IQ tests is dependent on reading ability, to some extent. In other words, students with poor reading skills have difficulty expanding their vocabularies and learning about the world. As a result, they get lower-than-average scores on IQ tests, which lessen the discrepancy between IQ and achievement. Also, some educators have pointed out that the idea of discrepancy is practically useless in the earliest elementary grades. In the first or second grade, a child isn't expected to have achieved very much in reading or math, so it's difficult to find a discrepancy. Because of this delay in identification, the IQ–achievement discrepancy approach has been called a "wait-to-fail" model.

Response to Intervention or Response to Treatment

On the basis of the previously mentioned criticisms of IQ–achievement discrepancy, researchers proposed an alternative means of identifying students as learning disabled: a

response-to-intervention (RTI) or **response-to-treatment approach.** As we noted in Chapter 2, no universally accepted RTI model exists. But, typically, it involves three tiers of progressively more intensive instruction, with monitoring of progress in each of the tiers. (See Figure 2.1.) Tier 1 involves instruction (which is supposed to be evidence based) that typically occurs in the general education classroom by the general education teacher. Those students who don't respond favorably move to Tier 2, in which they receive small-group instruction several times a week. Those not responding favorably to the small-group instruction are referred for evaluation for special education (Tier 3).

As we noted in Chapter 1, the jury is still out on the effectiveness of RTI in identifying students with disabilities, including learning disabilities (D. Fuchs, Fuchs, McMaster, Yen, & Svenson, 2004; D. Fuchs, Mock, Morgan, & Young, 2003; L. S. Fuchs, 2003; O'Connor & Sanchez, 2011; Vaughn & Fuchs, 2003). Some cautions raised have been the following:

- Little research evidence exists regarding the effectiveness of RTI in identifying students with learning disabilities, especially when implemented on a large scale.
- Most of what we do know about RTI is focused just on reading.
- Currently, many general education teachers are failing to use evidence-based instruction in Tier 1.
- Currently, considerable variability occurs in Tier 2 with respect to such things as type of instruction, duration of instruction, and who the instructor is (e.g., general education teacher, special education teacher, school psychologist, paraprofessional).
- Some students don't experience significant difficulties in reading until the third, fourth, or fifth grade, when skills required for reading become more complex; thus, the students go undiagnosed because most RTI models are implemented only in the early elementary grades.
- Some students referred to Tier 2 who do well enough to return to Tier 1 experience reading problems again and are referred back to Tier 2. This recycling between Tiers 1 and 2 may result in delaying them from what they really need, which is Tier 3.

Despite these cautions, most school administrators see RTI as promising a more reliable way of identifying students with learning disabilities. Virtually all states have implemented or are developing models of RTI for use by local school divisions (Berkeley, Bender, Peaster, & Saunders, 2009). And because the federal government has made funding of research on RTI a high priority over the next several years, there is hope that some of the concerns noted above can be ameliorated.

INTERNETRESOURCES

For more information on response to intervention, visit the National Center on Response to Intervention, http://www.rti4success.org/index.php?option=com_frontpage&Itemid=I and the RTI Action Network http://www.rtinetwork.org/

PREVALENCE

According to U.S. government figures, just under 5% of children between the ages of 6 and 17 years have been identified as learning disabled by the public schools. Learning disability is by far the largest category of special education. About half of all students identified by the public schools as needing special education have learning disabilities.

Increase and Decrease in Prevalence

Since 1976–1977, when the federal government first started keeping prevalence figures, the size of the learning disabilities category has more than doubled. Many authorities maintain that the rapid expansion of the learning disabilities category reflects poor diagnostic practices. They believe that children are being overidentified, that teachers are too quick to label students with the slightest learning problem as "learning disabled" rather than entertain the possibility that their own teaching practices are at fault. As we noted earlier, that's one of the reasons why the field has moved away from using the IQ–achievement discrepancy and toward RTI as a way of identifying students with learning disabilities. Others, however, argue that some of the increase might be due to social and cultural changes that have raised children's vulnerability to develop learning disabilities (Hallahan, 1992). For example, the number of children living in poverty doubled between 1975 and 1993. Although these numbers declined in the 1990s, they are on the rise again. Fourteen million children live in families below the federal poverty level (Wright, Chau, & Aratani, 2010), and poverty is associated with higher rates of social and learning problems. Furthermore, even families who aren't in poverty are under more stress than ever before, which takes its toll on the time children have for concentrating on their schoolwork and on their parents' ability to offer social support.

Still others maintain that a causal relationship exists between the decrease in the numbers of students who are being identified as having intellectual disabilities (mental retardation) and the increase in the numbers of students who are being identified with learning disabilities. Evidence suggests that, when faced with a student who could qualify as intellectually disabled, school personnel often bend the rules to apply the label of "learning disabilities" rather than the more stigmatizing label of "intellectually disabled" (MacMillan, Gresham, & Bocian, 1998; MacMillan & Siperstein, 2002).

Even though the prevalence of students identified as learning disabled has doubled since the 1970s, it's significant that after peaking at 5.66% in the late 1990s, the rate has been gradually, but steadily, decreasing to its current level of just under 5%. This turnabout may be due to a conscious effort to be more conservative in identifying learning disabilities because so much concern has been raised about its seemingly endless growth. How much this decrease might be due to the emergence of RTI as a replacement of IQ–achievement discrepancy as an identification tool is not yet known.

Gender Differences

Boys outnumber girls by about three to one in the learning disabilities category (Cortiella, 2009). Some researchers have suggested that the prevalence of learning disabilities among males is due to their greater biological vulnerability. The infant mortality rate for males is higher than that for females, and males are at greater risk than females for a variety of biological abnormalities. Other researchers have contended, however, that the higher prevalence of learning disabilities among males might be due to referral bias. They suggest that boys are more likely to be referred for special education when they do have academic problems because of other behaviors that bother teachers, such as hyperactivity. Research on this issue is mixed (Clarizio & Phillips, 1986; Leinhardt, Seewald, & Zigmond, 1982; S. E. Shaywitz, Shaywitz, Fletcher, & Escobar, 1990). At this point, it's probably safest to conclude that

> some bias does exist but that the biological vulnerability of males also plays a role. For example, the federal government's figures indicate that all disabilities are more prevalent in males, including conditions that are difficult to imagine resulting from referral or assessment bias, such as hearing impairment (53% are males), orthopedic impairment (54% are males), and visual impairment (56% are males). (Hallahan, Lloyd, Kauffman, Weiss, & Martinez, 2005, p. 35)

CAUSES

For years, many professionals suspected that neurological factors were a major cause of learning disabilities. When the field of learning disabilities was emerging, professionals noted that many of these children displayed behavioral characteristics (e.g., distractibility, hyperactivity, language problems, perceptual disturbances) similar to those exhibited by people who were known to have brain damage, such as those who had suffered a stroke or a head wound. (See Hallahan & Mercer, 2002, for a review.)

In the case of most children with learning disabilities, however, little neurological evidence exists of actual *damage* to brain tissues. Therefore, today, the term *dysfunction* has replaced *injury* or *damage*. A child with learning disabilities is now often referred to as having CNS dysfunction rather than brain injury. Dysfunction does not necessarily mean tissue damage; instead, it signifies a malfunctioning of the brain or CNS.

Researchers have documented neurological dysfunction as a probable cause of learning disabilities using neuroimaging techniques such as **magnetic resonance imaging (MRI), functional magnetic resonance imaging (fMRI), functional magnetic reso-**

nance spectroscopy (fMRS), and **positron-emission tomography (PET) scans**, as well as measuring the brain's electrical activity with **event-related potentials (ERPs**, also referred to as evoked potentials).

- An MRI sends magnetic radio waves through the head and creates cross-sectional images of the brain.
- fMRI and fMRS are adaptations of the MRI. Unlike an MRI, they are used to detect changes in brain activity while a person is engaged in a task, such as reading.
- A PET scan, like an fMRI or fMRS, is used while the person is performing a task. The subject is injected with a substance containing a low amount of radiation, which collects in active neurons. Using a scanner to detect the radioactive substance, researchers can tell which parts of the brain are actively engaged during various tasks.
- ERPs measure the brain's response to perceptual and cognitive processing. They result from the administration of an **electroencephalograph (EEG)**.

Using these neuroimaging techniques, researchers have accumulated evidence for structural and functional differences between the brains of people with and without learning disabilities, especially reading disabilities. *Structural differences* refer to such things as the size of the various areas of the brain. *Functional* refers to activity in the brain. Findings from these neuroimaging studies have been relatively consistent in identifying structural and/or functional differences in the **left temporal lobe** and areas around it in persons with dyslexia (see Gabrieli, 2009, for a review of this research). See Figure 6.1.

FIGURE 6.1 The left temporal lobe of the brain and some areas around it are closely associated with reading disabilities.

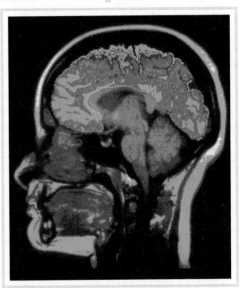

Using ERPs, researchers have determined that newborns' responses to speech stimuli are correlated with their language scores in preschool (Guttorm et al., 2005) and also predict whether they are reading disabled at 8 years of age (Molfese, 2000). Evidence also suggests that ERP measures might someday be reliable enough to be used, along with educational and psychological tests, to determine children at risk for later reading disabilities (Hoeft et al., 2007).

Taken as a whole, these studies are not definitive evidence of a neurological basis for *all* students who are identified as learning disabled. However, the results have turned many people who were formerly skeptical into believers that CNS dysfunction could be the cause of many, if not most, cases of learning disabilities.

Even in cases in which one can be fairly certain that the person with learning disabilities has neurological dysfunction, the question still remains: How did the person come to have the neurological dysfunction? Possible reasons fall into three general categories: genetic factors, toxins, and medical factors.

Genetic Factors

Over the years, evidence has accumulated that learning disabilities can be inherited. The two most common types of studies that researchers use to examine the genetic basis of learning disabilities are familiality studies and heritability studies.

Familiality studies examine the degree to which a certain condition, such as a learning disability, occurs in a single family (i.e., the tendency for it to "run in a family"). Researchers have found that about 35% to 45% of first-degree relatives (the immediate birth family: parents and siblings) of individuals with reading disabilities have reading disabilities (Hallgren, 1950; Olson, Wise, Conners, Rack, & Fulker, 1989; Pennington, 1990; Schulte-Korne et al., 2006), and the risk for having reading disabilities goes up for children who have both parents with reading disabilities (W. H. Raskind, 2001). The same degree of familiality has also been found in families of people with speech and language disorders (Beichtman, Hood, & Inglis, 1992; Lewis, 1992; Schulte-Korne et al., 2006) and spelling disabilities (Schulte-Korne, Deimel, Muller, Gutenbrunner, & Remschmidt, 1996; Schulte-Korne et al., 2006).

The tendency for learning disabilities to run in families may also be due to environmental factors. For example, it's possible that parents with learning disabilities will pass on their disabilities to their children through their child-rearing practices. A more convincing method of determining whether learning disabilities are inherited is **heritability studies** that compare the prevalence of learning disabilities in identical (monozygotic, from the same egg) versus fraternal (dizygotic, from two eggs) twins. Researchers have found that identical twins are more concordant than are fraternal twins for reading disabilities, speech and language disorders, and math disabilities (DeFries, Gillis, & Wadsworth, 1993; DeThorne et al., 2006; Lewis & Thompson, 1992; Reynolds et al., 1996; Shalev, 2004). In other words, if an identical twin and a fraternal twin each has a learning disability, the second identical twin is more likely to have a learning disability than the second fraternal twin.

With the rapid advances in molecular genetics, an expanding body of research is attempting to pinpoint the genes involved in learning disabilities. Virtually all geneticists agree that no single gene causes a learning disability. Thus far, researchers have identified at least four genes as candidates for being connected in some way with learning disabilities (Fisher & Francks, 2006; Galaburda, LoTurco, Ramus, Fitch, & Rosen, 2006; McGrath, Smith, & Pennington, 2006; Plomin & Kovas, 2005; Smith, 2007). And, interestingly, evidence suggests that some of these genes are associated with more than one type of learning disability. In other words, the same genes are linked to reading, math, and spelling disabilities (Hayworth et al., 2009; Plomin & Kovas, 2005).

It's important to keep in mind that, as exciting as these genetics findings are, just as was the case for intellectual disabilities (discussed in Chapter 5), the environment also plays an important role in learning disabilities. This is especially true in the early stages of learning, for example, early reading skills (Petrill, Deater-Deckard, Thompson, DeThorne & Schatschneider, 2006).

Toxins

Toxins are agents that can cause malformations or defects in the developing fetus. In Chapter 5, we discussed **fetal alcohol syndrome (FAS)**, **fetal alcohol spectrum disorders**, and lead as potential causes of intellectual disabilities. Authorities have also speculated that some people may be exposed to levels of these substances that are not high enough to result in intellectual disabilities/mental retardation but are high enough to cause learning disabilities.

Medical Factors

Several medical conditions can cause learning disabilities. Many of these can also result in intellectual disabilities, depending on the severity of the condition. For example, premature birth places children at risk for neurological dysfunction and learning disabilities (Aarnoudse-Moens, Weisglas-Kuperus, van Goudoever, & Oosterlaan, 2009), and pediatric AIDS can result in neurological damage resulting in learning disabilities.

PSYCHOLOGICAL AND BEHAVIORAL CHARACTERISTICS

Before discussing some of the most common characteristics of people with learning disabilities, we point out two important features of this population: People with learning disabilities exhibit a great deal of both interindividual and intraindividual variation.

Interindividual Variation

In any group of students with learning disabilities, some will have problems in reading, some will have problems in math, some will have problems in spelling, some will be inattentive, and so on. One term for such interindividual variation is *heterogeneity*. Although heterogeneity is a trademark of children from all the categories of special education, the old adage "No two are exactly alike" is particularly appropriate for students with learning disabilities. This heterogeneity makes it a challenge for teachers to plan educational programs for the diverse group of children they find in their classrooms.

Intraindividual Variation

In addition to differences among one another, children with learning disabilities also tend to exhibit variability within their own profiles of abilities. For example, a child might be 2 or 3 years above grade level in reading but 2 or 3 years behind grade level in math. Such uneven profiles account for references to *specific* learning disabilities in the literature on learning disabilities.

We now turn to a discussion of some of the most common characteristics of persons with learning disabilities.

Academic Achievement Problems

Academic deficits are the hallmark of learning disabilities. By definition, if an academic problem does not exist, a learning disability does not exist.

Reading Reading poses the most difficulty for most students with learning disabilities. Students with reading disabilities are likely to experience problems with three aspects of reading: decoding, fluency, and comprehension (Hallahan et al., 2005). **Decoding** is the ability to convert print to spoken language and is largely dependent on phonological awareness and phonemic awareness. **Phonological awareness** is the understanding that speech consists of small units of sound, such as words, syllables, and phonemes (Pullen, 2002; Troia, 2004). Phonemic awareness is particularly important (Blachman, 2001; Boada & Pennington, 2006). Children with **phonemic awareness** understand that words are made up of sounds, or phonemes. For example, the word *bat* consists of three phonemes: \b\, \a\, and \t\. The accompanying Success Stories feature describes the achievements of a fifth grader with learning disabilities.

Interestingly, evidence suggests that readers of English are more susceptible to problems with phonological awareness than are readers of some other languages. Some professionals have speculated that this is why reading disabilities are more prevalent in English-speaking countries than in some other countries (see the Focus on Concepts box, "Dyslexia," on page 148).

Students who have difficulty decoding invariably have problems with fluency. **Reading fluency** refers to the ability to read effortlessly and smoothly. Reading rate and the ability to read with appropriate expression are components of reading fluency.

Problems with reading fluency are a major reason why students have difficulties with reading comprehension (Good, Simmons, & Kame'enui, 2001). **Reading comprehension** refers to the ability to gain meaning from what one has read. In other words, reading too slowly or in a halting manner interferes with the ability to comprehend text.

Written Language People with learning disabilities often have problems in one or more of the following areas: handwriting, spelling, and composition (Hallahan et al., 2005). Although even the best students can have less-than-perfect handwriting, the kinds of problems that some students with learning disabilities exhibit are much more severe. These children are sometimes very slow writers, and their written products are sometimes illegible. Spelling can be a significant problem because of the difficulty (noted in the previous section) in understanding the correspondence between sounds and letters.

In addition to the more mechanical areas of handwriting and spelling, students with learning disabilities frequently have difficulties in the more creative aspects of composition (Graham & Harris, 2011). For example, compared to nondisabled peers, students with learning disabilities use less complex sentence structures; include fewer types of words; write paragraphs that are less well organized; include fewer ideas in their written products; and write stories that have fewer important components, such as introducing main characters, setting scenes, and describing a conflict to be resolved (Hallahan et al., 2005).

Spoken Language Many students with learning disabilities have problems with the mechanical and social uses of language. Mechanically, they have trouble with **syntax** (grammar),

Success Stories

HARD WORK AT HOME AND SCHOOL HELPS RANDY READ ON GRADE LEVEL

Special Educator Celia Gottesman:"Unless you work harder, faster, and more intensively, they won't catch up."

Ten-year-old Randy Daniels is reading on grade level as he starts fifth grade at Lake Forest Elementary School in Florida.

These are the keys to his success:

* ★ Intensive instruction in reading and math
* ★ Relentless progress monitoring
* ★ Specific incentives and parental support

RANDY DANIELS ended third grade reading at a second-grade level, 1 year behind many of his classmates. This year he has caught up, and he is proud of it. "I did it! I did it! I did it!" he said when he heard the good news. "Randy moved 2 years ahead in reading in 1 year with two intensive summer school experiences, and that's a tremendous achievement" says special educator Dr. Celia Gottesman. Hard work at home and at school helped Randy achieve success through intensive, relentless, and specific special education.

★ **Intensive Instruction in Reading and Math** Randy Daniels loves football and he likes to do his best, but last year he struggled to keep up in his regular class. In summer school Randy received intensive instruction for 90 minutes every day in a resource classroom with Celia Gottesman and Waltraud Schmid. Known to their students as Dr. G. and Mrs. Schmid, these special educators strengthened Randy's academic skills using a combination of formative assessment, direct instruction, and cognitive strategy training. "We also provided lots of positive reinforcement and personal attention," says Celia. The effective team of Gottesman and Schmid gets results, and this year their high-poverty school met its goals for adequate yearly progress (AYP). Celia Gottesman teaches reading and math to exceptional learners at Lake Forest Elementary. Waltraud Schmid also taught special education at the school before she retired. As a school volunteer, she now helps Celia plan and deliver systematic instruction 5 days a week. For Celia, teaching students with learning disabilities means accelerating progress as quickly as possible. "We assess frequently to see where students are, what academic and social skills they need, and how fast we can push them—and I'm a pusher," she says. She speaks candidly as the mother of three college graduates who have learning disabilities: "Unless you work harder, faster, and more intensively, they won't catch up."

To improve Randy's reading fluency and comprehension, Celia modified the pace of instruction, and taught him in small groups with other students who struggled with similar concepts and vocabulary. She also taught evidence-based learning strategies to help him anchor academic content. In addition Randy received supplemental one-on-one instruction daily from Waltraud Schmid, who inventoried his skill levels and charted his progress. "Mrs.

semantics (word meanings), and, as we have already noted, **phonology** (the ability to break words into their component sounds and blend individual sounds together to make words).

The social uses of language are commonly referred to as **pragmatics**. Students with learning disabilities are often inept in the production and reception of discourse. In short, they're not very good conversationalists. They cannot engage in the mutual give-and-take that conversations between individuals require. For instance, conversations of individuals with learning disabilities are frequently marked by long silences because they don't use the relatively subtle strategies that their nondisabled peers do to keep conversations going. They're not skilled at responding to others' statements or questions and tend to answer their own questions before their companions have a chance to respond. They tend to make task-irrelevant comments and make those with whom they talk uncomfortable. In one often cited study, for example, children with and without learning disabilities took turns playing the role of host in a simulated television talk show (Bryan, Donahue, Pearl, & Sturm, 1981). In contrast to children without disabilities, children with learning disabilities playing the host role allowed their guests without disabilities to dominate the conversation. Also, their guests exhibited more signs of discomfort during the interview than did the guests of hosts without disabilities.

tional Institute of Child Health and Human Development, 2000). This report identified five essential components of effective reading instruction: phonological awareness training, phonics instruction, fluency instruction, vocabulary instruction, and comprehension instruction. In addition, the most successful reading instruction is explicit and systematic.

As we noted earlier in this chapter, **phonological awareness** involves knowing that speech consists of small units of sound, such as words, syllables, and phonemes. **Phonemic awareness**, a component of phonological awareness, involves knowing that words are made up of sounds, or phonemes. Strong research evidence indicates that teaching students with reading disabilities to manipulate phonemes in words is highly effective in helping them acquire reading skills.

Phonics instruction involves learning the alphabetic system, that is, the pairing of letters and words with their sounds. Effective phonics instruction is explicit, systematic, with plentiful opportunities for practice (Mercer, Mercer, & Pullen, 2011).

Reading fluency refers to the ability to read effortlessly and smoothly. Successful interventions for problems with reading fluency typically involve having the student read aloud. An especially effective technique is **repeated readings**, whereby students repeatedly (several times a week) read the same short passages aloud until they are reading at an appropriate pace with few or no errors.

A variety of methods are available for increasing students' listening and reading vocabulary. Because much of a person's vocabulary is learned indirectly, proving ample opportunities for reading a wide range of materials is important. With respect to directly teaching vocabulary, the most effective methods include "reviewing new or unknown words in a text prior to reading, extending instruction on specific words over time and across different contexts" (Mercer et al., 2011, p. 269).

Numerous strategies can help students comprehend what they are reading. Some involve the types of cognitive training strategies that we've already discussed. And some involve content-enhancement strategies that we discuss later when describing approaches for content area instruction.

Instructional Approaches for Writing   The ability to read and write are closely linked. Students who exhibit reading disabilities also often have problems with writing. Researchers have determined that effective writing instruction for students with learning disabilities involves teaching students explicit and systematic strategies for planning, revising, and editing compositions (Graham & Harris, 2011).

Self-regulated strategy development (SRSD) (Graham & Harris, 2003; Harris, Graham, & Mason, 2003) is a research-based model that has been highly effective (Regan & Mastropieri, 2009). SRSD approaches writing as a problem-solving task that involves planning, knowledge, and skills. Within SRSD are several strategies focused on different aspects of writing. A good example is the story-writing strategy, *POW+WWW, What = 2, H = 2.* POW = **P**ick my idea; **O**rganize my notes; **W**rite and say more. WWW = **W**ho is the main character? **W**hen does the story take place? **W**here does the story take place? What = **W**hat does the main character do? and **W**hat happens then? H = **H**ow does the story end? and **H**ow does the main character feel?

Instructional Approaches for Math   Researchers have determined that certain principles characterize effective math instruction for students with learning disabilities. Probably the most important one is that the instruction needs to be explicit (L. S. Fuchs et al., 2011; Gersten et al., 2009). Constructivist, discovery-oriented approaches to math may succeed with students who don't experience learning problems, but students with learning disabilities need more structure and teacher direction. Some other principles are that the teacher should sequence the instruction to minimize errors, but when errors occur, they should be immediately rectified. The instruction should include cumulative review of concepts and operations, and the students' progress should be closely monitored.

Instructional Approaches for Science and Social Studies   Students with learning disabilities often have problems with content areas such as science and social studies, especially when the primary means of delivering the content is through textbooks. Unfortunately, the current climate of standards-based learning and high-stakes testing has resulted in heavy emphasis on textbook-based science and social studies instruction. And textbook-based instruction does not align well with the weaknesses of students with learning disabilities in prior knowledge, reading, vocabulary, and memory. At the same time, however, the need for structure experienced by students with learning disabilities makes the use of activities-oriented instruction problematic. When activities-based instruction is carefully structured and sequenced, however, with emphasis on cumulative review and monitoring of student progress, it can be effective for students with learning disabilities (Scruggs, Mastropieri, & Marshak, 2011).

When textbooks are used, researchers have found that enhancing the content of science and social studies materials is very effective for students with learning disabilities (Gajria, Jitendra, Sood, & Sacks, 2007). **Content enhancement** can take many forms. It's a way of making materials more salient or prominent. Two particularly effective ways of enhancing content are graphic organizers and mnemonics. **Graphic organizers** "are visual devices that employ lines, circles, and boxes to organize information: hierarchic, cause/effect, compare/contrast, and cyclic or linear sequences" (E. S. Ellis & Howard, 2007, p. 1). **Mnemonics** involve using pictures and/or words to help remember information. For a description of mnemonics and how it can be used in the classroom, see the accompanying Responsive Instruction feature, "Mnemonics."

Direct Instruction

INTERNETRESOURCES

For more information on DI, visit the Association for Direct Instruction Website: http://www.adihome.org/

Direct Instruction (DI) focuses on the details of the instructional process. Commercial DI programs are available for several academic areas, e.g., reading, math, science, social studies. Advocates of DI stress a systematic analysis of the concept to be taught, rather than analysis of the characteristics of the student. A critical component of DI is task analysis. **Task analysis** involves breaking down academic problems into their component parts so that teachers can teach the parts separately and then teach the students to put the parts together in order to demonstrate the larger skill.

Originally pioneered by Sigfried Engelmann and the late Wesley C. Becker, DI programs consist of precisely sequenced, scripted, fast-paced lessons taught to small groups of 4 to 10 students with a heavy emphasis on drill and practice. See the Responsive Instruction feature, "Direct Instruction," on page 157 for more information about DI in the classroom.

Direct Instruction programs, which consist of precisely sequenced, fast-paced lessons taught to small groups of 4 to 10 students, may bring both immediate and long-term academic gains in students with learning disabilities.

RESPONSIVE *INSTRUCTION*

MEETING THE NEEDS OF STUDENTS WITH LEARNING DISABILITIES

Mnemonics

WHAT ARE MNEMONICS?

The term *mnemonic* comes from the name of the Greek goddess of memory, Mnemosyne. Mnemosyne's name was derived from *mnemon*, meaning mindful. Today, a mnemonic refers to any memory-enhancing strategy. Almost everyone has used a mnemonic at one time or another. To remember the order of the planets, many students learn the phrase "My Very Educated Mother Just Served Us Nine Pizzas." Music students trying to remember scales learn "Every Good Boy Deserves Fudge." Rhymes are another form of mnemonic—"*I* before *E*, except after *C*, or when pronounced as *A* as in *neighbor* and *weigh*." Mnemonics come in a variety of forms, but what defines a mnemonic is its ability to aid in the retention of certain information.

WHAT THE RESEARCH SAYS

Researchers have studied mnemonics and students with learning disabilities in both laboratory settings (i.e., one-to-one with trained experimenters rather than classroom teachers) and classroom settings. Findings from these studies reveal the following gains made by students who were taught using mnemonics:

- Mnemonic keyword method resulted in increased recall of information.
- Small groups of students with learning disabilities could be taught using a variety of mnemonic strategies over a period of days without diminishing the effectiveness of the specific mnemonics.
- Mnemonic pictures aided in the comprehension and recall of information presented in science and history texts.
- Students with learning disabilities could be taught to create their own mnemonics and apply them successfully.
- Students with learning and behavior disorders benefited from teacher-created mnemonics and were able to retain the information longer than students who were not provided mnemonics.
- Mnemonics appeared to result in increased motivation, efficacy, and willingness to learn. (Mastropieri & Scruggs, 1998; Scruggs et al., 2011)

IMPLEMENTING MNEMONICS IN THE CLASSROOM

Two effective mnemonic techniques are the key-word and peg-word methods (Lasley, Matczynski, & Rowley, 2002). (See Figure A.)

FIGURE A Mnemonic representation of Franklin Pierce, 14th president of the United States.

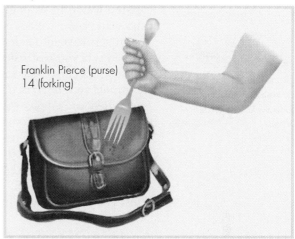

Franklin Pierce (purse)
14 (forking)

Source: Adapted from Mastropieri, M. A., Scruggs, T. E., & Whedon, C. (1997). Using mnemonic strategies to teach information about U.S. Presidents: A classroom-based investigation. *Learning Disability Quarterly, 20,* 13–21. Copyright 1994 by Thomas E. Scruggs and Margo A. Mastropieri.

When using a keyword approach, students are taught how to transform an unfamiliar word to a familiar word. For example, the word *accolade* could be associated with the keyword *Kool-Aid*. To associate *Kool-Aid* with the definition of *accolade*, students can think of someone making a toast to a guest of honor with a cup of Kool-Aid. Thus, the definition "giving praise" will be closely associated with accolade (Levin, 1993).

To use the peg-word strategy, students learn to correlate numbers with familiar rhyming words. The teacher creates a picture that incorporates the peg word along with the content associations. Teachers use this strategy when students need to remember the order of information or when a number is associated with the fact. For example, a student who is trying to remember that Monroe was the fifth president could combine the key word for Monroe and the peg word *hive* for five. The image of bees carrying money to a hive would be the mnemonic (Mastropieri & Scruggs, 1998).

• By Kristin L. Sayeski

Direct instruction programs are among the best-researched commercial programs available for students with learning disabilities. Use of these programs not only results in immediate academic gains, but also may bring long-term academic gains (A. K. Ellis & Fouts, 1997; Tarver, 1999).

Peer Tutoring

Teachers have successfully used several types of peer tutoring arrangements with students with learning disabilities. Two examples are **classwide peer tutoring (CWPT)** and **peer-assisted learning strategies (PALS)**. In Chapter 5, we discussed the use of CWPT for students with intellectual disabilities. (See the Responsive Instruction box on p. 119 in Chapter 5.) Researchers have also extensively documented CWPT as effective for students with learning disabilities or those at risk for learning disabilities (Kourea, Cartledge, & Musti-Rao, 2007; Maheady, Harper, & Mallette, 2003). CWPT consists of "students who are taught by peers who are *trained* and *supervised* by classroom teachers" (Maheady et al., 2003, p. 1). "Trained" and "supervised" are emphasized because it's imperative that the teachers carefully structure the tutoring experience. In other words, the instruction isn't just turned over to the students.

PALS is based on research-proven, best practices in reading, such as phonological awareness, decoding, and comprehension strategies (D. Fuchs & Fuchs, 2005; D. Fuchs, Fuchs, & Burish, 2000). PALS involves the pairing of a higher performing student with a lower performing student, with the pairs then participating in highly structured tutoring sessions. The students take turns being the "coach" (tutor) and the "reader" (tutee).

Service Delivery Models

For many years, the most common form of educational placement for students with learning disabilities was the special education resource room. In the mid-1990s, however, in keeping with the trend toward inclusion, the general education classroom surpassed the resource room as the most popular placement. In addition, the number of placements in separate classrooms has gradually diminished. As of 2007, 59% of students with learning disabilities between the ages of 6 and 21 were being educated primarily in the general education classroom, which is up from only 40% in 2000 (Cortiella, 2009).

As we discussed in Chapter 2, more and more schools are moving toward some kind of cooperative teaching arrangement, in which general and special education teachers work together in the general education classroom. Some advocates believe that this model is particularly appropriate for students with learning disabilities because it allows them to stay in the general education classroom for all or almost all of their instruction. However, the research base for cooperative teaching is still in its infancy (Cook, McDuffie, Oshita, & Cook, 2011; Murawski & Swanson, 2001). See the Making It Work feature on page 158 for a description of a co-teaching situation in an eighth-grade algebra class.

Because students with learning disabilities make up the largest category of special education students and because their academic and behavioral problems are not as severe as those of students with intellectual disabilities or behavior disorders, they are often candidates for full inclusion. However, all the major professional and parent organizations have developed position papers against placing all students with learning disabilities in full-inclusion settings. Research on the effectiveness of inclusion for students with learning disabilities also argues against using full inclusion for *all* students with learning disabilities (Zigmond & Kloo, 2011). Evidence indicates that the legal mandate of IDEA requiring the availability of a full continuum of placements is sound policy for students with learning disabilities.

ASSESSMENT OF PROGRESS

The notion of using assessment information to help plan educational strategies has gained much of its popularity from professionals working in the area of learning disabilities. For example, **curriculum-based measurement (CBM)** was developed largely by Deno and his colleagues (Deno, 1985; L. S. Fuchs, Deno, & Mirkin, 1984) of the University of Minnesota

INTERNETRESOURCES

For more information on PALS, visit their Website: http://www.kc.vanderbilt.edu/pals/

RESPONSIVE INSTRUCTION

MEETING THE NEEDS OF STUDENTS WITH LEARNING DISABILITIES

Direct Instruction

WHAT IS DIRECT INSTRUCTION?

Direct instruction (DI) is a highly structured, teacher-directed method of instruction. The main features of DI programs are as follows:

- Field-tested, scripted lesson plans
- Curriculum based upon the theory of mastery learning (i.e., students do not move on until they have mastered the concept)
- Rapid pace of instruction highly dependent upon frequent teacher questioning and student response
- Achievement grouping
- Frequent assessments

Siegfried Engelmann developed DI in the 1960s on the basis of studies of beginning reading. Since the development of his early DI programs such as DISTAR Reading I (Engelmann & Bruner, 1969), DI programs have been developed in the areas of reading, language arts, mathematics, science, and social studies. One of the defining features of DI programs is that virtually every aspect of instruction undergoes careful evaluation before it is approved for inclusion in the program. Researchers evaluate everything from group size to teacher directions to method of student response to achieve optimal effectiveness. As a result, DI programs have received the highest ranking for program effectiveness in an independent analysis of instructional programs (Ellis, 2001).

WHAT THE RESEARCH SAYS

To obtain an idea of the overall effectiveness of a program, researchers conduct what is called a meta-analysis. To conduct a meta-analysis, researchers identify all studies that have been conducted on a specific technique or program and statistically determine how effective the technique is as a whole. Since the inception of DI, several of these comprehensive evaluations have been conducted in regard to DI curriculum. A recent meta-analysis made over 173 comparisons between DI and other programs. Results showed that (1) 64% of the comparisons resulted in statistically significant differences in favor of the groups using DI, (2) 35% of the comparisons showed no differences among programs, and (3) 1% showed differences in favor of programs other than DI (Adams & Englemann, 1996). In short, the overall effectiveness of DI programs is among the highest in the field of education.

EXERCISE 3

Say the Sounds

***Note:* Do not write the words on the board. This is an oral exercise.**

1. Listen: fffe¯e¯e¯. (Hold up a finger for each sound.)
2. Say the sounds in (pause) fffe¯e¯e¯. Get ready. (Hold up a finger for each sound.) fffe¯e¯e¯. (Repeat until the students say the sounds without stopping.)
3. Say it fast. (Signal.) Fee.
4. What word? (Signal.) Fee. Yes, fee.
5. (Repeat steps 2–4 for if, fish, sam, at, me, rim, she, we, ship, fat, miff.)

FIGURE A

IMPLEMENTING THE CURRICULUM

To implement DI, teachers need to receive training in the program. Because of the highly structured nature of DI materials, many educators and administrators incorrectly assume that DI is "teacher-proof"; that is, anyone could be effective using the materials. Nothing could be further from the truth. Using the materials with ease, understanding the rationale for each component and therefore being able to communicate that to students, and pacing the instruction to meet the unique needs of a group of students all require teaching skills that cannot come from a script. After initial training, coaches or facilitators provide ongoing support for teachers who use DI programs to ensure that teachers are maximizing the effectiveness of the curriculum.

WHAT DOES DI LOOK LIKE?

The sample exercise in Figure A is an excerpt from Corrective Reading, an accelerated reading program for students in grades 3.5 through 12 who have not mastered the basics of decoding and comprehension. In this decoding lesson, students work on phonemic awareness, letter–symbol identification, and sounding out words. The use of choral response increases opportunities for student engagement, and individual questioning ensures individual mastery.

• By Kristin L. Sayeski

MAKING IT WORK
COLLABORATION AND CO-TEACHING FOR STUDENTS WITH LEARNING DISABILITIES

"How can she help me if she doesn't know algebra like I do?"

How can co-teaching with a special educator to meet the needs of students with learning disabilities work if the special educator is not as much of a content area specialist as the general educator? Though you might think that would mean an end to equal collaboration in, say, a biology or advanced literature course, teachers of students with learning disabilities have knowledge about learning that can help make them an active part of any co-teaching team.

WHAT DOES IT MEAN TO BE A TEACHER OF STUDENTS WITH LEARNING DISABILITIES?

Most programs for teachers of students with learning disabilities focus on the learning process and effective strategies for learning across the content areas. Specifically, the Council for Exceptional Children (2003) states that teachers of students with learning disabilities should be able to:

1. Use methods for teaching individuals to independently use cognitive processing to solve problems.
2. Use methods for guiding individuals in identifying and organizing critical content.
3. Use methods for ensuring individual academic success in one-to-one, small-group, and large-group settings.
4. Use instructional methods to strengthen and compensate for deficits in perception, comprehension, memory, and retrieval.
5. Identify and teach essential concepts, vocabulary, and content across the general curriculum.

SUCCESSFUL STRATEGIES FOR CO-TEACHING

Joan Hamilton is a former special educator who co-taught with general educators at the middle and high school level. She describes a situation in which she was not the content specialist but was able to provide explicit strategy instruction to all students because of a successful co-teaching arrangement.

> I was originally certified to teach social studies from 8th to 12th grades. When I began working in those classrooms, I realized that there were several students who really struggled to read the textbook I was using, and I became interested in learning disabilities.
>
> After earning a Masters in Special Education, one of my first positions required co-teaching in an 8th-grade pre-algebra classroom. I knew the material, but wasn't as confident that I knew the best way to teach it. My co-teacher and I ended up with a class of 18 students, 11 of whom were identified with disabilities (nine with learning disabilities) and the rest had done poorly in their previous math courses. The textbook prescribed a rigid plan for the classroom: review homework, teach the next lesson, do some practice problems. The pacing guide provided by the district (and part of my co-teacher's evaluation criteria) did not leave many opportunities for creativity in instruction. Though we were both on the same 8th-grade team, we could use very little of the team meeting time to plan together. So, after many philosophical discussions, we plunged into the course. After a few weeks, we found a rhythm that seemed to work with the students.
>
> First, my co-teacher taught the lesson as I took notes on the overhead for the students. I would often create a circle on the overhead with the example problem in the middle. As we worked the problem in the middle of the circle, I would use words to describe the step on the outside of the circle (see Rooney, 1998). This helped me understand how my co-teacher would teach the concept. And it provided the students with an annotated example problem.
>
> Next, we both moved around the room to help students as they completed practice problems.
>
> The next day, I did the homework review. This gave me the opportunity to return to the graphic organizers for review and to re-teach the steps of the problem as necessary (as my co-teacher had taught it earlier). It also allowed my co-teacher to circulate and to help individual students.
>
> This co-teaching plan is probably a combination of the structures described in articles and books about co-teaching. It provided us with what we felt was the best support for our students, given the conditions of the classroom and curriculum. We had a few students fail the course because they just didn't even attempt to do much of the work. The majority, however, made it through the material and on to algebra with a basic understanding of the concepts and of how to structure their notes and ask questions.

• By Margaret P. Weiss

Institute for Research on Learning Disabilities (IRLD). In addition to CBM, teachers may administer other forms of informal assessments to monitor students' progress and make instructional decisions. This section provides a brief overview of CBM and other informal measures to monitor progress in the areas of mathematics, reading, and written expression.

Curriculum-Based Measurement

Teachers of students with learning disabilities are using CBM increasingly as a means to monitor academic progress and to document students' responsiveness to instruction.

CBM involves direct and frequent samples of performance on items from the curriculum in which students are being instructed. Each curriculum-based measure has multiple forms of equivalent difficulty that are administered at regular intervals to determine whether a student is making progress toward a specified goal (McMaster & Espin, 2007). Teachers implement the measures as short probes that require only minutes.

In reading, for example, CBM typically focuses on oral reading fluency, which is determined by calculating the number of correct words per minute (CWPM) read on a graded passage. To monitor progress toward a specified goal, the teacher first gathers data to determine the student's current CWPM. The teacher then uses this information to calculate a **baseline data point**. Using data of **expected growth norms** (see e.g., Hosp, Hosp, & Howell, 2007), the teacher establishes a goal for the student and creates an **aim line** on a graph to depict where the student should be performing at a given point in time. The teacher assesses the student's reading on a CBM probe two or more times each week and graphs the data to determine if the student is on target to reach the specified goal.

Figure 6.2 illustrates a CBM graph for a student, Billy, a fourth grader with a learning disability. Billy's teacher had gathered the baseline data point and determined that he read 56 CWPM. She then created an aim line for 18 weeks of instruction (one semester). Based on expected growth norms (L. S. Fuchs et al., 1993; Hosp et al., 2007) and the baseline data point for CWPM, his teacher determined that Billy should be reading 79 CWPM by the end of the semester. After the first 5 weeks of instruction, Billy was on track to reach his goal by the end of the semester. However, during weeks 6 through 8, his CWPM began to decline, such that it looked like he wouldn't be able to reach his goal. At this point, the teacher

FIGURE 6.2 A progress-monitoring chart using curriculum-based measurement on oral reading fluency for Billy, a fourth grader with a learning disability.

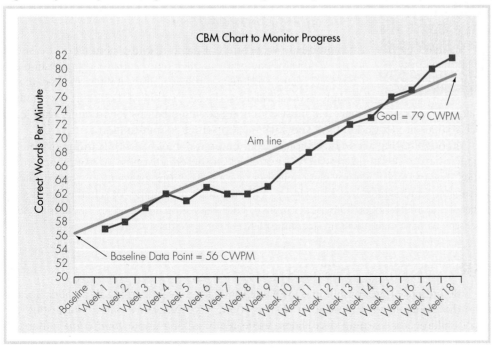

INTERNETRESOURCES

For more information on progress monitoring, visit the National Center on Student Progress Monitoring: http://www.studentprogress .org/

adjusted the instruction, by adding 15 minutes per day of peer tutoring, two times a week. From that point on, Billy improved and actually exceeded his goal, reading 82 CWPM by the end of the semester.

Although oral reading fluency probes are the most common form of CBM, teachers use additional methods to monitor student progress in other areas of reading (e.g., phonemic awareness, decoding, and comprehension), mathematics, spelling, and writing. In mathematics, researchers have developed CBMs that span topics in early mathematics through secondary skills. As early as prekindergarten, students may participate in CBM to demonstrate their knowledge of mathematics through various tasks (e.g., circling numbers to demonstrate numeral identification; Foegen, Jiban, & Deno, 2007). For school-age students, most CBMs focus on basic operations; however, CBM may be used for computation as well as conceptual knowledge.

Informal Assessment

In addition to CBM, teachers may also use other informal measures to monitor student progress and plan for instruction. In the area of reading, for example, teachers can use an **informal reading inventory (IRI)**, a series of reading passages or word lists graded in order of difficulty. The teacher has the student read from the series, beginning with a list or passage that is likely to be easy for the student. The student continues to read increasingly more difficult lists or passages while the teacher monitors the student's performance. After compiling the results of the IRI, the teacher can use them to estimate the appropriate difficulty level of reading material for the student.

Mathematics dynamic assessment (MDA) is another example of an informal assessment that can inform instruction. Using MDA, the teacher integrates research-based assessment techniques including (1) examining mathematical understanding at concrete, semi-concrete, and abstract levels, (2) assessing mathematical interests and experiences, (3) examining error patterns, and (4) using flexible interviews (Allsopp, Kyger, & Lovin, 2008). This informal, yet comprehensive assessment process allows teachers to design effective instruction to meet the unique needs of students with learning disabilities.

Some of the most accurate predictors of learning problems in preschool that may show up later are emergent literacy skills, such as counting and identifying letters, numbers, shapes, and colors.

Testing Accommodations

Accommodations for students with learning disabilities are similar to those for students with intellectual disabilities, as presented in Chapter 5. Many students with learning disabilities receive accommodations on standardized tests that alter scheduling, presentation format, and response format. The most common accommodations for students with learning disabilities are extended time and small-group setting administration.

Although testing accommodations are common for students with learning disabilities, particularly extended time, research is not clear on the effectiveness of testing accommodations. For example, it's not clear whether accommodations provide an opportunity for students to demonstrate their knowledge without unfair advantage, or whether the accommodations actually boost their performance. Likewise, more research is needed to determine how to best match testing accommodations for specific students.

EARLY INTERVENTION

Very little preschool programming is available for children with learning disabilities because of the difficulties in identification at such a young age. When we talk about testing preschool children for learning disabilities, we're really talking about *prediction* rather than *identification* because, strictly speaking, they haven't had much exposure to academics such as reading or math. Unfortunately, all other things being equal, prediction is always less precise than identification. In addition, in the preschool years some children do experience developmental delays. Some nondisabled children show slow developmental progress at this young age but soon catch up with their peers.

Even though it's wise to be cautious in identifying preschool children as learning disabled, researchers have determined that several risk factors are relatively good predictors of later learning disabilities. Table 6.1 provides a list of developmental milestones parents and teachers should monitor in the preschool years.

TRANSITION TO ADULTHOOD

A major difficulty faced by students with learning disabilities in the transition from high school to college is the decrease in the amount of guidance provided by adults, and the greater demand on self-discipline.

At one time, professionals thought that children outgrew their learning disabilities by adulthood. We now know that this is far from the truth. Although the long-term prognosis for individuals with learning disabilities is generally more positive than the prognosis for children with some other disabilities (e.g., behavior disorders), the potential for difficulty exists. Although the majority of students with learning disabilities don't drop out of school, their dropout rate of 25% is two to three times that of their peers without disabilities (Cortiella, 2009: Rojewski & Gregg, 2011). Also, many adults with learning disabilities have persistent problems in learning, socializing, holding jobs, and living independently (Scanlon, Patton, & Raskind, 2011). Even those individuals who are relatively successful in their transition to adulthood often must devote considerable energy to coping with daily living situations.

Factors Related to Successful Transition

How any particular adult with learning disabilities will fare depends on a variety of factors and is difficult to predict. Several researchers have addressed the topic of what contributes to successful adjustment of adults with learning disabilities (Bear, Kortering, & Braziel, 2006;

TABLE 6.1 Important developmental milestones

- Delay in comprehension and/or expression of spoken language
  - Limited receptive vocabulary
  - Reduced expressive vocabulary ("late talkers")
  - Difficulty understanding simple (e.g., one-step) directions
  - Monotone or other unusual prosodic features of speech
  - Reduced intelligibility
  - Infrequent or inappropriate spontaneous communication (vocal, verbal, or nonverbal)
  - Immature syntax
- Delay in emergent literacy skills
  - Slow speed in naming objects and colors
  - Limited phonological awareness (e.g., rhyming, syllable blending)
  - Minimal interest in print
  - Limited print awareness (e.g., book handling, recognizing environmental print)
- Delay in perceptual-motor skills
  - Problems in gross- or fine-motor coordination (e.g., hopping, dressing, cutting, stringing beads)
  - Difficulty in coloring, copying, and drawing

Source: Adapted from National Joint Committee on Learning Disabilities. (2006). *Learning disabilities and young children: Identification and intervention.* Retrieved from http://www.ldonline.org/about/partners/njcld

Gerber, Ginsberg, & Reiff, 1992; Kavale, 1988; Lindstrom & Benz, 2002; M. H. Raskind, Goldberg, Higgins, & Herman, 1999; Reiff, Gerber, & Ginsberg, 1997; Rojewski & Gregg, 2011; Spekman, Goldberg, & Herman, 1992). Although IQ and achievement would seem to be the best predictors of success, according to successful adults with learning disabilities, the things that set them apart from those who are not as successful are the following:

- An extraordinary degree of perseverance
- The ability to set goals for oneself
- A realistic acceptance of weaknesses coupled with an attitude of building on strengths
- Access to a strong network of social support from friends and family
- Exposure to intensive and long-term educational intervention
- High-quality on-the-job or postsecondary vocational training
- A supportive work environment
- Being able to take control of their lives

The last attribute, in particular, is a consistent theme among the successful. They have not let their disability rule them; rather, they have taken the initiative to control their own destiny. As one adult remarked, on looking back at his days in secondary school:

> Having an LD is much akin to being blind or losing the use of an appendage; it affects all aspects of your life. In dealing with this, you have two choices. One, you can acknowledge the parasitic relationship the LD has with you and consciously strive to excel despite its presence.
>
> . . . The other path let[s] the LD slowly dominate you and become[s] the scapegoat for all your failings. Can't find a good job? Must be the LD. Relationships always fail? It's the LD. If you follow this destructive path, you spend the remainder of your life being controlled by your LD. (Queen, 2001, p. 15)

Eric Breeden (see accompanying Peer Connections) is a good example of not allowing a learning disability to interfere with long-term goals.

Secondary Programming

Approaches to educating students with learning disabilities at the secondary level differ, depending on whether the goal is to prepare students for college or work. Students whose goal is to enter work after high school are taught basic academic skills in math, language arts, and reading. They're also taught functional skills, such as on-the-job behavior, filling out job applications, and balancing a checkbook. It's often combined with work–study—supervised work experiences during the school day. Ideally, the student can explore a variety of jobs that might be of interest. Engaging in paid work experiences during high school is also beneficial for successful employment upon graduation (Rojewski & Gregg, 2011).

Students intending to pursue college work receive continued support in their academic subjects. Compared to elementary school, in high school the role of the special education teacher typically shifts even more to one of consultation with the general education teachers in the content areas (e.g., math, history, science). The general education teacher teaches the content, and the special education teacher recommends modifications to the format of the content and teaches the student strategies for learning. For example, the learning strategies model developed at the University of Kansas Center for Research on Learning focuses on teaching students to overcome their metacognitive deficits by using learning strategies (Deshler et al., 2001). The Kansas group has developed a variety of strategies that students can use to help them organize information and learn it more efficiently.

Regardless of whether the focus is on transition to work or to college, a key element to successful transition programming is enabling students to make informed choices and to take responsibility for their futures (Cobb & Alwell, 2009). One way of achieving this is to ensure that students take part in their transition planning. In addition to a **transition plan** (see Chapter 2), federal law now requires that schools develop a

INTERNETRESOURCES

For more information on the University of Kansas Center for Research on Learning, visit http://www.ku-crl.org/

PEER CONNECTIONS: ERIC BREEDEN

ERIC BREEDEN was born in Charlottesville, Virginia. He is currently a high school senior at Albemarle High School. Eric was diagnosed with a learning disability in fifth grade. His mother initially had concerns about disruptive behavior that his teachers were noticing in the classroom. Once Eric was diagnosed, changes were made in the classroom, and this behavior disappeared. Since fifth grade, Eric has had optional services that include sitting in the front of the classroom and having notes taken for him, more time for tests, and a resource class and teacher. Eric has found some of these adaptations more beneficial than others and has gone on to have a successful high school career. Eric is an avid athlete and is looking forward to going to college, where he hopes to play football and pursue a degree in criminal justice.

What do you do for fun? I hang out with friends and play football.

What is your favorite way to relax? I like to hang out at the house and listen to music.

What is something that you excel at? Sports! I do football, wrestling, and track.

What is your pet peeve? Losing and failing, giving up. In sports and in school.

Can you recall one teacher in particular who has been a positive influence in your life? Yes, I guess my preschool teacher. She made me love school. She was a fun teacher, and I still remember her today.

Is there anyone else (celebrity, family member) whom you regard as a role model? Why are they a role model for you? The football player, Ray Lewis, who plays for the Ravens. I admire him because he's one of the best in the NFL, but he doesn't talk about it. He's not cocky and doesn't brag, even though he's a great player.

What is the most difficult thing for you about having a disability? When I was diagnosed with a learning disability, in fifth grade, I started having a resource class and teacher. This was helpful in some ways because the teacher helped me stay organized and on top of my work. But it was hard once I got to high school, because I couldn't really take any extra elective classes like my peers. Because of the resource class, I couldn't fit an arts class or a foreign language into my schedule. This was difficult, but in tenth grade I decided that I wanted to try school without having a resource class. It worked out well, and now I still receive guidance from a resource teacher but I rarely notice my learning disability because I'm not singled out as much. I feel that I can do all of my work without a lot of trouble.

Do you see your disability as affecting your ability to achieve what you want in your life? No, I think that I will still be able to graduate high school. When I had my resource class I wasn't going to be able to graduate with an advance diploma because I couldn't take a foreign language. But when they let me stop resource class, I took Spanish, and now I will graduate with an advance diploma. I also plan to go to college, and even hopefully play football in college.

Has your disability affected your social relationships? No, not at all.

Are there any advantages to having a disability that others might be surprised to know? Not really. I mean I have the option to have notes written for me in my classes, and I also can have different test formats, like written copies. But I don't find that I use a lot of these services right now.

How do you think others perceive you? I think as funny and outgoing … and an athlete.

What is one thing that you would like others to know about you? I want to play football in college. Right now I play linebacker, stage key, and receiver, but I really hope to play in college, too.

Where do you see yourself 10 years from now? Having a job, hopefully in criminal justice, and having a family. Also, probably living in New York, Florida, or California.

Please fill in the blank: I couldn't live without _____ . Sports!

CONNECT WITH ERIC— Eric welcomes you to contact him online at jbreeden@ charlottesvilledayschool.org

summary of performance (SOP) for each student with a disability as they exit secondary school, whether by graduating or exceeding the age of eligibility. SOPs are designed to provide a summary of relevant information, such as assessment reports; accommodations that have been provided; and recommendations for future accommodations, assistive technology, and support services for use in employment, training, or postsecondary schooling. SOPs also have a section for the student to provide input. Because SOPs only began implementation in 2007–2008, little research on their effectiveness exists (Gerber, 2009).

Postsecondary Programming

Postsecondary programs include vocational and technical programs as well as community colleges and 4-year colleges and universities. More and more individuals with learning disabilities are enrolling in colleges and universities, and more and more universities are establishing special programs and services for these students.

In selecting a college, students and their families should explore what kinds of student support services are offered. Section 504 of the Vocational Rehabilitation Act of 1973 (Public Law 93–112) requires that colleges make reasonable accommodations for students with disabilities so that they will not be discriminated against because of their disabilities. Some typical accommodations are extended time on exams, allowing students to take exams in a distraction-free room, providing tape recordings of lectures and books, and assigning volunteer note takers for lectures.

Even though students with disabilities are entitled to accommodations, they need to be much more proactive in order to receive these services than they were in the K–12 education system. Therefore, a potentially useful skill for college students with learning disabilities is *self-advocacy*: the ability to understand one's disability, be aware of one's legal rights, and communicate one's rights and needs to professors and administrators (Madaus & Banerjee, 2011). Although ideally, self-advocacy skills should be taught to students with learning disabilities in secondary school, many students come to college in need of guidance in how to advocate for themselves in a confident but nonconfrontational manner.

Much remains to be learned about programming effectively for students with learning disabilities in order for them to experience a rich, fulfilling adulthood. However, substantial strides are being made in the right direction. Since 1997, for individuals with learning disabilities, the high school dropout rate is down 40%, those graduating with a regular high school diploma are up 20% (Cortiella, 2009), and the numbers entering college are increasing.

SUMMARY

How do professionals define learning disabilities?

- The most common definition is that of the federal government, which has been in effect since 1975 (with a few minor wording changes in 1997).
- The National Joint Committee on Learning Disabilities (NJCLD) presented a definition that differs from the federal government's with respect to (1) no reference to psychological processes, (2) inclusion of intrinsic nature of learning disabilities, (3) inclusion of adults, (4) inclusion of self-regulation and social interaction problems, (5) omission of terms difficult to define, (6) purportedly less confusion regarding the exclusion clause, and (7) omission of spelling.

How do professionals identify students with learning disabilities?

- Since the late 1970s, the major method of identifying learning disabilities had been to look for an IQ–achievement discrepancy.
- More recently, professionals have proposed use of a response-to-intervention (RTI) approach.
  - RTI is based on a multi-tiered (typically three tiers) model of prevention.
  - A variety of RTI models have been proposed and implemented.
  - Many questions still remain regarding large-scale implementation of RTI.

What is the prevalence of learning disabilities?

- Just under 5% of school-age students are identified as learning disabled, making learning disabilities the largest category of special education by far.
- The prevalence of learning disabilities has more than doubled since the late 1970s, but it has begun to decline somewhat since the late 1990s.
  - Some believe the increase reflects poor diagnostic practices.
  - Some believe that some of the increase may be due to social and cultural changes as well as reluctance to label students "mentally retarded."
- Boys with learning disabilities outnumber girls about 3 to 1.
  - Some believe that this is due to gender bias in referrals.
  - Some believe that this is partly due to boys being more vulnerable biologically.

What causes learning disabilities?

- With the advance of neuroimaging techniques, most authorities now believe that central nervous system (CNS) dysfunction underlies learning disabilities.
- Strong evidence indicates that many cases of learning disabilities are inherited.
- Toxins (e.g., fetal alcohol syndrome) and medical factors (premature birth) can also result in learning disabilities.

What are some of the psychological and behavioral characteristics of learners with learning disabilities?

- Persons with learning disabilities exhibit interindividual and intraindividual variability.
- Academic deficits are the hallmark of learning disabilities.
  - Reading disabilities are the most common form of academic disability and can be manifested in decoding, fluency, and comprehension problems.
    - Phonological awareness, the understanding that speech consists of units of sound (words, syllables, phonemes), underlies the ability to decode.
    - Phonemic awareness—understanding that words are made up of sounds or phonemes—is particularly important for learning to decode.
  - Writing disabilities, including handwriting, spelling and composition, are common in students with learning disabilities.
  - Spoken language disabilities include problems with syntax (grammar), semantics (word meanings), phonology, and pragmatics (social uses of language).
  - Math disabilities include problems with computation and word problems.

- Some students with learning disabilities experience problems with perceptual, perceptual-motor, and general coordination.
- Many students with learning disabilities have problems with attention, and there is an overlap of 10% to 25% between learning disabilities and attention deficit hyperactivity disorder (ADHD).
- Memory problems include problems with short-term memory (STM) and working memory (WM).
- Metacognitive problems include deficits in recognizing task requirements, selecting and using appropriate strategies, and monitoring and adjusting performance.
- Social-emotional problems include peer rejection, poor self-concept, and poor social cognition.
  - Problems with social interaction are more prevalent in students with problems with math, visual-spatial and tactual tasks, and self-regulation; such students are sometimes referred to as having nonverbal learning disabilities.
  - Motivational problems can include having an external locus of control and learned helplessness.
  - Some authorities believe that a composite of many of the preceding characteristics indicates that many students with learning disabilities are passive rather than active learners.

What are some educational considerations for learners with learning disabilities?

- Cognitive training focuses on (1) changing thought processes, (2) providing strategies for learning, and (3) teaching self-initiative.
  - *Self-instruction* involves having students say out loud what it is they are to do.
  - *Self-monitoring* involves having students self-evaluate and self-record while they are doing academic work.
  - *Scaffolded instruction* involves providing students with teacher support while they perform academic work.
  - *Reciprocal teaching* involves teacher modeling correct performance and then having the student assume the role of co-teacher while using four strategies: predicting, questioning, summarizing, and clarifying.
- Effective instructional approaches for reading are explicit and systematic and focus on phonological awareness, phonics, fluency, vocabulary, and comprehension.
- Effective writing instruction is explicit and systematic; an example is the self-regulated strategy development (SRSD) model.
- Effective math instruction is explicit, systematic, and sequenced to minimize errors, but with errors immediately rectified.

- Carefully structured and sequenced science and social studies instruction is effective, and content enhancement (e.g., graphic organizers, mnemonics) is a technique that helps make textbook-based instruction more effective.
- *Direct instruction* (DI) focuses even more directly on academics than does cognitive training; a critical component of DI is task analysis, as well as the following:
  - Field-tested scripted lessons
  - Curricula based on mastery learning
  - Rapid instructional pace
  - Achievement grouping
  - Frequent assessments
- Using a peer tutoring strategy, students with learning disabilities are tutored by classmates without disabilities who are supervised and trained by the teacher.
- With respect to service delivery models, available research evidence indicates that a full continuum of placements is sound policy for students with learning disabilities.

How do professionals assess the academic progress of students with intellectual disabilities?

- Curriculum-based measurement (CBM) (brief samplings of academic performance) can be used to assess progress.
  - In reading, CBM typically focuses on correct words read per minute (CWPM).
  - CBM involves comparing the student's performance relative to a baseline point and an aim line based on expected growth norms.
- Informal reading inventories can be used to assess progress.
- Accommodations on standardized tests can include changes in scheduling and presentation and response formats.

What are some important considerations with respect to early intervention for learners with learning disabilities?

- Little preschool programming exists for children with learning disabilities because it's so hard to predict at that age which children will later develop academic problems.

- Even though prediction is not perfect, several developmental milestones are related to comprehension or expression of spoken language, emergent literacy skills, and perceptual skills that indicate risk for having learning disabilities.

What are some important considerations with respect to transition to adulthood for learners with learning disabilities?

- Factors related to successful transition include the following:
  - Extraordinary perseverance
  - Setting goals
  - Acceptance of weaknesses, combined with building on strengths
  - Strong network of social support
  - Intensive and long-term educational intervention
  - High-quality on-the-job or postsecondary vocational training
  - Supportive work environment
  - Taking control of one's life
- Secondary programming varies according to whether the goal is to prepare for work or college after graduation.
  - Those preparing for work receive training in basic academic skills, functional skills, and supervised work experiences.
  - Those preparing for college receive further academic training with support services from a special educator.
    - A key element to secondary programming is enabling students to make informed choices and to take responsibility for their futures.
    - In addition to a transition plan, the summary of performance (SOP) can be a potentially effective tool for transition to work or postsecondary education. The SOP includes information such as assessment reports, accommodations, recommendations for assistive technology and support services.
- Postsecondary programs include vocational and technical programs as well as community colleges and 4-year colleges and universities.
- More and more students with learning disabilities are attending college.

COUNCIL FOR EXCEPTIONAL CHILDREN

Addressing the Professional Standards

Council for Exceptional Children (CEC) Common Core Knowledge and Skills addressed in this chapter: ICC1K5, ICC1K6, ICC1K8, ICC2K1, ICC2K2, ICC2K5, ICC2K6, ICC3K1, ICC3K2, ICC4S2, ICC4S3, ICC4S4, ICC4S5, ICC4S6, ICC5K4, ICC5S8, ICC5S9, ICC8K2, ICC8K3, ICC8S2, ICC8S4, ICC8S6, ICC10K3, ICC10S4

Appendix: Provides a full listing of the CEC Common Core Standards and associated Knowledge and Skill Statements listed here.

MYEDUCATIONLAB

myeducationlab Now go to Topic 8: Learning Disabilities, in the MyEducationLab (www .myeducationlab.com) for your course, where you can:

- Find learning outcomes for the broad concepts covered in this chapter along with the national standards that connect to these outcomes.
- Complete Assignments and Activities that can help you more deeply understand the chapter content.
- Examine challenging situations and cases presented in the IRIS Center Resources.
- Apply and practice your understanding of the core concepts and skills identified in the chapter with the Building Teaching Skills and Dispositions learning units.
- Check your comprehension on the content covered in the chapter by going to the Study Plan in the Book-Specific Resources for your text. Here you will be able to take a chapter quiz, receive feedback on your answers, and then access Review, Practice, and Enrichment activities to enhance your understanding of chapter content.
- Watch video clips of CCSSO Teacher of the Year award winners responding to the question: "Why I teach?" in the Teacher Talk section.

Learners with Attention Deficit Hyperactivity Disorder

Let me see if Philip can
Be a little gentleman.
Let me see, if he is able
To sit still for once at table;
Thus Papa bade Phil behave;
And Mamma look'd very grave.
But fidgety Phil,
He won't sit still;
He wriggles
And giggles,
And then, I declare
Swings backwards and forwards
And tilts up his chair,
Just like any rocking horse;
"Philip! I am getting cross!"

Heinrich Hoffmann • *"The Story of Fidgety Philip,"* 1865

QUESTIONS to guide your reading of this chapter . . .

- What are the historical origins of attention deficit hyperactivity disorder (ADHD)?
- What is the current definition of ADHD?
- What is the prevalence of ADHD?
- What methods of assessment do professionals use to identify individuals with ADHD?
- What causes ADHD?
- What are some of the psychological and behavioral characteristics of learners with ADHD?
- What are some educational considerations for learners with ADHD?
- What are some medication considerations for learners with ADHD?
- How do professionals assess the academic, attention, and behavioral progress of students with ADHD?
- What are some important considerations with respect to early intervention for learners with ADHD?
- What are some important considerations with respect to transition to adulthood for learners with ADHD?

MISCONCEPTIONS ABOUT
Learners with Attention Deficit Hyperactivity Disorder

MYTH • All children with ADHD are hyperactive.

FACT • Psychiatric classification of ADHD attempts to account for the fact that some persons display only inattention, or only hyperactivity/impulsivity, or both.

MYTH • The primary symptom of ADHD is inattention.

FACT • Recent conceptualizations of ADHD place problems with behavioral inhibition, executive function, time awareness and management, and goal-directed behavior as the primary behavioral problems of ADHD.

MYTH • ADHD is a fad, a trendy diagnosis of recent times in the United States with little research to support its existence.

FACT • Literature indicates that physicians recognized the existence of attention problems and hyperactivity in the 18th, mid-19th, and early 20th centuries. Serious scientific study of attention problems began in the early and mid-20th century. A firmly established research base now supports its existence. And the prevalence of ADHD in several other countries is at least as high as it is in the United States.

MYTH • ADHD is primarily the result of minimal brain injury.

FACT • In most cases of ADHD, no evidence of actual damage to the brain exists. Most authorities believe that ADHD is the result of neurological dysfunction, which is often linked to hereditary factors.

MYTH • The social problems of students with ADHD are due to their not knowing how to interact socially.

FACT • Most people with ADHD know how to interact, but their problems with behavioral inhibition make it difficult for them to implement socially appropriate behaviors.

MYTH • Using psychostimulants, such as Ritalin, can easily turn children into abusers of other substances, such as cocaine and marijuana.

FACT • No evidence shows that using psychostimulants for ADHD leads directly to drug abuse. In fact, evidence shows that those who are prescribed Ritalin as children are less likely to turn to illicit drugs as teenagers. However, care should be taken to make sure that children or others do not misuse the psychostimulants prescribed for them.

MYTH • Psychostimulants have a "paradoxical effect" in that they subdue children rather than activate them. Plus, they have this effect only on children with ADHD.

FACT • Psychostimulants, instead of sedating children, actually activate parts of the brain responsible for behavioral inhibition and executive functions. In addition, this effect occurs in persons without ADHD, too.

MYTH • Because students with ADHD react strongly to stimulation, their learning environments should be highly unstructured in order to take advantage of their natural learning styles.

FACT • Most authorities recommend a highly structured classroom for students with ADHD, especially in the early stages of instruction.

Fidgety Phil, the character in the poem by the German physician Heinrich Hoffmann (1865) in this chapter's opening quote, is generally considered one of the first allusions in Western literature to what today is referred to as attention deficit hyperactivity disorder (ADHD) (Barkley, 2006c). Phil's lack of impulse control bears an uncanny similarity to today's conceptualization of ADHD as less a matter of inattention than a matter of regulating one's behavior. We discuss this conceptualization more fully later, but it's also important to point out here that Phil's excessive motor activity, or hyperactivity, may be characteristic of many children with ADHD but not all. Interestingly, Hoffman also wrote another poem, "The Story of Johnny Head-in-Air," about a child who fits to a *T* children with ADHD who do not have problems with hyperactivity.

BRIEF HISTORY

The fact that there's a substantial history to the recognition of attention deficits is important. Today, ADHD is often the subject of criticism, being referred to as a phantom or bogus condition—sort of a fashionable, trendy diagnosis for people who are basically lazy and unmotivated. Although undoubtedly a few people hide behind an inappropriate diagnosis of ADHD, evidence indicates that the condition is extremely real for those who have it. And, as we point out in the next section, ADHD is not a recently "discovered," trendy diagnosis.

Sir Alexander Chrichton's Treatise "On Attention and Its Diseases"

In addition to Hoffman's "poetic case study," two more early and scientifically oriented references to attention disorders are of interest; one pre-dates Hoffman, and one follows by about 40 years. Sir Alexander Chrichton (1798), a physician, is credited with being the first to address the issue of attention deficits in the professional literature (Barkley, 2008; Palmer & Finger, 2001). Many of Chrichton's notions regarding attention deficits are consistent with today's ideas. He noted that the ability to attend was not automatic but required active effort. And he theorized that a person could be born with attention disorders or could acquire them through diseases affecting the brain.

Dr. George F. Still's Children with "Defective Moral Control"

Writing much later than Chrichton but more than a century ago, Dr. George F. Still, a physician, provided an even more scientific account to the medical profession of what today we now call ADHD. Still delivered three lectures to the Royal College of Physicians of London in 1902 in which he described cases of children who displayed spitefulness, cruelty, disobedience, impulsivity, and problems of attention and hyperactivity. He referred to them as having "defective moral control" (Still, 1902, p. 1008). In the language of his day, Still was essentially saying that these children lacked the ability to inhibit or refrain from engaging impulsively in inappropriate behavior. (See Figure 7.1.)

Although Still's words are more than a century old, they still hold currency; one of the most influential current psychological theories is based on the notion that an essential impairment in ADHD is a deficit involving behavioral inhibition (Barkley, 1997, 2000a, 2000b, 2006e). Still's cases were also similar to today's population of persons with ADHD in at least five ways:

1. Still speculated that many of these children had mild brain pathology.
2. Many of the children had normal intelligence.
3. The condition was more prevalent in males than females.
4. There was evidence that the condition had a hereditary basis.
5. Many of the children and their relatives also had other physical or psychological problems, such as depression and tics.

myeducationlab

To check your comprehension on the content covered in Chapter 7, go to the Book-Specific Resources in the MyEducationLab (www .myeducation.lab.com) for your course, select your text, and complete the Study Plan. Here you will be able to take a chapter quiz, receive feedback on your answers, and then access review, practice, and enrichment activities to enhance your understanding of chapter content. ■

INTERNETRESOURCES

In 1998, The National Institutes of Health (NIH) brought together a panel of experts from a variety of disciplines, including medicine, psychology, and special education, to arrive at consensus regarding identification and treatment of ADHD. Although they concluded that more research was needed on various issues, they affirmed the validity of ADHD: "Although an independent diagnostic test for ADHD does not exist, there is evidence supporting the validity of the disorder" (NIH, 1998). Although much research has transpired since 1998, this is an important historical document. To see the complete NIH *Consensus Statement*, go to http:// consensus.nih.gov/1998/ 1998AttentionDeficit HyperactivityDisorder110html .htm NIH recommends that people go to Medline Plus for current information on ADHD: http://www.nlm.nih .gov/medlineplus/

FIGURE 7.1 A reproduction of Dr. George Still's opening remarks for his classic lectures on children with "defective moral control."

1008 THE LANCET,]   DR. G. F. STILL: ABNORMAL PSY

The Goulstonian Lectures

ON

SOME ABNORMAL PSYCHICAL CONDITIONS IN CHILDREN.

Delivered before the Royal College of Physicians of London on March 4th, 6th, and 11th, 1902,

BY GEORGE F. STILL, M.A., M.D. CANTAB., F.R.C.P. LOND.,

ASSISTANT PHYSICIAN FOR DISEASES OF CHILDREN, KING'S COLLEGE HOSPITAL; ASSISTANT PHYSICIAN TO THE HOSPITAL FOR SICK CHILDREN, GREAT ORMOND-STREET.

LECTURE I.

Delivered on March 4th.

MR. PRESIDENT AND GENTLEMEN,—The particular psychical conditions with which I propose to deal in these lectures are those which are concerned with an abnormal defect of moral control in children. Interesting as these disorders may be as an abstruse problem for the professed psychologist to puzzle over, they have a very real practical —shall I say social?—importance which I venture to think has been hardly sufficiently recognised. For some years past I have been collecting observations with a view to investigating the occurrence of defective moral control as a morbid condition in children, a subject which I cannot but think calls urgently for scientific investigation. It has long

Source: Still, G. F. (1902). Some abnormal psychical conditions in children. *The Lancet, 1,* 1008–1012.

INTERNETRESOURCES

You can see the "Fidgety Philip" and "Johnny-Head-in-Air" nursery rhymes complete with illustrations at www.fln .vcu.edu/struwwel/guck_e .html and http://home .earthlinknet/~mishal/phil1 .html

INTERNETRESOURCES

The National Institute of Neurological Diseases and Stroke has a Website with a variety of information pertaining to ADHD: http:// www.ninds.nih.gov/disorders/ adhd/adhd.htm

We return later to Barkley's theory and to these five points. Suffice it to say here that Still's children with "defective moral control" today would very likely be diagnosed as having ADHD by itself or ADHD with **conduct disorder**. Conduct disorder, which we discuss more fully in Chapter 8, is characterized by a pattern of aggressive, disruptive behavior.

Kurt Goldstein's Brain-Injured Soldiers of World War I

Kurt Goldstein reported on the psychological effects of brain injury in soldiers who had suffered head wounds in combat in World War I. Among other things, he observed in his patients the psychological characteristics of disorganized behavior, hyperactivity, **perseveration**, and a "forced responsiveness to stimuli" (1936, 1939). Perseveration, the tendency to repeat the same behaviors over and over again, is often cited today by clinicians as a characteristic of persons with ADHD. And their forced responsiveness to stimuli is akin to distractibility.

The Strauss Syndrome

Goldstein's work laid the foundation for the investigations of Heinz Werner and Alfred Strauss in the 1930s and 1940s (e.g., Werner & Strauss, 1939, 1941). Having emigrated from Germany to the United States after Hitler's rise to power, Werner and Strauss teamed up to try to replicate Goldstein's findings. They noted the same behaviors of distractibility and hyperactivity in some children with mental retardation (intellectual disabilities).

In addition to clinical observations, Werner and Strauss used an experimental task consisting of figure/background slides that were presented at very brief exposure times. The slides depicted figures (e.g., a hat) embedded in a background (e.g., wavy lines). Werner and Strauss found that the children with supposed brain damage, when asked what they saw, were more likely than those without brain damage to say that they had seen the background (e.g., "wavy lines") rather than the figure (e.g., "a hat") (Strauss & Werner, 1942; Werner & Strauss, 1939, 1941). After these studies, professionals came to refer to children who were apparently hyperactive and distractible as exhibiting the **Strauss syndrome**.

William Cruickshank's Work

William Cruickshank and colleagues, using Werner and Strauss's figure/background task, found that children with cerebral palsy were also more likely to respond to the background than to the figure (Cruickshank, Bice, & Wallen, 1957). This research extended the work of Werner and Strauss in two important ways. First, whereas Werner and Strauss had largely assumed that their children were brain damaged, Cruickshank's children all had **cerebral palsy**, a condition that's relatively easy to diagnose. Cerebral palsy is characterized by brain damage that results in impairments in movement (see Chapter 14). Second, the children Cruickshank studied were largely of normal intelligence, thus demonstrating that children without mental retardation (intellectual disabilities) could display distractibility and hyperactivity.

Cruickshank is also important historically because, as we discuss later in this chapter, he was one of the first to establish an educational program for children who today would meet the criteria for ADHD. At the time (the late 1950s), however, many of these children were referred to as "minimally brain injured."

Minimal Brain Injury and Hyperactive Child Syndrome

At about the same time as Cruickshank's extension of Werner and Strauss's work with children of normal intelligence, the results of a now classic study were published (Pasamanick, Lilienfeld, & Rogers, 1956). This study of the aftereffects of birth complications revived Still's (1902) notion that subtle brain pathology could result in behavior problems, such as hyperactivity and distractibility. Professionals began to apply the label of **minimal brain injury** to children of normal intelligence who were inattentive, impulsive, and/or hyperactive. Although popular in the 1950s and 1960s, the "minimal brain injury" label fell out of favor as professionals pointed out that it was difficult to document actual tissue damage to the brain (Birch, 1964).

"Minimal brain injury" was replaced in the 1960s by the label "hyperactive child syndrome" (Barkley, 2006c). **Hyperactive child syndrome** was preferred because it was descriptive of behavior and didn't rely on vague and unreliable diagnoses of subtle brain damage. This label's popularity extended into the 1970s. By the 1980s, however, it too had fallen out of favor as research began to point to inattention, not hyperactivity, as the major behavioral problem experienced by these children. In fact, some exhibited attention problems without excessive movement.

This recognition of inattention as more important than hyperactivity is reflected in the current definition of ADHD and its immediate predecessors. However, as we discuss later, some authorities are now recommending that deficits in behavioral inhibition replace inattention as the primary deficit in ADHD. In any case, most authorities do not view hyperactivity as the primary deficit in ADHD.

DEFINITION

Most professionals rely on the American Psychiatric Association's (APA's) *Diagnostic and Statistical Manual of Mental Disorders* (DSM) criteria to determine whether an individual has ADHD (American Psychiatric Association, 2010). The DSM is in the process of being revised as this textbook goes to press, with publication of the revision slated for 2012. The current DSM recognizes three subtypes of ADHD: (1) ADHD, Predominantly Inattentive Type; (2) ADHD, Predominantly Hyperactive-Impulsive Type; and (3) ADHD, Combined Type (American Psychiatric Association, 2000). Examples of criteria used to determine these subtypes include: (1) for inattention: trouble paying attention to details, difficulty sustaining attention, problems with organization, distractible; (2) for hyperactivity: fidgeting, leaving seat at inappropriate times, talking excessively; (3) for impulsivity: problems awaiting one's turn, interrupting others.

It's difficult to predict the exact changes that will be made to the new *DSM*, but some of the issues that have been discussed by working groups of the American Psychiatric Association (2010) are:

- Should "Attention-Deficit Disorder" be its own diagnostic category, or at least should the Primarily Inattentive subtype be divided into a "Predominantly Inattentive" and an "Inattentive (Restrictive)", with the latter reserved for those whose problems are all or virtually all related to inattention? (Professionals have commented that many individuals are purely inattentive.)

- Should the age for onset of symptoms be raised to 12 years instead of the current cutoff of 7 years? (Professionals have commented that some children's symptoms aren't severe enough to be considered ADHD until after they are 7.)

- Should fewer symptoms be required for adolescents and adults to meet the criteria for diagnosis? (Professionals have commented that the number of symptoms tends to reduce with age but the person's functioning is still significantly impaired.)

PREVALENCE

ADHD is widely recognized as one of the most frequent reasons, if not the most frequent reason, children are referred for behavioral problems to guidance clinics. Most authorities estimate that from 3% to 7% of the school-age population have ADHD (Barkley, 2006d).

INTERNETRESOURCES

Adults and Children with ADHD, as well as parents of children with ADHD, can find a wealth of useful information from organizations devoted to ADHD. The oldest organization devoted to ADHD is the Children and Adults with Attention-Deficit/Hyperactivity Disorder (CHADD). A more recent organization is the National Attention Deficit Disorder Association (National ADDA). Their respective Websites are www.chadd.org and www.add.org

However, because the U.S. Department of Education does not recognize ADHD as a separate category of special education, it's difficult to estimate how many students with ADHD are served in special education. When in the mid-1970s, the federal government began tracking the prevalence of students in all the major special education categories, ADHD was not included. This was due in part to two interrelated factors: (1) The research on this condition was still in its infancy, and (2) the advocacy base for children with ADHD was not yet well developed. In the early 1990s, advocacy groups lobbied for the inclusion of ADHD in these counts, but the U.S. Department of Education did not agree to add ADHD as a separate category. However, in 1991, it did determine that students with ADHD would be eligible for special education under the category "other health impaired" (OHI) "in instances where the ADD is a chronic or acute health problem that results in limited alertness, which adversely affects educational performance." Students with ADHD can also qualify for accommodations under another law: Section 504 of the Rehabilitation Act of 1973.

The growth of the OHI category since 1991 suggests that more and more students with ADHD are being identified as OHI. For example, since the mid-1990s the prevalence of students aged 6 to 17 years in the OHI category has quadrupled. However, the most recent published count of 1.22% for 2007-2008 is still well below the prevalence estimates of 3% to 7%. Many authorities think that fewer than half of students with ADHD are receiving special education services.

ADHD occurs much more frequently in boys than girls, with estimates of about 3 to 1 in community-based samples (Barkley, 2006d). Some have speculated that boys are identified more often than girls because boys tend to exhibit the highly noticeable hyperactive or impulsive type of ADHD, whereas girls are more likely to exhibit the inattentive type. Some gender bias in referral may exist, but our best research evidence suggests that it's not enough to account for the wide disparity in prevalence rates between boys and girls. Gender differences are likely due to constitutional, or biological, differences.

Some critics have asserted that ADHD is primarily a U.S. phenomenon, a result of our society's emphasis on achievement and conformity. However, statistics do not bear this out. Although it's difficult to compare prevalence rates cross-culturally because of differing diagnostic criteria, sampling techniques, and cultural expectations, the evidence strongly suggests that prevalence rates at least as high as those in the United States are found in several other countries. For example, a survey of the worldwide prevalence of ADHD, which included Africa, the Middle East, Oceania, South America, Asia, North America, and Europe, indicated an overall prevalence rate of 5.29% (Polanczyk, Silva de Lima, Horta, Biederman, & Rohde, 2007). And the highest rates were actually for South America and Africa, not North America. Furthermore, research on the behavioral characteristics of persons identified as ADHD in different countries indicates that they share the same core symptoms, which argues against ADHD being determined by cultural factors (Bauermeister, Canino, Polanczyk, & Rohde, 2010).

Some critics have also suggested that African American children, especially boys, are diagnosed disproportionately as ADHD. Unfortunately, there are no definitive, large-scale epidemiological studies on this topic. What scanty evidence does exist suggests that they are no more likely to be formally identified as ADHD than their white peers (Rowland et al., 2001). However, some evidence suggests that some cultural bias exists in how teachers view inattentive and hyperactive behaviors in children. For example, in one study, white teachers were more likely than African American teachers to rate African American students as highly inattentive and hyperactive (Reid, Casat, Norton, Anastopoulos, & Temple, 2001). In another study, compared to white teachers, Hispanic teachers were more likely to rate Hispanic, but not white children, as more hyperactive and impulsive (DeRamirez & Shapiro, 2005).

IDENTIFICATION

Findings like the preceding show that teachers and other professionals may not always be accurate in their ratings of attention and hyperactivity. Authorities therefore stress the importance of using several sources of information before arriving at a determination that an individual has ADHD. Most authorities agree that there are four important components to assessing whether a student has ADHD: a medical examination, a clinical interview, teacher and parent rating scales, and behavioral observations. The medical examination is necessary to rule out medical conditions, such as brain tumors, thyroid problems, or seizure disorders, as the cause of the inattention and/or hyperactivity (Barkley & Edwards, 2006).

The clinical interview of the parent(s) and the child provides information about the child's physical and psychological characteristics, as well as family dynamics and interaction with peers. Although the interview is essential to the diagnosis of ADHD, clinicians need to recognize the subjective nature of the interview situation. Some children with ADHD can look surprisingly "normal" in their behavior when in the structured and novel setting of a doctor's office.

In an attempt to bring some quantification to the identification process, researchers have developed rating scales to be filled out by teachers, parents, and, in some cases, the child. Some of the most reliable and popular are the Conners-3 (Conners, 2007) and the ADHD Rating Scale-IV (Du-Paul, Power, Anastopoulos, & Reid, 1998). Raters

In addition to medical exams and clinical interviews, rating scales filled out by teachers, parents, and in some cases children, can help quantify the process of identifying children who might have ADHD.

are asked such things as how often (never or rarely, sometimes, often, very often) the individual doesn't pay attention to details, is easily distracted, interrupts others, fidgets, and so forth. Whenever possible, the clinician should observe the student. This can be done in the classroom; clinicians who specialize in diagnosing and treating children with ADHD sometimes have specially designed observation rooms in which they can observe the child performing tasks that require sustained attention.

CAUSES

Probably because no simple diagnostic test, such as a blood test, is available for ADHD, much controversy has prevailed over what actually causes ADHD and over a history of questionable causal theories. (See the accompanying Focus on Concepts box, "Controversial Causal Theories of ADHD.") We now know, however, that strong evidence links neurological abnormalities to ADHD.

As we noted earlier, authorities in the early and middle parts of the 20th century attributed problems of inattention and hyperactivity to neurological problems resulting from brain damage. When researchers were unable to verify actual tissue damage in cases of ADHD, many professionals soured on the idea that ADHD was neurologically based. However, as we noted in our discussion of learning disabilities in Chapter 6, the development of neuroimaging techniques such as magnetic resonance imaging (MRI), positron emission tomography (PET) scans, and functional magnetic resonance imaging (fMRI) in the 1980s and 1990s allowed scientists for the first time to obtain more detailed and reliable measures of brain functioning. Using these techniques, researchers have made great strides in documenting the neurological basis of ADHD. As is the case with learning disabilities, research indicates that ADHD most likely results from neurological dysfunction rather than actual brain damage. Evidence also points to heredity as playing a very strong role in causing the neurological dysfunction, with teratogenic and other medical factors also implicated to a lesser degree.

Areas of the Brain Affected: Prefrontal Lobes, Frontal Lobes, Basal Ganglia, Cerebellum, and Corpus Callosum

Using neuroimaging techniques, several teams of researchers have found relatively consistent abnormalities in five areas of the brain in people with ADHD: the prefrontal lobes, frontal lobes, basal ganglia (specifically, the caudate and the globus pallidus), cerebellum,

FOCUS ON Concepts

CONTROVERSIAL CAUSAL THEORIES OF ADHD

Over the years, a number of myths have sprung up about what causes hyperactive behavior or ADHD. Most of these have little if any substantial scientific support. A good example is sugar. Parents and teachers have often complained that young children become more hyperactive when they ingest sugar in the form of soft drinks, cakes, and candies. However, careful research has demonstrated that this is not the case (Wolraich, Wilson, & White, 1995). The mistaken notion that sugar causes hyperactivity probably originated from the observation that children are hyperactive in situations where sweets are served. Relatively stimulating and unstructured, these situations, such as parties, are likely to elicit hyperactive behavior.

Another example is that of television and video games. Many people in the general public believe that by watching too much television or playing too many video games, children will become ADHD. One study did find that children who watch more television as preschoolers are rated as more inattentive at 7 years of age (Christakis, Zimmerman, DiGiuseppe, & McCarty, 2004). However, this isn't proof that watching television causes ADHD or even higher rates of inattention. Attention problems, themselves, might cause children to want to watch more television. Or parents might find that one way to control their child's hyperactive behavior, at least for a short period of time, is to put them in front of a TV. Or parents who let their children watch more television may contribute in some other ways to their chil-

dren's inattentive behavior. Perhaps they provide less supervision generally.

Other environmental agents that some believe cause ADHD are artificial food colorings and additives. The original proponent of this theory was Benjamin Feingold, a pediatric allergist (Feingold, 1975) who proposed a strict diet devoid of these additives. Although substantial research has shown that this diet is not beneficial for all children with ADHD (Kavale & Forness, 1983), a recent research study presents some provocative data suggesting that when young children are on a diet containing food colorings and additives, their parents rate them higher in inattention and hyperactivity than when they are on a diet free of colorings and additives (Bateman et al., 2004). A particular strength of this study is that the parents were "blind" to when the children's diet did or did not contain colorings and additives. However, a major caveat is that the children's behavior didn't differ with or without the diet on arguably more objective measures of inattention and hyperactivity administered by researchers in the clinic.

Another caveat is that this study (Bateman et al., 2004) still falls short of demonstrating a causal link between diet and formal ADHD diagnosis. Further research is definitely warranted to determine whether a subgroup of children with ADHD, however small, might benefit from a diet restricting certain food additives and colorings. In the meantime, no evidence supports automatically placing all children with ADHD on such restricted diets.

and corpus callosum (Arnsten, Berridge, & McCracken, 2009; Bender, Banaschewski, & Resch, 2010; Cherkasova & Hechtman, 2009; Shaw & Rabin, 2009; (see Figure 7.2).

Prefrontal, Frontal Lobes   Located in the front of the brain, the **frontal lobes**—and especially the very front portion of the frontal lobes, the **prefrontal lobes**—are responsible for *executive functions*. Among other things, executive functions involve the ability to regulate one's own behavior. (We discuss executive functions more fully later.)

Basal Ganglia   Buried deep within the brain, the **basal ganglia** consist of several parts: the **caudate** and the **globus pallidus** are the structures that are abnormal in persons with ADHD. The basal ganglia are responsible for the coordination and control of motor behavior (Pinel, 2006).

Cerebellum   The **cerebellum** is also responsible for the coordination and control of motor behavior. Although it's relatively small, constituting only about 10% of the mass of the brain, the fact that it contains more than half of all the brain's neurons attests to its complexity (Pinel, 2006).

Corpus Callosum   The **corpus callosum** consists of millions of fibers that connect the left and right hemispheres of the brain. Being responsible for communication between the hemispheres, it's important for a variety of cognitive functions.

FIGURE 7.2 Areas of the brain (frontal lobes, prefrontal lobes, cerebellum, globus pallidus and caudate of the basal ganglia, corpus callosum) that some researchers have identified as abnormal in people with ADHD.

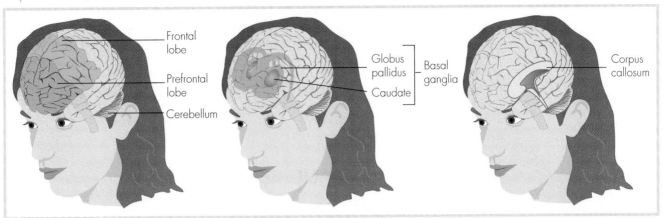

Neurotransmitters Involved: Dopamine and Norepinephrine

Much exciting research is being conducted on what neurotransmitter abnormalities might cause ADHD. **Neurotransmitters** are chemicals that help in the sending of messages between neurons in the brain. Researchers have found that abnormal levels of two neurotransmitters—**dopamine** and **norepinephrine**—are involved in ADHD (Barkley, 2006b; Tripp & Wickens, 2009; Volkow et al., 2007).

Hereditary Factors

Most authorities agree that ADHD has a hereditary basis. Research indicates that no single ADHD-gene exists. Rather, multiple genes (at least 20) are involved. And many of these genes are linked to how dopamine moves from neuron to neuron (Floet, Scheiner, & Grossman, 2010; Li, Sham, Owen, & He, 2006). Evidence for the genetic transmission of ADHD comes from at least three sources: family studies, twin studies, and molecular genetic studies.

Family Studies   Generally, studies indicate that if a child has ADHD, the chance of his or her sibling having ADHD is about 32% (Barkley, 2006b). Children of adults with ADHD run a 57% risk of having ADHD (Biederman et al., 1995). In addition, several studies demonstrate that parents of children with ADHD are two to eight times more likely to also be ADHD than are parents of non-ADHD children (Faraone & Doyle, 2001).

Twin Studies   Several researchers have compared the prevalence of ADHD in identical (monozygotic, from the same egg) versus fraternal (dizygotic, from two eggs) twins, when one of the members of the pair has ADHD. These studies consistently show that if an identical twin and a fraternal twin each have ADHD, the second identical twin is much more likely to have ADHD than is the second fraternal twin (Levy & Hay, 2001; Nigg, 2006; Nikolas & Burt, 2010).

Molecular Genetic Studies   With the mapping of the human genome have come advances in **molecular genetics**, the study of the molecules (DNA, RNA, and protein) that regulate genetic information. Molecular genetic research on ADHD is in its early stages, but the research is consistent with the idea that several genes contribute to ADHD.

Toxins and Medical Factors

In Chapters 5 and 6, we discussed **toxins**—agents that can cause malformations in the developing fetus of a pregnant woman—as the cause of some cases of intellectual disabilities or learning disabilities. Although the evidence for toxins is not as strong as that for heredity, some of these same substances have been shown to be related to ADHD. For example, research indicates that some children with ADHD have higher levels of lead in their blood, suggesting a greater exposure than non-ADHD children to this known toxin (Nigg, Nikolas, Knottnerus, Cavanagh, & Friderici, 2010).

Other medical conditions may also place children at risk for having ADHD. Again, the evidence is not as strong as it is for heredity, but complications at birth and low birthweight are associated with ADHD (Levy, Barr, & Sunohara, 1998; Milberger, Biederman, Faraone, Guite, & Tsuang, 1997). Smoking during pregnancy is associated with having babies of low birthweight. Evidence also suggests that smoking by mothers-to-be puts their children who are already genetically predisposed (based on their dopamine-related genes) at an even greater risk of being diagnosed with ADHD (Neuman et al., 2007).

PSYCHOLOGICAL AND BEHAVIORAL CHARACTERISTICS

The effects of ADHD on psychological and behavioral functioning can be pervasive, with a major impact on quality of life (Danckaerts et al., 2010). Although many areas of functioning are affected, a few are key. Surprisingly, even though most people believe that inattention is the key characteristic of ADHD, a growing consensus among researchers holds that inattention, hyperactivity, and impulsivity are actually the result of problems in behavioral inhibition.

Barkley's Model of ADHD

An abundance of research points to problems with behavioral inhibition in people with ADHD (Barkley, 1997, 2000a, 2006e; Schachar, Mota, Logan, Tannock, & Klim, 2000; Semrud-Clikeman et al., 2000; Willcutt, Pennington, et al., 2001). As we noted earlier, Russell Barkley, in particular, has proposed a model of ADHD in which behavioral inhibition is key. In its simplest form, this model proposes that problems in behavioral inhibition set the stage for problems in executive functions and time awareness and management, which then disrupt the person's ability to engage in persistent goal-directed behavior.

Behavioral Inhibition   **Behavioral Inhibition** involves the ability to:

1. delay a response,
2. interrupt an ongoing response, if one detects that the response is inappropriate because of sudden changes in the demands of the task, or
3. protect a response from distracting or competing stimuli (Lawrence et al., 2002).

Problems in behavioral inhibition can be reflected in the ability to wait one's turn, to refrain from interrupting conversations, to resist potential distractions while working, or to delay immediate gratification to work for larger, long-term rewards (Tripp & Alsop, 2001). In the classroom, difficulties with behavioral inhibition can present themselves during task switching or transitions. See the accompanying Responsive Instruction box for a description of research on this topic and how to apply this research to the classroom.

Executive Functions   Behavioral inhibition, along with goal-directed behavior, is the essential component of **executive functions** (Weyandt,

Students with ADHD may experience difficulties with behavioral inhibition, including the ability to wait one's turn, recognize inappropriate responses, or resist distractions.

RESPONSIVE *INSTRUCTION*
MEETING THE NEEDS OF STUDENTS WITH ADHD

Task Switching: Preparing Students with ADHD for Change

WHAT THE RESEARCH SAYS

Many researchers contend that the primary deficit of students with ADHD is deficient behavioral inhibition (e.g., Barkley, 1997, 2000a, 2006e; Willcutt, Pennington, et al., 2001). In other words, once students with ADHD begin a task, it is difficult for them to mentally switch to a new activity. Researchers hypothesize that the executive controls needed to "inhibit" the current activity and "start up" the next differ for students with ADHD compared to students who do not have ADHD.

RESEARCH STUDY

A group of researchers examined the task-switching ability of students with and without ADHD (Cepeda, Cepeda, & Kramer, 2000). Results from the study indicated that clear performance deficits existed for unmedicated students with ADHD in the first trial after a task switch, even when the tasks were considered compatible, such as both tasks involving numbers. All students with ADHD, unmedicated or medicated, had higher "switch costs"—increased response time—when the new task was incompatible with the old task (e.g., switching from a number-identification task to a word-identification task). This type of task required the inhibition of thinking about numbers and the preparation for thinking about letters and sounds. The findings suggest that differences do exist between students with and without ADHD in the ability to efficiently and effectively task switch.

APPLYING THE RESEARCH TO TEACHING

Studies such as the one presented here indicate the need to support students with ADHD as they transition from one activity to another. Cognitive support for such transitions can include the following:

- Allow for time between asking a student to do or say something and expecting the response (i.e., increasing wait time).
- Avoid overloading a students' working memory (Barkley, Murphy, & Kwasnik, 1996) by limiting the number of steps or sequence of procedures a student must keep in working memory or by providing a visual for students to refer to.
- Create routinized procedures for daily transitions.
- Prepare students for the type of response that will be required when answering a question.
- Divide instruction into consistent, predictable sequences throughout the day.

• By Kristin L. Sayeski

2009b). Executive functions permit individuals to self-regulate their behavior. The fact that a wealth of evidence indicates that executive functions are controlled by the prefrontal and frontal lobes of the brain fits nicely with the neuroimaging studies pointing to abnormality in these areas of the brain in persons with ADHD.

Overwhelming evidence shows that ADHD results in executive function deficits (Barkley, 1997; Goldstein & Kennemer, 2009; Weyandt, 2009b). In Barkley's model, persons with ADHD can exhibit problems with executive function in four general ways. First, they often have problems with working memory (WM). As we noted in Chapter 5, WM refers to a person's ability to keep information in mind that "can be used to guide one's actions either now or in the near future" (Barkley & Murphy, 1998, p. 2). In the case of students with ADHD, deficiencies in WM can result in forgetfulness, a lack of hindsight and forethought, and problems with time management.

Second, people with ADHD frequently have delayed inner speech. **Inner speech** is the inner "voice" that allows people to "talk" to themselves about various solutions when in the midst of solving a problem. Students with ADHD who have deficient inner speech have problems in guiding their behavior in situations that demand the ability to follow rules or instructions.

Third, children and adults with ADHD have problems controlling their emotions and their arousal levels. They often overreact to negative or positive experiences. On hearing good news, for example, children with ADHD might scream loudly, unable to keep their

Success Stories

DEVELOPING SELF-ADVOCACY SKILLS TO GET NEEDED ACCOMMODATIONS: KEY TO JOSH'S SUCCESS IN COLLEGE

Josh Bishop: "It's not like the work is hard; it's just getting it done!"

High school sophomore Josh Bishop hopes to play football on a team in the National Collegiate Athletic Association's Division I, despite his struggles with organization and time management.

These could be the keys to his success:

★ Intensive classroom structure and consistent expectations
★ Relentless positive reinforcement and behavioral support
★ Specific accommodations and self-advocacy

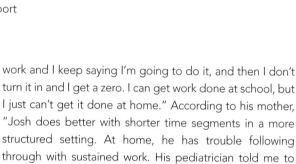

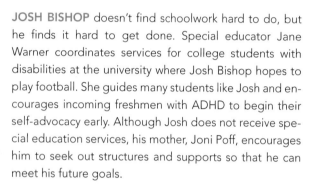

JOSH BISHOP doesn't find schoolwork hard to do, but he finds it hard to get done. Special educator Jane Warner coordinates services for college students with disabilities at the university where Josh Bishop hopes to play football. She guides many students like Josh and encourages incoming freshmen with ADHD to begin their self-advocacy early. Although Josh does not receive special education services, his mother, Joni Poff, encourages him to seek out structures and supports so that he can meet his future goals.

★ Intensive Classroom Structure and Consistent Expectations. Josh is a successful athlete, but in the classroom, he faces challenges. "I never have been very organized. I got by in elementary school, but middle school was a real wake-up call. In sixth grade, I'd get all my homework done in class. In seventh grade, I had homework due for every class."

Josh keeps an assignment book but admits that he doesn't use it faithfully. "When I've missed a deadline, sometimes I don't turn the work in at all. I know I need to do home-

work and I keep saying I'm going to do it, and then I don't turn it in and I get a zero. I can get work done at school, but I just can't get it done at home." According to his mother, "Josh does better with shorter time segments in a more structured setting. At home, he has trouble following through with sustained work. His pediatrician told me to back off. Josh takes medication during the day, and it's harder for him to concentrate in the evening."

Josh mentioned his medication but did not refer to his difficulties with completing written work, organizational skills, or attentiveness as being out of the ordinary. He would rather not be treated differently from other students, but he says that only a few teachers have provided the classroom structure that he needs. His mother thinks that the most successful teachers for Josh have been those who were very organized and made their expectations very clear. "They weren't wishy-washy. They were sympathetic that some things were difficult for Josh. They understood that he wasn't being purposefully lazy or disrespectful, but they still held high expectations for him."

emotions to themselves. Likewise, they are often quick to show their temper when confronted with frustrating experiences.

Fourth, children and adults with ADHD have difficulty analyzing problems and communicating solutions to others. They're less flexible when faced with problem situations, often responding impulsively with the first thing that comes to mind. Josh, the student described in the accompanying Success Stories feature, has many of the executive function difficulties we've just discussed. He has problems with completing homework, solving problems, and organizing himself to keep up with his work. Josh hopes to play sports in college, so he must figure out how to organize and study to get better grades.

Time Awareness and Management Barkley (2000a) sees the deficit in time awareness and management shown by people with ADHD as crucial:

> Understanding time and how we organize our own behavior within and toward it is a major key to the mystery of understanding ADHD. . . . I now believe that the awareness of themselves across time is the ultimate yet nearly invisible disability afflicting those with ADHD. (p. 30)

★ **Relentless Positive Reinforcement and Behavioral Support.** Josh was diagnosed by his pediatrician with ADHD when he was 7 years old. "Josh always had a high activity level," recalls his mother. "In kindergarten, he was put on a behavior contract with stickers as positive reinforcement, but his first-grade teacher didn't follow through with his behavior management." By second grade, medication was recommended. Josh's family moved to a small school district where the local high school he attends has only 650 students. Contact between home and school has been close. But as he has matured and the academic demands have increased, says his mother, "high school has been difficult for Josh. Recently, I asked him to take advantage of a tutor or some structured support to help reinforce his behavior, but he seems determined to do it alone."

★ **Specific Accommodations and Self-Advocacy.** Doing it alone is not always the answer, says Jane Warner. Students with ADHD frequently need support when they move from high school to college. "Study skills and time management are troublesome for students with ADHD. Things can start to fall apart. Students might miss several classes and think they can never go back, so they just sit out and their grades go down, their self-esteem starts to slip, and they hit the wall." Warner encourages students to disclose their learning needs confidently and make the primary contact with the office for disability services on campus. Students with ADHD who have not received special services in high school are advised to get the documentation they need for colleges to provide them with appropriate accommodations. "We prefer comprehensive evaluations that have been done by a qualified professional within the previous 3 years," says Warner. "IEPs are part of the puzzle, but IEPs can't be used as the only documentation for postsecondary accommodations."

Warner points out that current evaluations provide a clear picture of strengths and weaknesses, especially if the evaluator explains what the results mean in lay terms and makes specific educational recommendations. "Sometime between now and high school graduation," she says, "getting a current clinical evaluation will be a very important strategy for developing his self-advocacy and for moving Josh closer to reaching his goals."

CEC'S STANDARDS: PAVING THE WAY TO SUCCESS

Assess your steps to success in meeting the CEC Knowledge and Skill Base for All Beginning Special Education Teachers. Use the following questions to reflect on the growth of your own professional knowledge, skills, and dispositions.

REFLECTING ON YOUR OWN PROFESSIONAL DEVELOPMENT

If you were Josh's teacher . . .

- What are some areas about educating students with ADHD about which you would need to know more?
- What are some specific skills that would help you to address his academic and behavioral challenges?
- What personal dispositions do you think are most important for you to develop in teaching students with challenging behaviors posed by ADHD?

Using the CEC Standards

- How would you describe the psychological and social-emotional characteristics of individuals with ADHD? (GC2K4)
- What are the effects of various medications on individuals with ADHD? (CC2K7)
- What type of procedures would you use to increase self-awareness, self-management, self-control, self-reliance, and self-esteem in a student with ADHD? (CC4S5)

• By Jean B. Crockett

Persistent Goal-Directed Behavior The many problems with executive functions experienced by people with ADHD lead to deficits in engaging in sustained goal-directed activities:

> The poor sustained attention that apparently characterizes those with ADHD probably represents an impairment in goal- or task-directed persistence arising from poor inhibition and the toll it takes on self-regulation. And the distractibility ascribed to those with ADHD most likely arises from poor interference control that allows other external and internal events to disrupt the executive functions that provide for self-control and task persistence. The net effect is an individual who cannot persist in effort toward tasks that provide little immediate reward and who flits from one uncompleted activity to another as disrupting events occur. The inattention in ADHD can now be seen as not so much a primary symptom as a secondary one; it is the consequence of the impairment that behavioral inhibition and interference control create in the self-regulation or executive control of behavior. (Barkley, 1997, p. 84)

With diminished self-regulation or executive control abilities, students with ADHD find it exceedingly difficult to stay focused on tasks that require effort or concentration but that are not inherently exciting (e.g., many school-related activities). Substantial evidence shows that students with ADHD, indeed, have lower academic achievement than those without disabilities (Frazier, Youngstrom, Glutting, & Watkins, 2007).

Adaptive Behavior

The concept of **adaptive behavior skills** (e.g., self-help, community use, home use, and so forth) has traditionally been associated with the area of mental retardation or intellectual disabilities. The definition developed by the American Association on Intellectual and Developmental Disabilities, for example, stipulates that intellectual disabilities be defined as impairments in intelligence and adaptive behavior (see Chapter 5). In recent years, authorities in the ADHD field have discovered that many children and adults with ADHD also have difficulties in adaptive behavior (Barkley, 2006a; Whalen et al., 2006). A good example is that people with ADHD have more problems related to driving as adolescents and young adults: more accidents and traffic violations (Cox, Merkel, Kovatchev, & Seward, 2000; Fischer, Barkley, Smallish, & Fletcher, 2007; Woodward, Fergusson, & Horwood, 2000). It's logical to assume that poor behavioral inhibition would lead to driving problems, and evidence shows that these problems may also be related to poor anger control (Richards, Deffenbacher, Rosen, Barkley, & Rodricks, 2007).

Social Behavior Problems

Research suggests that students with ADHD are more disliked by their peers than are students with any other kind of disorder (Mikami, Jack, & Lerner, 2009). In social situations, it often doesn't take long for students with ADHD to be ostracized. Unfortunately, the negative social status experienced by students with ADHD is difficult to overcome and is usually long lasting. And adding to their socialization problems, many students with ADHD also have social difficulties with their parents, siblings, and teachers (Mikami et al., 2009). The enduring nature of social rejection easily leads to social isolation. The result is that many children and adults with ADHD have few friends, even though they may desperately want to be liked. This can set up a vicious circle in which they attempt to win friends by latching onto the least chance for interaction with others. But their frantic need for friendship, coupled with their deficient impulse control, ends up leading them to bother or pester the very people they are trying to befriend.

Given the problems in behavioral inhibition, it's not surprising that so many children and adults with ADHD end up socially ostracized. Unable to regulate their behavior and emotions, they are viewed as rude by others. It isn't that they don't know how to behave appropriately so much as that they are unable to do so (Landau et al., 1998). In other words, if asked what the appropriate behavior in a given situation should be, they can often give the socially acceptable answer. But when faced with choices in the actual situation, their deficits in behavioral inhibition lead them to make choices impulsively and to overreact emotionally.

Coexisting Conditions

ADHD often occurs simultaneously with other behavioral and/or learning problems, such as learning disabilities or emotional or behavioral disorders. In addition, persons with ADHD run a higher risk than the general population for substance abuse.

Learning Disabilities   Studies using careful diagnostic criteria have found an overlap of 10% to 25% between ADHD and learning disabilities (Forness & Kavale, 2002). Some authorities maintain that the relationship is strongest for students who have ADHD, Predominantly Inattentive Type (Marshall, Hynd, Handwerk, & Hall, 1997; Willcutt, Chhabildas, & Pennington, 2001).

Emotional or Behavioral Disorders   Estimates of the overlap with ADHD vary widely, but it's safe to say that 25% to 50% of people with ADHD also exhibit some form of emotional or behavioral disorder (Forness & Kavale, 2002; Hallahan & Cottone, 1997). Some people with ADHD can exhibit aggressive, acting-out behaviors, whereas others can have the types of withdrawn behaviors that accompany anxiety or depression. In fact, anxiety is evident in between 15% to 35% of children with ADHD, and they are especially vulnerable to having multiple anxiety disorders compared with children without disablities (Schatz & Rostain, 2007).

Substance Abuse   Adolescents with ADHD are more likely to experiment prematurely with alcohol, tobacco, or illicit drugs (Molina et al., 2007). Some reports in the popular media have claimed that the treatment of ADHD with psychostimulants such as Ritalin leads children to take up the use of illegal substances. However, very little research backs up this claim (Connor, 2006).

Children with ADHD who also have externalizing types of behavior disorders are especially vulnerable for early drug use.

Exactly why ADHD co-occurs with so many other learning and behavioral disabilities is unclear. Researchers are just beginning to tease out which of several possibilities are the most likely reasons for the extensive overlap between ADHD and other disabilities. For example, does having ADHD put one at risk for developing another disability, such as learning disabilities or depression? Or do ADHD and the other disability occur independent of each other? Is there a genetic basis to the coexistence of so many of these conditions? Research over the next few years should begin to provide more definitive answers to these questions.

EDUCATIONAL CONSIDERATIONS

In this section, we consider two aspects of effective educational programming for students with ADHD:

- Classroom structure and teacher direction
- Functional behavioral assessment and contingency-based self-management

Classroom Structure and Teacher Direction

As noted earlier, William Cruickshank was one of the first to establish a systematic educational program for children who today would meet the criteria for ADHD. Two hallmarks of Cruickshank's program were reducing stimuli irrelevant to learning and enhancing materials important for learning, and a structured program with a strong emphasis on teacher direction.

Because Cruickshank assumed that children with attention problems were susceptible to distraction, he reduced irrelevant stimuli as much as possible. For example, students' work spaces consisted of three-sided cubicles to reduce distractions. On the other hand, teachers were encouraged to use attractive, brightly colored teaching materials. The structure came in the form of a systematic schedule of activities for each child for virtually each minute of each day (Cruickshank, Bentzen, Ratzeburg, & Tannhauser, 1961).

It's rare today to see teachers using all the components of Cruickshank's program, especially the cubicles. Many authorities now believe that not all children with ADHD are distracted by things in their environment. For those who are distractible, however, some authorities recommend the use of things such as cubicles to reduce extraneous stimulation.

The degree of classroom structure and teacher direction advocated by Cruickshank is also rarely seen today. First, this intensity of structure could be achieved only in a self-contained classroom; most students with ADHD today are in general education settings.

Teacher-directed general education classes, with colorful visual aids, enclosed teaching areas, and proximity to the teachers have been successful learning environments for students with ADHD.

Second, most authorities today believe that a structured program is important in the early stages of working with many students with ADHD but that these students gradually need to learn to be more independent in their learning. Nevertheless, many of Cruickshank's ideas are still alive in the educational recommendations of today's professionals. For example:

> All children, and particularly, those with ADHD, benefit from clear, predictable, uncomplicated routine and structure. It helps if the day is divided into broad units of time and if this pattern is repeated daily. Within each block of lesson time there should be a similar breaking down of tasks and activities into subtasks/activities. Presenting the student with an enormously detailed list of tasks and subtasks should be avoided. An important goal should be to create a simple overarching daily routine that the student will eventually learn by heart. The number of tasks should be kept small and tight timelines should be avoided. Complexities of timetabling and working structures merely confuse students with ADHD, because a major difficulty that goes with this condition is a poorly developed ability to differentiate between and organize different bits of information. This clearly makes the formal curriculum difficult to manage, without having to struggle with the organizational arrangements that surround the curriculum. Once a workable daily timetable has been established this should be publicly displayed and/or taped to the student's desk or inside his or her homework diary. (Cooper, 1999, p. 146)

For more specifics about planning for students with ADHD in the classroom, see the accompanying Responsive Instruction box.

Functional Behavioral Assessment and Contingency-Based Self-Management

Functional behavioral assessment (FBA) is an important aspect of dealing with behavioral problems of students with intellectual disabilities. It's also extremely useful in educational programming for students with ADHD. FBA involves determining the consequences, antecedents, and setting events that maintain inappropriate behaviors (Horner & Carr,

RESPONSIVE *INSTRUCTION*
MEETING THE NEEDS OF STUDENTS WITH ADHD

Planning for Students with ADHD in the General Education Classroom

WHAT THE RESEARCH SAYS

The majority of students with ADHD are served in general education classrooms. Through adding key modifications or supports to their traditional instructional routines, teachers can address the needs of students with ADHD without diminishing the instruction of students without disabilities in their class.

The following lesson sequence includes a description of research-supported supports that teachers can provide at each stage of instruction and a rationale for how those supports meet the needs of students with ADHD.

APPLYING THE RESEARCH TO TEACHING

Stage I: Pre-planning—Divide Instruction into Meaningful "Chunks"

Description Before instruction, break your instructional sequence into meaningful chunks or steps (Rosenshine, 1995). By dividing your instructional sequence into small, meaningful sections, you ensure that all students do not move on until they understand and that ample practice and teacher feedback have been provided at each step.

Rationale Long tasks can be overwhelming for students with ADHD. Chunking allows for shorter periods of focused attention, activity changes as you move through the instructional sequence, focused practice, and reduced reliance on working memory (Kemp, Fister, & McLaughlin, 1995).

Stage II: Introduction

Description During this stage, the teacher introduces the day's instructional objectives. Information or activities that should be included in the introduction are (1) a rationale for the lesson, (2) an explanation or presentation of a model of what the end result of the lesson will be, and (3) an advance organizer that informs students of the sequence of instructional activity (Allsopp, 1999).

Rationale These activities provide a "road map" for students to follow. For students with ADHD who have difficulty focusing on the main task or goal (Barkley, 1997), explicit identification of lesson goals or outcomes and clearly delineated steps create an external goal-setting guide.

Stage III: Instruction and Modeling

Description After the teacher has set the stage for learning, the instructional part of the lesson begins. During this stage, a teacher might demonstrate a procedure or phenomenon, present students with a problem scenario to be solved, or have students engage in an activity that will then be linked to key instructional concepts. Regardless of the particular instructional method, students should have a clear understanding of

what the teacher is doing and what they should be doing in response. Effective teaching strategies include (1) think aloud while presenting the initial part of the lesson, (2) model the exact steps the students will complete, and (3) solicit feedback from students during the instructional phase.

Rationale A student with ADHD might have difficulty making connections between the instructional phase of a lesson and the activity, assignment, or worksheet that follows. By providing a clear model of what needs to be done, demonstrating the type of inner speech that should guide their thinking (via the think-aloud), and checking students for understanding, the teacher increases the likelihood of students' making connections between the instruction and the practice or application of the concept (Kucan & Beck, 1997).

Stage IV: Guided Practice

Description The guided practice (GP) stage is the critical transition stage between instruction and independent practice (IP). During GP, students have the opportunity to practice or work with the concept being taught while the teacher is actively providing feedback (Allsopp, 1999; Kemp et al., 1995). GP can consist of students working several problems at the board or on whiteboards at their desks, students explaining (in their own words) to the class what was previously presented, or groups of students doing the first part of a task and reporting their work to the class. The key element of GP is that the teacher has the opportunity to correct or reteach before students are engaged in IP.

Rationale The GP stage provides an important bridge for students with ADHD who may need to be actively engaged in the task to be receptive to instructional guidelines or recommendations provided during instruction (Kemp et al., 1995). GP also provides an opportunity for positive reinforcement as the student makes initial attempts at understanding. Given the chunking of the lesson, teachers could go through the instruction/modeling and GP stages two to three times during a given lesson. Providing frequent shifts in activity creates additional support for such ADHD characteristics as short attention span, task-completion difficulty, and short-term memory problems (Rooney, 1995).

Stage V: Independent Practice

Description Independent practice comes in many forms, ranging from individual to pair or small-group work to homework. The purpose of IP is for students to apply what was taught. At this point in the instructional sequence, students should understand the task requirements and be able to perform the task with competence (Rosenshine, 1995).

(continued)

Rationale Work presented at students' frustration level can be a trigger for common ADHD behaviors—out of seat or verbal or physical disruptions. By establishing clear expectations for IP, ensuring students are capable of the work, and providing support, teachers increase the likelihood of meaningful student engagement.

Stage VI: Closure and Review

Description At the end of every lesson, teachers should permit time to "recap" the main ideas of the lesson. For closure, teachers can review key vocabulary, have students state something they learned, or have students complete a brief journal activity. During closure, the teacher should reinforce the lesson's "big idea" as well as make connections to past and future learning (Kameenui & Carnine, 1998).

Rationale Students with ADHD may have difficulty synthesizing information (Barkley, 1994). Providing closure at the end of a lesson creates the support necessary for students to make connections among the day's concepts (Rosenshine, 1995).

In summary, teachers can serve many students with ADHD effectively within the general education setting, by providing instruction responsive to the unique needs of these students.

• By Kristin L. Sayeski

▪ ▪ ▪ ▪ ▪ ▪ ▪ ▪ ▪ ▪ ▪

1997). Examples of typical functions of inappropriate behavior of students with ADHD are to avoid work and to gain attention from peers or adults (DuPaul & Ervin, 1996).

Contingency-based self-management approaches usually involve having people keep track of their own behavior and then receive consequences, usually in the form of rewards, based on their behavior (Davies & Witte, 2000; DuPaul, Arbolino, & Booster, 2009; Shapiro, DuPaul, & Bradley-Klug, 1998). For example, the teacher might have students use self-monitoring to record how many times they left their seats during a class period. For directions about how to use self-monitoring in the classroom, see the accompanying Responsive Instruction box, and see Chapter 6.

A combination of FBA and contingency-based self-management techniques has proven successful in increasing appropriate behavior of elementary and secondary students with ADHD (DuPaul, Eckert, & McGoey, 1997; Ervin, DuPaul, Kern, & Friman, 1998; Shapiro et al., 1998). In one study, for instance (Ervin et al., 1998), a combination of FBA and contingency-based self-management increased the on-task behavior of two adolescents with ADHD. For one of the students, the FBA interviews with the teacher and observations in the classroom led the researchers and teachers to conclude that the adolescent boy's disruptive behavior was a function of gaining peer attention. They based this assumption on evidence that the antecedents to his inattentive behavior included peers' looking his way, calling out his name, and making gestures toward him and that the consequences of his inattention included the peers' laughing or returning comments to him.

The contingency-based self-management phase involved the student evaluating his on-task behavior on a 5-point scale (0 = unacceptable to 5 = excellent) at the end of each math class. The teacher also rated the student's behavior and awarded the student points based on how closely the ratings matched. During writing class, the teacher awarded negative or positive points to members of the class depending on whether or not they responded to attention-seeking behaviors from any member of the class. In both classes, the students could use the points for privileges.

The Role of Reinforcement Authorities have pointed to the crucial role that contingency plays in contingency-based self-management: reinforcement of some kind, such as social praise or points that can be traded for privileges, is especially im-

Programs that allow students to monitor their own behavior and performance may encourage them to maintain appropriate behavior at school.

RESPONSIVE *INSTRUCTION*
MEETING THE NEEDS OF STUDENTS WITH ADHD

The Benefits of Self-Monitoring and Group Contingency

WHAT THE RESEARCH SAYS

Many students with ADHD lack the ability to self-monitor. Self-monitoring requires the ability to appraise a situation and consider alternative ways of responding as well as possible outcomes associated with the various forms of responding (Shapiro, DuPaul, & Bradley-Klug, 1998). This inability to think before acting creates problems for students with ADHD in the areas of paying attention in class, responding to social situations appropriately, and finishing assigned tasks. To address these issues, teachers can help students learn to use self-management procedures to monitor, record, analyze, and reinforce their own behavior (Davies & Witte, 2000). Many studies have repeatedly demonstrated the effectiveness of teaching students such strategies (Cobb, Sample, Alwell, & Johns, 2006; Harris, Friedlander, Saddler, Frizzelle, & Graham, 2005; Lloyd, Hallahan, Kauffman, & Keller, 1998; Reid & Lienemann, 2006; Reid, Trout, & Schartz, 2005).

Although teaching self-management to students with ADHD has been proven to be effective, many teachers prefer whole-class or group-contingency plans. Within a group-contingency model, the behavior of one student is tied to the outcome of the whole group. Group-contingency models promote interdependence, as group members must work together to meet a goal (Tankersley, 1995). Under a group contingency, teachers can use the same behavior management approach for all students and don't have to differentiate their treatment of the few students who need help with self-management. Thus, group contingencies can be very effective for general education teachers whose classrooms include students with ADHD.

RESEARCH STUDY

One study examined the effects of a management program with third graders on the behaviors of students with ADHD in a general education classroom (Davies & Witte, 2000). All students—those with ADHD as well as nondisabled students—were responsible for monitoring their own behavior, and the researchers established contingencies for group performance. Procedures for the group intervention follow:

1. If any student displayed the target behavior [inappropriate verbalizations], she or he moved one dot from his/her group's chart from the green section into the blue section. If the child did not move the dot after about ten seconds, then the teacher moved a dot into the red section of the chart.

2. The rewards a group received were related to how many dots the group had in the green section of their chart at the end of the intervention period. Each group needed to have at least one dot left in the green section at the end of the intervention period to receive the reinforcer. [Each group started with five dots.] (Davies & Witte, 2000, p. 141)

RESEARCH FINDINGS

Results from the study demonstrated a decrease in talking out of turn for the four students with ADHD. In addition, no evidence showed possible negative side effects of peer pressure, such as threats or negative verbal comments (Davies & Witte, 2000).

APPLYING THE RESEARCH TO TEACHING

Findings from this study demonstrate the effectiveness of using self-management within the context of a group contingency. Teachers can implement similar management strategies through (1) targeting specific undesirable behaviors to be eliminated or specific desirable behaviors to be reinforced, (2) creating a chart for students to use for self-management, (3) communicating the procedures for recording behaviors on the chart (e.g., "If you do X, mark your chart" or "When the beeper beeps, check to see if you are doing X, then mark your chart accordingly"), or (4) connecting the self-management procedures to a group contingency (e.g., "If all students get over X points during the lesson, all students will get a homework pass").

• By Kristin L. Sayeski

▪ ▪ ▪ ▪ ▪ ▪ ▪ ▪

portant for self-management techniques to be effective. For example, an extensive review of research found that contingency-based self-management strategies were more effective than self-management strategies without contingencies in leading to positive behavioral changes in students with ADHD (DuPaul & Eckert, 1997).

The use of behavioral procedures such as reinforcement is somewhat controversial, and some are opposed to their use (Kohn, 1993). Many authorities, however, consider them almost indispensable in working with students with ADHD. For example, behavioral procedures are an integral part of a set of intervention principles advocated by one team of authorities (Pfiffner, Barkley, & DuPaul, 2006; see Table 7.1).

TABLE 7.1 Pfiffner, Barkley, and DuPaul's intervention principles for ADHD

1. Rules and instructions must be clear, brief, and often delivered through more visible and external modes of presentation.
2. Consequences must be delivered swiftly and immediately.
3. Consequences must be delivered more frequently [than for students without ADHD].
4. The types of consequences must often be of a higher magnitude, or more powerful [than for students without ADHD].
5. An appropriate and often richer degree of incentives must be provided.
6. Reinforcers, or particularly, rewards must be changed or rotated more frequently.
7. Anticipation is the key. Teachers must be mindful of planning ahead, particularly during phases of transition across activities or classes, to ensure that the children are cognizant of the shift in rules (and consequences) that is about to occur.

Source: Condensed from Pfiffner, L. J., Barkley, R. A., & DuPaul, G. J., (2006). Treatment of ADHD in school settings. In R. A. Barkley, *Attention-deficit hyperactivity disorder: A handbook for diagnosis and treatment* (3rd ed.). New York: Guilford Press, 2006, pp. 554–555. Adapted with permission.

Service Delivery Models

Because the U.S. Department of Education doesn't recognize ADHD as a separate special education category, we don't have statistics on how many of these students are served in different classroom environments. It's safe to assume, however, that one can find students with ADHD across the entire continuum of placements. But because, as we noted earlier, there is reason to believe that fewer than half receive any special education services, it's logical to assume that most students with ADHD spend most of their time in general education classrooms. The accompanying Making It Work feature describes different ways to use co-teaching to help meet the needs of these students, whether they receive special education services or not.

MAKING IT WORK
COLLABORATION AND CO-TEACHING FOR STUDENTS WITH ADHD

"How can I get this student focused?!"

WHAT DOES IT MEAN TO BE A TEACHER OF STUDENTS WITH ADHD?

Currently, the Council for Exceptional Children doesn't have specific competencies for teachers of students with attention deficit hyperactivity disorder (ADHD). As you read in this chapter, ADHD isn't recognized as a separate special education category by the U.S. Department of Education. These students, however, often have additional disabling conditions and are served by teachers with expertise in those areas. That expertise may include:

1. Understanding educational implications of characteristics of various exceptionalities
2. Understanding the effects of various medications on individuals with exceptional learning needs
3. Using procedures to increase the individual's self-awareness, self-management, self-control, self-reliance, and self-esteem

SUCCESSFUL STRATEGIES FOR CO-TEACHING

Co-teaching classroom configurations come in many forms, and all give teachers "more hands" to meet the needs of students with ADHD. Vaughn, Schumm, and Arguelles (1997) describe five basic models of co-teaching that provide co-teachers with opportunities to use the instructional strategies described in this chapter and in Table 7.1.

One Teach, One Drift

In this model, one teacher is responsible for instruction, and the other teacher drifts, monitoring students. This model allows the drifting teacher to redirect students who may be off task, to observe and mark student-monitoring forms, to provide feedback on individual student's attention and participation, and to deliver reinforcers or consequences on a frequent basis.

Station Teaching

In station teaching, co-teachers split content into two parts and students into three groups. Each teacher teaches one of the two content pieces at a station to a small group of students, and the other group works independently. The student groups rotate between stations. Teachers can break content down into smaller tasks that maintain the attention of all students. Each teacher can work with a small group of students, making it easier to ensure that they are focused and learning. It is also easier to help students work together and to provide reinforcers and consequences more frequently. The difficulty lies in making sure that students with ADHD can work appropriately in the independent station.

Parallel Teaching

In parallel teaching, the two teachers split the class into two groups and teach the same content to a smaller group of students. This model provides the same opportunities as station teaching, along with the chance to modify the instructional delivery of the same content material to meet the needs of the student.

Alternative Teaching

The alternative teaching model includes content instruction by one teacher to a large group of students and remedial or supplementary instruction by the other teacher to a small group of students. The teacher of the small group can modify delivery of content, control the delivery of consequences and rewards, and closely monitor and observe students. In addition, the teacher of the small group can incorporate instruction in strategies such as self-monitoring.

Team Teaching

In team teaching, co-teachers alternate or "tag team" in delivering instruction to the entire class. In this model, co-teachers can both be on the lookout for misconceptions, confusion, inattention, and disruption. Teachers can then address these issues during the flow of instruction rather than afterward or on an individual basis. In addition, co-teachers can work together to both present content and learning strategies in unison to better meet the needs of all students.

In All Models

Teachers working together can discuss and better evaluate whether rules and instructions are clear, brief, and delivered in appropriate formats for students with ADHD. Co-teachers can also work together to better anticipate "rough spots" for students with ADHD, particularly during transition times, changes in routines, or complex tasks (see Table 7.1). The varying models of co-teaching provide the flexibility for teachers to adjust instructional delivery to meet the objectives of the teachers and the needs of the students with ADHD.

CAUTIONARY NOTE

All too often, co-teachers fall into the habit of using one model to the exclusion of others. This is unfortunate in that it may mean that one teacher doesn't participate actively in instruction and/or planning. This nonparticipation can lead to a lack of interest on the teacher's part and a disregard for that teacher on the students' part. The models of co-teaching were developed to match the needs of instruction. Both teachers should participate in instruction in a way that matches their expertise.

• By Margaret P. Weiss

As with all students with disabilities, the best placement for students with ADHD should be determined on an individual basis. Although full inclusion in a general education classroom might be appropriate for some students with ADHD, for students with severe ADHD problems, one needs to keep in mind that the best research-based practices for students with ADHD—that is, classroom structure, teacher direction, functional behavioral assessment, and contingency-based self-management—can be a challenge to implement in the general education classroom.

MEDICATION CONSIDERATIONS

One of the most controversial topics in all of special education is the treatment of ADHD with medication. **Psychostimulants**, which stimulate or activate neurological functioning, are by far the most frequent type of medication prescribed for ADHD. However, promising research is emerging on a number of nonstimulants (Spencer, Biederman, & Wilens, 2010). **Strattera** is an example of a nonstimulant that is also sometimes prescribed for ADHD. The most common stimulant prescribed for ADHD is methylphenidate, or **Ritalin**. **Adderall** and **Vyvanse** are other stimulants that are sometimes prescribed. The fact that physicians would prescribe a psychostimulant for someone who exhibits hyperactivity is, at first blush, counterintuitive. In fact, for years professionals referred to the **paradoxical effect of Ritalin** because its effects appeared to be the opposite of those one would expect in the case of someone who does not have ADHD. Researchers have concluded, however, that Ritalin influences the release of the neurotransmitters dopamine and norepinephrine, thus enabling the brain's executive functions to operate more normally (Arnsten et al., 2009; Connor, 2006; Floet et al., 2010). Furthermore, it's now believed that Ritalin has the same chemical and behavioral effect on people who don't have ADHD as it does on those with ADHD (Solanto, 1998). Responsiveness to stimulants is highly individual, so the dosage level and number of doses per day vary from person to person.

INTERNETRESOURCES

The National Institutes of Mental Health (NIMH) has a Website devoted to medications for ADHD: http://www.nimh.nih.gov/health/publications/attention-deficit-hyperactivity-disorder/complete-index.shtml#pub6

Opposition to Ritalin

Not all professionals, parents, and laypeople are in favor of using pyschostimulants for ADHD. In fact, Ritalin has been the subject of numerous assaults in the media. Critics have appeared on nationally broadcast television shows such as *Oprah, Geraldo*, and *20/20*, as well as on evening and morning news shows. The Church of Scientology's objection to Ritalin has received much publicity due to Hollywood actor Tom Cruise's criticisms of Ritalin. Although some criticisms have been relatively mild, others have ranged from assertions that ADHD is a bogus diagnosis to claims that professionals are trying to control children with medication and make them overly docile.

The Research Evidence

Over the last 30 to 40 years, dozens of research teams around the world have studied the effects of several medications on ADHD. Most of this research has focused on the psychostimulant Ritalin.

Effectiveness   Despite all the negative publicity in the media, most ADHD authorities are in favor of Ritalin's use. After hundreds of studies, the research is overwhelmingly positive on the effectiveness of Ritalin in helping students to have more normalized behavioral inhibition and executive functioning (Connor, 2006; Meszaros et al., 2009; Spencer et al., 2010). Moreover, Ritalin not only leads to better results on parent and teacher rating scales, but also leads to improved academic achievement (Scheffler et al., 2009) as well as classroom behavior such as better note taking, on-task behavior, quiz scores, homework completion, and written-language work (Evans et al., 2001).

Nonresponders and Side Effects   Even though research has demonstrated the general effectiveness of Ritalin, it's important to point out that it's not effective for everyone. Somewhere around 30% of those who take Ritalin do not have a favorable response (Barbaresi et al., 2006). In addition, some side effects are possible, including insomnia, reduction in appetite, abdominal pain, headaches, and irritability. There has also been speculation on the possibility that in a very small number of cases, Ritalin causes tics or increases their intensity in those who already have tics (DuPaul, Barkley, & Connor, 1998). There have been many anecdotal reports of a "rebound effect," in which a child exhibits irritability as the Ritalin wears off. In most cases, these side effects are

Psychostimulants, especially Ritalin, have sparked a national controversy over the treatment of ADHD. Although Ritalin is not effective for everyone and can have side effects, the bulk of research evidence supports its effectiveness.

mild and can be controlled. For example, in the case of the two most common side effects—insomnia and reduction in appetite—care should be taken not to take the Ritalin too close to mealtime or bedtime. In the case of the rebound effect, some physicians recommend using a time-release form of Ritalin.

Drug Abuse   A popular misconception is that by taking Ritalin, children with ADHD are more likely to become abusers of drugs such as marijuana or cocaine as adolescents or young adults. Little if any documented evidence suggests that this occurs (Connor, 2006). In fact, evidence suggests that individuals with ADHD who are prescribed Ritalin as children are less likely to turn to illicit drugs as teenagers (Katusic et al., 2005). Some have speculated that perhaps those who are not medicated with Ritalin turn to other drugs to try to find "peace of mind" or to "chill out."

Cautions Regarding Medication

Although the research is overwhelmingly positive on the effectiveness of medication for increasing appropriate behavior, a number of cautions remain:

- Medication should not be prescribed at the first sign of a behavior problem. Only after careful analysis of the student's behavior and environment should medication be considered. The use of psychostimulants for ADHD in the United States increased approximately eight-fold from the 1970s to the 1990s (Wilens & Biederman, 1992), and in the first 5 years of the 21st century, the rate approximately doubled (Castle, Aubert, Verbrugge, Khalid, & Epstein, 2007). Although much of this increase in recent years can be attributed to an increase in prescriptions for females and adults coincident with the increase in diagnosis in these populations, it still should alert us to turning too quickly to medication as *the* answer to ADHD.
- Although research has demonstrated the effectiveness of medication on behavioral inhibition and executive functions, the results for academic outcomes have not been as dramatic. Thus, teachers shouldn't assume that medication will take care of all the academic problems these students face.
- Parents, teachers, and physicians should monitor dosage levels closely so that the dose used is effective but not too strong. Proper dosage levels vary considerably.
- Teachers and parents shouldn't lead children to believe that the medication serves as a substitute for self-responsibility and self-initiative.
- Teachers and parents shouldn't view the medication as a panacea; they, too, must take responsibility and initiative in working with the child.
- Parents and teachers should keep in mind that psychostimulants are a controlled substance. There is the potential for siblings, peers, or the child himself to attempt to experiment with them.
- The final key to the effective use of medication is communication among parents, physicians, teachers, and the child.

Medication Versus Behavior Management

Over the years, parents and professionals have considered the question of whether medication is more or less effective than, or equally effective as, behavior management. Unfortunately, research hasn't provided a definitive answer. The National Institute of Mental Health launched a large-scale study to address the question (MTA Cooperative Group, 1999). After 14 months of treatment, a combination of medication and behavior management was the most effective, followed by medication alone. Behavior management, while effective for some students, was a distant third. However, once the treatment groups were formally discontinued, leaving it to families and schools to decide whether to use medication and/or behavior management, follow-ups over 8 years showed that the treatment groups gradually lost most of their advantages (Molina et al., 2009; Swanson et al., 2008).

Based on these results and others (Fabiano et al., 2007; Majewicz-Hefley & Carlson, 2007), the best course of action appears to be a combination of medication and behavior management. The chances for continued improvement depend largely on the continued close monitoring of these treatments.

ASSESSMENT OF PROGRESS

Assessment of students with ADHD includes procedures for evaluating social and emotional behaviors and academic skills. Many of the procedures described in Chapter 6 on learning disabilities are also appropriate for students with ADHD.

Assessment of Academic Skills

As we discussed earlier, students with ADHD often experience difficulties with academic tasks as a result of inattention, impulsivity, and/or poor executive functioning skills. In addition, they're commonly diagnosed with learning disabilities as a co-existing condition.

Curriculum-based measurement (CBM), described in Chapter 6, is an appropriate method for monitoring academic progress for students with ADHD. An advantage of CBM for students with ADHD is that the measures take very little time to administer and are focused on a particular task. CBM should be implemented with students with ADHD to ensure that academic progress is adequate.

Assessment of Attention and Behavior

Two methods are commonly used to assess a student's attention to tasks and social/emotional behavior: rating scales and direct observation. An example of a rating scale that can be used to measure student outcomes or to monitor student progress is the Conners-3 (Conners, 2007). The Conners-3 includes measures of oppositional behavior, inattention, anxiety, and social problems.

Teachers should also directly observe students on a regular schedule to monitor attention, academic engaged time, and disruptive behavior. Behavioral recording systems provide a framework to conduct systematic observations. For example, **momentary time sampling** allows the teacher to conduct brief observations and collect data on a specific set of behaviors. In momentary time sampling, the observer determines the length of the observation and divides it into intervals (e.g., 15 minutes may be divided into 15 intervals of 1 minute each). At the beginning of each interval, the observer records whether the student is exhibiting the behavior of interest and then does not observe the student until the beginning of the next interval.

Figure 7.3 provides an example of a momentary time-sampling chart for a student, Susie, who is working to increase her time on task. The observation lasted for 15 minutes.

FIGURE 7.3 Momentary time sampling—an interval recording procedure to capture a representative sample of a target behavior over a specified period of time.

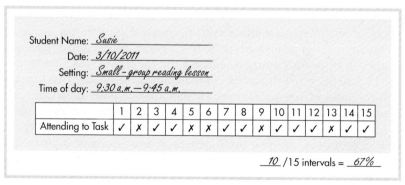

Glancing at Susie at the beginning of each minute, the observer placed a check mark in the box if Susie was attending to the task at the time sampled, and an *X* if she was not attending. At the end of the observation period, the teacher calculated the number of intervals Susie was on task to determine a percentage of on-task behavior for the 15-minute period. Susie was on task for 10 of the 15 intervals, or 67% of the time. Susie's teacher may use the momentary time-sampling procedure at regular intervals to monitor Susie's attention to tasks and modify interventions as needed.

A unique measure of student outcomes is the Telephone Interview Probe (TIP) (Corkum, Andreou, Schachar, Tannock, & Cunningham, 2007). This instrument uses brief telephone interviews of parents and teachers to determine the effects of interventions for students with ADHD. It's particularly useful for evaluating the effects of psychostimulant medications on an individual at a specific time of day or setting. Many common rating scales are limited to broader time frames and don't provide the specificity required to make decisions in regard to treatment with medications. The TIP provides ratings of inattention, impulsiveness, hyperactivity, oppositional behavior, and problem situations for three time points during the day (i.e., morning, afternoon, evening).

EARLY INTERVENTION

Diagnosis of young children with ADHD is particularly difficult because many young children who don't have ADHD tend to exhibit a great deal of motor activity and a lack of impulse control. However, in recent years the number of preschoolers identified as ADHD has increased; the prevalence rates of 2% to 6% for preschoolers now rival the rates of 3% to 7% for school-age students. And perhaps maybe even more significant, parents report that ADHD symptoms in their children first begin to appear between the ages of 2 and 4 years (Posner, Pressman, & Grennhill, 2009).

Behavioral inhibition and inattention in preschool are predictors of ADHD symptoms and early literacy skills, respectively, in early elementary school (Campbell & von Stauffenberg, 2009; Walcott, Scheemaker, & Bielski, 2009). Therefore, early intervention for preschoolers with ADHD is critically important.

Because excessive activity and impulsivity are relatively normal for young children, preschoolers with ADHD can be particularly difficult to manage. Those preschoolers who really do have ADHD are a great challenge to parents and teachers. The importance of the educational principles of classroom structure, teacher direction, functional behavioral assessment, and contingency-based self-management discussed previously in this chapter are all the more important for preschoolers. Given that even young children who don't have ADHD lack fully developed self-management skills, most professionals recommend an even stronger emphasis on the use of contingencies in the form of praise, points, and tangible rewards.

TRANSITION TO ADULTHOOD

Not too long ago, most professionals assumed that ADHD diminished in adolescence and usually disappeared by adulthood. However, authorities now recognize that, although the number of symptoms, especially those connected to hyperactivity (Weyandt, 2009a), may decrease, ADHD persists into adulthood for at least 50% of those affected. And an additional 25% may not have enough symptoms to be formally diagnosed as ADHD, but their residual symptoms have the potential to interfere with functioning (Ramsay, 2010). The accompanying Personal Perspectives relates an example of ADHD's effects on an adult.

Diagnosis in Adulthood

With the greater recognition of ADHD by the scientific community as well as by the popular media, many people are being diagnosed with ADHD in adulthood. However, the diagnosis of ADHD in adults can sometimes be controversial. Because of the long-held assumption that ADHD did not persist into adulthood, research on ADHD in adults is comparatively sparse. In recent years, however, professionals have begun to make progress in identifying and treating ADHD in adults. Because no diagnostic test exists for ADHD, most

 **Personal PERSPECTIVES**

An Adult with ADHD: Ann's Story

I grew up not feeling very good about myself. In school, it was hard for me to stay on the subject or to finish anything. . . . Teachers would be on my back. They said I was such a good child—they couldn't understand it. And I tried so hard. I just couldn't finish anything. . . . I was distracted very easily by practically everything. If someone sneezed, I'd look at him and my mind would go off in a million directions. I'd look out the window, wondering why he had sneezed. . . .

The situation has persisted into adulthood. I'm very disorganized. Take housekeeping, for example. After dinner, when I start the dishes, I'll wash a little, then run and wipe off the table, wipe the cabinet, talk on the phone, and never get anything completed. I have to really concentrate and tell myself, "You are going to get the dishes done." Then they get done, but I still get the urge to stop and go wash off the dining room table. Just like someone is pulling me. My closet and drawers are still a mess, just like when I was a kid. What's really hard is to stay with any kind of paper work—bills, for example. It's my husband's job to do the bills. If it were mine, we'd probably be in jail. . . . Only recently at age forty-five have I been able to sit down and write a letter. I usually write small postcards.

I'm the most impulsive person in the world. It gets me in trouble. If I see something I know I shouldn't buy, I'll buy it anyway. Or, I'll say something that I know the minute it comes out of my mouth I'm going to regret. . . .

I wish I could just slow down and relax. I have problems sitting still. . . . People say I make them nervous, but I don't even realize I'm doing anything. That hurts my feelings. I don't want to be different.

My dream has always been to be some kind of counselor, but I felt like I wasn't college material, so I got married and had two children. I have a real estate license now. I don't know how I passed the test. I must have guessed right. What I like about selling is that I'm always on the move and I love people. I'm tuned into them. But I'm too sensitive to have a sense of humor. I think I have a thin skin. I get my feelings hurt easily. When that happens, I cry and go into my shell.

My mood swings from high to low. I either feel very good or very down. I feel up if the house looks good. If I get everything done that I think I should, it makes me feel good about myself. I feel responsible for a lot of people. If my husband is in a bad mood, or if things aren't going right for my kids, my mother, or my sister, I feel bad. I don't know what's wrong with me.

By Ann Ridgley

Source: Weiss, L. (1992). *Attention deficit disorder in adults* (pp. 11–14). Lanham, MD: Taylor Publishing Co. Reprinted by permission.

authorities hold that the person's **clinical history** is of utmost importance. As one authoritative team has put it:

> Taking a history both from the identified patient (child or adult) and from someone else (parents, spouse, or significant other) constitute the crux of the evaluation. Although not usually considered a test, the history is the best method of assessment that we have. Sometimes it is the only "test" that will be needed. . . .
>
> The most common misconception about how to diagnose [ADHD], a misconception subscribed to by most schools and many professionals, is that there is a "test" for [ADHD], a psychological test or brain scan, that absolutely pins down the diagnosis. But there is no such test. The closest we have to it is the history. The history is more valuable than any paper-pencil test or brain scan.
>
> It is the individual's own story—what we doctors call the history—that makes or breaks the diagnosis of [ADHD]. (Hallowell & Ratey, 2006, pp. 117–118)

Within the history, the clinician looks for symptoms that are similar to those that children with ADHD display, although as mentioned, adults may have fewer symptoms, especially those related to hyperactivity. In addition, the symptoms may take a somewhat different form because they occur in a different context, for example, related to the work rather than the classroom environment or related to one's role as a spouse or parent rather than as a child in the family environment. For example, adults with ADHD may become bored easily with relatively routine work or have problems organizing their work schedule. Or they may have problems "tuning in" to what their spouse or children are saying or overcommit themselves to too many household projects, such that many of them remain undone.

Adult Outcomes

Overall, adults with ADHD tend to have a number of poorer outcomes with respect to educational attainment, psychiatric problems (e.g., depression and anxiety), marital difficulties, driving infractions, and addictive behaviors, such as substance abuse, gambling addiction (Barkley & Murphy, 2007; Biederman et al., 2010; Ramsay, 2010; Rucklidge, Brown, Crawford, & Kaplan, 2007; Weyandt & DuPaul, 2006). In addition, although people with ADHD are at risk for poorer outcomes, it's important to point out that many adults with ADHD have highly successful careers and jobs, and many have happy marriages and families. For example, Brittany Sanders (see the accompanying Peer Connections) appears to have coped very well with her ADHD and to be well on her way to a happy adult life.

Employment   One of the keys to successful employment, especially for persons with ADHD, is to select a job or career that maximizes the individual's strengths and minimizes weaknesses. Success often depends on pursuing a job that fits a person's needs for structure versus independence. It's recommended that those who work best with structure look for jobs with organizations that have a clear mission and lines of authority, with an emphasis on oversight from supervisors who have an understanding of ADHD. Those who find formal structures too confining should look for work environments that are flexible, have variety, and allow one to be independent (Hallowell & Ratey, 2006).

Marriage and Family   Given some of the behavioral characteristics of ADHD, it's not surprising that husbands and wives of people with ADHD frequently complain that their spouse is a poor listener, preoccupied, forgetful, unreliable, messy, and so forth. A person's ADHD can have a negative impact on the entire family. Parents who have ADHD may find it difficult to manage the daily lives of their children. As one parent put it, "I couldn't remember to brush my teeth when I was a kid, and now I can't remember to tell my kid to brush his teeth" (M. Weiss, Hechtman, & Weiss, 2000, p. 1060).

Many authorities recommend that the first step to treatment is to have all family members become educated about the facts associated with ADHD. Because ADHD is a family issue, they also recommend that all members of the family should be partners in its treatment.

Importance of Coaching

One highly recommended therapeutic technique is coaching (Hallowell & Ratey, 2006). **Coaching** involves identifying someone whom the person with ADHD can rely on for support. The coach, who can be a therapist or a friend, is someone who can regularly spend a few minutes to help keep the person with ADHD focused on goals. The coach provides the structure needed to plan for upcoming events and activities and heaps on praise when tasks are accomplished.

Although ADHD is a lifelong struggle for most people with the condition, with the appropriate combination of medical, educational, and psychological counseling, satisfactory employment and family adjustment are within the reach of most people with ADHD. Now that most authorities recognize that ADHD often continues into adulthood, more and more research will be focused on treatment of ADHD in adults. With this research should come an even more positive outlook for adults with ADHD.

PEER CONNECTIONS: BRITTANY SANDERS

BRITTANY SANDERS was diagnosed with ADHD in the fourth grade. She grew up in Louisa County, VA. Brittany currently attends Bennett College for Women in North Carolina and will graduate with a degree in Special Education in 2011. She spends her summers in Charlottesville, Virginia, teaching at a therapeutic camp for young children with disabilities.

What do you do for fun? I love to spend time with my friends. We enjoy going downtown and to the parks. I also like to go bowling with friends, and we love to go on trips together.

What is your favorite way to relax? I would have to say just having time all by myself helps me relax. I like having "me" time where nobody else is around.

What is something that you excel at? Working with kids. I love working with kids, especially kids with disabilities.

What is your pet peeve? I have several, kind of crazy pet peeves. The first is when people smack their mouth while they are eating. I also don't like it when someone says the same thing to me over and over again. Also, indecisive people, they drive me crazy.

Can you recall one teacher in particular who has been a positive influence in your life? Yes, my teacher-cadet mentor in high school. Her name was Ms. Steppe. She was the leader for the program I was in with other students who wanted to be teachers. She was more than a teacher though. She was like a friend—we could tell her anything, and she would listen and never judge us.

Is there anyone else (celebrity, family member) that you regard as a role model? Why are they a role model for you? My mom—she has always been there for me, especially my first year of college. I didn't do well, but she still supported me, and she still helps me work through hard times. Life has not always been easy, but she has always been there. She's a mental health counselor so we also have things in common in that we both love to help other people.

What is the most difficult thing for you about having a disability? When I was younger, I had a lot of trouble. I remember not being able to stay still. I couldn't sit in my seat. I was always up at the pencil sharpener or into something. As I've got-

ten older, I can sit in my seat and look focused. But I have a hard time focusing. Sometimes it may look like I'm paying attention, but my mind is often wandering. I also forget things a lot, it drives people crazy, but I just really can't help it sometimes. I take Adderall now, but when I haven't taken it I can definitely tell a difference. I've also learned to self-monitor.

Do you see your disability as affecting your ability to achieve what you want in your life? No, not at all, I'm still very social. My boyfriend sometimes gives me a hard time because I'm not always focused and forget things, but he and my friends have learned to accept me for me.

Has your disability affected your social relationships? If so, how? No. I can do whatever anyone else can do!

Are there any advantages to having a disability that others might be surprised to know? I don't know. I try to do the best that I can, but I don't always succeed. But most important, I always always try.

How do you think others perceive you? Hmmm . . . very happy, I smile a lot, very social. As a person that will do anything for anybody. I hope that's how others perceive me.

What is one thing that you would like others to know about you? I love Girl Scouts. I think it's such a great program. I started when I was in elementary school as a Brownie and participated in Girl Scouts all the way until I was a senior. I would love to have my own troop some day soon.

Please fill in the blank: I couldn't live without _____. My family. They are very accepting of me and the fact that I have ADHD. My mom has always made sure that I get the best care available!

Where do you see yourself 10 years from now? Married with kids. I hope to be someone's teacher somewhere, probably at an elementary school. I would love to be back in North Carolina.

CONNECT WITH BRITTANY— Brittany welcomes you to contact her online at BSanders@Bennett.edu

SUMMARY

What are the historical origins of ADHD?

- In the mid-19th century, Dr. Heinrich Hoffman wrote nursery rhymes about "Fidgety Phillip" and "The Story of Johnny Head-in-Air."
- In 1798, Sir Alexander Chrichton wrote a treatise on attention disorders.
- In 1902, Dr. George F. Still reported on children whom he referred to as having "defective moral control."
- In the 1930s, Kurt Goldstein reported on soldiers who had head wounds in World War I.
- In the 1930s and 1940s, Heinz Werner and Alfred Strauss reported on children with mental retardation (intellectual disabilities) who were assumed to be brain injured, referred to as having the "Strauss syndrome."
- In the 1950s, William Cruickshank extended Werner and Strauss's work to children with normal intelligence.
- In the 1950s and 1960s, professionals used the term *minimal brain injury* to refer to children who were of normal intelligence but who were inattentive, impulsive, and/or hyperactive.
- In the 1960s and 1970s, the term *hyperactive child syndrome* was popular.

What is the current definition of ADHD?

- Most professionals rely on the American Psychiatric Association's *Diagnostic and Statistical Manual of Mental Disorders* (DSM) for the definition of ADHD. Currently, the manual subdivides individuals into (1) ADHD, Predominantly Inattentive Type; (2) ADHD, Predominantly Hyperactive-Impulsive Type; and (3) ADHD, Combined Type. The revised manual, due to be published in 2012, may include changes related to recognition that (1) many individuals are *exclusively* inattentive with no hyperactivity; (2) some children don't exhibit ADHD until after the age of 7 years; and (3) adults often have fewer symptoms than children.

What is the prevalence of ADHD?

- The best estimates are that 3% to 7% of the school-age population has ADHD.
- Boys with ADHD outnumber girls, most likely owing to biological differences and perhaps some referral bias.

What methods of assessment do professionals use to identify individuals with ADHD?

- Professionals usually use four methods of assessment: (1) a medical examination, (2) a clinical interview, (3) teacher and parent rating scales, and (4) behavioral observations. The behavioral observations can be done in the classroom and/or in the clinician's office.

What causes ADHD?

- Neuroimaging studies have identified five areas of the brain that might be affected in people with ADHD: the prefrontal lobes, the frontal lobes, the basal ganglia, the cerebellum, and the corpus callosum.
  - The prefrontal and frontal lobes are responsible for executive functions, or the ability to regulate one's behavior.
  - The basal ganglia and cerebellum are involved in coordination and control of motor behavior.
  - The corpus callosum connects the left and right hemispheres of the brain and serves as a pathway for nerve signals between the two.
- Research has identified an imbalance in each of two neurotransmitters: dopamine and norepinephrine.
- Family studies, twin studies, and molecular genetic studies indicate that heredity may also be a significant cause of ADHD.
- Exposure to toxins such as lead, as well as medical factors such as complications at birth and low birth weight, can also be a cause of ADHD.

What are some of the psychological and behavioral characteristics of learners with ADHD?

- Barkley's theory of ADHD points to problems with (1) behavioral inhibition, (2) executive functioning, (3) time awareness and management, and (4) persistent goal-directed behavior.
- People with ADHD also often experience problems in adaptive behavior and in their relationships with peers.
- Several conditions often co-exist with ADHD: learning disabilities and emotional-behavioral problems, such as depression and anxiety; people with ADHD are also at risk for substance abuse problems.

What are some educational considerations for learners with ADHD?

- Good educational programming for students with ADHD involves a high degree of classroom structure and teacher-directed activities.
- Good educational programming for students with ADHD involves functional assessment and contingency-based self-management.
  - Functional behavioral assessment (FBA) involves determining the consequences, antecedents, and setting events that maintain inappropriate behaviors.
  - Such approaches might also include self-monitoring or self-management programs, with students recording their own behaviors.

What are some medication considerations for learners with ADHD?

- Psychostimulants, such as Ritalin, are prescribed most often; Strattera, a nonstimulant, is also often prescribed.
- Scientific studies (including a large-scale study sponsored by the National Institute for Mental Health) support the effectiveness of medication, and most authorities on ADHD favor its use.
- Some cautions about medication are that some people are nonresponders, dosage levels should be monitored closely, some people experience side effects (although these usually are not serious), children should not be encouraged to see the medication as a replacement for self-initiated behavioral control, and medication should not be the first response to problem behavior.

How do professionals assess the academic, attention, and behavioral progress of students with ADHD?

- Curriculum-based measurement can be used to assess progress in academics and attention and behavior.
  - Momentary time sampling is particularly useful for assessing behavioral progress.

- Testing accommodations often include small-group or individual administration in a quiet location, extended time, and frequent breaks.

What are some important considerations with respect to early intervention for learners with ADHD?

- Diagnosing ADHD in early childhood is difficult, partly because very young children typically have short attention spans and are motorically active.
- Principles of classroom structure, teacher direction, functional behavioral assessment, and contingency-based self-management are important for preschoolers with ADHD.
- Because young children typically do not have strong self-management skills, contingencies in the form of praise, points, and tangible rewards are important.

What are some important considerations with respect to transition to adulthood for learners with ADHD?

- A thorough clinical history is critical in diagnosing ADHD in adults.
- Although exceptions exist, adults with ADHD tend to have less positive outcomes than the general population in terms of employment, marriage and family, and general social well-being.
- Coaching is a therapeutic technique often recommended for adults with ADHD.

COUNCIL FOR EXCEPTIONAL CHILDREN

Addressing the Professional Standards

Council for Exceptional Children Council for Exceptional Children (CEC) Common Core Knowledge and Skills addressed in this Chapter: ICC1K5, ICC1K8, ICC2K1, ICC2K2, ICC2K3, ICC2K6, ICC2K7, ICC3K1, ICC4S6, ICC5S3, ICC5S8, ICC5S10, ICC5S11, ICC8K2, ICC8S3, ICC8S6, ICC9S2, ICC10K3, ICC10S2, ICC10S3

Appendix: Provides a full listing of the CEC Common Core Standards and associated knowledge and Skill Statements listed here.

MYEDUCATIONLAB

PEARSON
myeducationlab Now go the Topic 11: ADHD, in the MyEducationLab (www
.myeducationlab.com) for your course, where you can:

- Find learning outcomes for the broad concepts covered in this chapter along with the national standards that connect to these outcomes.
- Complete Assignments and Activities that can help you more deeply understand the chapter content.
- Examine challenging situations and cases presented in the IRIS Center Resources.
- Apply and practice your understanding of the core concepts and skills identified in the chapter with the Building Teaching Skills and Dispositions learning units.
- Check your comprehension on the content covered in the chapter by going to the Study Plan in the Book-Specific Resources for your text. Here you will be able to take a chapter quiz, receive feedback on your answers, and then access Review, Practice, and Enrichment activities to enhance your understanding of chapter content.
- Watch video clips of CCSSO Teacher of the Year award winners responding to the question: "Why I teach?" in the Teacher Talk Section.

Learners with Emotional or Behavioral Disorders

It has always been hard for me to have friends. I want friends, but I don't know how to make them. I always think people are being serious when they are just joking around, but I don't figure that out until a lot later. I just don't know how to adapt.

I get into fights with people all the time. I take their teasing seriously and get into trouble. I don't remember having as much trouble getting along with kids when I was little. They seemed to feel sorry for me or thought I was weird. I used to run away from kids and hide in the bathroom at school or under my desk.

After I got back from the hospital, I really couldn't get along with anyone. That was when kids first began calling me "retard." I am not retarded, but I get confused and can't figure out what is going on. At first I couldn't figure out what they were saying to me. Finally one girl in my special education class became my friend. She kind of took care of me. I had another friend in junior high who was also nice and kind to me. But my best friend is my dog Cindie. Even though I give her a hard time, she is always ready to love me.

I like to play by myself best. I make up stories and fantasies. My mother says it is too bad I have such a hard time writing, because with my imagination and all the stories I have created in my mind I could write a book.

—Anonymous

QUESTIONS to guide your reading of this chapter . . .

- What terminology is used to describe emotional or behavioral disorders?
- What is the definition of *emotional or behavioral disorder*?
- How are emotional or behavioral disorders classified?
- What is the prevalence of emotional or behavioral disorders?
- What are the causes of emotional or behavioral disorders?
- How are emotional or behavioral disorders identified?
- What are the most prominent characteristics of students with emotional or behavioral disorders?
- What are the major educational considerations regarding emotional or behavioral disorders?
- How do professionals assess the progress of students with emotional or behavioral disorders?
- What are important considerations in early intervention for learners with emotional or behavioral disorders?
- What are important considerations in transition to adulthood for learners with emotional or behavioral disorders?

MISCONCEPTIONS ABOUT
Learners with Emotional or Behavioral Disorders

MYTH • Most children and youths with emotional or behavioral disorders are not noticed by people around them.

FACT • Although it is difficult to identify the types and causes of problems, most children and youths with emotional or behavioral disorders, whether aggressive or withdrawn, are quite easy to spot.

MYTH • Students with emotional or behavioral disorders are usually very bright.

FACT • Some, but relatively few students with emotional or behavioral disorders, have high intelligence; in fact, most have below-average IQs.

MYTH • Most students who are seen by their teachers as a "pain in the neck" are not disturbed; they are disturbing to others, but they are not disturbed.

FACT • Most students who are disturbing to others are also disturbed. One of the signs of emotional health and good adjustment is behaving in ways that do not cause others concern, being neither unusually aggressive and disruptive nor overly reticent and socially withdrawn.

MYTH • Students with emotional or behavioral disorders exhibit problematic behavior constantly.

FACT • Most students with emotional or behavioral disorders often exhibit typical behavior most of the time.

MYTH • Most students with emotional or behavioral disorders receive special education and/or mental health services.

FACT • The vast majority of students with emotional or behavioral disorders are not identified and served in a timely fashion by either mental health or special education. Only a small percentage (perhaps 20%) are served by special education or mental health.

MYTH • Youngsters who exhibit shy, anxious behavior are more seriously impaired than those whose behavior is hyperaggressive.

FACT • Youngsters with aggressive, acting-out behavior patterns have less chance for social adjustment and mental health in adulthood. Neurotic, shy, anxious children and youths have a better chance of getting and holding jobs, overcoming their problems, and staying out of jails and mental hospitals, unless their withdrawal is extreme. This is especially true for boys.

MYTH • Most students with emotional or behavioral disorders need a permissive environment, in which they feel accepted and can accept themselves for who they are.

FACT • Research shows that a firmly structured and highly predictable environment is of greatest benefit for most students.

MYTH • Only psychiatrists, psychologists, and social workers can help children and youths with emotional or behavioral disorders overcome their problems.

FACT • Most teachers and parents can learn to be highly effective in helping youngsters with emotional or behavioral disorders, sometimes without extensive training or professional certification. Many of these children and youths do require services of highly trained professionals as well.

MYTH • Undesirable behaviors are only symptoms; the real problems are hidden deep in the individual's psyche.

FACT • The belief in hidden causes has no sound scientific basis; the behavior and its social context are the problems. Causes may involve thoughts, feelings, and perceptions.

MYTH • Juvenile delinquency and the aggressive behavior known as conduct disorder can be effectively deterred by harsh punishment if children and youths know that their misbehavior will be punished.

FACT • Harsh punishment, including imprisonment, not only does not deter misbehavior, but also creates conditions under which many individuals become even more likely to exhibit unacceptable conduct.

Children and youths with emotional or behavioral disorders aren't typically good at making friends. Their most obvious problem is failure to establish close and satisfying emotional ties with other people who can help them. As the youth in the chapter's opening quotation describes, it can be easier for these individuals to hide, both physically and emotionally. If they do have friends, their friends are often deviant peers (T. W. Farmer, 2000; T. W. Farmer, Quinn, Hussey, & Holahan, 2001; Kauffman & Landrum, 2009b; Landrum, 2011; Walker, Ramsey, & Gresham, 2004).

Some of these children are withdrawn. Other children or adults might try to reach them, but these efforts are usually met with fear or disinterest. In many cases, quiet rejection continues until those trying to be friends give up. Because close emotional ties are built around reciprocal social responses, people lose interest in others who don't respond to social overtures.

Many other children with emotional or behavioral disorders are isolated from others not because they withdraw from friendly advances but because they strike out with hostility and aggression. They're abusive, destructive, unpredictable, irresponsible, bossy, quarrelsome, irritable, jealous, defiant—anything but pleasant. Naturally, most other children and most adults choose not to spend time with children like this unless they have to. Some strike back at youngsters who show these characteristics. It's no wonder that these children and youths seem to be embroiled in a continuous battle with everyone. The reaction of most other children and adults is to withdraw to avoid battles, but rejected children then don't learn to behave acceptably. Teachers and well-behaved peers naturally tend to withdraw from them or avoid them, which reduces their opportunities to learn both academic and social skills.

A common but serious misunderstanding is that children with emotional or behavioral disorders aren't really disturbed, just a pain in the neck. Students can be both disturbed *and* disturbing, have an emotional or behavioral disorder *and* irritate the teacher. True, some irritating students don't have an emotional or behavioral disorder. However, most children with emotional or behavioral disorders are irritating to teachers, whereas most children are neither irritating nor have such a disorder. Moreover, students who are consistently irritating are at high risk of acquiring an emotional or behavioral disorder, if they don't already have one, or of encouraging such disorders in others, simply because the reactions of teachers and peers are likely to be negative and hostile.

Another widespread misunderstanding is that children and youths with emotional or behavioral disorders exhibit their problematic behavior all the time—24/7. Most people don't seem to understand the fact that such disorders tend to be episodic, highly variable, and sometimes situation specific (e.g., only when demands are placed on them to perform or only outside their home or family). People often don't understand the fact that their own observation may catch these students at a time when the impairment is *not* being exhibited. Many people also don't seem to realize that parents who are psychologically impaired may be very poor or unreliable reporters of the students' behavior at home. And often, people don't understand that a very good parent can have a really problematic child. Understanding the on-again, off-again nature of these disorders is critical. Expecting a youngster with an emotional or behavioral disorder to exhibit problem behavior all the time is somewhat like expecting someone with a seizure disorder to have seizures all the time. Emotional or behavioral disorders aren't exhibited as consistently as is intellectual disability or cerebral palsy.

myeducationlab

To check your comprehension on the content covered in Chapter 8, go to the Book-Specific Resources in the MyEducationLab (www .myeducationlab.com) for your course, select your text, and complete the Study Plan. Here you will be able to take a chapter quiz, receive feedback on your answers, and then access review, practice, and enrichment activities to enhance your understanding of chapter content. ■

Where does the problem start? Does it begin with behavior that frustrates, angers, or irritates other people? Or does it begin with a social environment so uncomfortable or inappropriate that the child can only withdraw or attack? These questions can't be answered fully on the basis of current research. The best thinking today is that the problem isn't always just in the child's behavior or just in the environment. The problem arises because the social interactions and transactions between the child and the social environment are inappropriate—both the behavior *and* responses to it are problematic. The issue is not just behavior that's appropriate and ways of reacting to it that are misguided, or behavior that's undesirable even though it's being handled well. This is an ecological perspective—an interpretation of the problem as a negative aspect of the child *and* the environment in which the child lives. And there are two equally serious mistakes people can make: First, assuming that the problem is only in the child who exhibits inappropriate behavior; second, assuming that the child's behavior is not the problem, only the context in which it occurs. Sometimes the problem may begin with misbehavior, and sometimes it may begin with mismanagement. However, by the time special educators are involved, the problem usually involves both misbehavior *and* mismanagement.

TERMINOLOGY

Many different terms have been used to designate children who have extreme social-interpersonal and/or intrapersonal problems, including *emotionally handicapped, emotionally impaired, behaviorally impaired, socially/emotionally handicapped, emotionally conflicted,* and *seriously behaviorally disabled.* These terms don't designate distinctly different types of disorders; that is, they don't refer to clearly different types of children and youths. Rather, the different labels appear to represent personal preferences for terms and slightly different theoretical orientations.

Until 1997, *seriously emotionally disturbed* was the term used in federal special education laws and regulations. *Seriously* was dropped from the terminology in 1997. *Emotionally disturbed* is the term used in the Individuals with Disabilities Education Act (IDEA). The term *behaviorally disordered* is consistent with the name of the Council for Children with Behavioral Disorders (CCBD, a division of the Council for Exceptional Children) and has the advantage of focusing attention on the clearly observable aspect of these children's problems: disordered behavior. Many authorities favor terminology indicating that these children may have emotional or behavioral problems or both (Cullinan, 2004, 2007; Kauffman & Brigham, 2009; Kauffman & Landrum, 2009b; Landrum, 2011). In 1990, the National Mental Health and Special Education Coalition, representing over 30 professional and advocacy groups, proposed the term *emotional or behavioral disorder* to replace *emotional disturbance* in federal laws and regulations (Forness & Knitzer, 1992).

DEFINITION

Defining emotional and behavioral disorders has always been problematic. Professional groups and experts have felt free to construct individual working definitions to fit their own professional purposes (Kauffman & Landrum, 2006, 2009b; Landrum, 2011). No one has come up with a definition that all professionals understand and accept.

Defining emotional and behavioral disorders is somewhat like defining a familiar experience—anger, loneliness, or happiness, for example. We all have an intuitive grasp of what these experiences are, but forming objective definitions of emotional or behavioral disorders is difficult. Mental health and normal behavior have been hard to define precisely. It's no wonder, then, that the definition of emotional or behavioral disorder presents a special challenge. Conceptual models—assumptions or theories about why people behave as they do and what we should do about it—may offer conflicting ideas about just what the problem is. Emotional or behavioral disorders tend to overlap a great deal with other disabilities, especially learning disabilities and intellectual disability. Finally, each professional group has its own reasons for serving individuals with emotional or behavioral disorders. For example, clinical psychologists, school psychologists, social workers, teachers, and juvenile justice authorities all have their particular concerns and language. Differences in the focuses of different professions tend to produce differences in definition as well.

Current Definitions

There is general agreement that emotional or behavioral disorder refers to the following:

- Behavior that goes to an *extreme*—not just slightly different from the usual
- A problem that is *chronic*—one that does not quickly disappear
- Behavior that is *unacceptable* because of social or cultural expectations

The Federal Definition   The federal rules and regulations governing the implementation of IDEA define the term *emotionally disturbed* as follows:

  i. The term means a condition exhibiting one or more of the following characteristics over a long period of time and to a marked extent, which adversely affects educational performance:
   A. An inability to learn that cannot be explained by intellectual, sensory, or health factors;
   B. An inability to build or maintain satisfactory relationships with peers and teachers;
   C. Inappropriate types of behavior or feelings under normal circumstances;
   D. A general pervasive mood of unhappiness or depression; or
   E. A tendency to develop physical symptoms or fears associated with personal or school problems.
  ii. The term includes children who are schizophrenic. The term does not include children who are socially maladjusted unless it is determined that they are emotionally disturbed. (45 C. F. R. 121a5[b][8][1978])

These inclusions and exclusions (in ii above) are unnecessary (Bower, 1982; Kauffman & Landrum, 2009b). Bower's five criteria (A–E above) for emotional disturbance indicate that schizophrenic children must be included and that socially maladjusted children cannot be excluded. Furthermore, the clause "which adversely affects educational performance" makes interpretation of the definition impossible, unless the meaning of educational performance is clarified. Does educational performance refer only to academic achievement? If so, then children with the behavioral characteristics listed but who achieve on grade level can be excluded.

One of the most widely criticized and controversial aspects of the definition is its exclusion of children who are socially maladjusted but not emotionally disturbed. Some states and localities have started to interpret social maladjustment as **conduct disorder**—aggressive, disruptive, antisocial behavior. The American Psychological Association and the CCBD have condemned this practice, which has no scientific basis (Kauffman & Landrum, 2009b; Landrum, 2011).

Developing objective criteria for defining emotional and behavioral disorders can be problematic, partly because feelings of unhappiness or anger are familiar—or "normal"—to all people.

An Alternative to the Federal Definition   The National Mental Health and Special Education Coalition proposed an alternative definition in 1990. The coalition's proposed definition is as follows:

  i. The term emotional or behavioral disorder means a disability characterized by behavioral or emotional responses in school so different from appropriate age, cultural, or ethnic norms that they adversely affect educational performance.

Educational performance includes academic, social, vocational, and personal skills. Such a disability:

A. is more than a temporary, expected response to stressful events in the environment;

B. is consistently exhibited in two different settings, at least one of which is school-related; and

C. is unresponsive to direct intervention in general education, or the child's condition is such that general education interventions would be insufficient.

ii. Emotional and behavioral disorders can co-exist with other disabilities.

iii. This category may include children or youths with schizophrenic disorders, affective disorder, anxiety disorder, or other sustained disorders of conduct or adjustment when they adversely affect educational performance in accordance with section (i). (Forness & Knitzer, 1992, p. 13)

Advantages of the proposed definition over the federal definition include the following:

- It uses terminology that reflects current professional preferences and concern for minimizing stigma.

- It includes both disorders of emotions and disorders of behavior, and it recognizes that they may occur either separately or in combination.

- It is school centered but acknowledges that disorders exhibited outside the school setting are also important.

- It is sensitive to ethnic and cultural differences.

- It does not include minor or transient problems or ordinary responses to stress.

- It acknowledges the importance of prereferral interventions but does not require slavish implementation of them in extreme cases.

- It acknowledges that children and youths can have multiple disabilities.

- It includes the full range of emotional or behavioral disorders of concern to mental health and special education professionals without arbitrary exclusions.

CLASSIFICATION

Researchers have identified two broad, pervasive dimensions of disordered behavior: externalizing and internalizing. **Externalizing behavior** involves striking out against others (see Furlong, Morrison, & Jimerson, 2004). **Internalizing behavior** involves mental or emotional conflicts, such as depression and anxiety (see Gresham & Kern, 2004). Some researchers have found more specific disorders, but all of the more specific disorders can be located on these two primary dimensions.

Individuals may show behaviors characteristic of both dimensions; the dimensions are not mutually exclusive. A child or youth might exhibit several behaviors associated with internalizing problems (e.g., short attention span, poor concentration) and several of those associated with externalizing problems as well (e.g., fighting, disruptive behavior, annoying others). Actually, **comorbidity**—the co-occurrence of two or more conditions in the same individual—is common. Few individuals with an emotional or behavioral disorder exhibit only one type of maladaptive behavior.

Children may exhibit any kind of troublesome behavior with any degree of intensity or severity. That is, any kind of problem behavior may be exhibited to a greater or lesser extent; the range may be from normal to severely disordered.

Researchers differentiate between the externalizing and internalizing dimensions of behavioral disorders. Externalizing behavior refers to striking out against others, damaging property, and other disruptive actions.

For example, an individual might have a severe conduct disorder, an externalizing problem defined by overt, aggressive, disruptive behavior or covert antisocial acts such as stealing, lying, and fire setting. Individuals with **schizophrenia** have a severe disorder of thinking, not a mild one. They might believe that they are controlled by alien forces or might have other delusions or hallucinations. Typically, their emotions are inappropriate for the actual circumstances, and they tend to withdraw into their own private worlds.

PREVALENCE

Credible studies in the United States and many other countries have consistently indicated that at least 6% to 10% of children and youths of school age exhibit serious and persistent emotional/behavioral problems (Kauffman & Landrum, 2009b; Landrum, 2011). However, less than 1% of schoolchildren in the United States are identified as emotionally disturbed for special education purposes (U.S. Department of Education, 2008). A report on children's mental health from the U.S. Surgeon General has also indicated that a very small percentage of children with serious emotional or behavioral disorders receive mental health services (U.S. Department of Health and Human Services, 2001). More recent studies confirm the Surgeon General's report (e.g., Costello, Foley, & Angold, 2005; Costello, Foley, & Angold, 2006). Costello et al. (2005) concluded:

> Substantively, we can say with certainty that only a small proportion of children with clear evidence of functionally impairing psychiatric disorder receive treatment. Once upon a time, when effective treatments for child and adolescent psychiatric disorders were rare, this was regrettable but not a major public health issue. Now it is. The tragedy is compounded by powerful evidence that most psychiatric disorders have their origins early in life: risk even for adult-onset disorders is often increased by childhood adversities, and disorders manifesting themselves in the early years often recur in adulthood. So the public health directive to intervene early is clear, . . . but the reality is different. (p. 982)

The gap between estimates of prevalence and services by mental health and special education is huge (Costello et al., 2006; Kauffman and Landrum, 2009b; Kauffman, Mock, and Simpson, 2007; Kauffman, Simpson, & Mock, 2009). The most common types of problems exhibited by students who are placed in special education for emotional or behavioral disorders are externalizing—aggressive, acting-out, disruptive behavior. Boys outnumber girls in displaying these behaviors by a ratio of five to one or more. Overall, boys tend to exhibit more aggression than girls do, although antisocial behavior in girls is an increasing concern (see Coutinho & Oswald, 2011; Furlong et al., 2004; Schaffner, 2006).

Juvenile delinquency and the antisocial behavior known as conduct disorder present particular problems in estimating prevalence. Disabling conditions of various kinds are much more common among juvenile delinquents than among the general population (Nelson, Leone, & Rutherford, 2004; O'Mahony, 2005). Moreover, the social and economic costs of delinquency and antisocial behavior are enormous. Students who exhibit serious antisocial behavior are at high risk for school failure as well as other negative outcomes (Kauffman & Landrum, 2009b; Walker et al., 2004).

CAUSES

Researchers have attributed the causes of emotional or behavioral disorders to four major factors:

1. Biological disorders and diseases
2. Pathological family relationships
3. Undesirable experiences at school
4. Negative cultural influences

Viewpoints differ as to whether juvenile delinquent youths should automatically be considered to have emotional or behavioral disorders.

Although in the majority of cases, no conclusive empirical evidence indicates that one of these factors is directly responsible, some factors might give a child a predisposition to exhibit problem behavior, and others might precipitate or trigger it. That is, some factors, such as genetics, influence behavior over a long time and increase the likelihood that circumstances will trigger maladaptive responses. Other factors (e.g., observing one parent beating the other) might have a more immediate effect and might trigger maladaptive responses in an individual who is already predisposed to problem behavior.

Another concept important in all theories is the idea that contributing factors heighten the risk of a disorder. It's extremely unusual to find a single cause leading directly to a disorder. Usually, several factors together contribute to the development of a problem. In almost all cases, the question of what specifically caused the disorder can't be answered because no one really knows. However, professionals often do know the factors that place children at risk—the circumstances or conditions that increase the chances that a child will develop the disorder (Sprague & Walker, 2000). Figure 8.1 illustrates how risk factors accumulate to place children and youths at risk for antisocial and violent behavior (often called *conduct disorder*), which is one of the most common and troubling emotional-behavioral problems of young people (see also Kazdin, 2008).

Biological Factors

Behaviors and emotions may be influenced by genetic, neurological, or biochemical factors, or by combinations of these. Certainly, a relationship exists between body and behavior, and it would therefore seem reasonable to look for a biological causal factor of some

FIGURE 8.1 Risk pathway to antisocial and violent behavior. It reflects the effects of exposure to known risk factors and developmental outcomes

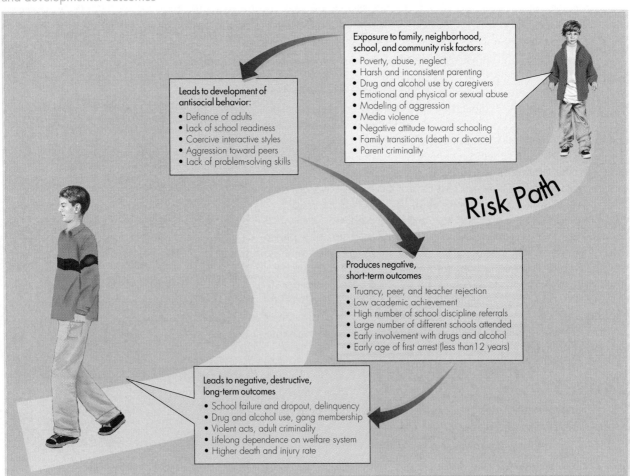

Source: From Early Identification and Intervention for Youth with Antisocial and Violent Behavior by J. Sprague and H. Walker. *Exceptional Children, 66*, p. 371. Copyright © 2000 by the Council of Exceptional Children. Reprinted with permission.

kind for certain emotional or behavioral disorders (Cooper, 2005; Forness & Kavale, 2001). For example, prenatal exposure to alcohol can contribute to many types of disability, including emotional or behavioral disorders. But only rarely is it possible to demonstrate a relationship between a specific biological factor and an emotional or behavioral disorder.

For most children with emotional or behavioral disorders, no real evidence shows that biological factors alone are at the root of their problems. For those with severe and profound disorders, however, evidence often suggests that biological factors contribute to their conditions. Moreover, increasing evidence shows that medications are helpful in addressing the problems of many or most students with emotional or behavioral disorders if they receive state-of-the-art psychopharmacology (Konopasek & Forness, 2004).

All children are born with a biologically determined behavioral style, or temperament. Although children's inborn temperaments may be changed by the way they are reared, some people have long believed that children with so-called difficult temperaments are predisposed to develop emotional or behavioral disorders. There is no one-to-one relationship between temperament and disorders, however. A difficult child might be handled so well or a child with an easy temperament so poorly that the outcome will be quite different from what one would predict on the basis of initial behavioral style (Keogh, 2003). Other biological factors besides temperament (e.g., disease, malnutrition, and brain trauma) can predispose children to develop emotional or behavioral problems. Substance abuse also can contribute to emotional and behavioral problems. Except in rare instances, it isn't possible to determine that these factors are direct causes of problem behavior (see Kauffman & Landrum, 2009b; Landrum, 2011).

Substance abuse may contribute to emotional and behavioral problems, but it is difficult to determine when or whether it is the direct cause.

Emotional and behavioral disorders are, in essence, social phenomena, whether they have biological causes or not. The causes of emotional and behavioral disorders are seldom exclusively biological or psychological. Once a biological disorder occurs, it nearly always creates psychosocial problems that then also contribute to the emotional or behavioral disorder. Medication may be of great benefit, but it is seldom the only intervention that is needed (Forness & Beard, 2007; Konopasek & Forness, 2004). The psychological and social aspects of the disorder must also be addressed.

Family Factors

Even in cases of severe emotional or behavioral disorders, it isn't possible to find consistent and valid research findings that allow blaming parents (Kauffman & Landrum, 2009b; Landrum, 2011). Very good parents sometimes have children with very serious emotional or behavioral disorders, and incompetent, neglectful, or abusive parents sometimes have children with no significant emotional or behavioral disorders. The relationship between parenting and emotional or behavioral disorders isn't simple, but some parenting practices are definitely better than others.

Educators must be aware that most parents of youngsters with emotional or behavioral disorders want their children to behave more appropriately and will do anything they can to help them. These parents need support—not blame or criticism—for dealing with very difficult family circumstances. The Federation of Families for Children's Mental Health was organized in 1989 to help provide such support and resources, and parents are organizing in many localities to assist each other in finding additional help.

School Factors

Some children already have emotional or behavioral disorders when they begin school; others develop such disorders during their school years, perhaps in part because of damaging

INTERNETRESOURCES

The home page of the Parent Advocacy Coalition for Educational Rights (PACER) Center is http://www.pacer.org

For the National Federation of Families for Children's Mental Health, see http://www.ffcmh.org

experiences in the classroom. Children who exhibit disorders when they enter school may become better or worse according to how they are managed in the classroom (Furlong, Morrison, & Fisher, 2005; Kauffman & Brigham, 2009; Kauffman & Landrum, 2009b; Landrum, 2011; Walker et al., 2004). School experiences are no doubt of great importance to children, but as with biological and family factors, we can't justify many statements about how such experiences contribute to the child's behavioral difficulties. A child's temperament and social competence can interact with the behaviors of classmates and teachers in contributing to emotional or behavioral problems.

A very real danger is that children who exhibit problem behavior will become trapped in a spiral of negative interactions, in which they become increasingly irritating to and irritated by teachers and peers. In considering how teachers might be contributing to disordered behavior, they must question themselves about their academic instruction, expectations, and approaches to behavior management. Teachers must not assume blame for disordered behavior to which they are not contributing, but it's equally important that teachers eliminate whatever contributions they might be making to their students' misconduct (see Kauffman & Brigham, 2009; Kauffman & Landrum, 2009b; Kauffman, Pullen, Mostert, & Trent, 2011).

Cultural Factors

Children, their families, and schools are embedded in cultures that influence them (see Anastasiou, Gardner, & Michail, 2011; Walker et al., 2004). Aside from family and school, many environmental conditions affect adults' expectations of children and children's expectations of themselves and their peers. Adults communicate values and behavioral standards to children through a variety of cultural conditions, demands, prohibitions, and models. Several specific cultural influences come to mind: the level of violence in the media (especially television and motion pictures), the use of terror as a means of coercion, the availability of recreational drugs and the level of drug abuse, changing standards for sexual conduct, religious demands and restrictions on behavior, and the threat of nuclear accidents, terrorism, or war. Peers are another important source of cultural influence, particularly after the child enters the upper elementary grades (T. W. Farmer, 2000; T. W. Farmer et al., 2001).

There is a danger that a child who exhibits problem behavior may become trapped in a spiral of negative interactions, resulting in worsening problems with teachers and peers.

IDENTIFICATION

It's much easier to identify disordered behaviors than it is to define and classify their types and causes. Most students with emotional or behavioral disorders don't escape the notice of their teachers. Occasionally, such students don't bother anyone and thus are invisible, but it's usually easy for experienced teachers to tell when students need help. Teachers often fail to assess the strengths of students with emotional or behavioral disorders. However, it's important to include assessment of students' emotional and behavioral competencies, not just their weaknesses or deficits (Epstein & Sharma, 1997; Jones, Dohrn, & Dunn, 2004).

The most common type of emotional or behavioral disorder is conduct disorder, an externalizing problem that attracts immediate attention, so identification is seldom a real problem. Students with internalizing problems might be less obvious, but they aren't difficult to recognize. Students with emotional or behavioral disorders are so readily identified by school personnel, in fact, that few schools bother to use systematic screening procedures. Also, the availability of special services for those with emotional or behavioral disorders lags far behind the need; and there isn't much point in screening for problems when no services are available to treat them. Children with schizophrenia are seldom mistaken for those who are developing normally. Their unusual language, mannerisms, and ways of relating to others soon become matters of concern to parents, teachers, and even many casual observers. Children with schizophrenia are a very small percentage of those with emotional or behavioral disorders, and problems in their identification aren't usually encountered. However, they might first be identified as having another disorder, such as attention deficit hyperactivity disorder or depression, and later be diagnosed with schizophrenia.

Even so, don't conclude that educators never have any question about whether a student has an emotional or behavioral disorder. The younger the child, the more difficult it is to judge whether the behavior signifies a serious problem. And some children's emotional or behavioral disorders are undetected because teachers aren't sensitive to the children's problems or because these children don't stand out sharply from other children in the environment who might have even more serious problems. Furthermore, cultural bias can work either way, leading educators to wrongly identify some children or fail to identify others. Even sensitive and unbiased teachers sometimes make errors of judgment. Also, keep in mind that some students with emotional or behavioral disorders don't exhibit problems at school.

Formal screening and accurate early identification for the purpose of planning educational intervention are complicated by the problems of definition we have already discussed (see Lane, Kalberg, & Menzies, 2009). In general, however, teachers' informal judgments have served as a reasonably valid and reliable means of screening students for emotional or behavioral problems (as compared with judgments of psychologists and psychiatrists). When more formal procedures are used, teachers' ratings of behavior have turned out to be quite accurate (Walker, Ramsey, & Gresham, 2003–2004a; Walker et al., 2004).

A teacher's judgment usually is a valid and cost-effective method of identifying children with emotional or behavioral disorders.

PSYCHOLOGICAL AND BEHAVIORAL CHARACTERISTICS

Describing the characteristics of children and youths with emotional or behavioral disorders is an extraordinary challenge because disorders of emotions and behaviors are extremely varied. Individuals may vary markedly in intelligence, achievement, life circumstances, and emotional and behavioral characteristics (Kauffman & Brigham, 2009).

Intelligence and Achievement

The idea that children and youths with emotional or behavioral disorders tend to be particularly bright is a myth. Research clearly shows that the average student with an emotional or behavioral disorder has an IQ in the dull–normal range (around 90) and that relatively few score above the bright–normal range. Compared to the normal distribution of intelligence, more children with emotional or behavioral disorders fall into the ranges of slow learner and mild intellectual disability. On the basis of a review of the research on the intelligence of students with emotional or behavioral disorders, Kauffman and Landrum (2009b) hypothesized distributions of intelligence as shown in Figure 8.2.

There are pitfalls in assessing the intellectual characteristics of a group of children by examining the distribution of their IQs. Intelligence tests aren't perfect instruments for measuring what we mean by intelligence, and it can be argued that emotional or behavioral difficulties might prevent children from scoring as high as they are capable of scoring. Still,

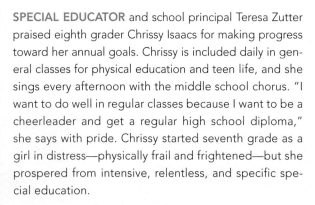

Success Stories

CHRISSY SUCCEEDS IN MIDDLE SCHOOL THROUGH SOCIAL SKILLS INSTRUCTION, POSITIVE BEHAVIORAL SUPPORTS, AND ACADEMIC INTERVENTIONS

School principal Teresa Zutter:"Chrissy, I've called you to my office because you are a star!"

Fourteen-year-old Christina Isaacs attends a special public middle school program for students with emotional and behavioral disorders. These are the keys to her success:

- ★ Intensive instruction in social skills and academics
- ★ Relentless positive behavioral support
- ★ Specific interventions for academic achievement, reducing reliance on adults, building friendships, and increasing her self-confidence

SPECIAL EDUCATOR and school principal Teresa Zutter praised eighth grader Chrissy Isaacs for making progress toward her annual goals. Chrissy is included daily in general classes for physical education and teen life, and she sings every afternoon with the middle school chorus. "I want to do well in regular classes because I want to be a cheerleader and get a regular high school diploma," she says with pride. Chrissy started seventh grade as a girl in distress—physically frail and frightened—but she prospered from intensive, relentless, and specific special education.

★ Intensive Instruction: Social Skills and Academics The Herndon Center serves 60 students in grades seven and eight with emotional and behavioral disorders. These students need close attention, and the program offers a small student–teacher ratio. In addition to Zutter, the center has 13 teachers and a psychologist, a social worker, a guidance counselor, a health awareness monitor, and a conflict-resolution teacher. Weekly clinical staff meetings address students' needs and provide a forum for educators and support staff to discuss problems. "This is such a spirited staff," says Zutter. "We laugh a lot and take care of each other."

Each classroom is equipped with a hot-line telephone connected to the main office. A carpeted quiet room serves as a time-out area for angry students. Zutter works closely with parents, alerting them to misbehaviors and sometimes calling them to take their sons or daughters home. Rules and policies are clear for students, teachers, and families. Gaining trust is critical. For these

the lower-than-normal IQs for these students do indicate lower ability to perform tasks that other students perform successfully, and the lower scores are consistent with impairment in other areas of functioning (e.g., academic achievement and social skills). IQ is a relatively

FIGURE 8.2 Hypothetical frequency distribution of IQ for students with emotional or behavioral disorders as compared to a normal frequency distribution

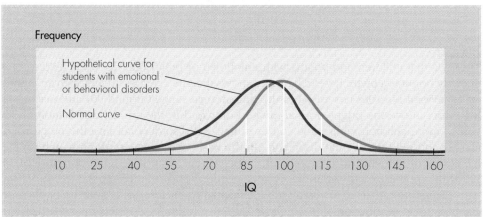

Source: Reprinted with permission of Merrill/Pearson from *Characteristics of Emotional and Behavioral Disorders of Children and Youth* (9th ed.), by J. M. Kauffman and T. J. Landrum. Copyright © 2009 by Pearson Education, Inc.

students, "there is an absolute need for structure and for individualization," says Zutter. "We have so many people here to help and to talk to students that no one has to hit to communicate."

★ Relentless Positive Behavioral Support: Coping with Stress The center's treatment model assumes that students thrive on positive reinforcement. Nonphysical punishment is used on occasion, but only to the degree necessary, and students are taught mechanisms to cope with their anxieties. "Girls and boys who are stressed can be made to feel better," says Zutter. "They are not just ED for a while but have entrenched behaviors; it's a life struggle. They won't be okay without interventions and without being taught how to cope with stress."

Chrissy is a good example. When she started seventh grade, she was out of touch with reality, staring at her own reflection whenever she could and slipping into the protection of fantasy. She was socially awkward and needed to learn how to act in various situations. When she was lost in her own thoughts, she would throw tantrums or provoke fights without seeing the impact her behaviors had on her relationships. She was also becoming oppositional.

As long as she is confronted gently and is not embarrassed in front of other students, Chrissy is responsive to correction. She takes pride in her appearance and musical talents. Socially, she tries to be everybody's friend, but peers are still afraid of her erratic and aggressive behaviors. "Chrissy tends to be overly sensitive to what oth-

ers are saying, whether it relates to her or not," says her mother. When she is angry, Chrissy resorts to profanity and physical threats. This year she managed to develop some stable and cherished friendships with a few girls.

★ Specific Interventions: Vocabulary Development, Increased Adult Attention, and Homework Accommodations Chrissy started seventh grade below grade level in most areas. She could decode words, but she couldn't comprehend what she read. She couldn't organize her thoughts. With frequent reassurance and lots of help to stay on task, Chrissy made gains and performed at grade level in all classes by the end of the year. Speech therapy helped Chrissy to develop vocabulary and use words with multiple meanings, like those in the jokes and riddles she couldn't understand. Accommodations included extra adult attention, additional time to complete class work and tests, shortened assignments, peer/work helpers, and directions stated several times. Although she daydreamed, Chrissy was willing to work hard and to focus when she was provided with support. She is now described as a conscientious student who worries about the quality of her work. According to Zutter, "Chrissy will always have some difficulties, but with help, she can be eased from her world of fantasy. Hopefully, she'll value herself and stay in reality."

• By Jean B. Crockett

good predictor of how far a student will progress academically and socially, even in cases of severe disorders.

Most students with emotional or behavioral disorders are also underachievers at school, as measured by standardized tests. Students with an emotional or behavioral disorder do not usually achieve at the level expected for their mental age; seldom are such students academically advanced. In fact, many students with severe disorders lack basic reading and arithmetic skills, and the few who seem to be competent in reading or math often cannot apply their skills to everyday problems (Kauffman & Landrum, 2009b; Lane & Menzies, 2010).

Social and Emotional Characteristics

Previously, we described two major dimensions of disordered behavior based on analyses of behavior ratings: externalizing and internalizing. The externalizing dimension is characterized by aggressive, acting-out behavior; the internalizing dimension is characterized by anxious, withdrawn behavior and depression. Our discussion here focuses on these two types.

A given student might, at different times, show both aggressive and withdrawn or depressed behaviors. Remember that most students with emotional or behavioral disorders have multiple problems. At the beginning of this chapter, we said that most students with emotional or behavioral disorders aren't well liked or they identify with deviant peers. Studies of the social status of students in regular elementary and secondary classrooms indicate that those who are identified as having emotional or behavioral disorders may be socially rejected. Early peer rejection and aggressive behavior place a child at high risk for later social and emotional problems. Many aggressive students who aren't rejected affiliate primarily with others who are aggressive (T. W. Farmer, 2000; T. W. Farmer, Farmer & Gut, 1999, 2001). The relationship between emotional or behavioral disorders and communication disorders is increasingly clear (Rogers-Adkinson & Griffith, 1999). Many children and youths with emotional or behavioral disorders have great difficulty in understanding and using language in social circumstances. Chrissy, the middle school student with emotional or behavioral disorders described in the Success Stories feature on pp. 212–213, has great difficulty understanding language. Her teachers focused on positive behavioral supports and increasing her vocabulary to help improve her social skills.

Aggressive, Acting-Out Behavior (Externalizing)   As we noted earlier, conduct disorder is the most common problem exhibited by students with emotional or behavioral disorders. Hitting, fighting, teasing, yelling, refusing to comply with requests, crying, destructiveness, vandalism, extortion—these behaviors, if exhibited often, are very likely to earn a child or youth the label "disturbed." Normal children cry, scream, hit, fight, become negative, and do almost everything else children with emotional or behavioral disorders do, but not as impulsively and not as often. Youngsters of the type we are discussing here drive adults to distraction. These youths aren't popular with their peers either, unless they are socialized delinquents who don't offend their delinquent friends. They typically don't respond quickly and positively to well-meaning adults who care about them and try to be helpful.

Aggression has been analyzed from many viewpoints. The analyses having the strongest support in empirical research are those of social learning theorists and behavioral psychologists (Colvin, 2004; Walker et al., 2004). Their studies take into account the child's experience and motivation, based on the anticipated consequences of aggression. In brief, these researchers view aggression as learned behavior and assume that it is possible to identify the conditions under which it will be learned.

Children learn many aggressive behaviors by observing parents, siblings, playmates, and people portrayed on television and in movies. Individuals who model aggression are more likely to be imitated if they are high in social status and are observed to receive rewards and escape punishment for their aggression—especially if they experience no unpleasant consequences or obtain rewards by overcoming their victims. If children are placed in unpleasant situations and they cannot escape from the unpleasantness or obtain rewards except by aggression, they are more likely to be aggressive, especially if this behavior is tolerated or encouraged by others. Aggression is encouraged by external rewards (social status, power, suffering of the victim, obtaining desired items), vicarious rewards (seeing others obtain desirable consequences for their aggression), and self-reinforcement (self-congratulation or enhancement of self-image). If children can justify aggression in their own minds (by comparison to the behaviors of others or by dehumanizing their victims), they are more likely to be aggressive. Punishment can actually increase aggression under some circumstances: when it is inconsistent or delayed, when there is no positive alternative to the punished behavior, when it provides an example of aggression, or when counterattack against the punisher seems likely to be successful.

Teaching aggressive children to be less so is no simple matter, but social learning theory and behavioral research do provide some general guidelines. In general, research doesn't support the notion that it is wise to let children act out their aggression freely. The most helpful techniques include providing examples (models) of nonaggressive responses to aggression-provoking circumstances, helping the child rehearse or role play nonaggressive behavior, providing reinforcement for nonaggressive behavior, preventing the child from obtaining positive consequences for aggression, and punishing aggression in ways that involve as little

INTERNETRESOURCES

Information about preventing violence in youths may be obtained from http://www .vida-health.com/node/127 You may want to begin with the general site, http://www .vida-health.com

Children who act out aggressively or impulsively with frequent negative confrontations often are not well liked by their peers.

counteraggression as possible (e.g., using time-out or brief social isolation rather than spanking or yelling; Colvin, 2004; Kauffman et al., 2011; Walker et al., 2003–2004b, 2004). The accompanying Responsive Instruction box provides a description of a schoolwide strategy to reduce aggression and bullying.

The seriousness of children's aggressive, acting-out behavior shouldn't be underestimated. It was believed for decades that although these children cause a lot of trouble, they aren't as seriously disabled as are children who are shy and anxious. Research has exploded this myth. When combined with school failure, aggressive, antisocial behavior in childhood generally predicts a gloomy future in terms of social adjustment and mental health, especially for boys. When we consider that conduct disorders and delinquency are highly correlated with school failure, the importance of meeting the needs of acting-out and underachieving children is obvious (Kauffman & Landrum, 2009b; Walker et al., 2004).

Immature, Withdrawn Behavior and Depression (Internalizing)   In noting the seriousness of aggressive, acting-out behavior, we don't intend to downplay the disabling nature of immaturity and withdrawal or depression. Such disorders not only have serious consequences for individuals in their childhood years, but also carry a very poor prognosis for adult mental health. The child whose behavior fits a pattern of extreme immaturity and withdrawal or depression cannot develop the close and satisfying human relationships that characterize normal development. Such a child will find it difficult to meet the pressures and demands of everyday life. The school environment is the one in which anxious and withdrawn adolescents in particular experience the most distress (Masia, Klein, Storch, & Corda, 2001).

As in the case of aggressive, acting-out behavior, withdrawal and depression can be interpreted in many different ways. Proponents of the psychoanalytic approach are likely to see internal conflicts and unconscious motivations as the underlying causes. Behavioral psychologists tend to interpret such problems in terms of failures in social learning; this view is supported by more empirical research data than other views (Kauffman & Landrum, 2009b; Landrum, 2011). A social learning analysis attributes withdrawal and immaturity to an inadequate environment. Causal factors may include overrestrictive parental discipline, punishment for appropriate social responses, reward for isolated behavior, lack of opportunity to learn and practice social skills, and models (examples) of inappropriate behavior. Immature or withdrawn children can be taught the skills they lack by arranging opportunities for them to learn and practice appropriate responses, showing models engaging in appropriate behavior, and providing rewards for improved behavior.

A particularly important aspect of immature, withdrawn behavior is depression. Only relatively recently have mental health workers and special educators begun to realize that depression is a widespread and serious problem among children and adolescents. Today, the consensus of psychologists is that the nature of depression in children and youths is quite similar in many respects to that of depression in adults. The indications of depression include disturbances of mood or feelings, inability to think or concentrate, lack of motivation, and decreased physical

Including students with emotional and behavioral disorders in general education classrooms may sometimes be problematic since social interactions are a primary area of concern.

RESPONSIVE *INSTRUCTION*
MEETING THE NEEDS OF STUDENTS WITH EMOTIONAL OR BEHAVIORAL DISORDERS

Approaches to Reducing Bullying in Schools

UNDERSTANDING BULLYING

Recent school tragedies directly or indirectly tied to bullying have resulted in increased attention on the part of administrators, teachers, and students to the issue of bullying in schools. One program recommended by researchers addresses bullying through involving key people who can help the aggressor learn more appropriate behaviors and help the victim learn options for responding. In addition to bringing all stakeholders together, the program addresses the issue from several vantage points (Garrity, Jens, Porter, Sager, & Short-Camilli, 1996, 2000).

A COMPREHENSIVE APPROACH TO REDUCING BULLYING

Garrity and colleagues' program involves the entire school (students, teachers, administrators, staff) as well as students' families. Staff members receive training in response procedures, and teachers then implement the program within their classes. A summary of this model follows.

WHO SHOULD BE INVOLVED?

1. *Teachers and other staff members.* All school personnel need to be informed of standard procedures and be willing to act. Students, including both the bully and the victim, must know that teachers and staff will respond.
2. *The caring majority.* The caring majority are those students who neither bully nor are bullied. These students know the bullying is occurring but often do not know whether or how to respond.
3. *The bullies.* The bullies need to be addressed in ways that stop their aggression toward other students and direct their need for power into more prosocial directions.
4. *The victims.* Victims need protection and support, but they also need the social and interpersonal skills critical for seeking outside and internal support.
5. *Parents.* Parents should be made aware of school policies and procedures. Informed parents will feel more secure about sending their child to school and know the type of response that will occur when their child is either the bully or the victim.

WHAT IS INVOLVED?

1. *Staff training.* All school personnel are involved in staff training, including bus drivers, after-school workers, me-

dia specialists, and others. During staff training, faculty members learn about the different manifestations of bullying (e.g., physical aggression, name calling, gossiping, intimidating phone calls, verbal threats, and locking in confined spaces); explore ways to address both the victim and bully; role play conflict resolution, particularly how to address the bully in a firm, no-nonsense manner; generate an antibullying curriculum, such as selecting literature on bullies and victims or creating skits or artwork with similar themes; and develop a comprehensive school plan for addressing instances of bullying.

2. *Classroom intervention.* Within the classroom, teachers instruct students in rules to eliminate bullying, strategies for reacting to bullying, and steps to follow if they see bullying occurring.

The following rules, strategies, and steps are recommended by Garrity and colleagues (1996, 2000):

a. Rules for Bully-Proofing Our Classroom:
   i. We will not bully other students.
   ii. We will help others who are being bullied by speaking out and by getting adult help.
   iii. We will use extra effort to include all students in activities at our school.

b. What I Can Do if I Am Being Bullied:
   i. HA = Help and assert
   ii. HA = Humor and avoid
   iii. SO = Self-talk and own it

c. What I Can Do if I See Someone Being Bullied:
   i. Creative problem solving
   ii. Adult help
   iii. Relate and join
   iv. Empathy

Finally, Garrity and colleagues suggest the following strategies for empowering victims: (1) Teach a repertoire of friendship-making skills, (2) develop an understanding that self-esteem affects friendships and how one handles bullying, and (3) teach skills that help victims to feel empowered and better able to handle bullies.

• By Kristin L. Sayeski

well-being. A depressed child or youth might act sad, lonely, and apathetic; exhibit low self-esteem, excessive guilt, and pervasive pessimism; avoid tasks and social experiences; and/or have physical complaints or problems in sleeping, eating, or eliminating. Sometimes depression is accompanied by such problems as bed-wetting (nocturnal **enuresis**), fecal soiling (**encopresis**), extreme fear of or refusal to go to school, failure in school, or talk of suicide or suicide attempts. Depression also frequently occurs in combination with conduct disorder.

Suicide is among the leading causes of death among young people ages 15 to 24. Depression, especially when severe and accompanied by a sense of hopelessness, is linked to suicide and suicide attempts. All adults who work with young people therefore must be able to recognize the signs of depression. Substance abuse is also a major problem among children and teenagers and may be related to depression.

Depression sometimes has a biological cause, and antidepressant medications have at times been successful in helping depressed children and youths to overcome their problems (Konopasek & Forness, 2004). In many cases, however, no biological cause can be found. Depression can also be caused by environmental or psychological factors, such as the death of a loved one, separation of one's parents, school failure, rejection by one's peers, or a chaotic and punitive home environment. Consider the boy's experience in the following account:

> One terrible morning at my house, my mother woke up next to my father, who had died in his sleep. It was Dec. 5, 1989, the day before my fourth birthday. . . . My dad's death hit us hard. My mother was left alone with two energetic little boys. She tried to be cheerful, but I knew she was crying every night, and I ached to be the man of the house. Within a few years, I had plunged into a massive depression. I didn't want to live. I couldn't get out of bed, and I stopped eating and playing. A couple of hospitalizations and a long recovery awaited me. (Godwin, 2004, p. C10)

Often, just having someone with whom to build a close relationship can be an important key in recovery from depression. In the case just described, a "big brother" volunteer was helpful to the narrator. Also, interventions based on social learning theory have often been successful in such cases (Gresham & Kern, 2004). These interventions include instructing children and youths in social interaction skills and self-control techniques and teaching them to view themselves more positively.

EDUCATIONAL CONSIDERATIONS

Students with emotional or behavioral disorders typically have low grades and other unsatisfactory academic outcomes, have higher dropout rates and lower graduation rates than other student groups, and are often placed in highly restrictive settings. Moreover, these students are disproportionately from poor and ethnic-minority families and frequently encounter the juvenile justice system. Consequently, their successful education is among the most important and challenging tasks facing special education today (Landrum, Tankersley, & Kauffman, 2003). Finding a remedy for the disproportionate representation of ethnic minorities in programs for students with emotional or behavioral disorders is a critical issue. However, finding effective intervention strategies for diverse students is equally important if we are really to have successful multicultural education (Ishii-Jordan, 2000; Kauffman, Conroy, Gardner, & Oswald, 2008; Kauffman et al., 2011; Kauffman & Landrum, 2009c; Landrum & Kauffman, 2003).

Unfortunately, special educators have never reached a consensus about how to meet the challenge of educating students with emotional or behavioral disorders. Although a national agenda has been written for improving services to students with emotional or behavioral disorders (Chesapeake Institute, 1994; see also Kauffman, 1997), it is so vaguely worded that it is of little value in guiding the design of interventions (Kauffman & Landrum, 2006, 2009a).

Educators have described several different conceptual models of education over the decades (Kauffman & Landrum, 2006). A combination of models now guides most educational programs (see Kauffman & Landrum, 2009a, 2009b, for a description and case illustrations of models). All credible conceptual models have two objectives: (1) controlling misbehavior and (2) teaching students the academic and social skills they need. The models don't focus on one objective to the exclusion of the other, and they recognize the need for integrating all the educational, psychological, and social services these students require.

INTERNETRESOURCES

You may want to read the following blog: http://ebdblog.com

Balancing Behavioral Control with Academic and Social Learning

Some writers have suggested that the quality of educational programs for students with emotional or behavioral disorders is often dismal. The focus is often said to be on external control of students' behavior, and academic instruction and social learning are too often secondary or almost entirely neglected. Teachers might not have knowledge and skills in teaching basic skills such as reading (Coleman & Vaughn, 2000). Although the quality of instruction is undoubtedly low in too many programs, examples can be found of effective academic and social instruction for students at all levels (Lane & Menzies, 2010).

Behavioral control strategies are an essential part of educational programs for students with externalizing problems (Colvin, 2004). Without effective means of controlling disruptive behavior, it's extremely unlikely that academic and social learning will occur. Excellent academic instruction will certainly reduce many behavior problems as well as teach important academic skills (Kauffman et al., 2011; see also Kerr & Nelson, 2010; Lane & Menzies, 2010). Nevertheless, even the best instructional programs won't eliminate the disruptive behaviors of all students. Teachers of students with emotional or behavioral disorders must have effective control strategies, preferably involving students as much as possible in self-control. In addition, teachers must offer effective instruction in academic and social skills that will allow their students to live, learn, and work with others. Teachers must also allow students to make all the choices they can—manageable choices that are appropriate for the individual student (Jolivette, Stichter, & McCormick, 2002; Kauffman et al., 2011).

Importance of Integrated Services

Children and youths with emotional or behavioral disorders tend to have multiple and complex needs. For most, life is coming apart in more ways than one. In addition to their problems in school, they typically have family problems and a variety of difficulties in the community (e.g., engaging in illegal activities, an absence of desirable relationships with peers and adults, substance abuse, difficulty finding and maintaining employment). Thus, children or youths with emotional or behavioral disorders might need, in addition to special education, a variety of family-oriented services, psychotherapy or counseling, community supervision, training related to employment, and so on. No single service agency can meet the needs of most of these children and youths, but it is clear that school plays an important role (E. M. Z. Farmer & Farmer, 1999; Kauffman & Landrum, 2009b). Integrating these needed services into a more coordinated and effective effort is now seen as essential.

Strategies That Work

Successful strategies at all levels, from early intervention through transition, balance concern for academic and social skills and provide integrated services. These strategies include the following elements:

- *Systematic, data-based interventions*. Interventions are applied systematically and consistently and are based on reliable research.
- *Continuous assessment and progress monitoring*. Teachers conduct direct, daily assessment of performance, with planning based on this monitoring.
- *Practice of new skills*. Skills are not taught in isolation but are applied directly in everyday situations through modeling, rehearsal, and guided practice.
- *Treatment matched to problems*. Interventions are designed to meet the needs of individual students and their particular life circumstances and are not general formulas that ignore the nature, complexity, cultural context, and severity of the problem.
- *Multicomponent treatment*. Teachers and other professionals use as many different interventions as are necessary to meet the multiple needs of students (e.g., social skills training, academic remediation, medication, counseling or psychotherapy, and family treatment or parent training).

- *Programming for transfer and maintenance*. Interventions promote transfer of learning to new situations; quick fixes nearly always fail to produce generalized change.
- *Sustained intervention*. Many emotional or behavioral disorders are developmental disabilities and will not likely be cured but demand life-long support.

Service Delivery

Only a relatively small percentage of children and youths with emotional or behavioral disorders are officially identified and receive any special education or mental health services (Costello et al., 2005). Consequently, the individuals who do receive special education tend to have very serious problems, although most have typically been *assumed* to have only mild disabilities. Perhaps students identified as having emotional or behavioral disorders (who may have intellectual disabilities or learning disabilities as well) tend to be placed in more restrictive settings than students in other high-incidence categories because their disabilities are more severe. As Mattison (2004) has written, research verifies what teachers of students with emotional and behavioral disorders understand, "they teach students who are among the most dysfunctional youths in their community" (p. 177).

Undeniably, the problems of typical students with emotional or behavioral disorders are often more serious than many people have assumed. The term *severe* doesn't apply only to schizophrenia; a child can have a severe conduct disorder or severe depression, for example, and its disabling effects can be extremely serious and persistent.

Trends Toward Inclusion   Regardless of the nature or severity of the disorder, the trend in programs for students with emotional or behavioral disorders is toward integration into regular schools and classrooms. Even when students are placed in separate schools and classes, educators hope for reintegration into the mainstream. Integration of these students is typically difficult and requires intensive work on a case-by-case basis. Furthermore, some educators, researchers, and parents have made the case that students with emotional or behavioral disorders who are at high risk for continued problems need the structure and support of a special class; being in a separate class can be better than being included in general education (Kauffman, Bantz, & McCullough, 2002; Kauffman, Mock, Tankersley, & Landrum, in 2008). The accompanying Making It Work feature provides suggestions as to how teachers can collaborate to implement positive behavioral supports for students with emotional or behavioral disorders in the general education classroom.

Different Needs Require Different Placements   Placement decisions for students with emotional or behavioral disorders are particularly problematic. Educators who serve students with the most severe emotional or behavioral disorders provide ample justification for specialized environments for these children and youths. That is, it's impossible to replicate in the context of general education in a neighborhood school the intensive, individualized, highly structured environments with very high adult–student ratios offered in special classes and facilities (see Brigham & Kauffman, 1998; Kauffman & Brigham, 2009).

Hence, it's extremely important to maintain the full continuum of placement options for students with emotional or behavioral disorders as well as to make placement decisions on an individual basis after designing an appropriate program of education and related services. Students must not be placed outside general education classrooms and schools unless their needs require it. However, students' needs for appropriate education and safety take priority over placement in a less restrictive environment.

Instructional Considerations   Before being identified for special education, many students with emotional or behavioral disorders have been in general education where they could observe and learn from appropriate peer models. In reality, though, these students usually fail to imitate these models. They are unlikely to benefit merely from being with other students who have not been identified as disabled, because incidental social learning is insufficient to address their difficulties. For students with emotional or behavioral disorders to learn from peer models of appropriate behavior, most will require explicit, focused instruction about whom and what to imitate (Hallenbeck & Kauffman, 1995). In addition,

MAKING IT WORK

COLLABORATION AND CO-TEACHING WITH A TEACHER OF STUDENTS WITH EMOTIONAL OR BEHAVIORAL DISORDERS

"I don't want him in my classroom if he can't follow the rules!"

Statewide standards to improve educational outcomes and policies of zero tolerance to increase the safety of public schools have placed increased pressure on all teachers. These two issues, combined with the fact that many general educators do not receive training in more than routine classroom management, often make a teacher hesitant to collaborate with special educators to include students with emotional or behavioral disorders, even though many students who create discipline problems are not identified as having a disability. The increase in disciplinary concerns in schools is actually a great reason for general educators to collaborate with teachers skilled in assessing and managing behavior.

WHAT DOES IT MEAN TO BE A TEACHER OF STUDENTS WITH EMOTIONAL OR BEHAVIORAL DISORDERS?

The expertise of a teacher of students with emotional or behavioral disorders includes understanding, assessing, and managing behavior to promote learning across the content areas. Specifically, the Council for Exceptional Children (2008) has identified the following as those skills necessary for beginning teachers of students with emotional or behavioral disorders:

1. Know a variety of prevention and intervention strategies for individuals who are at risk of emotional or behavioral disorders.

2. Use a variety of nonaversive techniques to control targeted behavior and maintain attention of individuals with emotional or behavioral disorders.

3. Establish a consistent classroom routine, and use skills in problem solving and conflict resolution.

4. Plan and implement individualized reinforcement systems and environmental modifications at levels equal to the intensity of the behavior.

5. Understand the advantages and limitations of instructional strategies and practices for teaching individuals with emotional or behavioral disorders.

6. Assess appropriate and problematic social behaviors of individuals.

SUCCESSFUL STRATEGIES FOR CO-TEACHING

Recent research has validated the use of positive behavioral support (PBS) for students with chronically challenging be-

haviors (U.S. Department of Education, 2009). According to the technical assistance positive behavior support

> is an application of a behaviorally-based systems approach to enhance the capacity of schools, families, and communities to design effective environments that improve the fit or link between research-validated practices and the environments in which teaching and learning occurs. Attention is focused on creating and sustaining primary (school-wide), secondary (classroom), and tertiary (individual) systems of support that improve lifestyle results (personal, health, social, family, work, recreation) for all children and youth by making problem behavior less effective, efficient, and relevant, and desired behavior more functional.

Lewis (2000) identifies six steps in developing PBS plans for individual students in any classroom (tertiary intervention). These steps provide a unique opportunity for collaboration among general and special education faculty. Special and general educators can work together on each step to lighten the workload, provide different perspectives, and improve consistency:

- Step 1. Define the behavior operationally. Each teacher can provide feedback to the others to pinpoint exactly what the student is doing in the classroom, not just stating, "He's disruptive."

- Step 2. Conduct a functional behavioral assessment (FBA). FBAs are time-consuming and include observing, analyzing, and hypothesizing about the behavior. Two (or more) teachers working together can observe the student at different times and in different situations, using both formalized and informal observation systems, without losing time with the rest of the class. They can also analyze data together to move to Step 3.

- Step 3. Develop a hypothesis about why the student engages in the behavior.

- Step 4. Target a replacement behavior. What do the teachers want the student to do instead of the unwanted behavior? Teachers who know the student well then work together to identify this behavior, task analyze it, and describe what skills the student has and does not have in order to set up a teaching scheme for this new behavior (Step 5).

- Step 5. The teachers work together to teach the student the new behavior, reinforce it in the classroom, and verify that it is achieving the goals for both student and teachers.

- Step 6. Modify the environment enough that the previous inappropriate behavior does not result in the same outcome. This can be the most difficult part and require the greatest amount of teamwork. The student will probably still try the old behavior. Teachers will hope not to see it again and can become discouraged if they do. It is at this point that teachers working together will need to support one another and to

enlist other collaborators, such as administrators, parents, and other teachers, to keep the plan going.

More information about PBS is available at the Office of Special Education Program's Technical Assistance Center on Positive Behavioral Interventions and Supports at www .pbis.org/

• By Margaret P. Weiss

they might need explicit and intensive instruction in social skills, including when, where, and how to exhibit specific types of behavior (Walker et al., 2004).

The academic curriculum for most students with emotional or behavioral disorders parallels that for most students. The basic academic skills have a great deal of survival value for any individual in society who is capable of learning them; failure to teach a student to read, write, and perform basic arithmetic deprives that student of any reasonable chance for successful adjustment to the demands of everyday life. Students who don't acquire academic skills that allow them to compete with their peers are likely to be socially rejected (Kauffman & Landrum, 2009b; Lane & Menzies, 2010).

Need for Social Skills   Most students with emotional or behavioral disorders need specific instruction in social skills. We emphasize two points: (1) Effective methods are needed to teach basic academic skills, and (2) social skills and affective experiences are as crucial as academic skills. How to manage one's feelings and behavior and how to get along with other people are essential features of the curriculum for many students with emotional or behavioral disorders. These children cannot be expected to learn such skills without instruction, because the ordinary processes of socialization obviously have failed (Walker et al., 2004).

Students with schizophrenia and other major psychiatric disorders vary widely in their behaviors and learning problems. Some might need hospitalization and intensive treatment; others might remain at home and attend regular public schools. Again, the trend today is away from placement in institutions or special schools and toward inclusion in regular public schools. In some cases, students with major psychiatric disorders who attend regular schools are enrolled in special classes.

Needs of Juvenile Delinquents   Educational arrangements for juvenile delinquents are hard to describe in general terms because *delinquency* is a legal term, not an educational distinction, and because programs for extremely troubled youths vary so much among states and localities. Special classes or schools are sometimes provided for youths who have histories of threatening, violent, or disruptive behavior. Some of these classes and schools are administered under special education law, but others aren't because the pupils assigned to them aren't considered emotionally disturbed. In jails, reform schools, and other detention facilities that house children and adolescents, educational practices vary widely. Education of incarcerated children and youths with disabilities is governed by the same laws that apply to those who are not incarcerated, but the laws aren't always carefully implemented. Many incarcerated children don't receive assessment and education appropriate for their needs because of lack of resources, poor cooperation among agencies, and the attitude that delinquents and criminals are not entitled to the same educational opportunities as law-abiding citizens (Kauffman & Landrum, 2009b; Nelson et al., 2004).

Special Challenges for Teachers   Given all this, it is clear that teachers of students with emotional or behavioral disorders need to be able to tolerate a great deal of unpleasantness and rejection without becoming counteraggressive or withdrawn. These students have been rejected by others; if kindness and concern were the only things they needed, they probably wouldn't be considered to have disabilities. Teachers cannot expect caring and decency always to be returned and must be sure of their own values and confident of their teaching and living skills. They must be able and willing to make wise choices for students who choose to behave unwisely (Kauffman & Landrum, 2009b; Kauffman et al., 2011; Kerr & Nelson, 2010).

Disciplinary Considerations

Classroom management and discipline are recognized as among the most difficult problems of teachers, both general and special education (Evertson & Weinstein, 2006; Kauffman et al., 2011). Students with emotional or behavioral disorders make behavior management even harder. Educators are now placing great emphasis on positive behavioral supports and behavior intervention plans for students with emotional and behavioral disorders. Increasingly, researchers recognize that problem behavior occurs less frequently in the classroom when the teacher is offering effective instruction, even though good instruction alone often isn't enough to resolve behavior problems.

Discipline is a controversial topic, especially for students with disabilities who exhibit behavior problems. Many teachers and school administrators are confused about what's legal. Special rules do apply in some cases to students who have been identified as having disabilities. In some instances, the typical school rules apply; in others, they don't. The issues are particularly controversial for students with emotional or behavioral disorders because, although their behavior might be severely problematic, the causes of their misbehavior are often difficult to determine.

Uncertainty or controversy usually surrounds a change in a student's placement or suspension or expulsion due to very serious misbehavior such as bringing a weapon or illegal drugs to school. IDEA discipline provisions for students with disabilities are intended to maintain a safe school environment without violating the rights of students with disabilities to fair discipline, taking the effects of their disability into consideration (see Mayer & Cornell, 2010; Yell, Katsyiannis, & Bradley, 2011).

Zero Tolerance   One of the most dramatic and controversial measures involving discipline for serious offenses is known as **zero tolerance** (Skiba & Rausch, 2006). School administrators and teachers have been assumed to abuse their discretion in determining the punishment for certain serious offenses, such as bringing a weapon to school. Therefore, higher authorities (e.g., boards of education) in many cases removed discretion from the hands of teachers and lower administrators. The higher authorities prescribed a given punishment such as long-term suspension or expulsion for a particular offense, regardless of the circumstances surrounding the act. For example, an elementary school child who accidentally takes a paring knife to school in her lunch box might be expelled. A high school student who forgets to remove a roofing knife from his pocket and turns it in at the office because he knows he should not have it in school might be expelled. A student with intellectual disability who brings a toy gun to school, even though he does not understand that a gun is a weapon and even toy weapons are forbidden in school, might be expelled. The zero-tolerance rationale simply does not allow any exceptions for extenuating circumstances.

Teachers and school administrators are often unsure of just what freedom and constraints the law allows them in disciplining students with disabilities, even if they have a policy of zero tolerance. They must struggle with balancing the rights of students with disabilities against the common good of maintaining a safe and orderly school environment.

Violence, disorder, and drugs in schools are serious problems that must be addressed (Mayer & Cornell, 2010). However, a fixed penalty for a given behavior without considering any circumstance or student characteristic presents particular problems for special education. All educators recognize the need for reasonable schoolwide discipline that brings a high degree of uniformity to consequences for particular acts (e.g., Fenning & Bohanon, 2006; Liaupsin, Jolivette, & Scott, 2004; Martella, Nelson, & Marchand-Martella, 2003). Nevertheless, special educators also argue for exceptions based on the relevance of the student's disability to the event in question, and note that zero tolerance has not made schools safer places (see Skiba & Rausch, 2006).

Manifestation Determination   Special rules apply to managing some of the serious misbehavior of students who are identified as having disabilities. Again, in some cases, the typical school rules apply, but in others, they don't (see Bateman & Linden, 2006; Huefner, 2006; Yell, 2006; Yell et al., 2011). In any case, much of the special education advocacy regarding discipline is based on finding alternatives to suspension and expulsion for bringing weapons or drugs to school or for endangering others. Keeping students out of school is not an effective way of helping them learn how to behave acceptably.

Three concepts and related procedures provide the basis for much of the controversy surrounding the discipline of students with disabilities:

1. Determine whether the behavior is or is not a manifestation of the student's disability.
2. Provide an alternative placement for the student's education for an interim period if temporary removal from the student's present placement is necessary.
3. Develop positive, proactive behavior intervention plans.

Deciding whether a student's misbehavior is or is not a manifestation of disability is called a **manifestation determination (MD)**, based on the idea that it would be unfair to punish students for engaging in misbehavior that is part of their disability. However, if the misbehavior is not a manifestation of disability, then the usual punishment for students without disabilities should apply. For example, if a misbehavior is the result of a seizure or other neurological disorder or a manifestation of intellectual incapacity or emotional disturbance, then the student should not be punished for it.

The manifestation determination is a highly controversial issue, and some writers believe that it is more political than educational in purpose (Sasso, Conroy, Stichter, & Fox, 2001). Some people argue that the process actually undermines fairness because the rules or procedures for the MD are not entirely objective, requiring subjective judgment about the causes of misbehavior (Sasso et al., 2001).

Functional Behavioral Assessment   IDEA calls for **functional behavioral assessment (FBA)** if the student's behavior is persistently a problem, but the meaning of *functional assessment* isn't entirely clear in the context of the law. FBA assists educators in determining and altering the factors that account for a student's misconduct. Nevertheless, precisely what the law requires of special educators and other school personnel regarding FBA is often uncertain (Landrum, 2000; Mueller, Edwards, & Trahant, 2003; Sasso et al., 2001; Sugai & Horner, 1999–2000). Apparently, the intent of the law is to require teachers to assess student behavior in ways that lead to the selection of effective intervention strategies and to figure out how to support desirable behavior. The accompanying Responsive Instruction feature offers suggestions about how teachers can use FBA in figuring out how best to manage problem behavior.

Supports for Desired Behavior

Perhaps the most critical part of the discipline provisions of IDEA is the requirement that schools must devise a **positive behavioral intervention plan (BIP)** for a student with disabilities who has behavior problems. The emphasis of this requirement is on creating proactive and positive interventions and avoiding punishment. When discipline is involved, the school must reevaluate the student's IEP and make efforts to address the misconduct that led to the problem, using positive (nonpunitive) means to the greatest extent possible.

An approach with support from research is **positive behavioral intervention and support (PBIS)** (Kauffman, Nelson, Simpson, & Mock, 2011). It integrates valued outcomes, the science of human behavior, validated procedures, and systems change to enhance quality of life and reduce problem behavior. Its primary goal is to improve the link between research-validated practices and the environments in which teaching and learning occur. This behaviorally based systems approach enhances the capacity of schools, families, and communities to design effective teaching and learning environments that improve lifestyle results (personal, health, social, family, work, recreation, etc.) for all children and youth. These environments apply contextually and culturally appropriate interventions to make problem behavior less effective, efficient, and relevant and to make desired behavior

INTERNETRESOURCES

If you search the Internet for "manifestation determination," you will find numerous sites describing what information is considered, what the law requires, and how the process should work.

INTERNETRESOURCES

Information about positive behavioral intervention and support (PBIS) and its role in school-wide discipline and teaching may be found at http://www.pbis.org

RESPONSIVE *INSTRUCTION*
MEETING THE NEEDS OF STUDENTS WITH EMOTIONAL OR BEHAVIORAL DISORDERS

Functional Behavioral Assessments

WHAT THE RESEARCH SAYS

Functional behavioral assessments (FBAs) have become standard practice in the development of Individualized Education Programs (IEPs), particularly the behavior intervention plan (BIP) component, for students with emotional or behavioral disabilities. Under IDEA, school districts are required to conduct an FBA and a BIP for any student who receives disciplinary action that results in more than 10 days' suspension or a change in placement due to disciplinary issues. Unfortunately, the implementation of these assessments varies greatly, as does, then, the efficacy of the tool (Fox & Davis, 2005; Sasso et al., 2001). When implemented correctly, research clearly demonstrates the effectiveness of the interventions employed based on FBAs (Fox & Davis, 2005). Thus, the burden is on school districts to ensure FBAs are implemented to the empirical standards established in the research.

RESEARCH STUDY

Van Acker and colleagues (Van Acker, Boreson, Gable, & Patterson, 2005) conducted an analysis of FBAs and BIPs created across a state to determine the prevalence of "best practices" in implementation. This analysis followed a 3-year effort on behalf of the state to provide FBA training to teachers in the form of 1- and 2-day workshops. More than 200 school districts and intermediary agencies participated in the training. It is important to note that many schools sent limited representatives to the state training. These representatives would then return to their home school and provide information to fellow IEP team members who had not attended the training. After completion of the training sessions, 71 IEP teams voluntarily submitted their FBA/BIPs for review for the study. Researchers scored each FBA/BIP using a standard rating scale.

RESEARCH FINDINGS

Despite the statewide initiative related to high-quality FBA/BIP development, the majority of plans reviewed exhibited serious flaws. The most prevalent issues follow:

1. *Failure to identify specific target behaviors.* The overarching goal of FBA/BIP is to reduce, eliminate, or replace challenging behaviors; thus, the failure to identify a clearly measurable target behavior results in an unfocused plan or a plan that was not directly connected to the behavior(s) of concern. A related flaw was to assume that a cluster of behaviors (e.g., hitting, swearing, and noncompliance) all re-

lated to the same function and therefore, different assessments for each behavior were not conducted.

2. *Failure to verify the hypothesized function of the behavior.* As teams are developing the FBA, they hypothesize the function of behavior of concern. In other words, they generate a hypothesis as to *why* the student is behaving in an undesirable manner. Teams can test the hypothesis through variable manipulation (e.g., if the hypothesized function was teacher attention, teacher attention could be removed to see if the behavior escalated). Similarly, teams could use data triangulation—the use of more than one data source in order to support the hypothesis. Teams typically did not show evidence of attempting to verify hypotheses before developing interventions.

3. *Failure to connect the function of the behavior to the specific interventions identified in the BIP.* In the study, the most significant (and problematic) flaw was that the BIPs failed to directly address the issues identified in the FBA. Researchers could clearly link only 25 of the interventions to the function of the behavior and the promotion of desirable and appropriate behaviors. Ideally, educators create BIPs using the principles of positive behavioral intervention and support—creating environmental conditions and reinforcers to promote desired behaviors. In contrast to positive intervention and behavioral support, 56 of the plans submitted included overreliance on aversive consequences. In some cases, these aversive consequences served the *same function* as the undesirable behavior. For example, if the FBA indicated that a student skipped class (i.e., "escaped") due to a skill deficit, the BIP would then call for suspension as the aversive consequence in response to skipping. Clearly, this consequence has the capacity to increase rather than decrease the undesired behavior!

APPLYING THE RESEARCH TO TEACHING

To avoid falling into the same pitfalls identified in their study, Van Acker and colleagues (2005) created the following checklist for teams to self-evaluate their plans:

1. Clearly identify target behavior.
2. Verify hypothesized target behavior function.
3. Develop clear BIP indicating function of the behavior met through alternative, desirable behavior.

4. Indicate positive behavioral supports.
5. Modify physical or social context as a part of BIP.
6. Plan for monitoring and evaluating BIP.

As a final note, Van Acker and colleagues did find that the higher quality FBA/BIPs were those submitted by teams who had

at least one member of the group with significant training (e.g., coursework in applied behavior analysis, district or state training in FBA). Thus, school districts and school personnel should actively seek out training and support for all IEP members.

• By Kristin L. Sayeski

■ ■ ■ ■ ■ ■ ■ ■ ■

more functional. However, it does recognize the value of nonviolent negative consequences (punishment) in managing behavior.

Interim Alternative Educational Setting   IDEA includes allowances for schools to use an **interim alternative educational setting (IAES)** in the discipline of a student with disabilities who can not be managed satisfactorily in the general education classroom or school. For example, an IAES might be a separate special school serving students with behavior problems, a separate arrangement within the public school similar to in-school suspension, or a self-contained classroom. IAES is intended to encourage schools to use such alternatives rather than suspension or expulsion. The law doesn't define what an IAES must be, but only what it must provide: a continuation of education and modifications spelled out in the student's individualized education program (IEP). The IAES must also include specific programming to address and prevent the recurrence of the behavior that prompted the placement. Schools might use such settings for students with serious behavior problems as a way of preserving order and manageability of the typical classroom and school. However, regardless of the setting in which a student with emotional or behavioral disorders is placed, special educators should try to provide the most positive and functional behavioral support they can offer (Yell et al., 2011).

How Successful Are MDs, FBAs, PBIS, and IAES?   The struggle to resolve discipline issues involving students with disabilities is ongoing. On the one hand, school administrators want the highest possible degree of uniformity of expectations (i.e., the same high expectations for all students). On the other hand, special educators and other advocates for students with disabilities see the absolute uniformity of disciplinary rules as failure to accommodate students' individual abilities and needs. The legal requirements regarding discipline, including suspension and expulsion, will continue to evolve as educators find more productive ways of dealing with serious misconduct. It is difficult to determine whether misbehavior is a function of a child's disability, and manifestation determinations will continue to be a matter of controversy for as long as the law requires them.

What are the components of a useful FBA? Can classroom teachers conduct such analyses without help from others? Some suggest that the FBA is considerably more complicated than many people think and that the law (IDEA) may have gotten considerably ahead of teachers' ability to do the necessary analyses. Although the idea is good, and a few educators may be able to perform a useful FBA, many functional analyses are poorly done (Fox & Gable, 2004). Can the manifestation of a disability always be found? What should we do if a disability's manifestation is unknown? In what settings can educators provide the necessary supports for positive behavior? With the proper behavioral supports, can a student with any emotional or behavioral disorder succeed in the general education environment? These and other questions will no doubt perplex educators for many decades to come.

ASSESSMENT OF PROGRESS

The ongoing assessment program for students with emotional or behavioral disorders should include measures that address several domains of social-emotional behavior that influence academic learning, including interpersonal skills, study skills, motivation, and engagement (DiPerna, 2006). Teachers typically use rating scales and direct observation to monitor students' progress in behavioral interventions.

Several rating scales are available to assess students' social skills. The School Social Behavior Scales (SSBS-2; Merrell, 2002) evaluates social competence and antisocial behavior and should be completed by teachers or other school personnel. Each of the two scales comprises 32 items divided into the following subscales: Peer Relations, Self-Management-Compliance, Academic Behavior, Hostile-Irritable, Anitsocial-Aggressive, and Defiant-Disruptive.

The Learning and Study Strategies Inventory (Weinstein, Palmer, & Schulte, 2002) is a self-report instrument appropriate for high school (LASSI-HS) and college students (LASSI) to assess learning and study strategies. LASSI scales include measures of attitude, motivation, time management, anxiety, concentration, study aids, and test strategies.

The Academic Competence Evaluation Scales (ACES; DiPerna & Elliott, 2000) is a measure that assesses both academic skills as well as social and behavioral skills that lead to academic success. The academic components of the ACES are reading and language arts, mathematics, and critical thinking. In addition to the academic skills, ACES measures motivation, engagement, study skills, and interpersonal skills. It's appropriate for students in K–12 settings as well as college students. A goal-attainment scale specifically measures the progress of students and helps evaluate the effects of an intervention.

EARLY INTERVENTION

Early identification and prevention are basic goals for any category of disability. For students with emotional or behavioral disorders, these goals present particular difficulties—yet also hold particular promise (Dunlap et al., 2006; Walker & Sprague, 2007). The difficulties are related to the definition and measurement of emotional or behavioral disorders, especially in young children; the particular promise is that young children's social-emotional behavior is quite flexible, so preventive efforts seem to have a good chance of success (Kauffman, 1999, 2005; Kauffman & Brigham, 2009).

As Thomas and Guskin remarked, "Diagnosis of disruptive behaviors in very young children is challenging because they appear to respond to a variety of risk factors with similar hyperactive, aggressive, and defiant behaviors" (2001, p. 50). Nevertheless, early identification and prevention of emotional or behavioral disorders—or, what some have termed "challenging behavior"—is possible (Qi & Kaiser, 2003). Table 8.1 suggests three ways in which parents and educators might prevent such behavior.

The patterns of behavior that signal problems for the preschool child are those that bring them into frequent conflict with, or keep them aloof from, their parents or caretakers and their siblings or peers. Many children who are referred to clinics for disruptive behavior when they are 7 to 12 years of age showed clear signs of behavior problems by the time they were 3 or 4—or even younger. Infants or toddlers who exhibit a very "difficult temperament"—who are irritable; have irregular patterns of sleeping, eating, and eliminating; have highly intense responses to many stimuli and negative reactions toward new situations—are at risk for developing serious behavior problems unless their parents are particularly skillful at handling them. Children of preschool age are likely to elicit negative responses from adults and playmates if they are much more aggressive or much more withdrawn than most children their age. (Remember the critical importance of same-age comparisons. Toddlers frequently grab what they want, push other children down, and throw things and kick and scream when they don't get their way; toddlers normally don't have much finesse at social interaction and often hide from strangers.)

TABLE 8.1 Prevention of challenging behavior

1. Children and their families who access mental and physical care are less likely to have behavioral and social problems.
2. Nurturing and positive parenting is associated with children who have healthy relationships and reduced challenging behavior.
3. High-quality early education environments and caregiver interactions are associated with fewer behavior problems and the development of social competence.

Source: From "Prevention and Intervention with Young Children's Challenging Behavior: Perspectives Regarding Current Knowledge," by G. Dunlap, P. S. Strain, L. Fox, J. J. Carta, M. Conroy, B. J. Smith, et al. *Behavioral Disorders, 32,* 29–45. Table 1, p. 33. Copyright © 2006 by the Council for Exceptional Children. Reprinted with permission.

Because children's behavior is quite responsive to conditions in the social environment and can be shaped by adults, the potential for primary prevention—preventing serious behavior problems from occurring in the first place—would seem to be great. If parents and teachers could be taught effective child management skills, perhaps many or most cases could be prevented. Furthermore, one could imagine that if parents and teachers had such skills, children who already have emotional or behavioral disorders could be prevented from getting worse (secondary prevention). But the task of primary prevention is not that simple. For one thing, the tremendous amount of money and personnel that are needed for training in child management are not available. For another, even if the money and personnel could be found, professionals would not always agree on what patterns of behavior should be prevented or on how undesirable behavior could be prevented from developing (Kauffman, 1999, 2005).

If overly aggressive or withdrawn behavior is identified in a preschooler, what kind of intervention program is most desirable? Behavioral interventions are usually effective. A behavioral approach implies defining and measuring the child's behaviors and rearranging the environment (especially adults' and other children's responses to the problem child) to teach and support more appropriate conduct. In the case of aggressive children, social rewards for aggression should be prevented. For example, hitting another child or throwing a temper tantrum might result in brief social isolation or time-out instead of adult attention or getting one's own way (see Kauffman & Brigham, 2009; Kazdin, 2008).

In summary, it is possible to identify at an early age those children who are at high risk for emotional or behavioral disorders. These children exhibit extreme aggression or social withdrawal and may be socially rejected or identify with deviant peers. They should be identified as early as possible, and their parents and teachers should learn how to teach them essential social skills and how to manage their problem behavior using positive, nonviolent procedures. If children with emotional or behavioral disorders are identified very early and intervention is sufficiently comprehensive, intense, and sustained, then there's a good chance that they can recover and exhibit developmentally normal patterns of behavior.

Nevertheless, research suggests that in practice early intervention typically doesn't occur (Dunlap et al., 2006; Kauffman, 2010). The primary reasons given for the rarity of early, comprehensive, intense, and sustained intervention include worry about labeling and stigma, optimism regarding the child's development (i.e., the assumption that the child will "grow out of it"), lack of resources required to address the needs of any but the most severely problematic children, and ignorance about the early signs of emotional or behavioral problems.

TRANSITION TO ADULTHOOD

Programs designed for adolescents with emotional or behavioral disorders vary widely in aims and structure (Cheney & Bullis, 2004; Nelson et al., 2004). Nelson and Kauffman (1977) describe the following types, which remain the basic options today:

- Regular public high school classes
- Consultant teachers who work with general education teachers to provide individualized academic work and behavior management
- Resource rooms and special self-contained classes to which students may be assigned for part or all of the school day
- Work-study programs in which vocational education and job experience are combined with academic study
- Special private or public schools that offer the regular high school curriculum in a different setting
- Alternative schools that offer highly individualized programs that are nontraditional in both setting and content
- Private or public residential schools

Incarcerated youths with emotional or behavioral disorders are an especially neglected group in special education (Nelson et al., 2004). The special educational needs of many (or most) of these teenagers who are in prison might be neglected because incarcerated youths are defined as socially maladjusted rather than emotionally disturbed. The current federal definition appears to allow denial of special education services to a large number of young people who exhibit extremely serious misbehaviors and have long histories of school failure.

It is difficult to design special education programs at the secondary level for students with emotional or behavioral disorders; this category of youths is so varied. Adolescents categorized for special education purposes as emotionally disturbed may have behavioral characteristics ranging from extreme withdrawal to aggressive delinquency, intelligence ranging from severely disabled to highly gifted, and academic skills ranging from preschool to college level. It's hardly realistic to suggest that any single type of program or model will be appropriate for all such youths. In fact, youths with emotional or behavioral disorders, perhaps more than any other category of exceptionality, need a highly individualized, creative, and flexible education. Programs may range from teaching daily living skills in a sheltered environment to advanced placement in college, from general education placement to hospitalization, and from the traditional curriculum to unusual and specialized vocational training (see Brolin & Loyd, 2004; Sitlington & Clark, 2006).

Transition from school to work and adult life is particularly difficult for adolescents with emotional or behavioral disorders. Many of them lack the basic academic skills necessary for successful employment. In addition, they often behave in ways that prevent them from being accepted, liked, and helped by classmates, employers, co-workers, and neighbors. It is not surprising that students with emotional or behavioral disorders are among the most likely to drop out of school and among the most difficult to train in transition programs (Cheney & Bullis, 2004; Sitlington & Clark, 2006).

Brolin and Loyd (2004) provide a case example of a student with "emotional/behavioral disturbance":

> Stephen is a 16-year-old boy who has difficulty building and maintaining satisfactory relationships with his peers and teachers. In most of his general education classes, he is inattentive and fails to complete class assignments, which has resulted in a lack of academic progress. Stephen functions at the eighth grade level in both reading and mathematics. Sometimes Stephen appears to be depressed and unhappy. His behavior in class and in nonacademic settings is often inappropriate and immature. (p. 240)

Many children and youths with emotional or behavioral disorders grow up to be adults who have real difficulties leading independent, productive lives. The outlook is especially grim for children and adolescents with conduct disorders. Contrary to popular opinion, the child or youth who is shy, anxious, or neurotic is not the most likely to have psychiatric problems as an adult. Rather, it is the conduct-disordered (hyperaggressive) child or youth whose adulthood is most likely to be characterized by socially intolerable behavior and lack of social competence (Walker et al., 2004). About half the children who are hyperaggressive will have problems that require legal intervention or psychiatric care when they are adults.

Successful transition to adult life is often complicated by neglectful, abusive, or inadequate family relationships. A high percentage of adolescents with conduct disorder have family relationships of this nature. However, the emphasis on punishment and imprisonment, particularly of African American males, appears to be counterproductive. The emphasis on punishment contributes to family deterioration and harsh conditions of life that perpetuate undesirable conduct.

Examples of relatively successful high school and transition programs are available, most of which employ a behavioral approach (Cheney & Bullis, 2004). However, it is important to stress the term *relatively*. Educators have known for decades that many adolescents and young adults with severe conduct disorder appear to have a true developmental disability that requires intervention throughout their life span (Wolf, Braukmann, & Ramp, 1987). By the time these antisocial youths reach high school, the aim of even the most effective program is to help them accommodate their disabilities. Rather than focusing on remediation of academic and social skills, these programs attempt to teach youths the skills they will need to survive and cope in school and community, to make a transition to work, and to develop vocations (Walker et al., 2004).

SUMMARY

What terminology is used to describe emotional or behavioral disorders?

- The current term in federal laws is *emotionally disturbed*.
- The terminology of various states and localities is varied and sometimes confusing; it includes a variety of combinations of terms such as *emotional disturbance*, *behavioral disorder*, and *social maladjustment*.

What is the definition of emotional or behavioral disorder?

- Any definition generally refers to behavior that goes to an extreme, a problem that is chronic, and behavior that is unacceptable because of social or cultural expectations.
- The current federal definition lists five characteristics, any one of which must be exhibited to a marked extent and over a period of time and adversely affect educational performance:
  - Inability to learn
  - Inability to establish satisfactory relationships
  - Inappropriate behavior
  - Pervasive unhappiness or depression
  - Physical symptoms, pains, or fears
- The major points of the definition of the National Mental Health and Special Education Coalition are that the behavior:
  - Is more than a temporary, expected response to stressful events in the environment
  - Is consistently exhibited in two different settings, at least one of which is school
  - Is unresponsive to direct intervention in general education, or the child's condition is such that general education interventions would be insufficient.

How are emotional or behavioral disorders classified?

- Psychiatric classifications are not very useful to teachers.
- The most useful and reliable classifications are based on the primary dimensions of externalizing (acting against others) and internalizing (acting against self).

What is the prevalence of emotional or behavioral disorders?

- Most studies suggest that 5% to 10% of the child population have such disorders.
- Special education and mental health serve only a fraction of those needing help for serious disorders (i.e., about 1% of the child population).

What are the causes of emotional or behavioral disorders?

- Causes are multiple and complex, and seldom can a single cause be identified.
- Major causal factors include biology, family, school, and culture.

How are emotional or behavioral disorders identified?

- Teacher judgment plays the most significant role.
- Most students are below average in tested intelligence and academic achievement.
- Students exhibit externalizing (aggressive toward others) or internalizing (immature, withdrawn, depressed) behavior or a combination of the two.

What are the major educational considerations regarding emotional or behavioral disorders?

- A balance between behavioral control and academic instruction is required.
- Integrated services are important.
- Strategies that work best include the following:
  - Systematic, data-based interventions
  - Continuous assessment and monitoring of progress
  - Provision for practice of new skills
  - Treatment matched to the problem
  - Multicomponent treatment
  - Programming for transfer and maintenance
  - Commitment to sustained intervention
- Service delivery emphasizes inclusion when appropriate and the importance of a full continuum of alternative placements.
- Instruction should be highly structured and relevant to the student's life.
- Special disciplinary considerations include functional behavioral assessment (FBA) and positive behavioral intervention and support (PBIS).

How do professionals assess the progress of students with emotional or behavioral disorders?

- Professionals may use a variety of standardized scales and observations to assess behavior; curriculum-based measurement is recommended for assessing academic progress.
- Testing accommodations might involve alterations in scheduling, such as extended time, or presentation, such as having directions read aloud.

What are important considerations in early intervention for learners with emotional or behavioral disorders?

- Early intervention is often suggested but seldom practiced.

What are important considerations in transition to adulthood for learners with emotional or behavioral disorders?

- Transition is difficult but particularly important because the long-term and employment outcomes for most students are not good.

COUNCIL FOR EXCEPTIONAL CHILDREN

Addressing the Professional Standards

Council for Exceptional Children (CEC) Common Core Knowledge and Skills addressed in this chapter: ICC1K2, ICC1K5, ICC1K6, ICC1K8, ICC2K1, ICC2K2, ICC2K3, ICC2K4, ICC2K5, ICC2K6, ICC3K1, ICC4S6, ICC5K2, ICC5K6, ICC5S4, ICC5S5, ICC5S10, ICC7S7, ICC8K4, ICC8S1, ICC8S2, ICC8S4, ICC8S6, ICC8S8, ICC9K3, ICC10K2, ICC10K3, ICC10S3, ICC10S6

Appendix: Provides a full listing of the CEC Common Core Standards and associated Knowledge and Skill Statements listed here.

MYEDUCATIONLAB

myeducationlab Now go to Topic 10: Emotional or Behavioral Disorders in the MyEducationLab (www.myeducationlab.com) for your course, where you can:

- Find learning outcomes for the broad concepts covered in this chapter along with the national standards that connect to these outcomes.
- Complete Assignments and Activities that can help you more deeply understand the chapter content.
- Examine challenging situations and cases presented in the IRIS Center Resources.
- Apply and practice your understanding of the core concepts and skills identified in the chapter with the Building Teaching Skills and Dispositions learning units.
- Check your comprehension on the content covered in the chapter by going to the Study Plan in the Book-Specific Resources for your text. Here you will be able to take a chapter quiz, receive feedback on your answers, and then access Review, Practice, and Enrichment activities to enhance your understanding of chapter content.
- Watch video clips of CCSSO Teacher of the Year award winners responding to the question: "Why I teach?" in the Teacher Talk section.

MISCONCEPTIONS ABOUT
Learners with Autism Spectrum Disorders

MYTH • Autism is a single, well-defined category of disability.

FACT • Autism comprises a wide spectrum of disorders and ranges from very severe to very mild.

MYTH • People with autism spectrum disorders are intellectually disabled and can't be involved in higher education or professions.

FACT • Autism spectrum disorders include people from the full range of intellectual capacity. Although a high percentage do have intellectual disabilities, many with milder forms, such as Asperger syndrome, are highly intelligent, earn graduate degrees, and are successful professionals.

MYTH • All people with autism are impaired in some cognitive areas but are highly intelligent or geniuses in other areas.

FACT • Only a very few people with autism have extraordinary skills. Called *autistic savants*, these individuals are not geniuses in the traditional sense, but they possess very highly developed splinter skills—skills that are in isolation from functional skills.

MYTH • There is an autism epidemic that must be due to something dangerous in our environment, such as a toxin or virus.

FACT • The number of diagnosed cases of autism has undoubtedly increased. Most authorities assert that this can be accounted for by three things: a widening of the criteria used to diagnose autism, including the recognition of milder forms such as Asperger syndrome; a greater awareness of autism in the general public as well as in the medical, psychological, and educational professions; and diagnosing people as autistic who previously would have received a different diagnosis, e.g., intellectually disabled (mentally retarded).

MYTH • The measles, mumps, and rubella (MMR) vaccine causes autism.

FACT • The Institute of Medicine of the National Academies commissioned a review of available evidence and concluded that the evidence favors rejection of a causal relationship between MMR vaccine and autism.

MYTH • Bad parenting, especially cold, nonresponsive mothering ("refrigerator moms") can cause autism.

FACT • No evidence indicates that bad parenting can cause autism. Furthermore, even if a parent is relatively unresponsive, this might be in reaction to the infant's low level of arousal or because of parental stress regarding the child's abnormal behavior.

myeducationlab

To check your comprehension on the content covered in Chapter 9, go to the Book-Specific Resources in the MyEducationLab (www.myeducationlab.com) for your course, select your text, and complete the Study Plan. Here you will be able to take a chapter quiz, receive feedback on your answers, and then access review, practice, and enrichment activities to enhance your understanding of chapter content. ■

As the poignant words of Tim Page attest, people with autism are often misunderstood. This misunderstanding often arises because, as Page describes, people with autism don't understand the social cues of others. They are, indeed, clueless about how odd their behavior appears and the effect it can have on others. It's important to point out that the peculiar behavior highlighted by Page—impaired ability to read social cues—is only one of myriad aberrant perceptual, cognitive, linguistic, and social behaviors that individuals with autism might display. And although some consistent patterns to the deficits accompany autism, a great deal of variation in symptoms also is exhibited by those who are autistic. Not only do the symptoms vary, but the severity of the symptoms can be wide ranging. Some have deficits so severe that communicating with them requires enormous effort. Others, like Page, a Pulitzer Prize-winning music critic for the *The Washington Post*, function in many respects at a very high level. Before turning to the definition of autism and its variants, such as Asperger syndrome, it's helpful to provide some historical context to the discussion.

HISTORICAL CONTEXT: KANNER'S AND ASPERGER'S PAPERS

The seminal work in the field of autism began with two scientific papers published 1 year apart (1943 and 1944) by physicians working independently: Leo Kanner (1943/1973) and Hans Asperger (1944/1991). Interestingly, both were born and raised in Vienna; however, Kanner came to the United States and wrote his historic paper in English. Asperger's work went largely ignored for many years, probably because it was published in German at the time of World War II.

Also interestingly, both Kanner and Asperger used the term *autistic* to refer to the children they were observing. Autism was a label that had been coined earlier in the 20th century (Bleuler, 1916/1951) and was used to refer to individuals who had an extremely narrow range of personal relationships and restricted interactions with their environment: "a withdrawal from the fabric of social life into the self. Hence the words 'autistic' and 'autism' from the Greek word autos meaning 'self'" (Frith, 2003, p. 5).

Kanner's Paper

Kanner (1943/1973) reported on the cases of 11 children from the Child Psychiatric Unit at Johns Hopkins University. Some of the major characteristics that distinguished these children were:

- An inability to relate to others in an ordinary manner
- An extreme autistic aloneness that seemingly isolated the child from the outside world
- An apparent resistance to being picked up or held by the parents
- Deficits in language including . . . echolalia. . . .
- Extreme fear reactions to loud noises
- Obsessive desire for repetition and maintenance of sameness
- Few spontaneous activities such as typical play behavior
- Bizarre and repetitive physical movement such as spinning or perpetual rocking

    (Scheuermann & Weber, 2002, p. 2)

A major conclusion that Kanner reached was that these children could be distinguished from children who had **schizophrenia** in at least three ways:

1. The children with schizophrenia tended to withdraw from the world, whereas the children with autism never seemed to have made any social connections to begin with.
2. The children with autism exhibited some unique language patterns, such as pronoun reversals (e.g., *I* for *it, he* for *she*) and **echolalia**, the repetition of words or phrases.
3. The children with autism did not appear to deteriorate in their functioning over time, as did some children with schizophrenia.

Asperger's Paper

Asperger (1944/1991) reported on four cases of children he observed in summer camp who preferred to play alone and not interact with other children. These children were similar to Kanner's cases with two notable exceptions. First, they had average intelligence, although they seemed to channel their intellectual pursuits into obsessive preoccupation in narrow areas, such as machinery or mathematical calculations. Second, their language was perceived as normal. (Later in this chapter, we'll discuss more recent research suggesting subtle language abnormalities.)

Asperger referred to his cases as having "autistic psychopathy." Nearly 40 years later, his work gained scientific notoriety when Lorna Wing (1981) published a paper that referred to Asperger's original paper and sparked interest in the topic. She was the one who

INTERNETRESOURCES

For a comprehensive overview of Asperger syndrome, including definition, causes, and treatments, see this National Institute of Neurological Disorders and Stroke Website: www.ninds.nih.gov/disorders/asperger/asperger.htm

suggested naming the syndrome after Asperger. And it was her paper that drew attention to the condition and was the catalyst for Asperger syndrome's becoming recognized as a condition meriting attention.

DEFINITION OF AUTISM SPECTRUM DISORDERS

Although autism has been a separate category under the Individuals With Disabilities Education Act (IDEA) since 1990, it and other similar disorders are now typically collected under a broader term: **autism spectrum disorders**. The American Psychiatric Association (APA) has been working on modifying the definition and diagnostic indicators for autism spectrum disorders and expects to publish a revised *Diagnostic and Statistical Manual* (DSM-V) in 2013. The APA recommends that in order to be diagnosed with autism spectrum disorder, the individual must meet the following three criteria:

1. Clinically significant, persistent deficits in social communication and interactions, as manifest by all of the following:
   a. Marked deficits in nonverbal and verbal communication used for social interaction;
   b. Lack of social reciprocity [give-and-take];
   c. Failure to develop and maintain peer relationships appropriate to developmental level
2. Restricted, repetitive patterns of behavior, interests, and activities, as manifested by at least TWO of the following:
   a. Stereotyped motor or verbal behaviors, or unusual sensory behaviors
   b. Excessive adherence to routines and ritualized patterns of behavior
   c. Restricted, fixated interests
3. Symptoms must be present in early childhood (but may not become fully manifest until social demands exceed limited capacities) (American Psychiatric Association: DSM-V Development, 2010)

Before the DSM-V is published, the preceding criteria may change slightly, based on comments from the field. Any changes, however, likely will be minor.

Table 9.1 lists the various disorders the APA revision work group is recommending be covered by the term *autism spectrum disorders*. By far the most prevalent of the disorders listed on the spectrum are autism and Asperger syndrome, so we confine our discussion to these two conditions.

PREVALENCE

In the past few years, the prevalence rate for autism spectrum disorder has become a moving target, with estimates increasing exponentially. Conducted in the 1960s, the first large-scale epidemiological survey of autism (Lotter, 1966) found a prevalence rate of about 0.04% (1 out of 2,500). Several other surveys in the 1970s and 1980s found similar rates. However, numerous surveys conducted since

INTERNETRESOURCES

An important and comprehensive report on autism and autism spectrum disorders is available from the National Academy of Sciences at http://www.nap.edu/catlog.php?record_id=10017

Children with autism spectrum disorders may be distinguished by many characteristics, often including an aversion to interaction with peers.

TABLE 9.1 Autism spectrum disorders classification recommended by DSM-V workgroup

- *Autism:* extreme social withdrawal and impairment in communication; often includes stereotyped movements, resistance to change, and unusual responses to sensory experiences; usually manifests before 3 years of age
- *Asperger syndrome (or Asperger disorder):* much like mild autism, but without significant impairments in cognition and language
- *Childhood disintegrative disorder:* normal development for at least 2 and up to 10 years, followed by significant loss of skills; much more prevalent in males
- *Pervasive developmental disorder not otherwise specified (PDD-NOS):* persons who display behaviors typical of autism but to a lesser degree and/or with an onset later than 3 years of age

2000 have found dramatically higher rates for autism spectrum disorder of anywhere from 1 in 333 to 1 in 91 (Kogan et al., 2009). If one is looking for an "official" prevalence figure, the rate of 1 in 110 provided by the U.S. Centers for Disease Control and Prevention (CDCP) is probably the best (CDCP, 2009). Even though these more recent studies have focused on the broader grouping of autism spectrum disorder rather than the earlier studies of just autism, the increase is incredible. Furthermore, figures for autism spectrum disorders have increased 57% just from 2002 to 2006. It's unclear how many of these individuals have autism, Asperger syndrome, or one of the other rarer varieties of autism spectrum disorder. However, what data do exist suggest that the majority of these cases are those with autism rather than Asperger syndrome.

A couple of important points should also be noted about prevalence rates of autism. First, the prevalence is 4 times higher for boys than girls. As with other disabilities (e.g., learning disabilities, attention deficit hyperactivity disorder), reasons for this disparity vary from males being biologically more susceptible to neurological dysfunction to professionals having a biased tendency to refer and/or diagnose males when they exhibit behaviors outside the range of normalcy. Second, the prevalence rate is higher for the European American population than it is for Latinos or African Americans (Mandell et al., 2009). At least two possible reasons for this ethnic disparity exist. It may be due to European Americans having better access to health services. Or it may be due to a bias to diagnose Latinos or African Americans who have low IQs in addition to autism as intellectually disabled instead of autistic.

Such growth in prevalence statistics for autism has led some to speculate that some mysterious toxin in our environment may be the culprit and that there is an "autism epidemic." Others point to the now widespread use of vaccinations for babies and toddlers (see the accompanying Focus on Concepts feature, "Is There a Link Between Vaccinations and Autism?"). Most scientists have ruled out vaccinations as the culprit. At this point, there are two scientifically tenable camps with respect to the increase in reported cases. The first believes that, in fact, there hasn't been an increase in the number of *true* cases (Fombonne, 2001; Frith, 2003; National Research Council, 2001; Shattuck, 2006; Wing & Potter, 2002). Instead, they argue, the reported increase is due to three factors:

1. A widening of the criteria used to diagnose autism, including the recognition of milder forms such as Asperger syndrome
2. A greater awareness of autism in the general public as well as the medical, psychological, and educational professions
3. "Diagnostic substitution," the phenomenon of persons now being identified as having an autism spectrum disorder who previously would have been diagnosed as mentally retarded (intellectually disabled) (Coo et al., 2008) or as having developmental language disorders (Bishop, Whitehouse, Watt, & Line, 2008)

The second scientifically valid position is that, even though the preceding factors may account for some of the increase, it might not account for all of the increase and, therefore, one can't rule out the possibility that some other yet unknown factors are causing a rise in the number of *true* cases (CDCP, 2009; Hertz-Picciotto & Delwiche, 2009).

Prevalence estimates for each of the autism spectrum disorders vary considerably, though studies are consistent in pointing to a higher prevalence in males than females.

CAUSES

With the rapid increase in autism has come an increase in research into its causes. This research has dramatically altered our understanding of the causes of the condition. Early speculative causal theories have been replaced by a more scientifically based set of theories.

IS THERE A LINK BETWEEN VACCINATIONS AND AUTISM?

A firestorm of controversy has been raging about whether the measles, mumps, rubella (MMR) vaccine can cause autism. In particular, assertions continue that the preservative thimerosal, which contains small traces of mercury, is the culprit.* In higher doses, mercury is known to cause neurological deficits. Thus far, evidence strongly indicates no connection between this vaccine and autism. How did this apparently specious theory come to be? How can we explain its influence on the public at large? It's an interesting lesson in how science, the media, and public policy sometimes interact.

The Original Wakefield Paper

In 1998, Andrew Wakefield, along with 12 coauthors, published a paper in one of the most prestigious medical journals, *The Lancet*, on 12 cases of children who had been referred to a clinic in England for gastrointestinal problems and language deficits. Wakefield and colleagues reported two major findings pertinent to the issue of autism. First, nine of the children were determined to be autistic. Second, parents or physicians of eight of the children attributed the onset of autistic symptoms to MMR vaccination; that is, the symptoms suddenly appeared a short time (48 hours to 2 weeks) after vaccination.

With respect to the latter finding, they concluded: "We did not prove an association between [MMR] vaccine and the syndrome [autism] described. . . . Studies are underway that may help resolve this issue" (Wakefield et al., 1998, p. 641).

In the same issue, the editors of *The Lancet* commissioned a commentary to the Wakefield paper that pointed out its limitations. One of the major limitations was that the onset of symptoms shortly after the immunization could very likely have been coincidental:

> A first dose of MMR vaccine is given to about 600,000 children every year in the UK, most during the second year of life, the time when autism first becomes manifest. Not surprisingly, therefore, some cases will follow MMR vaccination. (Chen & DeStefano, 1998, p. 612)

Public Reaction to the Wakefield Paper

Although Wakefield and colleagues stated that they did not *prove* that the MMR vaccine caused autism and although the

commentary cautioned readers against drawing that conclusion, these caveats were lost on much of the public. Once the possible connection between vaccines and autism was reported by the media, public fear spread quickly in Europe as well as North America.

This reaction, in turn, provoked concern that the public's loss of faith in the MMR vaccine could lead to an outbreak of measles. Many researchers and physicians wrote letters to the editors of *The Lancet* about this.

> We are now at a point when the elimination of measles is a real possibility. If, as a result of this paper, parents reject MMR vaccine, this could lead to a reemergence of measles infection with the associated deaths and permanent neurological damage among young children, and a resurgence of rubella infection leading to a rise in congenital rubella births and terminations of pregnancies. (Bedford et al., 1998, p. 907)

Reemergence of Measles Outbreaks

After publication of the Wakefield article and its attendant publicity, a substantial decrease in the percentage of children receiving the MMR vaccination occurred in the United States. And there's a strong probability that this decrease has been the cause of reported measles outbreaks in England and the United States. For example, in the United States an outbreak occurred in 2008, and 90% of those infected hadn't been vaccinated (Centers for Disease Control and Prevention, 2008).

Several Authors Submit Retraction

Ten of the thirteen authors of the Wakefield paper also voiced concerns about the public reaction and offered a retraction (Murch et al., 2004). They pointed out that the major focus of the paper was on the intestinal abnormalities of the children and that their data were "insufficient" to find a causal link between MMR vaccinations and autism. Furthermore, in light of the press coverage's potentially negative impact on public health, they considered that "now is the appropriate time that we should together formally retract the interpretation placed upon these findings in the paper" (Murch et al., 2004, p. 750).

Institute of Medicine's Commissioned Report

Since publication of the Wakefield paper, several epidemiological studies have investigated the possible autism–MMR vaccine link. In the United States, several federal agencies, including the prestigious Institute of Medicine of the National Academies, commissioned a review of the available evidence. In their third and final report, the committee con-

*In 1999, the American Academy of Pediatrics and the U.S. Public Health Service issued a joint statement recommending the removal of thimerosal from vaccines. Since that time, U.S. drug companies have stopped using thimerosal in vaccines, and it is estimated that no MMR vaccinations containing thimerosal have been given in the United States since 2001.

cluded "that the evidence favors rejection of a causal relationship between MMR vaccine and autism" (Institute of Medicine, 2004, p. 7; bold in the original). And studies published since the Institute of Medicine's report have continued to find no link between vaccines and autism. For example, researchers have demonstrated that, even after thimerosal was removed from the vaccine, the prevalence of autism has continued to rise (Schechter & Grether, 2008).

Lancet Issues Retraction

On February 2, 2010, the *Lancet* published a retraction of the Wakefield et al. study, citing methodological flaws (Editors of *The Lancet*, 2010).

Some Parents Remain Unconvinced: Most of Scientific Community Remain Convinced

Despite overwhelming scientific epidemiological evidence to the contrary, many parents remain unconvinced that MMR vaccinations did not cause their children's autism. However, most scientists studying the matter hold that no evidence links the vaccine, with or without thimerosal, to autism.

Early Causal Theories

Hans Asperger conjectured that there was a biological and hereditary basis for autism (Hewetson, 2002). Kanner also speculated that the cause of autism was biological, but he noted that the parents of these children were not "warmhearted":

> In the whole group, there are very few really warmhearted fathers and mothers. . . . Even some of the happiest marriages are rather cold and formal affairs. Three of the marriages were dismal failures. The question arises whether or to what extent this fact has contributed to the condition of the children. The children's aloneness from the beginning of life makes it difficult to attribute the whole picture exclusively to the type of the early parental relations with our patients.
>
> We must then assume that these children have come into the world with innate inability to form the usual, biologically provided affective contact with people. (Kanner, 1943/1973, pp. 42–43.)

Even though Asperger and Kanner came down on the side of a biological basis for autism, the prevailing **psychoanalytic** ideas of the 1960s held sway for several years for professionals who were groping to find an answer to the puzzling condition of autism. One psychiatrist in particular was extremely influential in promoting the idea that parents, especially mothers, were the cause of their children's autism. Perhaps influenced by Kanner's anecdotal reference to a handful of parents as not being warmhearted plus his later statement that "emotional refrigeration has been the common lot of autistic children" (Eisenberg & Kanner, 1956), Bruno Bettelheim (1967) conceived a theory that cold and unresponsive mothers caused autism. Most authorities attribute the term *refrigerator moms* (once used to refer to mothers of children with autism) to Bettelheim.

As we noted in Chapter 4, it wasn't too long ago that it was common to blame parents for the problems of their children, so Bettelheim's ideas were not viewed as radical. We now recognize that the direction of causation between child and adult behavior is

For much of the twentieth century, it was widely speculated that parents, especially mothers, were the cause of their children's autism.

a two-way street (Bell & Harper, 1977). It's reasonable to conclude that parents of a relatively unresponsive baby would over time come to display behaviors toward their infant that seemed cold and distant. Furthermore, we know that the families and parents of children with autism typically experience considerable stress because they are suddenly and unexpectedly confronted by the child's disability. Usually, their child does not look different from the typical child, and often the child has gone through a short period of months or years of apparently normal development before the parents recognize that something is wrong. It's therefore understandable that parents would behave in ways that reflect stress and concern.

Today's Causal Theories

Scientists don't yet know precisely what's wrong with the brain in autism spectrum disorders, but they have established unequivocally that the cause is neurological, not interpersonal (National Research Council, 2001; Muller, 2007; Strock, 2004). Furthermore, they have strong evidence that genetics plays a role in many cases. However, given the range of symptoms and levels of severity of autism spectrum disorders, it's a reasonable guess that no single neurological or genetic cause exists.

NEUROLOGICAL BASIS OF AUTISM SPECTRUM DISORDERS A neurological basis for autism spectrum disorders is suggested by the fact that people with autism have a high incidence of brain seizures and cognitive deficits (Volkmar & Pauls, 2003). Furthermore, postmortem studies and neurological imaging studies, using the same techniques that we discussed in earlier chapters on learning disabilities and attention deficit hyperactivity disorder (ADHD; e.g., positron emission tomography scans, computerized axial tomographic scans, and magnetic resonance imaging) have implicated a number of areas of the brain (Muller, 2007; Strock, 2004; Volkmar & Pauls, 2003). In fact, because so many areas are affected, many authorities now think that autism is better conceived as a disorder of neural networks rather than as being due to an abnormality in one specific part of the brain. In addition, research suggests that the brain cells of individuals with autism exhibit deficient connectivity that disrupts the cells' ability to communicate with each other (Glessner et al., 2009; Wang et al., 2009). Figure 9.1 depicts some of the major brain structures affected.

Another interesting line of neurological research involves the brain and head size of people with autism (Courchesne, Carper, & Akshoomoff, 2003; Courchesne et al., 2001; Elder, Dawson, Toth, Fein, & Munson, 2008; Fombonne, Roge, Claverie, Courty, & Fremoile, 1999; Fukomoto et al., 2008; Piven, Arndt, Bailey, & Andreason, 1996; Piven et al., 1995). Studies indicate that the brains and heads of young children with autism tend to grow suddenly and excessively starting perhaps as early as the first year of life. This is then followed by a deceleration, such that they are about normal in size by adolescence. The significance of abnormally high rates of brain growth in the first 2 years is underscored by the fact that this is a time of critical importance to brain organization:

> The organizational events in the brain during the first two years set the neurodevelopmental stage for the acquisition of language and the capacity for inference, a sense of self-awareness (Herschkowitz, 2000), and, eventually, complex information processing (Minshew, Sweeney, & Luna, 2002). (Lainhart, 2003, p. 394)

Theories vary, but some believe that the abnormal brain growth may be linked to elevated levels of growth hormones (Mills et al., 2007). Interestingly, another hormone-based theory of autism has drawn considerable attention among scientists as well as the popular media. Some researchers have claimed that those who, before birth, have high levels of **androgen** (a hormone that is responsible for controlling the development of male characteristics) in their mothers' amniotic fluid are more likely to exhibit autistic traits as children (Auyeung et al., 2009; Baron-Cohen, 2002, 2003; Baron-Cohen, Auyeung, Ashwin, & Knickmeyer, 2009). Based on these findings, some have come to refer to persons with autism as having an **extreme male brain (EMB)**. The theory remains plausible, but most of the sci-

FIGURE 9.1 Major brain structures implicated in autism

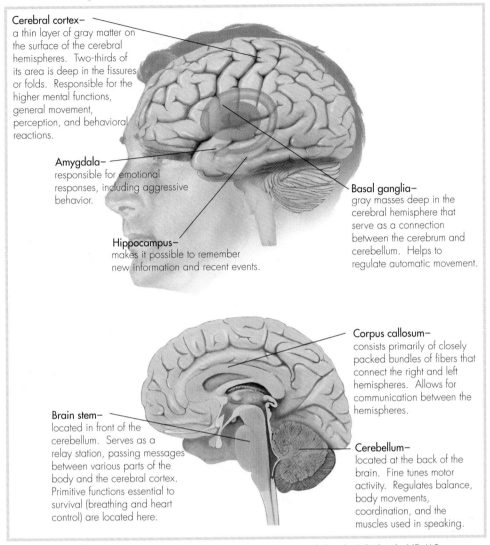

Cerebral cortex–
a thin layer of gray matter on the surface of the cerebral hemispheres. Two-thirds of its area is deep in the fissures or folds. Responsible for the higher mental functions, general movement, perception, and behavioral reactions.

Amygdala–
responsible for emotional responses, including aggressive behavior.

Hippocampus–
makes it possible to remember new information and recent events.

Basal ganglia–
gray masses deep in the cerebral hemisphere that serve as a connection between the cerebrum and cerebellum. Helps to regulate automatic movement.

Corpus callosum–
consists primarily of closely packed bundles of fibers that connect the right and left hemispheres. Allows for communication between the hemispheres.

Brain stem–
located in front of the cerebellum. Serves as a relay station, passing messages between various parts of the body and the cerebral cortex. Primitive functions essential to survival (breathing and heart control) are located here.

Cerebellum–
located at the back of the brain. Fine tunes motor activity. Regulates balance, body movements, coordination, and the muscles used in speaking.

Source: Strock, M. (2004). *Autism spectrum disorders (pervasive developmental disorders).* Bethesda, MD: U.S. Department of Health and Human Services, National Institutes of Health, National Institute of Mental Health. Retrieved from www.nimh.nih.gov/publicat/autism.cfm

entific community remain skeptical about its validity (Barbeau, Mendrek, & Mottron, 2009; Falter, Plaisted, & Davis, 2008; Skuse, 2009). One of many criticisms is that the theory is based on a relationship between androgen and autistic traits in the general population, not between androgen and those who have actually been diagnosed with autism.

GENETIC BASIS OF AUTISM SPECTRUM DISORDERS   Scientific evidence for autism having a hereditary component is very strong (Sutcliffe, 2008). Studies have shown that when a child is diagnosed with autism, the chances are 15% that his younger sibling will be also be diagnosed with autism. This percentage is 25 to 75 times higher than in the population as a whole (Sutcliffe, 2008). When a monozygotic (identical, one egg) twin has autism, the chances are much greater that the other twin will also have autism than is the case with dizygotic (fraternal, two eggs) twins. Furthermore, even if they aren't diagnosed as autistic, family members of those with autism are more likely to exhibit autistic-like characteristics at a subclinical level, such as a lack of close friends, a preoccupation with narrow interests, and a preference for routines (Stone, McMahon, Yoder, & Walden, 2007; Volkmar & Pauls, 2003).

In addition to a direct hereditary cause of autism spectrum disorders, evidence now shows that sporadic genetic mutations are involved in some cases. Researchers have found that tiny gene mutations—spontaneous deletions and/or duplications of genetic material—

INTERNETRESOURCES

For a comprehensive overview of autism spectrum disorders, including definition, causes, and treatments, see this National Institute of Mental Health Website: www.nimh.nih.gov/Publicat/autism.cfm

that can result in autism are sometimes passed down to children from one or both parents (Autism Genome Project Consortium, 2007; Sebat et al., 2007). This is similar to the way children with Down syndrome acquire an anomaly on the 21st chromosome. Also similar to Down syndrome, the frequency of these mutations increases with the age of the parent, especially the mother.

Research has yet to identify all the exact genes involved. However, researchers are overwhelmingly consistent in stating that no single "autism gene" exists; multiple genes are involved, and the same genes are not implicated in all people with autism.

IDENTIFICATION

The diagnosis of autism is often made by a psychiatrist using criteria established by the APA (2010) that focus on communication skills, social interactions, and repetitive and stereotyped patterns of behavior. In addition to observing the child in the examining room and taking a detailed history from parents, clinicians can use behavioral observation instruments and ask parents and/or teachers to fill out behavior checklists. Two instruments, both of which are standardized, are together generally considered the "gold standard" for diagnosing autism: the Autism Diagnostic Observation Schedule (ADOS) and the Autism Diagnostic Interview-Revised (ADI-R) (Conroy et al., 2011; Le Couteur, Haden, Hammal, & McConachie, 2008). Meant to be used together, the ADOS involves observing the child in several semi-structured play activities and the ADI-R is used to interview caregivers about the child's functioning in language/communication, reciprocal social interaction, and restricted, repetitive, and stereotyped behaviors.

Most children with autism can be diagnosed by the age of 3 years and sometimes earlier. Asperger syndrome can sometimes take longer to diagnose because the symptoms don't appear as severe. Researchers are hopeful that they will develop ways to diagnose these disorders even earlier, in infancy. Evidence shows that parents often start to notice the differences in their child with autism (Table 9.2) well before formal diagnosis, which is usually after the age of 3 (K. M. Gray, Tonge, & Bereton, 2006).

As noted in Table 9.2, an indicator for autism is loss or regression in babbling, speech, or social skills in a young child. Parents of some children with autism have often claimed that their child progressed normally for about the first 2 years and then abruptly began to regress in behavior. Estimates of this **autistic regression** range from about 20% to 47% of cases of children with autism (Werner & Dawson, 2005). Researchers have begun to document that these parents' perceptions are, in fact, valid (Landa, Holman, Garrett-Mayer, 2007; Werner & Dawson, 2005). In one study, for example, researchers compared the home videotapes of 1st-year and 2nd-year birthday parties and found that children whose parents said they had regressed had indeed shown signs of regression (Werner & Dawson, 2005). These

TABLE 9.2 Early signs of autism

6 Months
• No big smiles or other warm, joyful expressions
9 Months
• No back-and-forth sharing of sounds, smiles, or other facial expressions
12 Months
• No consistent response to own name
• No babbling
• No back-and-forth gestures, such as pointing, showing, reaching, waving, or three-pronged gaze (e.g., child looks at adult, looks at toy to indicate interest in it, looks back at adult to communicate something about the toy)
16 Months
• No words
24 Months
• No two-word meaningful phrases (without imitating or repeating)
Any loss of speech or babbling or social skills at any age

Sources: Cadigan & Estrem (2006/2007), Rogers (2000), Travis & Sigman (2000).

findings also help explain why some parents have believed that vaccinations caused their children's autism (see the preceding Focus on Concepts on feature, "Is There a Link Between Vaccinations and Autism?").

PSYCHOLOGICAL AND BEHAVIORAL CHARACTERISTICS

As noted earlier, some variation exists in the behavioral characteristics associated with the different autism spectrum disorders. This chapter focuses on autism and Asperger syndrome.

Autism

We noted that people with autism have deficits in social interaction and communication and have repetitive and stereotyped patterns of behavior. In addition, they display cognitive deficits, and some have abnormal sensory perceptions.

IMPAIRED SOCIAL INTERACTION   Many of the social interaction problems that individuals with autism exhibit involve deficits in social responsiveness. Parents of children with autism often notice that their babies or toddlers don't respond normally to being picked up or cuddled. The young child with autism might not show a differential response to parents, siblings, or their teachers compared to other strangers. They might not smile in social situations, or they might smile or laugh when nothing appears funny. Their eye gaze often differs significantly from that of others; they sometimes avoid eye contact with others or look out of the corners of their eyes. They might show little or no interest in other people but be preoccupied with objects. They might not learn to play normally. These characteristics persist and prevent the child from developing typical attachments to their parents or friendships with their peers.

IMPAIRED COMMUNICATION   Most children with autism lack **communicative intent**, or the desire to communicate for social purposes. As many as 50% are thought to be **mute**; they use no, or almost no, language (Scheuermann & Webber, 2002). Those who develop speech typically show abnormalities in intonation, rate, volume, and content of their oral language. Their speech sounds "robotic," or they might exhibit echolalia, parroting what they hear. They might reverse pronouns (e.g., confuse *you* and *I* or refer to themselves as *he* or *she* rather than *I* or *me*). Using language as a tool for social interaction is particularly difficult. If they do acquire language, they might have considerable difficulty using it in social interactions because they're unaware of the reactions of their listeners.

Strong research indicates that the impaired communication and impaired social skills of infants and young children with autism are linked to deficits in their ability to engage in joint attention (Adamson, Bakeman, Deckner, & Romiski, 2009; Clifford & Dissanayake, 2008; Murray et al., 2008). **Joint attention** is the process by which one alerts another to a stimulus via nonverbal means, such as gazing or pointing. For example, one person may gaze at another person, and then point to an object, and then return their gaze back to the other person. In this case, the pointing person is "initiating joint attention" by trying to get the other to look at the object. The person who looks to the referenced object is "responding to joint attention" (Joint Attention, n.d.).

REPETITIVE AND STEREOTYPED PATTERNS OF BEHAVIOR   Many people with autism display **stereotyped motor or verbal behaviors**: repetitive, ritualistic motor behaviors such as twirling, spinning objects, flapping the hands, and rocking, similar to those that are evident in some people who are blind (see Chapter 12). Another characteristic frequently seen in autism and related disorders is extreme fascination or preoccupation with objects and a very restricted range of interests. Children with autism might play ritualistically with an object for hours at a time or show excessive interest in objects of a particular type. They can become upset by any change in the environment (e.g., something out of place or something new in the home or classroom) or any change in routine; some individuals with autism seem intent on the preservation of sameness and have extreme difficulty with change or transition (Adreon & Stella, 2001; Myles & Simpson, 2001).

IMPAIRED COGNITION   Most individuals with autism display cognitive deficits similar to those of people with intellectual disabilities. However, some cognitive processing problems seem to be peculiar to autism:

> Children with autism are thought to display difficulty in coding and categorization of information, . . . relying on literal translations, and they seem to remember things by their location in space rather than concept comprehension (Schuler, 1995). For example, "shopping" means going to a particular store on a particular street, rather than the concept of visiting any type of store, browsing around, perhaps buying something . . . or various other aspects of the concept of "shopping." In fact, it has been speculated that individuals with autism employ an "echo box-like memory store" (Grandin, 1995; Hermelin, 1976). This would explain why autistic children may excel at putting puzzles together and building things out of blocks, matching tasks, or drawing replicas. However, they tend to perform poorly on tasks requiring verbal comprehension and expressive language. (Scheuermann & Webber, 2002, p. 9)

The striking difference in favor of visual and spatial abilities relative to language and conceptual abilities has been termed ***thinking in pictures*** by Temple Grandin, a designer of livestock handling facilities and a Professor of Animal Science at Colorado State University. Although Grandin is more typical of someone with Asperger syndrome, her description of heightened visual-spatial abilities is applicable to some with autism as well as to some with Asperger syndrome:

> I credit my visualization abilities with helping me understand the animals. . . . One of my early livestock design projects was to create a dip-vat and cattle-handling facility for a feed yard. . . . A dip vat is a long, narrow, 7-ft. deep swimming pool through which cattle move in single file. It is filled with pesticide to rid the animals of ticks, lice and other external parasites. . . . The animals often panicked because they were forced into the vat down a steep, slick decline. . . .
>
> The first thing I did when I arrived at the feedlot was put myself inside the cow's head and see with its eyes. Because their eyes are on the sides of their head, cattle have wide-angle vision. Those cattle must have felt as if they were being forced to jump down an airplane escape slide into the ocean.
>
> One of my first steps was to convert the ramp from steel to concrete. If I had a calf's body and hooves, I would be very scared to step on a slippery metal ramp. The final design had a concrete ramp at a 25° downward angle. Deep grooves in the concrete provided secure footing. The ramp appeared to enter the water gradually, but in reality it abruptly dropped away below the water's surface. The animals could not see the drop-off because the dip chemicals colored the water. When they stepped out over the water, they quietly fell in because their center of gravity had passed the point of no return. (Grandin, 2002, p. 56)

Some individuals with autism have such extraordinary skills that at first blush, one thinks they are geniuses. These individuals are referred to as autistic savants. **Autistic savants** might have relatively severe autism, in that they show serious developmental delays in overall social and intellectual functioning. However, people with this condition also show remarkable ability or apparent talent in particular splinter skills—skills that exist in apparent isolation from the rest of the person's abilities. An autistic savant might have extraordinary capabilities in playing music, drawing, or calculating. For example, when given a date that is far into the future, such as March 2, 2020, some autistic savants are immediately able to say that this will be a Monday. The same person, however, might not have the functional mathematical skills to be able to purchase items in a grocery store. The character Raymond, played by Dustin Hoffman, in the movie ***Rain Man*** (Guber & Levinson, 1988) was an autistic savant (see Sacks, 1995, and Treffert, 2006, for other examples).

Because the skills of individuals who are autistic savants are so extraordinary, they are often covered in the media. This fact—along with publicity that accompanies films such as ***Rain Man*** (Guber & Levinson, 1988), ***Shine*** (Scott & Hicks, 1996; a film loosely based on

INTERNETRESOURCES

The following Website contains a variety of information on autistic savants, including video clip profiles of several autistic savants: http://www .wisconsinmedicalsociety.org/ savant_syndrome   ■ ■ ■

INTERNETRESOURCES

Stephen Wiltshire, was diagnosed as autistic at age 3. From an early age, however, he displayed an incredible talent for drawing from memory, especially cityscapes. His Website contains more information on his fascinating life and talents: http:// www.stephenwiltshire .co.uk/   ■ ■ ■

the life of pianist David Helfgott), and *Mozart and the Whale* (Naess & Bass, 2005)—has led to the misconception in the general public that most, if not all, people with autism have amazing talents. Although precise figures are not available, most estimates are that only 10% of those who are autistic are autistic savants.

ABNORMAL SENSORY PERCEPTIONS Some people with autism are either hyperresponsive or hyporesponsive to particular stimuli in their environment (Ben-Sasson et al., 2009). For example, some experience hypersensitivity to visual stimuli, such as being overly sensitive to fluorescent lights, and others can be overly sensitive to touch. Interestingly, some people with autism are totally the opposite of hyperresponsive. They are very *un*responsive to auditory, visual, or tactile stimuli. In fact, to the casual observer, some appear to be deaf or blind. Still others have a combination of hypersensitivity and hyposensitivity, for instance, being oblivious to loud noises such as a fire alarm but overreacting to someone whistling at a great distance.

Some people with autism experience a neurological mixing of the senses, or synaesthesia. **Synaesthesia** occurs when the stimulation of one sensory or cognitive system results in the stimulation of another sensory or cognitive system. Daniel Tammet has Asperger syndrome and has phenomenal savant skills in memory and math, setting a British and European record for reciting Pi from memory, to 22,514 decimal places. Tammet describes his synaesthesia in his aptly titled memoir, *Born on a Blue Day*:

> I was born on 31 January 1979—a Wednesday. I know it was a Wednesday, because the date is blue in my mind and Wednesdays are always blue, like the number nine or sound of loud voices arguing. . . .
>
> Numbers are my friends and they are always around me. Each one is unique and has its own personality. Eleven is friendly and five is loud, whereas four is both shy and quiet—its my favorite number, perhaps because it reminds me of myself. Some are big—23, 667, 1179—while others are small: 6, 13, 581. Some are beautiful, like 333, and some are ugly, like 289. . . .
>
> No matter where I go or what I'm doing, numbers are never far from my thoughts. In an interview with chat show host David Letterman in New York, I told David he looked like the number 117—tall and lanky. Later outside, in the appropriately numerically named Times Square, I gazed up at the towering skyscrapers and felt surrounded by nines—the number I most associate with feelings of immensity. (Tammet, 2006, pp. 1–2)

Asperger Syndrome

People with Asperger syndrome are likely to display impairment or abnormalities in the same areas (i.e., social interaction, communication, repetitive and stereotyped patterns of behavior, cognitive processing, sensory perception) as those who have autism, but to a milder degree. We focus our discussion on impairments in social skills and communication skills because research suggests that social interaction is the biggest challenge of those with Asperger syndrome and because problems in communicating contribute to their social ineptitude.

IMPAIRED SOCIAL INTERACTION A major reason that people with Asperger syndrome have so much difficulty in social interactions is that they aren't adept at reading social cues. In fact, at times, they can appear clueless about what constitutes appropriate social behavior. Because they can be highly verbal and intelligent, others may get the impression that they are willfully disregarding social etiquette. By "turning off" those around them, they become further ostracized from their peer group, making it difficult to make and keep friends and to interact with others. See the accompanying Personal Perspectives feature ("Children's Book Author") for a unique way of helping peers and others understand the unusual characteristics of those with Asperger syndrome.

Many of the social interaction difficulties of those with Asperger syndrome are due to their inability to think about situations in a nuanced way. They are often overly literal in how they "read" the behavior and language of others. And they often interpret situations

Personal PERSPECTIVES

Children's Book Author Kathy Hoopmann Addresses Asperger Syndrome

Australian children's book author Kathy Hoopmann is known for her continuing "Asperger Adventure Series," *Blue Bottle Mystery* (2000), *Of Mice and Aliens* (2001), *Lisa and the Lacemaker* (2002), and *Haze* (2003), in which the main character has Asperger syndrome. Unlike her previous books, *All Cats Have Asperger Syndrome* (2006) appeals to a wide-ranging audience of preschoolers through adults, especially cat lovers. As one reviewer puts it, "[It's] a great addition for the coffee table for any residence. I would also suggest this for therapist, doctor, and school offices" (Sayers, 2010). Here are a few pages:

He likes to be near those he loves, but doesn't want them to hold him.

. . . preferring squishy places to a hug.

Instead of coming to people for comfort, he may be overly attached to a toy . . .

. . . or a pet.

Source: Hoopmann, K. (2006). *All cats have Asperger syndrome* (pp. 3–6). London: Jessica Kingsley. Reprinted by permission.

using logic to the exclusion of emotion or sentiment. Stephen Shore (2003) provides an example of his struggles with being overly literal:

> A friend of mine . . . said he felt "like a pizza." "What do you mean—'feel like a pizza'?" And it wasn't until college that I realized, "Oh, he meant he felt like EATING a pizza." At this time, idioms usually go zipping past me but I am often able to "pull them back" for further examination before I say something ridiculous. But it takes some additional thinking on my part, to figure out "Well, what's the meaning? How do I interpret this?" . . .

And John Elder Robison provides an example of his single-minded focus on logic over emotion:

> One time, my mother had invited her friend Betsy over. I wandered in as they sat on the sofa . . . .
>
> Betsy said, "Did you hear about Eleanor Parker's son? Last Saturday he got hit by a train and killed. He was playing on the tracks."
>
> I smiled at her words. She turned to me with a shocked expression on her face. "What! Do you think that's funny?"
>
> I felt embarrassed and humiliated. "No, I guess not," I said as I slunk away. . . .
>
> I didn't really know Eleanor. And I had never met her kid. So there was no reason for me to feel joy or sorrow. . . . Here is what went through my mind that summer day:
>
> ***Someone got killed.***
> ***Damn! I'm glad I didn't get killed.***
> ***I'm glad . . . my parents didn't get killed.***

I'm glad all my friends are okay.
He must have been a pretty dumb kid, playing on the train tracks.
I would never get run over by a train like that.
I'm glad I'm okay.

And at the end, I smiled with relief. Whatever killed that kid was not going to get me. I didn't even know him. It was all going to be okay, at least for me. Today my feelings would be exactly the same in that situation. The only difference is, now I have better control of my facial expressions. . . .

If ten people get killed in a bus crash in Brazil, I don't feel anything. I understand intellectually that it's sad, but I don't feel sad. . . .

Some people will cry and carry on, and I wonder . . . ***Do they really feel that, or is it just a play for attention?*** It is very hard for me to know. People die every minute, all over the world. If we tried to feel sorry for every death, our little hearts would explode. (Robison, 2007, pp. 29–31)

Another way of looking at the social problems for individuals with Asperger syndrome is captured by the notion of the hidden curriculum (Myles & Simpson, 2001, 2003). The **hidden curriculum** refers to the "dos and don'ts" of everyday living that most people learn incidentally or with very little instruction from others: behaviors or ways of acting that most of us take for granted. Recall Tim Page's "Sorry, Everyone" letter at the beginning of the chapter, in which he referred to commenting on his fellow student's monkey-like (simian) features. For people with Asperger syndrome, these rules of behavior remain hidden. What makes it all the more difficult for the person with Asperger syndrome is that the hidden curriculum can be different for different settings:

Everyone knows that Mrs. Robbins allows students to whisper in class as long as they get their work done, whereas Mrs. Cook does not tolerate any level of noise in her class. Similarly, everyone knows that Mr. Johnson, the assistant principal, is a stickler for following the rules, so no one curses or even slouches in his presence. Everyone also knows that the really tough guys (the ones who beat up unsuspecting kids) hang out behind the slide, just out of teachers' view—everyone knows these things—everyone, that is, except the student with Asperger syndrome.

Outside of school, the hidden curriculum is an even bigger issue. What is the hidden curriculum for talking to or taking rides from strangers? The bus driver is a stranger, but it is permissible to accept a ride from her. . . . It is okay to accept candy from the distributor who is giving free samples at Toys "R" Us, yet it is not prudent to take candy from a stranger standing on the street corner. (Myles & Simpson, 2003, p. 132)

All of these problems with social interaction are often misinterpreted as the person with Asperger syndrome's not wanting to engage socially with others. This may be true for some, but not for all people with autism. Numerous autobiographical accounts written by individuals with autism reveal that they often long to socialize with others (Causton-Theoharis, Ashby, & Cosier, 2009). They experience feelings of isolation. In addition, they often experience social anxiety about engaging socially with others (Kuusikko et al., 2008).

IMPAIRED COMMUNICATION SKILLS   People with Asperger syndrome may be able to express themselves using age-appropriate vocabulary and grammar, but they often exhibit numerous idiosyncratic language and language-related behaviors. They often have problems with **pragmatics**, the social uses of language (Colle, Baron-Cohen, Wheelwright, & van der Lely, 2008). For example, they might speak using an abnormal voice inflection, such as a monotone, talk too loudly or too quickly or slowly, not be adept at taking turns talking in a conversation, engage in monologues, or repeat the same thing over and over. In Chapter 6, we noted that people with learning disabilities can also experience problems with pragmatics; however, the deficits in pragmatic skills of those with Asperger syndrome are usually much more severe and pervasive.

INTERNETRESOURCES

John Elder Robison's Website (http://www.johnrobison.com/) is devoted to a variety of topics related to autism spectrum disorders. The site has links to Robison's blog, his Facebook page, and his Twitter account.

RESPONSIVE *INSTRUCTION*
MEETING THE NEEDS OF STUDENTS WITH AUTISM SPECTRUM DISORDERS

Social Stories for Adolescents

WHAT THE RESEARCH SAYS

Students with autism spectrum disorders experience challenges with communication, behavior, and social interactions. One promising intervention that has been successful in addressing these needs is social stories, which are brief, personalized narratives typically presented in a comic strip format that help students with ASDs to focus one particular skill in one context. For example, a student who becomes overwhelmed with the noise in the cafeteria may respond by yelling. The teacher would develop a social story with the following narrative:

1. Mary learns to "take deep breaths" and eat her lunch quietly. (picture of Mary eating at a lunch table);
2. Every day I go to the cafeteria for lunch. (picture of cafeteria filled with students);
3. Lots of kids eat lunch in the cafeteria and it is very noisy. (picture of kids at lunch table);
4. When I go to the cafeteria, I eat my lunch quietly and wait for the bell. (picture of Mary eating lunch);
5. When I eat my lunch quietly, it makes my teachers and friends happy. (picture of smiling students at lunch); and
6. My teacher says, "Great work, Mary!" when I eat my lunch quietly. (picture of smiling teacher).

Research indicates social stories can be an effective intervention for decreasing undesirable behaviors and increasing socially appropriate skills (Ali & Frederickson, 2006).

RESEARCH STUDY

Graetz, Mastropieri, and Scruggs (2009) investigated the effects of social stories on the behaviors of three adolescent students with autism. The majority of social story research has been conducted with younger students, and Graetz and colleagues were interested in finding out if (a) social stories were effective with older students, (b) new behaviors generalized to settings not included in the story, and (c) new behaviors were maintained after the social stories were no longer used. All three participants were classified in the average range of autism severity based on the Gilliam Autism Rating Scale (Gilliam, 1995). The target behaviors included standing independently (in contrast to falling on the ground refusing to stand during P.E.), using an appropriate voice (in contrast to using a high-pitched, falsetto voice in class), and keeping hands down (in contrast to sucking fingers or putting objects in mouth during instruction).

Researchers created modified social stories with photographs of the participants engaging in the target behavior. Teachers received training on how to use the stories (i.e., reading them during the appropriate time—before the target situation or in response to an undesirable behavior in the target situation) and give feedback to students about the stories.

RESEARCH FINDINGS

The use of social stories resulted in immediate decline in inappropriate behaviors for all three participants and appeared to be maintained after the intervention ended. Researchers also interviewed teachers and paraprofessionals about their perspectives on the use of social stories. These professionals indicated that they could competently create social stories and implement them successfully. In addition, the teachers and paraprofessionals felt confident about the potential of using social stories in support of students with autistic spectrum disorders in the future.

APPLYING THE RESEARCH TO TEACHING

Teachers can create their own social stories to address inappropriate social behaviors of students with autistic spectrum disorders. Each social story contains descriptive sentences that illustrate the situation of concern (e.g., circle time, free play, following a teacher or adult request); at least one directive sentence that clearly describes the desired behavior (e.g., sitting quietly, keeping hands to oneself, giving a desired response); and perspective sentences that relate the feelings of others in regard to the situation (Gray & Garand, 1993). Modified social stories can include pictures (photographs or cartoons) and callouts.

■ ■ ■ ■ ■ ■ ■ ■ ■

of these students are passive and disengaged from their environment, PRT focuses on teaching them to more actively initiate responses, such as asking simple questions as the situation dictates, for example, "What's that?" or "What happened?" Teaching the skill of responding to multiple cues targets the student with autism's tendency to focus on environmental stimuli in an overly selective manner, perhaps staring for long periods of time at just one or a few objects or focusing on only one aspect of an object. It brings to mind the old adage of "not seeing the forest for the trees." PRT encourages the training of multiple cues. For example,

> asking a child to get his or her green sweatshirt is requiring the child to make a conditional discrimination, when the child has another sweatshirt of a different color and other green articles of clothing. That is, the child must respond to both color (e.g., *green* as opposed to the *red* one) and object (e.g., green *sweatshirt* as opposed to green *shirt*). Subsequently, after a child has mastered a given number of cues, the number required for a correct response can be gradually and systematically increased (e.g., green sweatshirt to *new* green sweatshirt). (L. K. Koegel et al., 1999, p. 177)

Service Delivery Models

Currently, the most popular placement for students with autism is in a self-contained classroom. About 42% of students with autism are in separate classes, about 29% are primarily in general education classrooms, about 18% are in resource rooms, about 10% are in separate schools, and about 1% percent are in residential facilities.

Partly because of the emphasis on teaching children with autism spectrum disorders in the more naturalistic context of everyday interactions and environments, an increasing percentage of these students are being taught in neighborhood schools and general education classrooms, especially at younger ages. In this model, general educators and special educators work together to meet the individual needs of students with autism. However, little research describes how this collaboration should look in the classroom. One promising format might be the Autism Spectrum Disorder Inclusion Collaboration model (Simpson, deBoer-Ott, & Smith-Myles, 2003; (see the accompanying Making It Work feature, "Collaboration and Co-Teaching"). Nevertheless, some of the effective instruction of children with autism spectrum disorders requires one-on-one teaching or teaching in very small groups, and sometimes this can't be done effectively in the general education classroom.

Even when such intensive instruction is offered in specialized settings, state-of-the-art teaching emphasizes the most natural possible human interactions. At the preschool level, teachers emphasize natural interactions in general education classrooms with peers who do not have disabilities. At the elementary level, educators are including more children with autism spectrum disorders in cooperative learning groups in general education classrooms with their peers who do not have disabilities. For an example of intensive instruction in preparation for enrollment in a general education kindergarten classroom, see the Success Stories feature, "Intensive and Early Applied Behavior Analysis," on pp. 256–257.

INTERNETRESOURCES

More information about TEACCH can be found at www.teacch.com

ASSESSMENT OF PROGRESS

Two critical areas of assessment for students with autism spectrum disorders are progress in language development and social/adaptive behavior.

Monitoring Progress in Language Development

The language acquisition of individuals with autism spectrum disorders significantly affects their long-term life outcomes, and should, therefore, be a focus of intervention for most of these students. Furthermore, teachers should implement ongoing progress monitoring of language development to determine if the intervention is meeting the needs of the student. The National Institute on Deafness and Other Communication Disorders convened a work group that determined that assessment of expressive language, particularly for young children with autism spectrum disorders, should include measures from multiple sources (Tager-Flusberg et al., 2009). These sources include natural language samples collected in various communicative contexts, parent report via questionnaire or interviews, and direct assessment through standardized measures. The content of language assessments should be comprehensive, including measures of phonology, vocabulary, syntax, and pragmatics.

MAKING IT WORK
COLLABORATION AND CO-TEACHING WITH TEACHERS OF STUDENTS WITH AUTISM SPECTRUM DISORDER

"I don't know anything about students with autism spectrum disorder. How can this work?"

WHAT DOES IT MEAN TO BE A TEACHER OF STUDENTS WITH AUTISM SPECTRUM DISORDER?

The Council for Exceptional Children doesn't identify separate knowledge and skills requirements for teachers of students with autism spectrum disorders. In most cases, teachers working with these students are certified to teach in the area of emotional or behavioral disorders or in either the area of individualized general education or independence curriculum. Though no specific guidelines are available for the preparation of teachers of students with autism spectrum disorders, this is a new and growing area of study, and many universities (and other groups) offer specific training programs. The University of North Carolina's Treatment and Education of Autistic and related Communication-Handicapped CHildren (TEACCH) program is one example.

SUCCESSFUL STRATEGIES FOR COLLABORATION

Collaboration strategies for students with autism spectrum disorders are rather new, and few have been tested for effectiveness in the general education classroom. Nevertheless, researchers are working to create models that are effective and support both the general and special educators who are working "by the seat of their pants" at this point. One such model is the Autism Spectrum Disorder Inclusion Collaboration model (Simpson et al., 2003), which "emphasizes shared responsibility and shared decision making among general educators, special educators, and support personnel. The model also permits consideration of both learner behaviors and instructional factors" (p. 117). The model includes five main components: (1) environmental and curricular modifications, general education classroom support, and instructional methods; (2) attitudinal and social support; (3) coordinated team commitment; (4) recurrent evaluation of inclusion procedures; and (5) home–school collaboration. The model isn't prescriptive in its recommendations for how collaboration should look in the classroom, but it does list specific items that should be in place in each

component in order for collaboration to work. These items include:

Environmental and Curricular Modifications

- Availability of appropriately trained support personnel
- In-service Training
- Implementation of appropriate instructional methods
- Availability of paraeducators
- Adequate teacher planning time
- Reduced class size

Attitudinal and Social Support

- School administration has positive attitude toward inclusion
- Administrative support for those working to include students with autism spectrum disorders
- Dissemination of information about autism spectrum disorders
- Use of curricula and experiences to facilitate understanding and sensitivity toward students with autism spectrum disorders
- Social interaction training for students with autism spectrum disorders

Coordinated Team Commitment

- Clear definition of roles for service delivery personnel
- Effective communication
- Shared decision making

Recurrent Evaluation of Inclusion Practices

- Evaluating appropriate supplemental aides and services
- Evidence of benefit from participation and education
- Student demonstration of appropriate participation

Home–School Collaboration

- Meaningful participation
- Suitable administrative supports
- School's willingness to listen

• By Margaret P. Weiss

Teachers can use the MacArthur-Bates Communicative Development Inventory-Second Edition (CDI-II; Fenson et al., 2003) to monitor the progress of language development of very young children. Although this measure was designed for typically developing children, it's also been validated for children with disabilities, including children with autism spectrum disorders (Luyster, Lopez, & Lord, 2007; Luyster, Qiu, Lopez, & Lord, 2007). The CDI-II is appropriate for children ages eight to thirty months, and the CDI-III (Fenson, 2007) expands the measure for use with children up to thirty-seven months of age. Teachers may select the Clinical Evaluation of Language Fundamentals-4 (CELF 4; Semel, Wiig, & Secord, 2004) for older students. The CELF-4 measures receptive, expressive, grammatical, and semantic skills for individuals ages 5 to 21.

Monitoring Progress in Social/Adaptive Behavior

Comprehensive interventions for students with autism spectrum disorders invariably include a focus on social and adaptive behavior. The PDD Behavior Inventory (PDDBI) (Cohen & Sudhalter, 2005) is designed to monitor progress in social/adaptive behavior of students two to twelve years old. It includes parent and teacher versions and assesses the following domains of maladaptive behavior: (1) sensory/perceptual approach behaviors, (2) ritualisms/resistance to change, (3) social pragmatic problems, (4) semantic/pragmatic problems, (5) arousal regulation problems, (6) specific fears, and (7) aggressiveness. Adaptive behaviors assessed include (1) receptive social communication abilities and (2) expressive social communication abilities.

The Social Responsiveness Scale (SRS) (Constantino & Gruber, 2005) is a parent/teacher scale that may be used to monitor progress in social/adaptive behavior (social awareness, social information processing, reciprocal social communication, social anxiety, and avoidance). The SRS evaluates the severity of social impairment of individuals with autism spectrum disorders between the ages of four and eighteen.

The Autism Social Skills Profile (ASSP) (Bellini & Hopf, 2007) is a standardized outcome measure that examines social skills of children and adolescents with autism spectrum disorder. The ASSP is completed by teachers or parents and includes three subscales: (1) Social Reciprocity, (2) Social Participation/Avoidance, and (3) Detrimental Social Behaviors.

The Childhood Autism Rating Scale (CARS) (Schopler, Reichler, & Renner, 1988) is frequently used for screening and diagnostic purposes and can also be used to evaluate the effectiveness of interventions (Cohen et al., 2003). CARS focuses on behaviors that deviate from children developing typically and is appropriate for children over 2 years old.

EARLY INTERVENTION

Most early intervention programming focuses on children with relatively severe degrees of autism spectrum disorders, such as autism, rather than milder degrees, such as Asperger syndrome. (As previously noted, Asperger syndrome is usually not diagnosed until the child is beyond the preschool years.)

To be most effective, education and related interventions for students with autism must be early, intensive, and highly structured and should involve families. Early, intensive intervention may produce remarkable gains in many young children with autism spectrum disorders, although no intervention yet can claim universal success in enabling these children to overcome their disabilities completely. Education increasingly focuses on using natural interactions to teach students in natural environments, including general education classrooms to the extent possible. The National Research Council (NRC) (2001) reviewed research and practice and found strong consensus for the following essential features of effective preschool programs for children with autism spectrum disorders:

- Entry into intervention programs as soon as an autism spectrum diagnosis is seriously considered
- Active engagement in intensive instructional programming for a minimum of the equivalent of a full school day, 5 days (at least 25 hours) a week, with full-year programming varied according to the child's chronological age and developmental level

Success Stories

INTENSIVE AND EARLY APPLIED BEHAVIOR ANALYSIS PREPARE WESLEY FOR HIS GENERAL EDUCATION KINDERGARTEN CLASS

Ms. Gilmer, Wesley's mother: "His success has helped us feel more encouraged about his future."

Six-year-old Wesley Gilmer has attended a special elementary school program for students with autism. This year, Wesley will participate in the general education kindergarten with specialized supports.

These are the keys to his success:

★ Intensive, explicit instruction in social skills and academics

★ Relentless and structured positive behavioral support

★ Specific interventions for skill acquisition and communication

WESLEY GILMER takes his place as a student in the general education kindergarten program as special education coordinator Toni Elitharp glows with pride. Wesley has mastered his preschool goals, and he will continue to receive specially designed instruction as he learns the kindergarten curriculum. Wesley doesn't say much about his experiences, but the smile on his face tells the story. Wesley started preschool at 3 years of age with significant difficulties associated with autism, but he prospered from intensive, relentless, and specific special education.

★ Intensive, Explicit Instruction in Social Skills and Academics. Mountain View Elementary School serves neighborhood students in preschool through fifth grade. The school also provides specialized programming for children with autism who need intensive attention in classes with a small student–teacher ratio. The faculty and staff at Mountain View are active participants in creating a warm, caring, and cooperative climate for learning. "This school is child-centered," says Elitharp, who finds the key to working with students with autism is understanding their unique characteristics.

Toni Elitharp helps teachers learn to use applied behavior analysis (ABA), an educational model that targets individualized skill acquisition and behavior reduction. The ABA approach for teaching children with autism emphasizes the use of task analysis, discrete teaching, positive reinforcement, behavior intervention, and self-monitoring. "Visual strategies are also necessary to guide the students through the daily plan," says Elitharp. "It's a struggle for children with autism to know the sequence of their day without seeing the sequence in a visually explicit way." Mr. Gilmer says, "Wesley is a visual sponge."

★ Relentless and Structured Positive Behavioral Support. According to Elitharp, "children with autism live by rules, routine, and the predictability of their environment." She sees Wesley as an example of a child with autism who has thrived on relentless and structured support in coping with unpredictable events.

When he started preschool, Wesley had no parallel play skills or appropriate social skills for his age. "I knew there were some peculiarities," says Ms. Gilmer, "but he also had some unique talents." Now, as long as Wesley is

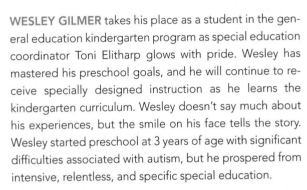

- Repeated, planned teaching opportunities generally organized around relatively brief periods of time for the youngest children (e.g., 15- to 20-minute intervals), including sufficient amounts of adult attention in one-to-one and very small group instruction to meet individualized goals
- Inclusion of a family component, including parent training
- Low student–teacher ratios (no more than two young children with autistic spectrum disorders per adult in the classroom)
- Mechanisms for ongoing program evaluation and assessments of individual children's progress, with results translated into adjustments in programming (p. 175)

Better understanding of the parental role has led to having parents work together with others as "co-therapists" in many treatment programs. If early intervention is to be as intensive and pervasive as required, family involvement is essential. A program that is based on the features recommended by the NRC, including emphasis on the role of parents as inter-

shown a picture schedule of his day and is made aware of any changes before they occur, he can participate in all activities. He now takes pride in his work, interacts with peers and adults, and shows a variety of appropriate emotions.

Wesley started preschool as a developmentally delayed child with autism. His communication skills, social skills, and readiness skills were very limited. Through the use of task analysis for each new skill, a predictable manner of presenting each skill, visual strategies, and consistent positive reinforcement, Wesley made gains and performed above grade level by the end of his preschool career.

★ Specific Interventions: Skill Acquisition and Communication. "ABA helps children learn how to learn," says Elitharp. She shows teachers how to break skills down into smaller units for easier understanding, how to practice the small units with each child, and then how to help the child connect the smaller units to something more meaningful. "The use of physical prompts reinforces correct learning, and then the prompts are gradually reduced until skills are self-maintained," she explains.

Elitharp also encourages teachers to use assistive technologies and a variety of communication systems to help children with autism gain the ability to generalize skills. Speech therapy has helped Wesley to develop his expressive vocabulary. "As he developed language, he became a happier little boy," says Ms. Gilmer. "He is now prompting us to help him learn what he wants to learn."

"When you first learn your child has autism, you want to find out what it means, and it's often discouraging," says Mr. Gilmer. "We tried to find encouraging stories. We had so many questions." Ms. Gilmer remembers, "We'd set little goals for Wesley, hoping they could be accomplished. They have been accomplished because of the willingness and patience of those who have worked with him." According to Toni Elitharp, Wesley has come far from where he began. "He has worked hard, and he will still have to work hard to progress in a world that is sometimes foreign to him." With continued effort and help from educators trained to provide specialized instruction, he should continue to succeed.

CEC'S STANDARDS: PAVING THE WAY TO SUCCESS

Assess Your Steps to Success in meeting the CEC Knowledge and Skill Base for All Beginning Special Education Teachers of Students in Individualized General Curriculums and of Students in Individualized Independence Curriculums. Use the following questions to reflect on the growth of your own professional knowledge, skills, and dispositions.

REFLECTING ON YOUR OWN PROFESSIONAL DEVELOPMENT

If you were Wesley's teacher . . .

- What are some areas about educating students with autism that you would need to know more about?
- What are some specific skills that would help you to address his academic and behavioral challenges?
- What personal dispositions do you think are most important for you to develop in teaching students with autism?

Using the CEC Standards

- What are some research-supported methods for teaching individuals with autism? (GC4S1)
- Describe how you might use task analysis in planning instruction for a student with autism. (CC7S5)
- What steps would you take in planning and implementing individualized reinforcement systems and environmental modifications for a student with autism? (IC7S1)

• By Jean B. Crockett

---

ventionists, is the **early intensive behavioral interventions (EIBI)** program. Anchored in the ABA tradition, EIBI requires considerable time commitments from therapists and parents in implementing very structured training on discrete skills. Some professionals therefore have been cautious in recommending it. Several extensive research reviews, however, have found it to be effective in improving language and functional skills in many, although not all, young children with autism (Eldevik et al., 2009; Howlin, Magiati, & Charman, 2009; Reichow & Wolery, 2009).

TRANSITION TO ADULTHOOD

Autism spectrum disorder is a condition that invariably continues into adulthood. We discuss transition to adulthood for student with more severe forms of autism spectrum disorders, such as autism, separately from students with the less severe form of Asperger syndrome.

Transition Programming for People with Autism

Although the outcomes for adults with autism are better than they once were, they are still a long way from what we should hope they'd be. For example, the majority don't live independently (Hendricks & Wehman, 2009). In many ways, their outcomes are similar to those with intellectual disabilities, and their outcomes depend to a certain degree on their level of cognitive functioning (Cederlund, Hagber, Billstedt, Gillberg, & Gillberg, 2008). Transition programming for people with autism therefore follows virtually the same principles as those for people with intellectual disabilities (see Chapter 5). Transition planning should begin as early as the elementary years and become gradually more intensive in the middle school and secondary years. The current prevailing philosophy is **person-centered planning**, whereby the person with the disability is encouraged to make her own decisions as much as possible. More and more people with autism are being integrated into the community in small **community residential facilities** and in **supported living** settings, such as their own homes or apartments. The goal for work settings is for people with autism to be in **competitive employment** or **supported competitive employment**.

Transition Programming for People with Asperger Syndrome

Much of the planning for transition to adulthood for people with Asperger syndrome addresses issues of social interaction. For example, in the accompanying Peer Connections, the transition planning for Kevin Lourens includes participation in supervised groups focused on social interactions. Research suggests that the social interaction issues for people with Asperger syndrome tend to increase as they reach adolescence and adulthood (Myles & Simpson, 2003). Unfortunately, this increase in difficulties in social interactions works against their achieving success in employment. Research also indicates that when people with Asperger syndrome do experience job difficulties, inappropriate social interactions rather than job performance are usually the cause (Gerhardt, 2003).

One way of approaching deficits in social interaction is to consider a continuum from social survival skills to social competence. Therapists or teachers of people with Asperger

Many persons with autism are being integrated into the community in small residential facilities and supported living settings, such as their own homes or apartments.

PEER CONNECTIONS: KEVIN LOURENS

KEVIN LOURENS was diagnosed with autism at around 4 years of age. He has Asperger syndrome and has been receiving services since Kindergarten. These services include speech therapy and social groups with school psychologists. He is a recent high school graduate and in the fall will attend Mira Costa Community College, where he plans to study marine biology. Currently, Kevin works for the Boys and Girls Club in San Diego, California.

1. What do you do for fun? I like to go the beach, play video games, and I'm also into cycling.

2. What is your favorite way to relax? My favorite way to relax is to listen to music, mostly 80s music.

3. What is something that you excel at? I'd have to say academics, especially math, in particular, Algebra.

4. What is your pet peeve? My pet peeve is people who have conditions similar to mine or others with my condition who refuse to accept them or get help; and also along with this, I can't stand when other people make fun of people who have disabilities.

5. Can you recall one teacher in particular who has been a positive influence in your life? Yes, my Spanish teacher in high school. His teaching style was very good. He was not like any other teacher. He rarely gave homework, but that's not the most important part. He was able to keep kids interested in what he taught by bringing it to life and teaching in different ways. He was willing to be different and take risks; he even brought his dog to school once.

6. Is there anyone else (celebrity, family member) whom you regard as a role model? Why are they a role model for you? Jeff Corwin, he is kind of like Steve Irwin. He is on TV and he goes on expeditions all around the world to find animals. He often discovers new species. He's a zoologist, and I want to go into a similar field. Right now, I'm really interested in marine biology.

7. What is the most difficult thing for you about having a disability? Knowing that I have it. I find it hard that I have to try and watch out for my symptoms that I display and express without even knowing it. For example, my hands often shake or I get really distracted, it's hard to deal with this sometimes.

8. Do you see your disability as affecting your ability to achieve what you want in your life? Career-wise, no. I'm going to college, and I find that I'm strong in academics. I plan on being a marine biologist, and I think I'll be able to achieve that goal.

9. Has your disability affected your social relationships? If so, how? Yes. It's been difficult. I didn't really want to interact with other kids during elementary school. But it wasn't until middle school that I realized they looked at me differently. Most other kids are not tolerant of my social interactions and sometimes just stay clear of me. I meet with a group of students and our school psychologist every 2 weeks. This is a time when we talk about life, school, and just anything.

10. Are there any advantages to having a disability that others might be surprised to know? I guess, I've been told by my parents that having Asperger's can kind of help me academically. It helps mathematically a lot; I can do many things. However, it's critical thinking that is really hard for me.

11. How do you think others perceive you? Well, not many people know that I have autism, so I guess that others would just see me as an average person, like everyone.

12. What is one thing that you would like others to know about you? Well, I love photography! Also, I bike 10 miles every day to and from the Boys and Girls Club where I work.

13. Please fill in the blank: I couldn't live without_____. Hmmmmm food! Pizza!

CONNECT WITH KEVIN— Kevin welcomes you to contact him online at kevinlourens@att.net

Kevin Lourens

syndrome using this approach focus first on social survival skills because they are the minimum necessary for independence (Gerhardt, 2003). For example, learning to have good manners and not be messy while eating is a more important skill than the more advanced skills involved in learning how to carry on a conversation while eating.

In transition programming for people with any kind of disability, it is always important that employers, college instructors, and those in similar positions have a solid understanding of the nature of the disability. In many cases, the person with Asperger syndrome may be misunderstood because he is intelligent but engages in eccentric behaviors.

It is fair to ask just how much the social eccentricities of people with Asperger syndrome should be tolerated or how much these behaviors actually interfere with the culture of the workplace. Most people would agree that there is room for improvement in society's attitudes toward those who behave differently from the norm but do not bother or harm others. In many cases, it's probably reasonable to ask how much it matters that an individual employee does not fit in socially with the rest of the workforce if she gets the job done. The following quote expresses well the tension between changing the individual with Asperger syndrome and changing society's reaction to people with the condition:

INTERNETRESOURCES

Alex Planck's Website
(http:www.wrongplanet.net/)
contains a variety of
information on autism
spectrum disorders, as well as
a weblog and a chatroom for
members.

A sentiment often expressed at the Douglass Group, a support group for adults with AS [Asperger syndrome] that I founded a number of years ago was "If you NTs [**neurotypicals**—a term coined by those with Asperger syndrome to describe those who do not have neurological disabilities] have all the skills, why don't you adapt for a while?" The perceived professional proclivity to focus solely on somehow "changing" the person with AS was often discussed as similar to expecting a person who is blind to see if only he or she would try harder. Given that, group members instead argued that while the primary focus of intervention should remain on the provision of skills to the learner with AS, the focus should be expanded to include comprehensive community education. (Gerhardt, 2003, p. 158)

Many people with Asperger syndrome, in fact, are becoming advocates for themselves and others who have their condition. For example, numerous Websites created by individuals with Asperger syndrome offer information and support (see the accompanying Personal Perspectives feature "Youth Uses Web to Help Others").

Personal PERSPECTIVES
Youth Uses Web to Help Others on "Wrong Planet"

People who suffer from Asperger syndrome often feel like they're on the "wrong planet" and don't fit in. One area teen, however, is trying to ensure they don't feel quite so out of this world. Alex Planck, an 18-year-old rising senior at Charlottesville High School, is the cofounder of a new Website for people with Asperger syndrome. . . .

The site, www.wrongplanet.net, was launched last month but already has close to 300 members. It features a chat room, member profiles, articles about Asperger's, personal Web logs, or "blogs," and an online store selling everything from shirts to mouse pads. . . .

"There were other Web sites . . . but they were kind of elitist," he said. His site fosters a sense of community and helps people fit in with society.

"They also didn't have as many features as our site," Planck added.

Creating and maintaining the site has been exciting for Planck. The site has received visits from such far off places as

Alex Planck

New Zealand, Australia, Denmark, and the Seychelles, a group of islands in the Indian Ocean. . . .

Although Planck says his greatest passion is learning new things, he confesses that computers are among his most enduring interests.

"It's easy to become obsessed with them because there's so much about them," he explained. Planck's partner in founding the site, Dan Grover, is a 15-year-old from Vermont who has already launched Wonderwarp, his own software group. Planck recently joined the group as a programmer.

Planck's mother, Mary, is a teacher . . . and his father, Doug, . . . is a lawyer.

"I think [the site] is such a neat resource. It's so hard to imagine what these kids deal with," his mother said.

Aside from computers and learning, the teen is also an enthusiastic mountain biker. He's hoping to attend the University of Virginia next year.

"When he wants to do something and he's focused on it, he's amazing," Mary Planck said, "We're proud of him."

Source: From Cannon, J. (2004, July 22). Youth uses Web to help others on "wrong planet." *Charlottesville Daily Progress.* Reprinted with permission.

SUMMARY

What is the history behind autism spectrum disorders?

- In 1943, Leo Kanner reported on cases of children, whom he labeled as "autistic," who had major problems in communication and social interactions, as well as bizarre repetitive movements and an obsessive dislike of change.
- In 1944, Hans Asperger reported on cases of children, whom he referred to as having "autistic psychopathy," who he thought had normal intelligence and language but who were socially isolated and had obsessive interests in extraordinarily narrow areas.

How do professionals define autism spectrum disorders?

- Autism spectrum disorder is characterized by clinically significant deficits in communication and interactions and by restricted, repetitive patterns of behavior, interests, and activities.
- People who have Asperger syndrome have higher cognitive and language skills than those with classic autism, but they have problems in the other areas, especially social interaction.

What is the prevalence of autism spectrum disorders?

- The U.S. Centers for Disease Control and Prevention estimates are that 1 out of 110 persons has an autism spectrum disorder.
- Males outnumber females 4:1 in autism spectrum disorders.
  - Prevalence is higher for European Americans than for Latinos or African Americans.
- Prevalence figures have risen dramatically for autism in the past 30 to 40 years, leading some to declare an autism "epidemic" and to claim that some mysterious toxin in our environment or the measles, mumps, rubella (MMR) vaccination may be a cause. The best scientific evidence indicates that the MMR vaccination does not cause autism.
- Most authorities maintain that the increase in autism is due to a widening of the criteria for identification as autism, a greater awareness of autism spectrum disorders, and diagnostic substitution (e.g., persons now identified as having an autism spectrum disorder previously might have been identified as intellectually disabled).

What causes autism spectrum disorders?

- Early causal theories were influenced by psychoanalytic thinking and blamed parents, often mothers, for causing autism by being too cold and unresponsive.
- Today's causal theories point to a neurological and genetic basis for autism.
  - Several areas of the brain are implicated, such as the cerebral cortex, basal ganglia, amygdala, hippocampus, corpus callosum, brain stem, and cerebellum; this has led authorities to view autism spectrum disorders as a disorder of neural networks.
  - Evidence indicates that heredity as well as spontaneous genetic mutations are involved in causing autism.
  - Evidence indicates that no single gene results in autism.

What methods are used to identify individuals with autism spectrum disorders?

- For autism, the clinician uses criteria that focus on communication skills, social interactions, and repetitive and stereotyped patterns of behavior.
  - Some early signs of autism are a lack of the following: joyful expressions at 6 months; back-and-forth sharing of sounds or facial expressions at 9 months; consistent response to his or her name, babbling, back-and-forth gestures at 12 months; words at 16 months; two-word meaningful phrases at 24 months; loss of speech or social skills at any age.
  - Clinicians often use two instruments that are considered the "gold standards" for diagnosing autism: the Autism Diagnostic Observation Scale (ADOS) and the Autism Diagnostic Interview—Revised (ADI-R)

What are some of the psychological and behavioral characteristics of learners with autism spectrum disorders?

- People with autism have deficits in social interaction, communication, and cognition; they also have repetitive and stereotyped patterns of behavior, and some have abnormal sensory perceptions.
  - Most lack communicative intent, the desire to communicate socially. Many infants and young children with autism display a lack of joint attention, the process of one person alerting another to a

stimulus via nonverbal means, such as gazing or pointing.

- They have cognitive deficits similar to those of people with intellectual disabilities; some have additional peculiarities, such as processing things visually and spatially rather than conceptually or linguistically.
- Some, who are called autistic savants, have extraordinary splinter skills.
- Examples of abnormal sensory perceptions are being hyperresponsive, hyporesponsive, or synaesthesia (a mixing of sensory information).

- Compared to people with autism, those with Asperger syndrome often display a milder degree of impairments or abnormalities in social interaction, communication, repetitive and stereotyped patterns of behavior, cognitive processing, and sensory perceptions.
  - People with Asperger syndrome often have difficulties with social interactions, understanding the hidden curriculum (the dos and don'ts of everyday living), and taking things too literally.
  - Another communication challenge in Asperger syndrome is in pragmatics, the social uses of verbal and nonverbal communication skills.

- Three theories have been proposed to account for many deficits in autism spectrum disorders. No one of them explains all the deficits of all the disorders, but together they begin to build a composite picture.
  - Problems with executive functions, including working memory, self-regulation of emotions, and the ability to plan ahead.
  - Problems with central coherence involve paying too much attention to details or parts in cognitive processing, thereby leading to impairments in conceptualizing coherent wholes.
  - Problems with a theory of mind lead to impairments in taking another person's perspective, or being able to "read" what they might be thinking.

What are some educational considerations for learners with autism spectrum disorders?

- Educational programming for students with autism includes direct instruction of skills, including applied behavior analysis (ABA); instruction in natural settings;

and behavior management, when needed, using functional assessment and positive behavioral intervention and support (PBIS).

- Examples of approaches for students with autism spectrum disorder include the Picture Exchange Communication System (PECS), social stories, and pivotal response teaching (PRT).

How do professionals assess the progress of students with autism spectrum disorders?

- Progress in language development and social/adaptive behavior can be monitored using one or more scales designed for such purposes.

What are some important considerations with respect to early intervention for learners with autism spectrum disorders?

- The most effective early intervention programs are intensive, highly structured, and involve families. One such program that has been effective for some, but not all, children is the Early Intensive Behavioral Interventions (EIBI) program.
- Early intervention programs often use natural interactions to teach students in natural environments, including general education classrooms to the extent possible.

What are some important considerations with respect to transition to adulthood for learners with autism spectrum disorders?

- For those with autism, the emphasis is on person-centered planning, with living arrangements in community residential facilities or supported living settings and placement in competitive employment or supported competitive employment situations.
- For those with Asperger syndrome, the focus is often on improving social interactions both in employment and in postsecondary school settings.

COUNCIL FOR EXCEPTIONAL CHILDREN

Addressing the Professional Standards

 Council for Exceptional Children (CEC) Common Core Knowledge and Skills addressed in this chapter: ICC1K5, ICC1K6, ICC1K7, ICC1K8, ICC2K1, ICC2K2, ICC2K4, ICC2K6, ICC3K2, ICC3K3, ICC3K4, ICC4S3, ICC4S6, ICC5K4, ICC5K8, ICC5S3, ICC6K4, ICC7K1, ICC7S2, ICC8K1, ICC8S2, ICC8S6, ICC10K3, ICC10S4,

Appendix: Provides a full listing of the CEC Common Core Standards and associated Knowledge and Skill Statements listed here.

MYEDUCATIONLAB

myeducationlab Now go to Topic 13: Autism, in the MyEducationLab (www .myeducationlab.com) for your course, where you can:

- Find learning outcomes for the broad concepts covered in this chapter along with the national standards that connect to these outcomes.
- Complete Assignments and Activities that can help you more deeply understand the chapter content.
- Examine challenging situations presented in the IRIS Center Resources.
- Apply and practice your understanding of the core concepts and skills identified in the chapter with the Building Teaching Skills and Dispositions learning units.
- Check your comprehension on the content covered in the chapter by going to the Study Plan in the Book-Specific Resources for your text. Here you will be able to take a chapter quiz, receive feedback on your answers, and then access Review, Practice, and Enrichment activities to enhance your understanding of chapter content.
- Watch video clips of CCSSO Teacher of the Year award winners responding to the question: "Why I teach?" in the Teacher Talk section.

Stutterers have a tendency to generalize their fear of one word that begins with a particular sound to a fear of all words that begin with the same sound. In the space of the summer I'd effectively eliminated every F from my vocabulary, with the exception of the preposition, "for," which for the time being was too small to incite terror. A few weeks later, my fear of F ended when another letter—I think it was L—suddenly loomed large.

David Shields • *Dead Languages (1990)*

QUESTIONS to guide your reading of this chapter . . .

- How are communication disorders defined?
- What is the prevalence of communication disorders?
- What is the difference between communicative differences and disorders?
- What are the major disorders of language?
- What are the major disorders of speech?
- What are the main educational considerations for communication disorders?
- What are the major features of assessment of progress for students with communication disorders?
- What are the major aspects of early intervention for communication disorders?
- What do educators emphasize in transition for students with communication disorders?

MISCONCEPTIONS ABOUT
Learners with Communication Disorders

MYTH • Children with language disorders always have speech difficulties as well.

FACT • It is possible for a child to have good speech yet not make any sense when he or she talks; however, most children with language disorders have speech disorders as well.

MYTH • Individuals with communication disorders always have emotional or behavioral disorders or intellectual disabilities.

FACT • Some children with communication disorders are normal in cognitive, social, and emotional development.

MYTH • How children learn language is now well understood.

FACT • Although recent research has revealed quite a lot about the sequence of language acquisition and has led to theories of language development, exactly how children learn language is still unknown.

MYTH • Stuttering is primarily a disorder of people with extremely high IQs. Children who stutter become stuttering adults.

FACT • Stuttering can affect individuals at all levels of intellectual ability. Some children who stutter continue stuttering as adults; most, however, stop stuttering before or during adolescence with help from a speech-language pathologist. Stuttering is primarily a childhood disorder, found much more often in boys than in girls.

MYTH • Disorders of phonology (or articulation) are never very serious and are always easy to correct.

FACT • Disorders of phonology can make speech unintelligible; it is sometimes very difficult to correct phonological or articulation problems, especially if the individual has cerebral palsy, intellectual disabilities, or emotional or behavioral disorders.

MYTH • There is no relationship between intelligence and communication disorders.

FACT • Communication disorders tend to occur more frequently among individuals of lower intellectual ability, although they may occur in individuals who are extremely intelligent.

MYTH • There is not much overlap between language disorders and learning disabilities.

FACT • Problems with verbal skills—listening, reading, writing, speaking—are often central features of learning disabilities. The definitions of language disorders and several other disabilities are overlapping.

MYTH • Children who learn few language skills before entering kindergarten can easily pick up all the skills they need, if they have good peer models in typical classrooms.

FACT • Early language learning is critical for later language development; a child whose language is delayed is unlikely to learn to use language effectively merely by observing peer models. More explicit intervention is typically required.

MYTH • English language learners who have acquired proficient social language will also succeed in academic tasks.

FACT • Basic interpersonal communication skills (BICS) do not ensure students' academic success. Students require proficiency in more advanced language skills, referred to as cognitive academic language proficiency (CALP), to succeed in academic areas.

ommunication is such a natural part of our everyday lives that we seldom stop to think about it. Social conversation with families, friends, and casual acquaintances is normally so effortless and pleasant that it is hard to imagine having difficulty with it. Consider the following description of speech by Hulit and Howard (2010):

> Speech is so much a part of the human experience that we truly take it for granted, but it is a wondrous human gift. The next time you engage in a conversation with one or more people, consider the speech chains that connect speakers to listeners. Marvel at the speed involved in the sending and receiving of messages. (p. 15)

Most of us have feelings of uncertainty about the adequacy of our speech or language only in stressful or unusual social situations, such as talking to a large audience or being interviewed for a job. If we always had to worry about communicating, we would worry about every social interaction we had.

For some people, however, communication is not effortless and pleasant. Their communication may take great effort. For instance, some individuals have serious problems producing a sufficiently clear voice quality, described as a *voice disorder*, and other individuals are unable to comprehend the language that others produce, described as a *receptive language disorder*. The young man David Shields (quoted in the chapter opening) was unable to produce fluent speech, or speech of an appropriate rhythm and rate; this is a *fluency disorder*, or stuttering.

Not all communication disorders involve disorders of speech. Not all speech disorders are as handicapping in social interactions as stuttering, nor is stuttering the most common disorder of speech. Stuttering affects only about 1 person in 20 children, and only about 1 in a 100 people stutter throughout their lives. Most cases of childhood stuttering are resolved by adulthood (Owens, Metz, & Farinella, 2010; Yairi & Ambrose, 2004).

Today, difficulty such as that described by Shields is viewed within the broad context of communication disorders because of the obstacle it presents to social interaction, which is the major purpose of language. The young man's stuttering resulted in an inability to convey his thoughts and feelings, not just a problem of being fearful and unable to say certain words. In thinking about communication disorders, three elements of communication must be considered: the contexts in which communication occurs (e.g., in a group, in the classroom), the functions expressed by communication or the reasons one communicates (e.g., to request, to comment, to reason), and the actual execution of communication comprehension and expression.

DEFINITIONS

Speech and language are tools used for communication. **Communication** is the process of sharing information and involves many **communicative functions**, such as seeking social interaction, requesting objects, sharing ideas, and rejecting an object or interaction. It requires sending messages in understandable form (encoding) and receiving and understanding messages (decoding). It always involves a sender and a receiver of messages, but it does not always involve oral language. Communication can also be nonverbal; in fact, much of the meaningful interaction among humans is nonverbal (Owens et al., 2010). Language (both verbal and nonverbal) and speech are important tools for human communication. A **communication disorder** impairs the ability to transmit or receive ideas, facts, feelings, and desires and may involve language or speech or both, including hearing, listening, reading, or writing.

Language is the communication of ideas—sending and receiving them—through an arbitrary system of symbols used according to certain rules that determine meaning. Encoding or sending messages is referred to as **expressive language**. Decoding or understanding messages is referred to as **receptive language**. When people think of language, they typically think of oral language. **Speech**—the neuromuscular activity of forming and sequencing the sounds of oral language—is the most common symbol system used in communication between humans. Without the rule-governed symbol system that we call language, we would have only grunts and groans, not speech.

myeducationlab

To check your comprehension on the content covered in Chapter 10, go to the Book-Specific Resources in the MyEducationLab (www.myeducationlab.com) for your course, select your text, and complete the Study Plan. Here you will be able to take a chapter quiz, receive feedback on your answers, and then access review, practice, and enrichment activities to enhance your understanding of chapter content. ■

INTERNETRESOURCES

On the *This American Life* radio show a college student who stutters discusses the challenges he faces as a result of his disability. Visit http://www.thisamericanlife.org/radio-archives/episode/203/recordings-for-someone and select ACT TWO. SPECIAL EFFECTS STORY to hear Kevin Murphy's story. Kevin describes how the National Stuttering Association changed his life. You can visit their website at http://www.westutter.org/

Some languages, however, are not based on speech. For example, American Sign Language (ASL) does not involve speech sounds; it is a manual language used by many people who cannot hear speech. **Augmentative or alternative communication (AAC)** for people with disabilities involving the physical movements of speech may consist of alternatives to the speech sounds of oral language (e.g., picture boards, ASL, gestures, and electronic devices that produce speech).

The American Speech–Language–Hearing Association (ASHA) provides definitions of disorders of communication, including speech disorders, language disorders, and variations in communication (differences or dialects and augmentative systems) that are not disorders (see the accompanying Focus on Concepts). **Speech disorders** are impairments in the production and use of oral language. They include disabilities in making speech sounds, producing speech with a normal flow, and producing voice.

Language disorders include problems in comprehension and expression. Remember that language is governed by rules. The problems—rule violations—may involve the form (phonology, morphology, syntax), content (semantics), or use of language (pragmatics).

- *Phonology* refers to the rules governing speech sounds—the particular sounds and how they are sequenced.
- *Morphology* refers to the rules that govern alterations of the internal organization of words, such as adding suffixes and other grammatical inflections to make proper plurals, verb tenses, and so on.
- *Syntax* refers to the rules of organizing sentences that are meaningful, including, for example, subject and predicate and placing modifiers correctly.
- *Semantics* refers to the rules about attaching meanings and concepts to words.
- *Pragmatics* refers to the rules about using language for social purposes.

Language disorders may involve any one or a combination of these five subsystems of language. Differences in speech or language that are shared by people in a given region, social group, or cultural/ethnic group should not be considered disorders. For example, African American English (Ebonics or Black English Vernacular), Appalachian English, and the Cajun dialect are varieties of English, not disorders of speech or language. These differences are governed by their own rules and reflect the cultural and linguistic diversity of North America. As long as speech and language are guided by consistent rules of a language community, they are not disorders, although they may differ from what we are accustomed to hearing and saying.

Similarly, the use of AAC systems does not imply that a person has a language disorder. Rather, such systems support people who have temporary or permanent inabilities to use speech satisfactorily for communication. Those who use AAC systems might or might not have language disorders in addition to their inability to use speech.

PREVALENCE

Establishing the prevalence of communication disorders is difficult because they are extremely varied, sometimes difficult to identify, and often occur as part of other disabilities (e.g., intellectual disabilities, brain injury, learning disability, or autism). About a million children—approximately one fifth of all children who are identified for special education—receive services primarily for language or speech disorders. Speech-language therapy is one of the most frequently provided related services for children with other primary disabilities (e.g., intellectual disabilities or learning disability).

About 8% to 9% of preschool children and about 5% of students in elementary and secondary grades have speech disorders; about 2% to 3% of preschoolers and about 1% of the school-age population have language disorders (Ehren & Nelson, 2005; National Institute on Deafness and Communication Disorders, 2010; Nelson, 1998; Onslow, Packman, & Payne, 2007). Communication disorders of all kinds are predicted to increase during the coming decades, as medical advances preserve the lives of more children and youths with severe disabilities that affect communication. Therefore, schools need more speech-language pathologists as well as greater knowledge of communication disorders by special and general ed-

FOCUS ON Concepts

DEFINITIONS OF THE AMERICAN SPEECH–LANGUAGE–HEARING ASSOCIATION

I. A communication disorder is an impairment in the ability to receive, send, process, and comprehend concepts or verbal, nonverbal, and graphic symbol systems. A communication disorder may be evident in the processes of hearing, language, and/or speech. A communication disorder may range in severity from mild to profound. It may be developmental or acquired. Individuals may demonstrate one or any combination of communication disorders. A communication disorder may result in a primary disability or it may be secondary to other disabilities.

  A. A speech disorder is an impairment of the articulation of speech sounds, fluency, and/or voice.

    1. An articulation disorder is the atypical production of speech sounds characterized by substitutions, omissions, additions, or distortions that may interfere with intelligibility.

    2. A fluency disorder is an interruption in the flow of speaking characterized by atypical rate, rhythm, and repetitions in sounds, syllables, words, and phrases. This may be accompanied by excessive tension, struggle behavior, and secondary mannerisms.

    3. A voice disorder is characterized by the abnormal production and/or absences of vocal quality, pitch, loudness, resonance, and/or duration, which is inappropriate for an individual's age and/or sex.

  B. A language disorder is impaired comprehension and/or use of spoken, written, and/or other symbol systems. The disorder may involve (1) the form of language (phonology, morphology, syntax), (2) the content of language (semantics), and/or (3) the function of language in communication (pragmatics) in any combination.

    1. Form of Language

      a. Phonology is the sound system of a language and the rules that govern the sound combinations.

      b. Morphology is the system that governs the structure of words and the construction of word forms.

      c. Syntax is the system governing the order and combination of words to form sentences, and the relationships among the elements within a sentence.

    2. Content of Language

      a. Semantics is the system that governs the meanings of words and sentences.

    3. Function of Language

      a. Pragmatics is the system that combines the above language components in functional and socially appropriate communication.

II. Communication Variations

  A. Communication difference/dialect is a variation of a symbol system used by a group of individuals that reflects and is determined by shared regional, social, or cultural/ethnic factors. A regional, social, or cultural/ethnic variation of a symbol system should not be considered a disorder of speech or language.

  B. Augmentative/alternative communication systems attempt to compensate and facilitate, temporarily or permanently, for the impairment and disability patterns of individuals with severe expressive and/or language comprehension disorders. Augmentative/alternative communication may be required for individuals demonstrating impairments in gestural, spoken, and/or written modalities.

Source: American Speech–Language–Hearing Association. (1993). *Definitions of communication disorders and variations, ASHA, 35*(Suppl. 10), pp. 40–41. Reprinted with permission.

ucation teachers and greater involvement of teachers in helping students learn to communicate effectively.

COMMUNICATION VARIATIONS

The fact that a student doesn't use the speech or language that is expected in school does not necessarily mean that she has a language disorder. The more important question is whether the student is an effective communicator in her speech and language community (see Goldstein & Iglesias, 2004; Justice, 2006; Owens, 2004). Someone with a language difference that is also a disorder has difficulty communicating in every language environment, including her home language community.

Systematic language variations that are rule governed are considered **dialects** (Vinson, 2007). A dialect may lead to a misdiagnosis of a language disorder. The speech or language of African American children, for example, might mistakenly be judged to indicate disorder when it is merely different from standard American English. Conversely, a speech or language deficit of an African American child may be attributed to the dialect, resulting in underdiagnosis (Stockman, 2010). Although a language variation or dialect does not constitute a language disorder, an individual may both have a language disorder and exhibit a variation that is not a disorder. Such an individual will be unable to communicate effectively even with others who use the same language variation.

Encouraging the communication of children whose cultural heritage or language patterns are not those of the professional's subculture is of increasing concern to classroom teachers and speech-language clinicians (see Chapter 3). On the one hand, care must be taken not to mistake a cultural or ethnic difference for a disorder; on the other hand, disorders that exist in the context of a language difference must not be overlooked. When assessing children's language, the professional must be aware of the limitations of normative tests and sources of potential bias.

A child might not have a language disorder yet have a communicative difference that requires special teaching to promote academic achievement and social communication. Children of nondominant cultures must be taught the rules for effective communication in the dominant culture. However, professionals must also understand and accept the effectiveness of a child's home language in its cultural context. Failure to teach children the skills they need to communicate effectively according to the rules of the dominant culture will deny them many opportunities. In effect, children of minority language groups might need to learn to live in two worlds: one in which their home language is used and one in which school language is used.

Many students for whom language difference is an issue do not speak entirely different languages, but variations peculiar to certain groups of speakers—that is, dialects. For example, one dialect that differs from standard American English (and is not a language disorder) is Appalachian English. People in Appalachia speak a variation of English with features that are not shared by other English dialects. Teachers must understand—and help their students understand—that other dialects are not inferior or limited language systems. Furthermore, teachers must recognize cultural differences regardless of the communication device being used. Multicultural issues arise in all communication interactions, including those in which AAC is used (Goldstein & Iglesias, 2004).

Families differ greatly in the ways they talk to children and in the language they expect children to use. Although students might not have language disorders, their language variations could put them at a disadvantage in using language in an academic context. Consequently, some people have suggested that children who come to school without mastery of the English of their textbooks should be taught it directly and consistently (e.g., Raspberry, 2001). Among the recommendations of Goldstein and Iglesias (2004, pp. 368–369) are the following:

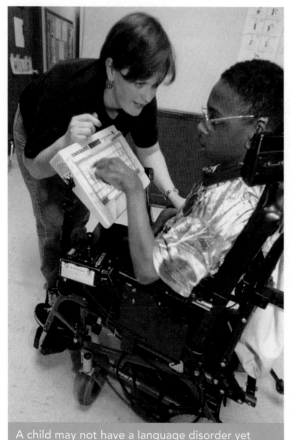

A child may not have a language disorder yet have a communication difference that demands special teaching. Such differences might be related to culture and/or disability.

- Take the student's cultural values and learning style into account.
- Ask for help from colleagues, parents, and others, if necessary.
- View the student in the naturalistic context of the classroom.
- Know the features of the community's dialects.
- Take the student's dialect into account.
- Use the least biased tools for assessment.

A major concern today in both special and general education is teaching children who are learning English as a second language, who are non-English proficient, or who have limited English proficiency. Bilingual education is a field of concern and controversy because of the rapidly changing demographics in many American communities. Spanish-speaking children make up a rapidly growing percentage of the students in many school districts. Moreover, a large number of children from various nations who do not speak English have immigrated to the United States during the past decade. Many of these children have no proficiency or limited proficiency in English, and some have disabilities as well. Bilingual special education is still a developing field. As we discussed in Chapter 3, finding the best way to teach children to become proficient in English, particularly when they have disabilities as well as language differences, is a special challenge for the 21st century.

LANGUAGE DISORDERS

Communication disorders cannot be understood without knowledge of normal language development. So before discussing the disorders of language and speech, we provide a brief description of normal language development. Language disorders are discussed first and more extensively than speech disorders, because the primary focus of speech-language pathologists and other specialists in communicative disorders has shifted from speech to language during the evolution of special education and related services (Owens, et al., 2010).

The newborn makes few sounds other than cries. Within a few years, however, the human child can form the many complex sounds of speech, understand spoken and written language, and express meaning verbally. The major milestones in this ability to use language are fairly well known by child development specialists, although the underlying mechanisms that control the development of language are still not well understood. What parts of the process of learning language are innate, and what parts are controlled by the environment? What is the relationship between cognitive development and language development? These and many other questions about the origins and uses of language cannot yet be answered definitively.

Table 10.1 describes typical development of speech, language, and communication. The child with a language disorder may eventually reach many or most of the milestones shown for normal development, but at a later age than typically developing children. It is important to note that children sometimes seem to "catch up" in language development, only to fall behind typical development again at a later age.

No one knows exactly how children learn language, but we do know that language development is related in a general way to physical maturation, cognitive development, and socialization. The details of the process—the particulars of what happens physiologically, cognitively, and socially in the learning of language—are still being debated. Nelson (1998) discusses six theories of language that have dominated the study of human communication at various times. The six theories and research based on them have established the following:

1. Language learning depends on brain development and proper brain functioning. Language disorders are sometimes a result of brain dysfunction, and ways to compensate for the dysfunction can sometimes be taught. The emphasis is on biological maturation.

2. Language learning is affected by the consequences of language behavior. Language disorders can be a result of inappropriate learning, and consequences can sometimes be arranged to correct disordered language. The emphasis is on behavioral psychology.

3. Language can be analyzed as inputs and outputs related to the way information is processed. Faulty processing may account for some language disorders, and more effective processing skills can sometimes be taught. The emphasis is on information processing.

4. Language is acquired by a biological process that dictates rules governing the form, content, and use of language. Language disorders are the result of a failure to acquire or employ rule-governed aspects of language, and these disorders may be overcome

TABLE 10.1 Development of speech, language, and communication

Age	Accomplishments
Newborn	Prefers human face and voice. Able to discriminate loudness, intonation, and phonemes.
3 months	Begins babbling. Responds vocally to partner.
6 months	Begins reduplicated babbling, "Ba-ba-ba".
8 months	Begins gesturing. Begins variegated babbling. Imitates tonal quality of adult speech, called *jargon*.
10 months	Adds phonetically consistent forms.
12 months	First word spoken. Words fill intentions previously signaled by gestures.
18 months	Begins combining words on the basis of word-order rules.
2 years	Begins adding bound morphemes. Average length or mean length of utterance (MLU) is 1.6–2.2 morphemes.
3 years	More adultlike sentence structure. MLU is 3.0–3.3 morphemes.
4 years	Begins to change style of talking to fit conversational partner. MLU is 3.6–4.7 morphemes.
5 years	90% of language form learned.
6 years	Begins to learn visual mode of communication with writing and reading.
8 years	All American English speech sounds acquired.
Adolescence	Able to competently participate in conversations and telling of narratives. Knows multiple meanings of words and figurative language. Uses a gender style, or genderlect, when talking.
Adult	Vocabulary has expanded to 30,000–60,000 words. Specialized styles of communicating with different audiences and for diverse purposes.

Source: Adapted with permission from Owens, R. E., Jr., Evans, D. E., & Haas, B. A. (2000). *Introduction to communication disorders: A life span perspective.* Boston: Allyn & Bacon.

by helping an individual induce or learn these rules. The emphasis is on a linguistic or nativist perspective.

5. Language is one of many cognitive skills. Language disorders reflect basic problems in thinking and learning, and sometimes these disorders can be addressed effectively by teaching specific cognitive skills. The emphasis is on cognitive development.

6. Language arises from the need to communicate in social interactions. Language disorders are a breakdown in ability to relate effectively to one's environment, and the natural environment can sometimes be arranged to teach and support more effective interaction. The emphasis is on social interaction.

All these theories contain elements of scientific truth, but none can explain the development and disorders of language completely. Each of the six theories has advantages and disadvantages for assessing language disorders and devising effective interventions. Advances in neurological imaging technology may lead to better understanding of the biological bases of language (Foundas, 2001). However, pragmatic or social interaction theory is widely viewed as having the most direct implications for speech-language pathologists and teachers because it focuses most directly on how communication skills can be fostered through adult–child interaction (Owens, 2004).

Language involves listening and speaking, reading and writing, technical discourse, and social interaction. Language problems are therefore basic to many of the disabilities discussed in this book, especially hearing impairment, intellectual disabilities, traumatic brain injury, autistic spectrum disorder, and learning disability.

Classification of Language Disorders

Language disorders can be classified according to two primary dimensions: domain (subsystem or type) and etiology (cause). The ASHA definitions in the Focus on Concepts on page 269 suggest a classification scheme involving five subsystems or types of language:

No one knows exactly how or why children learn language, but we do know language development is related in a general way to physical maturation, cognitive development, and socialization.

phonological (sounds), morphological (word forms), syntactical (word order and sentence structure), semantic (word and sentence meanings), and pragmatic (social use of language). Difficulty with one of these dimensions of language is virtually certain to be accompanied by difficulty with one or more of the others. However, children with language disorders often have particular difficulty with one dimension.

Another way of classifying language disorders is based on the presumed cause (etiology) or related conditions. Classification by etiology provides two subtypes: primary and secondary. A **primary language disorder** has no known cause. A **secondary language disorder** is caused by another condition, such as intellectual disabilities, hearing impairment, autistic spectrum disorder, cerebral palsy, or traumatic brain injury.

A scientific approach to problems demands classification, but human beings and their language are very difficult to categorize. Therefore, all classification systems contain ambiguities, and none can account for all cases. In a textbook devoted to language disorders, Owens (2004) notes:

> Many children with [language impairments] cannot be described easily by any of the categories discussed in this chapter. Such children may have either more than one primary diagnostic category or characteristics that do not fit into any category. Each child represents a unique set of circumstances, so language assessment and intervention should be individualized. (p. 20)

Ryan, the student described in the accompanying Success Stories feature, is a perfect example of this concept. He suffered a brain injury and, with the help of his family and involved professionals, he learned to communicate again. Ryan was fortunate enough to experience a full recovery, but his struggles with communication are fresh in his mind.

Children with language disorders often have difficulty with one of the following dimensions of language: phonology, morphology, syntax, semantics, or pragmatics.

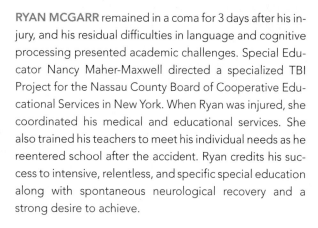

Success Stories

THROUGH COORDINATION OF MEDICAL AND EDUCATIONAL SERVICES, RYAN MOVES FROM REHABILITATION TO SCHOOL REENTRY SUCCESSFULLY

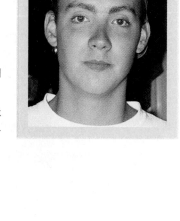

Ryan McGarr: "When I look back, I realize how slow I was as a result of the head injury."

College student Ryan McGarr was severely injured in a Thanksgiving Day car wreck during his junior year in high school. An innovative traumatic brain injury (TBI) project provided a bridge between his rehabilitation services and school reentry.

These are the keys to his success:

★ Intensive coordination of services and supports

★ Relentless instruction in academics and vocabulary development

★ Specific goals for compensatory strategies and teacher training

RYAN MCGARR remained in a coma for 3 days after his injury, and his residual difficulties in language and cognitive processing presented academic challenges. Special Educator Nancy Maher-Maxwell directed a specialized TBI Project for the Nassau County Board of Cooperative Educational Services in New York. When Ryan was injured, she coordinated his medical and educational services. She also trained his teachers to meet his individual needs as he reentered school after the accident. Ryan credits his success to intensive, relentless, and specific special education along with spontaneous neurological recovery and a strong desire to achieve.

★ **Intensive Coordination of Services and Supports.** Kathy McGarr was grateful that someone at the hospital told her about the TBI project: "Just the trauma, and trying to take care of your other children—the whole family tends to fall apart. I didn't have the concentration or anything to deal with this." According to Maher-Maxwell, "research suggests that kids who have this connection between rehabilitation and school reentry, along with ongoing staff support once they've returned, have greater success rates than those who don't."

Ryan returned to school part-time in April of his junior year. He went to an outpatient rehabilitation center for therapies in the morning and then to his local public high

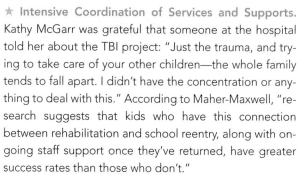

Primary Language Disorders

Specific language impairment (SLI) refers to a language disorder that has no identifiable cause; it is an unexpected and unexplained variation in the acquisition of language (Silliman & Scott, 2006). These disorders result in significant limitations in language and are not due to intellectual disabilities, the perceptual problems that characterize language learning disability, hearing problems, and so on (Owens et al., 2007). Often, SLI involves multiple aspects of language. Academic problems, particularly in the areas of reading and writing, are common for children with SLI (Choudhury & Benasich, 2003; Kohnert, Windsor, & Yim, 2006; Peterson, Pennington, Shriberg, & Boada, 2009; Tomblin, 2010).

Early expressive language delay (EELD) refers to a significant lag in expressive language (i.e., the child doesn't have a 50-word vocabulary or use 2-word utterances by age 2) that the child won't outgrow. About half the children whose language development is delayed at age 2 will gradually catch up developmentally with their age peers; however, the other half will not catch up and will continue to have language problems throughout their school years.

Language-based reading impairment involves a reading problem based on a language disorder. This disorder cannot be identified until the child begins learning to read and has problems. Research of such abilities as phonological awareness, alphabet knowledge, and grammatical speech have helped in identifying children who are vulnerable to this kind of disorder (Justice & Schuele, 2004; Vellutino, Fletcher, Snowling, & Scanlon, 2004). A significant percentage of children who show language impairments in kindergarten

school in the afternoon for English, social studies, art, and resource room. He returned full-time for his senior year, carrying a full program of academic courses with resource room support for 45 minutes daily.

★ **Relentless Instruction in Academics and Vocabulary Development.** Nancy Maher-Maxwell remembers that when she met Ryan 6 weeks after the accident, he was determined to graduate with his class and wanted tutoring. "The psychologist at the hospital, who evaluated him 9 weeks after the accident, told me Ryan would probably never finish school and that I was overwhelming him with academics," says Mrs. McGarr, "but it was what he wanted, and I had to let him try to do it." To start the process, Maher-Maxwell contacted Ryan's school district. His former English teacher agreed to be his home tutor. With Maher-Maxwell's help, her lessons were individualized, concentrating on vocabulary and word meanings. She used flash cards and together with Ryan made up funny sentences using mnemonics to help him remember information. Instead of giving him a chapter to read in history, she chunked material to be learned by breaking it up into smaller units.

★ **Specific Goals for Compensatory Strategies and Teacher Training.** The TBI Project coordinated Ryan's reentry into the regular educational environment by providing workshops as well as ongoing support for his teachers. Training emphasized Ryan's need to take in new information in a variety of ways. Teachers learned techniques to reinforce study skills, such as taking notes, outlining chapters, and organizing projects. "Often the typical high school teacher will lecture on the subject, expect the kids to take good notes, and evaluate them on a test. Because of the disruptions in the learning systems of students with TBI, there may be a slower rate in processing, so extended time is often necessary both in teaching and in testing," Nancy Maher-Maxwell says.

His mother recalls that it was hard to tell whether Ryan would regain his language abilities. "In speech therapy, he had a terrible time with categorization skills. His therapist asked him to name five green vegetables, and he couldn't do it! What was even more surprising was that he couldn't imagine that anyone could!"

TBI is an acquired injury that demands new adjustments. "If I hadn't spoken with Nancy," says Mrs. McGarr, "I wouldn't have known to put Ryan in a resource room, since he never needed special education before." Head injuries can also make the future harder to predict. "That early neuropsychological evaluation that said he could forget about his academic aspirations never took into account Ryan's determination and the compensatory strategies that special education could provide," says Maher-Maxwell.

Ryan still finds that he is more easily distracted than he used to be, and he continues to need extended time on some college exams. He remains confident about the future, saying, "I'll succeed in the world doing whatever I want to do. I have no doubts about that."

• By Jean B. Crockett

will have obvious reading problems by second grade (Catts, Adlof, Hogan, & Ellis Weismer, 2005; Catts, Fey, Zhang, & Tomblin, 2001; Sawyer, 2006). Although **phonological awareness** has garnered much of the attention for the past two decades, research also provides some evidence that pragmatic, syntactic, and semantic knowledge is predictive of later reading comprehension (Catts et al., 2001; DeThorne, Petrill, Schatschneider, & Cutting, 2010; Muter, Hulme, Snowling, & Stevenson, 2004; Silliman & Scott, 2006), again indicating significant risk for children with language impairment. Recent research also suggests that the magnitude of the reading impairment is greater when the language impairment is paired with a speech sound disorder (Peterson, Pennington, Shriberg, & Boada, 2009).

Secondary Language Disorders

The literature on language disorders often includes discussion of the particular communication impairments of individuals with other specific disabling conditions, such as intellectual disabilities or autism spectrum disorder (e.g., Owens, 2004). Difficulty in using language in social interactions and relationships is now seen as a basic problem in many disorders.

Emotional and behavioral disorders, for instance, may range from social reticence or withdrawal to severe acting out and aggression (McCabe & Marshall, 2006; Rogers-Adkinson & Griffith, 1999). Young children who have language disorders might have special difficulty in developing skills in social interaction because they do not interpret social circumstances correctly and have difficulty expressing themselves. Donahue, Hartas, and Cole (1999) provide an example.

> In a kindergarten classroom, there are two adjacent (unisex) bathroom doors, each sporting almost identical pumpkin face posters. Almost invisible to the adult eye, one pumpkin has the faintest suggestion of eyelashes (instead of triangle eyes, this pumpkin has rectangles with a jagged top). A boy identified as having a language disorder comes out of this bathroom and goes to his table. Another boy approaches him, saying:
>
>> Why did you go to the girls' bathroom? (pointing to the pumpkin face)
>> Huh?
>> You went to the girls' bathroom.
>> No—no—. That not girls'.
>> Yes it is.
>> No way—boys can too. (voice rising)
>> Yeah, there's a girl pumpkin on it.
>> But—but . . . that not a girl! (getting angry)
>> Yeah, look at those eyelashes.
>> But—but . . . NOT! (Splutters, jumps up and shoves the other boy. The teacher intervenes, and gives the child with the language disorder a time-out for fighting. He sits angrily, muttering to himself, "not a girl!") (p. 72)

Language impairment may also limit individuals' social interaction with peers. For example, in a study of adolescents' use of cell phone technology, students with SLI texted their friends less frequently than their peers without SLI, resulting in fewer opportunities to develop social networks (Conti-Ramsden, Durkin, & Simkin, 2010).

SPEECH DISORDERS

Speech disorders are very heterogeneous; that is, many different types, degrees, and combinations exist. Speech disorders pose a wide variety of challenges to the communication abilities of school children.

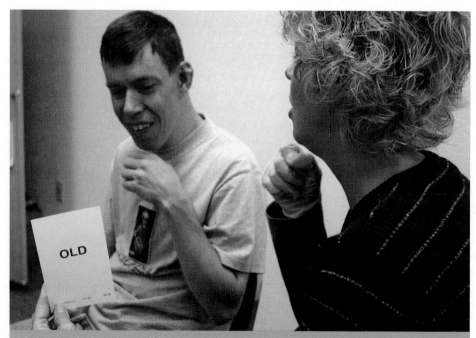

Most speech disorders will be treated primarily by speech-language pathologists, not classroom teachers. Teachers should be aware of possible speech disorders in order to be able to refer students properly.

We provide only brief descriptions of the major disorders affecting the speech of school-age children. Most speech disorders are treated primarily by a speech-language pathologist, not by a classroom teacher. However, both general and special education teachers are expected to work collaboratively with speech-language pathologists in assessment and intervention.

Phonological Disorders

Phonological disorders occur in children younger than 9 years of age. These disorders do not include the normally developing young child's inability to say words correctly. The cause of the disorder is often unknown, but for some reason children with phonological disorders do not understand the rules for producing the sounds of their language. Their speech sound production differs from age-appropriate, culturally based expectations. These children don't seem to understand how to differentiate and produce the phonemes or sounds of language to construct intelligible words. This disorder occurs in about 4 or 5 in 100 children, somewhat more often in boys than in girls.

Phonological disorders are difficult to distinguish conceptually from articulation disorders (Owens et al., 2007). Children with an articulation disorder simply have trouble producing sounds correctly. In contrast, children with a phonological disorder seem to have a poor inner representation of the sounds of language. They might not understand the contrasts between sounds or the distinctiveness of sound, which results in problems with how speech sounds are produced. For instance, children who do not have an internal representation of consonants at the end of words produce *hat* as *ha* and *dog* as *do*.

Phonology is critical to literacy. Learning to read requires an understanding of the alphabetic principle—that letters work systematically to represent sounds, and these sounds can be blended together to form words (Lane & Pullen, 2004). **Phonological awareness** is an understanding of the sound structure of language; it includes the abilities to blend sounds into words, to segment words into sounds, and to otherwise manipulate the sounds of spoken language. Without phonological awareness, a student cannot make sense of the alphabetic principle, which results in an inability to decode words. Some, but not all, children with phonological disorders lack phonological awareness. Some have serious problems with verbal working memory (remembering what was said or what they want to say) or word learning and word retrieval. Deficits in working memory and word retrieval are considered a phonological processing disorder. This disorder of the phonological system of language affects speech sound production and often affects literacy as well.

Articulation Disorders

Articulation disorders involve errors in producing sounds. The problem is not an underlying phonological problem but a disorder in which the individual omits, substitutes, distorts, or adds speech sounds. Lisping, for example, involves a substitution or distortion of the /s/ sound (e.g., *thunthine* or *shunshine* for *sunshine*). Missing, substituted, added, or poorly produced word sounds can make a speaker difficult to understand or even unintelligible. Such errors in speech production may also carry heavy social penalties, subjecting the speaker to teasing or ridicule.

When are articulation errors considered a disorder? That depends on a clinician's subjective judgment, which will be influenced by the clinician's experience, the number and types of errors, the consistency of these errors, the age and developmental characteristics of the speaker, and the intelligibility of the person's speech (see Bernthal & Bankson, 2004).

Young children make frequent errors in speech sounds when they are learning to talk. Many children do not learn to produce all the speech sounds correctly until they are 8 or 9 years old. Furthermore, most children make frequent errors until after they enter school. Thus, the age of the child is a major consideration in judging the adequacy of articulation. Another major consideration is the characteristics of the child's language community, because children learn speech largely through imitation. For instance, a child who is reared in the deep south might have speech that sounds peculiar to residents of Long Island, but this does not mean that the child has a speech disorder. Remember that there are differences that are not disorders.

Lack of ability to articulate speech sounds correctly can be caused by biological factors. For example, brain damage or damage to the nerves controlling the muscles that are used in speech may make it difficult or impossible to articulate sounds (Bernthal & Bankson, 1998; Cannito, Yorkston, & Beukelman, 1998). Among children with other disabilities, especially intellectual disabilities and neurological disorders such as cerebral palsy, the prevalence of articulation disorders is higher than that in the general population. Abnormalities of the oral structures, such as a cleft palate, can make normal speech difficult or impossible. Relatively minor structural changes, such as loss of teeth, can produce temporary errors. Poor articulation may also result from a hearing loss.

Most schools screen all new pupils for speech and language problems, and in most cases, a child who still makes many articulation errors in the third or fourth grade will be referred for evaluation. Older children and adults sometimes seek help on their own when their speech draws negative attention. The decision to include or not include a child in speech-language therapy depends on several factors, including the child's age, developmental characteristics, and the pathologist's assessment of the likelihood that the child will self-correct the errors and of the social penalties, such as teasing and shyness, the child is experiencing. If the child misarticulates only a few sounds but does so consistently and suffers social embarrassment or rejection as a consequence, an intervention program is usually called for.

Voice Disorders

People's voices are perceived as having pitch, loudness, and quality. Changes in pitch and loudness are part of the stress patterns of speech. Vocal quality is related not only to production of speech sounds, but also to the nonlinguistic aspects of speech. Voice disorders, though difficult to define precisely, are characteristics of pitch, loudness, and/or quality that are abusive of the **larynx**; hamper communication; or are perceived as markedly different from what is customary for someone of a given age, sex, and cultural background (Robinson & Crowe, 2001).

Voice disorders can result from a variety of causes and can be grouped into three primary categories including functional disorders, organic disorders, and neurological disorders (Anderson & Shames, 2006). Disorders that are a result of damage to the larynx (i.e., trauma) are considered functional disorders. A physical condition including growths in the larynx (e.g., nodules, polyps, or cancerous tissue) that has affected the structure or function of the larynx are considered organic disorders. Disorders that are a result of nervous system dysfunction are considered neurological disorders.

Misuse or abuse of the voice also can lead to a quality that is temporarily abnormal. High school cheerleaders, for example, frequently develop temporary voice disorders due to the formation of nodules (calluses) on their vocal cords (Campbell, Reich, Klockars, & McHenry, 1988). The same kind of problem can be caused by a child's screaming. Teachers and others who constantly use a very loud voice, whether expressing passionate beliefs, talking over noisy conditions, or speaking in a room with poor acoustics, may also develop voice problems.

Disorders resulting from misuse or abuse of the voice can damage the tissues of the larynx. So can smoking or inhaling substances that irritate the vocal folds. Sometimes a person has psychological problems that lead to a complete loss of voice (**aphonia**) or to severe voice abnormalities.

Voice disorders having to do with **resonance**—vocal quality—may be caused by physical abnormalities of the oral cavity (such as **cleft palate**) or damage to the brain or nerves controlling the oral cavity. Infections of the tonsils, adenoids, or sinuses can also influence how the voice is resonated. Most people who have severe hearing loss typically have problems in achieving a normal or pleasingly resonant voice. Finally, sometimes a person simply has not learned to speak with an appropriately resonant voice. This problem has no biological or deep-seated psychological causes; rather, it appears that the individual has learned faulty habits of positioning the organs of speech.

INTERNETRESOURCES

For more information about cleft lip, cleft palate, and other cranio-facial deformities and effects on speech, see SMILES at http://www.cleft.org/

Teachers need to observe children for common symptoms of voice disorders, such as hoarseness, aphonia, breathiness, odd pitch (voice too high or too low pitched), or an inappropriately loud or soft voice. A teacher who notes possible problems should ask a speech-language pathologist to conduct an evaluation. Teachers should also monitor their own voices for indications of vocal stress.

Fluency Disorders

Normal speech is characterized by some interruptions in speech flow. Especially when a child is learning to talk, we can expect normal **dysfluencies**. These are the hesitations, repetitions, and other interruptions of normal speech flow that are entirely normal parts of learning to use language. All of us occasionally get speech sounds in the wrong order (e.g., saying *revalent* for *relevant*), speak too quickly to be understood, pause at the wrong place in a sentence, use an inappropriate pattern of stress, or become dysfluent—that is, stumble and backtrack, repeating words or phrases, and fill in pauses with *uh* while trying to think of how to finish what we have to say. It is only when the speaker's efforts are so intense or the interruptions in the flow of speech are so frequent or pervasive that they prevent understanding or draw extraordinary attention that they are considered disorders. Besides, listeners have a greater tolerance for some types of dysfluencies than others. Most of us will more readily accept speech-flow disruptions that we perceive as necessary corrections of what the speaker has said or is planning to say than disruptions that appear to reflect the speaker's inability to proceed with the articulation of what he has decided to say (Robinson & Crowe, 2001).

The most frequent type of fluency disorder is stuttering. **Stuttering** is different from normal dysfluency in both the rate and the type of dysfluency. Children who stutter produce dysfluencies at a greater rate than children who do not stutter. The dysfluencies include part-word repetitions ("I wa-wa-want . . ."), sound prolongations ("It is at my hhhhhouse . . ."), and sound blocks ("My name is M≠ike . . ."). Stuttering can also consist of related secondary behaviors that are intended to avoid or escape the dysfluency, such as gestures, head nods, and eye blinks. It also includes negative feelings about communication on the part of those who stutter.

Stuttering is not a common disorder; about 1% of children and adults are considered stutterers. More boys than girls stutter. Many children quickly outgrow their childhood dysfluencies. These children generally use regular and effortless dysfluencies, appear to be unaware of their hesitancies, and have parents and teachers who are unconcerned about their speech patterns. Those who stutter for more than 1½ to 2 years appear to be at risk for becoming chronic stutterers (Conture, 2001).

A child who is thought to stutter should be evaluated by a speech-language pathologist. Early diagnosis is important to avoid the development of chronic stuttering. Unfortunately, many educators and physicians do not refer potential stutterers for in-depth assessment, because they are aware that dysfluencies are a normal part of speech-language development. Among experts, there is a lack of consensus on the optimal time and method for early identification and intervention (Onslow, Packman, & Payne, 2007). Persistent stuttering that goes untreated can result in a lifelong disorder that affects the ability to communicate, to develop positive feelings about oneself, and to pursue certain educational and employment opportunities (Conture, 2001).

Motor-Speech Disorders

The muscles that make speech possible are under voluntary control. When damage occurs to the areas of the brain that control these muscles or to the nerves leading to the muscles, the ability to speak normally is disturbed. These disorders may involve controlling speech sounds (**dysarthria**) or planning and coordinating speech (**apraxia**). Both dysarthria and apraxia affect the production of speech, slow its rate, and reduce intelligibility (Owens et al., 2000). Keep in mind, too, that dysarthria and apraxia are not mutually exclusive; that is, an individual can have both problems. Because these disorders are caused by a neurological problem, they are often called *neurogenic disorders of speech.*

INTERNETRESOURCES

The Stuttering Foundation of America (http://www .stuttersfa.org/) and the National Center for Stuttering (http://www.stuttering.com/) offer more information about stuttering.

INTERNETRESOURCES

Advance for Speech-Language Pathologists and Audiologists provides bi-weekly research updates available online at http:// speech-language-pathology-audiology .advanceweb.com/

Damage to the areas of the brain controlling the muscles used for speech can create a disturbance in the ability to speak normally in several ways.

By listening to the person's speech and inspecting her speech mechanism, the speech-language pathologist assesses the ability of the person with a motor-speech disorder or neurogenic speech disorder to control breathing, phonation, resonation, and articulatory movements. Medical, surgical, and rehabilitative specialists in the treatment of neurological disorders also must evaluate the person's problem and plan a management strategy. In cases in which the neurological impairment makes the person's speech unintelligible, an AAC system might be required.

DYSARTHRIA   Difficulties in speaking may occur because the individual cannot control precisely the muscles governing breathing, the larynx, the throat, the tongue, the jaw, and/or the lips. Depending on the nature of the injury to the brain, perceptual and cognitive functions may also be affected; the individual may have a language disorder in addition to a speech disorder.

Dysarthria is characterized by slow, labored, slurred, and imprecise speech. As a result of brain injury, the person's respiratory support for making speech sounds is affected, and his speech may be characterized by shallow breathing, hoarseness, and reduced loudness. The person might not be able to produce speech sounds precisely because of muscle weakness.

APRAXIA   Apraxia is characterized by a disruption of motor planning and programming so that speech is slow, effortful, and inconsistent. A person with this disorder may recognize that she is making errors and try to correct them, but the attempts at correction make it even harder to understand what the person intends to say. Owens and co-workers (2000) provide the following example of the speech of someone with apraxia:

> O-o-on . . . on . . . on cavation, cavation, cacation . . . oh darn . . . vavation, of, you know, to Ca-ca-caciporenia . . . no, Lacifacnia, vafacnia to Lacifacnion . . . On vacation to Va-cafornia, no darn it . . . to Ca-caliborneo . . . not bornia . . . fornia, Bornfifornia . . . no, Balliforneo, Ballifornee, Balifornee, Californee, California. Phew, it was hard to say Cacaforneo. Oh darn. (p. 416)

Developmental apraxia is a disorder of motor planning that emerges as the child develops speech and language skills. Children with this disorder show significant delays in the ability to produce speech sounds and to organize sounds into words for effective communication. **Acquired apraxia** has similar symptoms, but it occurs because of a stroke or other type of brain damage after learning speech. Usually, the person with apraxia knows that she is making errors, wants to correct them, knows what she wants to communicate, but simply cannot do so. Consequently, apraxia is an unusually frustrating disorder for the speaker.

EDUCATIONAL CONSIDERATIONS

Children with all types of disabilities are increasingly placed in general education classrooms. This means that all teachers must become aware of how they can address language problems in the classroom (Owens, 2004; Throneburg, Calvert, Sturm, Paramboukas, & Paul, 2000). Helping children overcome speech and language disorders is not the responsibility of any single professional. Rather, identification is the joint responsibility of the classroom teacher, the speech-language pathologist, and parents. The teacher can carry out specific suggestions for individual cases. By listening attentively and empathetically when children speak, providing appropriate models of speech and language for children to imitate, and encouraging children to use their communication skills appropriately, the classroom teacher can help not only to improve speech and language, but also to prevent some disorders from developing in the first place.

Facilitating the Social Use of Language

In considering language development, the primary role of the classroom teacher is to facilitate the social use of language. The fact that a student has a language or speech disorder does not necessarily mean that the teacher or clinician must intensify efforts to teach the student about the form, structure, or content of language. Rather, language must be taught as a way of solving problems by making oneself understood and making sense of what other people say.

The classroom offers many possibilities for language learning. It should be a place in which almost continuous opportunities exist for students and teachers to employ language and obtain feedback in constructive relationships. Language is the basic medium through which most academic and social learning occurs in school. Nevertheless, the language of school, in both classrooms and textbooks, is often a problem for students and teachers. The accompanying Responsive Instruction feature provides a strategy for enhancing one aspect of social language, personal narratives, for students who use AAC.

School language is more formal than the language many children use at home and with playmates. It is structured conversation, in which listeners and speakers or readers and writers must learn to be clear and expressive, to convey and interpret essential information quickly and easily. Without skill in using the language of school, a child is certain to fail academically and virtually certain to be socially unsuccessful as well.

The classroom offers many possibilities for language learning and should provide almost continuous opportunities for students and teachers to employ language and obtain feedback in constructive relationships.

Teachers need the assistance of speech-language specialists in assessing their students' language disabilities and in devising interventions. Specifics about how speech-language pathologists work to meet the needs of students with communication disorders form the topic of the accompanying Making It Work feature. Part of the assessment and intervention strategy must also examine the language of the teacher. Problems in classroom discourse involve how teachers talk to students as well as how students use language. Learning how to be clear, relevant, and informative and how to hold listeners' attention are problems not only for students with language disorders but also for their teachers. The Personal Perspectives feature on page 284 offers some general guidelines for how teachers should talk with students.

Question-Asking Strategies

One example of the role of the teacher's language in classroom discourse is asking questions. Teachers often ask students too many questions in areas of their identified weaknesses, thereby inadvertently curtailing the students' use of expressive language. For example, a teacher might ask a preschooler who does not know colors to identify colors repeatedly. Or a teacher may overuse yes/no questions (e.g., "Is this blue?" "Are you finished?"), which curtail the child's engagement in extended dialogues or provocative conversations. Unfortunately, teachers might not know how to modify their questions to teach concepts effectively, so their questions merely add to children's confusion.

Teachers can use alternative question-asking strategies to help students think through problems successfully. When students fail to answer higher-order questions because these are beyond their level of information or skill, the teacher should reformulate the problem at a simpler level. After students solve the intermediate steps, the teacher can return to the question that was too difficult at first.

RESPONSIVE *INSTRUCTION*
MEETING THE NEEDS OF STUDENTS WITH COMMUNICATION DISORDERS

Enhancing the Personal Narratives of Students who Use AAC

WHAT THE RESEARCH SAYS

Many students who use augmentative and alternative communication (AAC) experience difficulty in creating personal narratives (Soto, Solomon-Rice, Caputo, 2009). Personal narratives, stories about ideas or events one has experienced or is thinking about, can play an important role in shaping how young children understand the world around them and connect with others (Nelson, 1993). Through personal narratives, children organize and remember events; attach significance to events; share event knowledge with others, thus creating a shared experience; and attach adult values that shape their understanding of events. Children who use AAC can be restricted in their telling of personal narratives due to limitations of the AAC device or support used and by their lack of experience in creating narratives (Soto, Solomon-Rice, Caputo, 2009).

RESEARCH STUDY

Soto and co-workers (2009) sought to examine the effects of teaching personal narrative construction to students who used AAC on the organization and complexity of their narratives. Three elementary-aged students participated in the study. Two of the participants had cerebral palsy and used multimodal communicators (Vantage II™). The other participant had severe verbal apraxia and used a variety of modalities for communication including vocalizations, the use of Signing Exact English (SEE) signs (Gustason & Zawolkow, 1993), a picture communication system, and an 84-location Vantage II™.

For the intervention, three different interventionists worked individually with students for approximately 1 hour twice a week over a 6-month period. Each intervention session consisted of two activities: (a) personal photo description and (b) emotional states description. During each activity, the interventionist showed the student a photo of either a personal event such as birthday or vacation (for the personal photo activity) or a child displaying an emotional state such as happy, sad, or angry (for the emotional states activity). The interventionist asked the students if they remembered the event or could describe how the pictured child felt. The interventionist then used a variety of strategies to extend and validate the response. These included asking open-ended questions, fill-in-the-blank sentences, binary choices, modeling of strategic vocabulary including new words and wording formats, and visual story mapping. The interventionist wrote the narrative on a large piece of paper visible to the student and asked the student to edit the story as needed.

RESEARCH FINDINGS

Soto and colleagues (2009) used a variety of tools to evaluate the narratives generated by the participants. Each narrative was coded in terms of dimensions of discourse (e.g., topic maintenance, event sequencing, explicitness, referencing, conjunctive cohesiveness, and fluency), linguistic complexity (e.g., number of different words and total number of words), number of clauses, number of syntactical features, and story complexity (e.g., identification of characters, emotional states of characters, setting, initiating event, and resolution).

All three participants improved in their overall organization, ability to add descriptive detail, use of linguistic complexity, number of clauses expressed, and ability to create narratives with greater story complexity.

APPLYING THE RESEARCH TO TEACHING

Four features that have been shown to support personal narrative development are:

1. Interactive engagement during narrative development that includes the use of open-ended questions, verbal prompts, binary choices, verbal scaffolds, and modeling.
2. Use of a visual guide such as a story map and written record of the narrative.
3. Strategies to connect emotional state to an event as research has shown that children tend to remember events associated with an emotional experience.
4. Repeated opportunities to engage in personal narrative development.

Teachers can incorporate these features into instruction designed to teach and support the development of personal narratives in students with communication disorders.

MAKING IT WORK
COLLABORATION AND CO-TEACHING WITH SPEECH-LANGUAGE PATHOLOGISTS

"Answer me, Amanda. What? Has the cat got your tongue?"

Simple misunderstandings during discussion, reluctance to respond to questions for which they have the answer, and an inability to interpret directions are all problems students may have if they have communication disorders. These characteristics may be incorrectly interpreted by the general classroom teacher. Language delays are a thread that run through many disabilities, not just communication disorders (B. Lubker, personal communication). For these reasons, collaboration with a speech-language pathologist or language interventionist is important for students with communication disorders and their teachers.

WHAT DOES IT MEAN TO BE A TEACHER OF STUDENTS WITH COMMUNICATION DISORDERS?

The American Speech and Hearing Association (ASHA) is the professional organization that oversees the certification of speech-language pathologists. The Certificate of Clinical Competence: (CCC) requires a master's or doctoral degree. The CCC includes requirements in basic science courses, professional coursework, 375 clock hours of supervised clinical observation/practice, a clinical fellowship, and a national exam.

According to McCormick, Loeb, and Schiefelbusch (1997), the speech-language pathologist or language interventionist has the following responsibilities to general educators:

1. Provide information about delays and disorders of speech, language, or communication.
2. Collect information about speech, language, and communication strengths and intervention needs in order to maximize participation in the classroom and other school settings.
3. Interpret assessment information to others and help to develop intervention goals and objectives, plan activities, and select appropriate methods and materials.
4. Provide direct instruction for specific speech, language, and communication skills to individuals and small groups.
5. Demonstrate for, teach, and assist others to implement language and communication intervention procedures.
6. Work collaboratively with others to promote student participation in age-appropriate activities and natural environments. (p. 167)

SUCCESSFUL STRATEGIES FOR COLLABORATION

Kathleen Wright is a speech-language pathologist in several elementary schools. She has worked with many general educators and, because she is an itinerant teacher, she must work hard to schedule meaningful involvement in classroom instruction. Here is an example of one of her successful collaborations:

I worked with a second-grade class two times per week during the language arts block for 30 to 45 minutes each time. The teacher knew the days I would be available and planned activities on these days that would benefit from extra adult support. During the block, I would lead a "center" activity, assist groups with group projects, or work individually with students. I provided speech services to three students in the class: one student had mainly articulation deficits, which affected reading skills; one student had autism with language and social issues; and one student had a language deficit.

During the language arts block, I was able to address these three students' individual needs, and I was able to see firsthand how their speech and language deficits affected their performance in the general education classroom. The student who had articulation deficits was better able to monitor speech skills when I was present in the classroom. I was also able to work with other students who were not identified with speech-language disorders but who needed the added support and different instructional techniques.

The collaborating teacher was also able to observe my interactions with students and she was able to use some of the same strategies when I was not available.

Positives from collaboration

- I was able to become better known by students in the school, and I was also able to observe how students with and without disabilities perform in the classroom.
- It is a better way for me to assess skills in the natural environment.
- I learned more about classroom expectations and curriculum and can incorporate instruction in these skills into pull-out speech language sessions.

Negatives from collaboration

- In some class sessions, I was treated as an "aide," and my skills were not utilized to benefit instruction.
- I found I must have a good relationship with the general education teacher in order to collaborate.

Personal PERSPECTIVES
Suggestions for Talking with Students

- Choose a topic of interest to the student. Comment on the student's thinking, feelings, and experiences, as the student describes them by providing models of other words or phrases.
- After initiating the conversation, let the student take the lead. Show interest in and, if appropriate, excitement about what the student says.
- Try not to ask lots of questions, and when you do ask questions, ask open-ended ones for which explanations are appropriate.
- Use appropriate wait time with your questions; don't demand an immediate response, but give the student enough time to formulate an answer. Be comfortable with some open or empty spaces in the conversation; don't rush.
- Encourage question asking in return, and give honest and open answers (except, of course, decline politely to answer inappropriate or highly personal questions).

- Keep your voice at an appropriate level, keep your pace moderate, and keep the conversation light and humorous unless the topic of conversation is serious and humor is inappropriate.
- Avoid being judgmental or making snide remarks about the student's language. If the student thinks you are judgmental or if you correct every error, the student will stop talking to you. Demonstrate acceptance of the student's language.
- Do not interrupt the student when she is talking, and listen attentively to the student's ideas; show respect.
- Provide as many opportunities as you can for the student to use language in social situations, and respond appropriately to the student's attempts to use language to accomplish his goals.

Teachers sometimes do not clearly express their intent in questioning students or fail to explicitly delimit the topic of their questions. For example, a teacher might ask, "What are you going to tell me?" (not being clear about intention) or "How have you been feeling recently?" (asking a question that is too general or not sufficiently focused). Consequently, students become confused. Teachers must learn to clarify the problems under such circumstances. Teachers must also give unambiguous feedback to students' responses to their questions. Too often, teachers do not tell students explicitly that their answers are wrong, for fear of showing nonacceptance. Lack of accurate, explicit feedback, however, prevents students from learning the concepts involved in instruction. Our points here are these:

FIGURE 10.1 For children with developmental language disorders, the components of language can change over time. Here we can see how a single child's receptive and expressive language skills shift over time relative to typically developing peers.

- The teacher's role is not merely to instruct students about language but also to teach them how to use it. More specifically, the teacher must help students learn how to use language in the context of the classroom.
- The teacher's own use of language is a key factor in helping students learn effectively, especially if students have language disorders.

Teachers need to keep in mind, too, that language disorders can change with a child's development. Just because a child has receptive or expressive language within the normal range at one age doesn't mean that it will be within the same range at a later age. Figure 10.1 depicts changes with age for Troy, a child whose language problems are shown at various ages (Plante & Beeson, 2004). Language intervention can change the nature and course of a child's language abilities, but even with therapy, a child might have persistent language problems. Notice that Troy, who received speech-language services, did not achieve expressive language abilities close to the normal range until age 14, and only then did his expressive language ability exceed his receptive ability.

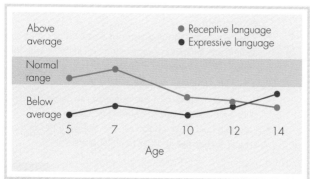

Source: Plante, E., & Beeson, P. M. (2004). *Communication and communication disorders: A clinical introduction* (2nd ed.). Boston: Allyn & Bacon, p. 182. Copyright © 2004. Reprinted/adapted by permission of Allyn & Bacon.

Teaching Literacy: Reading and Written Expression

Developing literacy is a special problem for many students with speech and language disorders. As noted earlier in this chapter, students with language impairments often have reading deficits in both word-recognition skills and comprehension. It is less common for individuals who have pure speech disorders to have difficulties with reading, but those with language, or language and speech problems are indeed at significant risk for reading disability (Snowling & Hayiou-Thomas, 2006). In particular, students who have poor phonological awareness are typically unable to learn how to decode without intervention. **Decoding** refers to the ability to transfer the written words into speech. For those students with language impairments who learn how to decode, many will still have difficulty with reading comprehension. Thus, it is critical for the classroom teacher, speech-language pathologist, and special education teacher to work together to provide explicit and systematic intervention in reading for children with language impairments.

In addition to reading problems, students with language impairment also have difficulty with written expression. As students progress through the grades, written language takes on increasing importance. Students are expected to read increasingly complex and difficult material and understand its meaning. In addition, they are expected to express themselves more clearly in writing. The interactions teachers have with students about their writing—the questions they ask to help students understand how to write for their readers—are critical to overcoming disabilities in written language (Graham, Harris, MacArthur, & Schwartz, 1998).

Finally, intervention in language disorders employs many of the same strategies used in intervention in learning disabilities. Metacognitive training, strategy training, and other approaches discussed in Chapter 6 are typically appropriate for use with students who have language disorders (see also Hallahan, Lloyd, Kauffman, Weiss, & Martinez, 2005; Mercer & Pullen, 2009).

ASSESSMENT OF PROGRESS

A primary purpose of language assessment is to inform instruction. An intervention plan based on assessment must consider the content, form, social context, and use of language. That is, it must consider the following:

- What the child talks about and should be taught to talk about
- How the child talks about things and how the child could be taught to speak of those things more intelligibly
- How the child functions in the context of the child's linguistic community
- How the child uses language and how the child's language use could be made to serve the purposes of communication and socialization more effectively

After developing the intervention plan, educators implement an ongoing assessment plan to monitor progress and identify outcome measures and to ensure that the student is meeting programmatic goals. Methods for monitoring the progress of students with language impairments may use a system of dynamic assessment that involves a cycle of teaching, followed by testing, and then reteaching as necessary (Ehren & Nelson, 2005). Teachers administer **dynamic assessments** during the learning process, and the **speech-language pathologist (SLP)** determines how the student performs with and without support (Anderson & Shames, 2006). This information guides intervention as the speech-language pathologist establishes what the student can do and where the student needs further intervention. Teachers can use dynamic assessments in the context of a response-to-intervention (RTI) program by speech-language pathologists (Ehren & Nelson).

Teachers can also use **curriculum-based language and communication assessment (CBLA)** to monitor students' progress. CBLA differs from curriculum-based measurement (CBM) discussed in Chapter 6 in that it measures a student's speech, language, and communication skills required to learn the school curriculum (Staskowski & Nelson, 2007). CBLA generally measures the communications skills required to participate in the school curriculum and the strategies the student employs to conduct curricular tasks. Based on the observations related to these two areas, the speech-language pathologist then determines what skills the student needs to acquire and how to modify the task to ensure success.

As in other areas of education, the current trend requires that service providers demonstrate the value of communication intervention in terms of student outcomes. Currently, speech-language pathologists may rely on the National Outcomes Measurement System (NOMS) to measure the outcomes of students in communication interventions. In an effort to assist speech-language pathologists in documenting treatment outcomes, the American Speech Language Hearing Association formed the National Center for Treatment Effectiveness in Communication in the early 1990s (Mullen & Schooling, 2010). A result of these efforts is the NOMS, an online database assessment system. The speech-language pathologist uses a series of scales that measure functional communication. The speech-language pathologist then uses these data, along with demographic and diagnostic data, to generate a report of outcomes based on the individual's intervention plan.

EARLY INTERVENTION

Early intervention is critically important for two primary reasons:

1. The older the child is when intervention is begun, the smaller the chance that he or she will acquire effective language skills (other things being equal).
2. Without having functional language, the child cannot become a truly social being (Warren & Abbaduto, 1992). Of all the skills in which a child may be lagging, language—communication—is the most important, as it is the foundation of academic and social learning.

Early Development and Early Intervention

The study of children's early development has shown that the first several years of life are a truly critical period for language learning. Educators have known for a long time that much of children's language, literacy, and social development depends on the nature and quantity of the language interactions they have with parents or other caregivers. In the homes of children who come to school ready to learn, the language interactions between parents and children have typically been frequent, focused on encouragement and affirmation of the children's behavior, emphasized the symbolic nature of language, provided gentle guidance in exploring things and relationships, and demonstrated the responsiveness of adults to children. By contrast, children who enter school at a disadvantage tend to have experienced much lower rates of language interaction; to have heard primarily negative, discouraging feedback on their behavior; and to have heard language that is harsh, literal, and emotionally detached.

In a now classic study, Hart and Risley (1995) compared the language experiences of children of professional parents, working-class parents, and parents on welfare. The contrasts in language experiences and the effects observed in children's academic achievement and behavior are stark, but the differences are unrelated to income or ethnicity. Rather, the differences are related to how and how much the parents talked to their children. As summed up by the authors:

> Our data showed that the magnitude of children's accomplishments depends less on the material and educational advantages available in the home and more on the amount of experience children accumulate with parenting that provides language diversity, affirmative

Milieu teaching is an approach that uses naturalistic language to teach functional language skills. In this approach, teaching is built around the child's interests.

feedback, symbolic emphasis, gentle guidance, and responsiveness. By the time children are 3 years old, even intensive intervention cannot make up for the differences in the amount of such experience children have received from their parents. If children could be given better parenting, intervention might be unnecessary. (p. 210)

Thus, it appears that the key to preventing many disabilities related to language development is to help parents improve how they relate to their children when they are infants and toddlers. Nevertheless, for many young children, intervention in the preschool and primary grades will be necessary. But such intervention must be guided by understanding of children's families, particularly the primary caretaker's, usually the mother's, views of language development (Hammer & Weiss, 2000). Preschoolers who require intervention for a speech or language disorder occasionally have multiple disabilities that are sometimes severe or profound.

Language is closely tied to cognitive development, so impairment of general intellectual ability is likely to have a negative influence on language development. Conversely, lack of language can hamper cognitive development. Because speech is dependent on neurological and motor development, any neurological or motor problem might impair ability to speak. Normal social development in the preschool years also depends on the emergence of language, so a child with language impairment is at a disadvantage in social learning. The preschool child's language therefore is seldom the only target of intervention.

Early Intervention in Delayed Language Development

Children with language disorders may follow the same sequence of development as most children but achieve each skill or milestone at a later-than-average age. Some children with language disorders reach final levels of development that are significantly below those of their peers who don't have disabilities. Still other children may be generally delayed in language development but show great discrepancies in the rate at which they acquire certain features of language.

Some children develop speech late but will eventually develop age-appropriate speech and language (Vinson, 2007). Yet many children whose language development is delayed show a developmental lag that they won't outgrow (Owens, 2004). They are frequently diagnosed as having intellectual disabilities or another developmental disability. Sometimes these children come from environments where they have been deprived of many experiences, including the language stimulation from adults that is required for normal language development, or they have been severely abused or neglected. Regardless of the reasons for a child's delayed language, however, it's important to understand the nature of the delay and to intervene to give him or her the optimal chance of learning to use language effectively.

Some children 3 years of age or older show no signs that they understand language and do not use language spontaneously. They might make noises, but they use them to communicate in ways that may characterize the communication of infants and toddlers before they have learned speech. In other words, they may use **prelinguistic communication**. For example, they may use gestures or vocal noises to request objects or actions from others, to protest, to request a social routine (e.g., reading), or to greet someone.

When assessing and planning intervention for children with delayed language, it is important to consider what language and nonlanguage behaviors they imitate, what they comprehend, what communication skills they use spontaneously, and what part communication plays in their lives. It's also important, particularly with young children, to provide intervention in the contexts in which children use language for normal social interaction. For example, parents or teachers may use **milieu teaching,** a strategy to teach functional language skills in the natural environment. In this approach, teaching is built around the child's interests. When the child requests some action, object, or activity from the adult, the adult prompts the child's language and gives access to what is requested contingent on an attempt to communicate. Milieu teaching is a naturalistic approach, in that it encourages designing interventions that are similar to the ordinary conversational interactions of parents

The first several years of life are truly critical for language learning.

and children. Prelinguistic communication may be a good indication of a child's later ability to use language (Calandrella & Wilcox, 2000). The effectiveness of a milieu teaching approach may depend, at least to some extent, on mothers' responsiveness to their children's prelinguistic communication (Yoder & Warren, 2001).

Involvement of Families

Researchers have become increasingly aware that language development has its beginning in the earliest mother–child interactions. Concern for the child's development of the ability to communicate can't be separated from concern for development in other areas. Therefore, speech-language pathologists are a vital part of the multidisciplinary team that evaluates an infant or young child with disabilities and develops an individualized family service plan (IFSP; see Chapters 2 and 4). Early intervention programs involve extending the role of the parent. This means a lot of simple play with accompanying verbalizations. It means talking to the child about objects and activities in the way most mothers talk to their babies. But it also means choosing objects, activities, words, and consequences for the child's vocalizations with great care to enhance the likelihood that the child will learn functional language (Fey, Catts, & Larrivee, 1995).

Early childhood specialists now realize that prelinguistic intervention is critical for language development—that is, intervention should begin before the child's language emerges. The foundations for language are laid in the first few months of life through stimulating experiences with parents and other caretakers (Koury, 2007). In the early years of implementing IFSPs, educators emphasized assessing families' strengths and needs and training parents how to teach and manage their children. More recently, professionals have come to understand that assessing families in the belief that professionals know best is often misguided. Parents can indeed be helped by professionals to play an important role in their children's language development. But the emphasis today is on working with parents as knowledgeable and competent partners whose preferences and decisions are respected (Hammer & Weiss, 2000; see also discussion in Chapter 4).

Intervention in early childhood is likely to be based on assessment of the child's behavior related to the content, form, and especially the use of language in social interaction. For the child who has not yet learned language, assessment and intervention will focus on imitation, ritualized and make-believe play, play with objects, and functional use of objects. At the earliest stages in which the content and form of language are interactive, it is important to evaluate the extent to which the child looks at or picks up an object when it is referred to, does something with an object when directed by an adult, and uses sounds to request or refuse things and call attention to objects. When the child's use of language is considered, the earliest objectives involve the child's looking at the adult during interactions; taking turns in and trying to prolong pleasurable activities and games; following the gaze of an adult; directing the behavior of adults; and persisting in or modifying gestures, sounds, or words when an adult does not respond. In the preschool, teaching discourse (conversation skills) is a critical focus of language intervention. In particular, preschool teachers emphasize teaching children to use the discourse that is essential for success in school. Children must learn, for example, to report their experiences in detail and to explain why things happen, not just add to their vocabularies. They must learn not only word forms and meanings but also how to take turns in conversations and maintain the topic of a conversation or change it in an appropriate way. Preschool programs in which such language teaching is the focus may include teachers' daily individualized conversations with children, daily reading to individual children or small groups, and frequent classroom discussions.

Current trends are directed toward providing speech and language interventions in the typical environments of young children. This means that classroom teachers and speech-language pathologists must develop a close working relationship. The speech-language pathologist might work directly with children in the classroom and advise the teacher about the intervention that he can carry out as part of the regular classroom activities. Alternatively, the speech-language pathologist might work with the teacher directly to help her incorporate effective instructional practices for these students. The child's peers may also be involved in intervention strategies. Because language is essentially a social activity, its facilitation requires involvement of others in the child's social environment—peers as well as adults (Audet & Tankersley, 1999; Fey et al., 1995; Prizant, 1999).

Normally developing peers have been taught to assist in the language development of children with disabilities by doing the following during playtimes: establish eye contact; describe their own or others' play; and repeat, expand, or request clarification of what the child with disabilities says. Peer tutors can help in developing the speech and language of their classmates who may use different dialects (McGregor, 2000). Another intervention strategy involving peers is sociodramatic play. Children are taught in groups of three, including a child with disabilities, to act out social roles such as those people might take in various settings (e.g., a restaurant or shoe store). The training includes scripts that specify what each child is to do and say, which the children can modify in creative ways.

TRANSITION TO ADULTHOOD

In the past, adolescents and adults in speech and language intervention programs generally fell into three categories: (1) the self-referred, (2) those with other health problems, and (3) those with severe disabilities. Adolescents or adults might refer themselves to speech-language pathologists because their phonology, voice, or stuttering is causing them social embarrassment and/or interfering with occupational pursuits. These are generally people with long-standing problems who are highly motivated to change their speech and obtain relief from the social penalties their differences impose.

Adolescents and adults with other health problems might have experienced damage to speech or language capacities as a result of disease or injury, or they might have lost part of their speech mechanism through injury or surgical removal. Treatment of these individuals always demands an interdisciplinary effort. In some cases of progressive disease, severe neurological damage, or loss of tissues of the speech mechanism, the outlook for functional speech is not good. However, surgical procedures, medication, and prosthetic devices are making it possible for more people to speak normally. Loss of ability to use language is typically more disabling than loss of the ability to speak. Traumatic brain injury may leave the individual with a seriously diminished capacity for self-awareness, goal setting, planning, self-directing or initiating actions, inhibiting impulses, monitoring or evaluating one's own performance, or problem solving. Recovering these vital language-based skills is a critical aspect of transition of the adolescent or young adult from hospital to school and from school to independent living (Klein & Moses, 1999).

Individuals with severe disabilities might need the services of speech-language pathologists to help them achieve more intelligible speech. They might also need to be taught an alternative to oral language or given a system of augmented communication. One of the major problems in working with adolescents and adults who have severe disabilities is setting realistic goals for speech and language learning. Teaching simple, functional language—such as social greetings, naming objects, and making simple requests—may be realistic goals for some adolescents and adults.

A major concern of transition programming is ensuring that the training and support provided during the school years are carried over into adult life. To be successful, the transition must include speech-language services that are part of the natural environment. That is, the services must be community based and integrated into vocational, domestic, recreational, consumer, and mobility training activities. Speech-language interventions for adolescents and young adults with severe disabilities must emphasize functional communication— understanding and making oneself understood in the social circumstances that are most likely

FOCUS ON Concepts

IDENTIFYING POSSIBLE LANGUAGE PROBLEMS RELATED TO TRANSITION

Older children and adolescents may need help from a communication specialist if they

- Fail to understand instructions in typical situations.
- Cannot use language effectively to meet their daily living needs.

- Frequently violate social rules involving politeness and interpersonal interactions.
- Cannot read important signs and symbols, complete forms, and write simple reports.
- Have problems speaking so that others understand.

to be encountered in everyday life (Justice, 2006). Developing appropriate conversation skills (e.g., establishing eye contact, using greetings, taking turns, and identifying and staying on the topic), reading, writing, following instructions related to recreational activities, using public transportation, and performing a job are examples of the kinds of functional speech-language activities that may be emphasized.

Today, educators are placing much more emphasis on the language disorders of adolescents and young adults who do not fit into other typical categories of disabilities. Many of these individuals were formerly seen as having primarily academic and social problems that were not language related. But now it is understood that underlying many or most of the school and social difficulties of adolescents and adults are basic disorders of language. These language disorders are a continuation of difficulties experienced earlier in the person's development.

Classroom teachers are in a particularly good position to identify possible language-related problems and to request help from a communication specialist. The accompanying Focus on Concepts describes several characteristics exhibited by older children and adolescents that may indicate a need for consultation and intervention. Addressing problems like these as early and effectively as possible is important in helping youngsters make successful transitions to more complex and socially demanding environments.

Some adolescents and adults with language disorders are excellent candidates for strategy training, which teaches them how to select, store, retrieve, and process information (see Hallahan et al., 2005; see also Chapter 6). Others, however, don't have the required reading skills, symbolic abilities, or intelligence to benefit from the usual training in cognitive strategies. Whatever techniques are chosen for adolescents and older students, the teacher should be aware of the principles that apply to intervention with these individuals.

SUMMARY

How are communication disorders defined?

- Communication involves sharing information between two individuals or among more than two individuals.
- Communicative functions include requesting, rejecting, commenting, arguing, reasoning, and so on.
- Communication disorders may involve language or speech or both, and they impair communicative functions.
- Language is sending and receiving ideas—expression and reception—through an arbitrary system of symbols used according to rules.

- Speech is the neuromuscular activity of forming and sequencing the sounds of oral language.

What is the prevalence of communication disorders?

- Reasonable estimates are that about 10% to 15% of preschool children and about 6% of students in elementary and secondary grades have speech disorders.
- Probably about 2% to 3% of preschoolers and about 1% of the school-age population have language disorders.

What is the difference between communicative differences and disorders?

- Differences include dialects, regional differences, language of ethnic minority groups, and nondominant languages.
- An individual with a difference that is not a disorder is an effective communicator in her language community, whereas someone with a disorder has impaired communication in all language environments.

What are the major disorders of language?

- There are many different theories of language development and the disorders of language.
- Language disorders may be primary (no known cause) or secondary (attributable to another condition or disability).
- Primary language disorders include specific language impairment (SLI), early expressive language delay (EELD), and language-based reading impairment.
- Secondary language disorders include those related to emotional or behavioral disorders or any other disability, such as intellectual disabilities or autistic spectrum disorder.

What are the major disorders of speech?

- Speech disorders are a very heterogeneous group of problems related to the production of oral language, including the following:
  - *Phonological disorders*—problems in understanding the sound system of language
  - *Articulation disorders*—problems in producing correct speech sounds
  - *Voice disorders*—problems in producing voice with appropriate pitch, loudness, or quality
  - *Fluency disorders*—problems in maintaining speech flow
  - *Motor-speech*—problems in speaking due to neuromotor damage, including the following:
    - *Dysarthria*—problems in controlling the production of speech sounds
    - *Apraxia*—problems in planning and coordinating speech

What are the main educational considerations for communication disorders?

- The classroom teacher needs to work with others in three main areas:
  - Facilitating the social uses of language
  - Question asking
  - Teaching literacy: Reading and written language

What are the major features of assessment of progress for students with communication disorders?

- A primary purpose of language assessment is to inform instruction.
- Assessment for intervention requires attention to the following:
  - What the child talks about and should be taught to talk about
  - How the child talks about things and how he could be taught to speak of those things more intelligibly
  - How the child functions in the context of his linguistic community
  - How the child uses language and how his or her use of it could be made to serve the purposes of communication and socialization more effectively
- Progress monitoring assessments are dynamic and should follow a cycle of teaching, testing, and reteaching.
- Progress monitoring assessments include curriculum-based language assessment (CBLA).
- Assessment of student outcomes should be implemented to confirm that learning has occurred.

What are the major aspects of early intervention for communication disorders?

- Early intervention is based on early language development.
- Early intervention usually involves working with delayed language.
- Early intervention requires working with families.

What do educators emphasize in transition for students with communication disorders?

- Transition involves helping students use the language demanded for successful employment.

COUNCIL FOR EXCEPTIONAL CHILDREN

Addressing the Professional Standards

Council for Exceptional Children (CEC) Common Core Knowledge and Skills addressed in this chapter: ICC1K5, ICC1K6, ICC1K8, ICC2K1, ICC2K2, ICC2K3, ICC2K4, ICC2K6, ICC3K1, ICC3K3, ICC4S5, ICC5S1, ICC6K4, ICC7K1, ICC7S2, ICC7S9, ICC8S2, ICC8S5, ICC8S8, ICC9K4, ICC9S7

Appendix: Provides a full listing of the CEC Common Core Standards and associated Knowledge and Skill Statements listed here.

MYEDUCATIONLAB

myeducationlab Now go to Topic 12: Communication Disorders, in the MyEducationLab (www.myeducationlab.com) for your course, where you can:

- Find learning outcomes for the broad concepts covered in this chapter along with the national standards that connect to these outcomes.
- Complete Assignments and Activities that can help you more deeply understand the chapter content.
- Examine challenging situations presented in the IRIS Center Resources.
- Apply and practice your understanding of the core concepts and skills identified in the chapter with the Building Teaching Skills and Dispositions learning units.
- Check your comprehension on the content covered in the chapter by going to the Study Plan in the Book-Specific Resources for your text. Here you will be able to take a chapter quiz, receive feedback on your answers, and then access Review, Practice, and Enrichment activities to enhance your understanding of chapter content.
- Watch video clips of CCSSO Teacher of the Year award winners responding to the question: "Why I teach?" in the Teacher Talk section.

Upon transitioning to high school, friends dispersed into separate crowds. The new school was much bigger.... I found myself becoming increasingly isolated. One afternoon, ... I sat on the sofa ... having a mutually desired but laborious conversation with my mother.... I asked her why I didn't have as many friends as the other kids.... She looked at me with a surprised expression on her face.

"You don't know why?" she asked.

"No."

"It's because you can't hear, and they don't understand that."

That was a revelation and turning point in my life. Until that moment, I had only understood my deafness in a blur. I had never understood this difference between myself and others to be such a determining factor in my life.... But still I did not realize all the implications regarding relationships, my future, language, and education. I did not know this wasn't just a hearing problem. The difficulties I faced were not because I had a hearing problem, but because the often-cruel world around me was full of barriers. That understanding was a long way off.

Martha Sheridan • *Inner Lives of Deaf Children: Interviews and Analysis*

QUESTIONS **to guide your reading of this chapter . . .**

- How do professionals define and classify individuals who are deaf or hard of hearing?
- What is the prevalence of hearing impairment?
- What are some basic anatomical and physiological characteristics of the ear?
- How is hearing impairment identified?
- What causes hearing impairments?
- What are some psychological and behavioral characteristics of learners with hearing impairments?
- What are some educational considerations for learners with hearing impairments?
- How do professionals assess the progress of students with hearing impairments?
- What are some important considerations with respect to early intervention for learners with hearing impairments?
- What are some important considerations with respect to transition to adulthood for learners with hearing impairments?

MISCONCEPTIONS ABOUT
Learners Who Are Deaf or Hard of Hearing

MYTH • People who are deaf are unable to hear anything.

FACT • Most people who are deaf have some residual hearing.

MYTH • Deafness is not as severe a disability as blindness.

FACT • Although it's impossible to predict the exact consequences of a disability on a person's functioning, in general, deafness poses more difficulties in adjustment than does blindness. This is largely due to the effects hearing loss can have on the ability to understand and speak oral language.

MYTH • It's unhealthy for people who are deaf to socialize almost exclusively with others who are deaf.

FACT • Many authorities now recognize that the phenomenon of a Deaf culture is natural and should be encouraged. In fact, some are worried that too much mainstreaming will diminish the influence of the Deaf culture.

MYTH • In learning to understand what is being said to them, people with a hearing impairment concentrate on reading lips.

FACT • *Lipreading* refers only to visual cues arising from movement of the lips. Some people who have a hearing impairment not only read lips but also take advantage of a number of other visual cues, such as facial expressions and movements of the jaw and tongue. They are engaging in what is referred to as *speechreading*.

MYTH • Speechreading is relatively easy to learn and is used by the majority of people with a hearing impairment.

FACT • Speechreading is extremely difficult to learn, and very few people who have a hearing impairment actually become proficient speechreaders.

MYTH • American Sign Language (ASL) is a loosely structured group of gestures.

FACT • ASL is a true language in its own right, with its own set of grammatical rules.

MYTH • People within the Deaf community are in favor of mainstreaming students who are deaf into general education classes.

FACT • Some within the Deaf community have voiced the opinion that general education classes are not appropriate for many students who are deaf. They point to the need for a critical mass of students who are deaf in order to have effective educational programs for these individuals. They see separate placements as a way of fostering the Deaf culture.

MYTH • Families in which both the child and the parents are deaf are at a distinct disadvantage compared to families in which the parents are hearing.

FACT • Research has demonstrated that children who are deaf who have parents who are also deaf fare better in a number of academic and social areas. Authorities point to the parents' ability to communicate with their children in ASL as a major reason for this advantage.

To be deaf, or even hard of hearing, often places a person in a difficult place somewhere between the world of the hearing and the world of the Deaf. Martha Sheridan's (2001) words in this chapter's opening reflect the isolation that can accompany a hearing impairment—an isolation caused primarily by communication problems. As we see in this chapter, even if the hearing impairment isn't severe enough for a child to be classified as "deaf," but rather as "hard of hearing," the child with a hearing impairment is at a distinct disadvantage in virtually all aspects of English language development. The importance of the English language in U.S. society, particularly in school-related activities, is obvious. Many of the problems that people with hearing impairment have in school are due primarily to their difficulties in English. We explore this issue in some depth in this chapter.

A related controversy inherent in Martha Sheridan's (2001) words is the debate about whether the child who is deaf should be educated to communicate orally or through manual sign language. Sheridan is typical of the approximately 90% of those who are deaf, in that both her parents are hearing (National Institute on Deafness and Other Communication Disorders [NIDCD], 2008) and had chosen not to learn sign language. Also common, unfortunately, is the difficulty that Sheridan had learning to speechread, or to use visual information (including lip movements) from a number of sources, to understand what is being said.

Again, like others in the same situation, Sheridan eventually went on to immerse herself in the Deaf community. She found her identity as a Deaf person through her experiences at Gallaudet University, the primary postsecondary institution for students with hearing impairment:

> Gallaudet was a major gateway for me. It was the pot of gold at the end of my search for self, and it represented the beginning of the rest of my life. It was at Gallaudet that I discovered what it means to be deaf. . . . Here, and with sign language, my love for learning blossomed. (Sheridan, 2001, pp. 7–8)

But not all people who are deaf elect to join the Deaf community. Some become fluent enough in spoken English to function in mainstream society. Others are able to straddle both the world of the hearing and the Deaf. But no matter what the outcome, virtually all people who are deaf, as well as their parents, struggle with critical choices about oral versus manual modes of communication and cultural identity. With respect to the latter, in fact, many members of the Deaf community consider themselves part of a cultural minority rather than disabled.

All of these thorny issues make deafness one of the most challenging fields of study in all of special education. As you would surmise from our discussion of other special education areas, this challenge is evident in attempts to arrive at a definition of hearing impairment.

DEFINITION AND CLASSIFICATION

By far the most common way of classifying hearing impairment is the distinction between *deaf* and *hard of hearing*. Although it's common to think that being deaf means not being able to hear anything and that being hard of hearing means being able to hear a little bit, this is generally not true. Most people who are deaf have some residual hearing. Complicating things is the fact that different professionals define the two categories differently. The extreme points of view are represented by those with a physiological orientation versus those with an educational orientation.

Those who maintain a strictly physiological viewpoint are interested primarily in the measurable degree of hearing impairment. Children who can't hear sounds at or above a certain intensity (loudness) level are classified as deaf; others with a hearing impairment are considered hard of hearing. Hearing sensitivity is measured in **decibels** (units of relative loudness of sounds). Zero decibels (0 dB) designates the point at which the average person with normal hearing can detect the faintest sound. Each succeeding number of decibels that a person cannot detect indicates a certain degree of hearing impairment. Those who maintain a physiological viewpoint generally consider people with hearing impairments of about 90 dB or greater to be deaf and people with impairments at lower decibel levels to be hard of hearing. For comparison purposes, 90 dB is the approximate loudness of a lawn mower (American Academy of Otolaryngology—Head and Neck Surgery, 2007).

People with an educational viewpoint are concerned with how much the hearing impairment is likely to affect the child's ability to speak and develop language. Because of the close causal link between hearing impairment and delay in language development, these professionals categorize primarily on the basis of spoken language abilities. *Hearing*

PEARSON
myeducationlab

To check your comprehension on the content covered in Chapter 11, go to the Book-Specific Resources in the MyEducationLab (www.myeducationlab.com) for your course, select your text, and complete the Study Plan. Here you will be able to take a chapter quiz, receive feedback on your answers, and then access review, practice, and enrichment activities to enhance your understanding of chapter content. ■

impairment is a broad term that covers individuals with impairments ranging from mild to profound; it includes those who are deaf or hard of hearing. Following are commonly accepted, educationally oriented definitions for *deaf* and *hard of hearing*:

- A deaf person is one whose hearing disability precludes successful processing of linguistic information through audition, with or without a hearing aid.
- A person who is hard of hearing generally, with the use of a hearing aid, has residual hearing sufficient to enable successful processing of linguistic information through audition (Brill, MacNeil, & Newman, 1986, p. 67).

Educators are extremely concerned about the age of onset of hearing impairment. Again, the close relationship between hearing impairment and language delay is the key. The earlier the hearing impairment occurs in life, the more difficulty the child will have developing the language of the hearing society (e.g., English). For this reason, professionals frequently use the terms **congenitally deaf** (those who are born deaf) and **adventitiously deaf** (those who acquire deafness at some time after birth).

Two other frequently used terms are even more specific in pinpointing language acquisition as critical: **Prelingual deafness** refers to deafness that occurs at birth or early in life before speech and language develop. **Postlingual deafness** is deafness that occurs after the development of speech and language. Experts differ about the dividing point between prelingual and postlingual deafness. Some believe that it should be at about 18 months; others think it should be lower, at about 12 months or even 6 months (Meadow-Orlans, 1987).

Some professionals find it useful to classify according to hearing threshold levels, such as mild (26 to 40 dB), moderate (41 to 55 dB), moderate-severe (56 to 70 dB), severe (71 to 90 dB), and profound (91 dB and above); (Andrews, Leigh, & Weiner, 2004). These levels of loss of hearing sensitivity cut across the broad classifications of deaf and hard of hearing, which stress the degree to which speech and language are affected rather than being directly dependent on hearing sensitivity.

Some authorities object to adhering too strictly to any of the various classification systems. Because these definitions deal with events difficult to measure, they're not precise. Therefore, it is best not to form any hard-and-fast opinions about an individual's ability to hear and speak solely on the basis of a classification of his hearing disability.

In considering issues of definition, it's important to point out the growing sentiment among people who are deaf that deafness should not even be considered a disability (Padden & Humphries, 2005). In the Focus on Concepts feature on page 300, note that Lane (2002) at times uses the term *Deaf* with a capital *D* and at other times does not. Although some variance occurs, the following is the distinction often used by those who view deafness as a cultural difference rather than as a disability:

> The lowercase "deaf" refers to those for whom deafness is primarily an audiological experience. It is mainly used to describe those who lost some or all of their hearing in early or late life, and who do not usually wish to have contact with signing Deaf communities, preferring to try to maintain their membership in the majority society in which they were socialized.
>
> "Deaf" refers to those born Deaf or deafened in early (sometimes late) childhood, for whom the sign languages, communities and cultures of the Deaf collective represents their primary experience and allegiance, many of whom perceive their experience akin to other language minorities. (Ladd, 2003, p. xvii)

Later in the chapter, we discuss more thoroughly the nature and purpose of the Deaf culture. For now, it's enough to be aware of the challenges that have been raised to the very notion of considering deafness a disability.

PREVALENCE

Estimates of the number of children with hearing impairment vary considerably, due to such factors as differences in definition, populations studied, and accuracy of testing. The U.S. Department of Education's statistics indicate that the public schools identify about 0.14% of

A current issue in defining deafness is that many people in the Deaf community do not want to be considered as having a disability. Instead, they want to be recognized as members of a cultural group with its own language—American Sign Language (ASL).

the population from 6 to 17 years of age as deaf or hard of hearing. Although the Department of Education doesn't report separate figures for the categories of deaf versus hard of hearing, strong evidence indicates that students who are hard of hearing are far more prevalent than those who are deaf (Mehra, Eavey, & Keamy, 2009). Furthermore, some authorities believe that many children who are hard of hearing who could benefit from special education are not being served.

An important statistic is that more than half of those students who receive special education services for hearing impairment come from diverse backgrounds (Andrews, Shaw, & Lomas, 2011), with close to 29% coming from Spanish-speaking homes (Gallaudet Research Institute, 2008). In addition, relatively large numbers of other non-English-speaking immigrants are deaf. The relatively high numbers of students who are deaf from non-English-speaking families creates significant challenges for the schools. Deafness by itself makes spoken language acquisition in the native language very difficult, let alone deafness plus attempting to learn a second language.

ANATOMY AND PHYSIOLOGY OF THE EAR

The ear is one of the most complex organs of the body. The many elements that make up the hearing mechanism are divided into three major sections: the outer, middle, and inner ear. The outer ear is the least complex and least important for hearing; the inner ear is the most complex and most important for hearing. Figure 11.1 shows these major parts of the ear.

The Outer Ear

The outer ear consists of the auricle and the external auditory canal. The canal ends with the **tympanic membrane (eardrum)**, which is the boundary between the outer and middle ears. The **auricle** is the part of the ear that protrudes from the side of the head. The part that the outer ear plays in the transmission of sound is relatively minor. Sound is collected by the auricle and is funneled through the external auditory canal to the eardrum, which vibrates, sending the sound waves to the middle ear.

INTERNETRESOURCES

More information on the anatomy of the ear, including drawings, can be found at a Website called Virtual Tour of the Ear: www.augie.edu/perry/ear/hearmech.htm The Virtual Tour of the Ear home page contains dozens of links to Websites devoted to many topics concerning hearing impairment: http://ctl.augie.edu/perry/ar/ar.htm Another excellent Website is maintained by the National Institute on Deafness and Other Communication Disorders of the National Institutes of Health. On this site you can access a number of interesting demonstrations, including a video that explains how the ear works: www.nidcd.nih.gov

FOCUS ON Concepts

DEAFNESS: DISABILITY OR CULTURAL DIFFERENCE?

For the vast majority of society, it seems fairly obvious that deafness is a disability. However, it is far from obvious to many people who are deaf, who argue that instead of being considered disabled, people who are deaf should be considered a cultural minority with a language of their own: sign language (Ladd, 2003; Lane, 2002; Padden & Humphries, 1988). As Harlan Lane puts it:

> What is the source of the belief that being a Deaf person entails an inherent biological limitation? Why is deaf associated with loss rather than difference or gain (different language, different culture, etc.)? I submit that it is because the society that has elaborated the concept of deaf is largely hearing and conceptualizes deaf as a loss of hearing. Indeed, the difference in hearing of a person born Deaf and one born hearing is called "hearing loss," although the Deaf person didn't lose anything. (Lane, 2002, p. 366)

Knowing that some within the Deaf community do not believe that deafness is a disability presents an interesting and challenging problem for educators and other professionals. Should their wishes be honored? Special educators, in particular, are trained to help remediate differences and to try to make people with such differences as "normal" as possible. Would it be professionally irresponsible not to find students who are deaf and who are eligible for special education services?

One team of authorities has acknowledged that historically, some behaviors of people who are deaf have been viewed as pathological. These behaviors include very expressive facial expressions and overt methods of getting someone's attention. In fact, these behaviors are merely cultural differences (Andrews et al., 2004). However, authorities also note that many within the Deaf community were advocates for equal rights protections under the Americans with Disabilities Act. They further state:

> The point to be made is that the hearing population, including professionals, need to focus on and recognize the . . . positive aspects of deaf people. . . . The pendulum has swung from the time when deafness was viewed as a pathology so severe that Alexander Graham Bell, in a paper published by the prestigious National Academy of Science, proposed that stringent eugenics should be applied to eradicate deafness through genetic and reproductive restrictions (Bell, 1883). This bears testimony to the conditions and attitudes deaf people have faced in the past. It makes understandable their desire to have their culture respected and the focus placed on their abilities, not limitations. (Andrews et al., 2004, p. 12)

FIGURE 11.1 Illustration of the outer, middle, and inner ear

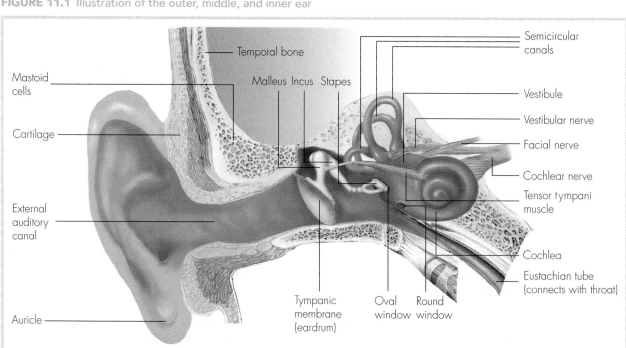

The Middle Ear

The middle ear comprises the eardrum and three very tiny bones (**ossicles**) called the **malleus** (hammer), **incus** (anvil), and **stapes** (stirrup), which are contained within an air-filled space. The chain of the malleus, incus, and stapes conducts the vibrations of the eardrum along to the **oval window**, which is the link between the middle and inner ears. The ossicles function to create an efficient transfer of energy from the air-filled cavity of the middle ear to the fluid-filled inner ear.

The Inner Ear

About the size of a pea, the inner ear is an intricate mechanism of thousands of moving parts. Because it looks like a maze of passageways and is highly complex, this part of the ear is often called a *labyrinth*. The inner ear is divided into two sections according to function: the vestibular mechanism and the cochlea. These sections, however, do not function totally independently of each other.

The **vestibular mechanism**, located in the upper portion of the inner ear, is responsible for the sense of balance. It's extremely sensitive to such things as acceleration, head movement, and head position. Information about movement is fed to the brain through the vestibular nerve.

By far the most important organ for hearing is the **cochlea**. Lying below the vestibular mechanism, this snail-shaped organ contains the parts necessary to convert the mechanical action of the middle ear into an electrical signal in the inner ear that is transmitted to the brain. In the normally functioning ear, sound causes the malleus, incus, and stapes of the middle ear to move. When the stapes moves, it pushes the oval window in and out, causing the fluid in the cochlea of the inner ear to flow. The movement of the fluid in turn causes a complex chain of events in the cochlea, ultimately resulting in excitation of the cochlear nerve. With stimulation of the cochlear nerve, an electrical impulse is sent to the brain, and sound is heard.

IDENTIFICATION OF HEARING IMPAIRMENT

There are four general types of hearing tests: screening tests, pure-tone audiometry, speech audiometry, and specialized tests for very young children. Depending on the characteristics of the examinee and the use to which the results will be put, the audiologist may choose to give any number of tests from any one or a combination of these four categories.

Screening Tests

Screening tests are available for infants and for school-age children. As a result of an initiative by the federal government, about 95% of all newborns are screened for hearing (Andrews et al., 2011). Ideally, a 1-3-6 rule is followed; babies are screened at the hospital by 1 month, with those who show signs of hearing loss followed up by 3 months and entering a family intervention program by 6 months. Unfortunately, many who are identified at 1 month slip through the cracks and aren't followed up and end up not receiving services until they reach school age (Brown, 2009).

Some of the screening tests involve computer technology to measure **otoacoustic emissions**. The cochlea not only receives sounds but also emits low-intensity sound when stimulated by auditory stimuli. These sounds emitted by the cochlea are known as *otoacoustic emissions*, and they provide a measure of how well the cochlea is functioning (Campbell & Mullin, 2006).

Many schools have routine screening programs in the early elementary grades. These tests, especially those that are group rather than individually administered, are less accurate than tests done in an **audiologist**'s office. Children detected through screening as having possible problems are referred for more extensive evaluation.

INTERNETRESOURCES

The National Institute on Deafness and Other Communication Disorders of the National Institutes of Health has been concerned about the fact that many infants with hearing impairment go undetected even though technology exists to identify such impairments. Information on early screening can be found on their Website: http://www.nidcd.nih.gov/health/hearing/screened.asp

Pure-Tone Audiometry

Pure-tone audiometry is designed to establish the individual's threshold for hearing at a variety of different frequencies. Frequency, measured in **hertz (Hz)** units, has to do with the number of vibrations per unit of time of a sound wave; the pitch is higher with more vibrations, lower with fewer. A person's threshold for hearing is simply the level at which she can first detect a sound; it refers to how intense a sound must be before the person detects it. As mentioned earlier, hearing sensitivity, or intensity, is measured in decibels.

Pure-tone audiometers present tones of varying intensities, or decibel levels, at varying frequencies, or pitch (hertz). Audiologists are usually concerned with measuring sensitivity to sounds ranging from 0 to about 110 dB. A person with average-normal hearing can barely hear sounds at a sound-pressure level of 0 dB. The zero-decibel level is frequently called *the zero hearing-threshold level,* or **audiometric zero**. Because the decibel scale is based on ratios, each increment of 10 dB is a tenfold increase in intensity. This means that 20 dB is 10 times more intense than 10 dB, and 30 dB is 100 times more intense than 10 dB. Whereas a leaf fluttering in the wind registers about 0 dB, normal conversation is about 60 dB, and, as we stated earlier, a power lawnmower is about 90 dB (American Academy of Otolaryngology—Head and Neck Surgery, 2007).

Hertz are usually measured from 125 Hz (low pitch) to 8,000 Hz (high pitch). Frequencies in speech range from 80 to 8,000 Hz, but most speech sounds have energy in the 500- to 2,000-Hz range.

Testing each ear separately, the audiologist presents a variety of tones within the range of 0 to about 110 dB and 125 to 8,000 Hz until she establishes the level of intensity (dB) at which the individual can detect the tone at a number of frequencies: 125 Hz, 250 Hz, 500 Hz, 1,000 Hz, 2,000 Hz, 4,000 Hz, and 8,000 Hz. For each frequency, the audiologist records a measure of degree of hearing impairment. A 50-dB hearing impairment at 500 Hz, for example, means the individual can detect the 500-Hz sound when it is given at an intensity level of 50 dB, whereas the average person would have heard it at 0 dB.

Speech Audiometry

Because the ability to understand speech is of prime importance, audiologists use **speech audiometry** to test a person's detection and understanding of speech. The **speech-reception threshold (SRT)** is the decibel level at which one can understand speech. One way to measure the SRT is to present the person with a list of two-syllable words, testing each ear separately. Audiologists often use the decibel level at which the person can understand half the words as an estimate of SRT level.

Tests for Young and Hard-to-Test Children

A basic assumption for pure-tone and speech audiometry is that the individuals tested understand what is expected of them. They must be able to comprehend the instructions and show with a head nod or raised hand that they have heard the tone or word. None of this might be possible for very young children (under about 4 years of age) or for children with certain disabilities.

Audiologists use a number of different techniques to test the hearing of young and hard-to-test children. For example, some use the otoacoustic emission testing mentioned earlier. Others use **conditioned play audiometry**. Using pure tones or speech, the examiner teaches the child to do various activities whenever he hears a signal. The activities are designed to be attractive to the young child. For example, the child might be required to pick up a

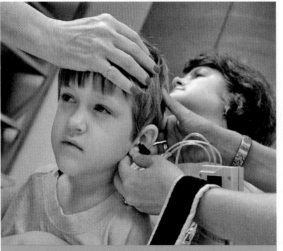

Tympanometry is used to assess the middle ear's response to pressure and sound.

block, squeeze a toy, or open a book. In **tympanometry**, a rubber-tipped probe is inserted in the ear, sealing the ear canal, and the effects of pressure and sound are then measured to assess the functioning of the middle ear. Still another method is **brain-stem–evoked response audiometry**, which measures electrical signals from the brain stem that are in response to an auditory stimulus, such as a click. It can be used with infants as well as young children. Clinicians can administer it while the child is asleep or sedated.

CAUSES

We discuss causes with respect to the type of hearing impairment (conductive, sensorineural, and mixed) as well as the location of the hearing impairment (outer, middle, or inner ear).

Conductive, Sensorineural, and Mixed Hearing Impairment

Professionals classify causes of hearing impairment on the basis of the location of the problem within the hearing mechanism. There are three major classifications: conductive, sensorineural, and mixed hearing impairments. A **conductive hearing impairment** refers to an interference with the transfer of sound along the conductive pathway of the middle or outer ear. A **sensorineural hearing impairment** involves problems in the inner ear. A **mixed hearing impairment** is a combination of the two. Audiologists attempt to determine the location of the dysfunction. The first clue may be the severity of the loss. A general rule is that hearing impairments greater than 60 or 70 dB usually involve some inner-ear problem. Audiologists use the results of pure-tone testing to help determine the location of a hearing impairment. They then convert the results to an audiogram—a graphic representation of the weakest (lowest-decibel) sound the individual can hear at each of several frequency levels. The profile of the audiogram helps to determine whether the loss is conductive, sensorineural, or mixed.

Hearing Impairment and the Outer Ear

Although problems of the outer ear are not as serious as those of the middle or inner ear, several conditions of the outer ear can cause a person to be hard of hearing. In some children, for example, the external auditory canal does not form, resulting in a condition known as *atresia*. Children may also develop **external otitis**, or "swimmer's ear," an infection of the skin of the external auditory canal. Tumors of the external auditory canal are another source of hearing impairment.

Hearing Impairment and the Middle Ear

Although abnormalities of the middle ear are generally more serious than problems of the outer ear, they, too, usually result in a classification as hard of hearing rather than deaf. Most middle-ear hearing impairments occur because the mechanical action of the ossicles is interfered with in some way. Unlike inner-ear problems, most middle-ear hearing impairments are correctable with medical or surgical treatment.

The most common problem of the middle ear is **otitis media**—an infection of the middle-ear space caused by viral or bacterial factors, among others. Otitis media is common in young children. At least 80% of children are diagnosed with otitis media at least once before they are 10 years old (Thrasher, 2009). It is linked to abnormal functioning of the eustachian tubes. If the eustachian tube malfunctions because of a respiratory viral infection, for example, it cannot do its job of ventilating, draining, and protecting the middle ear from infection. Otitis media can result in temporary conductive hearing impairment, and even these temporary losses can make the child vulnerable for having language delays (Feldman et al., 2003). If untreated, otitis media can lead to rupture of the tympanic membrane.

Hearing Impairment and the Inner Ear

The most severe hearing impairments are associated with the inner ear. In addition to problems with hearing sensitivity, a person with inner-ear hearing impairment can have additional problems, such as sound distortion, balance problems, and roaring or ringing in the ears.

Causes of inner-ear disorders can be hereditary or acquired. Genetic or hereditary factors are a leading cause of deafness in children. In fact, over 400 different varieties of hereditary deafness have been identified (Andrews et al., 2011). Scientists have identified mutation in the **connexin-26 gene** as the most common cause of congenital deafness.

Acquired hearing impairments of the inner ear include those due to bacterial infections (e.g., meningitis, the second most frequent cause of childhood deafness), prematurity, viral infections (e.g., mumps and measles), anoxia (deprivation of oxygen) at birth, prenatal infections of the mother (e.g., maternal rubella, congenital syphilis, and cytomegalovirus), Rh incompatibility (which can now usually be prevented with proper prenatal care of the mother), blows to the head, side effects of some antibiotics, and excessive noise levels.

Two of the preceding conditions deserve special emphasis because of their relatively high prevalence. **Congenital cytomegalovirus (CMV)**, a herpes virus, deserves special mention because it's the most frequent fetal viral infection (Kenneson & Cannon, 2007). And although not all infants born with CMV have a hearing loss, it's the most common nongenetic cause of deafness in infants. CMV can result in a variety of other conditions, such as intellectual disabilities and visual impairment.

In addition, repeated exposure to environmental factors such as loud music, gunshots, or machinery can result in gradual or sudden hearing impairment.

PSYCHOLOGICAL AND BEHAVIORAL CHARACTERISTICS

Hearing impairment can have profound consequences for some aspects of a person's behavior and little or no effect on other characteristics. Consider this question: If you were forced to choose, which would you rather be—blind or deaf? On first impulse, most of us would choose deafness, probably because we rely on sight for mobility and because many of the beauties of nature are visual. But in terms of functioning in an English language-oriented society, the person who is deaf is at a much greater disadvantage than is someone who is blind.

Spoken Language and Speech Development

By far the most severely affected areas of development in the person with a hearing impairment are the comprehension and production of the English language. We stress English because it is the predominant language in the United States of those who can hear. In other words, people who are hearing impaired are generally deficient in the language used by most people of the hearing society in which they live. The distinction is important, because people who are hearing impaired can be expert in their own form of language: sign language.

Nevertheless, it's an undeniable fact that individuals with hearing impairment are at a distinct disadvantage. This is true in terms of language comprehension, language production, and speech. Speech intelligibility is linked to (1) degree of hearing impairment and (2) the age of onset of the hearing impairment. Even after intensive speech therapy, it's rare for children with prelingual profound deafness to develop intelligible speech (Marschark, 2002). Infants who can hear their own sounds and those of adults before becoming deaf have an advantage over those born deaf. Children who are deaf are handicapped in learning to associate the sensations they feel when they move their jaws, mouths, and tongues with the auditory sounds these movements produce. In addition, these children have difficulty hearing adult speech, which nonimpaired children can hear and imitate.

TABLE 11.1 Degrees of hearing impairment and impact on communication

Hearing Level	Descriptor	Impact on Communication
10–15 dB	Normal	No impact on communication.
16–25 dB	Slight	In quiet environments, has no difficulty recognizing speech, but in noisy environments, has difficulty understanding faint speech.
26–40 dB	Mild	In quiet conversational environments where the topic is known and vocabulary is limited, has no difficulty in communicating. Has difficulty hearing faint or distant speech, even if the environment is quiet. Has challenges in following classroom discussions.
41–55 dB	Moderate	Can hear conversational speech only at a close distance. Group activities, such as classroom discussions, present a communicative challenge.
56–70 dB	Moderate-Severe	Can hear only loud, clear conversational speech and has much difficulty in group situations. Often, the individual's speech is noticeably impaired though intelligible.
71–90 dB	Severe	Cannot hear conversational speech unless it is loud, and even then, cannot recognize many of the words. Can detect, though not always identify, environmental sounds. The individual's speech is not altogether intelligible.
91 dB +	Profound	May hear loud sounds, but cannot hear conversational speech at all. Vision is the primary modality for communication. The individual's own speech, if developed at all, is not easy to understand.

Source: From Schirmer, B. R. (2001). *Psychological, social, and educational dimensions of deafness.* Boston: Allyn & Bacon. Adapted with permission.

Table 11.1 provides general examples of the possible effects of various degrees of hearing impairment on English language development. This is only a general statement of these relationships, because many factors interact to influence language development in the child with hearing impairment.

Sign Language

Although children who are deaf face extraordinary challenges in learning a spoken language, with exposure they can easily learn **sign language**. However, historically, sign language has suffered from several misconceptions, including the belief that it is not a true language. The notion that sign language is simply a primitive, visual representation of oral language similar to mime was first challenged by the pioneering work of William Stokoe at Gallaudet University. A linguist, Stokoe submitted that, analogous to the phonemes of spoken English, each sign in ASL consists of three parts: handshape, location, and movement (Stokoe, 1960; Stokoe, Casterline, & Croneberg, 1976). For many years, Stokoe's colleagues scoffed at him, but research in several areas has proved that he was correct in asserting that sign language is a true language.

Grammatical Complexity of Sign Language   Researchers have continued to refine Stokoe's (1960) work on sign language grammar, confirming its complexity. For example, like spoken language, sign language has grammatical structure at the sentence level (syntax) as well as the word or sign level (Goldin-Meadow, 2003). Handshapes, location, and movement are combined to create a grammar every bit as complex as that of spoken language.

Nonuniversality of Sign Language   Contrary to popular opinion, no single, universal sign language exists. Just as geographical or cultural separations result in different spoken languages, they also result in different sign languages. For example, people who are deaf in France communicate in French Sign Language, and those in the United States use American Sign Language (ASL). A person who is deaf visiting a foreign country has difficulties communicating with others who are deaf, much as a hearing person does. This is because sign languages, like spoken languages, evolve over time through common usage. In other words, sign language was not invented by any one person or a committee of people. The 18th-century French clergyman Charles-Michel de l'Eppe is often referred to as the "father of sign language." On hearing this, some people assume that de l'Eppe invented sign language. However, he did promote the usage of French Sign Language, which already existed within the Deaf community. This is not to diminish his profound impact on advocating for using sign language in educating students with hearing impairments.

FOCUS ON Concepts

THE BIRTH AND EVOLUTION OF NICARAGUAN SIGN LANGUAGE

For years researchers have claimed that sign languages evolve naturally over time wherever there is a critical mass of persons who are deaf. The need to communicate is a driving force in the development of sign language. Although these scholars' conclusions were compelling, much of their work was based on retrospective analyses of sign languages that were already in existence. However, beginning in the 1970s, researchers were presented with a rare opportunity to study and document the evolution of sign language in Nicaragua:

> Before the 1970s, there was no deaf community in Nicaragua. Deaf people were largely isolated from each other, and used simple home sign systems and gesture 'mímicas' to communicate with their families and friends. The conditions necessary for a language to arise occurred in 1977, when a center for special education established a program initially attended by 50 young deaf children. The number of students at the school . . . grew to 100 by 1979, the year of the Sandinista revolution.
>
> In 1980, a vocational school for adolescent deaf children was opened. . . . By 1983 there were over 400 deaf students enrolled in the two schools. Initially, the language program emphasized spoken Spanish and lipreading, and the use of signs by teachers limited to fingerspelling (using simple signs to sign the alphabet). The program achieved little success, with most students failing to grasp the concept of Spanish words. However, while the children remained linguistically disconnected from their teachers, the schoolyard, the street, and the bus to and from school provided fertile ground for them to communicate with each other, and by combining gestures and elements of their home-sign systems, a pidgin-like form, and then a creole-like language rapidly emerged. They were creating their own language. This "first-stage" pidgin . . . is still used by many of those who attended the school at this time.
>
> Staff at the school, unaware of the development of this new language, saw the children's gesturing as mime, and as a failure to acquire Spanish. Unable to understand what the children were saying to each other, they asked for outside help, and in June 1986, the Nicaraguan Ministry of Education contacted Judy Kegl, an American Sign Language linguist from Northeastern University. As Kegl and other researchers began to analyze the language, they noticed that the young children had taken the pidgin-like form of the older children to a higher level of complexity, with verb agreement and other conventions of grammar. This more complex sign language is now known as *Idioma de Señas de Nicaragua* (ISN). (*Nicaraguan Sign Language*, 2010)

One surprising finding has been that over time, the youngest signers have been the ones who have been most influential in changing the grammar of ISN (Kegl, Senghas, & Coppola, 1999). However, the complete development and perpetuation of ISN is dependent on a complex interplay between the generations (Senghas, 2003). The bottom line is that sign language, like spoken language, changes over time based on intergenerational interactions among users of the language.

Several studies have verified the evolutionary aspect of sign languages. For example, twins who are deaf born to parents who hear soon begin to develop a signing system to communicate with each other. However, even after several years of such communication, their means of communication is still extremely rudimentary and nowhere near as sophisticated as ASL. The Nicaraguan Sign Language Study has also documented how sign languages change over time and is described in the accompanying Focus on Concepts.

Developmental Milestones of Sign Language   Considerable evidence indicates that children who are deaf reach the same language development milestones in sign that children who can hear reach in spoken language, and do so at about the same time (Emmorey, 2002; Goldin-Meadow, 2003). For example, they manually "babble" at about the same time as infants who can hear verbally babble. And infants who are deaf sign their first words and two-word phrases at about the same time that hearing infants verbalize their first words and two-word phrases.

Neurological Foundations of Sign Language   Further evidence that sign language is a true language comes from studies showing that sign language has the same neurological underpinnings as does spoken language. In Chapter 6, we noted that areas within the left cerebral hemisphere of the brain are primarily responsible for language. However, we were referring to spoken language. Interestingly, using neuroimaging techniques, substantial evidence shows that the left hemisphere of the brain is also the primary site responsible for sign language acquisition and use (Campbell & MacSweeney, 2004; Emmorey, 2002; Waters et al., 2007). Also, stroke patients who are deaf are more likely to have deficits in signing if the stroke is to the left hemisphere than if the right hemisphere is damaged.

Intellectual Ability

For many years, professionals believed that the spoken language of individuals who are deaf was a sign that they also had intellectual deficiencies. As was noted earlier, however, we now know that they might not have a spoken language such as English, but if they use American Sign Language, they are using a true language with its own rules of grammar.

Any intelligence testing of people who are hearing impaired must take their English language deficiency into account. Performance tests, rather than verbal tests, especially if they are administered in sign, offer a much fairer assessment of the IQ of a person with a hearing impairment. When these tests are used, there is no difference in IQ between those who are deaf and those who are hearing (Prinz et al., 1996).

Academic Achievement

Unfortunately, most children who are deaf have large deficits in academic achievement. Reading ability, which relies heavily on English language skills and is probably the most important area of academic achievement, is most affected. For example, the average 15-year-old student who is hearing impaired has a deficit of at least 5 years in reading (Trezek, Wang, & Paul, 2010). Even in math, their best academic subject, students with hearing impairment trail their hearing peers by substantial margins.

Several studies have demonstrated that children who are deaf who have parents who are deaf have higher reading achievement and better language skills than do those who have hearing parents. Researchers do not agree about the cause (Powers, 2003). However, many authorities speculate that the positive influence of sign language is the cause. Parents who are deaf might be able to communicate better with their children through the use of ASL, providing the children with needed support. In addition, children who have parents who are deaf are more likely to be proficient in ASL, and ASL can aid these children in learning written English and reading.

Social Adjustment

Social development and personality development in the hearing population depend heavily on communication, and the situation is no different for those who are deaf. People who can hear have little difficulty finding people with whom to communicate. People who are deaf, however, can face problems in finding others with whom they can converse. Studies have demonstrated that many students who are deaf are at risk for loneliness (Cambra, 1996; Charlson, Strong, & Gold, 1992). Two factors are important in considering the possible isolation of students who are deaf: inclusion and hearing status of the parents.

Researchers have shown that in inclusionary settings, very little interaction typically occurs between students who are deaf and those who are not (Kluwin, Stinson, & Colarossi, 2002). Furthermore, in inclusionary settings, students who are deaf feel more emotionally secure if they have other students who are deaf with whom they can communicate (Stinson & Whitmire, 1992). This is not always possible, however, because of the low prevalence of hearing impairment. Some interventions using cooperative learning have succeeded in increasing the interactions between students who are deaf and their peers who can hear (Kluwin et al., 2002).

Some authorities believe that the child who is deaf and has parents who can hear runs a greater risk of being unhappy than the child who has parents who also are deaf. This is because many parents who can hear, as well as parents who are hard-of-hearing, don't become proficient in ASL (Mitchell & Karchmer, 2005) and are unable to communicate with their children easily. Given that about 90% of children who are deaf have hearing parents (Mitchell & Karchmer, 2004), this problem in communication might be critical.

The need for social interaction is probably most influential in leading many people with hearing impairment to associate primarily with others with hearing impairment. If their parents are deaf, children who are deaf are usually exposed to other deaf families from an early age. Nonetheless, many people who are deaf end up, as adults, socializing predominantly with others who are deaf, even if they have hearing parents and even if they didn't come into contact as children with many other children who were deaf. This phenomenon of socializing with others who are deaf is attributable to the influence of the Deaf culture.

INTERNETRESOURCES

Visit the National Theatre of the Deaf's Website to look for upcoming performances in your area: www.NTD.org

The Deaf Culture   In the past, most professionals viewed isolation from the hearing community on the part of many people who are deaf as a sign of social pathology. Now most professionals agree with the many people who are deaf who believe in the value of having their own Deaf culture. They view this culture as a natural condition emanating from the common bond of sign language.

The unifying influence of sign language is the first of six factors noted by Reagan (1990) as demarcating the Deaf community as a true culture:

1. *Linguistic differentiation* is at the heart of Deaf culture; many within the Deaf community view themselves as bilingual, with individuals possessing varying degrees of fluency in ASL and English (Ladd, 2003; Padden & Humphries, 2005). People who are deaf continually shift between ASL and English as well as between the Deaf culture and that of the hearing (Padden, 1996).

2. *Attitudinal deafness* refers to whether a person thinks of himself as deaf. It might not have anything to do with a person's hearing acuity. For example, a person with a relatively mild hearing impairment might think of herself as deaf more readily than does someone with a profound hearing impairment.

3. *Behavioral norms* within the Deaf community differ from those in hearing society. A few examples of these norms, according to Lane, Hoffmeister, and Bahan (1996), are that people who are deaf value informality and physical contact in their interactions with one another, often giving each other hugs when greeting and departing, and their leave-takings often take much longer than those of hearing society. Also, they are likely to be frank in their discussions, not hesitating to get directly to the point of what they want to communicate.

4. *Endogamous marriage* patterns are evident from surveys showing rates of in-group marriage as high as 90%. The Deaf community tends to frown on "mixed marriages" between people who are deaf and those who are hearing.

5. *Historical awareness* of significant people and events pertaining to people who are deaf permeates the Deaf community. They are often deferential to elders and value their wisdom and knowledge pertaining to Deaf traditions.

6. *Voluntary organizational networks* are abundant in the Deaf community. Some examples are the National Association of the Deaf, the World Games for the Deaf (Deaf Olympics), and the National Theatre of the Deaf.

Whereas professionals once viewed isolation from the hearing community as a sign of social pathology, many now recognize the value of having a Deaf culture.

Concern for the Erosion of Deaf Culture Many within the Deaf community and some professionals are concerned that the cultural status of children who are deaf is in peril (Lane et al., 1996; Padden & Humphries, 2005). They believe that the increase in inclusion is eroding the cultural values of the Deaf culture. In the past, much of Deaf culture was passed down from generation to generation through contacts made at residential schools, but if they attend local schools, today's children who are deaf may have little contact with other children who are deaf. Many authorities now recommend that schools involve members of the Deaf community in developing classes in Deaf history and culture for students who are deaf who attend local schools.

Deaf Activism: The Gallaudet Experience Considering all groups with exceptionalities, those who are deaf have been one of the most, if not the most, outspoken about their rights. Even though some might think that the Deaf community is in peril of losing its identity, it's still very active in advocating a variety of social, educational, and medical policies. Two good examples of this activism are Gallaudet's Deaf President Now and Unity for Gallaudet Movements (see the accompanying Personal Perspectives) and the debate over cochlear implants.

Deaf Activism: The Cochlear Implant Debate Deaf activists have also been aggressive in attacking what they consider an oppressive medical and educational establishment. An example of just how much this segment of the Deaf community is at odds with many professionals is its opposition to the medical procedure of cochlear implantation. This procedure involves surgically implanting electronic elements under the skin behind the ear and in the inner ear. A small microphone worn behind the ear picks up sounds and sends them to a small computerized speech processor worn by the person. The speech processor sends coded signals to an external coil worn behind the ear, which sends them through the skin to the implanted internal coil. The internal coil then sends the signals to electrodes implanted in the inner ear, and these signals are sent on to the auditory nerve. (See Figure 11.2.)

Ever since the U.S. Food and Drug Administration approved the use of cochlear implants for young children in 1990, thousands of operations have been performed both in the United States and the rest of the world. The technology is advancing rapidly, but not everyone with a hearing impairment is a candidate for implantation. Generally, it is recommended for those who have a severe to profound sensorineural loss in both ears. In

INTERNETRESOURCES

Two examples of publications devoted to issues of concern to the Deaf community are the magazines *Silent News* and *Deaf Life*. The former also has an online edition (www.silentnews.com/index .html). On the site, it presents itself as "a good glimpse into the Deaf community." Deaf Life's Website has chat rooms for adults and just for children: www .deaflife.com

 Personal PERSPECTIVES
Gallaudet's Deaf President Now
and Unity for Gallaudet Movements

DEAF PRESIDENT NOW MOVEMENT

A prominent and historic example of Deaf activism occurred in the 1980s at Gallaudet University, a liberal arts college for the deaf and hard of hearing, when students and faculty protested the board of trustees' selection of a hearing president. Since its founding in 1864, Gallaudet had never had a deaf president. But when on March 6, 1988, the trustees announced the appointment of yet another hearing president, faculty and students took to the streets and halls in protest. Having successfully shut down the university, organizers of the Deaf President Now Movement issued four demands:

1. that a deaf president be named immediately;
2. that the chair of the board resign;
3. that the board, which consisted of 17 hearing and 4 deaf members, be reconfigured to include a majority of deaf members; and
4. that there be no reprisals.

After 8 days of protest, the board acceded to all four demands, the most significant of which was the naming of a long-time faculty member who was deaf: I. King Jordan as president of the university.

UNITY FOR GALLAUDET MOVEMENT

Upon Jordan's retirement, the board announced on May 1, 2006, the appointment of the vice president of the university, Jane K. Fernandes, to be Jordan's successor. Students and faculty once again protested, holding rallies and blocking entrances to the school. The protests continued during the Fall semester, with more than 100 students arrested for blocking entrances.

Given that Fernandes is also deaf, accounts vary as to why such a negative reaction occurred (Christiansen, 2009; Tapper & Sandell, 2006; Takruri, 2006). Some cited what they considered a flawed, noninclusive selection process, but many pointed to concerns that Fernandes was not "deaf enough." They objected to her having stated that she wanted to be more inclusive by admitting more students with cochlear implants as well as those who had not grown up learning sign language. (Fernandes herself reportedly grew up using speech and speechreading and didn't learn sign language until she was in her 20s.)

In October 2006, Fernandes was removed as president by the board. In December, 2006, the board named Robert Davilla as an interim president. Deaf since the age of 8, Davilla had previously served in a number of high-level government and university positions. Also deaf, T. Alan Hurwitz became president in May, 2010. Hurwitz, whose background is engineering, came to the position after being president of the National Technical Institute for the Deaf.

children, most implants occur between the ages of 2 and 6 years (National Institute on Deafness and Other Communication Disorders, 2009). The FDA has not approved cochlear implants for children under the age of 12 months.

Although the manufacturers of these devices, as well as many within the medical community, view cochlear implants as miraculous, many within the Deaf community oppose them, viewing the process as physically and culturally invasive:

> I expect that most Americans would agree that our society should not seek the scientific tools or use them, if available, to change a child biologically so he or she will belong to the majority rather than the minority—even if we believe that this biological engineering might reduce the burdens the child will bear as a member of a minority. Even if we could take children destined to be members of the African American, or Hispanic American, or Native American, or Deaf American communities and convert them with bio-power into white, Caucasian, hearing males—even if we could, we should not. We should likewise refuse cochlear implants for young deaf children even if the devices were perfect. (Lane, 1992, p. 237)

FIGURE 11.2 A cochlear implant

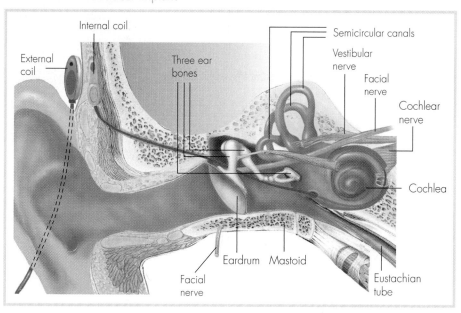

The Deaf community has not had to confront the issue raised by Lane: whether to have the surgery even if it were to result in perfect hearing. Although perfect hearing through cochlear implants might not be just around the corner, enormous strides in technology have resulted in many more cases than ever before of greatly improved hearing for people with implants. These more positive results are making it more difficult for those who are deaf, or their parents, to decide whether to choose cochlear implantation. One problem is that in order to reap the benefits of improved hearing from the implant, many professionals recommend intensive oral instruction. As we discuss later, many within the Deaf community favor manual (ASL) over oral teaching methods. So they are concerned that persons with implants may not gain enough exposure to sign language. Also, results still vary enormously from individual to individual (Andrews et al., 2011). See the accompanying Success Stories feature, "Bailea, a Kindergartener with a Cochlear Implant," for an example of a child whose cochlear implant has been relatively successful. In the case of children, research shows that the earlier the transplant takes place, the better the resulting ability to hear and speak (Geers, Moog, Biedenstein, Brenner, & Hayes, 2009). But the majority of children with implants still don't attain hearing and speaking skills within the range of hearing children. Again, this is a far cry from a cure, but for some, it's enough of an improvement to elect to undergo the surgery.

Deaf Activism: The Genetic Engineering Debate   Ironically, deaf activists can also put scientific discoveries to use to help sustain the Deaf culture but not without facing thorny ethical concerns (Emery, Middleton, & Turner, 2010; Middleton, Emery, & Turner, 2010). Earlier, we noted the discovery of the mutation of the connexin-26 gene as the leading cause of deafness in children. Parents could use such information to increase their chances of having a baby who is deaf. (Contrary to what many in hearing society assume, when both parents are deaf, they usually would prefer to have a baby who is deaf.) For example, they could use **in vitro fertilization**, a procedure that is usually used to help infertile couples, whereby egg cells from the mother are fertilized in the laboratory and then placed in the mother's uterus. Parents who are deaf could choose to retain only fertilized eggs that have the connexin-26 mutation. Another option that actually has been used by deaf couples is artificial insemination by a donor who has a high probability of carrying genes leading to deafness (Mundy, 2002; Sanghavi, 2006).

INTERNETRESOURCES

The National Association of the Deaf had for years been opposed to cochlear implants. However, in the fall of 2000, it issued a policy statement that was much more neutral in tone; see http://www.nad.org/issues/technology/assistive-listening/cochlear-implants
The Public Broadcasting Service (PBS) has established an excellent Website focused on the documentary *Sound and Fury*. Although the site focuses on the issue of cochlear implants, it also contains useful information pertaining to the Deaf culture and links to other interesting Websites: www.pbs.org/wnet/soundandfury

Success Stories

BAILEA, A KINDERGARTENER WITH A COCHLEAR IMPLANT, BENEFITS FROM EARLY INTERVENTION AND CO-TEACHING

Special Educator Heather Miles: *"Set expectations high, and really work to meet them."*

Five-year-old Bailea Kohler uses a cochlear implant in an inclusive kindergarten class.

These are the keys to her success:

★ intensive early intervention and structured routines
★ relentless focus on teamwork
★ specific interventions in auditory-verbal learning

"I JUST LOVE BAILEA," says special educator Heather Miles. "She's strong willed and very curious about things." Bailea's father says she's an energetic and happy 5-year-old. "She always has bumps and bruises from trying to keep up with her older sister, Madison." Bailea was born deaf to hearing parents, Stacia and Mike Kohler. She has a cochlear implant, and she has benefited from intensive, relentless, and specific special education.

★ **Intensive Early Intervention and Structured Routines.** At first, Bailea's doctors predicted her hearing would improve. "When she failed to hear doors slam or dogs bark, I reached out to everybody I could to find the best for her," says Stacia. When she was 12 months old, Bailea started intensive speech and language services 3 days a week at the Saginaw Hearing Center, in Saginaw, Michigan. An audiologist recommended a cochlear implant, but before surgery Bailea was required to wear hearing aids for 6 months. "It was a constant fight, and she tried to pull them out," recalls Stacia. "Bailea had surgery to implant the cochlear device when she was 19 months old. Her hearing specialist drove 3 hours to the University

of Michigan in Ann Arbor, in an ice storm to visit Bailea in the hospital. The professionals who worked with us were like family."

Structured routines have been important. "Bailea likes being in charge," says Heather, and she started kindergarten at age 5 with temper tantrums when she couldn't make her needs known. Classmates were positive models, but structured interactions and instruction helped her communicate. "We use a picture schedule to provide students with visual supports for learning. We also use tape to assign places for students to sit on the carpet during group time. Bailea's special place is near the front so she can scoot away if she needs to." Bailea's language skills are not strong, and her attention span is short in group settings. "Sometimes," says Heather, "the loudness of talking and laughter can get a bit much, and she needs to get away."

★ **Relentless Focus on Teamwork.** Coordinated teamwork is critical to Bailea's success. Heather Miles has collaborated for 7 years with Bailea's kindergarten teacher, Mrs. English, who also has experience as a special educa-

EDUCATIONAL CONSIDERATIONS

Formidable problems face the educator who works with students who are deaf or hard of hearing. One major problem is of course communication. Dating back to the 16th century, debate has raged about how individuals who are deaf should converse (Lane, 1984). This controversy is sometimes referred to as the **oralism–manualism debate**, to represent two very different points of view: oralism favors teaching people who are deaf to speak; manualism advocates the use of some kind of manual communication. Manualism was the preferred method until the middle of the 19th century, when oralism began to gain predominance. Currently, most professionals recommend both oral and manual methods in what is referred to as a **total communication** or **simultaneous communication** approach (Andrews et al., 2004). However, many within the Deaf community believe that even the total communication approach is inadequate, and they advocate for a **bicultural-bilingual approach**, which promotes ASL as a first language and promotes instruction in the Deaf culture.

We first discuss the major techniques that make up the oral approach and the oral portion of the total communication approach; then we explore total communication, followed by a discussion of the bicultural-bilingual approach.

tor. Their classroom is equipped with a portable FM speaker that amplifies sounds for any of the 19 students who might benefit. Heather spends 2 hours daily with Mrs. English, co-teaching reading and language arts in the morning, and writing in the afternoon. Sometimes Bailea joins Heather in a larger group for Direct Instruction (discussed in Chapter 6), and other times they work together in a separate classroom. Both teachers meet monthly with the speech and hearing specialists to ensure everyone is working toward the same goals. An audiologist sees Bailea weekly in the classroom and regularly attends team meetings. Says Heather, "She makes practical suggestions by telling us where the FM reception is best in the room, and she observes Bailea's behavior to monitor the volume and functioning of the cochlear implant." School personnel aren't responsible for adjusting implanted devices, so Bailea's parents let the medical team at the University of Michigan know about any problems that might be occurring with the implant in the classroom.

★ **Specific Interventions for Auditory-Verbal Learning.** The Kohlers credit the team with helping Bailea develop the desire to hear. At home, 11-year-old sister Madison patiently helps Bailea to communicate. It hasn't been easy. The fragile cochlear device breaks easily—three times in recent months—but her new implant is smaller and less bulky than the original device. The new technology seems to make a positive difference in her ability to distinguish sounds, says Heather. "When I work with her individually, she can develop a thought, and together we stretch the words into a sentence. Now, she can write phonetically in a manner that most people can read." Bailea's language skills are delayed, so Heather monitors the rate with which she speaks and takes extra time to explain things in detail. "Bailea mimics what others are doing but she doesn't always grasp the concept. If directions call for using scissors to cut out three characters and put them in

the story order, she would look at others cutting, but not really understand what she's supposed to do next." Heather uses a variety of assessments at least every 2 weeks to monitor Bailea's early literacy skills and to chart her progress. "We set expectations high," she says, "and really work to meet them."

CEC'S STANDARDS: PAVING THE WAY TO SUCCESS

Assess your steps to success in meeting the CEC Knowledge and Skill Base for All Beginning Special Education Teachers of Students Who Are Deaf and Hard of Hearing. Use the following questions to reflect on the growth of your own professional knowledge, skills, and dispositions.

REFLECTING ON YOUR OWN PROFESSIONAL DEVELOPMENT

If you were Bailea's teacher . . .

- What are some areas about educating students who are deaf and hard of hearing that you would need to know more about?
- What are some specific skills that would help you address her academic and behavioral challenges?
- What personal dispositions do you think are most important for you to develop in teaching students with hearing loss?

Using the CEC Standards:

- What are some ways that families influence the overall development of the individual who is deaf or hard of hearing? DH3K3
- How would you design a classroom environment that maximizes opportunities for visual and/or auditory learning for individuals who are deaf or hard of hearing? DH5S5
- What are some sources of specialized materials for individuals who are deaf or hard of hearing? DH4K1

• *By Jean B. Crockett*

Oral Approaches: The Auditory-Verbal Approach and the Auditory-Oral Approach

The Auditory-Verbal Approach The **auditory-verbal approach** focuses exclusively on using audition to improve speech and language development (Andrews et al., 2004). It assumes that most children with hearing impairment have some residual hearing that they can use to their benefit. It relies heavily on amplification technology, such as hearing aids and cochlear implants, and stresses that this amplification technology should be instituted at as young an age as possible. This approach also places a heavy emphasis on speech training. Because children with hearing impairments have problems hearing their own speech or that of others and often hear speech in a distorted fashion, they must be explicitly instructed in how to produce speech sounds.

The Auditory-Oral Approach The **auditory-oral approach** is similar to the auditory-verbal approach, but it also stresses the use of visual cues, such as speechreading and cued speech. Sometimes inappropriately called *lipreading*, **speechreading** involves teaching children to use visual information to understand what is being said to them. *Speechreading* is a more accurate term than *lipreading* because the goal is to teach students to attend to a variety of stimuli in addition to specific movements of the lips. For example, proficient speechreaders read contextual stimuli so that they can anticipate certain types of messages in certain types of situations. They use facial expressions to help them interpret what is being said to them. Even the ability to discriminate the various speech sounds that flow from a person's mouth involves attending to visual cues from the tongue and jaw as well as the lips. For example, to learn to discriminate among vowels, the speechreader concentrates on cues related to the degree of jaw opening and lip shaping.

Cued speech is a way of augmenting speechreading. In cued speech, the individual uses handshapes to represent specific sounds while speaking. Eight handshapes are cues for certain consonants, and four serve as cues for vowels. Cued speech helps the speechreader differentiate between sounds that look alike on the lips. Although it has some devoted advocates, cued speech is not used widely in the United States.

Criticisms of the Oral Approach   Several authorities have been critical of using an exclusively oral approach with students who have hearing impairment (Lane et al., 1996; Padden & Humphries, 2005). In particular, they object to the deemphasis of sign language in this approach, especially for children who are deaf. These critics assert that it's unreasonable to assume that many children with severe or profound degrees of hearing impairment have enough hearing to be of use. Therefore, denying these children access to ASL is denying them access to a language to communicate.

Critics of the oral approach also point out that speechreading is extremely difficult and that good speechreaders are rare (Andrews et al., 2004). It's easy to overlook some of the factors that make speechreading difficult. For instance, speakers produce many sounds with little obvious movement of the mouth. Another issue is that the English language has many **homophenes**—different sounds that are visually identical when spoken. For example, a speechreader cannot distinguish among the pronunciations of *p*, *b*, and *m*. Speakers also vary in how they produce sounds. Finally, factors such as poor lighting, rapid speaking, and talking with one's head turned are further reasons why good speechreading is a rare skill (Menchel, 1988).

Total Communication/Simultaneous Communication

As we noted previously, most schools have adopted the total communication approach, a combination of oral and manual methods. Total communication involves the simultaneous use of speech with one of the **signing English systems**. These signing systems are approaches that professionals have devised for teaching people who are deaf to communicate. **Fingerspelling**, the representation of letters of the English alphabet by finger positions, is also used occasionally to spell out certain words.

Dissatisfaction with total communication has been growing among some professionals and many within the Deaf community. The focus of the criticism has been on the use of signing English systems rather than ASL. Unlike ASL, signing English systems maintain the same word order as spoken English, thereby making it possible to speak and sign at the same time. Defenders of signing English systems state that the correspondence in word order between signing English systems and English helps students to learn English better. Advocates of ASL assert that the use of signing English systems is too slow and awkward to be of much benefit in learning English. They argue that word order is not the critical element in teaching a person to use and comprehend English.

INTERNETRESOURCES

The Internet has several sites with animated fingerspelling or American Sign Language dictionaries. An example for fingerspelling is: www.pbs .org/wnet/soundandfury/ culture/sign_basic.html An example for ASL, developed at Michigan State University, is: http:// commtechlab.msu.edu/sites/ aslweb

A total communication approach blends oral and manual methods.

Advocates of ASL believe that fluency in ASL provides students with a rich background of information that readies them for the learning of English. Furthermore, they argue that ASL is the natural language of people who are deaf and that it should be fostered because it is the most natural and efficient way for students who are deaf to learn about the world. Unlike ASL, signing English systems are not true languages. They have been invented by one or a few people in a short period of time, whereas true sign languages such as ASL have evolved over several generations of users. Many of the critics of the total communication approach advocate the bicultural-bilingual approach.

The Bicultural-Bilingual Approach

Although several variations of the bicultural-bilingual approach exist, most contain these three features (Schirmer, 2001):

1. ASL is considered the primary language, and English is considered the secondary language.
2. People who are deaf play an important role in the development of the program and its curriculum.
3. The curriculum includes instruction in Deaf culture.

Bilingual education for students who are deaf can be structured so that ASL is learned first, followed by English, or the two can be taught simultaneously.

Research directly bearing on the efficacy of bicultural-bilingual programs is in its infancy. At this point, we know that such programs hold great promise and that ASL may contribute to the reading and writing skills of students who are deaf (Simms, Andrews, & Smith, 2005). However, research comparing ASL, signing English systems, and the various approaches has been insufficient to conclude that only one approach should be used. Rather, it is probably safest to conclude that

> No fail-safe, success-guaranteed method exists for educating deaf children, though periodically through the history of deaf education various methods have been proposed as the pedagogical solution. In the 1960s and 1970s, total communication was considered to be the answer. In the 1980s and 1990s, bilingual education was touted as the solution. With the increase in cochlear implants, greater numbers of children are being educated orally/aurally . . . and oral/aural approaches have seen renewed interest. Ultimately, the profession may recognize that only a range of approaches can meet the needs of a range of deaf children. (Schirmer, 2001, p. 203)

Technological Advances

A number of technological advances have made it easier for persons with hearing impairment to communicate with and/or have access to information from the hearing world. This technological explosion has primarily involved five areas: hearing aids, captioning, telephones, computer-assisted instruction, and the Internet. The accompanying Responsive Instruction feature describes one way of using assistive technology to enhance literacy skills of children who are deaf or hard-of-hearing.

Hearing Aids   There are three main types of hearing aids: those worn behind the ear, those worn in the ear, and those worn farther down in the canal of the ear. The behind-the-ear hearing aid is the most powerful and is therefore used by those with the most severe hearing impairment. It's also the one that children most often use because it can be used with FM systems that are available in some classrooms. With an FM system, the teacher wears a wireless lapel microphone, and the student wears an FM receiver (about the size of a cell phone). The student hears the amplified sound either through a hearing aid that comes attached to the FM receiver or by attaching a behind-the-ear hearing aid to the FM receiver. Whether a student will be able to benefit from a hearing aid by itself depends a great deal on the acoustic qualities of the classroom.

RESPONSIVE *INSTRUCTION*
MEETING THE NEEDS OF STUDENTS WHO ARE DEAF OR HARD OF HEARING

Assistive Technology

WHAT THE RESEARCH SAYS

Historically, assistive technologies for students who are deaf or hard of hearing have focused on addressing hearing needs or aiding in communication. These traditional technologies include amplification systems, cochlear implants, captioning services, and telecommunication devices for the deaf (TDDs/TTYs). Newer assistive technologies, however, can go beyond simply supporting communication to address the unique *learning* needs of students who are deaf or hard of hearing. Videophones, webcams, 3D avatars, interactive white boards (e.g., Smart-Boards™), student response systems, and reading and writing software programs are some of the new technologies that can facilitate and enhance learning outcomes.

One learning challenge for many students who are deaf or hard of hearing is in learning to read (Paul, 1998). Some researchers hypothesize that because the majority of deaf children have hearing parents, these children may lack early literacy experiences, which contributes to later difficulties in learning to read. Research on typically developing children has demonstrated the benefits of shared reading on later reading development (Snow, Burns, & Griffin, 1998). Newer assistive technologies can assist parents and teachers in creating shared storybook reading experiences that provide opportunities for learning story grammar, internalizing concepts of print, and mastering complex syntax and vocabulary that are unique to the written language experience (Mueller & Hurtig, 2010).

RESEARCH STUDY

Mueller and Hurtig (2010) conducted a study to see if an electronic storybook with signing support enhanced the shared storybook reading experience. Four children under the age of 5 and their mothers participated in the study. For a period of 5 weeks, the mother–child dyads received five different e-books on a touch screen tablet PC to read together. The books, created using the Iowa Signing E-book, included interactive features such as embedded questions, clickable text (e.g., each word was linked to a video clip of the sign for that word), and page navigation. Parents received e-training for each book that included suggestions on how to engage their child during reading and video models on how to sign the story. Each week the story format would alternate between presentation of the story with a video of a signing narrator and presentation without the signing narrator. During both formats, mothers were expected to supplement the reading of the story through signing.

RESEARCH FINDINGS

Overall, participants spent more time engaged in shared storybook reading when the books included the signing narrator. Although this time was only an increase of a few minutes per book, this time resulted in 30% to 60% more time engaged in reading. In addition, the mothers interested in learning to sign spent more time with the parent training e-books during the nonsigning narrative weeks. Finally, both mothers and children increased their signed vocabulary over the course of the study.

APPLYING THE RESEARCH TO TEACHING

Shared storybook reading is an important component of early literacy experiences. Due to their lack of signing ability, many hearing teachers and parents are reluctant to engage in shared storybook reading with children who are deaf (Moeller & Luetke-Stahlman, 1990). E-books that include signing components can facilitate the shared reading experience by providing this necessary visual support for both students and their hearing facilitators. Teachers can extend the findings of this study and think about ways that new technologies, such as webcams and interactive whiteboards, can provide similar supports (i.e., a visual signing component) during the instruction and independent work of students who are deaf or hard of hearing.

• By Kristin L. Sayeski

■ ■ ■ ■ ■ ■ ■ ■ ■

Although hearing aids are an integral part of educational programming, some children who are deaf can't benefit from them because of the severity and/or nature of the hearing impairment. Generally, hearing aids make sounds louder, not clearer, so if a person's hearing is distorted, a hearing aid will merely amplify the distorted sound.

It is critical for the student, parents, and teachers to work together to ensure the maximum effectiveness of any device. This means that the teacher should be familiar with its proper operation and maintenance.

Television, Video, and Movie Captioning   At one time, viewers needed a special decoder to access captioned programs. Federal law now requires that TVs over 13 inches screen size must contain a chip to allow one to view captions without a decoder—and also stipulates that virtually all new programming must be captioned. However, advocates such as the National Association of the Deaf continue to press for more and better captioning. One need only watch a live news show on TV to see how inaccurate some of the captions can be.

Many videotapes and DVDs available from rental stores are captioned as well. The most recent innovation in captioning is the Rear Window captioning system, which displays captions on transparent acrylic panels that movie patrons can attach to the cup holders on their seats. The captions are actually displayed in reverse at the rear of the theater, and viewers see them reflected on their acrylic screen.

Telephone Adaptations   At one time, people with hearing impairments had problems using telephones, either because their hearing impairment was too great or because of acoustic feedback (noise caused by closeness of the telephone receiver to their hearing aids). However, ironically, text messaging with mobile phones has now become a very useful way for those with hearing impairments to communicate. Also, another primary means for communication are **text telephones (TT)**, sometimes referred to as *TTYs (teletypes)* or *TDDs (telecommunication devices for the deaf)*. People can use a TT connected to a telephone to type a message to anyone else who has a TT. A special phone adaptation allows people without a TT to use the pushbuttons on their phone to "type" messages to people with a TT.

The federal government now requires each state to have a relay service that allows a person with a TT to communicate with anyone through an operator, who conveys the message to a person who does not have a TT. The TT user can carry on a conversation with the non-TT user, or the TT user can leave a message.

Another expanding technology is **video relay service (VRS)**. VRS enables people who are deaf to communicate with people who hear through a sign language interpreter serving as an intermediary. For example, the person who is deaf can communicate in sign over television or video camera over the Internet to the interpreter, who then speaks to the hearing caller and also signs the response back to the person who is deaf.

Computer-Assisted Instruction   The explosion of microcomputer and related technology (e.g., DVDs, CD-ROMs) is expanding learning capabilities for people who are deaf and their families. For example, visual displays of speech patterns on a computer screen can help someone with hearing impairment to learn speech. DVD programs showing people signing are also available for use in learning ASL.

Another example of computer-based technology is C-Print. With C-Print, a person who hears uses an abbreviation system that reduces keystrokes to transcribe on a computer what is being said by, for example, someone lecturing. Students who are deaf can read a real-time text display on their computers as well as receive a printout of the text at a later time.

Researchers are also working on using gesture-recognition technology to help young children who are deaf practice ASL skills (Brashear et al., 2006; Lee,

Technological advances such as this state of the art video telephone system allow students who are deaf to converse with friends over dedicated Integrated Services Digital Network (ISDN) lines using their primary language, American Sign Language.

Henderson, & Brashear, 2005). The child sits in front of a monitor and wears special wireless gloves whose movement can be monitored by the computer to determine how accurately the child is signing.

The Internet   The information superhighway has opened up a variety of communication possibilities for people who are deaf. Besides e-mail, blogs, and instant messaging, which have been around for a while, the flow of new social networking sites, such as Facebook, Twitter, and so forth, seems constant. All of these can serve as vehicles for the Deaf community to stay connected and for people with and without hearing impairments to communicate with each other.

Service Delivery Models

Students who are deaf or hard of hearing can be found in settings ranging from general education classrooms to residential institutions. Since the mid-1970s, more and more of these students have been attending local schools in self-contained classes, resource rooms, and general education classes. Currently, about 86% of students with hearing impairments between the ages of 6 and 21 attend classes in local schools, and 52% spend the vast majority of their time in the general education classroom (Individuals With Disabilities Data Accountability Center, 2010). Even though students with hearing impairment are now included to a very high degree in general education classrooms, they are still served in special schools or residential settings more than most other disability categories, with about 9% in the former and 4% in the latter type of placement.

Many people within the Deaf community have been critical of the degree of inclusion that is occurring (Aldersley, 2002; Lane et al., 1996; Padden & Humphries, 2005; Siegel, 2000). For example, several national organizations, including the National Association for the Deaf, have issued statements supporting the full continuum of placements, including residential schools. They argue that residential schools (and, to a lesser extent, day schools) have been a major influence in fostering the concept of a Deaf culture and the use of ASL. Inclusion, they believe, forces students who are deaf to lose their Deaf identity and places them in a hearing and speaking environment in which it is almost impossible for them to succeed. In particular, critics of inclusion argue that when a student who is deaf is placed in a setting with children who do not have a disability, she is usually the only student with a hearing impairment in the class. This lack of a "critical mass" of students who are deaf can lead to two interrelated problems: (1) a lack of peers with whom the student who is deaf can communicate and (2) a high degree of social isolation. Some evidence shows that this social isolation is experienced most acutely at the middle and high school levels (Oliva, 2004).

Even though inclusion can present problems for many students who are deaf, by no means is it a negative experience for all students. Research on the effects of integrating students who are deaf with hearing peers has consistently found that social and academic outcomes vary depending on the individual. For some, full integration is beneficial; for others, a separate setting is best. Researchers have found that effective inclusive programming for students who are deaf is related to support from the school administration and parents and opportunities for instruction in the general education classroom by special educators trained in deaf education (Schirmer, 2001). For an example of how this can work, read the accompanying Making It Work feature.

Although students who are deaf or hard of hearing are included to a high degree in general education classrooms, they are still served in separate settings more than any other disability category.

MAKING IT WORK
COLLABORATION AND CO-TEACHING OF STUDENTS WHO ARE DEAF OR HARD OF HEARING

"If he can't hear me, how can I teach him?"

Working with a teacher of students who are deaf or hard of hearing may mean learning a new language or learning to work with interpreters. This may cause anxiety and initial reluctance on the part of the general education teacher to try to collaborate. In all cases, the general educator who is being asked to collaborate has a right to a thorough understanding of the abilities of the student (not just the disabilities) and of the goals the special educator has set for the collaboration.

WHAT DOES IT MEAN TO BE A TEACHER OF STUDENTS WHO ARE DEAF OR HARD OF HEARING?

The focus of training for teachers of the deaf or hard of hearing is not on content but on the assessment, characteristics, and management of hearing impairments. Again, these teachers have special skills that they can offer the general educator, such as:

1. An understanding of the communication features (e.g., visual cues, accommodations) that are necessary to enhance cognitive, emotional, and social development of students with hearing impairments.
2. An ability to modify incidental language experiences (e.g., communicating with other students and friends when working in groups) to fit the visual and other sensory needs of individuals who are deaf or hard of hearing.
3. A knowledge of strategies to facilitate cognitive and communicative development in individuals who are deaf or hard of hearing. (Council for Exceptional Children, 2003).

Tapping into these areas of expertise will certainly help in a collaborative situation, but it takes more than expertise in a teaching area to make a collaboration work, as evidenced by the following example.

SUCCESSFUL STRATEGIES FOR CO-TEACHING

Cindy Sadonis (a teacher of students who are deaf/hard of hearing) and Connie Underwood (a third-grade teacher) worked collaboratively to include Joe and Brittany. Joe used hearing aids but had language deficits, and Brittany had a profound hearing loss and used both sign and oral language.

Cindy: I teach nine students with hearing impairments in grades K through 5. The students receive a range of special education services. All students, however, are mainstreamed for library, music, PE, guidance, and special events.

Connie: I teach a general education third-grade class. There are 17 students. I had worked with students with hearing impairments in my general education classroom in the past, and although the experiences were positive in many ways, I felt that I was connecting with the students "at a distance."

Cindy: We were both apprehensive despite being friends, coworkers, and experienced teachers. I went into Connie's room, and she and her third-grade students came into my room.

Connie: I had three main fears. First, was I going to be able to communicate with Joe and Brittany without an interpreter? Yikes! My signing skills were labored, elementary, and painfully wrong at times. Second, how much more planning and time would this take? When I was lead teacher, Cindy interpreted and observed and was ready the following week with lessons on the same theme. I became a support in her room when she became the lead teacher. Third, I was concerned about student relationships. Without prompting, our students began signing as they tried to communicate, and by the latter part of the year it was amazing how much communication was going on at the lunch table, in PE, and even secretively (or so the kids thought) in the classroom.

There were times when Brittany and Joe still felt different and when my students found it much easier to engage in conversations with their friends without hearing losses.

Cindy: It's important to know that collaborative teaching to this degree is often difficult, largely due to schedule. Positive teacher attitudes are required if inclusion is to succeed. Challenges presented themselves along the way for us, too. Social interaction was always an area of need despite our best efforts. As teachers, we have highs and lows, too. Working through them has helped us continue to move in the right direction.

For more information on hearing impairments, visit the National Institute of Deafness and Other Communication Disorders at www.nidcd.nih.gov/health/kids/index.htm.

• By Margaret P. Weiss

ASSESSMENT OF PROGRESS

Many students who are deaf or hard of hearing are educated in inclusive settings with their peers who do not have a disability. As we noted earlier, however, these students characteristically underachieve in academic areas. To ensure that they receive appropriate instruction, it's critical to assess their progress and outcomes in academic subject areas. Additionally, students who are deaf or hard of hearing are often included in state- and district-wide assessments. Teachers should understand appropriate accommodations and alternate assessments specific to this population of students (Cawthon, 2009).

Assessing Academic Skills

Assessment of academic skills for students who are deaf or hard of hearing includes measures to monitor student progress and evaluate student outcomes. Progress monitoring measures are similar to those used to assess students who hear. Research suggests that the technical adequacy of various methods of curriculum-based measurement (CBM) is appropriate for students who are deaf or hard of hearing (Allinder & Eccarius, 1999; Cheng & Rose, 2009). Based on this research, teachers can feel confident in administering CBM probes to monitor progress in reading fluency and comprehension as well as written expression and math.

The STAR Reading, Math, and Early Literacy Assessments (Renaissance Learning, 2006) are also useful for monitoring the academic progress of students who are deaf or hard of hearing. These measures are computerized assessment tools that provide immediate information on student skills to assist with instructional planning. The National Center on Student Progress Monitoring evaluated this measure and found that it met high standards of rigor in progress monitoring (U.S. Department of Education, National Center on Progress Monitoring, 2006).

Performance on measures documenting academic outcomes has significant implications for students; these assessments, however, may not be technically appropriate for students who are deaf or hard of hearing. Unfortunately, most standardized assessments are biased toward the majority culture (Mason, 2005). Educators must consider these biases carefully when making decisions as a result of students' outcomes. Despite these concerns, it's important to have methods to evaluate students' academic achievement.

Testing Accommodations

As students who are deaf or hard of hearing are being included in standardized assessments at higher rates, states are developing guidelines for the use of accommodations (Thompson, Johnston, Thurlow, & Altman, 2005). The most common presentation accommodations for these students are sign interpretation for directions and for test questions, extended time, and small group or individual administration (Cawthon, 2010). Most states allow signing directions without restriction, but some states consider the accommodation for signing questions nonstandard (Lazarus, Thurlow, Lail, Eisenbraun, & Kato, 2006). A nonstandard accommodation often affects scoring and interpretation of the test. Students who are deaf or hard of hearing also receive response accommodations such as signing responses to an interpreter.

EARLY INTERVENTION

Education for infants and preschoolers with hearing impairments is of critical importance. Such programs not only can help facilitate the development of the children but also may be beneficial in reducing parents' stress levels (Lederberg & Golbach, 2002).

Because language development is such an issue for children who are hearing impaired and because early childhood is such an important time for the development of language, it's not surprising that many of the most controversial issues surrounding early intervention in the area of deafness focus on language. As indicated in our earlier discussion of oralism versus manualism, some people maintain that English language should be the focus of intervention efforts, and others hold that ASL should be used starting in infancy.

Children who are deaf who have parents who are deaf are likely to do better than children who are deaf who have hearing parents. For example, in infancy, they develop ASL at a rate similar to the rate at which hearing infants of hearing parents develop English. But infants who are deaf who have hearing parents don't develop either English or ASL at as fast a rate. This may be because day-to-day interactions between mothers and infants are more facilitative and natural when both the infant and parents are deaf than when the infant is deaf and the parents are hearing.

In addition to facility with ASL, parents who are deaf also have the advantage of being better prepared to cope with their infant's deafness (Meadow-Orlans, 1990). Most parents who are hearing are unprepared for the birth of a child with hearing impairment, whereas parents who are deaf can draw on their own experiences in order to offer helpful support to their child who is deaf.

Hearing parents, especially if they want to teach their infants sign language, may need help in understanding the importance of the visual modality in communicating with their infants (Bornstein, Selmi, Haynes, Painter, & Marx, 1999). Hearing parents need to understand, for example, that the eye gaze of the infant who is deaf is extremely important because it's her way of expressing interest and motivation.

Hearing parents of children who are deaf face a quandary over how to provide their children with appropriate sign language models. Both signed English and ASL, especially the latter, are difficult to learn to a high degree of fluency in a relatively short time. And like any language, ASL is harder to acquire as an adult and can rarely be learned to the same degree of fluency as that possessed by a native ASL signer.

The fact that about 90% of children who are deaf have parents who are hearing underscores the importance of intervention for many infants who are deaf. In fact, many authorities believe that the need for early intervention is far greater for families with hearing parents of a child who is deaf than for families in which both the parents and the child are deaf (Andrews & Zmijewski, 1997).

Educators have established preschool intervention projects to teach the basics of sign language to the parents of children who are deaf as well as to the children themselves. Such projects are generally successful at teaching the rudiments of sign to parents and infants. Once the child is ready to progress beyond one- and two-word signed utterances, however, it's important that native signers be available as models. Authorities recommend a practice that is popular in Sweden: adults who are deaf are part of early intervention efforts because they can serve as sign language models and can help hearing parents form positive expectations about their children's potential (Lane et al., 1996). Even though hearing parents might never be able to communicate fluently in sign language, it is important that they continue to sign with their child. Not only does signing allow parents a means of communicating with their child; it also demonstrates that they value the child's language and the Deaf culture.

TRANSITION TO ADULTHOOD

Unemployment and underemployment (being overqualified for a job) have been persistent problems for persons with a hearing impairment, especially women (Punch, Hyde, & Creed, 2004; Schirmer, 2001). Some evidence indicates, however, that this bleak picture is slowly beginning to change. The primary reason for this change has been the expansion of postsecondary programming for students with hearing impairment. A 15-year follow-up of graduates with hearing impairment from 2- and 4-year colleges found that a college education made a substantial difference in having a satisfying career and life (Schroedel & Geyer, 2000).

The reasons for the difficulty experienced by individuals with hearing impairments in finding appropriate and satisfying employment have a lot to do with a poor understanding among the members of the population who do not have hearing impairments of what it means to have a hearing impairment and of possible accommodations in the workplace

(Punch, Creed, & Hyde, 2006). Likewise, people with hearing impairments, themselves, often aren't prepared to ask for the right accommodations and have difficulties making good career choices (Punch et al., 2004).

Postsecondary Education

Before the mid-1960s, the only institution established specifically for the postsecondary education of students with hearing impairment was Gallaudet College (now Gallaudet University). Except for this one institution, these students were left with no choice but to attend traditional colleges and universities. However, traditional postsecondary schools were generally not equipped to handle the special needs of students with hearing impairment. It's little wonder, then, that a study by Quigley, Jenne, and Phillips (1968) identified only 224 people with hearing impairment who were graduates of regular colleges and universities in the United States between 1910 and 1965.

Findings such as these led to the expansion of postsecondary programs. The federal government has funded a wide variety of postsecondary programs for students with hearing impairment. The two best-known ones are Gallaudet University and the National Technical Institute for the Deaf (NTID) at the Rochester Institute of Technology. The NTID program, emphasizing training in technical fields, complements the liberal arts orientation of Gallaudet University. At NTID, some students with hearing impairment also attend classes at the Rochester Institute of Technology with students who hear.

In addition to Gallaudet and NTID, well over 100 postsecondary programs are now available in the United States and Canada for students with hearing impairment. By law, Gallaudet and NTID are responsible for serving students from all 50 states and territories. Others serve students from several states, from one state only, or from specific districts only.

Although many people who are deaf who enroll in higher education choose to attend Gallaudet, NTID, or colleges with special programs, some go to traditional colleges and universities. These students usually take advantage of the expanding roles of university programs that have been established to facilitate the academic experiences of students with disabilities. One of the accommodations often recommended is to provide sign language interpreters in the classes of students with hearing impairment. For example, Jasmine Saleh (see the accompanying Peer Connections), a recent graduate of the University

INTERNETRESOURCES

Deafcareers Magazine (www.deafcareers.com) offers a forum for practitioners and the Deaf community to address career preparedness.

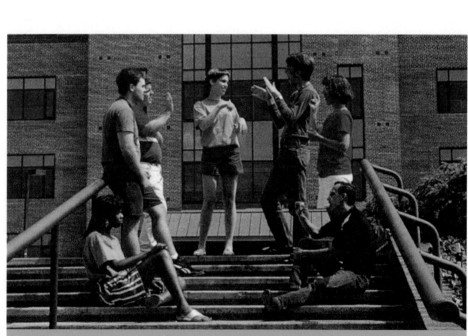

Over 100 postsecondary programs in the United States and Canada are now established for students who are deaf or hard of hearing. Many of these students choose to attend traditional colleges and universities as well.

PEER CONNECTIONS: JASMINE SALEH

JASMINE SALEH was in born in Toronto, Canada. She was diagnosed with profound deafness at 17 months of age. She lived in Canada for 9 years, and then she moved with her family to New York. She had no contact with other deaf people and received no services until she moved to Minnesota in middle school. In Minnesota she learned American Sign Language and had an interpreter. Her family then moved to Charlottesville, and Jasmine attended the University of Virginia. While at UVA, Jasmine's accommodations consisted of sign language interpreters, note taking by peers, and preferential seating. She graduated in May 2010, planning to attend medical school at the University of Illinois in fall 2010.

1. What do you do for fun? I hang out with my family and friends. We go to the movies. I'm also involved with the Deaf community in Charlottesville at UVA, which keeps me busy. We promote Deaf awareness and culture in Charlottesville. I also like to travel.

2. What is your favorite way to relax? Exercising! Lifting weights, running, and occasionally yoga.

3. What is something that you excel at? Hmm. . . . Academically, probably math. Otherwise, basketball, I played in high school.

4. What is your pet peeve? I hate when people cut into other traffic lanes when they are driving and don't use a signal!

5. Can you recall one teacher in particular who has been a positive influence in your life? Yes, Professor Christopher Krit. He teaches American Sign Language and English at UVA. He is severely hard of hearing, and he's actively involved with the Deaf community at UVA. He was never my teacher, but through my contacts with him he has shown me that deaf people can do anything!

6. Is there anyone else (celebrity, family member) whom you regard as a role model? Why are they a role model for you? My parents, their moral values of hard work ethic and perseverance have really helped me throughout my life.

7. What is the most difficult thing for you about having a disability? I think the most difficult thing is others' misinterpretation and assumptions, thinking that deaf are limited and that they can't do everything that hearing people can do; I have to show them otherwise.

8. Do you see your disability as affecting your ability to achieve what you want in your life? No, I mean there are obstacles to overcome, but it is about hard work. I can do anything with hard work.

9. Has your disability affected your social relationships? If so, how? My friends from college are more mature and realize that I am more mature than most 18-year-olds. However, I can relate to them more than my friends back home. It has been hard to keep in touch with friends back home. I skipped high school and it's hard to relate to friends who are just finishing high school. But I try to keep in touch and keep a balance.

10. Are there any advantages to having a disability that others might be surprised to know? I've learned to work hard and to prove and advocate for myself because of my disability.

11. How do you think others perceive you? I think that now people see me as an equal. I hope people see me as a smart, funny, beautiful person. Previously, people seemed more scared of me and looked down on me.

12. What is one thing that you would like others to know about you? I've never flown out of the country. However, this summer I'm going on a medical mission trip to Palestine with my father.

13. Where do you see yourself 10 years from now? I see myself with a small family, probably working at home or in the medical field. Paying taxes!

14. Please fill in the blank: I couldn't live without _____. The Internet, the best invention ever.

CONNECT WITH JASMINE— Jasmine welcomes you to contact her online at Jss6e@virginia.edu

of Virginia, was provided with sign language interpreters, along with note taking by peers, and preferential seating, as her accommodations.

Sign Language Interpreters Even though most authorities would agree that having a sign language interpreter is one of the best accommodations, it's important to keep in mind that this is a far cry from leveling the academic playing field for students with hearing impairments. First, there is a national shortage of adequately trained interpreters

(Schick, Williams, & Kupermintz, 2006). Even when students with hearing impairment have access to highly trained interpreters, the amount of information they can take in falls well below that of their hearing peers. In other words, when hearing students and students who are deaf hear and see (through interpretation) the same lecture, the students who are deaf don't learn as much of the material (Marschark, Pelz, et al., 2005; Marschark, Sapere, Convertino, & Seewagen, 2005; Marschark, Sapere, Convertino, Seewagen, & Maltzen, 2004).

The role of interpreters generates a debate over using ASL versus transliteration. **Transliteration,** which is similar to signed English, maintains the same word order as spoken English. ASL, by contrast, requires the interpreter to digest the meaning of what is said before conveying it through signs. Interestingly, according to Jasmine Saleh (in the accompanying Peer Connections box), her interpreters used both ASL and transliteration, depending on the difficulty of understanding and visualizing the concepts discussed in courses. For example, in physiology class, when her professor discussed blood circulation in the human body, her interpreters understood the concepts and therefore were able to use ASL. However, when her professor discussed the diffusion gradient in the kidneys, the interpreters didn't understand the concepts and just used transliteration.

Most college instructors have limited, if any, experience in working with sign language interpreters. Even so, it is critical that instructors and interpreters work closely together to provide the optimum learning experience for students who are deaf while not disrupting other students in the class (Seal, 2004).

Family Issues

With regard to raising a family, people who are deaf often face unique challenges. National statistics indicate that 95% of adults who are deaf choose deaf spouses, and 90% of the offspring of these marriages have normal hearing (Buchino, 1993). These hearing children often serve as interpreters for their parents. Being called on to interpret for one's parents can help to develop self-confidence around adult authority figures (e.g., doctors, lawyers, insurance agents), but it can also force one to face some unpleasant biases, as the following story from a hearing child of deaf parents demonstrates:

> Curled up in the seat, chin dug into my chest, I noticed there was a lull in the conversation. Dad was a confident driver, but Mom was smoking more than usual.
> "Something happened? That gas station?" Mom signed to me.
> "No, nothing," I lied.
> "Are you sure?"
> "Everything is fine." Dad and I had gone to pay and get directions. The man behind the counter had looked up, seen me signing and grunted, "Huh, I didn't think mutes were allowed to have driver's licenses." Long ago I'd gotten used to hearing those kind of comments. But I never could get used to the way it made me churn inside. (Walker, 1986, p. 9)

These children also sometimes resent that being called on to interpret for their parents has interfered with their social lives (Buchino, 1993).

There has been a long tradition of preparing students who are deaf for manual trades (Lane, 1992). But unskilled and semiskilled trades are fast disappearing from the workforce in favor of jobs requiring higher-level skills. As a result, adults who are deaf face even greater obstacles when they enter the job market.

Although the educational, work, and social opportunities for adults who are deaf are often limited, there are reasons to be optimistic about the future. With the continued expansion of transition programming, postsecondary education, and greater public awareness of the potential of people who are deaf, there is promise for a brighter outlook for adults who are deaf.

SUMMARY

How do professionals define and classify individuals who are deaf or hard of hearing?

- Professionals with a *physiological* perspective use a decibel loss of 90 dB or greater as the cutoff for deafness.
- Those with an *educational* perspective classify individuals as deaf if they can't process linguistic information, with or without a hearing aid; they classify individuals as hard of hearing if they can process this information with the help of a hearing aid.
- *Congenital versus adventitious deafness* refers to being born deaf versus acquiring deafness after birth; *prelingual deafness* versus postlingual deafness refers to deafness occurring before versus after speech and language development.
- Sentiment is growing in the Deaf community that those who are deaf should be considered as a cultural/linguistic minority rather than disabled.

What is the prevalence of hearing impairment?

- About 0.14% of students from 6 to 17 years of age are identified as hearing impaired; those classified as hard of hearing are more prevalent than those identified as deaf.
- More than half of students identified as hearing impaired are minorities, and close to 29% come from Spanish-speaking homes.

What are some basic anatomical and physiological characteristics of the ear?

- The outer ear consists of the auricle and external auditory canal.
- The middle ear consists of the eardrum and three tiny bones (ossicles): the malleus, incus, and stapes.
- The inner ear consists of the vestibular mechanism and the cochlea; the former monitors balance, and the latter is the most important for hearing because it is responsible for sending electrical impulses to the brain via the cochlear nerve.

How is hearing impairment identified?

- Screening tests for infants often measure otoacoustic emissions, low-intensity sound emitted from the cochlea when stimulated.
- Pure-tone audiometry assesses decibel (intensity) and hertz (frequency) levels.
- Speech audiometry assesses the ability to detect and understand speech.
- Specialized tests for young children and children who are hard to test include conditioned play audiometry, tympanometry, and brain-stem–evoked response audiometry.

What causes hearing impairments?

- Conductive hearing impairments involve the middle or outer ear, sensorineural hearing impairments involve the inner ear, mixed hearing impairments involve both.
- The causes of impairments of the outer ear include infections of the external canal or tumors.
- Impairments of the middle ear are often due to malfunctioning of the ossicles; otitis media is a common cause of temporary middle-ear hearing problems.
- Impairments of the inner ear usually result in greater hearing impairment than do those of the middle or outer ear; impairments of the inner ear can be hereditary or acquired, but the former are much more common. Genetic or hereditary factors are the leading cause of deafness in children, with mutation of the connexin-26 gene now considered the most common cause of congenital deafness.

What are some psychological and behavioral characteristics of learners with hearing impairments?

- The most severely affected area is comprehension and production of English.
- Sign language is the primary language of most people in the Deaf community.
  - Each sign consists of three parts: handshape, location, and movement.
  - Sign language is a true language, as evidenced by the facts that sign language is as grammatically complex as spoken language, there is no universal sign language, children who are deaf reach the same language milestones and at the same times as do those who can hear, and the neurological underpinnings of sign are the same as those for spoken language.
- Deafness doesn't affect intelligence.
- Most students who are deaf have extreme deficits in academics, especially reading.
  - Students who are deaf who have parents who are deaf do better academically.
  - A supportive home environment is associated with higher achievement.
- Students who are deaf might face limited opportunities for social interaction.

- The inclusion movement can result in students who are deaf not having peers who are deaf with whom to communicate.
- About 90% of children who are deaf have hearing parents, most of whom are not proficient in sign language.
- Many authorities recognize the Deaf culture as a means of healthy social communication. There is concern that the Deaf culture might be eroding owing to inclusionary programming. Deaf activists have raised issues with respect to cochlear implants and genetic engineering.

What are some educational considerations for learners with hearing impairments?

- The oral approach consists of the following:
  - The auditory-verbal approach, which focuses on using audition to improve speech and language development.
  - The auditory-oral approach, which is like the auditory-verbal approach with the addition of using visual cues such as speechreading and cued speech.
- The manual approach stresses sign language.
- Most educational programs use a total communication (simultaneous communication) approach, a blend of oral and manual techniques, the latter being a type of signing English system in which the English word order is preserved.
- Some advocate for a bicultural-bilingual approach, which consists of three features: ASL is considered the primary language, people who are deaf are involved in the development of the program and curriculum, and the curriculum involves instruction in Deaf culture.
- Educational placement of students who are deaf includes the full continuum, but more inclusive settings are becoming more and more popular, with about 86% of students who are deaf attending classes in regular schools and 52% spending the vast majority of their time in general education classrooms. Many within the Deaf community are concerned that the inclusion movement results in the absence of a "critical mass" of students who are deaf, which can result in social isolation.
- Numerous technological advances are occurring in hearing aids; television, video, and movie captioning; text telephone technology; computer-assisted instruction; and the Internet.

How do professionals assess the progress of students with hearing impairments?

- Using sign language, professionals can implement CBM to monitor progress in academics, such as reading fluency, reading comprehension, writing, and math.
- The most common accommodations for standardized assessments include sign interpretation for directions and for test questions, extended time, and small-group or individual administration.

What are some important considerations with respect to early intervention for learners with hearing impairments?

- Families of children who are deaf who have hearing parents might be in greater need of early intervention programming than families in which the parents are deaf.
- Because it is difficult for hearing parents to become fluent in sign language, native signers are a part of some intervention programs.

What are some important considerations with respect to transition to adulthood for learners with hearing impairments?

- In addition to Gallaudet University and the National Technical Institute for the Deaf, several postsecondary programs are now available for students with hearing impairment.
- A common accommodation in college is the use of sign language interpreters. Transliteration involves maintaining the same word order as English, whereas ASL does not.
- Ninety percent of the children of two parents who are deaf have normal hearing. These children often face challenges of negotiating between the Deaf community and hearing society.
- There has been a long tradition of preparing many students who are deaf for manual trades; however, these trades are disappearing.
- Expanded transition programming, postsecondary education, and public awareness promise a brighter outlook for adults who are deaf.

COUNCIL FOR EXCEPTIONAL CHILDREN

Addressing the Professional Standards

 Council for Exceptional Children (CEC) Common Core Knowledge and Skills addressed in this chapter: ICC1K5, ICC1K6, ICC1K8, ICC2K1, ICC2K2, ICC2K6, ICC3K1, ICC4S4, ICC4S6, ICC6K4, ICC7S1, ICC7S7, ICC7S8, ICC7S9, ICC8S2, ICC8S5, ICC8S7, ICC10K3

Appendix: Provides a full listing of the CEC Common Core Standards, and associated Knowledge and Skill Statements listed here.

MYEDUCATIONLAB

myeducationlab Now go to Topic 12: Sensory Impairments, in the MyEducationLab (www.myeducationlab.com) for your course, where you can:

- Find learning outcomes for the broad concepts covered in this chapter along with the national standards that connect to these outcomes.
- Complete Assignments and Activities that can help you more deeply understand the chapter content.
- Examine challenging situations presented in the IRIS Center Resources.
- Apply and practice your understanding of the core concepts and skills identified in the chapter with the Building Teaching Skills and Dispositions learning units.
- Check your comprehension on the content covered in the chapter by going to the Study Plan in the Book-Specific Resources for your text. Here you will be able to take a chapter quiz, receive feedback on your answers, and then access Review, Practice, and Enrichment activities to enhance your understanding of chapter content.
- Watch video clips of CCSSO Teacher of the Year award winners responding to the question: "Why I teach?" in the Teacher Talk section.

Ray, no one knows what it's like to carry water
The way your mother made you carry it—
Even the boy Pharaoh
Wore a yoke on his shoulders
Just to show he was a man.
History doesn't matter much,
At least until your child
"Done gone blind"—your Mama saw it—
"You always got to carry water," she said.
"This ain't no kidding around."
Long time
You carried water
In both hands,
Feeling for the path
With your feet.
Ray, your Mama knew—
A song comes that way—
Or else it never will.
Laugh or cry it's the same.
A Mockingbird listens from a telephone wire.
Long time, water, both hands.

Stephen Kuusisto • *"Elegy for Ray Charles and His Mother"*
Source: Stephen Kuusisto, "Elegy for Ray Charles" from
Ragged Edge (June 2004). Copyright © 2004 by Stephen Kuusisto.
Reprinted with permission of the author.

QUESTIONS **to guide your reading of this chapter . . .**

- How do professionals define and classify learners with blindness and low vision?
- What is the prevalence of visual impairment?
- What are some basic anatomical and physiological characteristics of the eye?
- How is visual ability measured?
- What causes visual impairments?
- What are some of the psychological and behavioral characteristics of learners with visual impairments?
- What are some educational considerations for learners with visual impairments?
- How do professionals assess the progress of students with visual impairments in academic and functional skills and make testing accommodations for them?
- What are some important considerations with respect to early intervention for learners with visual impairments?
- What are some important considerations with respect to transition to adulthood for learners with visual impairments?

MISCONCEPTIONS ABOUT
Learners with Blindness or Low Vision

MYTH • People who are legally blind have no sight at all.

FACT • Only a small percentage of people who are legally blind have absolutely no vision. Many have a useful amount of functional vision.

MYTH • People who are blind have an extra sense that enables them to detect obstacles.

FACT • People who are blind do not have an extra sense. Some can learn to develop an "obstacle sense" by noting the change in pitch of echoes as they move toward objects.

MYTH • People who are blind automatically develop better acuity in their other senses.

FACT • Through concentration and attention, individuals who are blind can learn to make very fine discriminations in the sensations they obtain. This is not automatic but rather represents learning to use received sensations better.

MYTH • People who are blind have superior musical ability.

FACT • The musical ability of people who are blind is not necessarily better than that of sighted people; however, many people who are blind pursue musical careers as one way in which they can achieve success.

MYTH • Stereotypic behaviors (e.g., body rocking, head swaying) are always maladaptive and should be totally eliminated.

FACT • Although more research is needed, some authorities maintain that these behaviors, except when they are extreme, can help persons who are blind regulate their levels of arousal.

MYTH • Braille is not very useful for the vast majority of people who are blind; it should only be tried as a last resort.

FACT • Very few people who are blind have learned braille, primarily due to fear that using it is a sign of failure and to a historical professional bias against it. Authorities acknowledge the utility of braille for people who are blind.

MYTH • Braille is of no value for those who have low vision.

FACT • Some individuals with low vision have conditions that will eventually result in blindness. More and more, authorities think that these individuals should learn braille to be prepared for when they can't read print effectively.

MYTH • If people with low vision use their eyes too much, their sight will deteriorate.

FACT • Only rarely is this true. Visual efficiency can actually be improved through training and use. Wearing strong lenses, holding books close to the eyes, and using the eyes often cannot harm vision.

MYTH • Mobility instruction should be delayed until elementary or secondary school.

FACT • Many authorities now recognize that even preschoolers can take advantage of mobility instruction, including the use of a cane.

MYTH • The long cane is a simply constructed, easy-to-use device.

FACT • The National Academy of Sciences has drawn up specifications for the manufacture of the long cane and its proper use.

MYTH • Guide dogs take people where they want to go.

FACT • The guide dog does not "take" the person anywhere; usually, the person must first know where he or she is going. The dog can be a protection against unsafe areas or obstacles.

Stephen Kuusisto, author of the poem reprinted in the chapter opener, was blind from birth but was well into his adult years before he stopped the charade of trying to "pass" as a sighted person. Once at peace with his blindness, he was able to turn his energies to more productive endeavors, such as being a successful author. As Kuusisto acknowledges in his elegy to Ray Charles, people vary in their response to being blind. Some actually gain an inner strength from adversity, for example, "She'd make me cut wood, wash clothes and build a fire under the pot. . . . People thought that was abusive. My mother had the attitude 'He's got to learn, and just because he's blind doesn't mean he's stupid'" (Interview with Ray Charles, reported June 11, 2004 by Reuters UK). However, a major impediment to being able to accept one's blindness is society's reactions to people who are blind. Visual impairments seem to evoke more awkwardness than most other disabilities. Why are we so uncomfortably aware of blindness? For one thing, blindness is visible. We often don't realize that a person has impaired hearing, for example, until we actually talk to her. The person with visual impairment, however, usually has a variety of symbols: a cane, thick or darkened glasses, a guide dog.

Another possible reason for being self-conscious around people who are blind is the role that eyes play in social interaction. Poets, playwrights, and songwriters have long recognized how emotionally expressive the eyes can be for people who are sighted. Those of us who are sighted know how uncomfortable it can be to talk with someone who doesn't make eye contact with us. Think how often we've heard someone say or have ourselves said that we prefer to talk face to face on an important matter, rather than over the telephone.

Another reason we fear loss of vision is that the sense of sight is linked so closely with the traditional concept of beauty. We derive great pleasure from our sight. Our feelings about others are often based largely on physical appearances that are visually perceived. Additionally, our use of language reinforces a negative view of blindness:

> The word blind has always meant more than merely the inability to see. . . . Throughout history of the language and in common usage today, the word [blind] connotes a lack of understanding, . . . a willful disregard or obliviousness, a thing meant to conceal or deceive. In fact, when you stop to listen, the word is far more commonly used in its figurative than its literal sense. And it comes up so often: blind faith, blind devotion, blind luck, . . . blind alley, . . . blind taste test, double-blind study, flying blind, . . . blind submission, blind side, blind spot. . . . Pick up any book or magazine and you will find dozens of similes and metaphors connecting blindness and blind people with ignorance, confusion, indifference, ineptitude. (Kleege, 1999, p. 21)

So although blindness is the least prevalent of all disabilities, at least in children, people dread it. It is reportedly the third most feared condition; only cancer and AIDS outrank it (Jernigan, 1992). With a bit of reflection, however, it becomes obvious that our anxieties about blindness are irrational. Most of our apprehension is because of our lack of experience interacting with individuals with visual impairment. It's not until we talk to people who are blind or read about their appreciation of sounds, smells, and touch that we begin to realize that sight is not the only sense that enables us to enjoy beauty or socialize with other people.

Like anyone with a disability, the person who is blind wants to be treated like everyone else. Most people who are blind do not seek pity or unnecessary help. In fact, they can be fiercely protective of their independence. The accompanying Personal Perspectives, "Social Interaction with People Who Are Blind," provides etiquette tips on interacting with someone who is blind.

In this chapter, we hope to dispel several myths about blindness. We start by presenting a fact that most sighted people do not know: The majority of people who are blind can actually see.

DEFINITION AND CLASSIFICATION

The two most common ways of describing someone with visual impairment are the legal and educational definitions. Laypeople and medical professionals use the former; the latter is the one educators favor. The two major classifications are blindness and low vision.

Legal Definition

The legal definition involves assessment of visual acuity and field of vision. A person who is **legally blind** has visual acuity of 20/200 or less in the better eye even with correction (e.g., eyeglasses) or has a field of vision so narrow that its widest diameter subtends an angular distance no greater than 20 degrees. The fraction 20/200 means that the person sees at 20 feet what a person with normal vision sees at 200 feet. (Normal visual acuity is thus 20/20.) The inclusion of a narrowed field of vision in the legal definition means that a person may have 20/20 vision in the central field but severely restricted peripheral vision. Legal blindness qualifies a person for certain legal benefits, such as tax advantages and money for special materials.

In addition to this classification of blindness, is a category referred to as **low vision** (sometimes referred to as *partially sighted*). According to the legal classification system, persons who have low vision have visual acuity falling between 20/70 and 20/200 in the better eye with correction.

Personal PERSPECTIVES
Social Interaction with People Who Are Blind: Points of Etiquette

The following letter to "Dear Abby" from the president of the American Foundation for the Blind lists some appropriate ways that people who are sighted can interact with those who are blind. Suggestions such as these help to avoid awkward social situations.

Dear Abby:

You recently ran a letter from a woman who gave a few tips on what sighted people should do when they meet a blind person. As president of the American Foundation for the Blind, and a blind person myself, I believe I can add a few more points of etiquette your readers may find helpful.

1. Speak to people who are blind or visually impaired using a natural conversational tone and speed. Do not speak loudly and slowly unless the person also has a hearing impairment.
2. Address blind people by name when possible. This is especially important in crowded places.
3. Immediately greet blind people when they enter a room or service area. This lets them know you are present and ready to assist.

4. Indicate the end of a conversation with a blind person in order to avoid the embarrassment of leaving a person speaking when no one is actually there.
5. Feel free to use words that refer to vision when conversing with blind people. Words such as "look," "see," "watching TV," are part of everyday communication. The words "blind" and "visually impaired" are also acceptable in conversation.
6. Do not leave a blind person standing in "free space" when you serve as a guide. Also, be sure that the person you guide has a firm grasp on your arm or is leaning against a chair or a wall if you have to be separated momentarily.
7. Be calm and clear about what to do if you see a blind person about to encounter a dangerous situation. For example, if the person is about to bump into something, calmly and firmly call out, "Wait there for a moment; there is an obstruction in your path."

By Carl R. Augusto
President, American Foundation for the Blind, New York

Source: Letter reprinted with permission of the American Foundation for the Blind.

Educational Definition

Many professionals, particularly educators, find the legal classification scheme inadequate. They have observed that visual acuity is not a very accurate predictor of how people will function or use whatever remaining sight they have. Although a small percentage of individuals who are legally blind have absolutely no vision, the majority can see to some degree.

Many who recognize the limitations of the legal definitions of blindness and low vision favor the educational definition, which stresses the method of reading instruction. For educational purposes, individuals who are blind are so severely impaired they must learn to read **braille**, a system of raised dots by which people who are blind read with their fingertips. It consists of quadrangular cells containing from one to six dots whose arrangement denotes different letters and symbols. Alternatively, they use aural methods (audiotapes and records). Those who have low vision can read print, even if they need adaptations such as magnifying devices or large-print books.

It's important to note that even though people with low vision can read print, many authorities believe that some of them can benefit from using braille. (We discuss this later in the chapter.) This is why we previously emphasized that those who are considered blind must use braille to read.

Some professionals think that both the legal definition and the educational definition are flawed because both focus on limitations rather than skills. Read about a skills definition of blindness in the accompanying Focus on Concepts box.

FOCUS ON Concepts

A SKILLS DEFINITION OF BLINDNESS

Focusing on Skills

Most definitions of disability, including blindness and low vision, focus on what the person *cannot* do. Carol Castellano, the mother of a child who is blind and the first vice president of the National Organization of Parents of Blind Children and president of New Jersey Parents of Blind Children, offers a different perspective. She proposes a *skills* definition of blindness:

> I propose that blindness/visual impairment simply means *using alternative skills and tools in place of, or in addition to, eyesight in order to gain information or perform tasks....*
>
> If the task is sorting laundry, the tool might be braille or tactile labels.... If the task is reading, the alternative tool might be braille or large print. (Castellano, 2005, p. 16)

Castellano also questions the utility of distinguishing between blindness and low vision, believing that equating blindness with braille reinforces the notion that braille is somehow inferior to visual techniques such as large print.

A skills definition is also reflected in the following statement by a man who lost his sight: "So am I blind? I think so.... For me to live my life the way I want to, I must use a combination of blindness skills, alternative techniques, and access technology to accomplish tasks I used to do using vision" (Pare, 2005, p. 412).

A Blindness Skills Quiz

Castellano (2005) notes that one of the challenges for teachers and parents is to identify skills that persons who are blind can use to perform everyday tasks. Here are some examples she uses:

How might a blind person . . .

1. keep track of where his/her toddler is?
2. shop at a supermarket?
3. grill meat on a barbeque?
4. go on the Internet?
5. pour a glass of juice?

Here are some possible solutions.

1. Attach bells to the baby's shoes (as many sighted parents do) or pay attention to the rustle of plastic diapers.
2. Write a shopping list in braille, make use of the store's courtesy service, ask a reader or driver to come along to assist, or shop online.
3. Use long oven mitts and a grilling basket.
4. Use a screen enlarging program or a screen reading program that makes the computer talk.
5. Use the sound of the liquid and the weight of the glass to tell when the glass is getting full, or hook one finger over the edge of the glass and stop pouring when the liquid reaches their finger. (Castellano, 2005, pp. 16–17)

PREVALENCE

Blindness is primarily an adult disability. Most estimates indicate that blindness is approximately one-tenth as prevalent in school-age children as in adults. The federal government classifies only about 0.05% of the population ranging from 6 to 17 years of age as "visually impaired," which includes those who are blind or who have low vision. This is probably an underestimate because many blind children also have other disabilities, and school systems are instructed to report only the "primary" condition. So, for example, some students who are both blind and intellectually disabled might be reported in the just the latter category. The fact remains, however, that visual impairment is one of the least prevalent disabilities in children.

ANATOMY AND PHYSIOLOGY OF THE EYE

The anatomy of the visual system is extremely complex, so our discussion here focuses on only basic characteristics. Figure 12.1 shows the functioning of the eye. The physical object being seen becomes an electrical impulse that is sent through the optic nerve to the visual center of the brain, the occipital lobes. Before reaching the optic nerve, light rays reflecting off the object being seen pass through several structures within the eye. The light rays do the following:

1. Pass through the **cornea** (a transparent cover in front of the iris and pupil), which performs the major part of the bending (refraction) of the light rays so that the image will be focused

2. Pass through the **aqueous humor** (a watery substance between the cornea and lens of the eye)

3. Pass through the **pupil** (the contractile opening in the middle of the **iris**, the colored portion of the eye that contracts or expands, depending on the amount of light striking it)

4. Pass through the **lens**, which refines and changes the focus of the light rays before they pass through the **vitreous humor** (a transparent gelatinous substance that fills the eyeball between the retina and lens)

FIGURE 12.1 The basic anatomical features of the eye and the visual process

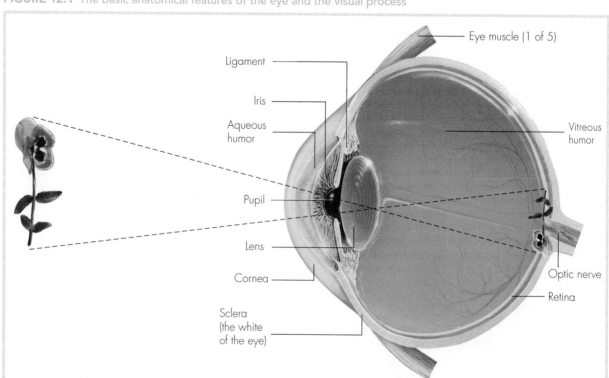

5. Come to a focus on the **retina** (the back portion of the eye, containing nerve fibers connected to the **optic nerve**, which carries the information back to the brain)

IDENTIFICATION OF VISUAL IMPAIRMENT

Visual acuity is most often measured with the **Snellen chart**, which consists of rows of letters (for individuals who know the alphabet). For the very young and/or those who cannot read, the chart has rows of the letter *E* arranged in various positions, and the person's task is to indicate in what direction the "legs" of the *E*'s face. Each row corresponds to the distance at which a person with normal vision can discriminate the letters or the directions of the *E*'s. (There are eight rows, one corresponding to each of the following distances: 15, 20, 30, 40, 50, 70, 100, and 200 feet.) People are normally tested at the 20-foot distance. If they can distinguish the letters in the 20-foot row, they are said to have 20/20 central visual acuity for far distances. If they can distinguish only the much larger letters in the 70-foot row, they are said to have 20/70 central visual acuity for far distances.

Although the Snellen chart is widely used and can be very useful, it does have some limitations. First, it's a measure of visual acuity for distant objects, and a person's distance and near vision sometimes differ. Assessing near vision usually involves naming letters that range in size from smaller to larger on a card that is at a typical reading distance from the person's eyes.

Second, and more important, visual acuity doesn't always correspond with how a student actually uses his vision in natural settings, which have variable environmental conditions (e.g., fluorescent lighting, windows that admit sunshine, highly reflective tile floors). Vision teachers, therefore, usually do a functional vision assessment. A **functional vision assessment** involves observing the student interacting in different environments (e.g., classroom, outdoors, grocery stores), under different lighting conditions to see how well the student can identify objects and perform various tasks (Zimmerman, 2011).

Teachers can sometimes play a key role in identifying students with visual impairments. So they should be alert to signs that children might have visual disabilities. Prevent Blindness America (2005) has listed a number of signs of possible eye problems on their Website, described in the accompanying Focus on Concepts feature.

INTERNETRESOURCES

Several Websites contain sample Snellen charts. Some examples are:
http://en.wikipedia.org/wiki/Snellen-chart
http://www.mdsupport.org/snellen.html
http://www.i-see.org/eyecharts.html
The Website of Prevent Blindness America contains an example of a Web-based measure of near vision: www.preventblindness.org/eye_tests/near_vision_test.html

---

FOCUS ON Concepts

SIGNS OF POSSIBLE EYE TROUBLE IN CHILDREN

If one or more of these signs appear, take your child to an eye doctor right away.

What do your child's eyes look like?

- eyes don't line up, one eye appears crossed or looks out
- eyelids are red-rimmed, crusted, or swollen
- eyes are watery or red (inflamed)

How does your child act?

- rubs eyes a lot
- closes or covers one eye
- tilts head or thrusts head forward
- has trouble reading or doing other close-up work, or holds objects close to eyes to see

- blinks more than usual or seems cranky when doing close-up work
- things are blurry or hard to see
- squints eyes or frowns

What does your child say?

- "my eyes are itchy," "my eyes are burning," or "my eyes feel scratchy."
- "I can't see very well."
- After doing close-up work, your child says "I feel dizzy," "I have a headache" or "I feel sick/nauseous."
- "Everything looks blurry," or "I see double."

Remember, your child may still have an eye problem even if he or she does not complain or has not shown any unusual signs.

Source: Retrieved from the World Wide Web: www.preventblindness.org/children/trouble_signs.html. Reprinted with permission from Prevent Blindness America ®. Copyright © 2005.

CAUSES

Causes Affecting Children and Adults

When considering both children and adults, the most common visual problems are the result of errors of refraction. **Refraction** refers to the bending of the light rays as they pass through the various structures of the eye. **Myopia** (nearsightedness), **hyperopia** (farsightedness), and **astigmatism** (blurred vision) are examples of refraction errors that affect central visual acuity. Although each can be serious enough to cause significant impairment (myopia and hyperopia are the most common impairments of low vision), wearing glasses or contact lenses usually can bring vision within normal limits.

Myopia results when the eyeball is too long. In this case, the light rays from the object in Figure 12.2a are in focus in front of, rather than on, the retina. Myopia affects vision for distant objects, but close vision may be unaffected. When the eyeball is too short, hyperopia (farsightedness) results (see Figure 12.2b). In this case, the light rays from the object in the diagram are in focus behind, rather than on, the retina. Hyperopia affects vision for close objects, but far vision may be unaffected. If the cornea or lens of the eye is irregular, the person is said to have astigmatism. In this case, the light rays from the object in the figure are blurred or distorted.

Among the most serious impairments are those caused by glaucoma, cataracts, and diabetes. These conditions occur primarily in adults, but each, particularly the latter two, can occur in children. See Figure 12.3 for simulations of how different eye conditions affect how people see.

Glaucoma is actually a *group* of eye diseases that causes damage to the **optic nerve**. At one time, it was thought to be due exclusively to excessive pressure inside the eyeball; we now know that some cases of glaucoma occur with normal pressure (Glaucoma Research Foundation, 2008). It is referred to as the "sneak thief of sight" because it often occurs with no symptoms. However, glaucoma can be detected through an eye exam; and because it occurs more frequently in older people (and in African Americans), professionals recommend increasingly frequent checkups, starting at age 35 (and even more frequently for African Americans).

Cataracts are caused by a clouding of the lens of the eye, which results in blurred vision. In children, the condition is called *congenital cataracts*, and distance and color vision are seriously affected. Surgery can usually correct the problems caused by cataracts.

Diabetes can cause **diabetic retinopathy**, a condition that results from interference with the blood supply to the retina.

FIGURE 12.2 Visual problems: (a) myopia, (b) hyperopia

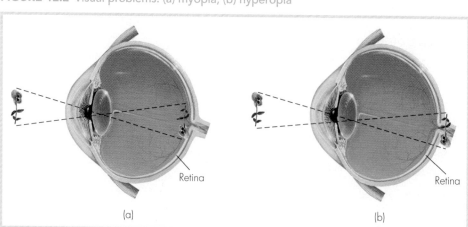

FIGURE 12.3 These are simulations of how people with certain visual impairments see the world: (a) normal vision; (b) glaucoma; (c) cataracts; (d) diabetic retinopathy; (e) retinitis pigmentosa

Causes Primarily Affecting Children

The three most common causes of blindness in children are cortical visual impairment, retinopathy of prematurity, and optic nerve hypoplasia (Zimmerman, 2011). For children, **cortical visual impairment (CVI)** is now the leading cause of visual impairment. CVI results from widespread damage to parts of the *brain* responsible for vision. The damage or dysfunction can be the result of a variety of causes, such as a head injury or infection. Although researchers are still refining a description of CVI, a unique pattern of visual responses appears to be associated with CVI. Some of these responses are an avoidance of looking at new visual information, a preference for looking at near objects, nonpurposeful gazing, distinct color preferences, attraction to rapid movements, and abnormal visual reflexes.

Retinopathy of prematurity (ROP) results in abnormal growth of blood vessels in the eye, which then causes the retina to detach. The discovery of the cause of ROP involved one of the most dramatic medical findings of the 20th century. ROP began to appear in the 1940s in premature infants. In the 1950s, researchers determined that excessive concentrations of oxygen often administered to premature infants were causing blindness. The oxygen was necessary to prevent brain damage, but it was often given at too high a level. Since then, hospitals have been careful to monitor the amount of oxygen administered to premature infants. Today, with medical advances, many more premature babies are surviving, but they need very high levels of oxygen and are thus at risk for ROP. Furthermore, ROP can result from factors other than excessive oxygen that are related to being born very prematurely (National Eye Institute, 2010).

Optic nerve hypoplasia (ONH) involves underdevelopment of the optic nerve. The underdevelopment is often associated with brain abnormalities, such that the child is also at risk for problems such as speech and cognitive disabilities. The exact cause or causes of ONH are still unknown.

Retinitis pigmentosa is an hereditary condition that results in degeneration of the retina. It can start in infancy, early childhood, or the teenage years. Retinitis pigmentosa usually causes the field of vision to narrow (**tunnel vision**) and also affects one's ability to see in low light (**night blindness**). Included in the "prenatal" category are infectious diseases that affect the unborn child, such as syphilis and rubella.

Strabismus and nystagmus, two other conditions resulting in visual problems, are caused by improper muscle functioning. **Strabismus** is a condition in which one or both eyes are directed inward (crossed eyes) or outward. Left untreated, strabismus can result in permanent blindness because the brain will eventually reject signals from a deviating eye. Fortunately, most cases of strabismus can be corrected with eye exercises or surgery. Eye exercises sometimes involve the person's wearing a patch over the good eye for periods of time to force use of the eye that deviates. Surgery involves tightening or loosening the muscles that control eye movement. **Nystagmus** is a condition in which rapid involuntary movements of the eyes occur, usually resulting in dizziness and nausea. Nystagmus is sometimes a sign of brain malfunctioning and/or inner-ear problems.

PSYCHOLOGICAL AND BEHAVIORAL CHARACTERISTICS

Language Development

Most authorities believe that lack of vision does not have a very significant effect on the ability to understand and use language (Rosel, Caballer, Jara, & Oliver, 2005). Because auditory more than

Infants and children who are blind may have serious delays in motor skills, such as sitting up, crawling, and walking. Therefore, adults should do as much as possible to encourage them to explore their environment.

visual perception is the sensory modality through which we learn language, it's not surprising that studies have found that people who are blind are not impaired in language functioning. The child who is blind can still hear language and might even be more motivated than the sighted child to use language because it's the main channel through which she communicates with others.

Intellectual Ability

PERFORMANCE ON STANDARDIZED INTELLIGENCE TESTS   At one time, it was popular for researchers to compare the intelligence of sighted people with that of persons with blindness. Most authorities now believe that such comparisons are virtually impossible because finding comparable tests is so difficult. From what is known, there is no reason to believe that blindness results in lower intelligence.

CONCEPTUAL ABILITIES   It is also very difficult to assess the performance of children with visual impairment on laboratory-type tasks of conceptual ability. Many researchers, using conceptual tasks originally developed by noted psychologist Jean Piaget, have concluded that infants and very young children who are blind lag behind their sighted peers. This is usually attributed to the fact that they rely more on touch to arrive at conceptualizations of many objects, and touch is less efficient than sight. However, these early delays don't last long, especially once the children begin to use language to gather information about their environment (Perez-Pereira & Conti-Ramsden, 1999). Touch, however, remains a very critical sense throughout life for those who are blind. As one person who is blind described it, he "sees with his fingers" (Hull, 1997).

An important difference between individuals with and without sight is that the latter need to take much more initiative to learn what they can from their environment. Sighted infants and children can pick up a lot of visual information incidentally. In a sense, the world comes to them; children who are visually impaired need to extend themselves out to the world to pick up some of the same information. Exploring the environment motorically, however, doesn't come easily for infants and young children with visual impairment, especially those who are blind. Many have serious delays in motor skills, such as sitting up, crawling, and walking (Celeste, 2002). Therefore, adults should do as much as possible to encourage infants and young children who are blind to explore their environment.

In addition to fostering a sense of exploration in children who are visually impaired, it is critical that teachers and parents provide intensive and extensive instruction, including repetition, in order to help them develop their conceptual abilities:

> When a student cannot see, . . . It can be mystifying to comprehend what the front and back of a store are when the student is inside of it. It is especially difficult if the student is thinking of the front and back of his or her own body that, as the student moves, are continually changing relationship to objects and their fronts and backs. . . . A gradual approach to teaching concepts, presenting many repetitions over time and in a variety of situations, with repeated opportunities for tactile exploration, will yield the most detailed mental image and the most thorough understanding. (Knott, 2002, p. 69)

Orientation and Mobility

Orientation and mobility skills are very important for the successful adjustment of people with visual impairment. **Orientation and mobility (O & M)** skills refer to the ability to have a sense of where one is in relation to other people, objects, and landmarks (orientation) and to move through the environment (mobility).

O & M skills depend to a great extent on spatial ability. Authorities have identified two ways in which persons with visual impairment process spatial information: as a sequential route or as a map depicting the general relation of various points in the environment (Webster & Roe, 1998). The latter method, referred to as **cognitive mapping**, is preferable because it offers more flexibility in navigating. Consider three sequential points—A, B, and C.

A sequential mode of processing spatial information restricts a person's movement so that the person can move from A to C only by way of B. But a person with a cognitive map of points A, B, and C can go from A to C directly without going through B. Although not impossible, it is more difficult for people who are blind to build these cognitive maps. Vision allows us to

> construct a coherent sense of the physical environment and our place in it, without struggling to remember. On entering an unfamiliar classroom, a sighted child is able to take in something of the whole at a glance, and perhaps work out the overall position of the room in relation to more familiar places, such as the library, computer room. . . . For the child with a visual impairment, constructing an inner map of this new classroom presents a problem of synthesizing information from the integration of small, local details to achieve a functional sense of the whole, which must then be largely memorised. (Webster & Roe, 1998, p. 69)

Mobility skills vary greatly among people with visual impairment. It is surprisingly difficult to predict which individuals will be the best travelers. For example, common sense seems to tell us that mobility would be better among those who have more residual vision and those who lose their vision later in life, but this is not always the case. How much motivation and how much proper instruction one receives are critical to becoming a proficient traveler.

OBSTACLE SENSE   Some persons who are blind, when walking along the street seem able to sense objects in their path. This ability has come to be known as the **obstacle sense**—an unfortunate term in some ways, because many laypeople have taken it to mean that people who are blind somehow develop an extra sense. It's easy to see why this misconception exists. Even people who are blind have a very difficult time explaining the phenomenon (Hull, 1997). A number of experiments have shown that with experience, people who are blind come to learn to detect subtle changes in the pitches of high-frequency echoes as they move toward objects. Actually, they are taking advantage of the **Doppler effect**, a physical principle wherein the pitch of a sound rises as a person moves toward its source.

Although obstacle sense can be important for the mobility of someone without sight, by itself it doesn't make its user a highly proficient traveler. Extraneous noises (e.g., traffic, speech, rain, wind) can render obstacle sense unusable. Also, it requires walking at a fairly slow speed to be able to react in time. However, some researchers continue to study the phenomenon in the hopes of developing mobility aids that can help sharpen the obstacle sense in those who are blind (Miura, Muraoka, & Ifukube, 2010).

THE MYTH OF SENSORY ACUTENESS   Along with the myth that people with blindness have an extra sense comes the general misconception that they automatically develop better acuity in their other senses. However, people who are blind don't have lowered thresholds of sensation in touch or hearing. What they can do is make better use of the sensations they obtain. Through concentration and attention, they learn to make very fine discriminations. It's easy to overlook just how much information can be picked up through listening and senses other than sight. The accompanying Personal Perspectives box gives an example of how much a person who is blind can appreciate about his or her surroundings through nonvisual information.

Another common belief is that people who are blind automatically have superior musical talent. Some do embark on musical careers, but this is because music is an area in which they can achieve success.

Academic Achievement

Most professionals agree that direct comparisons of the academic achievement of students who are blind with that of sighted students must be interpreted cautiously because the two groups must be tested under different conditions. Some achievement tests, however, are available in braille and large-print forms. The few studies that have been done suggest that both children with low vision and those who are blind are sometimes behind their sighted peers (Rapp & Rapp, 1992). Most authorities believe that when low achievement does oc-

Personal PERSPECTIVES
Stephen Kuusisto's Sensory World

People who are sighted often miss out on just how much information can be gained through other senses, such as hearing, touch, and smell. People who are blind, however, come to rely on these other senses. And for them, the world can consist of a rich array of sounds, textures, and smells. The following excerpt from Stephen Kuusisto's memoir, *Eavesdropping*, vividly demonstrates just how opulent these nonvisual sensations can be:

Maybe it was a Saturday. I remember that my parents were still sleeping. I had a plan and dressed quietly. When I was certain that no one was awake I slipped from the house. I loved to walk in the woods and follow the beams of light or depths of shade that fell between the trees. I remember that on this particular day I got lost while chasing light and found myself standing in front of the university's horse barn. I knew that somewhere in the cool space before me a horse was breathing. I stood in the door and listened to him breathe. He sounded like water going down a drain. Then I took one step forward into a pyramid of fragrances.

What a thing! To be a young boy smelling hay and leather and turds!

From his place in the dark the horse gurgled like water in the back of a boat.

Mice scurried like beaded curtains disturbed by the hand.

I stood in that magical nowhere and listened to a full range of barn sounds.

I was a blind child approaching a horse!

Behind me a cat mewed.

Who would guess that horses sometimes hold their breath?

The horse was eying me from his corner.

Stephen Kuusisto and his guide dog Corky.

Then two cats were talking.

Wind pushed forcefully at the high roof.

Somewhere up high a timber groaned.

My horse was still holding his breath.

When would he breathe again?

Come on boy!

Breathe for me!

Where are you?

I heard him rub his flank against a wall.

Then I heard him breathe again with great deflation!

He sounded like a fat balloon venting in swift circles.

And then I imitated him with my arm pressed to my mouth.

I made great, flatulent noises by pressing my lips to my forearm.

How do you like that, horse?

He snorted.

I noticed a ringing of silence. An insect traveled between our bursts of forced air.

Sunlight warmed my face. I was standing in a wide sunbeam.

I was in the luminous whereabouts of horse! I was a very small boy and I had wandered about a mile from home. Although I could see colors and shapes in sunlight, in the barn I was completely blind.

But I had made up my mind to touch a horse.

Judging by his breathing, his slow release of air, that sound of a concertina, judging by this I was nearly beside him. And so I reached out and there was a great wet fruit of his nose, the velvet bone of his enormous face. And we stood there together for a little while, all alive and all alone. (Kuusisto, 2006, pp. 7–8)

Source: Kuusisto, S. (2006). *Eavesdropping.* New York: W. W. Norton & Company. Reprinted by permission.

cur, it is due not to the blindness itself, but to such things as low expectations or lack of exposure to braille. Patrick, the student described in the accompanying Success Stories feature, has begun to learn braille as an older student. He enjoys reading braille instead of holding his book 2 inches from his right eye and struggling to use his remaining sight.

With respect to reading, we do know that learning to read braille is similar in some important ways to learning to read print. For example, **phonological awareness** (discussed in Chapter 6) is an important component of learning to read print or braille (Barlow-Brown & Connelly, 2002; Gillon & Young, 2002).

Social Adjustment

Most people with visual impairment are socially well adjusted. However, the road to social adjustment for people with visual impairment may be a bit more difficult for two reasons. First, social interactions among the sighted are often based on subtle cues, many of which

Success Stories

PATRICK PREPARES FOR TRANSITION FROM HIGH SCHOOL THROUGH FUNCTIONAL ACADEMICS AND VOCATIONAL EDUCATION

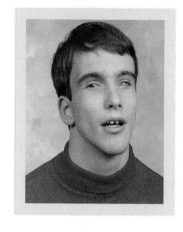

Patrick's mother, Audrey Pugh:*"All I want anyone to do is give him a fair chance."*

Nineteen-year-old Patrick Pugh is a high school junior with impaired vision and multiple disabilities. He is working toward his future with consistent and specialized support.

These are the keys to Patrick's success:

★ Intensive instruction from specialized personnel

★ Relentless persistence over time

★ Specific goals for transition and vocational education

SPECIAL EDUCATOR RICKI CURRY, an itinerant teacher of students with visual impairments, has worked closely with Patrick for 14 years. She credits much of his progress to a key ingredient—time. Since he was 5 years old, she has set high expectations for Patrick, who has no vision in his left eye and only partial sight in his right eye. His speech is slurred, and he does not have functional use of his left arm or leg. "Patrick is eager to learn new things," says Curry, who credits his success to intensive, relentless, and specific special education.

★ **Intensive Instruction from Specialized Personnel.** Patrick started vision and physical therapy when he was 2 years old. Ricki Curry remembers the little boy whose eyes would lift aimlessly to the ceiling, not using what vision he had. "Our basic goal was for Patrick to learn to use his sight by tracking objects and looking at pictures, but as a 5-year-old, he was stubborn, difficult, and noncompliant," she recalls. Despite his reluctance, Patrick successfully learned literal information and concrete routines. He

was highly distractible, and progress was very slow. His parents hoped that all he needed was extra time, so he stayed in a preschool for children with special needs until he was 7 years old.

Patrick spent first grade in a self-contained class for children with learning disabilities in the nearest physically accessible elementary school. Curry continued to provide weekly sessions and to supervise his vision services. He was also given a personal aide to assist with mobility and visual modifications. "In some ways, kids with personal aides never encounter problems, so they don't learn any problem-solving skills!" says Curry. "On the other hand, there are some effective strategies that can be used by paraeducators." Patrick's hand use was limited, so his aide assisted him with writing. His teachers broke math down into small steps, individualized his reading, and taught him to use a large-print word processor.

★ **Relentless Persistence Over Time.** Patrick finished elementary school 2 years older than most of his classmates

are visual. Second, sighted society is often uncomfortable in its interactions with those who are visually impaired (Erin, 2006).

SUBTLE VISUAL CUES   Most of us who are sighted take for granted how often we use visual cues to help us in our social interactions. In growing up, we learn most of these cues incidentally by observing others. Thus, children with visual impairment often need to be taught directly how to use these cues (Jindal-Snape, 2005; S. Z. Sacks, 2006). Facial expressions, such as smiling, are a good example of visual cues that don't come spontaneously for persons who are visually impaired. John M. Hull, whose eyesight deteriorated gradually over several years, kept a diary of his experiences. The following entry pertains to smiling:

> Nearly every time I smile, I am conscious of it. . . . Why is this? It must be because there is no reinforcement. There is no returning smile. . . . Most smiling is responsive. You smile spontaneously when you receive a smile. For me it is like sending dead letters. Have they been received, acknowledged? Was I even smiling in the right direction? (Hull, 1997, p. 30)

FIGURE 12.8 Human guide technique. (a) The child maintains a constant grip on the guide's arm while following the guide around obstacles as they travel through the environment. To maintain a grip that allows active participation in travel, the child must grasp the guide's arm so the thumb is placed on the outside, with the remaining fingers gripping the inside of the arm (b). The child is a half-step behind and to the side of the guide. A common adaptation for smaller students is to have the student grasp the guide's extended fingers, wrist, or forearm rather than maintaining a grip above the elbow (c). Effective guided travel involves a partnership between guide and child, with both participants actively involved.

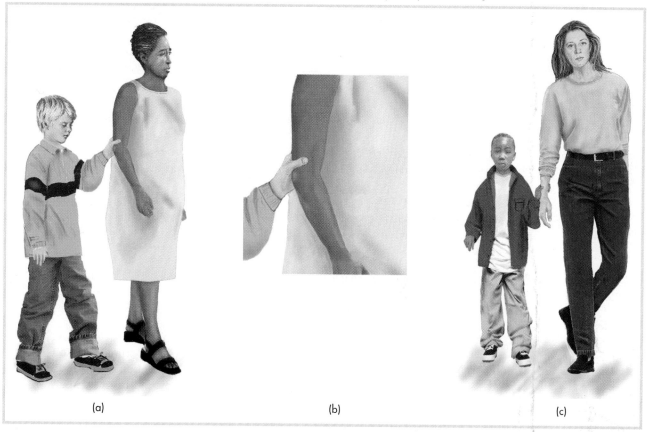

(a)   (b)   (c)

Source: Gense, D. J., & Gense, M. (2004, October, Revised). The importance of orientation and mobility skills for students who are deaf-blind. *DB-LINK Fact Sheet,* retrieved from http://nationaldb.org/NCDBProducts.php?prodID536 Copyright © 2004 DB-LINK. Reprinted with permission. Figure adapted from illustration by Rebecca Marsh-McCannell.

Technological Aids

Visual impairment is perhaps the disability area in which the most technological advances have been made. The infusion of technology has occurred primarily in two general areas: (1) communication and information access and (2) O & M. In addition, some highly experimental research has been conducted on artificial vision.

TECHNOLOGICAL AIDS FOR COMMUNICATION AND INFORMATION ACCESS

Computers and software are available that convert printed material into synthesized speech or braille. One such device is the **Kurzweil 1000**™. The user places the material on a scanner that reads the material with an electronic voice or renders it in braille. TheKurzweil 1000™ and other Kurzweil products can also be used by students with reading disabilities. The machines are compatible with MP3 players and other devices, such as portable braille notetakers, which we discuss next.

Portable **braille notetakers** can serve the same function as the Perkins Brailler or slate and stylus, but they offer additional speech-synthesizer and word-processing capabilities. The user enters information with a braille keyboard and can transfer the information into a larger computer, review it using a speech synthesizer or braille display, or print it in braille or text. Millions of people now own hand-held personal data assistants (PDAs) and

INTERNETRESOURCES

The Cellular Telecommunications & Internet Association has a Website that provides information on cell phone products and features for people with disabilities: www .accesswireless.org

cell phones. Some manufacturers have responded to the need to make these accessible for people with disabilities, such as blindness, by developing "talking" cell phones and PDAs. Some additional features they've included are voice recognition, audio cues for main functions, and keys more easily distinguishable by touch.

Two services available for those who are visually impaired are Newsline® and Descriptive Video Service. **NFB-Newsline**®, a free service available through the NFB, allows individuals to access magazines and newspapers 24 hours a day from any touch-tone telephone. Over 200 newspapers, including most of the major ones (e.g., *USA Today, The New York Times, The Wall Street Journal, The Washington Post, The Los Angeles Times*, and *The Toronto Globe and Mail*) are now available (National Federation of the Blind, 2006). **Descriptive Video Service**® inserts a narrated description of key visual features of programs on television. It is also available in some movie theaters as well as some movies on videotape or DVD.

Great strides have been made in recent years to make computers and the World Wide Web more accessible for people with disabilities, including those who have visual impairments. With respect to computer software, **screen readers** (such as JAWS® for Windows®) can magnify information on the screen, convert on-screen text to speech, or do both.

Designers of Web pages are also coming to understand that what might be attractive for the sighted can be problematic for those with visual impairments. An article with the clever title "[Image] [Image] [Image] [Link] [Link] [Link]: Inaccessible Web Design from the Perspective of a Blind Librarian" offered the following observations:

> During the past few years, advances in Internet technology have greatly enhanced librarian's access to information. Unfortunately, these same advances have made my job more complicated. Just a few years ago, I could surf the Web . . . without thinking twice. Those were the days when everything was text. . . .
>
> With the increased use of graphics, keyboard commands became beveled buttons or cute icons that could be activated with a click. Boring backgrounds became whimsical wallpapers. Important messages could blink or scroll across the screen. The Web became user-friendly. Unfortunately, this user-friendly Web was not very friendly to me. (V. Lewis & Klauber, 2002, p. 138.)

However, strides are being made to make the Web more accessible for people with visual impairments. And the NFB has established procedures for certifying Websites as being accessible to people who are blind.

TECHNOLOGICAL AIDS FOR ORIENTATION AND MOBILITY   Researchers have developed a number of sophisticated electronic devices for sensing objects in the environment, including the laser cane and the Miniguide. These devices operate on the principle that human beings can learn to locate objects by means of echoes, much as bats do. The laser cane can be used in the same way as the long cane or as a sensing device that emits beams of infrared light, which are converted into sound after they strike objects in the path of the traveler. The Miniguide is a small (2-ounces), hand-held device. Research has shown that the Miniguide is useful for such things as avoiding obstacles, locating doorways, avoiding park benches and poles, and detecting overhanging obstacles (J. Hill & Black, 2003). However, it doesn't detect dropoffs so it's not meant to be used alone without also using some other aid such as a long cane.

Software is available that allows people who are blind to take advantage of information obtained from the Global Positioning System (GPS). More than two dozen GPS satellites are constantly circling the earth and sending back signals, which can be picked up by hand-held receivers. Combining this information with an expanding data base of several million geographic points in the United States, the GPS allows users to determine their whereabouts with considerable accuracy. The BrailleNote GPS converts the GPS signals to braille. The makers of the BrailleNote GPS have entered 12 million points into the device. In addition, users can enter their own information into the device so that they can plan their routes to and from various sites.

Researchers have also made considerable progress in developing an artificial vision system for people who are blind. Several techniques are in the experimental stages, with different parts of the eye or brain the focus of the prosthesis, for example, the retina, the cornea, the visual cortex of the brain (Visual Prosthesis, 2010). These surgeries are extremely complicated, and the results are highly variable. Even when the surgery is successful, those who have been blind since birth or from a very young age can find it overwhelming to adjust to the flood of visual sensations. See the accompanying Personal Perspectives feature describing the experiences of Mike May, who underwent such a surgery.

CAUTIONS ABOUT TECHNOLOGY   Words of caution are in order in considering the use of computerized and electronic devices. Supporters of braille argue that although tape recorders, computers, and other technological devices can contribute much to reading and acquiring information, these devices cannot replace braille. For example, finding a specific section of a text and "skimming" are difficult with a tape recording, but these kinds of activities are possible when using braille. Taking notes for class, reading a speech, and looking up words in a dictionary are all easier when using braille than when using a tape recorder. Braille proponents are especially concerned that the slate and stylus be preserved as a viable method of taking notes. They point out that just as computers have not replaced paper and pen or pencil for people who are sighted, neither can computers take the place of the slate and stylus for people who are blind.

Technological devices designed for orientation and mobility also have limitations. They are best viewed as potential secondary O & M aids. They are not appropriate as substitutes for the long cane, for example.

Although technology might not be the answer to all the difficulties faced by people who are blind, there is no doubt that technology can make their lives easier and more productive. And as technologies develop for society in general, it is important that those who are visually impaired be able to take advantage of them.

Service Delivery Models

The four major educational placements for students with visual impairment, from most to least separate, are residential school, special class, resource room, and general education class with itinerant teacher help. In the early 1900s virtually all children who were blind were educated in residential institutions. Today, **itinerant teacher service**, wherein a vision teacher visits several different schools to work with students in their general education classrooms, is the most popular placement for students with visual impairment. The fact is, the number of students with visual impairment is so small that most schools find it difficult to provide services through special classes or resource rooms. The accompanying Making It Work feature illustrates how an itinerant teacher supports a fourth-grade student with a severe visual impairment.

Residential placement, however, is still a relatively popular placement model compared to other areas of disability. For example, approximately 6% of students with visual impairment between the ages of 6 and 21 are placed in a residential institution, whereas only about 1% of students with intellectual disabilities are so placed. The advantage of residential placement or special schools is that services can be concentrated to this relatively low-incidence population. For example, students in residential or special schools are more likely to receive O & M skills than those who are in regular schools (Cameto & Nagle, 2007). In the past, most children who were blind attended such institutions for several years; today some may attend on a short-term basis (e.g., 1 to 4 years). The prevailing philosophy of integrating children with visual impairments into classes with sighted children is also reflected in the fact that many residential facilities have established cooperative arrangements with local public schools wherein the staff of the residential facility usually concentrates on training for independent living skills such as mobility, personal grooming, and home management, whereas local school personnel emphasize academics.

Personal PERSPECTIVES
Mike May: An Adventure into the World of Sight

Founder of the Sendero Group (the manufacturer of the BrailleNote GPS), clocked at 65 miles per hour as the world's fastest blind skier, and hired as the first blind political risk analyst for the CIA, Mike May, blind since age 3, has never shied away from challenges. But perhaps his biggest challenge was his decision in 1999 to undergo stem cell transplant surgery to restore sight in his one operable eye. And it wasn't just the pain from the surgery or the fact that he might lose the miniscule amount of light perception he had in that eye, it was facing the prospect of leaving the world of blindness to which he had adapted so comfortably and successfully. Even more daunting was the fact that virtually every other known case of individuals who had been blind and then been given sight had resulted in harmful psychological consequences (Kurson, 2005, 2007).

Popular science writer Oliver Sacks (1996) was perhaps the first to introduce the general public to a case of someone whose sight was surgically restored after years of blindness. Virgil's case was typical of others who had preceded him. Overwhelmed at having to learn to process an entire new sense, he experienced frustration and depression. Virgil eventually lost his sight again, and ironically it seemed to release him from his state of despair:

> At the beginning, there was certainly amazement, wonder, and sometimes joy. . . . But then came the problems, the conflicts, of seeing but not seeing, not being able to make a visual world, and at the same time being forced to give up his own. He found himself between two worlds, at home in neither. . . . But then, paradoxically, a release was given, in the form of a second and now final blindness—a blindness he received as a gift. Now, at last, Virgil is allowed not to see, allowed to escape from the glaring, confusing world of sight and space, and to return to his own true being, the intimate, concentrated world of the other senses that had been his home for almost fifty years. (O. Sacks, 1996, pp. 151–152)

Fortunately, thus far, Mike May has been up to the challenge and has not been driven into the depths of despair experienced by so many before him. His biographer Robert Kurson attributes this to his extraordinarily adventurous attitude toward life. But it's important to note that his vision is still far from what sighted people experience:

He continued to struggle to see things in three dimensions, and his world stayed much like an abstract painting, a huge collection of colorful, flattened shapes that didn't always make sense. Information flooded his head, a never-ending flow that he could sometimes stem only by closing his eyes. High-speed events, such as the passing of cars and bicycles, became frightening; his brain simply didn't have time to interpret the information. Things often looked very close, scary close. Previous patients had been undone by these kinds of threats. May told himself that this was part of the adventure, that the leap forward wasn't really a leap at all if everything felt safe. (Kurson, 2005)

Kurson notes that scientists using neuron-imaging have studied May's brain and determined that those areas responsible for processing color, motion, and two-dimensional objects appear activated, but those used for spatial perception, judging faces, and processing three-dimensional objects are not. They theorize that this is because the former are more primitive and don't depend as much on experience to develop. What this means is that for May to be able to make sense of much of his world he would need to:

> use cumbersome work-arounds to see much of what sighted people see automatically. He would have to build a database of clues—earrings, long hair, plucked eyebrows—to help determine gender by face. He would have to employ usable context—an orange, round blob on a basketball court is most likely a basketball—to identify simple objects. He would have to spend time thinking about whether a skyscraper was a big thing far away or a little thing close up. All of it would require massive cognitive effort, the prospect of which had been enough to threaten the emotional well-being of May's predecessors. (Kurson, 2005)

Mike May continues to serve as a pioneer in helping scientists and others who are blind understand blindness, sightedness, and the complexity of the human brain and human emotions. For more information on Mike May's fascinating journey into sightedness, see Robert Kurson's *Crashing Through: A Story of Risk, Adventure, and the Man Who Dared to See* (Random House, 2007) and "Into the Light" (*Esquire*, June 2005). Sara Beck, a singer/song writer, has written and recorded "Crashing Through," and there is also a movie based on Kurson's book in production at Fox 2000.

MAKING IT WORK
COLLABORATING AND CO-TEACHING WITH TEACHERS OF STUDENTS WITH BLINDNESS OR LOW VISION

"I don't have time to learn braille!"

WHAT DOES IT MEAN TO BE A TEACHER OF STUDENTS WITH VISUAL IMPAIRMENTS?

Collaboration for students with visual impairments often takes the form of working with itinerant special education teachers. This can be frustrating for general educators in that they are left "on their own" when the special educator is at another building. Therefore, in planning for collaboration, it's important that the general educator and itinerant teacher have time to plan for student needs that may arise at any time. Working with the general educator to plan for instruction, the teacher of students with visual impairments can offer expertise in:

1. Strategies for teaching listening and compensatory auditory skills.
2. Techniques for modifying instructional methods and materials.
3. Design of multisensory learning environments that encourage active participation by individuals with visual impairments in group and individual activities.
4. Strategies for teaching basic concepts.
5. Strategies for teaching organization and study skills.
6. Strategies for teaching individuals with visual impairments to use thinking, problem-solving, and other cognitive strategies. (Council for Exceptional Children, 2003)

SUCCESSFUL STRATEGIES FOR CO-TEACHING

Ricki Curry (an itinerant teacher) and Jenny Garrett (a fourth-grade teacher) talk about how they collaborated to fully include Dennis, a student with a severe visual impairment.

Jenny: My fourth-grade class consisted of 23 nine- and ten-year-old students, including two children with learning disabilities, one with severe behavior disorders, and Dennis. They began the year reading on anywhere from a first- to a sixth-grade level.

Ricki: Although he has some usable vision, Dennis can see no details from a distance of more than about 2 feet and uses large-print texts for reading.

Jenny: Dennis has some difficulty making friends because of his immaturity, his compulsive talking, and his inability to listen. On the other hand, he's got a good sense of humor and is quick with language. Dennis was in my class all day long for every academic subject. Ricki worked with him during language arts block, teaching braille. She came to school during the last half of my planning period, which gave us a daily opportunity to discuss assignments, homework, curricular adaptations, equipment, and the like. Homework was an enormous issue. Ricki helped him set up a notebook with a homework contract enclosed and a special highlighter, which he used to mark off completed assignments. He had to write down the assignments himself, remember to take the notebook home, complete the assignments, get a parent's signature, and get it back to school.

The hardest part of working with Dennis was the start-up period. I had to get to know him, his visual capabilities, his strengths and weaknesses, his coping strategies. I began adapting my teaching style, using an easel rather than the blackboard so that he could scoot up to it. I had to decide how hard to push, what to expect from his parents, and what to demand from Dennis.

Ricki: I often found myself overwhelmed by the number of things that Jenny and/or Dennis needed help with in the short time that I was in the building. And so many things seemed to go wrong in the time between when I left one day and arrived again the next day! Although I was frustrated by the limitations imposed by time constraints, the beauty of the inclusion model was that I was very aware of the true gestalt of Dennis's program and knew exactly what he was involved in all the time. Had I not had an almost daily view of his classroom performance, I might not have believed how hard it was to integrate this very bright, verbal, personable child into Jenny's class.

Jenny: Collaboration works best when there is a match of personalities as well as energy, enthusiasm for teaching, and professionalism.

More information about visual impairments and their impact on the classroom is available at the Council for Exceptional Children's Division on Visual Impairments: www.cecdvi.org/

• By Margaret P. Weiss

ASSESSMENT OF PROGRESS

Teachers of students with visual impairments are required to assess both academic and functional skills. Academic assessments include braille skills for reading decoding and comprehension and Nemeth Code mathematics skills. Orientation and mobility skills are critical as part of a functional skills assessment.

Assessment of Academic Skills

The use of braille is a significant aspect of academic success for students with blindness or low vision, and IDEA requires inclusion of braille instruction in the IEP; thus, it's important for teachers to monitor the progress of these students in braille skills. **Curriculum-based measurement (CBM)** is an effective method for measuring the academic progress of students with visual impairments in the particular curriculum to which they are exposed. Braille versions of CBM reading passages have similar technical adequacy to CBM passages used with readers who are sighted (Morgan & Bradley-Johnson, 1995). Printed versions of passages can be translated into braille for use in monitoring students' braille reading rate and accuracy. However, teachers should modify standard CBM procedures for students with visual impairments because reading braille typically takes longer than reading print.

Teachers can also use CBM techniques in mathematics. Commercial CBM measures are available to monitor students' progress in computational fluency, and these measures can be translated into Nemeth Code for use with students with visual impairment. Standard CBM mathematics probes contain multiple items of one type (e.g., two-digit addition problems). A student who is sighted works for approximately 2 to 4 minutes (Thurber, Shinn, & Smolkowski, 2002), and the probe is scored by calculating the number of correct digits per minute. Students with blindness require longer for the same probes because Nemeth Code is more difficult to read and takes about twice the amount of time as reading standard print. Students with low vision may use large-print versions; these students may also need additional time; however, twice the time may not be necessary.

Assessment of Functional Skills

Orientation and mobility skills are critical to the successful adjustment of people with visual impairment, and thus should be the focus of assessment procedures. Common procedures for assessing O & M skills traditionally have comprised subjective checklists and self-report data. However, emerging technologies currently used for O & M training also offer promise for advancing progress-monitoring procedures. O & M instructors can use GPSs as a systematic way to monitor their clients' travel proficiency. The addition of GeoLogger to a GPS system gathers data such as travel times, travel modes, routes, and trip duration. Evaluating these data frequently can help O & M instructors improve their clients' travel proficiency through data-based planning.

Testing Accommodations

IDEA requires appropriate accommodations or alternate assessments for students with disabilities who need them. Among the most common accommodations for students with blindness and low vision are presentation accommodations (e.g., test in braille, test in regular print with magnification, large-print test) and response accommodations (e.g., use of brailler). Scheduling accommodations are also important to students with visual impairments, given that students' reading rate in braille is usually slower than that of a sighted student. However, little empirical evidence is available to determine the technical adequacy of these accommodations or alternate assessments for students with disabilities, particularly those with visual impairments (Zebehazy, Hartmann, & Durando, 2006). Furthermore, few states report having a representative on review teams qualified to examine test items to determine sources of potential bias for students with visual impairments (Thompson, Johnston, Thurlow, & Altman, 2005; Thompson & Thurlow, 2003). Despite the concerns with the reliability and validity of measures when accommodations are provided, more states are beginning to provide accommodations for students who are blind or have low vision, and including these students in tests of high-stakes accountability (Lazurus, Thurlow, Lail, Eisenbraun, & Kato, 2006).

EARLY INTERVENTION

Researchers have documented that immediately after birth infants begin processing a wealth of visual information in their environment (Berk, 2005). This fact makes it easy to understand why intensive intervention should begin as early as possible to help the infant with visual impairment begin to explore the environment. As we noted earlier, many infants who are blind lag behind their peers in motor development. Consequently, O & M training should be a critical component of preschool programming. At one time, O & M teachers thought that young children were not old enough to be taught mobility skills. Some parents, especially sighted parents, saw the use of a cane as too stigmatizing. As one person who is blind said:

> The cane was the thing that my parents put off for as long as they could, and they did it with the support of educators. For them the cane was the symbol. It transformed me from being their blind son—which was okay—to being somebody who might grow up to be a blind man. That wasn't okay. So I didn't see a cane until I was about eleven years old. (Wunder, 1993, p. 568)

Today, however, more and more preschoolers are learning cane techniques.

Although many people believe that preschoolers with visual impairments should be educated in inclusive settings with sighted children, it's critical that teachers facilitate interactions between the children. Given that the classmates of a student with visual impairment are almost always sighted, there is a potential for social isolation. We know from research that merely placing preschoolers who are visually impaired with preschoolers who are sighted doesn't lead to their interacting with one another (Celeste, 2006; D'Allura, 2002). Teachers must provide instruction in appropriate interactions using active engagement and repeated opportunities for learning.

Most authorities agree that it's extremely important to involve parents of infants with visual impairment in early intervention efforts. Parents can become actively involved in working at home with their young children, helping them with fundamental skills such as mobility and feeding, as well as being responsive to their infants' vocalizations. Parents, too, sometimes need support in coping with their reactions to having a baby with visual impairment.

TRANSITION TO ADULTHOOD

Two closely related areas are difficult for some adolescents and adults with visual impairment: independence and employment. The level of success attained by students with visual impairments in achieving independence and appropriate employment depends greatly on the kind of preparation and support they receive from their teachers and families. For example, Aaron (AJ) Faxon, Jr. (see the accompanying Peer Connections), has benefited greatly from the many years of instruction he's received from his vision teacher.

Independent Living

With proper training, preferably starting no later than middle school, most people who are blind can lead very independent lives. However, evidence shows that many students who are blind aren't receiving the necessary training in daily living skills (S. Lewis & Iselin, 2002; Wolffe et al., 2002). Ironically, some professionals have asserted that the movement toward including students with visual impairment in general education and providing them access to the general education curriculum has led to a diminished emphasis on teaching skills necessary for independence (Spungin, 2003). They say that itinerant teachers often do not have enough time to do much direct teaching of daily living skills.

Many authorities also point out that a major reason why adolescents and adults with visual impairment might have problems becoming independent is because of the way society treats people without sight. A common mistake is to assume that they are helpless.

PEER CONNECTIONS: AJ FAXON

AARON "AJ" FAXON, JR. was born with optic nerve hypoplasia (ONH) in both eyes. ONH is a medical condition that results in underdevelopment of the optic nerve. It affects AJ's visual acuity and visual field, causing a severe visual impairment. AJ knows how to read braille and has used a Perkins Braille Writer since Kindergarten. He is a senior in high school and plans to attend college in the fall. AJ aspires to be a teacher for students with vision impairments.

1. What do you do for fun? I love to play "goal ball." Goal ball is a game that you have to play in a gym and that you have to have extreme quiet for. Players are blindfolded, and there are balls with bells in them. The way it works is there is a triangle in the middle of the gym with flanks or boundaries set up on either side. Every player gets two rolls, and if you roll the ball and get it past the boundary, then you get a point. There are two 15-minute halves, and the player with the most points at the end of the game wins. There are U.S. tournaments for this game, and I actually introduced it to the students here at my high school.

2. What is your favorite way to relax? I like to fish with my family and friends. I also read and write braille and just finished reading *Pride and Prejudice* by Jane Austen

3. What is something that you excel at? I'd have to say I excel at braille—that and also interacting with other people.

4. What is your pet peeve? People who make fun of people who are different than themselves. I don't think that anybody has the right to judge.

5. Can you recall one teacher in particular who has been a positive influence on you? Ricki, my vision teacher, has been a huge influence on me, by just being there. She's my teacher, but we've also connected on a personal level. She's been there for me for so many things and has known me since Kindergarten; she's like a best friend.

6. Is there anyone else (celebrity, family member) whom you regard as a role model? Why are they a role model for you? My entire family as a whole is a role model because we complement each other's weaknesses. What I lack, they make up for in me, and I think what they lack, I make up for in them. My dad was in the National Guard for 11 years, so I get my toughness from him. My mom is so lighthearted and I get my sense of empathy from her. My older sister, Erica—we get along so well, and she sees the good in everyone and never judges anyone.

7. What is the most difficult thing for you about having a disability? Seeing my sister and others being able to drive makes me kind of sad because I think about what I'm missing out on. But at the same time, it's not all bad because I've learned to use my other senses better.

8. Do you see your disability as affecting your ability to achieve what you want in your life? Absolutely not! If you think about what it is that I want to do, I feel like I have an advantage. I've had a vision teacher for 13 years, and that's what I want to do—be a vision teacher. I've been given a lot, and being a vision teacher feels like a debt that I want and have to pay back. I have a passion for it and want to put all I have into it.

9. Has your disability affected your social relationships? If so, how? I just have a couple of friends that I go to school with. When I go to see other people who have visual impairments (like at camps), I have so many more friends. These people are more like me, and we have an understanding. When we're together, we have lots of fun, we pull pranks on each other, we also do a lot of teamwork activities, and act together in talent shows. Those are always awesome experiences.

10. Are there any advantages to having a disability that others might be surprised to know? I guess it's that I don't perceive my vision impairment as a chain that's holding me back. Instead, I feel like it's wind propelling me forward. Also, I think some people might be surprised to know that I do well despite it. It's hard because a lot of times people don't know that I even have a visual impairment by just looking at me.

11. How do you think others perceive you? I think some people feel sorry me. I don't need sympathy, because this to me is something that was given to me for a reason. I also think that some people perceive me, because of the technology that I get, as getting special treatment. But that's not it at all. Without technology, I'm a leg behind in a place called school, but with it I can catch up with everyone. Also, I guess that some people revere me and wonder what it would be like to spend a day in my shoes.

12. What is one thing that you would like others to know about you? One day no one will think of anyone who is vision impaired as different from the rest, that instead we could just blend in with the rest and be considered the same.

13. Please fill in the blank: I couldn't live without _____. My vision impairment, because without it things wouldn't have ended up the way they are, and I love the way things are.

CONNECT WITH AJ— AJ welcomes you to contact him online at Aj.faxon@gmail.com

Many people think of blindness as a condition to be pitied. People with visual impairment have a long history of arguing against paternalistic treatment by sighted society, often resisting governmental actions that were presumably designed to help them. For example, the NFB has passed resolutions opposing the *universal* installation of accessible pedestrian signals and underfoot raised dome detectable warnings. **Accessible pedestrian signals (APSs)** alert people who are blind to when it is safe to walk across an intersection. The most common types provide auditory or tactile cues or a combination of the two. The National Cooperative Highway Research Program (n.d.) has published a guide to best practices in implementing APSs. **Raised dome detectable warnings** alert people who are blind to unsafe areas, such as ledges next to tracks in subway stations.

The NFB has stated that APSs might be needed at some complex intersections, but that they are not needed universally (Maurer, 2003). They claim that APSs can be distracting and that continuously operating APSs add to noise pollution, which can interfere with the person's hearing traffic flow. The NFB asserts that the raised dome detectable warnings are also not needed in many instances and that they can lead to unstable walking conditions.

Underlying the NFB's objection to both of these travel aids is its concern that sighted society will view people who are blind as needing more accommodations than necessary, thus reinforcing the notion that they're helpless. Whether one agrees with the NFB or believes that it is being overly sensitive, there's no doubt that sighted society is inclined to view people who are blind in a paternalistic manner. The following account of a trip taken by students from the O & M Program of Louisiana Tech University to the World Trade Center in New York City points out—with considerable irony, given the tragedy of September 11, 2001—how misguided special treatment toward those who are blind can be. Presumably because of their blindness, the group experienced lax security in their trip up to the top of the building. Afterward, in the words of one of the students,

> we made jokes about lax security. If you want to bomb the trade center, just walk in with a white cane, and they will welcome you with open arms. There was a bit of irony in this. In 1993 the World Trade Center had been bombed, but at the moment I had forgotten one important detail about that event. . . .
>
> The thing which I had forgotten about that event was brought back to my attention. I don't remember if it was a graduate student, a center student, or a staff member who said it, but as soon as the words were out, a little piece of irony clicked into place. In a federal penitentiary outside my home town of Springfield, Missouri, sits a blind man. His crime? He masterminded the [1993] bombing of the World Trade Center. When will they ever learn?
>
> Society too loses something when it offers undeserved privileges to people it believes inferior. The general public loses the chance to experience the distinctiveness that we can add to society. . . . [T]hese people expect us all to be the same. They cannot tell the good guys from the bad guys in the blind minority. (Lansaw, 2000, pp. 964–965)

Compounding the problem of paternalism, the public also has a tendency to make superheroes out of people who are blind when they accomplish relatively mundane tasks. Although climbing mountains such as Mount McKinley or Mount Everest are no mundane feats, the sentiments of Erik Weihenmayer point out that the accolades can sometimes be way over the top:

> Not all of my time leading up to the climb [of Mount McKinley] was spent on the mountain; as part of their public-education campaign, the [American Foundation for the Blind] asked me to do some TV interviews. One was a cheesy daytime talk show, on which I was showcased among a group of blind people deemed "amazing and inspirational." All the blind people were led onto the stage, canes tapping and dogs' tails wagging, and seated in a row in front of the crowd. I was featured first, and the host opened with, "A blind mountain climber. Isn't that incredible? Even I, who can see just fine, wouldn't think of climbing a mountain." This wasn't the first time I had heard the "even I" statement. It was always meant as a compliment, but it never failed to annoy me. There might be a dozen other factors that prevented the host from excelling in the sport of mountain climbing.

Erik Weihenmayer receives accolades for his mountain climbing, but bristles when praise for the accomplishments of blind persons appears to mask low expectations.

She might be fifty pounds overweight, wheezing with every breath, and might never have even set foot on a mountain, but in her mind, success or failure was automatically attributed to one factor: sight or no sight. . . .

Throughout the rest of the segment, I squirmed in my seat. . . . I was simply a blind person who planned to climb a mountain and nothing more. But people sensationalize the lives of blind people when, often, all they did was exhibit a semblance of normalcy. I had been receiving these accolades my whole life: give someone directions to my house—incredible. Make eye contact in a conversation—amazing. Pour a glass of milk without spilling it all over the table—inspiring. Each of us on the panel was being honored for our heroic tales, but the recognition spoke more loudly of low expectations than of accomplishment. My heart burned with the memory of my heroes, people like Helen Keller, who took the world's perceptions about the disabled and shattered them into a million pieces, people whose stories made me hunger for the courage to live in their image. (Weihenmayer, 2001, pp. 166–168)

Even though people who are blind can achieve virtually the same degree of independence as people who are sighted, it would be a mistake to assume that this comes naturally or easily. Many independent living skills that people who are sighted learn incidentally need to be taught explicitly to those who are visually impaired. The NFB's Website has a number of products and resources offering practical suggestions for living more independently.

Employment

Many working-age adults with visual impairment are unemployed, and those who do work are often overqualified for the jobs they hold. For example, surveys indicate that adults who are blind are employed at about half the rate of those who are sighted (Capella-McDonnall, 2005; Houtenville, 2003), and data show that they are paid the lowest average hourly rate of all the disability categories (Kirchner & Smith, 2005). This unfortunate situation is due to a history of inadequate transition programming at the secondary school level rather than to the visual impairment itself. With proper transition programming, students with visual impairment, even those who are totally blind, can go on to hold jobs at every level of preparation—teachers, laborers, physicians, engineers. Proper transition programming, however, must be intensive and extensive, including numerous well-supervised work experiences or internships while still in secondary school. Research indicates that having previous work experience of some kind enhances the employment prospects for adults who are blind (McDonnall & Crudden, 2009; Zimmerman, 2011)

High on the list of ways to improve employment possibilities for those who are blind are job accommodations. Employees who are blind report that relatively minor adjustments can go a long way toward making it easier for them to function in the workplace. Suggested adaptations include improved transportation (e.g., car pools), better lighting, tinted office windows to filter light, prompt snow removal, regularly scheduled fire drills to ensure spatial orientation, hallways that are free of obstacles, and computer software (e.g., screen magnification programs) and reading machines that convert print into braille (Rumrill, Roessler, Battersby-Longden, & Schuyler, 1998; Rumrill, Schuyler, & Longden, 1997).

Visual impairment no doubt poses a real challenge for adjustment to everyday living. However, people with visual impairment have many similarities with people in the rest of society. Special and general educators need to achieve the delicate balance between providing special programming for students with visual impairment and treating them in the same manner as they do the rest of their students.

SUMMARY

How do professionals define and classify learners with blindness and low vision?

- Those using a legal definition use visual acuity and field of vision:
  - Blindness is visual acuity of 20/200 or less in the better eye with correction; low vision is 20/70 to 20/200.
  - Blindness is a field of vision no greater than 20 degrees.
- Those using an educational definition use method of reading:
  - Blindness is needing to use braille or aural methods.
  - Low vision is being able to read print (enlarged or magnified).
- Some advocate a skills definition of visual impairment—a focus on what methods other than, or in addition to, sight the individual needs in order to gain information or perform tasks.

What is the prevalence of visual impairment?

- Blindness is primarily an adult disability.
- Fewer than 0.05% of students from age 6 to 17 are identified as visually impaired.

What are some basic anatomical and physiological characteristics of the eye?

- Objects are seen when an electrical impulse travels from the optic nerve at the back of the eye to the occipital lobes of the brain.
- Light rays pass through the cornea, aqueous humor, pupil, lens, vitreous humor, and retina before reaching the optic nerve at the back of the brain.

How is visual ability measured?

- Visual acuity for far distances is most often measured by using the Snellen chart.
- Measures are also available for measuring visual acuity for near distances.
- Vision teachers can perform functional assessments to determine how students use their vision in everyday situations.

What causes visual impairments?

- The most common visual problems result from errors of refraction:
  - Myopia (nearsightedness)
  - Hyperopia (farsightedness)
  - Astigmatism (blurred vision)

- Some conditions affect both adults and children:
  - Glaucoma is a group of diseases causing damage to the optic nerve.
  - Cataracts cause clouding of the lens of the eye.
  - Diabetic retinopathy results from interference of the blood supply to the retina.
- Some conditions affect primarily children:
  - The three most common causes in children are cortical visual impairment, retinopathy of prematurity, and optic nerve hypoplasia.
    - Cortical visual impairment results from brain damage or dysfunction.
    - Retinopathy of prematurity can be caused by excessive concentrations of oxygen or other factors.
    - Optic nerve hypoplasia involves underdevelopment of the optic nerve
  - Retinitis pigmentosa, another cause primarily in children, usually causes tunnel vision and night blindness.
- Improper muscle functioning can cause visual problems:
  - *Strabismus* refers to the eyes being turned inward (crossed eyes) or outward.
  - *Nystagmus* refers to rapid involuntary movements of the eyes.

What are some of the psychological and behavioral characteristics of learners with visual impairments?

- Language development is largely unaffected, although subtle developmental delays can occur, especially in infancy.
- Individuals may experience early delays in conceptual development, which do not last long.
- Motor delays in infancy are common; it is important that adults encourage infants to explore their environment to help overcome these delays.
- Orientation and mobility (O & M) skills depend on spatial abilities:
  - People with visual impairment can process spatial information either sequentially or as a cognitive map; the latter is more efficient.
  - Some people with visual impairment have the obstacle sense, the ability to detect objects by noting subtle changes in high-frequency echoes (the Doppler effect).
  - Two myths are that people who are blind have an extra sense and that they automatically develop better acuity in their other senses.

- Studies suggest that some students who are blind experience low academic achievement, which is most likely due to low expectations or lack of exposure to braille.
- Phonological awareness is important for learning to read print or braille.
- Any social adjustment problems that people with visual impairment have are largely due to sighted society's reactions to blindness.
- Some people with visual impairment engage in stereotypic (repetitive) behaviors.
  - Most authorities attribute stereotypic behaviors to an attempt to stabilize arousal levels.
  - Professionals disagree about whether to intervene with these behaviors.

What are some educational considerations for learners with visual impairments?

- The ability to read braille is a crucial skill.
  - Many authorities believe that the use of braille has slipped to dangerously low levels.
  - Braille bills have helped to ensure that students receive instruction in braille.
  - Federal law requires that braille be available if any member of the IEP team, including parents, thinks it necessary.
  - Authorities point out that many people with low vision can benefit from braille instruction.
- The use of remaining sight is an important skill.
  - Large-print books are useful, although the need for storage space is a drawback.
  - Magnifying devices can be used for close or distance vision.
- Listening skills are important.
- O & M skills are of critical importance.
  - Learning to use a long cane is very important.
  - Unfortunately, some individuals with blindness or low vision resist using a long cane because they think it stigmatizing.
  - Preschoolers and young children can learn cane techniques.
  - There is debate about whether those who are blind can be good mobility instructors.
- Some find using a guide dog very helpful.
  - Guide dogs are much more practical for adults than for children, and they and their owner need extensive training in order to be useful.
  - Guide dogs do not take people anywhere; people usually need to know where they are going.
  - Guide dogs can alert their owners to dangerous areas.

- Tactile maps can be very helpful.
- Human guides, although not recommended as a primary means of mobility, can be helpful at times.
- Technological aids are becoming increasingly important.
  - Technological aids are available for communication and information access. These include braille notetakers, personal data assistants, Newsline®, Descriptive Video Service®, and screen readers for computers.
  - Technological aids are available for O & M. These include obstacle-detection devices and the Global Positioning System (GPS).
  - Learners with visual impairments should not become so dependent on technology that they neglect basic techniques, such as braille, the slate and stylus, and the long cane.
- Itinerant teacher service is the most common service delivery model, and compared to other areas of disability residential placement is relatively popular.

How do professionals assess the progress of students with visual impairments in academic and functional skills and make testing accommodations for them?

- Teachers can monitor progress in braille skills involved in reading and mathematics using curriculum-based measurement (CBM).
- O & M instructors can monitor travel skills using GPS devices.
- Professionals can assess academic outcomes using braille versions of standardized academic tests.
- Testing accommodations often include testing in braille, large-print, or extended time.

What are some important considerations with respect to early intervention for learners with visual impairments?

- Intensive intervention should begin as early as possible.
- Inclusive settings can be beneficial, but it is important that the teacher facilitate interactions between students with visual impairments and sighted students.
- It is important to try to involve parents.
- Many authorities now recommend that preschoolers be taught cane techniques

What are some important considerations with respect to transition to adulthood for learners with visual impairments?

- Most people who are blind can lead very independent lives.

- The current emphasis on inclusion needs to be viewed with caution to make sure it does not come at the expense of learning independent living skills.
- Sighted society needs to be careful not to treat those with visual impairments as helpless.
- Explicit teaching of independent living skills is essential.
- Many working-age adults with visual impairments are unemployed or are overqualified for the jobs they hold.

- Previous work experience is important for obtaining employment.
- Transition programming should be intensive and extensive.
- Job accommodations are essential.

COUNCIL FOR EXCEPTIONAL CHILDREN

Addressing the Professional Standards

Council for Exceptional Children

Council for Exceptional Children (CEC) Common Core Knowledge and Skills addressed in this chapter:

ICC1K5, ICC1K6, ICC1K7, ICC1K8, ICC2K1, ICC2K2, ICC2K4, ICC2K5, ICC3K2, ICC4S3, ICC4S4, ICC4S5, ICC4S6, ICC5K5, ICC5S3, ICC5S11, ICC7S7, ICC7S9, ICC8S2, ICC9K4, ICC9S2, ICC9S5, ICC10K3, ICC10S6

Appendix: Provides a full listing of the CEC Common Core Standards and associated Knowledge and Skill Statements listed here.

MYEDUCATIONLAB

PEARSON
myeducationlab

Now go to Topic 15: Sensory Impairments, in the MyEducationLab (www.myeducationlab.com) for your course, where you can:

- Find learning outcomes for the broad concepts covered in this chapter along with the national standards that connect to these outcomes.
- Complete Assignments and Activities that can help you more deeply understand the chapter content.
- Examine challenging situations presented in the IRIS Center Resources.
- Apply and practice your understanding of the core concepts and skills identified in the chapter with the Building Teaching Skills and Dispositions learning units.
- Check your comprehension of the content covered in the chapter by going to the Study Plan in the Book-Specific Resources for your text. Here you will be able to take a chapter quiz, receive feedback on your answers, and then access Review, Practice, and Enrichment activities to enhance your understanding of chapter content.
- Watch video clips of CCSSO Teacher of the Year award winners responding to the question: "Why I teach?" in the Teacher Talk section.

Learners with Low-Incidence, Multiple, and Severe Disabilities

Accidents divide things into the great Before and After.

"Even before his brain injury, Alan had a hard time remembering names," I'll say. "Since Daddy's accident, I have to work more," I tell our daughter, Kelly. The brain injury community marks time by asking how long someone has been "out of" injury, the same way bereavement counselors ask how long your loved one has been dead.

Out of what, exactly?

Out of the giant crevice that has been exploded into the bedrock of your life.

Here's how I see it: One day, you and your family are hiking across a long, solid plain, when out of the sky comes a blazing meteor that just happens to hit one family member on the head. The meteor creates a huge rift in the landscape, dragging the unlucky one down to the bottom of the crevice it has made. You spend the next year on a rescue mission, helping him climb to the top, but when he gets up there, you realize that he has been greatly changed by the hardship. He doesn't know a meteor has hit him. He will never know, really. He only knows that he has spent a lot of time in a dark, confusing place. He left a lot of stuff behind, the stuff he was carrying with him, down in the big hole, and it's impossible to get it all back.

Cathy Crimmins • *Where Is the Mango Princess? (2000)*

QUESTIONS to guide your reading of this chapter . . .

- What is the definition of low-incidence, multiple, and severe disabilities, and what is the prevalence?
- What is traumatic brain injury, and how might it affect education?
- How is deaf-blindness defined, and what are the special educational problems it entails?
- What educational considerations apply to many students with low-incidence, multiple, and severe disabilities?

MISCONCEPTIONS ABOUT

Learners with Low-Incidence, Multiple, and Severe Disabilities

MYTH • People with severe and multiple disabilities have problems so severe that the best they can hope for is employment in a sheltered workshop.

FACT • With intensive and extensive instruction, many people with severe and multiple disabilities can now be employed in more integrated work settings.

MYTH • People with severe and multiple disabilities have problems so severe that the best they can hope for is to live under close supervision in a large residential facility.

FACT • With intensive and extensive instruction, many people with severe and multiple disabilities can now live independently or semi-independently by themselves or in a small community residential facility (CRF).

MYTH • A person with traumatic brain injury (TBI) can be expected, with time, to recover completely and function without disabilities.

FACT • Some people with TBI do recover completely, but many do not. Usually, a person with TBI has long-term disabilities that may be compensated for in many ways, but these disabilities don't ordinarily disappear completely, even with the best treatment and rehabilitation.

MYTH • For students with Usher syndrome whose vision will deteriorate over time, it's best not to introduce braille and training with the long cane while their vision is still relatively good because to do so stigmatizes them.

FACT • Braille and orientation and mobility training should not wait until the later stages of vision loss. Getting a head start on learning these complex skills almost always outweighs any stigmatization that might occur.

MYTH • People who can't speak have extreme difficulty making themselves understood to others.

FACT • With an appropriate augmentative or alternative communication (AAC) system, people who can't speak can carry on a normal conversation, sometimes very near the rate of speakers without disabilities. The flexibility, speed, and usefulness in communication of AAC are increasing rapidly with new technologies, and they now often allow a user to approximate the typical verbal exchanges between speakers.

MYTH • The only really effective way of controlling the undesirable behavior of people with severe and multiple disabilities is to use punishment.

FACT • Functional behavioral assessment and positive behavioral supports are finding more and more ways of replacing undesirable with desirable behavior without the use of punishment. Often, the key is finding out what the person with severe and multiple disabilities is trying to communicate and helping him or her find a more effective, efficient way of communicating that to others.

MYTH • Braille is only for people who are blind.

FACT • It is helpful to teach braille to two groups of individuals who are not blind: (1) those who have visual impairments so severe that they can't read print reliably and (2) those whose condition will worsen with time to the point at which braille will be their only option.

The definition of low-incidence, severe, and multiple disabilities, like the definition of all other categories of disabilities, is controversial. Disabilities are particularly mystifying when they are seldom seen, multiple, or severe. The causes and meanings of such disabilities and the life course of the people who have them, may be particularly difficult to understand.

DEFINITION AND PREVALENCE

TASH (originally the Association for Persons with Severe Handicaps) uses the following definition of severe disabilities:

> *individuals with disabilities of all ages, races, creeds, national origins, genders and sexual orientations who require ongoing support in more than one major life activity in order to participate in an integrated community and enjoy a quality of life similar to that available to all citizens. Support may be required for life activities such as mobility, communication, self-care, and learning as necessary for community living, employment, and self-sufficiency.* (Snell & Brown, 2006, pp. 69–70, italics in original)

People with a severe disability in any area typically have more than one disability. Furthermore, a combination of mild disabilities may present severe educational problems (Kauffman, 2008). As noted in the Individuals with Disabilities Education Improvement Act of 2004 (IDEA): "Multiple disabilities means concomitant impairments . . . the combination of which causes such severe educational problems that they cannot be accommodated in special education programs solely for one of the impairments" (34 CFR, Sec. 300 (b)(6)). IDEA also states that

> The term "children with severe disabilities" refers to children with disabilities who, because of the intensity of their physical, mental, or emotional problems, need highly specialized education, social, psychological, and medical services in order to maximize their full potential for useful and meaningful participation in society and for self-fulfillment. The term includes those children with severe emotional disturbance (including schizophrenia), autism, severe and profound mental retardation, and those who have two or more serious disabilities, such as deaf-blindness, mental retardation and blindness, and cerebral palsy and deafness.
>
> Children with severe disabilities may experience severe speech, language, and/or perceptual-cognitive deprivations, and evidence abnormal behaviors, such as failure to respond to pronounced social stimuli, self-mutilation, self-stimulation, manifestation of intense and prolonged temper tantrums, and the absence of rudimentary forms of verbal control, and may also have intensely fragile physiological conditions. (34 CFR, Sec. 315.4(d))

Low-incidence, severe, and multiple disabilities are often linked conceptually. They occur in only a relatively small percentage of cases of disability (Kauffman, 2008). Furthermore, nearly any low-incidence, severe disability will involve extensive and ongoing support in more than one major life activity. That is, low-incidence, severe, and multiple disabilities tend to go together. All of the low-incidence, severe, and multiple disabilities that we discuss in the chapter probably affect fewer than 1% of the population.

With these considerations in mind, in this chapter, we first discuss the categories and problems of traumatic brain injury and deaf-blindness. Then we discuss issues that apply to all categories of low-incidence, multiple, and severe disabilities: augmentative and alternative communication, behavior problems, early intervention, and transition to adulthood.

We mentioned severe and profound intellectual disability in Chapter 5 and discussed autism spectrum disorders in Chapter 9. However, much of what we present in this chapter applies to some individuals with autism and to those with severe or profound intellectual disability as well. Remember, though, that autism spectrum disorders can range from mild to severe, as is the case in all other categories of disability.

TRAUMATIC BRAIN INJURY

Since 1990, when IDEA recognized the category of **traumatic brain injury (TBI)**, students with TBI may be found eligible for special education and related services. Today, there is much greater understanding of the nature of TBI and the educational needs of students with TBI (e.g., search the Internet using the term "traumatic brain injury" or "tbi"

PEARSON
myeducationlab

To check your comprehension on the content covered in Chapter 13, go to the Book-Specific Resources in the MyEducationLab (www.myeducationlab.com) for your course, select your text, and complete the Study Plan. Here you will be able to take a chapter quiz, receive feedback on your answers, and then access review, practice, and enrichment activities to enhance your understanding of chapter content. ∎

Justin Greenwood, who suffered a brain injury during a football game, works on his short-term memory during a therapy session.

INTERNETRESOURCES

More information about TBI may be found at the Brain Injury Association of America: www.biausa.org
You may also want to visit traumaticbraininjury.com/ and Google "traumatic brain injury."

or go to www.ninds.nih.gov/disorders/tbi/tbi.htm). Unlike cerebral palsy, TBI is brain damage that is acquired by trauma after a period of normal neurological development. As Cathy Crimmins suggests in this chapter's opening quotation, TBI is a life-altering experience. It presents unique educational problems that often have been poorly understood and mismanaged. Recent medical advances have greatly improved diagnosis and treatment.

Historically, recognition and treatment of disabilities are often encouraged by the return of injured soldiers to civilian life. Because TBI is one of the most common injuries of the wars in Iraq and Afghanistan, perhaps the public will become more aware of and demand better treatment of those with TBI.

Definition and Characteristics

Commonly accepted definitions of TBI specify the following:

1. There is injury to the brain caused by an external force.
2. The injury is not caused by a degenerative or congenital condition.
3. There is a diminished or altered state of consciousness.
4. Neurological or neurobehavioral dysfunction results from the injury.

Most definitions also specify that the injury is followed by impairments in abilities required for school learning and everyday functioning.

TBI can result from two categories of injury: open or closed. **Open head injuries** involve a penetrating head wound, from such causes as a fall, gunshot, assault, vehicular accident, or surgery. Individuals with **closed head injuries** have no open head wound but may have brain damage caused by internal compression, stretching, or other shearing motion of neural tissues within the head. Soldiers serving in Iraq and Afghanistan often acquire TBI as a result of improvised explosive devices (IEDs). They may experience either open head injuries, in which something penetrates their heads or removes part of their brains, or closed head injuries, in which the concussive force of the explosion or their being thrown against an object damages their brains without creating an open wound. The effects of damage to their brains and the resulting symptoms can be severe with either type of injury.

The educational definition of TBI focuses on impairments in one or more areas important for learning. The federal (IDEA) definition of TBI states that it is

an acquired injury to the brain caused by an external physical force, resulting in total or partial functional disability or psychosocial impairment, or both, that adversely affects a child's educational performance. The term applies to open or closed head injuries resulting in impairments in one or more areas, such as cognition; language; memory; attention; reasoning; abstract thinking; judgment; problem-solving; sensory, perceptual, and motor abilities; psychosocial behavior; physical functions; information processing; and speech. The term does not apply to injuries that are congenital or degenerative, or brain injuries induced by birth trauma. (34 CFR, Sec. 300.7(6)(12))

The effects of TBI range from very mild to profound, and TBI is often a part of or accompanied by other medical issues (Best, Heller, & Bigge, 2010). Often, the effects are immediate, and these immediate effects set TBI apart from most other disabilities—the child or youth is literally changed overnight. The sudden change presents particular difficulties to families and teachers, not to mention the individual sustaining the injury (Ashley, 2004). However, sometimes the effects of TBI are not seen immediately after the injury but appear months or even years afterward. The possible effects of TBI include a long list of learning and psychosocial problems, such as:

- Problems remembering things
- Problems learning new information
- Speech and/or language problems
- Difficulty sequencing things
- Difficulty in processing information (making sense of things)
- Extremely uneven abilities or performance (able to do some things but not others)
- Extremely uneven progress (quick gains sometimes, no gains other times)
- Inappropriate manners or mannerisms
- Failure to understand humor or social situations
- Becoming easily tired, frustrated, or angered
- Unreasonable fear or anxiety
- Irritability
- Sudden, exaggerated swings of mood
- Depression
- Aggression
- Perseveration (persistent repetition of one thought or behavior)

One of the great difficulties with TBI is that it's often "invisible." True, in some cases, a person with TBI has paralysis, slurred speech, or some other indicator of brain damage that is quickly apparent, as in Ronald's Story in the accompanying Personal Perspectives feature. But in many cases, the person with TBI looks just like everyone else. The casual observer doesn't see anything obvious, like the person with TBI drooling or being in a wheelchair.

Prevalence

The exact prevalence of TBI is difficult to determine, but we do know that TBI occurs at an alarming rate among children and youths. Males are more prone to TBI than females are, and the age range in which TBI is most likely to occur for both males and females is late adolescence and early adulthood. The Council for Exceptional Children (2001) refers to TBI as a "silent epidemic." It's considered an epidemic because of its increasing prevalence; it's "silent" because many serious head injuries are unreported, and many cases of TBI go undetected or are mistaken for other disabilities. The prevalence of TBI is disconcerting because so many of

 **Personal PERSPECTIVES**   *Ronald's Story*

Ronald is a 15-year-old who sustained a traumatic brain injury in a car crash. At the time of his injury, he was a 13-year-old seventh grader who earned top grades and was very athletic. Ronald has been in hospital and rehabilitation facilities since the time of his accident. Ronald has significant physical and cognitive disabilities as a result of his TBI. He presents with articulation difficulties and poor saliva management. Strength and coordination are moderately to severely im-

paired, and he is in a wheelchair. Significant short-term memory issues cause difficulty with new learning. He has nystagmus [involuntary eye movements] and is fully dependent for his toileting needs. Ronald fatigues easily, is sensitive to loud noises, is demonstrating periods of depression as he mourns his former self, and engaging in inappropriate social behaviors. Current assessments indicate an IQ of 88, with peaks and valleys in his abilities. . . .

Source: Grandinette & Best (2009, p. 137).

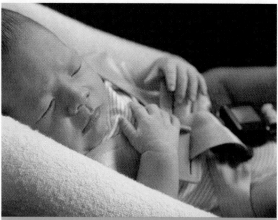

The prevalence of TBI is disconcerting because so many of the causes of TBI are entirely preventable or avoidable by following ordinary safety precautions, such as properly securing infants and children in car safety seats.

the causes of TBI are entirely preventable or avoidable by following ordinary safety precautions. Moreover, the prevalence of TBI has increased so much in recent years that it is now sometimes discussed as a high-incidence (frequent) rather than a low-incidence (uncommon) disability (see Grandinette & Best, 2009; Stichter, Conroy, & Kauffman, 2008).

Causes

Among children less than 5 years old, accidental falls are the dominant cause of TBI, with vehicular accidents and child abuse causing substantial injuries as well. After age five, and increasingly through adolescence, vehicular accidents (including accidents involving pedestrians, bicycles, motorcycles, and cars) account for the majority of TBI; assaults and gunshot wounds are increasingly prevalent among youths at older ages. Closed head injuries may be caused by a variety of events besides vehicular accidents, including a fall or abuse such as violent shaking of a child by an adult (see Lajiness-O'Neill & Erdodi, 2011).

Educational Considerations

The educational implications of TBI are varied and depend on the nature and severity of the injury and the age and abilities of the individual at the time of injury. A significant issue in educating someone who has experienced TBI is helping family members, teachers, and peers to respond appropriately to the sudden and sometimes dramatic changes that may occur in the student's academic abilities, appearance, behavior, and emotional states (Lajiness-O'Neill & Erdodi, 2011). Both general and special education teachers need training about TBI and its ramifications if students are to be reintegrated successfully into the schools and classrooms they attended before the injury (DePompei & Tyler, 2004; Grandinette & Best, 2009; Stichter et al., 2008). The following characteristics are essential features of appropriate education for students with TBI:

1. Transition from a hospital or rehabilitation center to the school.
2. A team approach involving regular and special educators, other special teachers, guidance counselor, administrators, and the student's family.
3. An individualized education program (IEP) concerned with cognitive, social/behavioral, and sensorimotor domains.
4. Educational procedures to help students solve problems in focusing and sustaining attention for long periods, remembering previously learned facts and skills, learning new things, dealing with fatigue, and engaging in appropriate social behavior.
5. Emphasis on the cognitive processes through which academic skills are learned, not just curriculum content.
6. Plans for addressing long-term needs in addition to immediate and annual IEP goals.

It's critical that educators understand the implications of the brain injury for structuring the student's psychological and social environments in school (Best, Heller, & Bigge, 2010).

The teacher must focus on helping the student with TBI to recover cognitive abilities because these are most critical to academic and social progress. The abilities to remember and to make sense of academic information and social circumstances are key to the student's long-term success. The teacher must help the student learn to use coping mechanisms and alternative strategies, such as using a tape recorder, a planner, or other organizational devices and memory aids for whatever abilities cannot be recovered.

A major problem in reentry to school after TBI—at least if the consequences are serious—is that the students tend to see themselves as not having changed, whereas peers and teachers are likely to notice that the student with TBI is not the same. Dell Orto and Power (2000) note that our societal emphasis on productiveness, organization, independence, and achievement can contribute to negative attitudes toward a student with TBI. "Academic deficits displayed by survivors of TBI conflict with achievement values, not only causing discomfort in teachers, but frustration and perhaps a sense of rejection in the young person" (p. 22). Many teachers apparently don't want students with TBI in their classrooms, probably because these students exhibit characteristics that teachers find troublesome (just consider the bulleted list of learning and psychosocial problems on p. 371). Thus, a student's returning to school after TBI is a major issue that typically requires a team approach involving a variety of professionals, as we mentioned in our list of essential features of appropriate educational programs. Collaboration and problem solving by this team are essential to the success of the student's reentry. (See the accompanying Making It Work feature for more on team problem solving.)

The assessment of a student's academic and social skills following TBI is tricky because it's often difficult or impossible to separate physiological causes or reasons for difficulty with a task from other causes. More important than knowing precisely what difficulties have a physiological cause is pinpointing just what the student's academic and social learning difficulties are. Here again, a team approach is essential. Neurologists can often provide information about the consequences of TBI that helps teachers to set reasonable expectations and teach coping skills that help the student to compensate for abilities that will not return.

LANGUAGE DISORDERS   A student with TBI might acquire a language disorder after a period of normal development, or acquire a more severe language disorder than existed before the injury (see Chapter 10). Individuals with TBI are a very diverse population, although a disproportionate number of students with TBI have a pretrauma history of learning problems or delayed speech and language.

Language or speech disorders are the greatest complicating factor in most students' return to school following TBI. A loss of ability to understand and formulate language due to brain injury is sometimes referred to as a **motor-speech disorder**, which we discussed in Chapter 10. The student may have trouble finding or saying words or constructing sentences that are appropriate for the topic of conversation or social context. Problems like these can be a source of frustration, anger, and confusion for students with TBI.

The language problems associated with TBI are primarily related to the cognitive and social demands of communication. The student might have problems with tasks that demand responding quickly, organizing, dealing with abstractions, sustaining attention (especially if there are distractions), learning new skills, responding appropriately in social situations, and showing appropriate affect. In fact, TBI can potentially disrupt all aspects of the give-and-take of social interaction that are required for effective communication.

The effects of TBI on language are extremely variable, and careful assessment of the given individual's abilities and disabilities is critically important. Interventions may range from making special accommodations, such as allowing more response time or keeping distractions to a minimum, to focusing on instruction in the social uses of language.

Depending on the site and degree of brain damage, a person with TBI may have motor control problems that interfere with communication, including the cognitive and social aspects of communication. Some students with TBI cannot communicate orally using the muscles of speech and must rely on alternative or augmentative communication systems, which we describe later in the chapter.

SOCIAL AND EMOTIONAL PROBLEMS   Brain injury may be accompanied by a variety of serious social and emotional effects. We know that TBI can cause violent aggression, hyperactivity, impulsivity, inattention, and a wide range of other emotional or behavioral problems, depending on just what parts of the brain are damaged. The possible effects of TBI include a long list of other psychosocial problems, some of which we listed previously as general characteristics.

The emotional and behavioral effects of TBI are determined by more than the physical damage; they also depend on the student's age at the time of injury and the social environment before and after the injury. Home, community, or school environments that foster misbehavior of any child or youth are known to be associated with increased risk for acquiring TBI. Such environments are extremely likely to worsen any emotional or behavioral problem resulting from TBI. Creating an environment that is conducive to and supportive

MAKING IT WORK
COLLABORATION AND CO-TEACHING OF STUDENTS WITH LOW-INCIDENCE, MULTIPLE, AND SEVERE DISABILITIES

"We may have different goals for students. How can we solve that problem?"

WHAT DOES IT MEAN TO BE A TEACHER OF STUDENTS WITH THESE DISABILITIES?

The Council for Exceptional Children (CEC) does not have a specific set of standards for the training of teachers who work with students with low-incidence, multiple, or severe disabilities. Instead, CEC has a set of standards for teachers who work with students who require an individualized, independent curriculum. A teacher with expertise in this area would:

1. Be able to identify the impact of learners' academic and social abilities, attitudes, interests, and values on instruction and career development.
2. Be able to use appropriate adaptations and assistive technology.
3. Identify and teach basic structures and relationships within and across curricula.

SUCCESSFUL STRATEGIES FOR COLLABORATION

Students with severe disabilities often require a wide range of services at school. Many professionals, including teachers, nurses, aides, etc., must collaborate to provide those services. With so many people involved in a student's education, problems are likely to arise, and everyone should be ready to engage in collaborative problem solving.

Partners in collaborative settings should develop a plan to attack problems before they arise. Problems can be related to the student response to settings and personnel, the student's environment, differences in professional goals, discrepancies in professional philosophies, and so on. Though the causes may be different, a similar step-by-step process can be used to address each one. Mostert (1998) describes the following steps for successful problem solving:

1. *Is there a problem to solve?* This step involves reflection on the questions: Is there really a problem here? Who owns it? Is the problem solvable?
2. *What is the problem?* Once a problem is identified, participants define it in specific, objective terms. Statements such as "I don't like his attitude" must be refined to describe the situation specifically, "John makes inappropriate comments about other students when I ask him a question in class." After the problem is defined, partners gather data on the frequency, duration, and degree of the problem in a variety of environments.
3. *How can the problem be solved?* All participants generate solutions to the problem. This is the brainstorming step, so all suggestions should be welcomed.

4. *Which solution or combination is best?* Personnel working together must be able to discuss the solutions presented and evaluate them without emotional attachment. Interventions for students should be judged as to whether there is evidence of previous success (research based, not anecdotal), whether there are appropriate supports and resources, whether the participants can/will fully implement it, and whether the intervention is truly appropriate for the student. The solutions that do not fit these criteria should be abandoned.
5. *Which solution should we select?* After evaluating all solutions, the partners choose the one to implement.
6. *How will we implement the solution?* This step requires delegating responsibilities for the solution to members of the team. It means specifically stating what the team hopes will happen, setting up how the partners will know if the solution worked, and scheduling a time to reconvene to share data.
7. *Did it work?* This step requires data collection again. Partners must be able to present information as to whether the solution achieved its goals. If not, it is time to start the process again. If the solution worked, the team can move on to another problem!

Problem solving with other professionals requires that participants develop an environment with open communication, overcoming barriers by using effective communication skills. According to Walther-Thomas, Korinek, McLaughlin, and Williams (2000), these skills include:

1. *Listening.* Attend to the speaker, paraphrase content, reflect feelings, and summarize.
2. *Repetition.* Send the same message to partners repeatedly and through different channels.
3. *Empathy.* Make predictions about how a partner will respond to a message you send.
4. *Understanding.* Make sure that the language you use is clear and concise.

When collaborating with other professionals and even with students, there is no way to avoid problems. But, to avoid conflict, partners should discuss and set up problem-solving strategies *before* these situations occur. Problem-solving strategies, along with effective communication skills, will help collaborators provide continuous, appropriate services to students.

• By Margaret P. Weiss

The emotional issues involved in TBI can be especially complex. Eileen Vosper, 12, enjoys holding Kelli, a 6-year-old collie who serves in a pet therapy program for children and adults with brain-injury–related disabilities. The visits with the dogs are short but meaningful.

of appropriate behavior is one of the great challenges of dealing effectively with the results of brain injury.

Many of the typical **behavior modification** or **behavior management** strategies that are used with other students who have emotional or behavioral difficulties are appropriate for use with students who have TBI. Consistency, predictability, and reinforcement (praise, encouragement, and other rewards) are particularly important (Persel & Persel, 2004), as is developing rapport with the student. Developing a good personal relationship with a student with TBI can be particularly challenging, as such students can be unpredictable, irritable, and angry with those who are trying to help (see Kauffman, Pullen, Mostert, & Trent, 2011).

TBI often shatters an individual's sense of self. Recovering one's identity can require a long period of rehabilitation and can be a painstaking process requiring multidisciplinary efforts (Best et al., 2010; Grandinette & Best, 2009). Effective education and treatment often require not only classroom behavior management, but also family therapy, medication, cognitive training, and communication training.

DEAF-BLINDNESS

In Chapters 11 and 12, we noted that, depending on the level of severity, blindness or deafness can have a substantial impact on a person's ability to function independently. For those who are both deaf and blind, the impact can be even more profound than simply adding the effects of each disability. Because the primary avenues for receiving information—sight and sound—are limited, those who are deaf-blind are at risk for having extensive problems in communicating and in navigating their environments.

Although being cut off from the sights and sounds of daily life makes deaf-blindness one of the most challenging of all multiple disabilities, this doesn't mean that a person with deaf-blindness is doomed to a poor-quality life. In general, outcomes for individuals with deaf-blindness depend on at least three factors:

1. *The quality and intensity of instruction the person receives are critical.* Teachers of students with deaf-blindness "must make the most of every opportunity for learning.

INTERNETRESOURCES

A variety of information about deaf-blindness is found at www.deafblind.com and at http://nationaldb.org/

All interactions with adults and all aspects of the environment will be harnessed to help the child overcome the restrictions imposed by sensory impairments" (Hodges, 2000, p. 167).

2. ***The degree and type of visual impairment and auditory impairment can vary dramatically in individuals with deaf-blindness.*** The term *deaf-blindness* covers those with visual impairments ranging from low vision (20/70 to 20/200 in the better eye with correction) to those who are totally blind. Likewise, the term covers those with hearing impairments ranging from mild to profound. Despite some very notable exceptions, in general, the more severe the impairments, the greater is the impact on a person's ability to adapt.

3. ***The vast majority of students who are deaf-blind have other disabilities and medical conditions.*** For example, they can be intellectually disabled, autistic and/or have physical disabties.

Definition

As we discussed in Chapters 11 and 12, considerable controversy exists over the definitions of deafness and blindness. As one might expect, this means that defining deaf-blindness is even more controversial than defining deafness or blindness by itself. The Individuals with Disabilities Education Improvement Act (2004) describes deaf-blindness as an individual

> (1)(i) Who has a central visual acuity of 20/200 or less in the better eye with corrective lenses, or a field defect such that the peripheral diameter of visual field subtends an angular distance no greater than 20 degrees, or a progressive visual loss having a prognosis leading to one or both of these conditions:
>
> (ii) Who has a chronic hearing impairment so severe that most speech cannot be understood with optimum amplification, or a progressive hearing loss having a prognosis leading to this condition; and
>
> (iii) For whom the combination of impairments described in paragraphs (1)(i) and (ii) of this definition causes extreme difficulty in attaining independence in daily life activities, achieving psychosocial adjustment, or obtaining a vocation;
>
> (2) Who, despite the inability to be measured accurately for hearing and vision loss due to cognitive or behavioral constraints, or both, can be determined through functional and performance assessment to have severe hearing and visual disabilities that cause extreme difficulty in attaining independence in daily life activities, or obtaining vocational objectives; or
>
> (3) Who meets any other requirements that the Secretary may prescribe. (34 CFR, Sec. 396.4 (c)(2))

Prevalence

Because the definitions and criteria of deaf-blindness vary from state to state, and because so many students with deaf-blindness also have other disabling conditions, obtaining an accurate prevalence rate is very difficult. We do know that it's a much rarer condition than either deafness or blindness alone. For example, the federal government reported that students receiving special education services in 2007 included 529 students with deaf-blindness from age 6 through 11 compared to almost 32,000 with deafness and 12,000 with blindness. (National Data Accountability Center, 2010).

Causes

Causes of deaf-blindness can be grouped into three broad categories: (1) genetic/chromosomal syndromes, (2) prenatal conditions, and (3) postnatal conditions.

GENETIC/CHROMOSOMAL SYNDROMES   Researchers are making enormous strides in discovering genetic/chromosomal syndromes involved in deaf-blindness. Some of these syndromes are inherited, and some result from damaged genetic and/or chromosomal material. Dozens of genetic/chromosomal syndromes are now known to be associated with deaf-blindness. The most common are CHARGE syndrome, Usher syndrome, and Down syndrome.

CHARGE Syndrome   CHARGE syndrome is characterized by a number of physical anomalies that are present at birth. The letters in CHARGE refer to some of the most common characteristics of this condition: C = coloboma, cranial nerves; H = heart defects; A = atresia of the choanae; R = retardation in growth and mental development; G = genital abnormalities; E = ear malformation and/or hearing loss. Strong evidence now indicates that most cases of CHARGE are caused by a mutation in one particular gene (CHD7) (Zentner, Layman, Martin, & Scacheri, 2010).

Coloboma refers to a condition in which the child is born with an abnormally shaped pupil and/or abnormalities of the retina or optic nerve. Coloboma can result in a variety of visual problems, including deficits in visual acuity and extreme sensitivity to light. The **cranial nerves** supply information between the brain and various muscles and glands in the body. Individuals with CHARGE syndrome often have paralysis or weakness of facial muscles as well as swallowing problems because of abnormal development of some of the cranial nerves.

An **atresia** is the absence or closure of a body opening present at birth. The **choanae** are air passages from the nose to throat. When the choanae are blocked or narrowed, the ability to breathe is affected. Surgery can help to correct these breathing problems.

Usher Syndrome   Usher syndrome, an inherited condition, is characterized by hearing impairment and **retinitis pigmentosa**. As mentioned in Chapter 12, retinitis pigmentosa can result in vision problems starting in infancy, early childhood, or the teenage years, with the condition becoming progressively worse. It results in problems in seeing in low light, referred to as **night blindness**, and as it progresses, it results in a narrowing of the field of vision, referred to as **tunnel vision**.

The three types of Usher syndrome vary with respect to the type and time of occurrence of the major symptoms of hearing loss, vision loss, and balance problems. For example, depending on the type of Usher syndrome, the person can be born profoundly deaf, hard of hearing, or with normal hearing that deteriorates over time. Some experience night blindness starting in infancy; others have night blindness starting in the teenage years. Some have severe balance problems, due to inner-ear problems, starting in infancy; some have no balance problems; and some are born with normal balance that deteriorates over time.

Thus far, researchers have found that a mutation in any one of about 11 genes can result in Usher syndrome (National Institute on Deafness and Other Communication Disorders, 2010). Although Usher syndrome is one of the most common hereditary conditions causing deaf-blindness, its overall prevalence is very low. Estimates suggest that about 16,000 people in the United States have Usher syndrome (Wrong Diagnosis, 2010). The genetics of Usher syndrome show an interesting demographic pattern (see the accompanying Focus on Concepts).

Down Syndrome Most often noted as a cause of intellectual disability (see Chapter 5), **Down syndrome** is also sometimes associated with deaf-blindness. Unlike Usher syndrome, which is inherited, Down syndrome results from damaged chromosomal material.

PRENATAL CONDITIONS Like Down syndrome, two of the most common types of **prenatal** conditions—**rubella**, sometimes referred to as **German measles**, and **congenital cytomegalovirus (CMV)**—can cause intellectual disability and/or deaf-blindness. When rubella occurs in a pregnant woman, especially in the first trimester, it can lead to a variety of disabilities, including deaf-blindness. Children born with CMV, a herpes virus, are also at risk for a variety of disabilities, including deaf-blindness.

POSTNATAL CONDITIONS Among the most common **postnatal** conditions that can cause deaf-blindness are **meningitis** and TBI. As we learned in Chapter 5, meningitis, which is an infection of the covering of the brain, can also cause intellectual disability. TBI, as we discussed earlier in this chapter, can result in a variety of other disabilities, as well as deaf-blindness.

FOCUS ON Concepts

THE GENETICS OF USHER SYNDROME AND ITS GEOGRAPHIC DISTRIBUTION

About 1 in 75 people carries an Usher gene, but most don't realize they have it. Usher syndrome is an *autosomal-recessive disorder*, meaning that for a child to have the condition, both parents must be carriers of the gene. And with each such pregnancy, there is a one-in-four chance of the child having Usher syndrome. Thus, the chance of having a child with Usher syndrome is relatively rare even among those who carry the gene, and that is why the prevalence of Usher syndrome is so low. However, the odds of producing an offspring with Usher syndrome rise dramatically among people who are related:

> Each of us, regardless of family history, is thought to silently carry five or more recessive genes that have the potential to cause genetic disorders in the next generation. But the chance of conceiving a child with a recessive disorder is low because most unrelated couples do not carry the exact same recessive genes. Conversely, because members of one's immediate or extended family share a similar genetic makeup, it becomes easier for two autosomal recessive genes to match up to cause a particular disorder. Thus, children conceived by parents who are related to each other are at higher than average risk for being affected by autosomal recessive disorders. And in certain cultures in which marriages between relatives are the norm or in which many people preferentially choose partners with the same inherited trait (e.g., marriage between two people with deafness), recessive conditions occur more commonly than expected. (Dykens, Hodapp, & Finucane, 2000, p. 46)

Unfortunately, social forces have operated historically to make the likelihood of intermarriage higher among a certain cultural group: the Acadian French of south Louisiana. This has resulted in a relatively higher number of people with Usher syndrome in this area of the country. The high prevalence of Usher syndrome in south Louisiana is also the subject of a video narrated by the well-known neurologist Oliver Sacks, *The Ragin' Cajun Usher Syndrome*, produced by the British Broadcasting Company. Following is an excerpt from a retired teacher who had worked at the Louisiana School for the Deaf for 27 years:

> To begin with, Usher syndrome among the Acadian French people in south Louisiana was something people knew the "about" of, but not the "what" or "why" of. They knew that

generation after generation of children were struck mysteriously with deafness and eventually with partial-to-full blindness. It was something that was dreaded, but had to be endured. Again and again, cousins, aunts, uncles, and sometimes two or three children in a family were found to have the condition, but no one knew what to do, or what to call it.

> The "what" and "why" of it was that the Acadian parishes of south Louisiana have a far higher percentage of Usher syndrome than anywhere else in the United States. This extraordinarily high percentage has been documented in several studies. . . . For example, [Kloepfer, Laguaite, & McLaurin, 1966] estimated that 30 percent of the deaf population in the parishes of Lafayette, Vermillion, and Acadia had Usher syndrome. The high incidence is a result of several hundred years of intermarriage among this close-knit ethnic group. Inevitably, two individuals, both carrying a recessive gene for Usher syndrome transmitted to them by a common ancestor, marry and have children with this condition.

> The Acadians, or Cajuns, as they are called, were originally from Acadia (Nova Scotia) in Canada. In the 1700s they were expelled from that area by the English. They moved down along the east-coast of America, finally settling along the bayous of several south Louisiana parishes. At first they were not readily accepted by people in the area and were somewhat isolated both by language and by culture. With time, however, the Cajuns came into their own and have won admirers around the world for their music, love of fun, and never-to-be-forgotten cuisine.

> Many students at the Louisiana School for the Deaf (LSD) come from the Acadian parishes resulting in a high incidence of Usher syndrome at the school. . . . Fifteen to twenty percent of children on the Louisiana deaf-blind census for children birth through age 21 are known to have Usher syndrome [Type 1] as compared to an average of 3 percent for all other states in the nation. (Melancon, 2000, p. 1)

Ironically, events of the early 21st century may serve to reverse some of the social forces that led to a high incidence of Usher syndrome among Acadians. It's too early to tell, but Hurricane Katrina and the British Petroleum oil spill have resulted in a population displacement in the Louisiana Gulf Coast. It's possible that such dispersion will result in a decrease in intermarriage, which in turn would result in fewer offspring with Usher syndrome.

Psychological and Behavioral Characteristics

People who are deaf-blind can have significant problems in at least three areas: (1) accessing information, (2) communicating, and (3) navigating the environment (Aitken, 2000).

PROBLEMS ACCESSING INFORMATION For people who are deaf-blind, access to the usual sources of information (e.g., Internet, television, newspapers) is more difficult than for those who are sighted. And because communication depends largely on the availability of information, restricted access to information can have a negative impact on the ability to communicate:

> The consequence of not being able to access information is that life experiences are reduced. Lack of everyday ordinary experiences—how to make a sandwich, knowing that water comes from a tap—makes it more difficult for the person who is deaf-blind to build up a store of world knowledge. Without that store of world knowledge what is there to communicate about? (Aitken, 2000, p. 3)

PROBLEMS COMMUNICATING Most authorities agree that the biggest obstacle faced by people with deaf-blindness is communication (Aitken, 2000; Miles, 1998). Without a strong commitment by teachers and other professionals and parents to providing a variety of opportunities for communication, the child who is deaf-blind can easily become socially isolated. The pattern for this isolation can begin at birth. The baby

> may not be able to make and sustain eye contact or to respond to a soothing voice. His mother's face may be invisible or only a blur and her speech only a low sound which he cannot pick out from the background of other noises. The deafblind baby may register little of the world around him, or may find it a frightening place full of half-registered shapes and sounds. He will not hold his mother's attention with a ready gaze and will not be able to play the games of sight, sound and movement which other babies enjoy. If his vision and hearing are so seriously damaged that he cannot use visual or auditory cues to warn him that someone is coming to pick him up, or that a particular activity is about to happen, contact with other people may even become threatening. (Pease, 2000, p. 38)

Once this pattern of isolation has been established, it's difficult to reverse. Therefore, it's critical that professionals and parents work together to provide an environment that's as supportive and rich in communication opportunities as possible. One such way of helping enrich communication opportunities is through the judicious use of social networking sites such as Facebook (Fagbemi, 2009). Such networking tools allow people with deaf-blindess to find and interact with those other rare individuals with deaf-blindness as well as with the broader population.

No better example of the importance of providing a language-rich environment exists than the classic case of Helen Keller (1880–1968) and her teacher Annie Sullivan (1866–1936). Popularized by the classic movie *The Miracle Worker* (Green & Penn, 1962), Helen Keller's accomplishments are now familiar to most of us. Having lost her sight and hearing at the age of 19 months, Keller went on to extraordinary achievements, including graduating cum laude from Radcliffe College in 1904; publishing essays and books (including the much acclaimed *The Story of My Life*, 1905, written while she was in college and available in over 50 languages); touring the country lecturing on blindness; being a spokesperson for women's right to vote; and receiving the Presidential Medal of Freedom, the nation's highest civilian award.

Helen Keller is testimony to the power of the human spirit to overcome overwhelming odds. However, just as important, she is testimony to the power of intensive and extensive special education instruction. As remarkable as she was, it's doubtful that Keller would have conquered her condition without the prolonged instruction from Annie Sullivan, who devoted nearly 50 years to being Keller's teacher and constant companion. Sullivan, herself born blind, had had some of her sight restored through several operations. She

INTERNETRESOURCES

The Perkins School for the Blind's Perkins Museum maintains a lot of historical information on blindness and deaf-blindness. For information on Laura Bridgman and Anne Sullivan, visit: http://perkins.pvt.k12 .ma.us/museum/section .php?id=213
For information on Helen Keller, visit: http://perkins.pvt .k12.ma.us/museum/section .php?id=218
The American Foundation for the Blind also maintains material on Helen Keller, including many of her letters and papers: www.afb.org/ section.asp?sectionid =1

arrived at the home of the Kellers in 1887 to meet a not yet 7-year-old Helen, who had some rudiments of communication but who was prone to severe tantrums. Through persistence and intensive instruction, Sullivan was able to set Helen's mind free to learn language and higher concepts.

Sullivan and Keller are not the only famous teacher–student team to demonstrate the importance of intensive instruction of the deaf-blind. See the accompanying Personal Perspectives feature for the story of Laura Bridgman and Samuel Gridley Howe.

PROBLEMS NAVIGATING THE ENVIRONMENT   As we discussed in Chapter 12, people who are blind or who have low vision can have significant difficulties with mobility. For people who are deaf-blind, these problems are often even more pronounced. Individuals who are blind and hearing can pick up auditory cues that help them in navigation. For example, being able to hear approaching traffic can be very helpful when crossing an intersection, and being able to hear such things as buses, trains, and construction noises, can help a person who is blind to identify her location. However, people who are both deaf and blind are restricted in their ability to make use of auditory signals for navigating the environment.

Educational Considerations

The major educational needs of infants and preschoolers, as well as of older students, who are deaf-blind fall generally under the categories of communication and orientation and mobility. Both abilities, but especially communication, are required for social interaction. If these skills are taught effectively, then the social interaction of deaf-blind individuals is enhanced considerably (Janssen, Riksen-Walraven, & van Dijk, 2004).

In addressing needs for communication and orientation and mobility, practitioners and parents should keep in mind at least two important principles: direct teaching and structured and predictable routines.

THE IMPORTANCE OF DIRECT TEACHING   Many students with disabilities (e.g., intellectual disability, learning disabilities, blindness, deafness) are more reliant than those without disabilities on having teachers teach them directly. Whereas students without disabilities can learn a great deal incidentally (e.g., from seeing or hearing things that happen around them), students with disabilities are often in greater need of having material taught to them directly (see Kauffman, 2002; Kauffman & Hallahan, 2005). Because of their restricted sensory input, this need for direct teaching of information is even more pronounced for students who are deaf-blind than it is for children with other disabilities.

THE IMPORTANCE OF STRUCTURED AND PREDICTABLE ROUTINES   To create a successful environment for learning, it's also critical that teachers and other professionals and parents provide a sense of security for students who are deaf-blind. One of the best ways to create this sense of security is through the use of predictable, structured routines (Chen, Alsop, & Minor, 2000; Miles, 1998; Smith, Smith, & Blake, 2010), discussed in detail in the Responsive Instruction feature on page 382.

COMMUNICATION   The hands play a critical role in communication for most students who are deaf-blind. In effect, the hands become the "voice, or the primary means of expression" (Miles, 1999, p. 1). Professionals use a number of modes of communication that involve touch with people who are deaf-blind. **Braille** is the most obvious one. Some other common tactile learning strategies are **hand-over-hand guidance**, **hand-under-hand guidance**, **adapted signs**, and **touch cues** (Chen, Downing, & Rodriguez-Gil, 2000/2001).

Hand-Over-Hand Guidance   Hand-over-hand guidance involves the adult placing his or her hand(s) over the child's hand(s) while exploring an object or signing. Although this technique may be necessary, especially for children who have physical disabilities that interfere with movement of their hands, it does have some disadvantages (Chen et al., 2000/2001; Miles, 1999). Some children are resistant to this technique, apparently because they don't like the feeling of loss of control over their hands. Furthermore, some children can become too passive, waiting for someone else's hands to be placed over theirs rather than reaching out on their own.

Personal PERSPECTIVES
Laura Bridgman and Her Teacher, Samuel Gridley Howe

Although most people are familiar with the story of Helen Keller, Laura Bridgman (1829–1889) was actually the first documented case of a deaf-blind person to learn language. Laura was struck at the age of 2 with scarlet fever and left deaf and blind.

Samuel Gridley Howe (1801–1876) was one of the 19th century's most daring social activists, reforming schools, prisons, and mental institutions as well as being a member of the "Secret Six," who lent financial support to John Brown's campaign to end slavery in the United States with his ill-fated launching of the raid at Harper's Ferry in 1859. Howe received his medical degree from Harvard University in 1824. After serving a 7-year stint as a surgeon in the Greek civil conflict, he returned to Boston. In 1832, he was named head of the Perkins Institution and Massachusetts School for the Blind (now named the Perkins School for the Blind).

After reading a newspaper account of Laura, Howe visited her parents and convinced them to send the 8-year-old to Perkins in 1837. There, he and his teachers worked painstakingly with Laura for several years. In addition to the goals of teaching her to communicate, Howe viewed Bridgman as a philosophical and religious experiment. By showing that she could learn to communicate, he was debunking the materialists, who held that sensory input was necessary in order to form concepts: "As Laura reached out to the world around her, Howe thrilled to witness the triumph of mind over matter" (Freeberg, 2001, p. 41). With respect to religion, Howe hoped to show that Laura possessed an innate moral consciousness that was intact despite her sensory losses.

Howe held open houses for the public to see the accomplishments of the students at Perkins. Laura soon became the major attraction, drawing hundreds of onlookers. One of the early visitors was Charles Dickens, whose account

Laura Bridgman with Samuel Gridley Howe.

of his meeting with Laura, which he described in *American Notes*, further publicized the accomplishments of Howe's work with her.

Howe eventually became discouraged because Laura did not progress as far as he had hoped. Although she was able to communicate well, her personality, characterized by immaturity and occasional fits of rage, kept her from becoming the ideal case to prove his philosophical and theological theories.

Although her achievements were not as spectacular as Keller's, Bridgman's accomplishments were extraordinary for the time, a time when many authorities believed that to be deaf-blind was to be mentally retarded. Furthermore, had it not been for Bridgman, Keller might never have received the instruction that unlocked her intellect. Helen's parents were alerted to the potential of teaching their own daughter after reading about Bridgman's accomplishments. Furthermore, Helen's teacher, Annie Sullivan, herself a former student at Perkins, consulted Howe's reports on Laura before embarking on her journey to tutor Helen.

Perhaps most important, Laura Bridgman's dramatic story drew the public's attention to the wider reform movement that was transforming the lives of many disabled people in nineteenth century America. Howe and other educators invented teaching tools, experimented with curriculum, and built new institutions that helped thousands of people with sensory handicaps to overcome the physical barriers that had always deprived them of an education. . . . Chipping away at centuries of accumulated prejudice and misunderstanding, these students and their teachers began to dismantle one of the greatest barriers faced by the blind and the deaf, the deep-rooted misconception that people with sensory handicaps are unreachable and somehow less than fully human. In the crucial early years of this important reform movement, no person did more to challenge those assumptions and inspire new respect for the disabled than Laura Bridgman. (Freeberg, 2001, pp. 220–221)

RESPONSIVE *INSTRUCTION*
MEETING THE NEEDS OF STUDENTS WITH LOW-INCIDENCE, MULTIPLE, AND SEVERE DISABILITIES

The Importance of Establishing Predictable, Structured Routines

WHAT THE RESEARCH SAYS

Researchers and practitioners from Project PLAI* (Promoting Learning Through Active Interaction) have developed several modules for working with infants who have multiple disabilities and their families (Chen, Alsop, & Minor, 2000; Klein, Chen, & Haney, 2000). One of the modules focuses on establishing predictable routines. Specifically, for infants who are deaf-blind, they have recommended the following objectives:

- Create a predictable routine by identifying at least five daily activities that can be scheduled in the same sequence each day.
- Identify predictable sequences within specific activities (i.e., "subroutines").
- Identify and use specific auditory, visual, tactile, olfactory, and kinesthetic cues to help the infant anticipate familiar activities. (Chen et al., 2000, p. 6)

The following describes how they implemented these objectives with 14-month-old Michael, his mother, Cecelia, and older sister, Kate. Michael was born prematurely and only weighed 1 pound, 8 ounces at birth. He was diagnosed with severe ROP (retinopathy of prematurity), cerebral palsy, and a hearing loss of undetermined severity.

> An early interventionist helped Cecelia realize that Michael could better understand what was going on around him if his daily events were more predictable. In addition to the early morning and evening routines, Cecelia decided to try to increase the predictability of Michael's routines in several ways. After he finished his morning bottle, he would always get a bath. After the bath, Cecelia would put lotion on him and give him a shoulder and back massage. At bedtime, she would give him his bottle and then Kate would rock him while watching TV. Cecelia also realized that she and Michael had developed "subroutines." For example, after removing Michael's diaper and cleaning him, she would blow on his tummy and say, "Okay, all dry. All dry." Then she would sprinkle powder and put a new diaper on him, say "All done," and give him a kiss while picking him up.
>
> Other predictable routines and subroutines followed. Before going into Michael's room, Cecelia would always announce loudly, "Here comes Mommy." She would touch his shoulders before picking him up. Before putting him in the bath, she would put his foot in the water a couple of times, which helped him to stop screaming when he was placed in the tub. Before Cecelia gave Michael his back massage, she would rub some lotion on her fingers and let him smell it. (Chen et al., 2000, pp. 6–7)

APPLYING THE RESEARCH TO TEACHING

Although the preceding example pertains to infants, predictable, structured routines are no less important for school-age children who have multiple disabilities, including deaf-blindness. School routines are particularly important for students who are deaf-blind because the only way for these children to learn is by doing. The students will be unable to learn through visually observing or hearing stimuli that will assist them in making sense of the world. Therefore, they will depend on the creation of a safe learning environment and trust with the primary instructor (Moss & Hagood, 1995). School routines that would benefit students who are deaf-blind follow:

- *Turn-taking routines.* By keeping interactions balanced ("me, then you"), students will consistently know when to respond and be more active in their learning.
- *Travel or movement routines.* If students do not feel comfortable moving around the classroom or school, they may choose to not move. Lack of mobility decreases opportunities for exploration, social interaction, and independence.
- *Communication routines.* Students who are deaf-blind will rely on tactile communication. Students will be unable to make connections among input without direct interaction with others. Therefore, it is important to establish routines for communication as these students move from objects to gestures for communication.

• By Kristin L. Sayeski

*Project PLAI was a 4-year collaborative project involving California State University-Northridge, SKI-HI Institute at Utah State University, and several early intervention programs, funded by the Office of Special Education Programs, U.S. Department of Education.

■ ■ ■ ■ ■ ■ ■ ■

Hand-Under-Hand Guidance   Hand-under-hand guidance is often recommended as an alternative to hand-over-hand guidance. This technique involves the adult gently slipping her hand(s) underneath part of the child's hand(s) while the child is exploring an object. It becomes the tactile equivalent to pointing (Miles, 1999). One of the main advantages of hand-under-hand guidance is that it is noncontrolling.

Adapted Signs   Signs used by the Deaf community, such as American Sign Language and signed English, are visually based, which makes them difficult or impossible to use by people who are deaf-blind, depending on the severity of their visual impairment. A variety of tactual versions of signing therefore have been created (Chen et al., 2000/2001). For example, for the reception of signs, the person who is deaf-blind can place his hands on the hands of the signer; for the expression of signs, the teacher or parent can hold the hands of the person who is deaf-blind and guide him to produce signs.

Touch Cues   Touch cues are tactual signals that can convey a number of messages depending on the situation and context. It is important that the touch cues be consistent; a child will not be able to decipher the meaning of a touch cue if different people use it for a variety of messages. For example, patting or tapping a child on the shoulder may express:

- positive feedback ("Great job")
- a request or directive ("Sit down")
- information ("Your turn")
- comfort or reassurance ("Don't cry, you're OK")

Touch cues should be used selectively, conservatively, and consistently so that the child can develop an understanding of what they represent (Chen et al., 2000/2001, p. 3).

ORIENTATION AND MOBILITY   For people who have both visual impairment and hearing impairment, the need for **orientation and mobility (O & M)** training is even more important than for those who are only blind because they are at even greater risk of being unable to navigate their environment.

O & M training for people who have both visual and hearing impairment differs in at least two ways from O & M training for those with only visual impairment. First, adaptations are needed to communicate with people with deaf-blindness (Gense & Gense, 2004). The O & M instructor might need to use adaptations such as an interpreter, adapted signs, and/or touch cues to communicate with the student who is deaf-blind.

Second, it's sometimes necessary to alert the public that a traveler is deaf-blind. Even the best travelers with deaf-blindness occasionally become temporarily disoriented and need assistance. People with visual impairment who can hear can ask for assistance relatively easily. However, people who have both hearing and visual impairment may have a more difficult time communicating their needs to the public, and it won't always be obvious to the public that the person has both a visual and hearing impairment. A long cane can signal vision loss, but it does not indicate hearing impairment. Therefore, some professionals advocate the use of assistance cards. **Assistance cards** are usually relatively small (e.g., 3″×6″) and can be held up by the person who is deaf-blind at a busy or unfamiliar intersection. The words on the card indicate that the person is asking for assistance—for example, "Please help me to CROSS STREET. I am both DEAF and VISUALLY IMPAIRED, so TAP ME if you can help. Thank you" (Franklin & Bourquin, 2000, p. 175).

SPECIAL CONSIDERATIONS FOR STUDENTS WITH USHER SYNDROME   Students with Usher syndrome present some special educational challenges because most of them have progressive visual impairment. They might start out having relatively good vision, but their vision inevitably declines to the point at which they are legally, if not totally, blind. The effects of retinitis pigmentosa, which accompanies Usher syndrome, can sometimes be erratic and change rapidly, thus catching the student and his or her family off guard (Miner & Cioffi, 1999). Even when the deterioration occurs slowly over the course of several years, parents and teachers of children with Usher syndrome might neglect the importance of preparing the child for the fact that he will one day have substantial visual impairment. Sometimes, they fear that the early introduction of braille and O & M training will stigmatize the child and damage his self-concept. However, most authorities now agree that braille and O & M training should not wait until the student can no longer function as a seeing individual.

EDUCATIONAL CONSIDERATIONS FOR MANY STUDENTS WITH LOW-INCIDENCE, MULTIPLE, AND SEVERE DISABILITIES

Some of the devices and methods that we describe here might apply to any of the disabilities we discuss in this chapter. Communication, behavior management, early intervention, transition, employment, family involvement, and normalization are all frequent concerns with any of these disabilities.

Augmentative or Alternative Communication

For some individuals with severe and multiple disabilities, oral language is out of the question; they have physical or cognitive disabilities, usually as a result of neurological damage, that preclude their learning to communicate through normal speech. Educators and professionals must design a system of **augmentative or alternative communication (AAC)** for them.

AAC includes any manual or electronic means by which such a person expresses wants and needs, shares information, engages in social closeness, or manages social etiquette (Beukelman, Yorkston, & Reichle, 2000; Gerenser & Forman, 2007; Heller & Bigge, 2010). Students for whom AAC must be designed range in intelligence from highly gifted to profoundly intellectually disabled, but they all have one characteristic in common: the inability to communicate effectively through speech because of a physical impairment. Some of these individuals cannot make any speech sounds at all; others need a system to augment their speech when they cannot make themselves understood because of environmental noise, difficulty in producing certain words or sounds, or unfamiliarity with the person with whom they want to communicate.

Manual signs or gestures are useful for some individuals. But many individuals with severe physical limitations cannot use their hands to communicate through the usual sign language; they must use another means of communication, usually involving special equipment. Dr. Nikki Kissane, now a surgeon, developed a simplified sign language system while a University of Virginia undergraduate student. Children and adults with limited speech capabilities can learn and use her simplified signs more easily than traditional signs (see the accompanying Focus on Concepts).

The problems to be solved in helping individuals communicate in ways other than signing include selecting a vocabulary and giving them an effective, efficient means of indicating elements in their vocabularies. Although the basic ideas behind AAC are quite simple, selecting the best vocabulary and devising an efficient means of communication for many individuals with severe disabilities are extraordinarily challenging. As one AAC user put it, "The AAC evaluation should be done with the AAC user involved in the process from step one. It is the augmented speaker who will be using the device every day, both personally and professionally, not the AAC specialist" (Cardona, 2000, p. 237).

A variety of approaches to AAC have been developed, some involving relatively simple or so-called low-technology solutions and some requiring complex or high-technology solutions. Many different direct-selection and scanning methods have been devised for AAC, depending on individual capabilities. The system that is used may involve pointing with the hand or a head-stick, eye movements, or operation of a microswitch by foot, tongue, or head movement or breath control. Sometimes, the individual can use a typewriter or computer terminal that is fitted with a key guard so that keys are not likely to be pressed accidentally or use an alternative means for selecting keystrokes. See the Success Stories feature on pages 386–387 about David Womack, a teenager who uses an alternative-access keyboard. Other students use communication boards, which offer an array of pictures, words, or other symbols and can be operated with either a direct-selection or scanning strategy. The content and arrangement of the board will vary, depending on the person's capabilities, preferences, and communication needs.

Today, researchers are finding increasingly innovative and creative technological solutions to the problem of nonvocal communication. At the same time, they are recognizing

FOCUS ON Concepts

SIMPLIFIED SIGN LANGUAGE

Figuring out how to communicate effectively with simple gestures has not been an easy task for U. Va. student Nikki Kissane. But thanks to her research efforts, mute children and adults or those with limited speech capabilities have a new simplified communication system that is easier to learn, produce, and understand than existing sign languages. . . .

After witnessing her grandfather suffer a series of strokes and seeing the physiological and emotional difficulties he experienced, Kissane approached psychology professor John Bonvillian to see if she could participate in his ongoing research on sign-language communication for nonspeaking but hearing individuals. . . .

Kissane studied more than 20 sign language dictionaries to identify signs that are "iconic," those clearly resembling the object or action they represent, or "transparent," those that easily convey their meaning. To illustrate, cradling one's arms while gently rocking back and forth would be a transparent sign for "baby," whereas gesturing throwing a ball would be an iconic gesture for "throw."

From her research, Kissane identified about 900 signs for such everyday words as "comb," "book" and "reach" that have the potential of being easily understood and communicated through simple hand and arm gestures. She also created numerous new signs to supplement those she found in her search.

To determine if such signs could be incorporated into a simplified system, she had volunteer U. Va. students view different groups of signs to see which ones they could remember and repeat easily. All signs recalled perfectly by at least 70 percent of the participants were added to a lexicon.

Kissane also observed some classes led by her mother, who teaches elementary school art to children, including several with autism. She gained pointers from her mother on how to draw the gestures.

"I observed a few of the classes to see where autistic children struggle in motor and cognitive skills," Kissane said.

Eye

Celebrate

Sleep

Source: Wooten, I. L. (2001, May 18). Student develops new sign language system. *Inside UVA, 31*(18), 12. Reprinted with permission. Photos from *The Daily Progress,* Charlottesville, VA. Reprinted with permission.

the importance of making decisions that are highly individualized and evidence-based. No one is well served by AAC that is not highly reliable from a scientific point of view. Researchers are attempting to make it possible for young AAC users to talk about the same kinds of things that other youngsters do. Other efforts are directed at training AAC users to tell those with whom they communicate how to interact with them more effectively—that is, to train AAC users in pragmatics. The Personal Perspectives box on page 388, "Life with Cerebral Palsy," was written by Chris Featherly when he was an 18-year-old high school student. His story and others written by AAC users (Oken-Fried & Bersani, 2000) illustrate the

DAVID GAINS INDEPENDENCE AND ACADEMIC ACHIEVEMENT THROUGH ASSISTIVE TECHNOLOGY AND PROFESSIONAL COLLABORATION

Mrs. Womack, David's mother: "When some teachers hear that ventilator, their tendency is to pamper the child, but I want him treated like a student."

Sixteen-year-old David Womack attends an academic day school for students with severe physical disabilities.

These are the keys to his success:

★ Intensive collaboration

★ Relentless emphasis on technology

★ Specific goals for independence and academic achievement

ON THE SECOND DAY OF SECOND GRADE, 7-YEAR-OLD DAVID WOMACK was hit by a car as he stepped off the school bus. The accident injured his spinal cord, leaving him with no movement below his neck and with an inability to breathe on his own. After 2 years of rehabilitation, David was ready to leave the hospital and reenter school. His parents and other members of the IEP team made the decision to enroll 9-year-old David in a special day school for students with intense medical and physical needs. David's achievements are the result of intensive, relentless, and specific special education.

★ **Intensive Collaboration.** David's specialized day school is staffed with medical and therapeutic personnel and with teachers who are dually certified as special and general educators. David was the first student dependent on a ventilator to attend the school. He entered his third-grade classroom in a large electronic sip-and-puff wheelchair that he propelled by blowing air through a strawlike mouthpiece. His life-support system, called "the vent," was mounted on the back of his chair and made a loud rhythmic sound. Never more than several feet away was a private-duty nurse who monitored him at all times. "It was so scary," recalls Mrs. Womack. "I could tell everybody was nervous."

The school's task included helping the Womack family adjust to a different life and stimulating David to discover his new potential. Even though the staff was experienced in dealing with difficult physical issues, David presented a challenge, and the presence of the ventilator and the private nurse emphasized his fragility. Says occu-

value of AAC and issues involved in its use. The fact that Chris Featherly has cerebral palsy, a congenital neurological condition that we discuss in Chapter 14, is beside the point here. The important thing is that some people have physical limitations that preclude their efficient use of oral language and need an augmented or alternative means of communicating.

Users of AAC encounter three particular challenges that are not faced by natural communicators:

1. AAC is often much slower than natural communication—perhaps 1/20th the typical rate of speech. This can result in great frustration for both AAC users and natural communicators.

2. Users of AAC who are not literate must rely on a vocabulary and symbols that are selected by others. If the vocabulary and symbols, as well as other features of the system, are not well chosen, AAC will be quite limited in the learning and personal relationships it allows.

3. AAC must be constructed to be useful in a variety of social contexts, allow accurate and efficient communication without undue fatigue, and support the individual's learning of language and academic skills.

Progress in the field of AAC requires that all of these challenges be addressed simultaneously. AAC is increasingly focused on literacy and the right to use print, including writing, for communication. In many ways the emphasis on basic literacy skills parallels the emphasis on literacy for all students, regardless of disabilities (Yoder, 2001).

pational therapist Ginette Howard, "We had to raise everybody's expectations by treating David like a student instead of a patient!"

The school's technology team supported David's classroom learning. Howard and computer teacher Maryann Cicchillo combined their knowledge of instructional software and sophisticated technologies to provide David with the tools to read, write, and compute. Classroom teachers followed their lead, and so did his nurse, Gail Nolan, who was committed to his academic and social growth. David's progress was built slowly but steadily on a foundation of trust.

★ Relentless Emphasis on Technology. David was frightened to leave the hospital, so the first task was securing his ventilator equipment for classroom use. "We made sure there was a plastic casing over the dials because he was afraid someone might play with the settings," Howard recalls. The second year, he became more confident and more willing to try new technologies. David progressed from being withdrawn and fearful to trusting and to developing an interest in computer applications. Providing him with computer access became the challenge.

"David has chin supports to keep his head erect, and he can move his mouth," says Howard. She and Cicchillo selected a small alternative-access keyboard that was worked by an electronic wand. With much effort, David would clench a mouthstick in his teeth and gently tap the attached wand on the miniature impulse-sensitive keyboard. Cicchillo ensured that appropriate software was available to David's teachers through the school's network.

Gradually, David became accustomed to using the mouthstick and to the expectation that he was independently responsible for his school work.

★ Specific Goals for Independence and Academic Achievement. David's technology sessions have increased his independence as a student. He uses a word-prediction and abbreviation/expansion program to reduce the number of keystrokes and to increase his speed in writing assignments. He is eager to try new technologies that challenge his accuracy and increase his speed. "I can't tell you how many times we've explored technology to support homework assignments, to take tests, or complete a paper," says Cicchillo.

"Science is my favorite subject," says David, a quiet young man who speaks in a soft, breathy voice. Dorothy Vann's science lab is fully accessible, with adjustable tables and low sinks. The lab is also equipped with instructional technology that David needs to fully participate. In biology, he views slides through a stereo microscope that utilizes a small attached camera to project video images. "I knew David was capable of doing more than he initially showed us," says Vann.

Working with David has been an evolving process for each of the collaborators. In reflecting on their work with David, Howard and Cicchillo identify a breaking-in period when teachers and the child who is newly ventilator-dependent have to overcome their fears. According to Dorothy Vann, "It takes a while for a child to accept goals for achievement and to believe in his or her own success."

• By Jean B. Crockett

The remarkable increase in the power and availability of microcomputers is radically changing the ability to provide AAC and make sure that the user's words are communicated. New applications of microcomputers may lead to breakthroughs that will allow people with severe disabilities to communicate more effectively, even if they have extremely limited muscle control. Furthermore, existing microcomputer software suggests ways of encouraging children to use their existing language skills.

Much information about AAC is now available on various Websites. The International Society for Augmentative and Alternative Communication (ISAAC) publishes the professional journal *Augmentative and Alternative Communication* and maintains a Website. Parents need to be aware of the availability of AAC and demand equipment and training that are effective for their child.

Behavior Problems

Some individuals who have certain severe or multiple disabilities engage in problematic behaviors such as self-stimulation, self-injury, tantrums, aggression toward others, or some combination of these. We caution that not all people with low incidence, severe, or multiple disabilities exhibit the behavior problems we discuss here. Many people who are deaf-blind and many who have TBI, autism, or other severe or multiple disabilities do not engage in these behaviors. Nevertheless, most of the people who do exhibit these problems to a significant extent have severe and multiple disabilities. Moreover, behaviors of the type that

Personal PERSPECTIVES
Life with Cerebral Palsy: Chris Featherly

My name is Christopher Glen Featherly, and I'm going to try to give you a little overview of life with cerebral palsy as I know it.

I'm 18 years old and was born in Fort Worth, Texas. I'm currently attending Bremen High School in Midlothian, Illinois. . . .

When I came from Texas to live with my grandparents at the age of 5, I only had five generic signs for communication. My grandmom wouldn't put up with that, and so she went to the library for a sign language book. Now she learned that there really was something upstairs! The school system wanted me to use a 48-page, three-ring binder of pictures for my communication. Can you see me, using my right hand, to flip between 48 pages to talk to someone? I don't think so! My grandmom took me to Siegel Institute in downtown Chicago for a speech evaluation. They said, "This kid needs a TouchTalker [an AAC device; see www.prentrom.com for descriptions of other devices]. . . ." Well, guess what! The school speech clinician said, "No. He doesn't have language, and if he has it [Touch Talker] he won't use his own voice to talk." So guess what grandmom did? She took me to Homewood to see another speech therapist. What do you think she said? You got it! She said, "TouchTalker." So back to school, and again the answer was, "No." Grandmom then told them she was going to take me to Shriners. If they said TouchTalker, that would be the mode of communication I would have. Well, what do you think they said? Yup! It was TouchTalker. Now, we knew how school felt about it, which meant it was in our ball park. It was time to save money and purchase it so that I could get stuff out of my head and stuff into it. By now, do you sorta have an idea what kind of grandmom I have?

[Chris also describes software and hardware upgrades that he needed as he progressed, and his use of online resources.]

Source: From Featherly, C. (2000). Life with cerebral palsy. In M. Oken-Fried & H. A. Bersani (Eds.), *Speaking up and spelling it out: Personal essays on augmentative and alternative communication* (pp. 189–193). Baltimore: Paul H. Brookes. Reprinted with permission.

INTERNET RESOURCES

For management of behavior problems, see www.pbis.org

we discuss here add a level of complexity and seriousness to any disability. Thus, finding solutions to these behavior problems is critical to treating the individual with respect and helping the person to participate in typical school and community activities (see Best et al., 2010; Heller et al., 2009).

Much controversy exists regarding the behavior problems of people with severe disabilities. Some educators and professionals assume that such problems simply will not occur if appropriate programs of instruction are provided. Others suggest that **functional behavioral assessment (FBA)**, **positive behavioral support (PBS)**, and nonaversive treatments (i.e., treatments in which punishment has no place) will be sufficient in all cases. However, others claim that positive behavioral supports and nonaversive treatments are insufficient in some cases to overcome behavior problems (e.g., Cullen & Mudford, 2005; Mulick & Butter, 2005; Newsom & Kroeger, 2005).

SELF-STIMULATION   **Self-stimulation** can be defined as any repetitive, stereotyped behavior that seems to have no immediately apparent purpose other than providing sensory stimulation. Self-stimulation (a form of stereotyped movement) may take a wide variety of forms, such as swishing saliva, twirling objects, hand-flapping, fixed staring, and the like. Repetitive, stereotyped behavior (sometimes called ***stereotypy***) may have multiple causes, including social consequences, in addition to sensory stimulation (Bodfish, 2007).

Nearly everyone sometimes engages in some form of self-stimulation, such as lip-biting, hair-stroking, and nail-biting, but not at the high rate that characterizes a disability. Nondisabled infants engage in self-stimulation, and so do nondisabled adults, particularly when they are tired or bored. Only the high rate, lack of subtlety, and social inappropriateness of such self-stimulation differentiate it from the norm.

Self-stimulation becomes problematic when it occurs at such a high rate that it interferes with learning or social acceptability or when it occurs with such intensity that it does injury. Some individuals with autism or other pervasive developmental disabilities engage in self-stimulation to the exclusion of academic and social learning. In most of these cases, it appears that only intrusive, directive intervention will be successful in helping the individual learn academic and social skills (Kauffman & Landrum, 2009).

SELF-INJURY   **Self-injurious behavior (SIB)** is repeated physical self-abuse, such as biting, scratching, or poking oneself, head-banging, and so on. Unchecked, SIB often results in self-mutilation. Self-stimulation can be so frequent and intense that it becomes SIB. Hand-mouthing is self-stimulation of the kind that all infants do; even some nondisabled adults can be seen occasionally mouthing their hands. However, hand-mouthing becomes self-injurious for some people with severe developmental disabilities, resulting in serious skin lesions.

TANTRUMS   Severe tantrums can include a variety of behaviors, including self-injury, screaming, crying, throwing or destroying objects, and aggression toward others. Sometimes, the event that sets off a tantrum is unknown, at least to the casual observer. Often, however, a tantrum is precipitated by a request or demand that the individual do something (perhaps a self-care task or some academic work), and the consequence of the tantrum is that the demand is withdrawn, thus reinforcing the tantrum behavior.

Tantrums impose a handicap on the individual who uses them to avoid learning or doing important things. They stymie socialization, as most people want to avoid interacting with someone who is likely to have a tantrum. Teachers and others who work most successfully with individuals who have tantrums do not withdraw reasonable demands for performance. What they do is modify their demand or circumstances in some way or alternate their demands for performance in ways that are less likely to set off a tantrum.

AGGRESSION TOWARD OTHERS   Not all aggression toward others is associated with tantrums. Some individuals with severe or multiple disabilities engage in calculated physical attacks that threaten or injure others (Gardner, 2007). Sometimes these attacks come without warning or only after subtle indications of imminent assault that only someone who knows the individual well is likely to perceive.

LACK OF DAILY LIVING SKILLS   Lack of daily living skills refers to the absence or significant impairment of the ability to take care of one's basic needs, such as dressing, feeding, or toileting. Many people with severe and multiple disabilities must be taught the adaptive behavior that is expected of older children and adults. These adaptive behaviors include a wide variety of tasks involving clothing selection and dressing, food preparation and eating, grooming, socializing, using money, using public transportation, playing games or other recreation, and so on (Snell & Brown, 2006).

FUNCTIONAL BEHAVIORAL ASSESSMENT AND POSITIVE BEHAVIORAL INTERVENTION AND SUPPORT   Problem behaviors are often related to a brain disorder or brain injury, even if the disorder is not understood. An example is severe autism, which often includes self-stimulation, self-injury, tantrums, or all of these. However, professionals and educators are increasing emphasis on analyzing and changing the environments in which problem behavior is exhibited; that is, focusing on the immediate and alterable influences on behavior rather than on immutable or historical reasons for behavior (Best et al., 2010; Bodfish, 2007; Snell & Brown, 2006).

In earlier chapters, we introduced the ideas of **functional behavioral assessment (FBA)** and **positive behavioral intervention and support (PBIS)**, primarily as they apply to students with less severe disabilities (see Chapters 7 to 9). However, these procedures may be particularly important for students with severe and multiple disabilities. FBA entails finding out why or under what circumstances problem behavior is exhibited, and PBIS involves creating an environment that supports appropriate behavior.

FBA often reveals how a student uses self-stimulation, SIB, tantrums, or aggression against others. A student might behave inappropriately to escape or avoid unpleasant or nonpreferred activities or tasks (see Kauffman & Landrum, 2009). In many instances, researchers and practitioners find that the student has no other effective and efficient means of communication. The task, therefore, is to figure out how the student is using unacceptable communication and teach her a more effective, efficient, and acceptable means of letting others know what she wants or is feeling. FBA has led to the discovery that sometimes

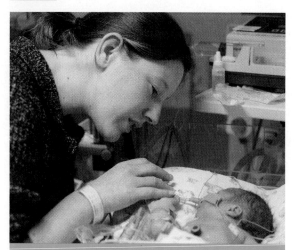

Authorities agree that parents should be encouraged to spend as much time as possible with the infants being cared for in neonatal intensive care units (NICUs).

people with severe and multiple disabilities use inappropriate behavior to communicate a variety of their wants or needs (e.g., "Pay attention to me," "Let me out of here," "There's nothing to do," "There's too much to do," or "I don't want to do that now").

PBIS is the vehicle for teaching students how to behave more appropriately, making appropriate behavior "work" for their communication. In the case of students with severe and multiple disabilities, making PBIS a part of managing behavior across school, home, neighborhood, and community is particularly important. The accompanying Responsive Instruction box provides a more detailed discussion of PBIS for students with multiple or severe disabilities.

Early Intervention

Most children with multiple and severe disabilities are identified at birth or soon thereafter because their disabilities are very noticeable to parents, physicians, and/or nurses. Some newborns with severe and multiple disabilities require extensive medical treatment and therefore are immediately placed in **neonatal intensive care units (NICUs)**. NICUs are the equivalent of intensive care units (ICUs) for older children and adults, providing around-the-clock monitoring of bodily functions. The NICU staff consists of several specialists, often including specially trained nurses, physicians, respiratory care practitioners, occupational therapists, and social workers. Because NICUs are expensive to staff and administer, not all hospitals have them; therefore, newborns are sometimes transported from one hospital to another that has an NICU. Even though the infant is under constant medical supervision, most authorities agree that parents should be allowed to spend as much time as possible with their newborns to promote parent–infant bonding. Some NICUs allow parents to "room in" with their babies.

Other children with severe and multiple disabilities might seem typical at birth but are recognized as having pervasive developmental disabilities within the first couple of years of their lives. In the case of very serious TBI, an individual might actually be developing normally until the event that causes severe brain damage. Early intervention therefore should be seen as having two meanings: (1) early in the child's life and (2) as soon as possible after the disability is detected.

The Division for Early Childhood (DEC) of the Council for Exceptional Children (CEC) recommends practices based on six criteria that are considered essential to early intervention programs in special education: (1) research- or value-based practices, (2) family-centered practices, (3) a multicultural perspective, (4) cross-disciplinary collaboration, (5) developmentally and chronologically age-appropriate practices, and (6) adherence to the principle of normalization (see Dunst, 2011; Noonan & McCormick, 2006).

RESEARCH- OR VALUE-BASED PRACTICES   Early intervention programs should be based as much as possible on techniques that research has shown to be effective (Dunst, 2011; Morris & Mather, 2008). Unfortunately, it is not always possible to conduct all the necessary research before an approach or technique is adopted. The CEC task force recommends that when research has not provided definitive evidence of an approach's effectiveness, the approach should be based on values held by the early childhood special education community. Some of these value-based practices are providing individualized practices for each child and family, communicating with family members in a nonpaternalistic manner and with mutual respect and caring, making center environments safe and clean, and providing opportunities for families to have access to medical decision making.

FAMILY-CENTERED PRACTICES   At one time, the prevailing philosophy in early childhood special education programming ignored parents and families at best or viewed them primarily as potential negative influences on the child with disabilities. When early intervention programs did involve parents, the assumption often was that the parents had little

RESPONSIVE *INSTRUCTION*
MEETING THE NEEDS OF STUDENTS WITH LOW-INCIDENCE, MULTIPLE, AND SEVERE DISABILITIES

Positive Behavioral Intervention and Support

WHAT IS POSITIVE BEHAVIORAL INTERVENTION AND SUPPORT?

Recent reauthorizations of the Individuals with Disabilities Education Act require teachers, school systems, and those involved with students who exhibit challenging behaviors to approach problematic behavior through a mechanism called positive behavioral intervention and support (PBIS). PBIS refers to the process of identifying alternative, acceptable ways to communicate through teaching more appropriate behaviors and/or changing the environment to reduce the likelihood of prompting the undesirable behavior (Kogel, Kogel, & Dunlap, 1996). This approach to behavior management differs fundamentally from traditional behavior modification plans that focus on the elimination of target behaviors, yet do not take into account possible environmental or personal triggers when doing so. For example, a student's undesirable behavior of banging his head on his desk might be eliminated by placing a baseball cap on his head. Although this might appear to be an acceptable solution, if the student's banging was a sign of boredom or an anxiety-producing peer in the vicinity, the baseball cap solution does not address the function of the behavior, and it is likely that another behavior will manifest in response to the original source of the behavior.

PBIS, by contrast, is guided by two fundamental assumptions: (1) Each behavior carries a communicative intent, and (2) typically, multiple factors influence the presence of specific behavior. Interventions based on these assumptions, therefore, include a functional behavioral assessment (FBA) (Horner, Vaughn, Day, & Ard, 1996). FBA seeks to identify the purpose of the behavior and supporting environmental conditions. The results of such assessment lead to the development of multifaceted plans that can include changing situational events, altering events that immediately precede the behavior, teaching alternative responses to the situation, and providing meaningful reinforcers to promote acceptable responses (Horner et al., 1996).

APPLYING THE RESEARCH TO TEACHING

The following support strategies are all involved in implementing PBIS:

- Remove high-frustration activities (e.g., difficult assignments, undesirable directives).
- Select functional and meaningful (from the student's perspective) curricula.
- Reduce fear or anxiety about a situation through precorrection (e.g., a teacher might suggest what to do when feeling frustrated).
- Teach more appropriate ways to make requests or express oneself.
- Use behavior modification to reinforce desired behaviors and communicate nonacceptability.
- Create activities that build on student interest and strength.

• By Kristin L. Sayeski

■ ■ ■ ■ ■ ■ ■ ■ ■ ■

to offer and were in need of training to improve their parenting skills. Although it's true that some parents do need to be educated about how to be better parents, to assume that this is always the case is paternalistic and off-putting to the majority of parents, who are very capable. For this reason, authorities now recommend that one not assume that parents have little or nothing to offer with respect to how to work with their children. Instead, they emphasize that parents, siblings, and extended family can be a valuable and integral part of the educational process for young children with disabilities.

As we discussed in Chapters 1, 2, and 4, IDEA also recognizes that parents and families should be central to the educational process for infants and toddlers. The requirement for individualized family service plans (IFSPs), in fact, dictates that the family be central in the decision-making process for the child. A family-centered philosophy means taking into account the particular priorities and needs of the family when developing an educational intervention plan for the child.

MULTICULTURAL PERSPECTIVE   Given the changing ethnic demographics in the United States, it is critical that all special education programming be culturally sensitive. It's particularly important that early intervention professionals adopt a multicultural perspective because parents are often still coping with the stress of having had their child diagnosed with a disability (Dunst, 2011; Noonan & McCormick, 2006). Having at least someone in the program who can speak the family's language is important. So is communicating respect, caring, and sensitivity. And it's important to provide services that are unbiased and nondiscriminatory with regard to disability, gender, race, religion, and ethnic and cultural orientation. Perhaps the most important multicultural factor, however, is providing services that are effective (Kauffman, Conroy, Gardner, & Oswald, 2008).

CROSS-DISCIPLINARY COLLABORATION   Because infants and young children with multiple and severe disabilities by definition have needs in multiple areas, best practice dictates the involvement of professionals from several disciplines. It's critical that these professionals collaborate in a coordinated way to provide high-quality services. Cross-disciplinary models vary, but the most essential feature for success is that the professionals in each of the disciplines work collaboratively, not independently. Some authorities also recommend that professionals should be willing to share roles.

DEVELOPMENTALLY AND CHRONOLOGICALLY AGE-APPROPRIATE PRACTICES   The term **developmentally appropriate practice (DAP)** was first used by the National Association for the Education of Young Children, an organization that focuses on early childhood education for children without disabilities. DAP refers to the practice of using educational methods that are at the developmental levels of the child and that meet the child's individual needs. Many early childhood special educators agree with the notion of DAP, but they believe that it should be balanced with the need for using educational methods that are also chronologically age appropriate. They believe that young children with disabilities should be educated as much as possible alongside their same-age nondisabled peers rather than with much younger nondisabled peers.

Transition to Adulthood

Transition to adulthood is a critical time for most people with severe and multiple disabilities. Special education has made great strides in developing transition services for people with disabilities. Much of this progress has been made because of a change in philosophy about how people with disabilities are treated, and this change is nowhere more evident than in the treatment of people with severe and multiple disabilities. For example, not long ago, the best employment that individuals with severe and multiple disabilities could hope for was in a **sheltered workshop**. Now, however, a much wider range of options is available, including, for some people, **competitive employment** alongside workers who are nondisabled.

CHANGING PHILOSOPHY   We can point to at least two principles of transition programming that reflect the change in philosophy toward treating people with severe disabilities with more dignity (Westling & Fox, 2000). First, as we noted in Chapter 5, is the emphasis on **self-determination**. As part of this emphasis on self-determination, professionals have developed a number of **person-centered plans**, which focus on the student's preferences and those of her or his family in planning for the future (Snell & Brown, 2006). Although person-centered planning is now part of most programs for people with severe disabilities, some have suggested that such plans are not particularly beneficial (e.g., Osborne, 2005).

Second, authorities now recommend that natural supports be an integral part of transition planning. Rather than always creating new services for a person's particular needs, using **natural supports**, professionals first try to find the available resources already existing in the workplace or the community. With respect to work, the use of natural supports might mean training co-workers to provide assistance rather than immediately assuming that a **job coach** is required. With respect to community living, the use of natural supports might mean the person with a disability could live in an apartment, with assistance in **daily living skills** from a neighbor, family member, or paid attendant, rather than living in a residential facility with attendants.

VOCATIONAL PROGRAMMING   A student's IEP must contain a transition plan, beginning no later than age 16 (and by age 14 when appropriate). The transition plan should contain recommendations for how to ready the student for the world of work and/or for postsecondary education or training.

For many students with severe and multiple disabilities, vocational training should begin in elementary school, because they might need several years to acquire all the skills needed to hold down a job successfully. In elementary school, the training might consist of learning to keep on schedule, building social skills, performing work-like tasks (e.g., helping to take attendance, collecting lunch money), and beginning to learn about different types of jobs.

In secondary school, the focus shifts to involving students in actual work situations in the community with the help of a job coach. The students should be involved in selecting these placements, which should vary sufficiently that the students experience a good sample of the kinds of jobs available and what they are good at and enjoy. In the early stages, this might involve the students' volunteering in several different types of placements. Later, it's preferable for students to engage in paid work placements. Being paid adds to the reality of the experience and provides an opportunity for students to learn how to handle finances.

COMMUNITY AND DOMESTIC LIVING SKILLS   As we noted in Chapter 5, community living skills involve using transportation, shopping, using telephones, managing money, and using the Internet. Domestic living skills include preparing meals, doing laundry, housekeeping, yard maintenance, and so forth. Because students aren't that far away from the time when they will move out of their parents' home and because teaching domestic skills is often done in small groups, there are some advantages to using a setting other than their own home. Thus, domestic living skills are often taught in a school setting, such as the home economics classroom and the school cafeteria.

Another reason for using the school as the instructional setting some of the time is to ensure that the student with disabilities has a chance to interact with peers who do not have disabilities. Inclusion in regular school programs provides social opportunities for students, and social skills are critical for successful integration into the community and workplace (see Everson & Trowbridge, 2011; Inge & Moon, 2011).

The last 30 to 40 years have brought enormous strides in preparing people with multiple and severe disabilities to lead productive lives as adults. It wasn't that long ago that people with multiple and severe disabilities were housed in large residential institutions and had minimal contact with the public. Today, with intensive and extensive instruction and the support of professionals and the community, many people with multiple and severe disabilities can aspire to work alongside persons without disabilities and live independently or semi-independently by themselves or in a small **community residential facility (CRF)**.

SUMMARY

What is the definition of low-incidence, multiple, and severe disabilities, and what is the prevalence?

- Low-incidence, multiple, and severe disabilities are those that occur relatively infrequently and require extensive support in more than one major life activity, such as mobility, communication, self-care, independent living, employment, and self-sufficiency. Probably 1% or fewer of all learners have such low-incidence, multiple, or severe disabilities.

What is traumatic brain injury, and how might it affect education?

- Traumatic brain injury (TBI) is injury to the brain resulting in total or partial disability or psychosocial maladjustment that affects educational performance.
  - It may be the result of closed head injuries or open head injuries.
  - It may affect cognition, language, memory, attention, reasoning, abstract thinking, judgment, problem.

solving, sensory or perceptual and motor disabilities, psychosocial behavior, physical functions, information processing, or speech—all of which are important in school.

How is deaf-blindness defined, and what are the special educational problems it entails?

- Deaf-blindness is defined by significant impairments in both hearing and seeing, although the individual may have some residual hearing or sight.

  - Deaf-blindness may be caused by a variety of genetic and chromosomal syndromes, prenatal conditions, and postnatal conditions.
  - The person who is deaf-blind has difficulty accessing information, communicating, and navigating the environment.
  - Deaf-blindness requires direct teaching, predictable, structured routines, and emphasis on communication and mobility.

What educational considerations apply to many students with low-incidence, multiple, and severe disabilities?

- Communication, behavior management, early intervention, and transition to adulthood are concerns that apply to many learners with these disabilities.

- Augmentative or alternative communication (AAC) is important for those who can't communicate effectively through speech.
- Common behavior problems requiring special management include self-stimulation, self-injury, tantrums, aggression toward others, lack of daily living skills, all of which may require functional behavioral assessment and positive behavioral support.
- Early intervention should be based on both research and values and be family-centered, multicultural, cross-disciplinary, age-appropriate, and feature normalization.
- Transition to adulthood should honor the concepts of person-centered planning and natural supports, feature vocational programming, and include community and domestic living skills.

COUNCIL FOR EXCEPTIONAL CHILDERN

Council for Exceptional Children

Addressing the Professional Standards

Council for Exceptional Children (CEC) Common Core Knowledge and Skills addressed in this chapter: ICC1K5, ICC1K5, ICC1K7, ICC2K1, ICC2K6, ICC3K1, ICC3K3, ICC4S3, ICC5K4, ICC5K6, ICC5S3, ICC5S10, ICC5S16, ICC6S1, ICC7S1, ICC7S7, ICC7S9, ICC8S2, ICC10S1, ICC10S6

Appendix: Provides a full listing of the CEC Common Core Standards and associated Knowledge and Skill Statements listed here.

MYEDUCATIONLAB

PEARSON
myeducationlab Now go to Topic 14: Physical Disabilities and Health Impairments, and Topic 16, Multiple Disabilities and Traumatic Brain Injury, in the MyEducationLab (www.myeducationlab.com) for your course, where you can:

- Find learning outcomes for the broad concepts covered in this chapter along with the national standards that connect to these outcomes.
- Complete Assignments and Activities that can help you more deeply understand the chapter content.
- Examine challenging situations presented in the IRIS Center Resources.
- Apply and practice your understanding of the core concepts and skills identified in the chapter with the Building Teaching Skills and Dispositions learning units.
- Check your comprehension on the content covered in the chapter by going to the Study Plan in the Book-Specific Resources for your text. Here you will be able to take a chapter quiz, receive feedback on your answers, and then access Review, Practice, and Enrichment activities to enhance your understanding of chapter content.
- Watch video clips of CCSSO Teacher of the Year award winners responding to the question: "Why I teach?" in the Teacher Talk section.

Learners with Physical Disabilities and Other Health Impairments

Jim trudged down the steps and across the yard. He felt mad at the world. He was angry at the uncles for bringing him up here, and mad at Mama for letting him come. He thought about going to wait in the truck for the uncles to come back, but his legs wouldn't stop moving down the slope of the yard. Penn had been to the top of the Empire State Building. Penn had been to Independence Hall. Jim had no idea what to say to a boy who had seen the things Penn had seen. And he had no idea what to say to a boy who had polio. When he walked past the rocking chairs, his stomach dropped as if he had jumped off of something high. He took a deep breath and turned around. "Hey, Penn," he said.

"Hey, Jim," said Penn.

The two boys stared at each other and grinned, then shook hands awkwardly, as if a grown-up were making them do it. Jim looked down at Penn's legs before he could stop himself. Penn slapped his right leg twice with an open palm.

"It's this one," he said. "I can't move this one."

"Oh," Jim said. "I'm sorry."

Penn shrugged. "It's okay," he said. "It could've been a lot worse." He kicked his left leg straight out. "This one's fine."

Tony Earley • *Jim the Boy, 2000*

QUESTIONS **to guide your reading of this chapter . . .**

- How are physical disabilities defined and classified?
- What is the prevalence of physical disabilities, and what is the need for special education?
- What are some major neuromotor impairments?
- What are some major orthopedic and musculoskeletal disorders?
- What other conditions affect health or physical ability?
- How can physical disabilities be prevented?
- What are the psychological and behavioral characteristics of individuals with physical disabilities?
- What are prosthetics, orthotics, and adaptive devices?
- What are the major educational considerations for students with physical disabilities?
- Why is early intervention important, and on what should it focus?
- What are the major issues in transition for students with physical disabilities?

MISCONCEPTIONS ABOUT
Learners with Physical Disabilities and Other Health Impairments

MYTH • Cerebral palsy is a contagious disease.

FACT • Cerebral palsy is not a disease. It's a nonprogressive neurological injury. It's a disorder of muscle control and coordination caused by injury to the brain before or during birth or in early childhood.

MYTH • Physical disabilities of all kinds are decreasing because of medical advances.

FACT • Because of advances in medical technology, the number of children with physical disabilities is increasing. The number of survivors of serious medical conditions who develop normally or have mild impairments, such as hyperactivity and learning disabilities, is also increasing.

MYTH • The greatest educational problem involving children with physical disabilities is highly specialized instruction.

FACT • The greatest educational problem is teaching people without disabilities about what it's like to have a disability and how disabilities can be accommodated.

MYTH • The more severe a person's physical disability, the lower is his intelligence.

FACT • A person can be severely physically disabled by cerebral palsy or another condition but have a brilliant mind.

MYTH • People with epilepsy are mentally ill.

FACT • People with epilepsy (seizure disorder) aren't any more or less disposed to mental illness than are those who don't have epilepsy.

MYTH • Arthritis is found only in adults, particularly those who are elderly.

FACT • Arthritic conditions are found in people of any age, including young children.

MYTH • People with physical disabilities have no need for sexual expression.

FACT • People with physical disabilities have normal sexual urges and need outlets for sexual expression.

MYTH • Physical disabilities shape people's personalities.

FACT • People with physical disabilities have the full range of personality characteristics found among those who don't have physical disabilities. No particular personality characteristics are associated with physical disability.

MYTH • If a child with a physical disability such as cerebral palsy or spina bifida learns to walk as a young child, then she will maintain that ability throughout life.

FACT • Continuing intervention through adolescence and adulthood—the entire life span—is required in many cases. Unless they have continued support for ambulation, adolescents or adults might find walking much more difficult or might give up walking, even if they learned to walk as children.

In Western culture, many people are almost obsessed with their bodies. They don't just want to be healthy and strong; they want to be beautiful—well formed and attractive to others. In fact, some people seem to be more concerned about the impression their bodies make than they are about their own well-being. They might even endanger their health in an effort to become more physically alluring. It isn't really surprising, then, that people with physical disabilities must fight two battles: the battle to overcome the limitations imposed by their physical conditions and the battle to be accepted by others.

Individuals with physical disabilities or differences are often stared at, feared, teased, socially rejected, or treated cruelly. This has been the case throughout history, and it remains true today (see Holmes, 2004, and Metzeler, 2006, for historical perspectives). Sometimes people feel embarrassed about someone else's disability and don't seem to understand the feelings of the person who has the disability. Or people might feel that an acquired physical disability must change someone's personality dramatically. In some cases involving traumatic brain injury, this is indeed the case. However, in most cases it is not.

In Tony Earley's (2000) story (in this chapter's opening quotation) about Jim and his friend Penn, who had polio, we see Jim's mixed feelings of anger and fear when seeing his pal for the first time after Penn was paralyzed. We probably expect Jim's mixture of anger, fear, and inquisitiveness from a 10-year-old—wondering about death, the permanence of disability, how it feels to have the disability, and so on. But most of us have such feelings and questions, regardless of our age. And most people with physical disabilities share Penn's matter-of-factness and eagerness to be accepted and get on with life.

Although polio has been virtually eradicated by vaccination, many other causes of partial paralysis and other physical disabilities haven't been eliminated. Traumatic brain injury is an example of a cause of physical disability that is actually increasing. Attitudes toward physical disabilities have not changed much in many ways, nor have the problems of having physical disabilities. Children with physical disabilities often face more than the problem of acceptance. For many, accomplishing the simple tasks of everyday living seems a minor—or major—miracle.

DEFINITION AND CLASSIFICATION

In this chapter, we consider children whose primary distinguishing characteristics are health or physical problems. *Children with physical disabilities or other health impairments* are those whose physical limitations or health problems interfere with school attendance or learning to such an extent that they require special services, training, equipment, materials, or facilities.

Children with physical disabilities might also have other disabilities of any type or special gifts or talents. Thus, the characteristics of children with physical disabilities are extremely varied. The child's physical condition is the proper concern of the medical profession, but when physical problems have obvious implications for education, teaching specialists are needed. The fact that the primary distinguishing characteristics of children with physical disabilities are medical conditions, health problems, or physical limitations highlights the necessity of interdisciplinary cooperation (Best, Heller, & Bigge, 2010).

Children may have **congenital anomalies** (defects they are born with), or they may acquire disabilities through accident or disease after birth. Some physical disabilities are comparatively mild and transitory; others are profound and progressive, ending in total incapacitation and early death. Some are increasingly common chronic diseases. Discussing physical disabilities in general is difficult because the variety of these disabilities is so great. We've organized this chapter around specific conditions that fall into one of three categories: neuromotor impairments, orthopedic and musculoskeletal disorders, and other conditions that affect health or physical ability.

It's important to make distinctions between acute or chronic conditions. It's also important to understand the difference between episodic or progressive problems.

An **acute** illness or condition may be very serious or severe, but with treatment (which may include hospitalization or medication) it resolves, and the person recovers. Someone with a serious infection or who has a serious accident may, for example, become acutely ill or be in critical condition for a time but recover. However, a **chronic** condition is ongoing. It does not resolve, even with the best treatment; it is an incurable condition. Cerebral palsy is chronic; it can't be cured.

An **episodic** condition occurs repeatedly, although most of the time the individual can function quite normally. Its occurrence is limited primarily to successive episodes. The episodes don't necessarily become more serious or severe over time. Asthma and seizure disorders (epilepsy), for example, tend to be episodic. However, a **progressive** condition is one that becomes more and more serious or severe over time, usually involving more and more complications or deterioration. Muscular dystrophy is an example of a physical problem that is usually progressive.

myeducationlab

To check your comprehension on the content covered in Chapter 14, go to the Book-Specific Resources in the MyEducationLab (www.myeducationlab.com) for your course, select your text, and complete the Study Plan. Here you will be able to take a chapter quiz, receive feedback on your answers, and then access review, practice, and enrichment activities to enhance your understanding of chapter content. ∎

PREVALENCE AND NEED

Roughly 1% of the school-age population (about half a million children and youths) are classified as having physical disabilities. About 75,000 of these have orthopedic disabilities, but the vast majority have other health problems. This doesn't include students with traumatic brain injury or multiple disabilities or young children with developmental delays. Statistics show a dramatic increase in the percentage of the school population served by special education due to health problems (see, e.g., annual reports to Congress on implementation of federal special education law). However, the needs of many students with physical disabilities are unmet because the number of children and youths with such disabilities is growing, and health and social service programs aren't keeping up.

Increases in the prevalence might be due in part to improvements in the identification of, and medical services to, children with certain conditions. Ironically, medical advances have not only improved the chances of preventing or curing certain diseases and disorders, but also assured the survival of more children with severe medical problems—just as improved medical care means that more combat soldiers are surviving grievous wounds. Many children with severe and multiple disabilities and those with severe, chronic illnesses or severe injuries, who in the past wouldn't have survived long, today can have a normal life span. Declining mortality rates don't necessarily mean that there will be fewer individuals with disabilities. Moreover, improvements in medical care might not lower the number of individuals with disabilities unless there is also a lowering of risk factors in the environment—factors such as accidents, toxic substances, poverty, malnutrition, disease, and interpersonal violence.

NEUROMOTOR IMPAIRMENTS

Neuromotor impairment is caused by injury to the brain or spinal cord (neurological damage) that also affects the ability to move parts of one's body (motor impairment). It may be associated with injury to the brain before, during, or after birth. **Traumatic brain injury (TBI)**, which we discussed in Chapter 13, involves brain damage with an identifiable external cause (trauma) after birth (see Lajiness-O'Neill & Erdodi, 2011). However, brain injury can be acquired from a variety of nontraumatic causes as well: hypoxia (reduced oxygen to the brain, as might occur in near drowning), infection of the brain or its linings, stroke, tumor, metabolic disorder (such as may occur with diabetes, liver disease, or kidney disease), or toxic chemicals or drugs.

In many cases of brain damage, it's impossible to identify the exact cause of the neuromotor impairment. The important point is that when a child's nervous system is damaged, no matter what the cause, muscular weakness or paralysis is often one of the symptoms. Because these children usually can't move about like most others, their education typically requires special equipment, special procedures, or other accommodations for their disabilities.

Cerebral Palsy

Cerebral palsy (CP) is not a disease. It's not contagious, it's not progressive (although improper treatment can lead to complications), and there are no remissions. Martin (2006) offers a succinct definition:

> Cerebral palsy is a disorder of movement and posture. It is caused by a brain injury that occurred before birth, during birth, or during the first few years after birth. The injury hinders the brain's ability to control the muscles of the body properly. The brain tells our muscles how to move and controls the tension of the muscles. Without the proper messages coming from the brain, infants with cerebral palsy have difficulty learning basic motor skills such as crawling, sitting up, or walking. (p. 2)

Cerebral palsy is more complicated than an impairment of movement and posture, as Martin (2006) and others recognize. For practical purposes, CP can be considered part of a syndrome that includes motor dysfunction, psychological dysfunction, seizures, and emotional or behavioral disorders due to brain damage (see also Best & Bigge, 2010).

INTERNETRESOURCES

The United Cerebral Palsy Association provides information and resources for people with cerebral palsy and their families at www.ucp.org

Some individuals with CP show only one indication of brain damage, such as motor impairment; others show combinations of symptoms. The usual definition of CP refers to paralysis, weakness, lack of coordination, and/or other motor dysfunction because of damage to the child's brain before it has matured. Symptoms can be so mild that they are detected only with difficulty or so profound that the individual is almost completely incapacitated. Because CP includes such a heterogeneous group of children, the label *cerebral palsy* has been called into question by some who have noted that the label "defines groups of children who are desperately in need of a service, and this seems an adequate ground" for continuing to use the label (Bax, 2001, p. 75).

Although no cure for CP is available, advances in medical and rehabilitation technology offer increasing hope of overcoming the disabilities resulting from neurological damage. For example,

Advances in medical and rehabilitation technology offer increasing hope of overcoming disabilities associated with cerebral palsy.

intensive long-term physical therapy in combination with a surgical procedure in which the surgeon cuts selected nerve roots below the spinal cord that cause spasticity in the leg muscles allows some children with spastic CP to better control certain muscles. Such treatment allows some nonambulatory children to walk and helps others to walk more normally.

CAUSES AND TYPES   Anything that can damage the brain during its development can cause CP. Before birth, maternal infections, chronic diseases, physical trauma, or maternal exposure to toxic substances or X-rays, for example, can damage the brain of the fetus. During the birth process, the brain can be injured, especially if labor or birth is difficult or complicated. Premature birth, hypoxia, high fever, infections, poisoning, hemorrhaging, and related factors can cause harm after birth. In short, anything that results in oxygen deprivation, poisoning, cerebral bleeding, or direct trauma to the brain can be a possible cause of CP.

Although CP occurs at every social level, it is more often seen in children born to mothers in poor socioeconomic circumstances. Children who live in such circumstances have a greater risk of incurring brain damage because of factors such as malnutrition of the mother, poor prenatal and postnatal care, environmental hazards during infancy, and low birthweight. However, the prevalence of CP in children with very low birthweight has declined in recent years due to better treatment of premature infants (Robertson, Watt, & Yasui, 2007).

The two most widely accepted means of classification of CP specify the limbs that are involved and the type of motor disability. Some individuals have a mixture of various types of CP. Classification according to the extremities involved applies not just to CP but to all types of motor disability or paralysis. The most common classifications are **quadriplegia** (all four limbs are involved) and **paraplegia** (only the legs are involved).

Likewise, classification by type of movement applies not only to CP, but also to other types of neuromotor disabilities. **Spasticity** refers to stiffness or tenseness of muscles and inaccurate voluntary movement. **Choreoathetoid** is the term applied to abrupt, involuntary movements and difficulty maintaining balance. **Atonic** refers to floppiness or lack of muscle tone.

The important point about CP is that the brain damage affects strength and the ability to move parts of the body normally. The difficulty of movement may involve the limbs as well as the muscles involving facial expressions and speech. As a result, someone with CP might have difficulty moving or speaking or might exhibit facial contortions or drooling. But these results of brain damage don't necessarily mean that the person's intelligence or emotional sensitivity has been affected by the damage affecting muscle control.

ASSOCIATED DISABILITIES AND EDUCATIONAL IMPLICATIONS   CP is a developmental disability—a multidisabling condition that is far more complex than a motor disability alone. When the brain is damaged, sensory abilities, cognitive functions, and emotional responsiveness as well as motor performance are usually affected. A high proportion of children with CP are found to have hearing impairments, visual impairments, perceptual disorders, speech problems, emotional or behavioral disorders, intellectual disability (mental retardation), or some combination of several of these disabling conditions in addition to motor disability. They might also exhibit such characteristics as drooling or facial contortions.

Some individuals with CP have normal or above-average intellectual capacity, and a few test within the gifted range. Nevertheless, the average tested intelligence of children with CP is lower than the average for the general population. We must be very cautious in interpreting the test results of children with CP, however, because many standardized tests of intelligence and achievement might be inappropriate for individuals with special difficulties in perception, movement, or response speed. Furthermore, the movement problems of a child with CP might become more apparent when the child is in a state of emotional arousal or stress; this can complicate using typical testing procedures, which tend to be demanding and stressful.

The educational problems of children who have CP are as multifaceted as their disabilities. Not only do these children need special equipment and procedures because of their physical disabilities, but they often require the same special educational procedures and equipment as children with vision, hearing, or communication disorders, learning disabilities, emotional or behavioral disorders, or intellectual disability. Careful and continuous educational assessment of the individual child's capabilities is particularly important. Teaching the child who has CP demands competence in many aspects of special education and experience in working with a variety of disabling conditions in a multidisciplinary setting (Best et al., 2010; Heller, Alberto, Forney, & Schwartzman, 2009).

Seizure Disorder (Epilepsy)

A person has a **seizure** when an abnormal discharge of electrical energy occurs in certain brain cells. The discharge spreads to nearby cells, and the effect may be loss of consciousness, involuntary movements, or abnormal sensory phenomena. The effects of the seizure depends on the location of the cells in which the discharge starts and how far the discharge spreads.

About 1 in 10 children has a seizure at some time, usually associated with a high fever or serious illness (Weinstein, 2002). However, this doesn't mean that 1 in 10 children has epilepsy. A person with **epilepsy** has a chronic neurological condition and has *recurrent* seizures (Arzimanoglou, Guerrini, & Aicardi, 2004; Weinstein, 2002). Because seizures reflect abnormal brain activity, it's not surprising that they occur more often in children with developmental disabilities (e.g., intellectual disability or cerebral palsy) than in children without disabilities (Best et al., 2010).

INTERNETRESOURCES

For more information about epilepsy, go to the site of the Epilepsy Foundation of America at www.efa.org ▪▪▪

CAUSES AND TYPES   Seizures are caused by damage to the brain. As brain imaging and molecular biology advance, scientists are arriving at a better understanding of risk for epilepsy (Barkovich, 2005). The most common immediate causes include lack of sufficient oxygen (hypoxia), low blood sugar (hypoglycemia), infections, and physical trauma. Certain conditions, such as those just listed, tend to increase the chances that neurochemical reactions will be set off in brain cells. In many cases, the causes are unknown. Some types of seizures may be progressive; that is, they may damage the brain or disrupt its functioning in such a way that having a seizure increases the probability of having another. Even though the cause of seizures isn't well understood, it's important to note that with proper medication, most people's seizures can be controlled.

Seizures can take many forms; neurologists debate the best way to classify seizures. However, educators should note that seizures may differ along at least the following dimensions:

- *Duration:* Seizures may last only a few seconds or for several minutes.
- *Frequency:* Seizures may occur as frequently as every few minutes or only about once a year.
- *Onset:* Seizures may be set off by certain identifiable stimuli or may be unrelated to the environment, and they may be totally unexpected or be preceded by certain internal sensations.

- *Movements:* Seizures may cause major convulsive movements or only minor motor symptoms (e.g., eye blinks).
- *Causes:* Seizures may be caused by a variety of conditions, including high fever, poisoning, trauma, and other conditions mentioned previously; but in many cases, the causes are unknown.
- *Associated disabilities:* Seizures may be associated with other disabling conditions or may be unrelated to any other medical problem or disability.
- *Control:* Seizures may be controlled completely by drugs, so that the individual has no more seizures, or they may be only partially controlled.

EDUCATIONAL IMPLICATIONS   About half of all children with seizure disorders have average or higher intelligence—just as is true for the general population. Among children with seizure disorders who do not also have intellectual disability, however, the incidence of learning disabilities seems to be higher than among children who do not have seizure disorders (Arzimanoglou et al., 2004). Although many children with seizure disorders have other disabilities, some don't. Consequently, both general and special education teachers can expect to encounter children who have seizures.

Besides obtaining medical advice about management of the child's particular seizure disorder, teachers should know first aid for epileptic seizures (see the accompanying Focus on Concepts, "First Aid for Epileptic Seizures"). Ignorance about the causes of seizures and about first aid are among the most common misconceptions about epilepsy (Arzimanoglou et al., 2004; Best et al., 2010).

Seizures are primarily a medical problem and require primarily medical attention. The responsibilities of educators follow:

1. General and special education teachers need to help dispel ignorance, superstition, and prejudice toward people who have seizures and provide calm management for the occasional seizure the child may have at school.

FOCUS ON Concepts

FIRST AID FOR EPILEPTIC SEIZURES

First aid for epilepsy is basically very simple. It keeps the person safe until the seizure stops naturally by itself. It is important for the public to know how to respond to all seizures, including the most noticeable kind—the generalized tonic clonic seizure, or convulsions.

When providing seizure first aid for generalized tonic clonic (grand mal) seizures, these are the key things to remember:

Keep calm and reassure other people who may be nearby.
Don't hold the person down or try to stop his movements.
Time the seizure with your watch.
Clear the area around the person of anything hard or sharp.
Loosen ties or anything around the neck that may make breathing difficult.

Put something flat and soft, like a folded jacket, under the head.
Turn him or her gently onto one side. This will help keep the airway clear. Do not try to force the mouth open with any hard implement or with fingers. It is not true that a person having a seizure can swallow his tongue. Efforts to hold the tongue down can injure teeth or jaw.
Don't attempt artificial respiration except in the unlikely event that a person does not start breathing again after the seizure has stopped.
Stay with the person until the seizure ends naturally.
Be friendly and reassuring as consciousness returns.
Offer to call a taxi, friend or relative to help the person get home if he seems confused or unable to get home by himself.

Source: From http://www.epilepsyfoundation.org/answerplace/Medical/firstaid/

2. Special education teachers who work with students with severe intellectual disability or teach children with other severe developmental disabilities need to be prepared to manage more frequent seizures as well as to handle learning problems. The teacher should record the length of a child's seizure and the type of activity the child was engaged in before it occurred. This information will help physicians in diagnosis and treatment. If a student is being treated for a seizure disorder, the teacher should know the type of medication and its possible side effects. (Best et al., 2010)

Some children who don't have intellectual disability but have seizures exhibit learning and behavior problems. These problems might result from damage to the brain that causes other disabilities as well, or they might be the side effects of anticonvulsant medication or the result of mismanagement by parents and teachers. Teachers must be aware that seizures of any type can interfere with the child's attention or the continuity of education. Brief seizures might require the teacher to repeat instructions or allow the child extra time to respond. Frequent major convulsions might prevent even a bright child from achieving at the usual rate.

Many students with epilepsy have no learning problems at all. However, some do have learning disabilities, and children with epilepsy have emotional or behavioral disorders more often than those without epilepsy. If children with epilepsy do have problems in school, their school adjustment can be improved dramatically if they are properly assessed, placed, counseled, taught about seizures, and given appropriate work assignments. The quality of life of children with epilepsy is related to the same risk factors that affect quality of life for others with disabilities, including problems with **executive function** (see Chapter 7), problems with **adaptive behavior** (see Chapter 5), low IQ, psychosocial difficulties, low family income, and early age of onset (Sherman, Slick, & Eyrl, 2006).

Spina Bifida and Other Spinal Cord Injuries

Neurological damage can involve only the spinal cord, leaving the brain unaffected. Spinal cord injury can occur before or after birth, affecting the individual's ability to move or control bodily functions below the site of the injury (Best et al., 2010).

During early fetal development, the two halves of the embryo grow together or fuse at the midline. Incomplete closure results in congenital midline defects such as cleft lip and cleft palate. **Spina bifida** is a congenital midline defect that results from failure of the bony spinal column to close completely during fetal development. It is one type of **neural tube defect** (a malformation of the spine, spinal cord, or brain; see Barkovich, 2005; Liptak, 2002). The defect may occur anywhere from the head to the lower end of the spine. Because the spinal column is not closed, the spinal cord (nerve fibers) can protrude, resulting in damage to the nerves and paralysis and/or lack of function or sensation below the site of the defect.

Spina bifida is often accompanied by paralysis of the legs and of the anal and bladder sphincters because nerve impulses cannot travel past the defect. Surgery to close the spinal opening is performed in early infancy, but this doesn't repair the nerve damage. Although spina bifida is one of the most common birth defects resulting in physical disability, its causes are not known.

Spinal cord injuries resulting from accidents after birth are also a major cause of paralysis. The basic difference between spina bifida and other spinal cord injuries is that the individual who is injured after birth has gone through a period of normal development and must adjust to an acquired disability.

EDUCATIONAL AND SOCIAL IMPLICATIONS   The extent of the paralysis resulting from a spinal cord injury depends on how high or low on the spinal column the injury is. Some children with spinal cord injuries can walk independently, some need braces, and others have to use wheelchairs. Lack of sensation and ability to control bodily functions also depend on the nature of the injury. Therefore, the implications for education are extremely varied. However, factors other than muscle weakness or paralysis alone affect a child's ability to walk. Careful analysis of motivation and other environmental inducements to walk are critically important.

Some children will have acute medical problems that might lead to repeated hospitalizations for surgery or treatment of infections. Lack of sensation in certain areas of the skin can increase the risk of burns, abrasions, and pressure sores. The child might need to be repositioned periodically during the school day and monitored carefully during some activities that involve risk of injury.

Because the student with spina bifida has deficiencies in sensation below the defect, he may have particular problems in spatial orientation, spatial judgment, sense of direction and distance, organization of motor skills, and body image or body awareness. Lack of bowel and bladder control in some children will require periodic **catheterization**. Many children can be taught to do the procedure known as clean intermittent catheterization themselves, but teachers should know what to do or obtain help from the school nurse.

Enormous progress has been made in treating spina bifida and in including those who have paralysis as a result of the condition in schools and the larger society. Nevertheless, controversies sometimes arise regarding just what appropriate inclusion in school activities might entail. For example, a high school athlete with spina bifida took legal action to be included with nondisabled runners, even though she had to use a wheelchair on the track because her legs were paralyzed (Saslow, 2007).

ORTHOPEDIC AND MUSCULOSKELETAL DISORDERS

Some children are physically disabled because of defects or diseases of the muscles or bones. Even though they don't have neurological impairments, their ability to move is affected. Most of the time, muscular and skeletal problems involve the legs, arms, joints, or spine, making it difficult or impossible for the child to walk, stand, sit, or use his hands. The problems may be congenital or acquired after birth, and the causes can include genetic defects, infectious diseases, accidents, or developmental disorders.

Two of the most common musculoskeletal conditions affecting children and youths are **muscular dystrophy** and **juvenile rheumatoid arthritis**. Muscular dystrophy is a hereditary disease that is characterized by progressive weakness caused by degeneration of muscle fibers. No cure exists yet for muscular dystrophy, but advances in pharmacology are promising (Welch et al., 2007). Juvenile rheumatoid arthritis is a potentially debilitating disease in which the muscles and joints are affected; the cause and cure are unknown (Best et al., 2010). It can be a very painful condition and is sometimes accompanied by complications such as fever, respiratory problems, heart problems, and eye infections. Among children with other physical disabilities, such as cerebral palsy, arthritis may be a complicating factor that affects the joints and limits movement. These and other conditions can significantly affect a student's social and academic progress at school.

A wide variety of other congenital conditions, acquired defects, and diseases also can affect the musculoskeletal system. These include the spinal curvature known as **scoliosis** or missing or malformed limbs (see Best et al., 2010; Heller, Alberto, Forney, & Schwartzman, 2009). In all these conditions, as well as in cases of muscular dystrophy and arthritis, the student's intelligence is unaffected unless additional disabilities are present. Regarding the musculoskeletal problem itself, special education is necessary only to improve the student's mobility, to ensure that the student maintains proper posture and positioning, to provide for education during periods of confinement to hospital or home, and to make the educational experience as normal as possible.

OTHER CONDITIONS AFFECTING HEALTH OR PHYSICAL ABILITY

In addition to the conditions we've discussed, an extremely wide array of diseases, physiological disorders, congenital malformations, and injuries can affect students' health and physical abilities and create a need for special education and related services. Chronic diseases and health conditions of children have increased dramatically during recent decades (Perrin, Bloom, & Gortmaker, 2007). These diseases and health-related conditions include childhood obesity, diabetes, and asthma, for example.

Special educators need to be familiar with the range of physical disabilities and the types of accommodations that might be necessary to provide an appropriate education and related services (see Best et al., 2010; Heller et al., 2009). Moreover, teachers should understand that chronic diseases make many children's lives complicated and difficult because of possible hospitalizations, restrictions of activity, medications, teasing, and other consequences that, essentially, rob children of the experiences most of us associate with being kids (Zylke & DeAngelis, 2007).

Asthma is an increasingly common lung disease characterized by episodic inflammation or obstruction of the air passages such that the person has difficulty in breathing. Usually, the difficulty in breathing is reversible (i.e., is responsive to treatment). Severe asthma can be life-threatening, and in some cases it severely restricts a person's activities. The disease can also get better or worse for poorly understood reasons, and the unpredictability of the condition can be difficult to deal with.

Congenital malformations and disorders can occur in any organ system, and they may range from minor to fatal flaws in structure or function. In many cases, the cause of the malformation or disorder is not known; other conditions are known to be hereditary or caused by maternal infection or substance use, including alcohol, by the mother during pregnancy.

More children die in accidents each year than are killed by all childhood diseases combined. Millions of children and youths in the United States are seriously injured and disabled temporarily or permanently in accidents each year. Many of those who don't acquire TBI receive spinal cord injuries that result in partial or total paralysis below the site of the injury. Others undergo amputations or are incapacitated temporarily by broken limbs or internal injuries.

Children with **acquired immune deficiency syndrome (AIDS)** often acquire neurological problems, including intellectual disability, cerebral palsy, seizures, and emotional or behavioral disorders. Infants may contract the disease during the birth process. Although HIV does often result in neurological damage and cognitive impairment, it appears that at least in some cases the damage may be reversible with state-of-the-art drug therapies (Willen, 2006).

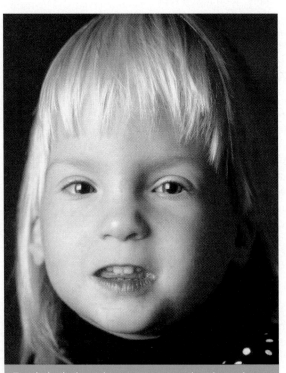

Fetal alcohol syndrome, associated with mothers' alcohol use during pregnancy, results in distinct physical and developmental abnormalities.

As children and youths with AIDS and other viral and bacterial infections live longer, owing to improved medical treatments, the need for special education and related services will increase. Teachers should be aware that if reasonable procedures are followed for preventing infections, no serious concern exists regarding transmission of HIV in the classroom (Best et al., 2010).

Fetal alcohol syndrome results in disabilities acquired by children of mothers who abuse alcohol during pregnancy. The abuse of other substances by mothers also has negative implications for their children. If the mother is a substance abuser, then the probability of neglect and abuse by the mother after her baby is born is also high. Many women who are intravenous drug users not only risk chemical damage to their babies, but also might give them venereal diseases such as syphilis, which can result in disabilities. Children of mothers who are intravenous drug users are also at risk for being born with AIDS. If the number of substance-abusing mothers increases, then the number of infants and young children with severe and multiple disabilities will increase as well. In spite of the multiple causal factors involved, the prospects of effective early intervention with children who are exposed prenatally to drugs are much better than previously thought.

Some students have conditions that require particularly careful treatment because seemingly minor mistakes or oversights can have very serious consequences for them. Programs for students who are medically fragile must be particularly flexible and open to revision. Daily health care plans and emergency plans are essential, as are effective lines of communication among all who are involved with the student's treatment, care, and schooling. Decisions regarding placement of these students must be made by a team that includes health care providers and school personnel as well as the students and their parents.

More frequently, children are returning home from hospitalization able to breathe only with the help of a ventilator (a mechanical device that forces oxygen into the lungs through a tube inserted into the trachea). Whether it's appropriate for children who are dependent on ventilators or other medical technology to attend general education is debatable. Educators and parents together must make decisions in each individual case, weighing medical judgment about danger to the child as well as the interest of the child in being integrated with peers into as many typical school activities as possible.

PREVENTION OF PHYSICAL DISABILITIES

Although some physical disabilities aren't preventable by any available means, many or most are. For instance, failure to wear seat belts and other safety devices accounts for many disabling injuries. Likewise, driving under the influence of alcohol or other drugs, careless storage of drugs and other toxic substances, careless storage of firearms, use of alcohol and other drugs during pregnancy, and a host of unsafe and unhealthful practices that could be avoided cause many disabilities. For example, lowering the incidence of obesity and increasing healthful diet and healthful physical activity could do much to prevent health complications of children, particularly diabetes (see Torpy, 2010).

Teenage mothers are more likely than older women to be physically battered. Teens are also more likely than older women to give birth to premature or low-birthweight babies, and these babies are at high risk for a variety of psychological and physical problems when they reach school age. Thus, preventing adolescent pregnancies would keep many babies from being born with disabilities. Inadequate prenatal care, including maternal infections and inadequate maternal nutrition during pregnancy, also contributes to the number of babies born with disabilities. And for young children, immunization against preventable childhood diseases could lower the number of those who acquire disabilities (see Heller et al., 2009). Although science is clear on the lack of any relationship between vaccinations and autism and vaccination is very clearly advantageous from a scientific point of view, vaccination against common childhood illnesses is declined by some parents (see Specter, 2009).

Child abuse is a significant contributing factor in creating physical disabilities in the United States, and its prevention is a critical problem. Many thousands of children, ranging from newborns to adolescents, are battered or abused each year. Teachers can play an extremely important role in detecting, reporting, and preventing child abuse and neglect because, next to parents, they are the people who spend the most time with children.

Children who are already disabled physically, intellectually, or emotionally are more at risk for abuse than are nondisabled children (Vig & Kaminer, 2002). Because children with disabilities are more vulnerable and dependent, abusive adults find them easy targets. Moreover, some of the characteristics of children with disabilities are sources of additional stress for their caretakers and may be contributing factors in physical abuse. These children often require more time, energy, money, and patience than children without disabilities. Parenting any child is stressful; parenting a child with a disability can demand more than some parents are prepared to give. It isn't surprising that children with disabilities are disproportionately represented among abused children and that the need for training is particularly great for parents of children with disabilities.

We mentioned in Chapters 1 and 5 that **phenylketonuria (PKU)** is now understood to be an inborn metabolic disorder that, untreated with a special diet, causes intellectual disability. PKU is

Teenage girls are more likely than older women to give birth to premature or low-birthweight babies, who will be at high risk for learning problems when they reach school age.

generally thought of as a problem associated with intellectual disability, but it is also an issue of health and prevention of disabilities. Inborn metabolic disorders can result not only in intellectual disability but in other disabilities associated with brain damage. Metabolic disorders may result in the buildup of **neurotoxins**, which can cause any of the disabilities associated with brain damage, including intellectual disability.

PKU isn't the only genetically determined metabolic disorder (see Batshaw & Tuchman, 2002), and it is not simply a metabolic disorder that results in intellectual disability if it is untreated in early childhood. Effective treatment of PKU does require a special diet free of or very low in phenylalanine for the infant, but the individual must remain on such a diet. Furthermore, women must continue the diet during pregnancy to avoid damaging the fetus.

PSYCHOLOGICAL AND BEHAVIORAL CHARACTERISTICS

Academic Achievement

It's impossible to make many valid generalizations about the academic achievement of children with physical disabilities because they vary so widely in the nature and severity of their conditions. The environmental and psychological factors that determine what a child will achieve academically also are extremely varied, and generalizations about academic outcomes aren't possible (see Batshaw, 2002; Best et al., 2010; Heller et al., 2009).

Many students with physical disabilities have erratic school attendance because of hospitalization, visits to physicians, bed-rest requirements, and so on. Some learn well with ordinary teaching methods; others require special methods because they have intellectual disability or sensory impairments in addition to physical disabilities. Because of the frequent interruptions in their schooling, some fall considerably behind their age peers in academic achievement, even though they have normal intelligence and motivation. The two major effects of a physical disability, especially if it is severe or prolonged, are that a child might be deprived of educationally relevant experiences and that he or she might not be able to learn to manipulate educational materials and respond to educational tasks the way most children do.

Some children with mild or transitory physical problems have no academic deficiencies at all; others have severe difficulties. Some students who have serious and chronic health problems still manage to achieve at a high level. Usually, these high-achieving children have high intellectual capacity, strong motivation, and teachers and parents who make every possible special provision for their education. Children with neurological impairments are, as a group, most likely to have intellectual and perceptual deficits and therefore to be behind their age peers in academic achievement.

Personality Characteristics

Research does not support the notion a certain personality type or self-concept is associated with any physical disability. Children and youths with physical disabilities are as varied in their psychological characteristics as nondisabled children, and they are apparently responsive to the same factors that influence the psychological development of other children. How children adapt to their physical limitations and how they respond to social-interpersonal situations greatly depend on how parents, siblings, teachers, peers, and the public react to the children (Best et al., 2010; Heller et al., 2009).

PUBLIC REACTIONS   Public attitudes can have a profound influence on how children with physical disabilities see themselves and on their opportunities for psychological adjustment, education, and employment. If the reaction is one of fear, rejection, or discrimination, these children might spend a great deal of energy trying to hide their stigmatizing differences. If the reaction is one of pity and an expectation of helplessness, people with disabilities will tend to behave in a dependent manner. To the extent that other people can see children with physical disabilities as people who have certain limitations but are otherwise just like everyone else, children and youths with disabilities will be encouraged to become independent, productive members of society.

Several factors seem to be causing greater public acceptance of people with physical disabilities. Professional and civic groups encourage support and decrease fear of people who are disabled through information and public education. People with physical disabilities are increasingly visible in the media, and they are often portrayed in a more realistic and positive light. Government insistence on the elimination of architectural barriers that prevent citizens with disabilities from using public facilities serves to decrease discrimination. Programs to encourage hiring workers with disabilities help the public to see those with physical disabilities as constructive, capable people. Laws that protect every child's right to public education bring more individuals into contact with people who have severe or profound disabilities. But many children with physical disabilities are still rejected, feared, pitied, or discriminated against. The more obvious the physical flaw, the more likely it is that the person will be perceived in negative terms by the public.

Public policy regarding children's physical disabilities has not met the needs of most of these children and their families. In particular, as successful medical treatment prolongs the lives of more and more children with severe, chronic illnesses and other disabilities, issues of who should pay the costs of treatment and maintenance (which are often enormous) and which children and families should receive the limited available resources are becoming critical.

CHILDREN'S AND FAMILIES' REACTIONS   As we have suggested, children's reactions to their own physical disabilities are largely a reflection of how others respond to them (see Olrick, Pianta, & Marvin, 2002; Singh, 2003). Shame and guilt are learned responses; children will have such negative feelings only if others respond to them by shaming or blaming them (and those who are like them) for their physical differences. Children will be independent and self-sufficient (within the limits of their physical disabilities) rather than dependent and demanding only to the extent that they learn how to take care of their own needs. And they will have realistic self-perceptions and set realistic goals for themselves only to the extent that others are honest and clear in appraising their conditions.

Children's feelings about their own disabilities are largely a reflection of how they are treated by others, and also of the attitude that their own families take toward them. They are more likely to see themselves as "normal" if they are treated that way, and encouraged to participate in regular activities.

However, certain psychological reactions are inevitable for children with physical disabilities, no matter how they are treated. The wish to be nondisabled and to participate in the same activities as most children and the fantasy that the disability will disappear are to be expected. With proper management and help, children can be expected eventually to accept their disability and live a happy life, even though they know the true nature of their condition. Fear and anxiety, too, can be expected. It's natural for children to be afraid when they are separated from their parents, hospitalized, and subjected to medical examinations and procedures that might be painful. In these situations, too, proper management can minimize emotional stress. Psychological trauma is not a necessary effect of hospitalization. The hospital environment may, in fact, be better than the child's home in the case of abused and neglected children.

Other important considerations regarding the psychological effects of a physical disability include the age of the child and the nature of the limitation (e.g., whether it is congenital or acquired, progressive or not). But even these factors are not uniform in their effects. A child with a relatively minor and short-term physical disability might become more maladjusted, anxious, debilitated, and disruptive than another child with a terminal illness because of the way the child's behavior and feelings are managed. Certainly, understanding the child's and the family's feelings about the disability is important. But it's also true that managing the consequences of the child's behavior is a crucial aspect of education and rehabilitation. Adolescence is a difficult time for most parents, and the fact that a child has a physical disability does not necessarily mean that the family will find a youngster's adolescence more difficult or less difficult.

Family support, school experiences, medical treatment, and attitudes have a very significant effect on the life of a child with a chronic health problem. Besides the school and society at large, the family and its cultural roots are important determinants of how and what children with physical disabilities will learn; therefore, it's important to take cultural values into account in teaching children not only about the academic curriculum but about their disability as well.

PROSTHETICS, ORTHOTICS, AND ADAPTIVE DEVICES FOR DAILY LIVING

INTERNETRESOURCES

The Northwestern University Prosthetics-Orthotics Center (NUPOC) is dedicated to the improvement of prostheses and orthoses. Information about the program can be found at www.nupoc .northwestern.edu ▪▪▪

Many individuals with physical disabilities use prosthetics, orthotics, and other adaptive devices to help them function better on a daily basis. A **prosthesis** is an artificial replacement for a missing body part (e.g., an artificial hand or leg); an **orthosis** is a device that enhances the partial function of a part of a person's body (a brace or a device that allows a person to do something). **Adaptive devices** for daily living include a variety of adaptations of ordinary items found in the home, office, or school—such as a device to aid bathing or hand washing or walking—that make performing the tasks required for self-care and employment easier for the person who has a physical disability.

The most important principles to keep in mind are use of residual function, simplicity, and reliability. For example, the muscles of the arm, shoulder, or back operate an artificial hand. This might be too complicated or demanding for an infant or young child with a missing or deformed upper limb. Depending on the child's age, the length and function of the amputated limb, and the child's other abilities, a passive "mitt" or a variety of other prosthetic devices might be more helpful. Choice of the most useful prosthesis will depend on careful evaluation of each individual's needs. A person without legs may be taught to use her arms to move about in a wheelchair or to use her torso and arms to get about on artificial legs (perhaps also using crutches or a cane). Again, each individual's abilities and preferences must be evaluated in designing the prosthesis (see Best et al., 2010; Heller et al., 2009).

Two points regarding prosthetics, orthotics, and residual function must be kept in mind:

1. *Residual function is often important even when a prosthesis, orthosis, or adaptive device is not used*. For example, it may be crucial for the child with cerebral palsy or muscular dystrophy to learn to use the affected limbs as well as possible without the aid of any special equipment because using residual function alone will make the child more independent and can help to prevent or retard physical deterioration.

Moreover, it's often more efficient for a person to learn not to rely completely on a prosthesis or orthosis, as long as he can accomplish a task without it.

2. ***Spectacular technological developments often have very limited meaning for the immediate needs of the majority of individuals with physical disabilities***. It might be years before expensive experimental equipment is tested adequately and marketed at a cost that most people can afford, and a given device might be applicable only to a small group of individuals with an extremely rare condition. Even though a device may provide greater ability to participate in ordinary childhood activities, the current cost of some technological devices is clearly a barrier to their widespread use. Common standby prostheses, orthoses, and other equipment adapted to the needs of individuals will continue to be the most practical devices for a long time to come.

We don't mean to downplay the importance of technological advances for people with physical disabilities. Advances in technology and applications have provided extraordinary help for many students with disabilities (Best et al., 2010; DeFord, 1998; Levy & O'Rourke, 2002; Lindsey, 2000). Our point here is that the greatest significance of a technological advance often lies in how it changes seemingly ordinary items or problems. For example, technological advances in metallurgy and plastics have led to the design of much more functional braces and wheelchairs. The heavy metal-and-leather leg braces that were formerly used by many children with cerebral palsy or other neurological disorders were cumbersome, difficult to apply, and not very helpful in preventing deformity or improving function. Those braces have been largely supplanted by braces constructed of thermoform plastic. Wheelchairs are being built of lightweight metals and plastics and redesigned to allow users to go places that are inaccessible to the typical wheelchair. And an increasing number of computerized devices are improving the movement and communication abilities of people with disabilities.

The greatest problem today isn't in devising new or more sophisticated assistive technology but rather in accurately evaluating children and youths to determine what would be most useful and then making that technology available. Most schools do not now make maximum use of available technology. Many children and youths who need prostheses or other assistive devices, such as computers, special vehicles, and self-help aids, are not carefully evaluated and provided with the most appropriate equipment.

Two social issues involving prosthetics are social acceptance and participation in sports. Returning war veterans are sure to expose more people than ever to prosthetic limbs (see McGrath, 2007). Furthermore, as a story in the May 13, 2007, issue of ***The New York Times*** Sunday Style section illustrated, people with disabilities, including those with prosthetic limbs, are increasingly, unashamedly exposing them to the public (Navarro, 2007). In sports, a growing controversy over prosthetic limbs and surgical enhancements has become a matter of general public concern (see Goodman, 2007). Some are questioning whether prosthetic limbs and surgical enhancement (e.g., Lasik surgery and, inevitably, we predict, other prosthetic devices, including artificial computer-operated gadgets of all kinds) give competitors an unfair advantage (Longman, 2007; see also Howe, M., n.d.). In a sense, the controversy may parallel that of performance-enhancing drugs: what is fair and what is not, in athletic competitions? Some of these issues are considered in the accompanying Focus on Concepts, "Prosthetics."

INTERNETRESOURCES

You can find information on world-class rehabilitation tools and assistive devices at www.rehabtool.com

INTERNETRESOURCES

At Adrian's Adaptive Closet (www.adrianscloset.com), you will find links to sites that offer clothes adapted for individuals who use wheelchairs.

People with physical disabilities can learn to do many of the things most nondisabled persons do, although sometimes they must perform these tasks in different ways.

EDUCATIONAL CONSIDERATIONS

Too often, we think of people who have physical disabilities as being helpless or unable to learn. It's easy to lower our expectations for them because we know that they are indeed unable to do some

FOCUS ON Concepts

PROSTHETICS

People with disabilities, particularly those with prostheses, are increasingly participating in society without trying to hide their disabilities. Even the cartoon *Doonesbury* features a character who acquired a prosthetic lower limb after his leg was amputated following his injury in the Iraq war. Prosthetics are becoming more stylish as well as more sophisticated and useful with the increasing use of technologies in their design and engineering, and these advances in the development of prosthetics require society to confront new ethical issues.

Some people who rely on prosthetics, such as South African racing phenomenon Oscar Pistorius, who has no lower legs and runs on J-shaped carbon fiber blades known as Cheetahs, do not think of themselves as disabled (see Goodman, 2007; Longman, 2007). The people who control sporting competitions need to consider not only the possible unfair advantage of people in wheelchairs compared to runners using their feet but also the possible advantage of those

who use Cheetahs or other prostheses rather than natural body parts.

You might consider the competitions under which you would feel a prosthetic device offers an unfair advantage. For example, under what conditions would you consider wrestling unfair, were one of the wrestlers using a prosthesis? Under what conditions would you consider an intellectual competition unfair were a competitor using a form of prosthetic intelligence? These questions and others like them may seem silly at this point, but remember that the questions now being raised about running on prostheses would have seemed silly a few years ago. Ethical issues will grow along with miniaturization of computerized components, new materials, new engineering ideas, new surgical and control techniques, and other advances in prostheses (not to mention more accepting social attitudes). It takes considerable imagination to hypothesize all of the possible issues that society will face in the next few decades (see Cascio, 2007; McGrath, 2007).

INTERNETRESOURCES

For information about wheelchair technology, go to www.wheelchairnet.org or to www.whirlwindwheelchair .org/ralf.htm

things. We forget, though, that many people with physical disabilities can learn to do many or all of the things that most nondisabled people do, although sometimes they must perform these tasks in different ways (e.g., a person who does not have the use of the hands might have to use the feet or mouth). Accepting the limitations imposed by physical disabilities without trying to see how much people can learn or how the environment can be changed to allow them to respond more effectively is an insulting and dehumanizing way of responding to physical differences. This is true in academics, but it is also the case in physical education. Adapted physical education is now a special educational feature of all school programs that make appropriate adaptations for students with disabilities (Kelly & Block, 2011).

Educating students with physical disabilities isn't so much a matter of special instruction for children with disabilities as it is of educating the nondisabled population (Best et al., 2010). People with physical disabilities solve many of their own problems, but their lives are often needlessly complicated because people without disabilities give no thought to what life is like for someone with specific physical limitations. Design adaptations in buildings, furniture, household appliances, and clothing can make it possible for someone with a physical disability to function as efficiently as a person without disabilities in a home, school, or community.

The objectives of educators and other professionals who work with children and youths with physical disabilities should include autonomy and self-advocacy (Best et al., 2010; Heller, 2009). Children with physical disabilities typically want to be self-sufficient, and they should be encouraged and taught the skills they need to take care of themselves to the maximum extent possible. This requires knowledge of the physical limitations created by the disability and sensitivity to the child's social and academic needs and perceptions—understanding the environmental and psychological factors that affect classroom performance and behavior.

Individualized Planning

Students with complex physical disabilities typically require a wide array of related services as well as special education. The individualized education programs (IEPs) for these students tend to be particularly specific and detailed. The instructional goals and objectives often include seemingly minute steps, especially for young children with severe disabilities (see Best et al., 2010; Heller et al., 2009). Many of the children under age 3 who need special education and related services are children with physical disabilities. These children, under federal law, have an **individualized family service plan (IFSP)** rather than an IEP (see Chapter 4 and Dunst, 2011).

Educational Placement

Children with physical disabilities may be educated in any one of several settings, depending on the type and severity of the condition, the services available in the community, and the medical prognosis for the condition, but most are in general education settings (Best et al., 2010; Nabors & Lehmkuhl, 2004). If children with physical disabilities ordinarily attend general education classes but must be hospitalized for more than a few days, they may be included in a class in the hospital itself. If they must be confined to their homes for a time, a visiting or homebound teacher can provide tutoring until they can return to general education. In these cases, which usually involve children who have been in accidents or who have conditions that are not permanently and severely disabling, relatively minor, common-sense adjustments are required to continue the children's education and keep them from falling behind their classmates. At the other extreme, usually involving serious or chronic disabilities, the child might be taught for a time in a hospital school or a special public school class designed specifically for children with physical disabilities.

Today, most children with disabilities are being integrated into the public schools because of advances in medical treatment; new developments in bioengineering, allowing them greater mobility and functional movement; decreases in or removal of architectural barriers and transportation problems; and the movement toward public education for all children. Any placement has positive and negative features, and the best decision for a particular child requires weighing the pros and cons. Working with a special educator to better understand a student's needs and how to meet those needs is imperative. For an example of how teachers can work together, read the accompanying Making It Work box. Sometimes the benefits of a particular type of placement are either greatly exaggerated or almost completely dismissed.

Educational Goals and Curricula

Educational goals and curricula cannot be prescribed for children with physical disabilities as a group because their individual limitations vary so greatly. Even among children with the same condition, goals and curricula must be determined after assessment of each child's intellectual, physical, sensory, and emotional characteristics. A physical disability, especially a severe and chronic one that limits mobility, may have two implications for education: (1) The child might be deprived of experiences that children without disabilities have, and (2) the child might find it impossible to manipulate educational materials and respond to educational tasks the way most children do. For example, a child with severe CP can't take part in most outdoor play activities and travel experiences and might not be able to hold and turn pages in books, write, explore objects manually, or use a typewriter without special equipment. This student might require adapted physical education. Read the accompanying Responsive Instruction box, "Adapted Physical Edication," for more on this topic (see also Kelly & Block, 2011).

INTERNETRESOURCES

The Attainment Company creates resources to help people identify the emerging issues in special education and access the educational materials that will allow them to meet such issues effectively. The Website is www.attainmentcompany .com

MAKING IT WORK
COLLABORATION AND CO-TEACHING FOR STUDENTS WITH
PHYSICAL DISABILITIES AND OTHER HEALTH IMPAIRMENTS

"But I'm not a nurse!"

Students with physical disabilities often require complex systems of care, including services from health care professionals, related service personnel, and special educators. It is easy for everyone to forget about the students' cognitive and social needs because of the day-to-day physical needs. Even though a student with physical disabilities may have a wide range of services, the least restrictive environment for them may be the general education classroom. It is in this situation that collaboration with a special educator is important for the general education teacher to understand and meet the needs of these students.

WHAT DOES IT MEAN TO BE A TEACHER OF STUDENTS WITH PHYSICAL DISABILITIES?

Special educators who work with students with physical disabilities must have skills related to learning and instruction, as well as skills in determining appropriate assistive technology devices, positioning, and socialization. According to the Council for Exceptional Children, special educators should be adept at the following:

1. Use adaptations and assistive technology to provide individuals with physical and health disabilities full participation and access to the general curriculum.
2. Identify instructional practices, strategies, and adaptations necessary to accommodate the physical and communication characteristics of individuals with physical and health disabilities.
3. Communicate adaptations of educational environments necessary to accommodate individuals with physical and health disabilities.
4. Implement specialized health care interventions.

These skills require a broad range of training for special educators, including medical management and extensive collaboration with health care providers and families. With this knowledge, special educators can collaborate with general education teachers to adjust instruction, change the physical environment of the classroom, and communicate successfully with students.

SUCCESSFUL STRATEGIES FOR CO-TEACHING

Jo is a special education teacher of 5- and 6-year-olds with CP and spina bifida. Charlotte is a general education teacher with a group of 28 kindergarten-aged students, some of whom have never had any school experiences. They describe their collaboration experiences.

Jo: We combined the children into two groups. Each group was made up of half my children and half of Charlotte's children. We'd occasionally put the two groups together. I became an expert in a certain content area. I taught it to two groups, and Charlotte did the same.

Charlotte: Our classes are scheduled for music together because of our collaboration. We had a music teacher come in who taught music to both classes as a large group; however, Jo and I did stay in the classroom to facilitate management needs because it was such a large group for one teacher to handle. In fact, we had to teach the music teacher some management ideas.

Charlotte: It was a good experience for her [the music teacher]; she was able to see how you can work with a range and variety of children. It's important to find someone who has a similar philosophy and treats children the way you do, but it also must be someone you can get along with, who has the same tolerance that you do. Had we not been friendly, liked each other, and respected the way each other did things, we would not have been successful. We have seen collaborations that were not as successful as ours because they did not develop out of commonalities.

Jo: One of the most demanding things about our collaboration was keeping up with the kids, keeping them on pace, and trying to make it valuable for them educationally. As much as I want this very worthwhile social experience for my special-needs kids, am I giving them the multisensory nuts-and-bolts special education that they need? I constantly have to try to strike a balance between the social needs of the children and the intense requirements of their special needs.

Charlotte: The most demanding thing about our collaboration was not working together ourselves, but effectively meeting the needs of the children. That's really the most demanding thing: living up to them.

• By Margaret P. Weiss

RESPONSIVE *INSTRUCTION*

MEETING THE NEEDS OF STUDENTS WITH PHYSICAL DISABILITIES AND OTHER HEALTH IMPAIRMENTS

Adapted Physical Education

WHAT IS ADAPTED PHYSICAL EDUCATION?

Adapted physical education (APE) is an instructional service, not a setting or placement. Students receive APE when their disability necessitates a physical education program different from their peers. The difference can be in the form of an alternative activity, an instructional modification or adaptation, or different criteria for success. APE can be part of an integrated program, for students with and without physical disabilities, or can be a stand-alone program for students with disabilities only.

WHO QUALIFIES FOR ADAPTED PHYSICAL EDUCATION?

Any student with an IEP may be eligible for APE. The Individuals with Disabilities Education Act (IDEA) requires that "physical education services, specially designed if necessary, must be made available to every child with a disability receiving a free appropriate public education." Necessary adaptations are determined by IEP team members. Any student with gross motor skill deficits or limitations in strength, flexibility, or physical fitness should be considered for APE services.

STRATEGIES FOR MAKING ACCOMMODATIONS

Strategies for making accommodations to general physical education classes include (Auxter, Pyfer, & Huettig, 2005):

- Reduce the size of the playing field through reducing the size of the soccer field, goal area, basketball court, or length of a race.
- Change the size of equipment by using larger or more colorful balls, increasing the size of the bat but decreasing weight, using larger rackets, lighter bows, or scoops for catching.
- Reduce the playing area by adding more players to the field or court.
- Modify basic rules such as everyone plays seated, less mobile players get two or three bounces to get to the ball in tennis, rest periods or frequent substitutions are allowed, shorten the game, or partner activities.
- Use specialized equipment such as a ramp or bumpers for bowling, a batting tee, or a sit-ski for skiing.

The overarching aim for APE is for students to have access to activities that will support physical, recreational, and/or leisure goals. APE should take place in the least restrictive environment (LRE). Determining the LRE involves considerations of safety as well as opportunities for meaningful participation. For many students, the LRE will be the general education physical education class.

• By Kristin L. Sayeski

For children with an impairment that is only physical, curriculum and educational goals should ordinarily be the same as those for nondisabled children: reading, writing, arithmetic, and experiences designed to familiarize them with the world around them. In addition, special instruction might be needed in mobility skills, daily living skills, and occupational skills. Because of their physical impairments, these children might need special, individualized instruction in the use of mechanical devices that will help them to perform tasks that are much simpler for people without disabilities. Children with other disabilities in addition to physical limitations will require further adaptation of curricula (Best et al., 2010; Heller et al, 2009).

Educational goals for students with severe or profound disabilities must be related to their functioning in everyday community environments. Only recently have educators and professionals begun to address the problems of analyzing community tasks (e.g., crossing streets, using money, riding public transportation, greeting neighbors) and planning efficient instruction for individuals with severe disabilities. Efficient instruction in such skills requires that teaching occur in the community environment.

The range of educational objectives and curricula for children with physical disabilities is often extended beyond the objectives and curricula typically provided for other students in school. For example, very young children and those with severe neuromuscular problems might need objectives and curricula focusing on the most basic self-care skills

INTERNETRESOURCES

For ideas and guidance about independent living, see one of the following: Canine Companions at www.caninecompanions.org Computer-related products at www.closingthegap.com Independent Living Research Utilization Center at www.ilru.org Institute on Independent Living at www. independentliving.org

RESPONSIVE *INSTRUCTION*
MEETING THE NEEDS OF STUDENTS WITH PHYSICAL DISABILITIES AND OTHER HEALTH IMPAIRMENTS

Integrating Physical and Occupational Therapy in General Education Settings

The majority of students with physical disabilities receive related services as a part of their educational program. Related services can include anything from speech-language pathology to counseling to transportation. Two common related services for students with physical disabilities are occupational and physical therapy. Researchers have found that the more integrated these types of services are into education settings, the more effective the outcomes (see Heller et al., 2009).

PHYSICAL AND OCCUPATIONAL THERAPY

Understanding the differences between physical and occupational therapy can be confusing. Yet a clear understanding of the skills that are supported through these therapies is fundamental for creating the necessary bridge between out-of-class therapy and integrated therapy that supports student learning.

Physical therapy addresses sensory and gross motor functions. Physical therapists can assist students by identifying optimal positions for various tasks; teach students how to move within the classroom and school environment; and develop students' movement, strength, and coordination. Occupational therapists provide support for daily living skills such as dressing, bathing, and toileting as well as fine motor skills (handling small objects, handwriting, oral-motor skills).

CLASSROOM IMPLICATIONS

As a classroom teacher, multidisciplinary collaboration among all service providers is a must. When planning for the integration of physical or occupational services in the classroom, the classroom teacher should consider the following questions:

- *What are educationally relevant services versus medically relevant services?* For example, an educationally relevant service would be to work on transfer and handling techniques with the teacher and paraprofessional to position a student for instruction. A medically relevant therapy would be strength building.

- *What are the educationally relevant IEP goals, and how can therapy support progress toward those goals?* For example, mobility independence, ability to operate assistive technology, improved posture, and improved upper extremity coordination are all therapy goals that directly relate to improved educational outcomes.

- *What type of service is necessary: direct, indirect, or both?* Direct services involve hands-on treatment provided directly by the therapist. Preferably, these treatments occur within the natural environment (classroom, playground, gym) where the skill is expected. Indirect services, on the other hand, involve consultation or monitoring support. Under a consultation model, the therapist makes recommendations for instructional modifications, activity enhancement, environmental modifications, adaptation of materials, or schedule alterations. The therapist may even train the classroom teacher in ways to provide direct services. Monitoring involves periodic evaluations of student progress and related training for team members. A combination of direct and indirect services provides both direct services for certain goals or skills and consultation support for others.

- *Is peer support appropriate?* As students become more skilled, peer support can be solicited. This reduces the dependence a student has on any one individual and encourages interdependence—an important skill as students mature.

By working with therapists to identify ways to support therapy within the classroom, teachers learn ways to reduce the physical challenges students can encounter within general education settings, while fostering the development of necessary physical and occupational skills.

• By Kristin L. Sayeski

■ ■ ■ ■ ■ ■ ■ ■ ■

(e.g., swallowing, chewing, self-feeding). Older students might need not only to explore possible careers in the way all students should, but also to consider the special accommodations their physical limitations demand for successful performance (see Best et al., 2010).

Although all students can profit from a discussion of death and dying, education about these topics might be particularly important in classrooms in which a student has a terminal illness. Teachers should be direct and open in their discussion of death and dying. Death shouldn't be a taboo subject; nor should teachers deny their own feelings or squelch the feelings of others. Confronted with the task of educating a child or youth with a terminal illness, teachers should seek available resources and turn to professionals in other disciplines for help (Heller et al., 2009).

Links with Other Disciplines

Children seldom have a single disability, and many children with physical disabilities have other disabilities as well. Therefore, multiple disciplines are often required, and special education is only one of many services required (see Batshaw, 2002).

Many children with physical disabilities will need the services of a physical therapist and/or occupational therapist. (For a description of classroom implications, see the Responsive Instruction box, "Integrating Physical and Occupational Therapy in General Education Settings on the opposite page.") Both professionals can give valuable suggestions about helping children use their physical abilities to the greatest extent possible, continuing therapeutic management in the classroom, and encouraging independence and good work habits. The teacher should be particularly concerned with handling and positioning the child to minimize risk of further physical disability and to maximize efficient independent movement and manipulation of educational materials to enhance learning.

Specialists in prosthetics and orthotics design and build artificial limbs, braces, and other devices that help individuals who are physically disabled to function more conventionally. By conferring with specialists, the teacher will better understand the function and operation of a child's prosthesis or orthosis and know what the child can and cannot be expected to do.

Cooperation with psychologists and social workers can be particularly important in the case of a child with a physical disability. Working with the child's family and community agencies is often necessary to prevent lapses in treatment. The child may also be particularly susceptible to psychological stress, so the teacher might need to consult the school psychologist to obtain an accurate assessment of intellectual potential.

Speech-language therapists are often called on to work with children with physical disabilities, especially those with cerebral palsy. The teacher will want advice from the speech-language therapist on how to maximize the child's learning of speech and language. Individuals of all ages need access to play and recreation, regardless of their physical abilities. Any adequate program for children or youths with physical disabilities will provide toys, games, and physical exercise to stimulate, amuse, and teach recreation skills and provide the youngster with options for productive leisure (Kelly & Block, 2011). Physical education that is adapted to the abilities and disabilities of students is an important part of every sound school program.

EARLY INTERVENTION

All people who work with young children with physical disabilities have two concerns: (1) early identification and intervention and (2) development of communication. Identifying signs of developmental delay so that intervention can begin as early as possible is important in preventing further disabilities that can result from lack of teaching and proper care. Early intervention also maximizes the outcome of therapy (see Dunst, 2011). Communication skills are difficult for some children with physical disabilities, and they are a critical objective of any preschool program (see Chapter 9). See the accompanying Success Stories box featuring Danielle, a 4-year-old who has received intensive language instruction as well as other modifications to her environment.

Besides communication, the first concern of teachers of young children with physical disabilities should be handling and positioning. *Handling* refers to how the child is picked up, carried, held, and assisted; *positioning* refers to providing support for the child's body and arranging instructional or play materials in certain ways. Proper handling makes the child more comfortable and receptive to education. Proper positioning maximizes physical efficiency and ability to manipulate materials; it also inhibits undesirable motor responses while promoting desired growth and motor patterns (Best et al., 2010). Proper positioning for one child might not be appropriate for another.

Success Stories

DANIELLE PROSPERS DUE TO INTENSIVE EARLY INTERVENTION AND INTRAPROFESSIONAL AND PARENTAL COMMUNICATION

Jennifer Durrance, Danielle's mother: "Her teacher wrote me notes daily because she knew Danielle couldn't tell me about her day."

After 3 years of early intervention services, 4-year-old Danielle Durrance receives early childhood special education in an inclusive preschool program.

These are the keys to her success:

★ Intensive early intervention
★ Relentless communication
★ Specific goals addressing physical delays and academic readiness

SPECIAL EDUCATOR LEIGH ANNE WILLIAMS teaches typically developing youngsters as well as 3- and 4-year-olds with disabilities or developmental delays. Danielle Durrance is the only child in her class who uses a wheelchair. Danielle's mother, Jennifer Durrance, communicates frequently with Williams to ensure that Danielle receives appropriate instruction and related services in her inclusive preschool program. Since she was 9 months old, Danielle has prospered from intensive, relentless, and specific special education.

★ Intensive Early Intervention. Danielle has cerebral palsy (CP), a neurological condition that limits her mobility, speech, and social interactions. On the day before Halloween, she dabbed white finger-painted ghosts and

goblins on black paper. Danielle finished her creation at her standing table, a piece of adaptive equipment that provides her with vertical support for up to 60 minutes each day. While her nine classmates washed their hands, Danielle transferred to her wheelchair with the help of one of the classroom's three instructional assistants. "My assistants take turns lifting Danielle and positioning her to use her walker or the vestibular swing that hangs from the classroom ceiling. They also help with her personal hygiene and we keep a chart on the bathroom door to be sure we're sharing her physical support," says Williams.

Danielle was born prematurely at 34 weeks' gestation and experienced a lack of oxygen during delivery. She weighed only 4 pounds, 4 ounces, at birth and spent 11 days in the hospital. When she was 4 months old, her

The teacher of young children with physical disabilities must know how to teach gross motor responses (e.g., head control, rolling over, sitting, standing, and walking) and must understand how abnormal reflexes that may be a part of developmental disabilities can interfere with learning basic motor skills. If the child has severe neurological and motor impairments, the teacher might need to begin by focusing on teaching the child to eat (e.g., how to chew and swallow) and to make the oral movements that are required for speech (Best et al., 2010; Martin, 2006). Fine motor skills, such as pointing, reaching, grasping, and releasing, can be critically important. These motor skills are best taught in the context of daily lessons that involve self-help and communication.

Motor skills shouldn't be taught in isolation but as part of daily living and learning activities that will increase the child's communication, independence, creativity, motivation, and future learning. Learning social responsiveness, appropriate social initiation, how to play with others, and problem solving are other important goals for which the teacher must develop instructional strategies.

TRANSITION

Transition involves a turning point, a change from one situation or environment to another. When special educators speak of transition, they typically refer to change from school to work or from adolescence to adulthood. For children with physical disabilities, however, transition is perhaps a more pervasive concern than it is for children with other disabilities.

mother suspected something was wrong. "She couldn't roll over and find a toy that was near her in the crib. You know how babies look at their hands a lot? Well, she would mostly look at one hand; she kept her other hand down." At 6 months, Danielle was not sitting up, and it was clear that her eyes were crossed. When she was 9 months old, developmental tests, including an MRI, confirmed that Danielle had CP, and early intervention services began. A special education teacher came to the house to work with Danielle, and her parents drove her to physical and occupational therapy several times a week. They also made visits to an ophthalmologist.

★ Relentless Communication. Mrs. Durrance credits effective communication between parents and professionals for Danielle's smooth transition from early intervention services to preschool special education. "At the transition meeting, someone asked if I had a picture of Danielle with me. I really appreciated that. There was nothing in particular that caused me to feel stressed, but I think teachers should know that many parents feel very nervous at these meetings."

Jennifer Durrance also advises teachers to learn as much as they can about how a child's disability affects her life and her learning:

- *Know the IEP*, especially when a child is served in the regular classroom.
- *Keep communication a priority*. Teachers need to know the parents of the child, too.
- *Seek information*. Know that parents are knowledgeable about their child's disability.

★ Specific Goals Addressing Physical Delays and Academic Readiness. Danielle attended the Green Valley Preschool Program. According to evaluations using the Carolina Curriculum for Preschoolers with Special Needs, Danielle has progressed in all developmental areas, although her delays in cognition and social adaptation place her approximately 1 year to 1 1/2 years behind her age peers. She remembers objects that have been hidden, understands concepts like "empty/full," and "add one more." Socially, she follows directions, expresses enthusiasm for work or play, plays games with supervision, and enjoys being with other children. According to her IEP, Danielle's social interactions are limited by her physical delays. Danielle's fine and gross motor skills place her closer to 2 years behind her age peers. She receives occupational and physical therapy to enhance her manipulative and visual motor skills and to improve her mobility and endurance. She also receives speech-language therapy. Receptively, Danielle appears to understand many age-appropriate concepts and vocabulary, but she doesn't often initiate communication, nor does she imitate consistently.

In Spring the IEP team will make decisions for Danielle's programming for the next school year. Together, her parents and her multidisciplinary team will decide if Danielle should start Kindergarten with her age peers or whether she would benefit more from extended preschool support.

• By Jean B. Crockett

It may involve discharge from intensive care or transition from hospital to home at any age. In fact, transition begins for some newborns immediately after they have been treated with sophisticated medical procedures. Nevertheless, we focus here on the transition concerns of adolescents and young adults with physical disabilities. Clearly, transition planning for many students with physical disabilities, including those who are supported by medical technology, is inadequate (see Moon, 2011; Scanlon, 2011).

Two areas of concern for transition stand out clearly for adolescents and young adults with physical disabilities: careers and sociosexuality. Adolescents begin contemplating and experimenting with jobs, social relations, and sexuality in direct and serious ways. For the adolescent with a physical disability, these questions and trial behaviors are often especially perplexing, not just to themselves but also to their families: Can I get and hold a satisfying job? Can I become independent? Will I have close and lasting friendships? Will anyone find me physically attractive? How can I gratify my sexual needs? Ordinary adolescents have a hard time coming to grips with these questions and the developmental tasks they imply; adolescents with physical disabilities often have an even harder time (see White, Schuyler, Edelman, Hayes, & Batshaw, 2002).

As we pointed out in discussing psychological characteristics, no formula predicts the emotional or behavioral problems a person with a given physical disability might have. The fact that children are enabled to walk doesn't mean that they will be able to walk all their lives. They might require continued services if they are to continue walking as adults (Bottos, Feliciangeli, Sciuto, Gericke, & Vianello, 2001). Much depends on the management and training the person has received and continues to receive as an adolescent and as an adult. Bottos and colleagues provide the following caution about interventions for CP: "Services for individuals with CP should be planned keeping in mind an entire life perspective rather than just the child-focused approach. Reduced contact when children grow up often results in a general deterioration of the quality of life of adults with disabilities and their careers" (2001, p. 526).

Choosing a Career

In working out an occupational goal for the adolescent or young adult with physical disabilities, it's important to carefully assess the individual's specific abilities, disabilities, and motivation. Postsecondary education must be considered in light of the individual's interests, strengths, demands, and accessibility. Some disabilities clearly rule out certain occupational choices. With other disabilities, high motivation and full use of residual function can make it possible to achieve unusual professional status.

One of the greatest problems in dealing with adolescents who have physical disabilities is helping them to attain a realistic employment outlook. Intelligence, emotional characteristics, motivation, and work habits must be assessed at least as carefully as physical limitations. Furthermore, the availability of jobs and the demands of certain occupations must be taken into account. The child who has moderate intellectual disability and severe spastic quadriplegia, for instance, is highly unlikely to have a career as a lawyer, a laboratory technician, or a clerk-typist. But what of a child who is physically disabled because of CP but who has a bright mind and is highly motivated? Such a person might well overcome both the physical limitation and the associated social stigma and succeed in a wide variety of fields in which the work is more mental than physical. For instance, consider Tyler Rich, the young man introduced in the accompanying Peer Connections feature, who's on the path to a very bright career.

The occupational outlook for students with physical disabilities is as varied as the students themselves. Students with mild or transitory disabling conditions might not be affected at all in their occupational choices. Yet some with relatively mild physical disabilities might be unemployed or even unemployable because of inappropriate social and emotional behavior or poor work habits; they might need vocational rehabilitation training to function even in a vocation with limited demands. Some people with severe physical disabilities can use their intelligence, social skills, and residual physical abilities to the fullest and become competitive employees (or employers) in demanding occupations.

The outlook for employment of students with physical or multiple and severe disabilities has been improved dramatically by legislation and research and demonstration projects. More accessible transportation and buildings, increased skill in using technology to allow people to accomplish tasks at work, and greater commitment to preparing people with disabilities for work are resulting in more personal independence, economic self-sufficiency, and social acceptance, which benefit not only people with disabilities, but the economy and society as well.

We now recognize that preparing for work begins in childhood. Long before adolescence, children, including those with physical disabilities, need to be taught about and to explore various careers. They need to be thinking about what they like to do as well as what they are particularly good at and about the demands and rewards of various kinds of jobs. The objective should be to help students select appropriate training and enter a career that makes maximum use of their abilities in ways that they find personally gratifying.

Supported employment for people with severe disabilities is a relatively new concept that is being adopted widely. In this approach, a person with a severe disability works in a regular work setting. She becomes a regular employee, performs a valued function in the same workplace as employees without disabilities, and receives fair remuneration. Training and continued support are necessary—hence the term *supported employment*. For example, a person with disabilities might be hired as a greeter at a store but might need training and continued support in such skills as making eye contact, smiling, welcoming shoppers to the store, and offering a shopping cart or information to customers. Training and continued support might also be required to help the person with disabilities know when to leave people alone and not insist on providing information or assistance that the customer does not want.

TYLER RICH was born with cerebral palsy, which affects the use of his legs. After using a walker for most of his life, he discovered the Segway Personal Transporter as a high school sophomore, joining a growing community of persons with disabilities who use Segways to enhance their mobility. Tyler's interest in engineering prompted him to approach SegVator, a company that made aftermarket products designed to enhance the functionality of the Segway Personal Transporter. He now tests many of their products, including car lifts and customized seating.

1. What do you do for fun? I love fly fishing, sailing, anything on the water. My grandfather lived on a sailboat, and I think love of the water is in my blood. I also work out several days a week. I used to use a walker, but now I put that energy towards going to the gym and working out to target specific muscles in my legs. It makes me feel good, and developing core strength also helps me to better control my Segway—although even before I had core strength I could still use it.

2. What is your favorite way to relax? I enjoy playing video games. And I read a lot; my favorite genre is satire.

3. What is your pet peeve? Ignorance. I try to educate people who are ignorant. If it doesn't work, I just go on about my business.

4. You mention that your pet peeve is ignorance. Is this ignorance about anything in particular? Ignorance in general? Could you tell us a bit more about this? By ignorance I'm referring to general closed-mindedness. When I approach someone I don't make judgments based on outward appearances. I get to know them and discover who they are as a person. If people were more accepting I think the world would be a lot better off.

5. Can you recall one teacher in particular who has been a positive influence in your life? Mr. Coughlin, my shop teacher in high school. Engineering is a real area of interest for me. Mr. Coughlin noticed that I was more experienced than most of the class and allowed me to work on my own projects instead of having to follow the curriculum. As a senior, I got to be a teaching assistant in his class.

6. Is there anyone else (celebrity, family member) whom you regard as a role model? Why are they a role model for you? Both of my grandfathers were role models for me. My mother's father was a woodworker, and I think that's where some of my interest in design and engineering came from. He lived on a sailboat, and my passion for sailing and other water activities probably comes from him. My dad's father designed machines and was always tinkering with something. I definitely take after him, too!

7. What is the most difficult thing for you about having a disability? Honestly, it's just not that big a deal for me.

I was born with cerebral palsy, so I've never known life any other way. I can do anything in the world, but I might just do it differently from other people.

8. What are some of the misperceptions others have about your disability? Cerebral palsy is such a broad term. I'm very active and high functioning, but people sometimes think that I am paralyzed. Some people also assume that I have cognitive impairment, but in my case cerebral palsy only affects my mobility.

9. Has your disability affected your social relationships? If so, how? In order to be friends with me, someone has to be an accepting person—accepting of people's differences. Since this is the type of person I'd want to be friends with anyway, it works out well. I've made a lot of good friends through a program I participate in at a nearby ski resort. I am very active and don't want to be handled with kid gloves because of my cerebral palsy, and my friends in Wintergreen Adaptive Skiing Program understand that.

10. Are there any advantages to having a disability that others might be surprised to know? I really appreciate the value of hard work, and I don't feel entitled to things that I haven't earned. I've gotten to do a lot of very cool things in my life because I have been willing to work hard to reach my goals.

11. How do you think others perceive you? I think there can be a stigma of the Segway as a lazy person's device. People see me riding it, and think that I just don't want to walk. It's ironic, because I work so hard every day.

12. Please fill in the blank: I couldn't live without _____. My wits. I like thinking, of being cognizant of where I am.

13. What do you see your life looking like 10 years from now? In 10 years, I see myself working in Engineering. As an undergrad I plan to focus on studying mechanical engineering, and in graduate school I would like to explore biomedical engineering. Before I'm 35 years old I'd like to own a company that makes medical engineering products that make life easier for people with disabilities. Oh, and I'd also love fractional ownership of a jet plane.

CONNECT WITH TYLER— Tyler welcomes you to contact him online at pearson.connect .tyler.rich@gmail.com

New technologies, especially in computing and other electronic devices, offer great promise for enabling students with physical disabilities to achieve personal independence, to acquire education and training that will make them employable, and to find employment. In some cases, the technology is readily available, and educators only need to become aware of the software (e.g., software that allows the functions of keys to be altered), find ways in which keystrokes can be saved through subprogramming routines (e.g., macros or find-and-replace features in word processing), or provide substitutions for physical manipulation of materials (e.g., computer graphics programs as substitutes for paper paste-ups or model construction).

Sometimes an individual's ability to use standard equipment is greatly enhanced by a simple modification such as orientation or location. Simply placing a keyboard in a vertical position over a monitor can enhance the ability of someone who uses a headstick to use a computer. (A headstick is an adaptive device that allow people who can't use their hands or feet, but who have control of neck muscles, to use a computer or accomplish other tasks). Teachers must always look for simple, inexpensive, or cost-free ways to facilitate the performance of students with disabilities—to prevent an environment designed for people without disabilities from handicapping those who must do things a different way. Overlooking the seemingly obvious is perhaps the way in which we most frequently handicap people with disabilities.

Sociosexuality

Until fairly recently, physical disabilities were assumed to cancel human sexuality. People who were not typical physically, especially if they had limited mobility, were thought of as having no sex appeal for anyone and as having little or no ability or right to function sexually.

Fortunately, attitudes and experiences are changing. It's now recognized that people with disabilities have a right to family life education, including sex education, and to a full range of human relationships, including appropriate sexual expression. Sociosexual education for students with physical disabilities, as for all other children and youths, should begin early, continue through adulthood, and include information about the structures and functions of the body, human relationships and responsibilities, and alternative modes of sexual gratification. Youths with physical disabilities need to experience close friendships and warm physical contact that is not sexually intimate. But it is neither realistic nor fair to expect people with physical disabilities to keep all their relationships platonic or to limit themselves to fantasy. Most physical disabilities, even if severe, don't in themselves kill sexual desire or prevent sexual gratification, nor do they preclude marriage and children. The purpose of special education and rehabilitation is to make exceptional individuals' lives as full and complete as possible. In the case of youths with physical disabilities, this might involve teaching or providing alternative means of sexual stimulation and accepting sexual practices and relationships that are different from the norm. With sensitive education and rehabilitation, satisfying sociosexual expression can be achieved by all but a small minority of people with disabilities.

SUMMARY

How are physical disabilities defined and classified?

- Physical disabilities are physical limitations or health problems that interfere with school attendance or learning to such an extent that special services, training, equipment, materials, or facilities are required.
  - May be congenital or acquired.
  - May be acute or chronic, episodic or progressive.

- May be accompanied by other disabilities, such as intellectual disability and emotional or behavioral disorders, or special gifts or talents.

- Major categories are neuromotor impairments, orthopedic or musculoskeletal disorders, and other conditions that affect health or physical abilities.

What is the prevalence of physical disabilities, and what is the need for special education?

- About 1% of the child population has a physical disability or health impairment.
  - About a fifth of these have multiple disabilities.
  - About one-tenth of these have orthopedic problems.
  - About 80% of these have chronic health problems.

What are some major neuromotor impairments?

- All involve damage to the brain before, during, or soon after birth or damage to the spinal cord.
  - Cerebral palsy, characterized by paralysis, weakness, uncoordination, and/or other motor dysfunction, sometimes by intellectual disability or other disabilities
  - Seizure disorder, an abnormal electrical discharge in the brain
  - Spina bifida, the failure of the spinal column to close during fetal development

What are some major orthopedic and musculoskeletal disorders?

- Muscular dystrophy, a degenerative disease causing a progressive weakening and wasting away of muscle
- Juvenile rheumatoid arthritis, acute inflammation around the joints that may cause chronic pain and other complications

What other conditions affect health or physical ability?

- Fetal alcohol syndrome (FAS), now one of the most common causes of malformation and intellectual disability, caused by the mother's abuse of alcohol during pregnancy
- AIDS, a life-threatening viral infection that often involves neurological complications such as intellectual disability, seizures, cerebral palsy, and emotional or behavioral disorders
- Accidents

How can physical disabilities be prevented?

- Safety precautions, better health care, prevention of pregnancy in early teens, prevention of child abuse, prevention of conditions that cause brain or spinal injury

What are the psychological and behavioral characteristics of individuals with physical disabilities?

- No generalizations are possible.
- Much depends on the reactions of family and the public.

What are prosthetics, orthotics, and adaptive devices?

- Prosthetics are artificial body parts.
- Orthotics enhance the function of a body part.
- Adaptive devices aid daily activity.

What are the major educational considerations for students with physical disabilities?

- Education must make the most of the student's assets.
- Education should be as normal as possible and equip the student for daily living as well as employment or further education.

Why is early intervention important, and on what should it focus?

- Early intervention is important in preventing further disability and maximizing the child's development.
- Early intervention should focus on communication, handling, positioning, and social skills.

What are the major issues in transition for students with physical disabilities?

- Transition may involve movement from one setting to another as well as preparation for adulthood.
  - Choice of and preparation for a career are important issues.
  - Sociosexuality is another critical issue.

COUNCIL FOR EXCEPTIONAL CHILDREN

Addressing the Professional Standards

 Council for Exceptional Children

Council for Exceptional Children (CEC) Common Core Knowledge and Skills addressed in this chapter: ICC1K5, ICC1K8, ICC2K4, ICC2K5, ICC3K5, ICC4S3, ICC4S4, ICC4S6, ICC5S1, ICC5S2, ICC5S3, ICC5S15, ICC6S1, ICC7K2, ICC7S1, ICC7S5, ICC7S7, ICC7S9, ICC8K2, ICC8K4, ICC8S2, ICC8S4, ICC8S6, ICC10K2, ICC10K4, ICC10S6

Appendix: Provides a full listing of the CEC Common Core Standards and associated Knowledge and Skill Statements listed here.

MYEDUCATIONLAB

PEARSON **myeducationlab** Now go to Topic 16: Multiple Disabilities and TBI in the MyEducationLab (www.myeducationlab.com) for your course, where you can:

- Find learning outcomes for the broad concepts covered in this chapter along with the national standards that connect to these outcomes.
- Complete Assignments and Activities that can help you more deeply understand the chapter content.
- Examine challenging situations presented in the IRIS Center Resources.
- Apply and practice your understanding of the core concepts and skills identified in the chapter with the Building Teaching Skills and Dispositions learning units.
- Check your comprehension on the content covered in the chapter by going to the Study Plan in the Book-Specific Resources for your text. Here you will be able to take a chapter quiz, receive feedback on your answers, and then access Review, Practice, and Enrichment activities to enhance your understanding of chapter content.
- Watch video clips of CCSSO Teacher of the Year award winners responding to the question: "Why I teach?" in the Teacher Talk section.

MISCONCEPTIONS ABOUT
Learners with Special Gifts and Talents

MYTH • People with special intellectual gifts are physically weak, socially inept, narrow in interests, and prone to emotional instability and early decline.

FACT • Wide individual variations exist among individuals with special intellectual gifts, and most are healthy, well adjusted, socially attractive, and morally responsible.

MYTH • People who have special gifts or talents are in a sense superhuman.

FACT • People with special gifts or talents are not superhuman; rather, they are human beings with extraordinary gifts in particular areas. And like everyone else, they may have particular faults.

MYTH • People with special gifts or talents tend to be mentally unstable.

FACT • Those with special gifts or talents are about as likely to be well adjusted and emotionally healthy as those who do not have such gifts.

MYTH • We know that 3% to 5% of the population has special gifts or talents.

FACT • The percentage of the population that is found to have special gifts or talents depends on the definition of *giftedness* used. Some definitions include only 1% or 2% of the population; others, over 20%.

MYTH • Giftedness is a stable trait, always consistently evident in all periods of a person's life.

FACT • Some of the remarkable talents and productivity of people with special gifts develop early and continue throughout life; in other cases, a person's gifts or talents are not noticed until adulthood. Occasionally, a child who shows outstanding ability becomes a nondescript adult.

MYTH • People who have special gifts do everything well.

FACT • Some people who are characterized as having a special gift have superior abilities of many kinds; others have clearly superior talents in only one area.

MYTH • People have special intellectual gifts if they score above a certain level on intelligence tests.

FACT • IQ is only one indication of one kind of giftedness. Creativity and high motivation are as important as general intelligence. Gifts or talents in some areas, such as the visual and performing arts, are not assessed by IQ tests.

MYTH • Students who have a true gift or talent for something will excel without special education. They need only the incentives and instruction that are appropriate for all students.

FACT • Some children with special gifts or talents will perform at a remarkably high level without special education of any kind, and some will make outstanding contributions even in the face of great obstacles to their achievement. But most will not come close to achieving at a level commensurate with their potential unless their talents are deliberately fostered by instruction that is appropriate for their advanced abilities.

People who have special gifts or the potential for gifted performance can go through life unrecognized. As Mark Twain pointed out in this chapter's opening quotation, they might seem unremarkable to their closest associates. Sometimes the special talents or gifts of children and youths aren't discovered because their families and intimates place no particular value on their special abilities. And sometimes they aren't recognized because these young people are not given opportunities or training. Especially in the case of those who are poor or members of minority groups, students with extraordinary gifts or talents may be deprived of chances to demonstrate and develop their potential. How many more outstanding artists and scientists would we have if every talented child had the opportunity and the training necessary to develop her talents to the fullest possible extent? We know that we would have more, but we don't know how many.

Unlike disabilities, gifts and talents are abilities that nearly everyone believes should be fostered deliberately. Yet giftedness is not without risk of stigma and rejection. Many people have a low level of tolerance for those who eclipse ordinary individuals in some area of achievement, especially in areas of academic knowledge or achievement. Children who achieve far beyond the level of their average peers may be subjected to criticism, social isolation, or unhelpful social pressure by their parents, other children, or school personnel (Callahan, 2011; Freeman, 2000, 2005).

Some of the problems of giftedness parallel those of disabling conditions. For instance, defining and identifying children with special gifts or talents involve the same difficulties as defining and identifying children with intellectual disability or emotional or behavioral disorders (see Kauffman & Hallahan, 2005). But an underlying philosophical question regarding giftedness makes us think differently about this exceptionality: Most of us feel a moral obligation to help people who are at some disadvantage compared to the average person, who have differences that prevent them from achieving ordinary levels of competence unless they are given special help. But we may not feel the same moral obligation to help people who have special gifts, who are already ahead of most of us, to become even better and distinguish themselves further by fulfilling their highest promise.

The desirability or necessity of helping the highest-achieving students to become even better is often questioned. Today, the emphasis is on programs to develop the talents of *all* students, with less special attention to those who might be identified as gifted or talented. As some researchers have noted, this trend toward downplaying or neglecting giftedness, especially as affected by the No Child Left Behind Act of 2002 (NCLB), might not be very wise (Gallagher, 2000b; Gentry, 2006; Goodkin, 2005; Kauffman & Konold, 2007; Mendoza, 2006; Van Tassel-Baska, 2006). DiGennaro (2007) describes the neglect of our most talented students as an ugly secret of contemporary American education policy.

DEFINITION

Students with special gifts excel in some way compared to other students of the same age. Beyond this almost meaningless statement, however, little agreement exists among educators about how giftedness should be defined. School systems have widely differing practices regarding the education of students with special gifts or talents, because the term *gifted* has no clearcut definition. Disagreements about definition are due primarily to differences of opinion regarding the following questions:

1. *In what ways do students with a special gift or talent excel?* Do they excel in general intelligence, insight, creativity, special talents, and achievements in academic subjects or in a valued line of work, moral judgment, or some combination of factors? Perhaps nearly everyone is gifted in some way or other. What kind of giftedness is most important? What kind of giftedness should be encouraged?

2. *How is giftedness measured?* Is it measured by standardized tests of aptitude and achievement, teacher judgments, past performance in school or everyday life, or some other means? If it's measured in any one particular way, some individuals will be overlooked. If past performance is the test, giftedness is being defined after the fact. What measurement techniques are valid and reliable? What measurements will identify those students who have the potential to develop special gifts or talents?

3. *To what degree must a student excel to be considered to have a special gift or talent?* Must the student do better than 50%, 80%, 90%, or 99% of the comparison group? The number of individuals with special gifts will vary depending on the criterion (or criteria) for giftedness. What percentage of the population should be considered to have special gifts?

4. *Who should be in the comparison group?* Should the comparison group comprise every student of the same chronological age, the other students in the same school, all

myeducationlab

To check your comprehension on the content covered in Chapter 15, go to the Book-Specific Resources in the MyEducationLab (www.myeducationlab.com) for your course, select your text, and complete the Study Plan. Here you will be able to take a chapter quiz, receive feedback on your answers, and then access review, practice, and enrichment activities to enhance your understanding of chapter content. ■

INTERNETRESOURCES

You may want to visit the site of the National Association for Gifted Children at www.nagc.org

students of the same ethnic or racial origin, or some other grouping? Almost everyone is the brightest or most capable in some group. What group should set the standard?

5. *Why should students with special gifts be identified?* What social or cultural good is expected to come from their identification? Is it important to meet individual students' educational needs? Are national economic or security issues at stake? Does identifying these individuals maintain an elite group or social power? By providing special educational opportunities for these students, will others reap personal or social benefits? What criteria will be used to judge whether identifying students with special gifts or talents pays off?

Giftedness, or *talent*, like *intellectual disability*, is whatever we choose to make it. Someone can be considered gifted (or intellectually disabled) one day and not the next, simply because an arbitrary definition has been changed. The definitions that professionals use have no inherent rightness or wrongness. Some definitions might be more logical, more precise, or more useful than others, but we are still unable to say that they are more correct in some absolute sense. We have to struggle with the concepts of gift and talent and the reasons for identifying individuals with gifts or talents before we can make any decisions about definition. Any definition of giftedness is shaped to a large extent by what the surrounding culture believes is most useful or necessary for its survival. Giftedness is defined, not discovered (see Callahan, 2011; Gallagher, 2000a, 2000b, 2002; Heller, Monks, Sternberg, & Subotnik, 2000; Lohman, 2006).

Even the terminology of giftedness can be rather confusing. Besides the word *gifted*, a variety of other terms have been used to describe individuals who are superior in some way: talented, creative, insightful, genius, and precocious, for example.

- **Precocity** refers to remarkable early development. Precocious children develop gifts in such areas as language, music, or mathematics at a very young age.
- **Insight** may be defined as separating relevant from irrelevant information, finding novel and useful ways of combining relevant bits of information, or relating new and old information in a novel and productive way.
- **Genius** has sometimes been used to indicate a particular aptitude or capacity in any area. More often, it has been used to indicate extremely rare intellectual powers (often assumed to be indicated by IQ) or creativity.

Children who are gifted may have superior cognitive abilities that allow them to compete with adults of average intellect.

- **Creativity** refers to the ability to express novel and useful ideas, to sense and elucidate novel and important relationships, and to ask previously unthought of, but crucial, questions.
- **Talent** ordinarily has been used to indicate a special ability, aptitude, or accomplishment.
- **Giftedness**, as we use the term in this chapter, refers to cognitive (intellectual) superiority (not necessarily of genius caliber), creativity, and motivation in combination and of sufficient magnitude to set children apart from the vast majority of their age peers and make it possible for them to contribute something of particular value to society.

The lack of consensus about what giftedness means poses problems for government definitions. No federal law requires special education for students with special gifts or talents, although federal legislation encourages states to develop programs and support research. The federal mandate for special education applies only if the student has a disability in addition to giftedness (see Huefner, 2006; Zirkel, 2003). However, most states mandate programs, and the most common elements of state definitions are (1) general intellectual ability, (2) specific academic aptitude, (3) creative thinking ability, (4) advanced ability in the fine arts and performing arts, and (5) leadership ability.

The field of special education is beginning to appreciate the different ways in which giftedness can be expressed in various areas of human endeavor. Likewise, educators are starting to acknowledge the extent to which the meaning of giftedness is rooted in cultural values (Gallagher, 2002; Karnes & Bean, 2001; Lohman, 2006; Sternberg, 1998, 2000). There are many different abilities and many different ways of measuring them. What's considered giftedness and how it's measured depend to a large extent on what a culture values and believes. Most experts now acknowledge that intelligence isn't all there is to giftedness (Lohman, 2006).

Recognizing the many facets of human intelligence has led to dissatisfaction with previous conceptualizations of general intelligence that reduced it to a single number (IQ) that was assumed to be unchangeable (Gould, 1996). Sternberg (1997) describes a theory of intelligence that suggests three main kinds of giftedness: analytic, synthetic, and practical:

- *Analytic giftedness* involves being able to take a problem apart—to understand the parts of a problem and how they are interrelated, which is a skill typically measured by conventional intelligence tests.
- *Synthetic giftedness* involves insight, intuition, creativity, or adeptness at coping with novel situations, skills that are typically associated with high achievement in the arts and sciences.
- *Practical giftedness* involves applying analytic and synthetic abilities to the solution of everyday problems, the kinds of skills that characterize people who have successful careers.

A popular idea today is that individuals have "multiple intelligences" (Gardner & Hatch, 1989; see also Chan, 2006). However, the concept of multiple intelligences is scientifically untenable because it is not supported by research (Lloyd & Hallahan, 2007; Willingham, 2009). The theory of multiple intelligences is widely held to be legitimate, but few, if any, reliable applications of the theory to teaching exist (see Lloyd & Hallahan, 2007).

Today, most experts in educating students with special gifts and talents suggest that giftedness refers to superior abilities in specific areas of performance, which may be exhibited under some circumstances but not others. Even though giftedness is believed to be a remarkable ability to do something that society values, it's not an inherent, immutable trait that a person necessarily carries for life (Reis & Renzulli, 2009). Moreover, having a special gift at one thing doesn't mean that a person is good at everything—or even that someone who is a good thinker about one thing is a good thinker about all things. People become extraordinarily good at something only by developing their ability to do that particular thing. Ability is not "a mental tool that can be applied at will to different intellectual content . . . all cognitive tests measure developed abilities. There are no exceptions" (Lohman, 2006, p. 37).

INTERNETRESOURCES

An interesting site to explore for educating students with special gifts and talents is www .hoagiesgifted.org/

Research has shown that the home and family, especially in a child's younger years, are extremely important.

PREVALENCE

Federal reports and legislation have assumed that 3% to 5% of the U.S. school population could be considered to have special gifts or talents. The prevalence of giftedness is a function of the definition that is used; if giftedness is defined as the top x percent on a given criterion, the question of prevalence has been answered. Of course, if x percent refers to a percentage of a national sample, the prevalence of gifted pupils in a given school or cultural group may vary from that of the comparison group, regardless of the criteria that are used to measure performance (see Callahan, 2011).

ORIGINS OF GIFTEDNESS

As defined today, giftedness isn't something that sets people apart in every way from people who are average. Instead, it refers to specific, valued, and unusual talents that people may exhibit during some periods of their lives. The main factors that contribute to giftedness therefore are really much the same as those that foster any type of behavior, whether typical or exceptional:

1. Genetic and other biological factors, such as neurological functioning and nutrition.
2. Social factors, such as family, school, the peer group, and community.

We are all combinations of the influences of our genetic inheritances and social and physical environments. What environments foster gifted performance? We can often change students' environments; we cannot change their genetic makeup.

Although giftedness may be determined in part by one's genetic inheritance, whatever genetic combinations are involved are exceedingly complex and not distributed according to race or social class. The idea that giftedness is entirely inherited is one of the worst ideas associated with gifted education (Gallagher, 2006). However, children are not born with equal capabilities:

> There are some youngsters who are born with the capability to learn faster than others those ideas or concepts that modern societies value in children and adults. Such youngsters and their abilities are subject to many social influences and must interact with their environmental context. Therefore, it often becomes difficult to find students with these special talents in a multicultural society. (Gallagher, 2000b, p. 6)

Families, schools, peer groups, and communities have a profound influence on the development of giftedness. Stimulation, opportunities, expectations, demands, and rewards for performance all affect children's learning.

How can families, schools, and the larger culture nurture children's giftedness? Research has shown that parents differ greatly in their attitudes toward and management of the giftedness of their children (Renzulli & Park, 2002). Home and family are critically important, especially in the child's younger years (see Muratori et al., 2006). In the families of highly successful persons:

- Someone in the family (usually one or both parents) had a personal interest in the child's talent and provided great support and encouragement for its development.
- The parents were role models (at least at the start of their child's development of talent), especially in terms of lifestyle.
- There was specific parental encouragement of the child to explore, to participate in home activities related to the area of developing talent, and to join the family in related activities. Small signs of interest and capability by the child were rewarded.

- Parents took it for granted that their children would learn in the area of talent, just as they would learn language.
- The family exhibited expected behaviors and values related to the talent, holding to clear schedules and standards for performance appropriate for the child's stage of development.
- Teaching was informal and occurred in a variety of settings. Early learning was exploratory and much like play.
- The family interacted with a tutor/mentor and received information to guide the child's practice—including specific tasks to be accomplished, information or specific points to be emphasized or problems to be solved, a set time by which the child could be expected to achieve specific goals and objectives, and the amount of time to be devoted to practice.
- Parents observed practice, insisted that the child put in the required amount of practice time, provided instruction where necessary, and rewarded the child for doing something especially well or meeting a standard.
- Parents sought special instruction and special teachers for the child.
- Parents encouraged participation in events (recitals, concerts, contests, etc.) in which the child's capabilities were displayed in public.

How schools can nurture children's giftedness has received too little attention (Robinson, Shore, & Enersen, 2007). Yet the ways in which schools identify giftedness, group children for instruction, design curricula, and reward performance have profound effects on what the most able students achieve. When schools facilitate the performance of all students who can achieve at a superior level in specific areas, giftedness is found among children of all cultural and socioeconomic groups.

IDENTIFICATION OF GIFTEDNESS

Measuring giftedness is a complicated matter (Lohman, 2006). Appropriate methods of early identification will help children with special talents achieve self-fulfillment and aid them in developing their special potential to make a unique and valuable contribution to society.

The most common methods of identifying giftedness include IQ (based on group or individual tests), standardized achievement test scores, teacher nominations, parent nominations, peer nominations, self-nominations, and evaluations of student work or performance. In fact, strong arguments can be made not to disregard the traditional psychometric test-score approach altogether (Robinson, 2005). Typically, some combination of several of these methods is used.

In devising identification procedures that are fair to individuals from all cultural and ethnic groups and all social classes, educators must take into account the varied definitions of giftedness and recognize the effects of cultural variation on children's behavior (McCluskey, Baker, & McCluskey, 2005; Tomlinson, Ford, Reis, Briggs, & Strickland, 2004). In addressing multicultural differences, it's important to recognize the variations of socioeconomic status, language, and values that occur within various ethnic and cultural groups, not just between them. Hunsaker and Callahan (1995) propose eight general identification principles to help ensure fairness:

1. Assessments exceed a narrow conception of talent.
2. Separate and appropriate identification strategies are used to identify different aspects of giftedness.
3. Reliable and valid instruments and strategies are used to assess talent.
4. Appropriate instruments are employed for underserved populations.
5. Each child is viewed as an individual, recognizing the limits of a single score on any measure.
6. A multiple-measure/multiple-criteria approach is followed.
7. Appreciation is shown for the value of the individual case study and the limitations of combinations of scores.

8. Identification and placement are based on individual students' needs and abilities rather than on the numbers who can be served.

Identification methods should focus on balancing concern for identifying only those students whose capabilities are markedly above average, with concern for including all who show promise for gifted performance (see Robinson, 2005).

PSYCHOLOGICAL AND BEHAVIORAL CHARACTERISTICS

Giftedness has been recognized in some form in every society throughout recorded history. In many societies, individuals with special gifts have been stereotyped in one of two ways: (1) as physically weak, socially inept, narrow in interests, and prone to emotional instability and early decline or, in the opposite direction, (2) as superior in intelligence, physique, social attractiveness, achievement, emotional stability, and moral character and immune to ordinary human frailties and defects. Although it might be possible to find a few individuals who seem to fit one stereotype or the other, the vast majority of people with special gifts or talents fit neither.

Nevertheless, stereotypes persist. A still-common misperception is that genius predisposes people to mental illness. The idea that giftedness and insanity are linked is one of the worst misconceptions of the field (Gallagher, 2006). Some people with special gifts and talents accomplish remarkable things in spite of, not because of, mental illness or physical disability (see Goldsmith, 2005; Martin, Burns, & Schonlau, 2010; Mueller, 2009).

Perhaps it shouldn't be surprising that the majority of students who show giftedness enter occupations that demand greater-than-average intellectual ability, creativity, and motivation. Most find their way into the ranks of professionals and managers, and many distinguish themselves among their peers in adulthood. But not all such students enjoy occupational success in demanding jobs; some choose career paths that do not make use of their talents, or they otherwise fail to distinguish themselves (Manstetten, 2000).

Contrary to myth, most students who are gifted are not constantly bored with and antagonistic toward school, if they are given work that is challenging.

The self-concepts, social relationships, and other psychological characteristics of students with special gifts or talents have been matters of considerable interest (Assouline & Colangelo, 2006; Robinson et al., 2007). Many of these students are happy, well liked by their peers, emotionally stable, and self-sufficient. They may have wide and varied interests and perceive themselves in positive terms. Nevertheless, some gifted students experience bullying and are traumatized by it (Peterson & Ray, 2006). Furthermore, as Maria Hernandez mentions in the accompanying Peer Connections box, being known as gifted can be stigmatizing.

Students with intellectual gifts are often acutely sensitive to their own feelings and those of others and highly concerned about interpersonal relationships, intrapersonal states, and moral issues. Using their advanced cognitive abilities appears to help many of these children develop at a young age the social and emotional adjustment strategies used by most adults. In short, many (but not all) students with high intellectual gifts are self-aware, self-assured, socially skilled, and morally responsible. For example, note that the prodigy Gregory Smith (described later in this chapter, in the Personal Perspectives box, "Child Prodigy Now U. Va. Grad Student") is also very concerned about other children and issues of social justice.

However, assuming that gifted students never need education in morality is a terrible mistake. Students identified as gifted sometimes bully others (Peterson & Ray, 2006). Moreover, individuals can and have used their special gifts for nightmarish purposes, as Tannenbaum

PEER CONNECTIONS: MARIA HERNANDEZ

MARIA HERNANDEZ was born and raised in Greenville, South Carolina. Her parents are both from Costa Rica. Maria is a gifted student. She started reading at a very young age. She taught herself to read at about age 3. She recently graduated from Mary Baldwin College at the age of 18. Maria majored in International Relations with a minor in Economics. This fall Maria will begin Law School and also work on her MBA in a dual degree program at the University of South Carolina.

1. What do you do for fun? *I love to read. I read a lot of fiction books that aren't really normal but that capture my attention. I also like to spend time with my family and friends.*

2. What is your favorite way to relax? *Reading! I've been reading since I was really little and love to sit down with a good book.*

3. What is something that you excel at? *I excel at reading and just recently I learned how to excel at writing. I was not a good writer until I came to college and now I excel at it. I also excel at math; it has always been a favorite subject for me in school.*

4. What is your pet peeve? *When people try to organize my things. I have my own organization system that works for me and it's hard and confusing when people come and change things around.*

5. Can you recall one teacher in particular who has been a positive influence in your life? *Yes, my economics teacher. At first I had to take economics classes for my major and I didn't think I would like them at all. But my teacher was amazing; she was really great at explaining things and was always available for questions. She had an open door policy, and she was always happy. Eventually, I ended up really connecting with her and became a teacher assistant for her class. Through this she helped me and taught me how to deal with other people in positive ways. I admire her a lot.*

6. Is there anyone else (celebrity, family member) that you regard as a role model? Why are they a role model for you? *My mother, she is one of the strongest people I know. I am an only child, and she let me go to college when I was only 14 years old, which was really hard for her. But she saw it as a wonderful opportunity for me. I also admire her strength. She was born in Costa Rica and had to work really really hard to gain a scholarship so she could come to the United States. She came to the states all by herself and is in general just a very strong person.*

7. What is the most difficult thing for you about having a special gift? *The stigma that comes attached to the label of being "gifted." I don't consider myself to be a genius.*

People always assume that because I'm gifted I have no friends and must spend all my time studying. I've learned to not tell people that I'm gifted until I give them a chance to get to know me. At Mary Baldwin College, we were allowed to move out of the dorms at age 16 and I began to interact with older students. It was hard at first, and I still don't tell people until they know me for ME. Sometimes when I do tell them, they don't believe me, but they still see me for the person they became friends with.

8. Do you see your special talent as affecting your ability to achieve what you want in your life? *Well, when I first went to college, I wanted to be a doctor. A lot of times gifted students are pushed to go into math and science fields. When I got into some of my science classes, I found them to be difficult. I could do the work, but I realized that I did not enjoy science. I did a 180 and decided to be pre-law instead of pre-med.*

9. Has your giftedness affected your social relationships? If so, how? *My friends from college are more mature and realize that I am more mature than most 18 year olds. However, I can relate to them more than my friends back home. It has been hard to keep in touch with friends back home. I skipped high school, and it's hard to relate to friends that are just finishing high school. But I try to keep in touch and keep a balance.*

10. How do you think others perceive you? *For the most part, I think people see me as being a normal person. I don't try to be a know-it-all. I don't feel like I have anything to prove. I think people perceive me as a happy, bubbly friend that loves to tell jokes and laugh.*

11. What is one thing that you would like others to know about you? *I played basketball for 7 years, which surprises some people because they assume that gifted students are not into sports, but I love sports. Also, I don't think that being gifted is about being smart. It's about applying yourself and working hard.*

12. Where do you see yourself 10 years from now? *Working at the top of a legal department at a large International Business Corporation. I would love to work in China, since they have so many new business ideas going on right now. I hope to be traveling back and forth a lot between international countries and the states.*

13. Please fill in the blank: I couldn't live without _____. *Music and books.*

(2000b) has described. Therefore, it's important to recognize the enormous potential for both good and evil purposes to which special gifts and talents can be put and to help individuals who have such gifts and talents see the value of using them in the service of what is morally right.

Giftedness includes a wide variety of abilities and degrees of difference from average (Callahan, 2011). Moreover, the nature and degree of an individual's giftedness may affect his or her social and emotional adjustment and educational and psychological needs. Consider, for example, that categorizing only people with IQs of 180 or higher as "gifted" is roughly like categorizing as "intellectually disabled" only those individuals with IQs of 20 or less. In fact, children who are exceptionally precocious—those whose talents are extremely rare—may constitute a group for which extraordinary adaptations of schooling are required (just as extraordinary adaptations are required for children with very severe intellectual disabilities; see Gross, 2000, 2002; von Karolyi & Winner, 2005). Child prodigies are children whose development and accomplishments meet or exceed those of adults with extraordinary talent. They often astonish others by their talent at an early age, and they often need opportunities that more typical students don't need and would find intimidating. An example of a musical prodigy is Geoff Gallante, described in the accompanying Personal Perspectives box, "A Child Prodigy on Trumpet."

CULTURAL VALUES REGARDING STUDENTS WITH SPECIAL GIFTS AND TALENTS AND THEIR EDUCATION

In American culture, it's difficult to elicit sympathy and next to impossible to arrange sustained public support for education that meets the needs of children with special gifts, especially intellectual gifts (Gallagher, 2000a, 2002, 2004; Murray, 2005). This is not a peculiarly American problem, but there's something self-limiting, if not self-destructive, about a society that refuses to acknowledge and nourish the special talents of its children who have the greatest gifts (see DiGennaro, 2007; De Hahn, 2000; Murray, 2005; Tannenbaum, 1993, 2000a).

Gallagher (2000a) describes American society's ambivalence toward students with special gifts or talents. Our society loves the good things that people with extraordinary gifts produce, but it hates to acknowledge superior intellectual performance. Opponents of special education for students with special gifts argue that it's inhumane and un-American to segregate such students for instruction and to allocate special resources for educating those who are already advantaged. There is the danger of leaving some children out when only the ablest are selected for special programs. However, it seems impossible to argue against special education for students with special gifts and talents without arguing against special education in general, because all special education involves recognizing and accommodating unusual individual differences (Kauffman & Hallahan, 2005).

NEGLECTED GROUPS OF STUDENTS WITH SPECIAL GIFTS AND TALENTS

Students who are disadvantaged by economic needs, racial discrimination, disabilities, or gender bias are often overlooked in programs for gifted and talented students. In fact, many groups of gifted learners are neglected in a diverse, multicultural society (Callahan, 2011). Two facts cannot be ignored:

1. Children from higher socioeconomic levels already have many of the advantages, such as more appropriate education, opportunities to pursue their interests in depth, and intellectual stimulation, that special educators recommend for those with special gifts or talents.

2. Far too many individuals with special gifts or talents are disadvantaged by life circumstances or disabilities and have been overlooked and discriminated against, resulting in a tremendous waste of human potential.

Personal PERSPECTIVES
Geoff Gallante: A Child Prodigy on Trumpet

FIRST-GRADER BLOWS AWAY AUDIENCES

Geoff Gallante has played with Wynton Marsalis, jammed with Maynard Ferguson, played the National Anthem at numerous pro basketball games and on Sunday will join the University of Virginia Wind Ensemble for a rendition of "Trumpeter's Lullaby."

That's not a bad resume for a 6-year-old.

"It's pretty amazing, really," said William Pease, the wind ensemble's director. "It's not 'Carnival of Venice' but 'Trumpeter's Lullaby' is a good high school-level concerto and he's only 6."

Geoff, of Fairfax County, who has been featured in Washington newspapers and television broadcasts, is a bit of a rarity: He's a young child who plays a brass instrument well.

"You find child prodigies who play piano and violin and other stringed instruments but it's a lot different when you're talking about brass," Pease said, "It takes an enormous amount of air to play a brass instrument. If you change the amount of air you use when you're playing, you can actually change the note you're playing."

Add to that the complexities of brass embouchure—the position and use of lips and mouth on the instrument to create tone—and trumpet becomes a difficult instrument to play for most people under the age of 10.

"It's quite amazing when you see his size—he's small—and the size of the trumpet and then you hear him play," Pease said. "He has a very mellow sound, a dark and warm sound and that's good."

Geoff's playing has surprised people since he first picked the instrument up at the age of 4. He was at his grandmother's house, found his older brother's horn and took a quick lesson on lip placement from his mother.

Geoff Gallante began playing the trumpet at age 4. After two years of playing, he has racked up an impressive resume.

"He made a sound with it and his eyes lit up," said his father, David Gallante. "He walked around with that trumpet blowing it for about a month or two. He'd put some CDs he owned in the [stereo] and try and play the trumpet with them."

Gallante tried to convince trumpet teachers to teach his son, but most begged off.

"They thought I was crazy and totally dismissed it out of hand. They couldn't imagine that a 4-year-old could play a trumpet. They thought it would be a waste of time," said Gallante, who estimated that he approached eight teachers. "I finally convinced one to hear him play and he agreed to take Geoff as a student."

His first time at band camp, the pre-kindergarten Geoff auditioned with middle school students and was placed in the symphonic band, the band that plays the most difficult music. That's also where he met members of the UVa Wind Ensemble who served as camp counselors.

"They thought it would be fun for us to play with him," Pease said. "It is, too. It's amazing how good he sounds at his age."

Age: 6
Grade: First
Residence: Fairfax County
Age started playing trumpet: 4
Featured in: *The Washington Post, Downbeat Magazine,* various BBC radio broadcasts, CBS's "The Early Show," NBC's "Tonight Show with Jay Leno" and NBC's "Today" show
Played with: The Tonight Show Band, Arturo Sandoval, Phill Driscoll, Wynton Marsalis, Maynard Ferguson, Chuck Mangione and Doc Severinsen. He has also performed with The Washington Symphonic Brass, 257th Army Band, Metropolitan Jazz Orchestra, U.S. Army Blues Jazz Ensemble, George Mason University symphony orchestra and jazz ensemble. He has played the National Anthem for NBA games in Oakland, Phoenix, Salt Lake City, and Detroit.

Source: "First-grader blows away audiences" by Byran McKenzie. *Charlottesville Daily Progress,* Charlottesville, VA, February 24, 2007, p. A2. Reprinted with permission.

Underachievers

Monks and Katzko (2005) define underachievement as "a discrepancy between potential and achievement" (p. 189). Students can fail to achieve at a level consistent with their abilities for a variety of reasons, including low expectations, lack of motivation, family trauma, and other causes (Robinson et al., 2007). Many females achieve far less than they might because of social or cultural barriers to their selection or progress in certain careers. Students who are members of racial or ethnic minorities also are often underachievers because of bias in identifying or programming for their abilities. Likewise, students with obvious disabilities are frequently overlooked or denied opportunities to achieve.

Underachievement of children with special gifts or talents can result from any of the factors that lead to underachievement in any group, such as emotional conflicts or a chaotic, neglectful, or abusive home environment. A frequent cause is inappropriate school programs—schoolwork that is unchallenging and boring because these students have already mastered most of the material or because teachers have low expectations or mark students down for their misbehavior. A related problem is that underachievers with special gifts or talents often develop negative self-images and negative attitudes toward school. When students show negative attitudes toward school and self, any special abilities they might have will likely be overlooked.

One way of preventing or responding to underachievement is allowing students to skip grades or subjects so that school becomes more nurturing and provides greater interest and challenge. However, acceleration is not always appropriate, nor is it typically sufficient by itself to address the problems of the underachieving student with exceptional abilities. Counseling, individual and family therapy, and a variety of supportive or remedial strategies are possible alternatives or additions to acceleration.

Underachievement must not be confused with nonproductivity. A lapse in productivity doesn't necessarily indicate that the student is underachieving. Students with extraordinary ability should not be expected to be constantly producing something remarkable. But this highlights the difficulty in defining giftedness: How much time must elapse between episodes of creative productivity before we say that someone no longer exhibits giftedness or has become an underachiever? We noted earlier that giftedness is in the performance, not the person. Yet we know that the unrelenting demand for gifted performance is unrealistic and can be inhumane.

Students Low in Socioeconomic Status or Living in Remote Areas

Children who are reared in poverty might not have toys, reading materials, opportunities for travel and exploration, good nutrition and medical care, and many other advantages that more affluent families typically provide. Lack of basic necessities and opportunities for learning can mask intelligence and creativity. Families of children in inner-city areas don't have the financial resources to provide the opportunities and early experiences to foster talent. Yet support for gifted students from low-income families often appears to be an easy target for elimination in tight budgets (see Murray, 2005).

Children who live in remote areas might not have access to many of the educational resources typically found in more populated regions. Many of those who live in remote areas also experience economic deprivation and lack the advantages that affluent families have (Davis & Rimm, 2004).

Cultural- and Ethnic-Minority Groups

Some ethnic groups, such as many ethnic minorities from Asian countries, are included in programs for gifted students more often than would be suggested by their percentage of the general population. However, other ethnic groups, especially African Americans and Spanish-speaking students, are underrepresented in programs for gifted students (Yoon & Gentry, 2009).

Among the greatest challenges in the field today are identifying culturally diverse and disadvantaged students with special abilities and including and retaining these students in special programs (Moore, Ford, & Milner, 2005; Robinson et al., 2007). Some cultural and ethnic groups have been sorely neglected in programs for students with special gifts or talents. Many ethnic minority students with special gifts or talents remain underachievers, even if they recognize the importance of achievement in American society (Borland, 2004;

Bridglall & Gordon, 2005; Lohman, 2005; Tomlinson et al., 2004).

Appropriate identification and programming for students with special gifts or talents can be assumed to result in approximately equal proportions among all ethnic groups. However, this proportionality will likely occur only if educators renew efforts to achieve the following:

- Devise and adopt culturally sensitive identification criteria.
- Provide counseling to raise the educational and career aspirations of students in underrepresented groups.
- Make high-achieving models from all ethnic groups available.
- Retain underrepresented ethnic students in programs for gifted students.
- Adopt a workable system to ensure the inclusion of underrepresented groups.
- Build relationships with the families of minority children.

Students whose disabilities prevent them from speaking or physically expressing themselves may have potential that is not obvious through casual observation.

Ultimately, the larger social-environmental issue of making families and communities safe, as well as intellectually stimulating, for children and youths of all cultural and ethnic backgrounds must be addressed (Borland, 2004; Gallagher, 1998, 2000a; Gordon & Bridglall, 2005). Equal opportunity for development outside the school environment would help address the underrepresentation of minority students in programs for students with extraordinary abilities (see Davis & Rimm, 2004; Ford & Moore, 2006).

Students with Disabilities

The education of students with both disabilities and special gifts or talents is emerging as a field. The idea that students can be **twice exceptional** (meaning that they have both a disability and a special gift or talent) is, as Gallagher (2006) notes, one of the best ideas in gifted education.

The major goals of special education for twice-exceptional students are identifying gifted and talented students with specific disabilities, research and development, preparing teachers and other professionals to work with such children and youths, improving interdisciplinary cooperation for the benefit of such children and youths, and preparing students for adult living. Educators should consider the full range of programs for gifted and talented students for those who are twice exceptional, including acceleration. The accompanying Responsive Instruction, "Who Are Twice-Exceptional Students?" provides a summary of the early stages of the research on instructional strategies for these students.

Our stereotypic expectations of people with disabilities frequently keep us from recognizing their abilities. For example, if a child lacks the ability to speak or to be physically active or presents a demeanor associated with intellectual dullness (e.g., drooling, slumping, dull eyes staring), we tend to assume that the child has intellectual disability. The fact is, students with physical characteristics typically associated with severe intellectual disabilities might be intellectually brilliant; unless this is acknowledged, however, the talents of students with cerebral palsy and other physical disabilities can be easily overlooked. Students with special gifts or talents and impaired hearing also can be overlooked if their communication skills are poorly developed, if their teachers are not looking for signs of talent, or if they are taught by teachers who have limited competence in communicating with people who are deaf. Students with learning disabilities involving written language may be overlooked (Assouline, Nicpon & Whiteman, 2010). In fact, students with disabilities associated with communication problems, such as autism spectrum disorder or mental disorders, may be found to be gifted (Assouline, Nicpon, & Doobay, 2009; Martin et al., 2010). And people with

INTERNETRESOURCES

For resources for gifted, advanced, and special needs learners, one site is The Prufrock Press at www.prufrock.com

RESPONSIVE *INSTRUCTION*
MEETING THE NEEDS OF STUDENTS WITH SPECIAL GIFTS AND TALENTS

Strategies for the Identification and Instruction of Twice-Exceptional Students

WHO ARE "TWICE-EXCEPTIONAL" STUDENTS?

The term *twice exceptional* refers to any student who is both gifted and has a disability, such as a learning disability or cerebral palsy. Unfortunately, the identification of gifts or talents can be challenging, as the "disability" characteristics often take center stage. Researchers have identified specific barriers to the identification of giftedness in populations of students with disabilities (Cline & Hegeman, 2001). Challenges can include:

- Focus on assessment of the disability without attention to possible talents
- Stereotypic expectations associated with physical or global intelligence expectations
- Developmental delays particularly evident in certain areas of cognitive ability such as abstract thinking or verbal ability
- Lack of worldly experiences due to disability limitations
- Narrow views of giftedness as global, high intelligence only
- Disability-specific concerns overshadowing possible gifts or talents

To overcome these barriers, these researchers recommend that (1) assessment batteries include information about participation in extracurricular activities, (2) patterns of strengths should be noted in addition to disability-specific reporting, (3) ability should be viewed in terms of experiential opportunities, (4) adaptations and accommodations should be made during testing (e.g., omitting questions about color for a blind student or allowing extended time for a student with learning disabilities), (5) comparisons should be made with other students with similar disabilities, and (6) areas unaffected by the disability should be weighed more heavily (Cline & Hegeman, 2001; Willard-Holt, 1999).

STRATEGIES FOR MEETING THE NEEDS OF TWICE-EXCEPTIONAL STUDENTS

To address the issue of underidentification of giftedness in individuals with disabilities, schools need to become advocates for the identification of gifts in all populations of students. Parents, school personnel, and the community should take an active role in supporting the unique needs of students with gifts.

Instructional strategies to foster the development of gifts in twice-exceptional students include the following:

- Focus on the development of strengths, interests, and intellectual gifts.
- Teach and encourage the use of compensatory strategies.
- Reduce communication limitations, and develop alternative means for communicating.
- Help students shape a healthy, realistic self-concept in which students acknowledge their strengths and weaknesses through open discussions.
- Emphasize high-level abstract thinking, creativity, and problem-solving approaches.
- Provide for individual pacing in areas of giftedness and disability.
- Establish high expectations, and promote avenues for self-direction.
- Offer instructional options that capitalize on students' strengths. (Willard-Holt, 1999)

• By Kristin L. Sayeski

■ ■ ■ ■ ■ ■ ■ ■ ■ ■

physical disabilities may be found to have an extraordinary talent that we might not expect, as illustrated by the example of Doug Landis, an artist whose work we featured in Chapter 1.

Giftedness occurs in combination with disabilities of nearly every description. Marie Curie, twice the winner of the Nobel Prize (physics and chemistry), suffered from profound depression (Goldsmith, 2005). Consider also Evelyn Glennie, a deaf percussionist, and Timothy Cordes, a blind medical student. They don't fit the stereotypes we hold. True, they are not typical of people with their disabilities—or of people who do not have their disabilities, for that matter. Fortunately, their disabilities did not preclude their pursuit of their areas of special talent.

We don't want to foster the myth that giftedness is found as often among students with disabilities as among those who do not have disabilities. But clearly, students with special gifts or talents and disabilities have been a neglected population. A key factor in meeting these students' needs is the collaboration of a variety of disciplines and institutions to provide appropriate technology and training.

Females

Females comprise the largest group of neglected students with special gifts or talents. Females with extraordinary capabilities today have many opportunities for education and choice of careers that were denied to females a generation ago (see Callahan, 2011; Goldsmith, 2005).

Cultural factors work against the development and recognition of females with special gifts or talents. Females simply have not had equal opportunity and motivation to enter many academic disciplines or careers that have by tradition been dominated by males, such as chemistry, physics, medicine, and dentistry. When females have entered these fields, they have often been rewarded inappropriately (according to irrelevant criteria) for their performance. English literature has tended to portray females as wives, mothers, or "weaker" sisters, who are either dependent on males or sacrifice themselves for the sake of males. Such barriers to giftedness in females have only recently been brought forcefully to public attention (see Davis & Rimm, 2004).

Cultural factors work against the development and recognition of females with special gifts and talents. Barriers to giftedness in females haven't always been recognized.

Females with special gifts or talents lag behind males in many measures of achievement and aptitude (e.g., professional and career achievement, standardized test scores, grades) and tend not to pursue courses of study or careers involving science, engineering, and math (Lubinski, Benbow, & Morelock, 2000). In short, they are underrepresented in many fields of advanced study and in professions and careers that carry high status, power, and pay. We can only presume to know the reasons for their underrepresentation (Kerr, 2000). Factors that have contributed to the situation might include lower parental expectations for females, overemphasis on and glamorization of gender differences, school and societal stereotypes of gender roles, and educational practices that are detrimental to achievement (e.g., less attention to high-achieving girls, expectations of less independence of girls).

Research suggests that the problems of neglect and underrepresentation of females with exceptional abilities are much more complex than was previously believed. Like underrepresentation of ethnic and cultural minorities, the problems involving females are closely tied to cultural, social, and political issues, and they do not have simple or easy solutions. Nevertheless, the education of females with special gifts or talents might be improved by encouraging females to take risks by enrolling in challenging courses, to make career choices appropriate for their abilities, and to explore avenues that break stereotypical female roles.

EDUCATIONAL CONSIDERATIONS

The focus of education is now on talent development across the full spectrum of abilities in particular areas of functioning (see Callahan, 2011; Heller et al., 2000; Robinson et al., 2007; Tomlinson et al., 2002). However, this point of view includes the recognition that equity for many students with special gifts and talents may require special education. Although no federal requirement exists for special education for gifted students, the National Association for Gifted Children has published program standards that states and localities can use to assess the quality of their services (Landrum, Callahan, & Shaklee, 2001). Nevertheless, state and local policies are uneven and often inadequate (Van Tassel-Baska, 2006).

All students at all ages have relative talent strengths, and schools should help students to identify and understand their own best abilities. Students whose talents are at exceptionally higher levels than those of their peers should have access to instructional resources and activities commensurate with their talents (Davis & Rimm, 2004). The one-size-fits-all mentality that is at least partly an outgrowth of the inclusion movement reflects a mistaken view of human

Success Stories

NOSHUA EXCELS IN A RESIDENTIAL ACCELERATION PROGRAM

Noshua: "I felt I could finally be myself!"

Eighteen-year-old Noshua Watson is enrolled in a Ph.D. program in economics at Stanford University. She completed high school and college through a residential acceleration program for gifted students.

These are the keys to her success:

★ Intensive and accelerated programming

★ Relentless, individualized, academic challenges

★ Specific attention to personal growth and unique abilities

AT AGE 13, NOSHUA WATSON enrolled in the Program for the Exceptionally Gifted, known as PEG, an acceleration program at Mary Baldwin College in Virginia. Combining high school and college, Noshua was challenged in a supportive environment that encouraged her personal growth. She thrived on campus activities, assisting with research and helping to teach an economics course during her senior year. Noshua credits her success to intensive, relentless, and specific instruction geared to her exceptional learning needs.

★ **Intensive and Accelerated Programming.** "Acceleration programs like PEG challenge our culture," says Celeste Rhodes, the program's director. "Parents and students must

be courageous in their ability to accept uniqueness," she says. Rhodes describes the PEG program as an alternative for the motivated student who might have teenage interests but demonstrates a serious sense of purpose. "You see it in the interviews," she says. "There is an energy, a spark, a drive."

To Rhodes, giftedness is not defined narrowly by IQ but includes multiple measures including consistent achievement over time. "We are accelerating students by 4 years. That requires a history of discipline, hard work, and high grades." Through a lengthy essay and interview process, PEG seeks an optimal match between student and program. Says Rhodes, "Since we are residential, emotional stability is extremely important." Noshua agrees, "As PEG students, we were ready and eager for

development. Highly talented young people suffer boredom and negative peer pressure in heterogeneous classrooms. Students at all ages and grade levels are entitled to challenging and appropriate instruction if they are to develop their talents fully. For some, like Noshua Watson, this instruction might be available only in a setting apart from her age mates. Read about Noshua's success in college courses in the accompanying Success Stories feature.

The belief that students with special gifts or talents don't need special education designed for their needs is, according to Gallagher (2006), one of the worst ideas of educators and works against talent development. "Such an idea justifies a 'Do Nothing' approach by educators. It encourages acceptance of such ideas as *inclusion* as doing no real mischief to gifted students and lowers the expectations for the performance of such students" (Gallagher, 2006, p. 10). As we noted earlier, family support plays a crucial role in the development of talent (Freeman, 2000). However, many students also need special school supports if they are to achieve to their full potential. The consensus of leaders in the field is that special education for students with special gifts or talents should have three characteristics:

1. A curriculum designed to accommodate the students' advanced cognitive skills (see Van Tassel-Baska & Stambaugh, 2006).

2. Instructional strategies consistent with the learning of students with extraordinary abilities in the particular content areas of the curriculum (see Davis & Rimm, 2004; Dixon & Moon, 2006).

3. Administrative arrangements facilitating appropriate grouping of students for instruction (see Callahan, 2000, 2001, 2011; Robinson et al., 2007; Tomlinson et al., 2002).

the academic rigors, but emotionally and physically, we were not as mature. We were still teenagers with a lot of special needs."

★ **Relentless, Individualized, Academic Challenges.** Noshua was supported by an individualized curriculum that matched her advanced cognitive skills. Small-group instruction was combined with personal mentoring and alternatives such as independent study and accelerated pacing. Noshua was free to choose among the college's liberal arts offerings but was required to take two PEG-level courses—one in literature and one in mathematics. She also took study skills workshops taught by veteran PEG students designed to prepare novices for college-level learning and campus life. Says Noshua, "I was intellectually challenged, but I could socially mature at my own rate, and for me that was really key."

★ **Specific Attention to Personal Growth and Unique Abilities.** For her first 2 years, Noshua lived in a special dormitory for younger PEG students. Social activities were sponsored and friendships nurtured through residence life. Residential coordinators were sensitive to the needs of adolescents, and they also served as academic advisors. For her last 2 years, Noshua lived independently in a regular dorm, and her academic advisor was a faculty member in her chosen major of economics.

Selecting educational alternatives to meet her unique abilities is a familiar practice for Noshua and her family. As a youngster, she attended a magnet school and was described as an avid learner who was strong-willed and knew her own mind. She experienced gifted education for the first time in a regional public school program for third through fifth graders. Noshua's family moved in her sixth-grade year; her new district had no specialized programs for gifted students. Enrichment classes were held only before and after school, and transportation problems prevented Noshua from attending.

Junior high was not a positive experience. "I was frustrated academically because my guidance counselor said if I wanted to take both French and Spanish, I also had to take an honors math course one level beyond my grade. Socially, I was frustrated because most kids at school just wanted to "hang out." My parents wouldn't allow me to do this, and it was hard for me to relate. I guess you could say I was sort of a geek!" she says playfully.

Noshua felt that she could finally be herself after spending three happy summers at a residential camp for gifted students. In eighth grade, she and her parents looked for programs that offered alternatives to conventional high schools. "That's when I heard about PEG, and so did a fellow camper. We graduated from college together last June." As for starting graduate school, she says, "I just love being at Stanford. My life experience has been different, and I'm used to a lot more independence than other people my age."

• By Jean B. Crockett

States and localities have devised a wide variety of plans for educating students with special gifts or talents. Generally, the plans can be described as providing **enrichment** (additional experiences provided to students without placing them in a higher grade) or **acceleration** (placing the students ahead of their age peers).

Many variations of enrichment and acceleration have been invented, ranging from general education placement with little or no assistance for the teacher to special schools offering advanced curricula in special areas such as science and mathematics or the arts. STEM high schools—special high schools emphasizing science, technology, engineering, and mathematics—are appropriate for some gifted students (see Ambrose, 2010). Between the extremes of regular classrooms in which the teacher tries to go it alone and special schools for gifted students are consulting teacher programs, resource rooms, community mentor programs (in which highly talented students work individually with professionals), independent study programs, special classes, and rapid advancement of students through the usual grades, including early admission to high school or college.

Accelerated educational programs, particularly in mathematics, have been evaluated favorably and may support early college entrance for some students who are gifted.

443

INTERNETRESOURCES

For information about STEM high schools, go to www.hsalliance.org/stem/index.asp

Not every community offers all possible options. The types of services offered vary greatly within the school systems of given states and from state to state. As one might expect, large metropolitan areas typically offer more program options than small towns or rural areas.

Some of the educational options for students with high ability, such as acceleration and inclusion, are extremely controversial. No single type of program option meets the needs of all students who have special gifts or talents. Ideally, assessment, identification, and instruction are closely linked, whether students have disabilities or special gifts and talents—or both. When including students with disabilities and special gifts and talents, it is important to use strategies that meet the needs of both types of students. The accompanying Making It Work feature provides a description of one such strategy, called fractured fairy tales.

Advances in telecommunications, the presence of computers in the home and classroom, and the call for excellence in U.S. education are three developments with implications for educating the most able students. The possible uses of computers for enhancing the education of extraordinarily high-performing students are enormous. Using software tutorials, accessing data banks, playing or inventing intellectually demanding computer games, writing and editing in English and foreign languages, learning computer languages, and solving advanced problems in mathematics are only a few of the possibilities (see Robinson et al., 2007).

EARLY INTERVENTION

The giftedness of young children presents special problems of definition, identification, programming, and evaluation (Brighton & Jarvis, 2011; Porter, 2005; Robinson et al., 2007; Ruf, 2005). Although educators have made progress in building model programs and providing better services for young children with special gifts, negative attitudes toward such efforts persist. Barriers inhibiting the development of better education for these children include lack of parental advocacy, lack of appropriate teacher training, an emphasis on older students of extraordinary ability, financial constraints, and legal roadblocks such as laws preventing early admission to school. The barriers to early identification and programming for students with special gifts or talents include school policies and ideologies that refuse to advance students in grade beyond their chronological age peers.

Ruf (2005) describes the early signs of giftedness and provides descriptions of children's typical abilities for each of her five levels of giftedness. Her descriptions are those of parents when their children were birth to 9 years of age and older. Table 15.1 contains sample descriptions of one child at age 4 to 5 years from each level. In Ruf's classification scheme, Level One designates children who test between approximately the 90th and the 98th percentiles in general ability (meaning that they score higher than 90% to 98% of children taking the test). Each higher level in her system represents higher performance and a smaller percentage of the general population of children.

Many questions remain unanswered about the education of young children who have special gifts. Relatively little is known about how advantageous it is to identify and program for such children before they are in third or fourth grade or how best to train parents and teachers to work with preschoolers with special abilities. Young children with disabilities need the best possible early intervention to make sure that all of their abilities, including any special gifts they might have, are not overlooked (see Odom & Wolery, 2006; Porter, 2005).

Although not a panacea, early admission to school and acceleration through grades and subjects offer significant advantages for some young students with special gifts or talents. What many young children with special abilities need most is the freedom to make full and appropriate use of school systems as they now exist. They need the freedom to study with older children in specific areas in which their abilities are challenged. Such children need to be able to get around the usual eligibility rules so that they can go through the ordinary curriculum at an accelerated rate. Unfortunately, relatively few preschoolers with special gifts receive the kind of educational programming appropriate for their abilities. See the Responsive Instruction, "Acceleration: *A Nation Deceived* Report," on pages 446–447 for information on the research supporting acceleration.

INTERNETRESOURCES

You may want to do a search of the web using the search term "educational acceleration."

MAKING IT WORK
COLLABORATION AND CO-TEACHING OF STUDENTS WITH SPECIAL GIFTS AND TALENTS

"How can I challenge him when half of my students have difficulty reading?"

Working with students with gifts and talents can be especially challenging for classroom teachers considering the wide range of achievement levels in today's classrooms. Collaboration with a teacher of students with special gifts and talents can help general education teachers challenge all students.

WHAT DOES IT MEAN TO BE A TEACHER OF STUDENTS WITH SPECIAL GIFTS AND TALENTS?

The Council for Exceptional Children (2003) requires that teachers of students with special gifts and talents be able to:

1. Identify sources of differentiated materials for individuals with gifts and talents.
2. Provide effective management of teaching and learning for students with gifts and talents.
3. Identify grouping practices that support differentiated learning environments.
4. Teach individuals to use self-assessment, problem solving, and other cognitive strategies.

SUCCESSFUL STRATEGIES FOR CO-TEACHING OR COLLABORATION

Instruction in a differentiated classroom is based on student readiness and includes constant assessment of student skill and knowledge, varying of activities or assignments for individuals, and the active exploration of topics at varying levels by individuals or groups of students (Tomlinson, 1995). This can be quite difficult to manage as a single classroom teacher with between 20 and 30 students with a wide variety of skills. Teachers of students with gifts and talents can facilitate this process by helping to manage the classroom when groups and individuals are working, by helping to assess student progress, and by helping to collect resources.

For example, take a look at the following differentiated activity. The instructional objective is to help all students learn the water cycle (Trank, 2006, p. 327).

Independent water cycle activities differentiated by interest and learning profile.

Distribute the **Water Cycle Activity Option.** Students choose one of six possible activities to complete in class (time permitting) or as homework.

A. Design a cartoon that illustrates your journey as a water droplet. Include an appropriate caption.
B. Draw an accurate version of the water cycle that includes all steps. Be sure to show the processes that get a water droplet from one step to another.
C. Create a fictional story about the journey of a water droplet. Base it on your water droplet's journey.
D. Design a similar game using another cycle we have studied (e.g., the carbon cycle or the nitrogen cycle). Write out or sketch one possible journey. How does this journey differ from your journey as a water droplet?
E. Create a bar graph of your journey and the journey of two other droplets, based on the amount of time spent at each station. For data, refer to your paper clip chain and the chains of two classmates.
F. Create a local version of the water cycle. Be sure to include the names of local rivers, bays, oceans, mountains, and so on.

TEACHER REFLECTIONS

These differentiated activities are designed to appeal to a variety of interests and learning styles as defined by both Gardner (1993) and Sternberg (1988). My goal was to encourage students to solidify their understanding of water and cycles in nature. Observing the activity choices students made here gave me further insight into their learning preferences. Note that some of the activities are more difficult than others. I also watched to see which students took on the extra challenge (Trank, 2006, p. 327).

This lesson can be used with students of all achievement levels; however, the instructional support necessary for all students to understand the lesson varies. Collaborating with a teacher of students with special gifts and talents would allow both teachers to provide instructional support, observe student work, and develop subsequent lessons. Differentiation to this extent may not be possible without this collaboration.

• By Margaret P. Weiss

TABLE 15.1 Examples of gifted children at ages four to five years

Level One

Johnathan Truett—At four, Johnathan read *Hop on Pop* and other Dr. Seuss books that we'd read to him. He started sounding out simple words, so we read the text and stopped at words we thought he could recognize or figure out. He then did this with harder words.

Level Two

Debra Sund—At four, Debra read the label on the graham cracker box. Before she turned five, she read long words like "elevator." She didn't seem to learn to read by sounding out the letters. Instead, when she saw a word she didn't know, she would ask what it was. After she heard and saw the word once, she knew it on sight. At 4½, while walking home from the park, Debra asked about wind and what we needed in order to live. Her father explained there was something in the air that we needed to breathe. Debra replied, "You mean oxygen?" Where she heard that is anyone's guess.

Level Three

Brennan Ahlers—Brennan started to read chapter books when he was about four. He did simple division and multiplication in his head at 4½. When he started preschool, I didn't know enough to ask for any adjustments to be made for him. His teacher tried to keep him challenged, but he complained that it was boring. He was already reading and writing while many students couldn't write their names. He was puzzled at having to memorize his address and phone number, because it seemed so basic. He thought every kid knew that.

Level Four

Rebecca Renick—When she was four, Rebecca's babysitter played school with her and gave her addition and subtraction worksheets. Rebecca filled them out correctly. Her teacher said that she always had more complex and interesting ideas for play than the other kids. When she got frustrated that "they didn't get it," she went to the bookrack and read. She was really into jokes and told one joke after another to my mother on the phone. She also loved colored beads and made perfect geometric patterns with them.

Level Five

Jacob Jones—By the age of 4½, we'd go to the library and Jacob would head to the section with computer manuals. Nobody imagined that he was really reading them, but he was. We allowed him access to any level book, which led to some interesting questions when this five-year-old was reading about human reproduction in a large book with pictures during church.

Source: Ruf, D. L. (2005). *Losing our minds: Gifted children left behind.* Scottsdale, AZ: Great Potential Press, pp. 63, 88, 113–114, 144, 178.

RESPONSIVE *INSTRUCTION*

MEETING THE NEEDS OF STUDENTS WITH SPECIAL GIFTS AND TALENTS

Acceleration: A Nation Deceived Report

Nothing is so unequal as the equal treatment of unequal people.

—*Thomas Jefferson*

WHAT THE RESEARCH SAYS

In 2004, *A Nation Deceived: How Schools Hold Back Its Brightest Students* was released (Colangelo, Assouline, & Gross). This report summarized 50 years of research on the various forms of acceleration and came to the singular conclusion that acceleration, in many of its forms and under many different circumstances, benefits gifted students both academically and socially. Unfortunately, concern over ability tracking (an extreme form of ability grouping that sorts students based on global measures such as IQ or GPA) has spilled over into concern about acceleration programs. Acceleration, not a form of tracking, is any ed-

ucational program that moves students through at a faster rate or younger than typical age. Effective acceleration programs match the level and complexity of the curriculum to the readiness and motivation of the student (Colangelo et al., 2004).

The report dispels many myths associated with acceleration including the belief that the majority of students are not socially mature enough to advance grades, holding students to their grade level is the "safer" educational route, and acceleration results in gaps in students' knowledge. The report touches upon the 18 types of acceleration found in schools today and reviews the relevant research associated with each practice. The types of acceleration are early admission to kindergarten, early admission to first grade, grade skipping, continuous progress, self-paced instruction, subject-matter acceleration/partial acceleration, combined classes, curriculum compacting, telescoping curriculum, mentoring, extracurricular programs, correspondence courses, early graduation, concurrent/dual enrollment, advanced placement, credit by examination, acceleration in college, and early entrance into middle school, high school, or college.

SUMMARY OF THE FINDINGS

A synthesis of the research highlights important aspects related to successful acceleration. Some of the main findings follow:

1. Acceleration is more effective in raising student achievement than most successful school reforms.
2. Accelerated students are more likely than nonaccelerated students to aspire to advanced educational degrees.
3. When the curriculum moves at a slow pace, boredom and discontent frequently ensue.
4. Problems that stem from acceleration can frequently be traced to incomplete (poor) planning.
5. Almost *all* forms of acceleration result in academic growth (from a review of 380 studies).
6. Few early college entrants experience social or emotional difficulties—when difficulties do arise, they are typically short-term and part of an overall adjustment period.
7. Gifted students tend to be socially and emotionally more mature than their same-age mates—thus, acceleration can provide a better personal maturity match.
8. The Iowa Acceleration Scale (IAS) is a proven instrument for making acceleration decisions.
9. Many alternatives to full-time early college entrance are available today, including advanced placement (AP) courses, dual-enrollment classes, distance education, and summer programs.

IOWA ACCELERATION SCALE

A consistent theme throughout the report is that the positive benefits of acceleration are associated with students who have been appropriately evaluated for the purposes of acceleration.

One tool used to assess the "readiness" of students for grade-skipping acceleration is the IAS. The IAS was designed for child-study teams to use to review objective data regarding a child's potential for successful acceleration. The survey includes 20 items divided into 4 subscales: (1) Academic Ability and Achievement, (2) School Information, (3) Interpersonal Skills, and (4) Attitude and Support. The Grand Total, a sum of the four subscales, translates into one of the following recommendations: (a) excellent candidate, (b) good candidate, (c) marginal candidate, and (d) poor candidate. Studies that have examined the efficacy of the IAS find that it is a useful tool for schools and families (Assouline et al., 2003).

WHAT CAN SCHOOLS DO?

The report encourages school professionals to consider the following three questions when making acceleration decisions:

1. Have we assessed the student's ability correctly so that we know this child is ready for an advanced, fast-paced curriculum?
2. Given the results of our assessment, what might be the best form of acceleration for this child?
3. We know that in a few cases acceleration has not been effective. What can we do as a school to ensure success for the accelerated student? (Colangelo et al., 2004, p. 69)

The message of the report is clear: parents, teachers, administrators, and colleges of education need to be familiar with the research on acceleration to meet the needs of gifted students. Borland (1989) summarizes the current conundrum of resistance to acceleration:

> Acceleration is one of the most curious phenomena in the field of education. I can think of no other issue in which there is such a gulf between what research has revealed and what most practitioners believe. The research on acceleration is so uniformly positive, the benefits of appropriate acceleration so unequivocal, that it is difficult to see how an educator could oppose it. (p. 185)

• By Kristin L. Sayeski

■ ■ ■ ■ ■ ■ ■ ■ ■ ■ ■

TRANSITION TO ADULTHOOD

For students with special gifts or talents who are achieving near their potential and are given opportunities to take on adult roles, the transitions from childhood to adolescence to adulthood and from high school to higher education or employment are typically not very problematic. Particularly by adolescence, these students tend to be aware of their relative strengths and weaknesses. This means that they might not see themselves as gifted in their areas of relative weakness even though they perform as well as or better than the majority of their age peers in those areas (Plucker & Stocking, 2001; Robinson et al., 2007).

In many ways, transitions for these youths tend to mirror the problems in transitions faced by adolescents and young adults with disabilities (see Kohler & Field, 2006). Not all adolescents and young adults with special gifts or talents take transitions in stride. Many need personal and career counseling and a networking system that links students to school and community resources (Herbert & Kelly, 2006; Neihart et al., 2002).

If there is a central issue in the education of adolescents with special gifts or talents, it is that of acceleration versus enrichment. Proponents of enrichment believe that these students need continued social contact with their age peers. They argue that such students should follow the curriculum of their age peers and study topics in greater depth. Proponents of acceleration believe that the only way to provide challenging and appropriate education for students with special gifts and talents is to let them compete with older students. These educators argue that because the cognitive abilities of these students are advanced beyond their years, these students should proceed through the curriculum at an accelerated pace.

Acceleration for adolescents with special gifts or talents can mean enrollment in advanced placement courses, early entrance to college, or enrollment in college courses while they are attending high school (see Callahan, 2003; Colangelo et al., 2004b; Muratori et al., 2006). Some of the most highly gifted students might even be admitted early to graduate study. In the case of the child prodigy who is now a graduate student at the University of Virginia, described in the accompanying Personal Perspectives, radical acceleration seems to have been an obvious choice. It's difficult to argue against early admission to college and gradu-

Personal PERSPECTIVES
Child Prodigy Now U. Va. Grad Student

Gregory R. Smith completed one goal May 31 when he received his bachelor's degree from Randolph-Macon College at the age of 13. Now the child prodigy is aiming at another by jumping into the University's graduate studies program.

Smith started the first of two summer classes Tuesday, the day after his 14th birthday. He is pursuing a Ph.D. in mathematics, the first of several doctoral degrees he plans to obtain.

"The University of Virginia has been my first choice all along," Smith said in announcing his decision last week. "It has been my plan since I graduated from high school to apply to U. Va. for my graduate work. I am so excited to have this wonderful opportunity to study at one of our country's best universities."

U. Va. officials have been equally excited about Smith's selection. Gene Block, vice president and provost, said, "Greg will be a wonderful addition to our graduate studies program. His record of intellectual achievement, combined with his dedication to international service, fit well into the U. Va. tradition. We realize that it's important not only to challenge Greg academically but also to provide an environment where he feels at home among peers."

Smith has been recognized as a prodigy since early childhood. Born in West Reading, Pa., he was solving math problems at 14 months and reading by age 2. The family moved to Florida, where he completed his K–12 education in five years, then to Virginia, where at age 10 he enrolled at Randolph-Macon College in Ashland. He graduated cum laude with a degree in mathematics and was a member of Phi Beta Kappa and five other honor fraternities.

Along the way Smith has used the media attention generated by his blazing academic pace to become a vocal advocate for the pursuit of peace and for children's rights around the world. He founded International Youth Advocates and has served as youth ambassador for the Christian Children's Fund and youth spokesperson for World Centers of Compassion for Children. During the past year, he has traveled throughout the United States and visited six countries on four continents. Humanitarian aid efforts are benefiting orphans in East Timor and youth in Sao Paulo, Brazil, and Smith is helping people in Rwanda build their first public library.

He has met with presidents, including former President Bill Clinton and former Soviet Union President Mikhail Gorbachev, as well as Nobel Peace laureates, such as Ireland's Betty Williams and South Africa's Archbishop Desmond Tutu. His efforts have brought him before the United Nations Security Council and several state legislatures.

One of Smith's goals is to create an international symbol for the child, so that child-occupied buildings in conflict zones can be marked and protected. In addition, he hopes to create recognized safe havens in embattled areas so children will have shelters sanctioned by international law.

"I believe all children are born pure and innocent and only act with violence because we teach them hate and violence," he said. "There must be peaceful parenting to have a peaceful future. It is up to us to create an environment that makes it possible for children to resist the corruptions that take us down violent and immoral paths."

Nominated in 2002 and '03 for the Nobel Peace Prize, Smith has been tapped to co-chair the World of Children Awards with Muhammad Ali. He is among 43 students in the nation to receive scholarships up to $50,000 a year for six years from the Jack Kent Cooke Foundation for his graduate studies.

Source: Graves, L. (June 13, 2004). Child prodigy now U. Va. grad student. *Inside UVA.* Reprinted with permission.

ate school for an adolescent with Gregory Smith's very unusual intellectual gifts, social maturity, and moral commitments. Other students with special gifts or talents who are nonetheless less dramatically different from their age peers may not benefit from radical acceleration.

Acceleration programs, particularly in mathematics, have been evaluated very favorably (see Assouline & Lupkowski-Shoplik, 2003; Brody & Stanley, 2005; Muratori et al., 2006). In fact, early entrance to college on a full-time or part-time basis appears to work very well for adolescents, as long as it is done with care and sensitivity to the needs of individual students. It's important to provide counseling and support services for students who enter college early to ensure that they have appropriate, rewarding social experiences that enhance their self-esteem, as well as academic challenges and successes.

Beyond acceleration and enrichment, adolescents with special gifts or talents often need attention to social and personal development if they are to make successful and gratifying transitions to adulthood and careers (Assouline & Colangelo, 2006). Like other groups of students with special characteristics and needs, they may benefit from opportunities to socialize with and learn from other students who have similar characteristics and face similar challenges. They may be able to obtain particular benefit from reflecting on the nature and meaning of life and the directions they choose for themselves. Given proper supports, they can often make use of self-determination and survival skills (see Neihart et al., 2002).

SUMMARY

How is giftedness defined?

- Students with special gifts excel in some way compared to others of the same age. However, little agreement exists about how giftedness should be defined. Disagreements about definition include:
  - What is to be measured
  - How it is to be measured
  - The degree to which one must excel
  - The comparison group
  - Reasons for identifying giftedness
- Giftedness is actually whatever we wish to make it.
- There may be different kinds of giftedness, such as analytic, synthetic, and practical intelligence.

What is the prevalence of giftedness?

- Prevalence depends on definition; school systems across the nation typically identify about 3% to 5% of students as gifted.

What are the origins of giftedness?

- Both biological (primarily genetic) and social factors (e.g., family, school, peer group, community) are involved.
  - No one knows precisely how much each of these two factors contributes to giftedness, especially in the individual case.
  - We can alter many social factors but not genetic factors, and more attention needs to be given to how schools foster giftedness.

How is giftedness identified?

- Individual intelligence tests have been the traditional means of identifying giftedness.
- More attention is being given now to additional, culturally sensitive identification procedures, including nomination by peers, parents, teachers, and self as well as to interests and accomplishments.

What are the psychological and behavioral characteristics of students with special gifts and talents?

- Gifted students typically learn to read at an early age and achieve other developmental milestones earlier than most children.
- Gifted students are typically good at many things.
- Gifted students typically like school and like learning.
- Gifted students are subject to the same psychological and physical problems of other students.

How do cultural values affect the education of students with special gifts and talents?

- American culture is ambivalent about giftedness, liking the good things that giftedness brings but disliking intellectual superiority and identifying individuals with intellectual gifts.

What groups of students with special gifts and talents are neglected?

- Underachievers are often overlooked.
- Students who are low in socioeconomic status and those living in remote areas are often unrecognized.
- Students from cultural- and ethnic-minority groups are often neglected.
- Students who also have disabilities are often not identified.
- Females are underrepresented.

What are the major educational considerations for students with special gifts and talents?

- Acceleration and enrichment are the two most common ways of accommodating gifted students; and both have advantages and disadvantages, proponents and opponents.

What are the major problems of early intervention for children with special gifts and talents?

- Lack of research to indicate effective ways of identifying giftedness in young children (i.e., before third or fourth grade) is a major problem.

What provisions are made for transition of students with special gifts and talents?

- The problems of gifted adolescents tend to mirror those of students with disabilities of the same age, and many will need personal counseling about further education and career paths.
- Acceleration (including early admission to college) and enrichment (including advanced placement courses) are the two primary accommodations.

COUNCIL FOR EXCEPTIONAL CHILDREN

Addressing the Professional Standards

 Council for Exceptional Children

Council for Exceptional Children (CEC) Common Core Knowledge and Skills addressed in this chapter: ICC1K4, ICC1K5, ICC1K7, ICC1K8, ICC2K4, ICC2K5, ICC2K6, ICC3K1, ICC3K2, ICC3K4, ICC4S3, ICC5K3, ICC5S2, ICC7S1, ICC7S9, ICC8S4, ICC8S5, ICC8S6

Appendix: Provides a full listing of the CEC Common Core Standards, and associated Knowledge and Skill Statements listed here.

MYEDUCATIONLAB

PEARSON myeducationlab Now go to Topic 17: Gifted & Talented in the MyEducationLab (www.myeducationlab.com) for your course, where you can:

- Find learning outcomes for the broad concepts covered in this chapter along with the national standards that connect to these outcomes.
- Complete Assignments and Activities that can help you more deeply understand the chapter content.
- Apply and practice your understanding of the core concepts and skills identified in the chapter with the Building Teaching Skills and Dispositions learning units.
- Check your comprehension on the content covered in the chapter by going to the Study Plan in the Book-Specific Resources for your text. Here you will be able to take a chapter quiz, receive feedback on your answers, and then access Review, Practice, and Enrichment activities to enhance your understanding of chapter content.
- Watch video clips of CCSSO Teacher of the Year award winners responding to the question: "Why I teach?" in the Teacher Talk section.

CEC KNOWLEDGE AND SKILL STANDARDS COMMON CORE

Standard I: Foundations

ICC1K1: Models, theories, and philosophies, and research methods that provide the basis for special education practice.

ICC1K2: Laws, policies, and ethical principles regarding behavior management planning and implementation.

ICC1K3: Relationship of special education to the organization and function of educational agencies.

ICC1K4: Rights and responsibilities of students, parents, teachers, and other professionals, and schools related to exceptional learning needs.

ICC1K5: Issues in definition and identification of individuals with exceptional learning needs, including those from culturally and linguistically diverse backgrounds.

ICC1K6: Issues, assurances, and due process rights related to assessment, eligibility, and placement within a continuum of services.

ICC1K7: Family systems and the role of families in the educational process.

ICC1K8: Historical points of view and contributions of culturally diverse groups.

ICC1K9: Impact of the dominant culture on shaping schools and the individuals who study and work in them.

ICC1K10: Potential impact of differences in values, languages, and customs that can exist between the home and school.

ICC1S1: Articulate personal philosophy of special education.

Standard II: Development and Characteristics of Learners

ICC2K1: Typical and atypical human growth and development.

ICC2K2: Educational implications of characteristics of various exceptionalities.

ICC2K3: Characteristics and effects of the cultural and environmental milieu of the individual with exceptional learning needs and the family.

ICC2K4: Family systems and the role of families in supporting development.

ICC2K5: Similarities and differences of individuals with and without exceptional learning needs.

ICC2K6: Similarities and differences among individuals with exceptional learning needs.

ICC2K7: Effects of various medications on individuals with exceptional learning needs.

Standard III: Individual Learning Differences

ICC3K1: Effects an exceptional condition(s) can have on an individual's life.

ICC3K2: Impact of learner's academic and social abilities, attitudes, interests, and values on instruction and career development.

ICC3K3: Variations in beliefs, traditions, and values across and within cultures and their effects on relationships among individuals with exceptional learning needs, family, and schooling.

ICC3K4: Cultural perspectives influencing the relationships among families, schools, and communities as related to instruction.

ICC3K5: Differing ways of learning of individuals with exceptional learning needs including those from culturally diverse backgrounds and strategies for addressing these differences.

Standard IV: Instructional Strategies

ICC4K1:   Evidence-based practices validated for specific characteristics of learners and settings.

ICC4S1:   Use strategies to facilitate integration into various settings.

ICC4S2:   Teach individuals to use self-assessment, problem-solving, and other cognitive strategies to meet their needs.

ICC4S3:   Select, adapt, and use instructional strategies and materials according to characteristics of the individual with exceptional learning needs.

ICC4S4:   Use strategies to facilitate maintenance and generalization of skills across learning environments.

ICC4S5:   Use procedures to increase the individual's self-awareness, self-management, self-control, self-reliance, and self-esteem.

ICC4S6:   Use strategies that promote successful transitions for individuals with exceptional learning needs.

Standard V: Learning Environments and Social Interactions

ICC5K1:   Demands of learning environments.

ICC5K2:   Basic classroom management theories and strategies for individuals with exceptional learning needs.

ICC5K3:   Effective management of teaching and learning.

ICC5K4:   Teacher attitudes and behaviors that influence behavior of individuals with exceptional learning needs.

ICC5K5:   Social skills needed for educational and other environments.

ICC5K6:   Strategies for crisis prevention and intervention.

ICC5K7:   Strategies for preparing individuals to live harmoniously and productively in a culturally diverse world.

ICC5K8:   Ways to create learning environments that allow individuals to retain and appreciate their own and each other's respective language and cultural heritage.

ICC5K9:   Ways specific cultures are negatively stereotyped.

ICC5K10:   Strategies used by diverse populations to cope with a legacy of former and continuing racism.

ICC5S1:   Create a safe, equitable, positive, and supporting learning environment in which diversities are valued.

ICC5S2:   Identify realistic expectations for personal and social behavior in various settings.

ICC5S3:   Identify supports needed for integration into various program placements.

ICC5S4:   Design learning environments that encourage active participation in individual and group settings.

ICC5S5:   Modify the learning environment to manage behaviors.

ICC5S6:   Use performance data and information from all stakeholders to make or suggest modifications in learning environments.

ICC5S7:   Establish and maintain rapport with individuals with and without exceptional learning needs.

ICC5S8:   Teach self-advocacy.

ICC5S9:   Create an environment that encourages self-advocacy and increased independence.

ICC5S10:   Use effective and varied behavior management strategies.

ICC5S11:   Use the least intensive behavior management strategy consistent with the needs of the individual with exceptional learning needs.

ICC5S12:   Design and manage daily routines.

ICC5S13:   Organize, develop, and sustain learning environments that support positive intracultural and intercultural experiences.

ICC5S14:   Mediate controversial intercultural issues among students within the learning environment in ways that enhance any culture, group, or person.

ICC5S15:   Structure, direct, and support the activities of paraeducators, volunteers, and tutors.

ICC5S16:   Use universal precautions.

Standard VI: Communication

ICC6K1:   Effects of cultural and linguistic differences on growth and development.

ICC6K2:   Characteristics of one's own culture and use of language and the ways in which these can differ from other cultures and uses of languages.

ICC6K3:   Ways of behaving and communicating among cultures that can lead to misinterpretation and misunderstanding.

ICC6K4:   Augmentative and assistive communication strategies.

ICC6S1:   Use strategies to support and enhance communication skills of individuals with exceptional learning needs.

ICC6S2:   Use communication strategies and resources to facilitate understanding of subject matter for students whose primary language is not the dominant language.

Standard VII: Instructional Planning

ICC7K1:   Theories and research that form the basis of curriculum development and instructional practice.

ICC7K2:   Scope and sequences of general and special curricula.

ICC7K3:   National, state or provincial, and local curricula standards.

ICC7K4:   Technology for planning and managing the teaching and learning environment.

ICC7K5:   Roles and responsibilities of the paraeducator related to instruction, intervention, and direct service.

ICC7S1:   Identify and prioritize areas of the general curriculum and accommodations for individuals with exceptional learning needs.

ICC7S2:   Develop and implement comprehensive, longitudinal individualized programs in collaboration with team members.

ICC7S3:   Involve the individual and family in setting instructional goals and monitoring progress.

ICC7S4:   Use functional assessments to develop intervention plans.

ICC7S5:   Use task analysis.

ICC7S6:   Sequence, implement, and evaluate individualized learning objectives.

ICC7S7:   Integrate affective, social, and life skills with academic curricula.

ICC7S8:   Develop and select instructional content, resources, and strategies that respond to cultural, linguistic, and gender differences.

ICC7S9:   Incorporate and implement instructional and assistive technology into the educational program.

ICC7S10:   Prepare lesson plans.

ICC7S11:   Prepare and organize materials to implement daily lesson plans.

ICC7S12:   Use instructional time effectively.

ICC7S13:   Make responsive adjustments to instruction based on continued observations.

ICC7S14:   Prepare individuals to exhibit self-enhancing behavior in response to societal attitudes and actions.

ICC7S15:   Evaluate and modify instructional practices in response to ongoing assessment data.

Standard VIII: Assessment

ICC8K1:   Basic terminology used in assessment.

ICC8K2:   Legal provisions and ethical principles regarding assessment of individuals.

ICC8K3:   Screening, prereferral, referral, and classification procedures.

ICC8K4:   Use and limitations of assessment instruments.

ICC8K5:   National, state or provincial, and local accommodations and modifications.

ICC8S1:   Gather relevant background information.

ICC8S2:   Administer nonbiased formal and informal assessments.

ICC8S3:   Use technology to conduct assessments.

ICC8S4:   Develop or modify individualized assessment strategies.

ICC8S5:   Interpret information from formal and informal assessments.

ICC8S6:   Use assessment information in making eligibility, program, and placement decisions for individuals with exceptional learning needs, including those from culturally and/or linguistically diverse backgrounds.

ICC8S7:   Report assessment results to all stakeholders using effective communication skills.

ICC8S8:   Evaluate instruction and monitor progress of individuals with exceptional learning needs.

ICC8S9:   Develop or modify individualized assessment strategies.

ICC8S10:   Create and maintain records.

Standard IX: Professional and Ethical Practice

ICC9K1:   Personal cultural biases and differences that affect one's teaching.

ICC9K2:   Importance of the teacher serving as a model for individuals with exceptional learning needs.

ICC9K3:   Continuum of lifelong professional development.

ICC9K4:   Methods to remain current regarding research-validated practice.

ICC9S1:   Practice within the CEC Code of Ethics and other standards of the profession.

ICC9S2:   Uphold high standards of competence and integrity and exercise sound judgment in the practice of the professional.

ICC9S3:   Act ethically in advocating for appropriate services.

ICC9S4:   Conduct professional activities in compliance with applicable laws and policies.

ICC9S5:   Demonstrate commitment to developing the highest education and quality-of-life potential of individuals with exceptional learning needs.

ICC9S6:   Demonstrate sensitivity for the culture, language, religion, gender, disability, socioeconomic status, and sexual orientation of individuals.

ICC9S7:   Practice within one's skill limit and obtain assistance as needed.

ICC9S8:   Use verbal, nonverbal, and written language effectively.

ICC9S9:   Conduct self-evaluation of instruction.

ICC9S10:   Access information on exceptionalities.

ICC9S11:   Reflect on one's practice to improve instruction and guide professional growth.

ICC9S12:   Engage in professional activities that benefit individuals with exceptional learning needs, their families, and one's colleagues.

ICC9S13:   Demonstrate Commitment to engage evidence-based practice.

Standard X: Collaboration

ICC10K1:   Models and strategies of consultation and collaboration.

ICC10K2:   Roles of individuals with exceptional learning needs, families, and school and community personnel in planning of an individualized program.

ICC10K3:   Concerns of families of individuals with exceptional learning needs and strategies to help address these concerns.

ICC10K4:   Culturally responsive factors that promote effective communication and collaboration with individuals with exceptional learning needs, families, school personnel, and community members.

ICC10S1:   Maintain confidential communication about individuals with exceptional learning needs.

ICC10S2:   Collaborate with families and others in assessment of individuals with exceptional learning needs.

ICC10S3:   Foster respectful and beneficial relationships between families and professionals.

ICC10S4:   Assist individuals with exceptional learning needs and their families in becoming active participants in the educational team.

ICC10S5:   Plan and conduct collaborative conferences with individuals with exceptional learning needs and their families.

ICC10S6:   Collaborate with school personnel and community members in integrating individuals with exceptional learning needs into various settings.

ICC10S7:   Use group problem-solving skills to develop, implement, and evaluate collaborative activities.

ICC10S8:   Model techniques and coach others in the use of instructional methods and accommodations.

ICC10S9:   Communicate with school personnel about the characteristics and needs of individuals with exceptional learning needs.

ICC10S10:   Communicate effectively with families of individuals with exceptional learning needs from diverse backgrounds.

ICC10S11:   Observe, evaluate, and provide feedback to paraeducators.

GLOSSARY

A

Acceleration An approach in which students with special gifts or talents are placed in grade levels ahead of their age peers in one or more academic subjects.

Accessible pedestrian signal (APSs) Devices for people who are blind to let them know when the "walk" signal is on at intersections; can be auditory, tactile, or both.

Accommodations Changes in the delivery of instruction, type of student performance, or method of assessment which do not significantly change the content or conceptual difficulty of the curriculum.

Acquired apraxia As in Developmental apraxia, there are problems in motor planning such that the child has difficulty in producing speech sounds and organizing words and word sounds for effective communication. However, the problem is known to be caused by neurological damage.

Acquired immune deficiency syndrome (AIDs) A virus-caused illness resulting in a breakdown of the immune system; currently, no known cure exists.

Acute A serious state of illness or injury from which someone often recovers with treatment.

Adaptations Changes in curricular content or conceptual difficulty or changes in instructional objectives and methods.

Adapted signs Signs adapted for use by people who are deaf-blind; tactually based rather than visually based, such as American Sign Language for those who are deaf but sighted.

Adaptive behavior The social and practical intelligence used in people's everyday lives; along with IQ, is considered in making a determination of intellectual disability.

Adaptive behavior skills Skills needed to adapt to one's living environment (e.g., communication, self-care, home living, social skills, community use, self-direction, health and safety, functional academics, leisure, and work); usually estimated by an adaptive behavior survey; one of two major components (the other is intellectual functioning) of the AAMR definition.

Adaptive devices Special tools that are adaptations of common items to make accomplishing self-care, work, or recreation activities easier for people with physical disabilities.

Adderall A psychostimulant for ADHD; its effects are longer acting than those of Ritalin.

Adventitiously deaf Deafness that occurs through illness or accident in an individual who was born with normal hearing.

Affective disorder A disorder of mood or emotional tone characterized by depression or elation.

Aggression Behavior that intentionally causes others harm or that elicits escape or avoidance responses from others.

Aim Line Used in CBM; based on expected growth norms, a line drawn from the baseline data point to the anticipated end of instruction.

Americans with Disabilities Act (ADA) Civil rights legislation for persons with disabilities ensuring nondiscrimination in a broad range of activities.

Amniocentesis A medical procedure that allows examination of the amniotic fluid around the fetus; sometimes recommended to determine the presence of abnormality.

Androgen A hormone that is responsible for controlling the development of male characteristics.

Anoxia Deprivation of oxygen; can cause brain injury.

Anxiety disorder A disorder characterized by anxiety, fearfulness, and avoidance of ordinary activities because of anxiety or fear.

Aphonia Loss of voice.

Applied behavior analysis (ABA) Highly structured approach that focuses on teaching functional skills and continuous assessment of progress; grounded in behavioral learning theory.

Apraxia The inability to plan and coordinate speech.

Aqueous humor A watery substance between the cornea and lens of the eye.

Asperger syndrome One of five autistic spectrum disorders; a milder form of autism without significant impairments in language and cognition; characterized by primary problems in social interaction.

Assistance card A relatively small card containing a message that alerts the public that the user is deaf-blind and needs assistance in crossing the street.

Asthma A lung disease characterized by episodic difficulty in breathing, particularly exhaling, due to inflammation obstruction of the air passages.

Astigmatism Blurred vision caused by an irregular cornea or lens.

Atonic Lack of muscle tone; floppiness.

Atresia Absence or closure of a part of the body that is normally open.

Attention deficit hyperactivity disorder (ADHD) A condition characterized by severe problems of inattention, hyperactivity, and/or impulsivity; often found in people with learning disabilities.

Audiologist An individual trained in audiology, the science dealing with hearing impairments, their detection, and remediation.

Audiometric zero The lowest level at which people with normal hearing can hear.

Auditory-oral approach A method of teaching communication to people who are deaf that stresses the use of visual cues, such as speechreading and cued speech.

Auditory-verbal approach Part of the oral approach to teaching students who are hearing impaired; stresses teaching the person to use his or her remaining hearing as much as possible; heavy emphasis on use of amplification; heavy emphasis on teaching speech.

Augmentative or alternative communication (AAC) Alternative forms of communication that do not use the oral sounds of speech or that augment the use of speech.

Auricle The visible part of the ear, composed of cartilage; collects the sounds and funnels them via the external auditory canal to the eardrum.

Autism One of five autistic spectrum disorders; characterized by extreme social withdrawal and impairment in communication; other common characteristics are stereotyped movements, resistance to environmental change or change in daily routines, and unusual responses to sensory experiences; usually evident before age of 3 years; a pervasive developmental disability characterized by extreme withdrawal, cognitive deficits, language disorders, self-stimulation, and onset before the age of 30 months.

Autism or autistic spectrum disorder A pervasive developmental disability characterized by extreme withdrawal, cognitive deficits, language disorders, self-stimulation, and onset before the age of 30 months.

Autism spectrum disorders Five similar conditions: autism, Asperger syndrome, Rett syndrome, childhood disintegrative disorder, and pervasive developmental disorder not otherwise specified; all involve varying degrees of problems with communication skills, social interactions, and repetitive and stereotyped patterns of behavior.

Autistic regression Phenomenon whereby a child appears to progress normally until about 16 to 24 months of age and, then, begins to show signs of being autistic and ultimately is diagnosed as autistic.

Autistic savant A person with severe autism whose social and language skills are markedly delayed but who also has advanced skills in a particular area, such as calculation or drawing.

B

Basal ganglia A set of structures within the brain that include the caudate, globus pallidus, and putamen, the first two being abnormal in people with ADHD; generally responsible for the coordination and control of movement.

Baseline Data Point Used in CBM; the beginning score gathered before an intervention begins, e.g, the number of correct words per minute that a student reads before receiving a fluency intervention.

Behavior management Strategies and techniques used to increase desirable behavior and decrease undesirable behavior. May be applied in the classroom, home, or other environment.

Behavior modification Systematic control of environmental events, especially of consequences, to produce specific changes in observable responses. May include reinforcement, punishment, modeling, self-instruction, desensitization, guided practice, or any other technique for strengthening or eliminating a particular response.

Behavioral inhibition The ability to stop an intended response, to stop an ongoing response, to guard an ongoing response from interruption, and to refrain from responding immediately; allows executive functions to occur; delayed or impaired in those with ADHD.

Behavioral phenotype A collection of behaviors, including cognitive, language, and social behaviors as well as psychopathological symptoms, that tend to occur together in people with a specific genetic syndrome.

Bicultural-bilingual approach An approach for teaching students with hearing impairment that stresses teaching American Sign Language as a first language and English as a second language and promotes the teaching of Deaf culture.

Braille A system in which raised dots allow people who are blind to read with their fingertips; each quadrangular cell contains from one to six dots, the arrangement of which denotes different letters and symbols.

Braille bills Legislation passed in several states to make braille more available to students with visual impairment; specific provisions vary from state to state, but major advocates have lobbied for (1) making braille available if parents want it, and (2) ensuring that teachers of students with visual impairment are proficient in braille.

Braille notetakers Portable devices that can be used to take notes in braille, which are then converted to speech, braille, or text.

Brain stem-evoked response audiometry Measures electrical signals from the brain stem that are in response to an auditory stimulus, such as a click.

C

Cataracts A condition caused by clouding of the lens of the eye; affects color vision and distance vision.

Caudate A structure in the basal ganglia of the brain; site of abnormal development in persons with ADHD.

Center-based program A program implemented primarily in a school or center, not in the student's home.

Central coherence The inclination to bring meaning to stimuli by conceptualizing it as a whole; thought to be weak in people with ASD.

Cerebellum An organ at the base of the brain responsible for coordination and movement; site of abnormal development in persons with ADHD.

Cerebral palsy (CP) A condition characterized by paralysis, weakness, lack of coordination, and/or other motor dysfunction; caused by damage to the brain before it has matured.

CHARGE syndrome A genetic syndrome resulting in deaf-blindness; characterized by physical anomalies, often including coloboma (abnormalities of the pupil, retina and/or optic nerve), cranial nerves, heart defects, atresia (absence or closure) of the chonae (air passages from nose to throat), retardation in growth and mental development, genital abnormalities, ear malformation and/or hearing loss.

Choanae Air passages from the nose to the throat.

Choreoathetoid Characterized by involuntary movements and difficulty with balance; associated with choreoathetoid cerebral palsy.

Chorionic villus sampling (CVS) A method of testing the unborn fetus for a variety of chromosomal abnormalities, such as Down syndrome; a small amount of tissue from the chorion (a membrane that eventually helps form the placenta) is extracted and tested; can be done earlier than amniocentesis but the risk of miscarriage is slightly higher.

Chromosomal disorder Any of several syndromes resulting from abnormal or damaged chromosome(s); can result in intellectual disabilities.

Chromosome A rod-shaped entity in the nucleus of the cell; contains genes, which convey hereditary characteristics; each cell in the human body contains 23 pairs of chromosomes.

Chronic A long-lasting condition; not temporary.

Chronological age Refers to how old a person is; used in comparison to mental age to determine IQ. IQ = (mental age ÷ chronological age) × 100.

Classwide peer tutoring (CWPT) An instructional procedure in which all students in the class are involved in tutoring and being tutored by classmates on specific skills as directed by their teacher.

Cleft palate A condition in which there is a rift or split in the upper part of the oral cavity; may include the upper lip (cleft lip).

Clinical history A history both from the patient and from a close contact such as parents, spouse, or significant other.

Closed head injury Damage to the brain that occurs without penetration of the skull; might be caused by a blow to the head or violent shaking by an adult.

Coaching A technique whereby a friend or therapist offers encouragement and support for a person with ADHD.

Cochlea A snail-shaped organ that lies below the vestibular mechanism in the inner ear; its parts convert the sounds coming from the middle ear into electrical signals that are transmitted to the brain.

Cochlear implantation A surgical procedure that allows people who are deaf to hear some environmental sounds; an external coil fitted on the skin by the ear picks up sound from a microphone worn by the person and transmits it to an internal coil implanted in the bone behind the ear, which carries it to an electrode implanted in the cochlea of the inner ear.

Cognition The ability to solve problems and use strategies; an area of difficulty for many persons with learning disabilities.

Cognitive mapping A nonsequential way of conceptualizing the spatial environment that allows a person who is visually impaired to know where several points in the environment are simultaneously; allows for better mobility than does a strictly sequential conceptualization of the environment.

Cognitive training A group of training procedures designed to change thoughts or thought patterns.

Collaborative consultation An approach in which a special educator and a general educator collaborate to come up with teaching strategies for a student with disabilities. The relationship between the two professionals is based on the premises of shared responsibility and equal authority.

Coloboma A condition of the eye in which the pupil is abnormally shaped and/or there are abnormalities of the retina or optic nerve; can result in loss of visual acuity and extreme sensitivity to light.

Communication The process of sharing information.

Communication disorders Impairments in the ability to use speech or language to communicate.

Communicative function Acts of communication, such as requesting, rejecting, commenting, arguing, and reasoning.

Communicative Intent The need to communicate for social reasons; thought to be lacking in most children with autism.

Community residential facility (CRF) A place, usually a group home, in an urban or residential neighborhood where about 3 to 10 adults with intellectual disabilities live under supervision.

Comorbidity Co-occurrence of two or more conditions in the same individual.

Competitive employment A workplace that provides employment that pays at least minimum wage and in which most workers are nondisabled.

Comprehension monitoring The ability to keep track of one's own comprehension of reading material and to make adjustments to comprehend better while reading; often deficient in students with learning disabilities.

Conditioned play audiometry Using pure tones or speech, the examiner teaches the child to do various activities whenever he hears a signal.

Conduct disorder A disorder characterized by overt, aggressive, disruptive behavior or covert antisocial acts such as stealing, lying, and fire setting; may include both overt and covert acts.

Conductive hearing impairment A hearing impairment, usually mild, resulting from malfunctioning along the conductive pathway of the ear (i.e., the outer or middle ear).

Congenital A characteristic or condition that is present at birth; might or might not be due to genetic factors.

Congenital anomaly An irregularity (anomaly) that is present at birth; might or might not be due to genetic factors.

Congenital cytomegalovirus (CMV) The most frequently occurring viral infection in newborns; can result in a variety of disabilities, especially hearing impairment.

Congenitally deaf Deafness that is present at birth; can be caused by genetic factors, by injuries during fetal development, or by injuries occurring at birth.

Connexin-26 gene A gene, the mutation of which causes deafness; the leading cause of congenital deafness in children.

Constant time delay An instructional procedure whereby the teacher makes a request while simultaneously prompting the student and then over several occasions makes the same request and waits a constant period of time before prompting; often used with students with intellectual disabilites.

Content enhancement The modification of curriculum materials to make them more salient or prominent, e.g., graphic organizers and mnemonics.

Continuous performance test (CPT) A test measuring a person's ability to sustain attention to rapidly presented stimuli; can help in the diagnosis of ADHD.

Cooperative learning A teaching approach in which the teacher places students with heterogeneous abilities (for example, some might have disabilities) together to work on assignments.

Cooperative teaching An approach in which general educators and special educators teach together in the general classroom; it helps the special educator know the context of the general education classroom better.

Cornea A transparent cover in front of the iris and pupil in the eye; responsible for most of the refraction of light rays in focusing on an object.

Corpus callosum A part of the brain, consisting of millions of fibers connecting the left and right hemispheres; responsible for communication between the two hemispheres; site of abnormal development in persons with ADHD.

Cortical visual impairment (CVI) A poorly understood childhood condition that apparently involves dysfunction in the visual cortex; characterized by large day-to-day variations in visual ability.

Co-teaching A special educator working side-by-side with a general educator in a classroom, both teachers providing instruction to the group.

Cranial nerves Twelve pairs of nerves that connect the brain with various muscles and glands in the body.

Creativity The ability to express novel and useful ideas, to sense and elucidate new and important relationships, and to ask previously unthought of, but crucial, questions.

Cued speech A method to aid speechreading in people with hearing impairment; the speaker uses hand shapes to represent sounds.

Curriculum based measurement (CBM) A formative evaluation method designed to evaluate performance in the curriculum to which students are exposed; usually involves giving students a small sample of items from the curriculum in use in their schools; proponents argue that CBM is preferable to comparing students with national norms or using tests that do not reflect the curriculum content learned by the students.

Customized employment Based on an assessment of the individual's strengths, weaknesses, and interests, the job matches the person's profile of interests and skills.

Cystic fibrosis An inherited disease affecting primarily the gastrointestinal (GI) tract and respiratory organs; characterized by thick, sticky mucous that often interferes with breathing or digestion.

D

Daily living skills Skills required for living independently, such as dressing, toileting, bathing, cooking, and other typical daily activities of nondisabled adults.

Decibels Units of relative loudness of sounds; zero decibels (0 dB) designates the point at which people with normal hearing can just detect sound.

Decoding The ability to convert print to spoken language; dependent on phonemic awareness and understanding of the alphabetic principles; a significant problem for many people with reading disabilities.

Deinstitutionalization A social movement starting in the 1960s whereby large numbers of persons with intellectual disabilities and/or mental illness are moved from large mental institutions into smaller community homes or into the homes of their families; recognized as a major catalyst for integrating persons with disabilities into society.

Descriptive Video Service® A service for use of people with visual impairment that provides audio narrative of key visual elements; available for several public television programs and some videos of movies.

Developmental apraxia A disorder of speech or language involving problems in motor planning such that the child has difficulty in producing speech sounds and organizing words and word sounds for effective communication. The cause may be unknown.

Developmentally appropriate practice (DAP) Educational methods for young children that are compatible with their developmental levels and that meet their individual needs; coined by the National Association for the Education of Young Children.

Diabetic retinopathy A condition resulting from interference with the blood supply to the retina; the fastest-growing cause of blindness.

Dialects A variation of a language that differs from that standard language based on phonology, vocabulary, or grammar. Dialects may be distinct to members of a particular group (e.g., ethnic group, regional group).

Direct Instruction (DI) A method of teaching academics, especially reading and math; emphasizes drill and practice and immediate feedback; lessons are precisely sequenced, fast-paced, and well-rehearsed by the teacher.

Dopamine A neurotransmitter, the levels of which may be abnormal in people with ADHD.

Doppler effect A term used to describe the phenomenon of the pitch of a sound rising as the listener movies toward its source.

Down syndrome A condition resulting from an abnormality with the 21st pair of chromosomes; the most common abnormality is a triplet rather than a pair (the condition sometimes referred to as trisomy 21); characterized by intellectual disability and such physical signs as slanted-appearing eyes, hypotonia, a single palmar crease, shortness, and a tendency toward obesity.

Due process hearing A non-court proceeding held before an impartial hearing officer.

Dynamic assessments An interactive assessment process that involves ongoing analysis of student learning in response to an intervention.

Dysarthria A condition in which brain damage causes impaired control of the muscles used in articulation.

Dysfluencies Hesitations, repetitions, and other disruptions of normal speech flow.

E

Early expressive language delay (EELD) A significant lag in the development of expressive language that is apparent by age 2.

Early intensive behavioral intervention (EIBI) A program anchored in the applied behavioral analysis tradition that emphasizes the role of parents as interventionists, and requires considerable time commitments from therapists and parents in implementing very structured training on discrete skills. Some researchers have found it to be effective in improving language and functional skills in many, although not all, young children with autism.

Echolalia The parroting repetition of words or phrases either immediately after they are heard or later; often observed in individuals with autistic spectrum disorders.

Education for All Handicapped Children Act Also known as Public Law 94-142, which became law in 1975 and is now known as the Individuals with Disabilities Education Act (IDEA). Retitled in 1990 and reauthorized in 1997 and 2004.

Electroencephalography (EEG) A method of measuring the electrical activity of the brain.

Emotional disturbance The term used in federal special education laws and regulations for problematic behavior that interferes with education; the federal term used to indicate the problems of emotionally disturbed students.

Emotional or behavioral disorders The terminology proposed by the National Mental Health and Special Education Coalition to replace the federal terminology "emotional disturbance."

Encephalitis An inflammation of the brain; can affect the child's mental development adversely.

Encopresis Bowel incontinence; soiling oneself.

Enrichment An approach in which additional learning experiences are provided for students with special gifts or talents while the students remain in the grade levels appropriate for their chronological ages.

Enuresis Urinary incontinence; wetting oneself.

Epilepsy A pattern of repeated seizures.

Episodic Occurring in episodes; a temporary condition that will pass but may recur.

Executive functions The ability to regulate one's behavior through working memory, inner speech, control of emotions and arousal levels, and analysis of problems and communication of problem solutions to others; delayed or impaired in people with ADHD.

Expected growth norms Used with CBM; the rate at which the average student is expected to learn given typical instruction.

Expressive language Encoding or sending messages in communication.

External otitis An infection of the skin of the external auditory canal; also called swimmer's ear.

Externalizing Acting-out behavior; aggressive or disruptive behavior that is observable as behavior directed toward others.

Extreme male brain A description sometimes applied to persons with autism based on some researchers claims that high levels of androgen (a hormone that is responsible for controlling the development of male characteristics) in amniotic fluid are more likely to result in autistic traits in children.

F

Familiality studies A method of determining the degree to which a given condition is inherited; looks at the prevalance of the condition in relatives of the person with the condition.

Family activity settings Activities that families routinely engage in, such as mealtimes and seasonal celebrations; can be focal points for the implementation of PBSs.

Family-centered model A consumer-driven model that encourages the family to make its own decisions with respect to services while mobilizing resources and supports for the family's goals.

Family characteristics A component of the Turnbulls' family systems model; includes type and severity of the disability as well as such things as size, cultural background, and socioeconomic background of the family.

Family functions A component of the Turnbulls' family systems model; includes such things as economic, daily care, social, medical, and educational needs.

Family interaction A component of the Turnbulls' family systems model; refers to how cohesive and adaptable the family is.

Family life cycle A component of the Turnbulls' family systems model; consists of birth and early childhood, childhood, adolescence, and adulthood.

Family systems theory Stresses that the individual's behavior is best understood in the context of the family and the family's behavior is best understood in the context of other social systems.

Fetal alcohol spectrum disorders (FASD) A range of disorders in children whose mothers consumed large quantities of alcohol during pregnancy.

Fetal alcohol spectrum (FAS) Abnormalities associated with the mother's drinking alcohol during pregnancy; defects range from mild to severe, including growth retardation, brain damage, intellectual disability, hyperactivity, anomalies of the face, and heart failure; also called *alcohol embryopathy*.

Fingerspelling Spelling the English alphabet by various finger positions on one hand.

Fragile X syndrome A condition in which the bottom of the X chromosome in the twenty-third pair of chromosomes is pinched off; can result in a number of physical anomalies as well as intellectual disabilities; occurs more often in males than females; thought to be the most common hereditary cause of intellectual disabilities.

Free appropriate public education (FAPE) The primary intent of federal special education law, that the education of all children with disabilities will in all cases be free of cost to parents (i.e., at public expense) and appropriate for the particular student.

Frontal lobes Two lobes located in the front of the brain; responsible for executive functions; site of abnormal development in people with ADHD.

Functional Behavioral Assessment (FBA) Evaluation that consists of finding out the consequences (what purpose the behavior serves), antecedents (what triggers the behavior), and setting events (contextual factors) that maintain inappropriate behaviors.

Functional magnetic resonance imaging (fMRI) An adaptation of the MRI used to detect changes in the brain while it is in an active state; unlike a PET scan, it does not involve using radioactive materials.

Functional magnetic resonance spectroscopy (fMRS) An adaptation of the MRI used to detect changes in the brain while it is in an active state; unlike a PET scan, it does not involve using radioactive materials.

Functional vision assessment An appraisal of an individual's use of vision in everyday situations.

G

Genius A word sometimes used to indicate a particular aptitude or capacity in any area; rare intellectual powers.

Giftedness Refers to cognitive (intellectual) superiority, creativity, and motivation of sufficient magnitude to set the child apart from the vast majority of age peers and make it possible for the child to contribute something of particular value to society.

Glaucoma A condition often, but not always, due to excessive pressure in the eyeball; the cause is unknown; if untreated, blindness results.

Globus pallidus A structure in the basal ganglia of the brain; site of abnormal development in people with ADHD.

Graphic organizers A way of enhancing content visual displays using lines, circles, and boxes to organize information.

Guardianship A legal term that gives a person the authority to make decisions for another person; can be full, limited, or temporary; applies in cases of parents who have children who have severe cognitive disabilities.

Gullibility An inclination to believe highly questionable statements or claims, despite scanty evidence; considered by some to be a key characteristic of persons with intellectual disabilities, especially those who are mildly intellectually disabled.

H

Hand-over-hand guidance A tactile learning strategy for persons who are deaf-blind; the teacher places his or her hands over those of the person who is deaf-blind and guides them to explore objects.

Hand-under-hand guidance A tactile learning strategy for persons who are deaf-blind; the teacher places his or her hands underneath part of the student's hand or hands while the child is exploring objects.

Heritability studies A method of determining the degree to which a condition is inherited; a comparison of the prevalence of a condition in identical (i.e., monozygotic, from the same egg) twins versus fraternal (i.e., dizygotic, from two eggs) twins.

Herpes simplex A viral disease that can cause cold sores or fever blisters; if it affects the genitals and is contracted by the mother-to-be in the later stages of fetal development, it can cause mental subnormality in the child.

Hertz (Hz) A unit of measurement of the frequency of sound; refers to the highness or lowness of a sound.

Hidden curriculum The dos and don'ts of social interactions that most people learn incidentally or with little instruction but that remain hidden for those with Asperger syndrome.

History A patient's "story" of his or her functioning in life with respect to strengths and weaknesses; considered crucial by many physicians in the diagnosis of ADHD.

Homophenes Sounds that are different but that look the same with regard to movements of the face and lips (i.e., visible articulatory patterns).

Human immunodeficiency virus (HIV) The virus that leads to AIDS; a type of retrovirus that gradually disables the body's immune system, eventually leading to AIDS. The virus has been detected in the bloodstream of a person who is said to be "HIV positive."

Hydrocephalus A condition characterized by enlargement of the head because of excessive pressure of the cerebrospinal fluid.

Hyperactive child syndrome A term used to refer to children who exhibit inattention, impulsivity, and/or hyperactivity; popular in the 1960s and 1970s.

Hyperopia Farsightedness; vision for near objects is affected; usually results when the eyeball is too short.

I

In vitro fertilization The procedure of removing eggs from the mother, fertilizing them with the father's sperm in a laboratory, then returning them to the mother's uterus; used to help infertile couples conceive.

Inborn errors of metabolism Deficiencies in enzymes used to metabolize basic substances in the body, such as amino acids, carbohydrates, vitamins, or trace elements; can sometimes result in intellectual disabilities; PKU is an example.

Inclusion Mainstreaming; the idea of placing students with disabilities in general education classes and other school activities.

Incus The anvil-shaped bone in the ossicular chain of the middle ear.

Individualized education program (IEP) IDEA requires an IEP to be drawn up by the educational team for each exceptional child; the IEP must include a statement of present educational performance, instructional goals, educational services to be provided, and criteria and procedures for determining that the instructional objectives are being met.

Individualized family service plan (IFSP) A plan mandated by PL 99-457 to provide services for young children with disabilities (under three years of age) and their families; drawn up by professionals and parents; similar to an IEP for older children.

Individuals with Disabilities Education Act (IDEA) The Individuals with Disabilities Education Act was enacted in 1990 and reauthorized in 1997 and 2004; it replaced PL 94-142, enacted in 1975. This federal law requires that to receive funds under the act, every school system in the nation must provide a free, appropriate public education for every child between the ages of three and twenty one, regardless of how or how seriously he or she may be disabled.

Individuals with Disabilities Education Improvement Act (IDEIA) The Individuals with Disabilities Education Act is a federal law that guarantees services to individuals with disabilities. That law was reauthorized in 2004 and titled at that time the Individuals with Disabilities Education Improvement Act.

Informal reading inventory (IRI) A method of assessing reading in which the teacher has the student read progressively more difficult series of word lists and passages; the teacher notes the difficulty level of the material read and the types of errors the student makes.

Insight The ability to separate and/or combine various pieces of information in new, creative, and useful ways.

Intellectual disabilities The newer term for "mental retardation"; a disability in intelligence and adaptive behavior.

Interim alternative educational setting (IAES) A temporary placement outside general education for students whose behavior is extremely problematic, but in which their education is continued.

Internalizing Acting-in behavior; anxiety, fearfulness, withdrawal, and other indications of an individual's mood or internal state.

IQ-achievement discrepancy Academic performance markedly lower than would be expected on the basis of a student's intellectual ability.

Iris The colored portion of the eye; contracts or expands, depending on the amount of light striking it.

Itinerant teacher services Services for students who are visually impaired in which the special education teacher visits several different schools to work with students and their general education teachers; the students attend their local schools and remain in general education classrooms.

J

Job coach A person who assists adult workers with disabilities (especially those with intellectual disabilities), providing vocational assessment, instruction, overall planning, and interaction assistance with employers, family, and related government and service agencies.

Joint attention The process by which one person alerts another to a stimulus via nonverbal means, such as gazing or pointing.

Juvenile rheumatoid arthritis A systemic disease with major symptoms involving the muscles and joints.

K

Kurzweil 1000 A computerized device that converts print into speech for persons with visual impairment; the user places the printed material over a scanner that then reads the material aloud by means of an electronic voice.

L

Language An arbitrary code or system of symbols to communicate meaning.

Language disorders Oral communication that involves a lag in the ability to understand and express ideas, putting linguistic skill behind an individual's development in other areas, such as motor, cognitive, or social development.

Language-based reading impairment A reading problem that is based on a language problem.

Large-print books Books having a font-size that is larger than the usual 10-point type; a popular size for large print books is 18-point type.

Larynx The structure in the throat containing the vocal apparatus (vocal cords); laryngitis is a temporary loss of voice caused by inflammation of the larynx.

Learned helplessness A motivational term referring to a condition in which a person believes that no matter how hard he or she tries, failure will result.

Least restrictive environment (LRE) A legal term referring to the fact that exceptional children must be educated in as normal an environment as possible.

Left temporal lobe An area on the left side of the brain; neuroimaging studies indicate it is responsible for speech, language, and reading abilities and is dysfunctional in persons with reading disabilities.

Legally blind A person who has visual acuity of 20/200 or less in the better eye even with correction (e.g.; eyeglasses) or has a field of vision so narrow that its widest diameter subtends an angular distance no greater than 20 degrees.

Lens A structure that refines and changes the focus of the light rays passing through the eye.

Literary braille Braille symbols used for most writing situations.

Locus of control A motivational term referring to how people explain their successes or failures; people with an internal locus of control believe that they are the reason for success or failure, whereas people with an external locus of control believe that outside forces influence how they perform.

Long cane A mobility aid used by individuals with visual impairment, who sweep it in a wide arc in front of them;

proper use requires considerable training; the mobility aid of choice for most travelers who are blind.

Low birth weight (LBW) Babies who are born weighing less than 5.5 pounds; usually premature; at risk for behavioral and medical conditions, such as intellectual disabilities.

Low vision A term used by educators to refer to individuals whose visual impairment is not so severe that they are unable to read print of any kind; they may read large or regular print, and they may need some kind of magnification.

M

Magnetic resonance imaging (MRI) A neuroimaging technique whereby radio waves are used to produce cross-sectional images of the brain; used to pinpoint areas of the brain that are dysfunctional.

Magnifying devices Often recommended for people with low vision; can be for close vision (e.g., handheld magnifier) or distance vision (e.g., monocular telescope or binocular telescope mounted on eyeglass frames).

Malleus The hammer-shaped bone in the ossicular chain of the middle ear.

Manifestation determination Determination that a student's misbehavior is or is not a manifestation of a disability.

Maternal serum screening (MSS) A method of screening the fetus for developmental disabilities such as Down syndrome or spina bifida; a blood sample is taken from the mother and analyzed; if it is positive, a more accurate test such as amniocentesis or CVS is usually recommended.

Meningitis A bacterial or viral infection of the linings of the brain or spinal cord; can cause a number of disabilities.

Mental age Age level at which a person performs on an IQ test; used in comparison to chronological age to determine IQ. IQ = (mental age ÷ chronological age) × 100.

Metacognition One's understanding of the strategies available for learning a task and the regulatory mechanisms needed to complete the task.

Microcephalus A condition causing development of a small, conical-shaped head; proper development of the brain is prevented, resulting in intellectual disabilities.

Mild mental retardation or intellectual disability A classification used to specify an individual whose IQ is approximately 50–70.

Milieu teaching A naturalistic approach to language intervention in which the goal is to teach functional language skills in a natural environment.

Minimal brain injury A term used to describe a child who shows behavioral but not neurological signs of brain injury; the term is not as popular as it once was, primarily because of its lack of diagnostic utility (i.e., some children who learn normally show signs indicative of minimal brain injury); a term used to refer to children who exhibit inattention, impulsivity, and/or hyperactivity; popular in the 1950s and 1960s.

Mixed hearing impairment A hearing impairment resulting from a combination of conductive and sensorineural hearing impairments.

Mnemonics The use of memory-enhancing cues to help one remember something; techniques that aid memory, such as using rhymes, songs, or visual images to remember information.

Moderate mental retardation or intellectual disabilities A classification used to specify an individual whose IQ is approximately 35–50.

Modifications Changes made in instruction or assessment to make it possible for a student with a disability to respond more normally.

Momentary time sampling An interval recording procedure used to capture a representative sample of a target behavior over a specified period of time.

Morphology The study within psycholinguistics of word formation; how adding or deleting parts of words changes their meaning.

Motor-speech disorder Loss or impairment of the ability to understand or formulate language because of accident or illness.

Multicultural education Aims to change educational institutions and curricula so they will provide equal educational opportunities to students regardless of their gender, social class, ethnicity, race, disability, or other cultural identity.

Muscular dystrophy A hereditary disease characterized by progressive weakness caused by degeneration of muscle fibers.

Mute Possessing no, or almost no, language; characteristic of many with autism.

Myopia Nearsightedness; vision for distant objects is affected; usually results when eyeball is too long.

N

Native-language emphasis An approach to teaching language-minority pupils in which the student's native language is used for most of the day and English is taught as a separate subject.

Natural supports Resources in person's environment that can be used for support, such as friends, family, co-workers.

Nemeth Code Braille symbols used for mathematics and science.

Neonatal intensive care unit (NICU) A special unit in a hospital designed to provide around-the-clock monitoring and care of newborns who have severe physical problems; staffed by professionals from several disciplines, such as nursing, social work, occupational therapy, respiratory therapy, and medicine; similar to an intensive care unit for older children and adults.

Neural tube defect Any defect involving the spinal cord.

Neurotoxin A substance known to damage nerve cells.

Neurotransmitters Chemicals involved in sending messages between neurons in the brain.

Neurotypicals A term coined by people with Asperger syndrome to describe people who do not have neurological disabilities.

NFB-Newsline® A free service available through the National Federation of the Blind, allows individuals to access magazines and newspapers 24 hours a day from any touch-tone telephone.

Night blindness A condition characterized by problems in seeing at low levels of illumination; often caused by retinitis pigmentosa.

Nonverbal learning disabilities A term used to refer to individuals who have a cluster of disabilities in social interaction, math, visual-spatial tasks, and tactual tasks.

Norepinephrine A neurotransmitter, the levels of which may be abnormal in people with ADHD.

Nuchal translucency sonogram A method of screening for Down syndrome; fluid from behind the fetus's neck and protein from the mother's blood are analyzed.

Nystagmus A condition in which there are rapid involuntary movements of the eyes; sometimes indicates a brain malfunction and/or inner-ear problems.

O

Obstacle sense A skill possessed by some people who are blind, whereby they can detect the presence of obstacles in their environments; research has shown that it is not an indication of an extra sense, as popularly thought; it is the result of learning to detect subtle changes in the pitches of high-frequency echoes.

Open head injury A brain injury in which there is an open wound in the head, such as a gunshot wound or penetration of the head by an object, resulting in damage to brain tissue.

Optic nerve The nerve at the back of the eye, which sends visual information back to the brain.

Optic nerve hypoplasia (ONH) A condition resulting in underdevelopment of the optic nerve; often accompanied by brain abnormalities, which can result in other problems (e.g., speech and/or cognitive disabilities); one of the most common causes of childhood blindness.

Oralism–manualism debate The controversy over whether the goal of instruction for students who are deaf should be to teach them to speak or to teach them to use sign language.

Orientation and mobility (O & M) skills The ability to have a sense of where one is in relation to other people, objects, and landmarks and to move through the environment.

Orthosis A device designed to restore, partially or completely, a lost function of the body (e.g., a brace or crutch).

Ossicles Three tiny bones (malleus, incus, and stapes) that together make possible an efficient transfer of sound waves from the eardrum to the oval window, which connects the middle ear to the inner ear.

Otitis media Inflammation of the middle ear.

Otoacoustic emissions Low-intensity sounds produced by the cochlea in response to auditory stimulation; used to screen hearing problems in infants and very young children.

Oval window The link between the middle and inner ears.

P

Paradoxical effect of Ritalin The now discredited belief that Ritalin, even though a stimulant, acts to subdue a person's behavior and that this effect of Ritalin is evident in people with ADHD but not in those without ADHD.

Paraplegia A condition in which both legs are paralyzed.

Partial participation An approach in which students with disabilities, while in the general education classroom, engage in the same activities as nondisabled students but on a reduced basis; the teacher adapts the activity to allow each student to participate as much as possible.

Peer-assisted learning strategies (PALS) Based on research-proven, best practices in reading, such as phonological awareness, decoding, and comprehension strategies. PALS involves the pairing of a higher performing student with a lower performing student, with the pairs then participating in highly structured tutoring sessions. The students take turns being the "coach" (tutor) and the "reader" (tutee).

Peer confederates Peers who assist the teacher.

Peer tutoring A method that can be used to integrate students with disabilities in general education classrooms, based on the notion that students can effectively tutor one another. The role of learner or teacher may be assigned to either the student with a disability or the nondisabled student.

Peer-mediated instruction The deliberate use of a student's classroom peer(s) to assist in teaching an academic or social skill.

Perinatal The time of birth.

Perkins Brailler A system that makes it possible to write in braille; has six keys, one for each of the six dots of the cell, which leave an embossed print on the paper.

Perseveration A tendency to repeat behaviors over and over again; often found in people with brain injury, as well as those with ADHD.

Person-centered plan A method of planning for people with disabilities that places the person and his family at the center of the planning process.

Pervasive Developmental Disorder not Otherwise Specified (PDD-NOS) One of five autistic spectrum disorders; pervasive delay in development that does not fit into any of the other diagnostic categories.

Phenylketonuria (PKU) A metabolic genetic disorder caused by the inability of the body to convert phenylalanine to tyrosine; an accumulation of phenylalanine results in abnormal brain development.

Phonemic awareness One's ability to understand that words are made up of sounds or phonemes.

Phonological awareness The ability to understand that speech flow can be broken into smaller sound units such as words, syllables, and phonemes; lack of such awareness is generally thought to be the reason for the reading problems of many students with learning disabilities.

Phonological disorders A phonological disorder is a disorder that occurs in children who are younger than 9 years old. The disorder results in the impaired ability to produce sounds in his or her own language.

Phonology The study of how individual sounds make up words.

Pivotal response teaching (PRT) Based on the assumption that some skills are critical, or pivotal, in order for the individual to be able to function in other areas.

Positive behavior intervention plan (BIP) A plan for changing behavior with an emphasis on positive reinforcement (rewarding) procedures.

Positive behavioral intervention and support (PBIS) Systematic use of the science of behavior to find ways of supporting desirable behavior rather than punishing the undesirable behavior; positive reinforcement (rewarding) procedures that are intended to support a student's appropriate or desirable behavior.

Positive behavioral support (PBS) Positive reinforcement (rewarding) procedures intended to support a student's appropriate or desirable behavior.

Positron emission tomography (PET) scans A computerized method for measuring bloodflow in the brain; during a cognitive task, a low amount of radioactive dye is injected in the brain; the dye collects in active neurons, indicating which areas of the brain are active.

Postlingual deafness Deafness occurring after the development of speech and language.

Postnatal The time after birth.

Practical intelligence Ability to solve everyday problems.

Prader-Willi syndrome Caused by inheriting from one's father a lack of genetic material on the fifteenth pair of chromosomes; leading genetic cause of obesity; degree of intellectual disabilities varies, but the majority fall within the mildly intellectually disabled range.

Pragmatics The study within psycholinguistics of how people use language in social situations; emphasizes the functional use of language rather than the mechanics.

Precocity Remarkable early development.

Prefrontal lobes Two lobes located in the very front of the frontal lobes; responsible for executive functions; site of abnormal development in people with ADHD.

Prelingual deafness Deafness that occurs before the development of spoken language, usually at birth.

Prelinguistic communication Communication through gestures and noises before the child has learned oral language.

Prenatal The time before birth.

Prereferral teams (PRTs) Teams made up of a variety of professionals, especially general and special educators, who work with general education teachers to come up with strategies for teaching difficult-to-teach children. Designed to influence general educators to take ownership of difficult-to-teach students and to minimize inappropriate referrals to special education.

Primary language disorder A language disorder that has no known cause.

Profound mental retardation or intellectual disabilities A classification used to specify an individual whose IQ is below approximately 20.

Progressive A disease or condition that worsens over time and from which one seldom or never recovers with treatment.

Progressive time delay An instructional procedure whereby the teacher makes a request while simultaneously prompting the student and then over several occasions gradually increases the latency between the request and the prompt; often used with students with intellectual disabilities.

Prosthesis A device designed to replace, partially or completely, a part of the body (e.g., artificial teeth or limbs).

Psychoanalytic Related to psychoanalysis, including the assumptions that emotional or behavior disorders result primarily from unconscious conflicts and that the most effective preventive actions and therapeutic interventions involve uncovering and understanding unconscious motivations.

Psychostimulants Medications that activate dopamine levels in the frontal and prefrontal areas of the brain that control behavioral inhibition and executive functions; used to treat persons with ADHD.

Pupil The contractile opening in the middle of the iris of the eye.

Pure-tone audiometry A test whereby tones of various intensities and frequencies are presented to determine a person's hearing loss.

Q

Quadriplegia A condition in which all four limbs are paralyzed.

R

Raised dome detectable warnings Bumps in the pavement that are designed to alert people who are blind to unsafe areas.

Reading comprehension The ability to understand what one has read.

Reading fluency The ability to read effortlessly and smoothly; consists of the ability to read at a normal rate and with appropriate expression; influences one's reading comprehension.

Receptive language Decoding or understanding messages in communication.

Reciprocal teaching A cognitive teaching strategy whereby the student gradually assumes the role of co-instructor for brief periods; the teacher models four strategies for the students to use: (1) predicting, (2) questioning, (3) summarizing, and (4) clarifying; a method in which students and teachers are involved in a dialogue to facilitate learning.

Refraction The bending of light rays as they pass through the structures (cornea, aqueous humor, pupil, lens, vitreous humor) of the eye

Repeated readings Students repeatedly (several times a week) read the same short passages aloud until they read at an appropriate pace with few or no errors.

Resonance The quality of the sound imparted by the size, shape, and texture of the organs in the vocal tract.

Response-to-intervention (RTI) or response-to-treatment approach A way of determining whether a student has a learning disability; increasingly intensive levels of instructional intervention are delivered, and if the student does not achieve, at some point, he or she is determined to have a learning disability or is referred for special education evaluation.

Retina The back portion of the eye, containing nerve fibers connected to the optic nerve.

Retinitis pigmentosa A hereditary condition resulting in degeneration of the retina; causes a narrowing of the field of vision and affects night vision.

Retinopathy of prematurity (ROP) A condition resulting from administration of an excessive concentration of oxygen at birth; causes scar tissue to form behind the lens of the eye.

Ritalin The most commonly prescribed psychostimulant for ADHD; its generic name is methylphenidate.

Rubella (German measles) A serious viral disease, which, if it occurs during the first trimester of pregnancy, is likely to cause a deformity in the fetus.

S

Scaffolded instruction Teachers provide assistance to students when they are first learning tasks and then gradually reduce it so that eventually students do the tasks independently.

Scoliosis An abnormal curvature of the spine.

Screening instruments Quick measures administered to determine who may need further assessment.

Screen reader Software for computers that magnifies images on the screen and/or converts text on the screen to speech.

Secondary language disorder A language disorder that is caused by another disorder or disability, such as intellectual disabilities, hearing impairment, or brain injury.

Seizure (convulsion) A sudden alteration of consciousness, usually accompanied by motor activity and/or sensory phenomena; caused by an abnormal discharge of electrical energy in the brain.

Self-determination Having control over one's life, not having to rely on others for making choices about one's quality of life; develops over one's life span.

Self-injurious behavior (SIB) Behavior causing injury or mutilation of oneself, such as self-biting or head-banging; usually seen in individuals with severe and multiple disabilities.

Self-instruction A type of cognitive training technique that requires individuals to talk aloud and then to themselves as they solve problems.

Self-monitoring A type of cognitive training technique that requires individuals to keep track of their own behavior.

Self-regulation Refers generally to a person's ability to regulate his or her own behavior (e.g., to employ strategies to help in a problem-solving situation); an area of difficulty for persons who are intellectually disabled.

Self-stimulation Any repetitive, stereotyped activity that seems only to provide sensory feedback.

Semantics The study of the meanings attached to words and sentences.

Sensorineural hearing impairment A hearing impairment, usually severe, resulting from malfunctioning of the inner ear.

Severe mental retardation or intellectual disabilities A classification used to specify an individual whose IQ is approximately 20–35.

Sheltered workshop A facility that provides a structured environment for people with disabilities in which they can learn skills; can be either a transitional placement or a permanent arrangement.

Sheltered-English approach A method in which language-minority students are taught all their subjects in English at a level that is modified constantly according to individuals' needs.

Short-term memory (STM) The ability to recall information after a short period of time.

Sign language A manual language used by people who are deaf to communicate; a true language with its own grammar.

Signing English systems Used simultaneously with oral methods in the total communication approach to teaching students who are deaf; different from American Sign Language because the signs maintain the same word order as spoken English.

Simultaneous communication The use of both manual and oral communication by people who are deaf.

Slate and stylus A method of writing in braille in which the paper is held in a slate while a stylus is pressed through openings to make indentations in the paper.

Sleep apnea Cessation of breathing while sleeping.

Snellen chart Used in determining visual acuity; consists of rows of letters or Es arranged in different positions; each row corresponds to the distance at which a normally sighted person can discriminate the letters; does not predict how accurately a child will be able to read print.

Social support Emotional, informational, or material aid provided to a person or a family; this informal means of aid can be very valuable in helping families of children with disabilities.

Spasticity Characterized by muscle stiffness and problems in voluntary movement; associated with spastic cerebral palsy.

Specific language impairment (SLI) A language disorder with no identifiable cause; language disorder not attributable to hearing impairment, intellectual disabilities, brain dysfunction, or other plausible cause; also called specific language disability.

Speech The formation and sequencing of oral language sounds during communication.

Speech audiometry A technique that tests a person's detection and understanding of speech, rather than using pure tones to detect hearing loss.

Speech disorders Oral communication that involves abnormal use of the vocal apparatus, is unintelligible, or is so inferior that it draws attention to itself and causes anxiety, feelings of inadequacy, or inappropriate behavior in the speaker.

Speech-language pathologist (SLP) Speech-language pathologists work with individuals who have disorders related to speech, language, communication, swallowing, voice, or fluency. SLPs may work in the heath care profession or in schools. SLPs assess, diagnose, and treat individuals with speech and language disorders.

Speech-reception threshold (SRT) The decibel level at which a person can understand speech.

Speechreading A method that involves teaching children to use visual information from a number of sources to understand what is being said to them; more than just lipreading, which uses only visual clues arising from the movement of the mouth in speaking.

Spina bifida A congenital midline defect resulting from failure of the bony spinal column to close completely during fetal development.

Stapes The stirrup-shaped bone in the ossicular chain of the middle ear.

Stereotyped motor or verbal behaviors Repetitive, ritualistic motor behaviors such as twirling, spinning objects, flapping the hands, and rocking, similar to those that are evident in some people who are blind.

Strabismus A condition in which the eyes are directed inward (crossed eyes) or outward.

Strattera A nonstimulant medication for ADHD; affects the neurotransmitter norepinephrine.

Strauss syndrome Behaviors of distractibility, forced responsiveness to stimuli, and hyperactivity; based on the work of Alfred Strauss and Heinz Werner with children with intellectual disabilities.

Stuttering Speech characterized by abnormal hesitations, prolongations, and repetitions; may be accompanied by grimaces, gestures, or other bodily movements indicative of a struggle to speak, anxiety, blocking of speech, or avoidance of speech.

Subculture A culture that is associated with or part of a larger culture; a culture that is not the entire culture of a nation or other entity. Sometimes called "microculture," but a subculture is not necessarily small or a minority of a larger culture.

Summary of performance (SOP) Now required by federal law, schools must develop an SOP for each student with a disability as the student exits secondary school whether by graduating or exceeding the age of eligibility. SOPs are designed to provide a summary of relevant information, such as assessment reports; accommodations that have been provided; and recommendations for future accommodations, assistive technology, and support services for use in employment, training, or postsecondary schooling.

Supported competitive employment A workplace where adults who are disabled earn at least minimum wage and receive ongoing assistance from a specialist or job coach; the majority of workers in the workplace are nondisabled.

Supported employment A method of integrating people with disabilities who cannot work independently into competitive employment; includes use of an employment specialist, or job coach, who helps the person with a disability function on the job.

Supported living An approach to living arrangements for those with disabilities and/or intellectual disabilities that stresses living in natural settings rather than institutions, big or small.

Supports Resources and strategies that promote a person's development, education, interests, and personal well-being; critical to the AAIDD's conceptualization of intellectual disabilities.

Synaesthesia Occurs when the stimulation of one sensory or cognitive system results in the stimulation of another sensory or cognitive system.

Syntax The way words are joined together to structure meaningful sentences; grammar.

Syphilis A venereal disease that can cause mental subnormality in a child, especially if it is contracted by the mother-to-be during the latter stages of fetal development.

Systematic instruction Teaching that involves instructional prompts, consequences for performance, and transfer of stimulus control; often used with students with intellectual disabilities.

T

Tactile map An embossed representation of the environment that people who are blind can use to orient themselves to their surroundings.

Talent Ordinarily has been used to indicate a special ability, aptitude, or accomplishment.

Task analysis The procedure of breaking down an academic task into its component parts for the purpose of instruction; a major feature of Direct Instruction.

Text telephone (TT) A device connected to a telephone by a special adapter; allows communication over the telephone between people who are hearing impaired and those with hearing; sometimes referred to as a TTY (teletype) or TTD (telecommunication device for the deaf).

Theory of mind The ability to take another's perspective in a social exchange; the ability to infer another person's feelings, intentions, desires, etc.; impaired in those with ASD.

Tiered assignment Assignments varying in difficulty but on a single topic.

Total communication approach An approach for teaching students with hearing impairment that blends oral and manual techniques.

Touch cues Tactual signals used to communicate with persons who are deaf-blind; can be used to signify a variety of messages.

Toxins Poisons in the environment that can cause fetal malformations; can result in cognitive impairments.

Transition plan A plan defined in the student's IEP that specifies a students' goals and services related to transitioning from high school to post-high school experiences. The Individuals with Disabilities Education Act requires that the IEP include the transition plan before the age of 16.

Transliteration A method used by most sign language interpreters in which the signs maintain the same word order as that of spoken English; American Sign Language (ASL) is also used by some interpreters.

Traumatic brain injury (TBI) Injury to the brain (not including conditions present at birth, birth trauma, or degenerative diseases or conditions) resulting in total or partial disability or psychosocial maladjustment that affects educational performance; may affect cognition, language, memory, attention, reasoning, abstract thinking, judgment, problem solving, sensory or perceptual and motor disabilities, psychosocial behavior, physical functions, information processing, or speech.

Traveling notebook A system of communication in which parents and professionals write messages to each other by way of a notebook or log that accompanies the child to and from school.

Trisomy 21 A type of Down syndrome in which the twenty-first chromosome is a triplet, making forty-seven, rather than the normal forty-six, chromosomes in all.

Tunnel vision A condition characterized by problems in peripheral vision, or a narrowing of the field of vision.

Twice exceptional Possession of both a disability and a special gift or talent.

Tympanic membrane (eardrum) The anatomical boundary between the outer and middle ears; the sound gathered in the outer ear vibrates here.

Tympanometry A method of measuring the middle ear's response to pressure and sound.

U

Unified English Braille A combination of literary braille and braille codes for technical fields, such as the Nemeth Code for science and mathematics; not yet widely adopted.

Universal design The design of new buildings, tools, and instructional programs to make them usable by the widest possible population of potential users.

Universal Design for Learning (UDL) Designing lessons that are appropriate for all learners.

Usher syndrome An inherited syndrome resulting in hearing loss and retinitis pigmentosa, a progressive condition characterized by problems in seeing in low light and tunnel vision; there are three different types of Usher syndrome, differing with respect to when it occurs developmentally and the range of the major symptoms of hearing impairment, vision impairment, and balance problems.

V

Vestibular mechanism Located in the upper portion of the inner ear; consists of three soft, semicircular canals filled with a fluid; sensitive to head movement, acceleration, and other movements related to balance.

Video relay service (VRS) A service, using a sign language interpreter, a video camera or computer, and an internet connection, that allows persons who are deaf to communicate with those who are hearing.

Visual acuity The ability to see fine details; usually measured with the Snellen chart.

Vitreous humor A transparent, gelatinous substance that fills the eyeball between the retina and the lens of the eye.

Vyvanse A stimulant that is sometimes prescribed to treat symptoms of attention deficit hyperactivity disorder in children.

W

Williams syndrome A condition resulting from deletion of material in the seventh pair of chromosomes; often results in mild to moderate intellectual disabilities, heart defects, and elfin facial features; people affected often display surprising strengths in spoken language and sociability while having severe deficits in spatial organization, reading, writing, and math.

Working memory (WM) The ability to remember information while also performing other cognitive operations.

Wraparound service systems Involve using not only educational services but available community services (e.g., mental health, social welfare, juvenile justice, and so forth) in order to meet the individualized needs of children and their families.

Z

Zero tolerance A school policy, supported by federal and state laws, that having possession of any weapon or drug on school property will automatically result in a given penalty (usually suspension or expulsion) regardless of the nature of the weapon or drug or any extenuating circumstances.

REFERENCES

CHAPTER 1

Bateman, B. D. (2007). Law and the conceptual foundations of special education practice. In J. B. Crockett, M. M. Gerber, & T. J. Landrum (Eds.), *Achieving the radical reform of special education: Essays in honor of James M. Kauffman* (pp. 95–114). Mahwah, NJ: Erlbaum.

Bateman, B. D. (2011). Individual education programs for children with disabilities. In J. M. Kauffman & D. P. Hallahan (EDs.), *Handbook of special education.* New York: Routledge.

Bateman, B. D., & Linden, M. A. (2006). *Better IEPs: How to develop legally correct and educationally useful programs* (4th ed.). Verona, WI: Attainment.

Board of Education of Hendrick Hudson v. Rowley, 484 US 176 (1982).

Bolger, K. E., & Patterson, C. J. (2001). Developmental pathways from child maltreatment to peer rejection. *Child Development, 72,* 549–568.

Carr, M. R. (2004, January 4). My son's disability, and my own inability to see it. *The Washington Post,* p. B5.

Crockett, J. B., & Kauffman, J. M. (1999). *The least restrictive environment: Its origins and interpretations in special education.* Mahwah, NJ: Erlbaum.

Crockett, J. B., & Kauffman, J. M. (2001). The concept of the least restrictive environment and learning disabilities: Least restrictive of what? Reflections on Cruickshank's 1977 guest editorial for the *Journal of Learning Disabilities.* In D. P. Hallahan & B. K. Keogh (Eds.), *Research and global perspectives in learning disabilities: Essays in honor of William M. Cruickshank* (pp. 147–166). Mahwah, NJ: Erlbaum.

Dupre, A. P. (1997). Disability and the public schools: The case against "inclusion." *Washington Law Review, 72,* 775–858.

Earley, P. (2006). *Crazy: A Father's search through America's mental health madness.* New York: Penguin.

Gelman, J. A., Pullen, P. L., & Kauffman, J. M. (2004). The meaning of highly qualified and a clear roadmap to accomplishment. *Exceptionality, 12,* 195–207. dio:10.1207/s15327035ex1204_2

Gerber, M. M. (2011). History. In J. M. Kauffman & D. P. Hallahan (Eds.), *Handbook of special education.* New York: Routledge.

Gladwell, M. (2008). *Outliers: The story of success.* New York: Little, Brown.

Goin, M. K. (2007, July 8). The wrong place to treat mental illness. *The Washington Post,* p. B7.

Gresham, T. (2007, May 7). Something to cheer about. *The Daily Progress,* pp. E1, E6. Charlottesville, VA.

Hallahan, D. P., & Kauffman, J. M. (1977). Labels, categories, behaviors: ED, LD, and EMR reconsidered. *Journal of Special Education, 11,* 139–149. doi: 10.1177/002246697701100202

Hallahan, D. P., Lloyd, J. W., Kauffman, J. M., Weiss, M., & Martinez, E. (2005). *Introduction to learning disabilities* (3rd ed.). Boston: Allyn & Bacon.

Hart, B., & Risley, T. R. (1995). *Meaningful differences in the everyday experience of young American children.* Baltimore: Brookes.

Hendrick, I. G., & MacMillan, D. L. (1989). Selecting children for special education in New York City: William Maxwell, Elizabeth Farrell, and the development of ungraded classes, 1900–1920. *Journal of Special Education, 22,* 395–417. doi: 10.1177/00224669890220040

Heward, W. L. (2003). Ten faulty notions about teaching and learning that hinder the effectiveness of special education. *The Journal of Special Education, 36,* 186–205. doi: 10.1177/00224690303600401

Holmes, M. S. (2004). *Fictions of affliction: Physical disability in Victorian culture.* Ann Arbor, MI: University of Michigan Press.

Huefner, D. S. (1994). The mainstreaming cases: Tensions and trends for school administrators. *Educational Administration Quarterly, 27,* 55. doi: 10.1177/0013161X94030001004

Huefner, D. S. (2006). *Getting comfortable with special education law: A framework for working with children with disabilities* (2nd ed.). Norwood, MA: Christopher Gordon.

Hungerford, R. (1950). On locusts. *American Journal of Mental Deficiency, 54,* 415–418.

Itard, J. M. G. (1962). *The wild boy of Aveyron.* (G. Humphrey & M. Humphrey, Trans.). Upper Saddle River, NJ: Pearson.

Kanner, L. (1964). *A history of the care and study of the mentally retarded.* Springfield, IL: Charles C. Thomas.

Kauffman, J. M. (1999a). Today's special education and its messages for tomorrow. *The Journal of Special Education, 32,* 244–254. doi: 10.1177/002246699903200405

Kauffman, J. M. (1999b). How we prevent the prevention of emotional and behavioral disorders. *Behavioral Disorders, 65,* 448–468.

Kauffman, J. M. (2004). The President's commission and the devaluation of special education. *Education and Treatment of Children, 27,* 307–324.

Kauffman, J. M. (2005). Waving to Ray Charles: Missing the meaning of disability. *Phi Delta Kappan, 86*(6), 520–521, 524.

Kauffman, J. M. (2007). Conceptual models and the future of special education. *Education and Treatment of Children, 30*(4), 1–18.

Kauffman, J. M. (2008). 44: Special education. In T. L. Good (Ed.), *21st Century education: A reference handbook* (pp. 405–413). Thousand Oaks, CA: Sage.

Kauffman, J. M. (2010). *The tragicomedy of public education: Laughing, crying, thinking, fixing.* Verona, WI: Attainment.

Kauffman, J. M., & Brigham, F. J. (2009). *Working with troubled children.* Verona, WI: Attainment.

Kauffman, J. M., & Hallahan, D. P. (1974). The medical model and the science of special education. *Exceptional Children, 41,* 97–102.

Kauffman, J. M., & Hallahan, D. P. (2005a). *Special education: What it is and why we need it.* Boston: Allyn & Bacon.

Kauffman, J. M., & Hallahan, D. P. (Eds.). (2005b). *The illusion of full inclusion: A comprehensive critique of a current special education bandwagon* (2nd ed.). Austin, TX: Pro-Ed.

Kauffman, J. M., & Hallahan, D. P. (2009). Parental choices and ethical dilemmas involving disabilities: Special education and the problem of deliberately chosen disabilities. *Exceptionality, 17,* 45–62. doi:10.1080/09362830802667835

Kauffman, J. M., & Hallahan, D. P. (Eds.). (2011). *Handbook of special education.* New York: Routledge.

Kauffman, J. M., & Hung, L. Y. (2009). Special education for intellectual disability: Current trends and perspectives. *Current Opinion in Psychiatry, 22,* 452–456. doi: 10.1097/YCO .0b013e32832eb5c3

Kauffman, J. M., & Konold, T. R. (2007). Making sense in education: Pretense (including NCLB) and realities in rhetoric and policy about schools and schooling. *Exceptionality, 15,* 75–96. doi:10 .1080/09362830701294151

Kauffman, J. M., & Landrum, T. J. (2006). *Children and youth with emotional and behavioral disorders: A history of their education.* Austin, TX: Pro-Ed.

Kauffman, J. M., & Landrum, T. J. (2007). Educational service interventions and reforms. In J. W. Jacobson, J. A. Mulick, & J. Rojahn (Eds.), *Handbook of intellectual and developmental disabilities* (pp. 173–188). New York: Springer.

Kauffman, J. M., & Landrum, T. J. (2009). Politics, civil rights, and disproportional identification of students with emotional and behavioral disorders. *Exceptionality.* doi: 10.1080/ 09362830903231903

Kauffman, J. M., Mock, D. R., Tankersley, M., & Landrum, T. J. (2008). Effective service delivery models. In R. J. Morris & N. Mather (Eds.), *Evidence-based interventions for students with learning and behavioral challenges* (pp. 359–378). Mahwah, NJ: Erlbaum.

Kauffman, J. M., & Wiley, A. L. (2004). How the president's Commission on Excellence in Special Education (PCESE) devalues special education. *Learning Disabilities: A Multidisciplinary Journal, 13,* 3–6.

Lamb, H. R., & Weinberger, L. E. (Eds.). (2001). *Deinstitutionalization: Promise and problems.* San Francisco: Jossey-Bass.

Lloyd, J. W., Forness, S. R., & Kavale, K. A. (1998). Some methods are more effective than others. *Intervention in School and Clinic, 33,* 195–200.

MacMillan, D. L., & Forness, S. R. (1998). The role of IQ in special education placement decisions: Primary and determinative or peripheral and inconsequential? *Remedial and Special Education, 19,* 239–253.

Metzler, I. (2006). *Disability in medieval Europe: Thinking about physical impairment during the Middle Ages, c. 1100–1400.* New York: Routledge.

National Research Council. (2001). *Educating children with autism.* Washington, DC: National Academy Press.

Nomani, A. Q. (2007, April 29). My brother's battle— and mine. *The Washington Post,* p. B2.

Palmer, D. S., Fuller, K., Arora, T., & Nelson, M. (2001). Taking sides: Parent's views on inclusion for their children with severe disabilities. *Exceptional Children, 67,* 467–484.

Pinel, J. P. J. (2006). *Biopsychology* (5th ed.). Boston: Allyn & Bacon/Pearson.

Pinker, S. (2002). *The blank slate: The modern denial of human nature.* New York: Viking.

Rothstein, R., Jacobsen, R., & Wilder, T. (2006, November). *"Proficiency for all"—An oxymoron.* Paper presented at symposium on "Examining America's commitment to closing achievement gaps: NCLB and its alternatives." Teachers College, Columbia University, New York.

Rozalski, M., Miller, J., & Stewart, A. (2011). Least restrictive environment. In J. M. Kauffman & D. P. Hallahan (Eds.), *Handbook of special education.* New York: Routledge.

Sarason, S. B. (1990). *The predictable failure of educational reform: Can we change course before it's too late?* San Francisco: Jossey-Bass.

Sitlington, P. L., & Clark, G. M. (2006). *Transition education and services for students with disabilities* (4th ed., p. 83). Boston: Allyn & Bacon/Pearson. Reprinted with permission.

Stichter, J. P., Conroy, M. A., & Kauffman, J. M. (2008). *An introduction to students with high-incidence disabilities.* Upper Saddle River, NJ: Merrill/Pearson.

Torrey, E. F., & Zdandowicz, M. T. (1999, July 9). Deinstitutionalization hasn't worked: "We have lost effectively 93 percent of our state psychiatric hospital beds since 1955." *The Washington Post.* Retrieved from www.psychlaws.org/generalresources/article17.htm

Turnbull, H. R. (2007). A response to Professor Vitello. *Remedial and Special Education, 28,* 69–71. doi: 10.1177/07419325070280020501

U.S. Department of Education. (2008). *Thirtieth annual report to Congress on implementation of the Individuals with Disabilities Education Act.* Washington, DC: Author.

Vitello, S. J. (2007). Shared responsibility reconsidered: A response to Professor Turnbull on IDEIA 2004 accountability and personal responsibility. *Remedial and Special Education, 28,* 66–68. doi: 10.1177/07419325070280020401

Walker, H. M., & Sprague, J. R. (2007). Early, evidence-based intervention with school-related behavior disorders: Key issues, continuing challenges, and promising practices. In J. B. Crockett, M. M. Gerber, & T. J. Landrum (Eds.), *Achieving the radical reform of special education: Essays in honor of James M. Kauffman* (pp. 37–58). Mahwah, NJ: Erlbaum.

Warnock, M. (2005). *Special educational needs: A new look. Impact No. 11.* London: Philosophy of Education Society of Great Britain.

Welch, E. M., Barton, E. R., Zhuo, J., Tomizawa, Y., Friesen, W. J., Trifillis, P., et al. (2007). PTC124 targets genetic disorders caused by nonsense mutations. Retrieved from www.nature.com/nature/journal/vaop/ncurrent/abs/nature05756.html

Winzer, M. A. (1993). *The history of special education: From isolation to integration.* Washington, DC: Gallaudet University Press.

Wolfensberger, W. (1972). *The principle of normalization in human services.* Toronto: National Institute on Mental Retardation.

Yell, M. L. (2006). *The law and special education* (2nd ed.). Upper Saddle River, NJ: Pearson.

Yell, M. L., & Drasgow, E. (2005). *No child left behind: A guide for professionals.* Upper Saddle River, NJ: Merrill/Pearson.

Yell, M. L., Katsiyannis, A., & Bradley, M. R. (2011). The Individuals with Disabilities Education Act: The evolution of special education law. In J. M. Kauffman & D. P. Hallahan (Eds.), *Handbook of special education.* New York: Routledge.

Yell, M. L., Rogers, D., & Rogers, E. L. (1998). The legal history of special education: What a long,

strange trip it's been! *Remedial and Special Education, 19,* 219–228.

Zelder, E. Y. (1953). Public opinion and public education for the exceptional child—court decisions 1873–1950. *Exceptional Children, 19,* 187–198.

Zigmond, N. (2007). Delivering special education is a two-person job: A call for unconventional thinking. In J. B. Crockett, M. M. Gerber, & T. J. Landrum (Eds.), *Achieving the radical reform of special education: Essays in honor of James M. Kauffman* (pp. 115–137). Mahwah, NJ: Erlbaum.

Zigmond, N., & Kloo, A. (2011). General and special education are (and should be) different. In J. M. Kauffman & D. P. Hallahan (Eds.), *Handbook of special education.* New York: Routledge.

Zigmond, N., Kloo, A., & Volonino, V. (2009). What, where, and how? Special education in the climate of full inclusion. *Exceptionality, 17,* 189–204. doi: 10.1080/09362830903231986

CHAPTER 2

Anastasiou, D., & Keller, C. (2011). International differences in provision for exceptional learners. In J. M. Kauffman & D. P. Hallahan (Eds.), *Handbook of special education.* New York: Routledge.

Bateman, B. D. (2007). Law and the conceptual foundations of special education practice. In J. B. Crockett, M. M. Gerber, & T. J. Landrum (Eds.), *Achieving the radical reform of special education: Essays in honor of James M. Kauffman* (pp. 95–114). Mahwah, NJ: Erlbaum.

Bateman, B. D. (2011). Individual education programs for children with disabilities. In J. M. Kauffman & D. P. Hallahan (Eds.), *Handbook of special education.* New York: Routledge.

Bateman, B. D., & Linden, M. A. (2006). *Better IEPs: How to develop legally correct and educationally useful programs* (4th ed.). Verona, WI: Attainment.

Boardman, A. G., & Vaughn, S. (2007). Response to intervention as a framework for prevention and identification of learning disabilities: Which comes first, identification or intervention? In J. B. Crockett, M. M. Gerber, & T. J. Landrum (Eds.), *Achieving the radical reform of special education: Essays in honor of James M. Kauffman* (pp. 15–35). Mahwah, NJ: Erlbaum.

Brolin, D. E., & Loyd, R. J. (2004). *Career development and transition services: A functional life-skills approach* (4th ed.). Upper Saddle River, NJ: Pearson.

Browder, D. M., Wood, W. M., Test, D. W., Karvonen, M., & Algozzine, B. (2001). Reviewing resources on self-determination: A map for teachers. *Remedial and Special Education, 22,* 233–244. doi:10.1177/074193250102200407

Chambers, C. R., Wehmeyer, M. L., Saito, Y., Lida, K. M., Lee, Y., & Singh, N. (2007). Self-determination: What do we know? Where do we go? *Exceptionality, 15,* 3–15. doi: 10.1207/s15327035ex1501_2

Cheney, D., Flower, A., & Templeton, T. (2008). Applying Response to Intervention metrics in the social domain for students at-risk of developing emotional or behavioral disorders. *Journal of Special Education, 42*(2), 108–126.

Cook, B. G., & Friend, M. (1998). Co-teaching: Guidelines for creating effective practices. In E. L. Meyen, G. A. Vergason, & R. J. Whelan (Eds.), *Educating students with mild disabilities: Strategies and methods* (2nd ed., pp. 453–479).

Cook, B. G., McDuffie, K. A., Oshita, L., & Cook, S. C. (2011). Co-teaching for students with

disabilities: A critical analysis of the empirical literature. In J. M. Kauffman & D. P. Hallahan (Eds.), *Handbook of special education.* New York: Routledge.

Council for Exceptional Children. (1998). *What every special educator must know* (3rd ed.) Reston, VA: Author.

Crockett, J. B., & Kauffman, J. M. (1999). *The least restrictive environment: Its origins and interpretations in special education.* Mahwah, NJ: Erlbaum.

Crockett, J. B., & Kauffman, J. M. (2001). The concept of the least restrictive environment and learning disabilities: Least restrictive of what? Reflections on Cruickshank's 1977 guest editorial for the *Journal of Learning Disabilities.* In D. P. Hallahan & B. K. Keogh (Eds.), *Research and global perspectives in learning disabilities: Essays in honor of William M. Cruickshank* (pp. 147–166). Mahwah, NJ: Erlbaum.

Cronin, M. E. (2000). Instructional strategies. In P. L. Sitlington, G. M. Clark, & O. P. Kolstoe (Eds.), *Transition education and services for adolescents with disabilities* (3rd ed., pp. 255–283). Boston: Allyn & Bacon/Pearson.

Cruickshank, W. M. (1977). Guest editorial. *Journal of Learning Disabilities, 10,* 193–194. doi:10.1177/002221947701000401

Duhon, G. J., Mesmer, E. M., Atkins, M. E., Greguson, L. A., & Olinger, E. S. (2009). Quantifying intervention intensity: A systematic approach to evaluating student response to increasing intervention frequency. *Journal of Behavioral Education, 18,* 101–118.

Earley, P. (2006). *Crazy: A father's search through America's mental health madness.* New York: Penguin.

Esquith, R. (2007). *Teach like your hair's on fire: The methods and madness inside room 56.* New York: Viking.

Everson, J. M., & Trowbridge, M. H. (2011). Preparing students with low-incidence disabilities for community living opportunities. In D. P. Hallahan & J. M. Kaufman (Eds.), *Handbook of special education.* New York: Routledge.

Fairbanks, S., Sugai, G., Guardino, D., & Lathrop, M.(2007). Response to intervention: Examining classroom behavior support in second grade. *Exceptional Children, 73,* 288–310.

Falk, K. B., & Wehby, J. H. (2001). The effects of peer-assisted learning strategies on the beginning reading skills of young children with emotional or behavioral disorders. *Behavioral Disorders, 26,* 344–359.

Finn, C. E., Jr., Rotherham, A. J., & Hokanson, C. R., Jr. (Eds.). (2001). *Rethinking special education for a new century.* New York: Thomas B. Fordham Foundation.

Fuchs, D., & Fuchs, L. S. (1994). Inclusive schools movement and the radicalization of special education reform. *Exceptional Children, 60,* 294–309.

Fuchs, D., Fuchs, L. S., & Stecker, P. M. (2010). The "blurring" of special education in a new continuum of general education placements and services. *Exceptional Children, 76,* 301–323.

Fuchs, D., Fuchs, L. S., Thompson, A., Svenson, E., Yanb, L., Otaiba, S. A., et al. (2001). Peer-assisted learning strategies in reading: Extensions for kindergarten, first grade, and high school. *Remedial and Special Education, 22,* 15–21. doi:10.1177/074193250102200103

Fuchs, D., Mock, D., Morgan, P. L., & Young, C. L. (2003). Responsiveness-to-intervention: Definitions, evidence, and implications for the learning disabilities construct. *Learning Disabilities Research and Practice, 18,* 157–171. doi:10.1111/1540-5826.00072

Fuchs, L. S., Fuchs, D., Compton, D. L., Bryant, J. D., Hamlett, C. L., & Seethaler, P. M. (2007). Mathematics screening and progress monitoring at first grade: Implications for responsiveness-to-intervention. *Exceptional Children, 73,* 311–330.

Fulk, B. M., & King, K. (2001). Classwide peer tutoring at work. *Teaching Exceptional Children, 34*(2), 49–53.

Gardner, R., Cartledge, G., Seidl, B., Woolsey, M. L., Schley, G. S., & Utley, C. A. (2001). Mt. Olivet after-school program: Peer-mediated interventions for at-risk students. *Remedial and Special Education, 22,* 22–33. doi:10.1177/074193250102200104

Gibb, G. S., & Dyches, T. T. (2007). *Guide to writing quality individualized education programs* (2nd ed.). Boston: Allyn & Bacon/Pearson.

Gliona, M. F., Gonzales, A. K., & Jacobson, E. S. (2005). Dedicated, not segregated: Suggested changes in thinking about instructional environments and the language of special education. In J. M. Kauffman & D. P. Hallahan (Eds.), *The illusion of full inclusion: A comprehensive critique of a current special education bandwagon* (2nd ed., pp. 135–146). Austin, TX: Pro-Ed.

Goin, M. K. (2007, July 8). The wrong place to treat mental illness. *The Washington Post,* p. B7.

Goodman, E. (2007, May 29). Wheels competing with feet. *The Charlottesville Daily Progress,* p. A8.

Greene, G., & Kochhar-Bryant, C. A. (2003). *Pathways to successful transition for youth with disabilities.* Upper Saddle River, NJ: Pearson.

Greenwood, C. R., Arrega-Mayer, C., Utley, C. A., Gavin, K. M., & Terry, B. (2001). Classwide peer tutoring learning management system: Applications with elementary-level English language learners. *Remedial and Special Education, 22,* 34–47. doi:10.1177/074193250102200105

Hallahan, D. P. (2007). Learning disabilities: Whatever happened to intensive instruction? *LDA Newsbriefs, 42*(1), 1, 3–4, 24.

Hallahan, D. P., Lloyd, J. W., Kauffman, J. M., Weiss, M., & Martinez, E. (2005). *Introduction to learning disabilities* (3rd ed.). Boston: Allyn & Bacon/Pearson.

Hockenbury, J. C., Kauffman, J. M., & Hallahan, D. P. (1999–2000). What's right about special education? *Exceptionality, 8*(1), 3–11.

Hoover, J. J., & Patton, J. R. (2004). Differentiating standards-based education for students with diverse needs. *Remedial and Special Education, 25,* 74–78. doi:10.1177/07419325040250020101

Huefner, D. S. (2006). *Getting comfortable with special education law: A framework for working with children with disabilities* (2nd ed.). Norwood, MA: Christopher Gordon.

Hughes, W., Wood, W. M., Konrad, M., & Test, D. W. (2006). Get a life: Students practice being self-determined. *Teaching Exceptional Children, 38*(5), 57–63.

Hungerford, R. (1950). On locusts. *American Journal of Mental Deficiency, 54,* 415–418.

Itard, J. M. G. (1962). *The wild boy of Aveyron* (G. Humphrey & M. Humphrey, Trans.). Upper Saddle River, NJ: Pearson.

Johns, B. H. (2003). NCLB and IDEA: Never the twain should meet. *Learning Disabilities: A Multidisciplinary Journal, 12*(3), 89–91.

Jones, M. (2006). Teaching self-determination: Empowered teachers, empowered students. *Teaching Exceptional Children, 39*(1), 12–17.

Kauffman, J. M. (1995). Why we must celebrate a diversity of restrictive environments. *Learning Disabilities Research and Practice, 10,* 225–232.

Kauffman, J. M. (1999–2000). The special education story: Obituary, accident report, conversion experience, reincarnation, or none of the above? *Exceptionality, 8*(1), 61–71.

Kauffman, J. M. (2002). *Education deform: Bright people sometimes say stupid things about education.* Landham, MD: Scarecrow Education.

Kauffman, J. M. (2004). The president's commission and the devaluation of special education. *Education and Treatment of Children, 27,* 307–324.

Kauffman, J. M. (2005). *Characteristics of emotional and behavioral disorders of children and youth* (8th ed.) Upper Saddle River, NJ: Pearson.

Kauffman, J. M. (2007). Conceptual models and the future of special education. *Education and Treatment of Children, 30*(4), 1–18. doi:10.1353/etc.2007.0024

Kauffman, J. M., Bantz, J., & McCullough, J. (2002). Separate and better: A special public school class for students with emotional and behavioral disorders. *Exceptionality, 10,* 149–170.

Kauffman, J. M., & Hallahan, D. P. (1997). A diversity of restrictive environments: Placement as a problem of social ecology. In J. W. Lloyd, E. J. Kame'enui, & D. Chard (Eds.), *Issues in educating students with disabilities* (pp. 325–342). Mahwah, NJ: Erlbaum.

Kauffman, J. M., & Hallahan, D. P. (2005a). *Special education: What it is and why we need it.* Boston: Allyn & Bacon/Pearson.

Kauffman, J. M., & Hallahan, D. P. (Eds.) (2005b). *The illusion of full inclusion: A comprehensive critique of a current special education bandwagon* (2nd ed.) Austin, TX: Pro-Ed.

Kauffman, J. M., & Hallahan, D. P. (2009). Parental choices and ethical dilemmas involving disabilities: Special education and the problem of deliberately chosen disabilities. *Exceptionality, 17,* 1–18.

Kauffman, J. M., & Konold, T. R. (2007). Making sense in education: Pretense (including NCLB) and realities in rhetoric and policy about schools and schooling. *Exceptionality, 15,* 75–96.

Kauffman, J. M., & Landrum, T. J. (2007). Educational service interventions and reforms. In J. W. Jacobson, J. A. Mulick, & J. Rojahn (Eds.), *Handbook of intellectual and developmental disabilities* (pp. 173–188). New York: Springer.

Kauffman, J. M., McGee, K., & Brigham, M. (2004). Enabling or disabling? Observations on changes in the purposes and outcomes of special education. *Phi Delta Kappan, 85,* 613–620.

Kauffman, J. M., Mock, D. R., Tankersley, M., & Landrum, T. J. (2008). Effective service delivery models. In R. J. Morris & N. Mather (Eds.), *Evidence-based interventions for students with learning and behavioral challenges* (pp. 359–378). Mahwah, NJ: Erlbaum.

Kauffman, J. M., Mostert, M. P., Trent, S. C., & Pullen, P. L. (2006). *Managing classroom behavior: A reflective case-based approach* (4th ed.). Boston: Allyn & Bacon/Pearson.

Kauffman, J. M., & Pullen, P. L. (1996). Eight Myths about special education. *Focus on Exceptional Children, 28*(5), 7–8. Reprinted with permission.

Kauffman, J. M., & Sasso, G. M. (2006a). Certainty, doubt, and the reduction of uncertainty: A rejoinder. *Exceptionality, 14,* 109–120.

Kauffman, J. M., & Sasso, G. M. (2006b). Toward ending cultural and cognitive relativism in special education. *Exceptionality, 14,* 65–90.

Kauffman, J. M., & Wiley, A. L. (2004). How the President's Commission on Excellence in Special Education (PCESE) devalues special education. *Learning Disabilities: A Multidisciplinary Journal, 13,* 3–6.

Kavale, K. A., Kauffman, J. M., & Bachmeier, R. J. (2007). *The politics of response-to-intervention and reality surrounding the identification of specific learning disability.* Manuscript submitted for publication.

Kourea, L., Cartledge, G., & Musti-Rao, S. (2007). Improving reading skills of urban elementary students through total class peer tutoring. *Remedial and Special Education, 28,* 95–107. doi: 10.1177/07419325070280020801

Lamb, H. R., & Weinberger, L. E. (Eds.). (2001). *Deinstitutionalization: Promise and problems.* San Francisco: Jossey-Bass.

Landrum, T. J., & Kauffman, J. M. (2006). Behavioral approaches to classroom management. In C. M. Evertson & C. S. Weinstein (Eds.), *Handbook of classroom management: Research, practice, and contemporary issues* (pp. 47–71). Mahwah, NJ: Erlbaum.

Lazarus, S. S., Thurlow, M. L., Lail, K. E., & Christensen, L. (2009). A longitudinal analysis of state accommodations policies: Twelve years of change 1993–2005. *Journal of Special Education, 43*(2), 67–80.

Lloyd, J. W., & Hallahan, D. P. (2007). Advocacy and reform of special education. In J. B. Crockett, M. M., Gerber, & T. J. Landrum (Eds.), *Achieving the radical reform of special education: Essays in honor of James M. Kauffman* (pp. 245–263). Mahwah, NJ: Erlbaum.

Maheady, L., Harper, G. F., & Mallette, B. (2001). Peer-mediated instruction and interventions with students with mild disabilities. *Remedial and Special Education, 22,* 4–14. doi:10.1177/074193250102200102

Martin, E. W. (1995). Case studies on inclusion: Worst fears realized. *The Journal of Special Education, 29,* 192–199.

Mercer, C. D., Mercer, A. R., & Pullen, P. C. (2011). *Teaching students with learning problems, eighth edition.* Upper Saddle River, NJ: Pearson.

Miller, S. P. (2002). *Validated practices for teaching students with diverse needs and abilities.* Boston: Allyn & Bacon/Pearson.

Mock, D. R., & Kauffman, J. M. (2002). Preparing teachers for full inclusion: Is it possible? *The Teacher Educator, 37,* 202–215. doi:10.1080/08878730209555294

Mock, D. R., & Kauffman, J. M. (2005). The delusion of full inclusion. In J. W. Jacobson, J. A. Mulick, & R. M. Fuchs (Eds.), *Fads: Dubious and improbably treatments for developmental disabilities* (pp. 113–128). Mahwah, NJ: Erlbaum.

Moon, M. S. (2011). Section X editor: Transition of adults with low incidence disabilities. In J. M. Kauffman & D. P. Hallahan (Eds.), *Handbook of special education.* New York: Routledge.

Moon, M. S., & Inge, K. (2000). Vocational preparation and transition. In M. E. Snell & F. Brown (Eds.), *Instruction of students with severe disabilities* (5th ed., pp. 591–628). Upper Saddle River, NJ: Merrill/Pearson.

Moore, T. (2007, January 19). Classroom distinctions. *The New York Times,* p. A27.

Mostert, M. P., Kavale, K. A., & Kauffman, J. M. (Eds.). (2008). *Challenging the refusal of reasoning in special education.* Denver, CO: Love.

Nomani, A. Q. (2007, April 29). My brother's battle—and mine. *The Washington Post,* p. B2.

Noonan, M. J., & McCormick, L. (2006). *Young children with disabilities in natural environments: Methods and procedures.* Baltimore: Brookes.

O'Connor, R. E., & Sanchez, V. (2011). Responsiveness to intervention models for reducing reading difficulties and identifying learning disability. In J. M. Kauffman & D. P. Hallahan (Eds.), *Handbook of special education.* New York: Routledge.

Osborne, J. G. (2005). Person-centered planning: a *faux fixe* in the service of humanism? In J. W. Jacobson, J. A. Mulick & J. Rojahn (Eds.), *Handbook of intellectual and developmental disabilities* (pp. 313–329). New York: Springer.

Palmer, S. B., & Wehmeyer, M. L. (2003). Promoting self-determination in early elementary school: Teaching self-regulated problem-solving and goal-setting skills. *Remedial and Special Education, 24,* 115–126. doi:10.1177/07419325030240020601

Pierangelo, R., & Giuliani, G. A. (2006). *Assessment in special education: A practical approach* (2nd ed.). Boston: Allyn & Bacon/Pearson.

Pisha, B., & Coyne, P. (2001). Smart from the start: The promise of universal design for learning. *Remedial and Special Education, 22,* 197–203. doi:10.1177/074193250102200402

Powers, L. E., Garner, T., Valnes, B., Squire, P., Turner, A., Couture, T., et al. (2007). Building a successful adult life: Findings from youth-directed research. *Exceptionality, 15,* 45–56. doi:10.1207/s5327035ex1501_5

Pugach, M. C., & Warger, C. L. (2001). Curriculum matters: Raising expectations for students with disabilities. *Remedial and Special Education, 22,* 194–196. doi:10.1177/074193250102200401

Rothstein, R., Jacobsen, R., & Wilder, T. (2006, November). *"Proficiency for all"—An oxymoron.* Paper presented at symposium on *Examining America's commitment to closing achievement gaps: NCLB and its alternatives.* Teachers College, Columbia University, New York.

Rozalski, M., & Miller, J. (2011). Least restrictive environment. In J. M. Kauffman & D. P. Hallahan (Eds.), *Handbook of special education.* New York: Routledge.

Sasso, G. M. (2001). The retreat from inquiry and knowledge in special education. *The Journal of Special Education, 34,* 178–193.

Sasso, G. M. (2007). Science and reason in special education: The legacy of Derrida and Foucault. In J. B. Crockett, M. M. Gerber, & T. J. Landrum (Eds.), *Achieving the radical reform of special education: Essays in honor of James M. Kauffman* (pp. 143–167). Mahwah, NJ: Erlbaum.

Scanlon, D. J. (2011). Section IX editor: Transition of adults with high incidence disabilities. In J. M. Kauffman & D. P. Hallahan (Eds.), *Handbook of special education.* New York: Routledge.

Schwartz, A. A., Jacobson, J. W., & Holburn, S. C. (2000). Defining person centeredness: Results of two consensus methods. *Education and Training in Mental Retardation and Developmental Disabilities, 35,* 235–249.

Scruggs, T. E., Mastropieri, M. A., & McDuffie, K. A. (2007). Co-teaching in inclusive classrooms: A metasynthesis of qualitative research. *Exceptional Children, 73,* 392–416.

Shogren, K. A., Wehmeyer, M. L., Palmer, S. B., Soukup, J. H., Little, T. D., Garner, N., et al. (2007). Examining individual and ecological predictors of the self-determination of students with disabilities. *Exceptional Children, 73,* 488–509.

Simpson, R. L., & Kauffman, J. M. (2007). Inclusão de alunos deficientes em salas de aula regulares (Inclusion of students with disabilities in general education). In J. M. Kauffman & J. A Lopes (Eds.), *Pode a educação especial deixar de ser especial?* (pp. 167–190). Braga, Portugal: Psiquilíbrios Edições.

Siperstein, G. N., Parker, R. C., Bardon, J. N., & Widaman, K. F. (2007). A national study of youth attitudes toward the inclusion of students with intellectual disabilities. *Exceptional Children, 73,* 435–455.

Sitlington, P. L., & Clark, G. M. (2006). *Transition education and services for students with disabilities* (4th ed.). Boston: Allyn & Bacon/ Pearson.

Spooner, F., Baker, J. N., Harris, A. A., Ahlgrim-Delzell, L., & Browder, D. M. (2007). Effects of training in universal design for learning on lesson plan development. *Remedial and Special Education, 28,* 108–116. doi:10.1177/07419325070280020101

Thurlow, M. L. (2000). Standards-based reform and students with disabilities: Reflections on a decade of change. *Focus on Exceptional Children, 33*(3), 1–16.

Thurlow, M. L. (2010). Special issue: Testing students with disabilities. *Applied Measurement in Education, 23,* 121–131.

Thurlow, M. L., Nelson, J. R., Teelucksingh, W., & Draper, I. L. (2001). Multiculturalism and disability in a results-based educational system: Hazards and hopes for today's schools. In C. A. Utley & F. E. Obiakor (Eds.), *Special education, multicultural education, and school reform: Components of quality education for learners with mild disabilities* (pp. 155–172). Springfield, IL: Charles C. Thomas.

Thurlow, M. L., & Quenemoen, R. F. (2011). Standards-based reforms and students with disabilities. In J. M. Kauffman & D. P. Hallahan (Eds.), *Handbook of special education.* New York: Routledge.

Tomlinson, C. A. (2001). *How to differentiate instruction in mixed-ability classrooms* (2nd ed.). Alexandria, VA: Association for Supervision and Curriculum Development.

Torrey, E. F., & Zdandowicz, M. T. (1999, July 9). Deinstitutionalization hasn't worked: "We have lost effectively 93 percent of our state psychiatric hospital beds since 1955." *The Washington Post.* Retrieved from www.psychlaws.org/ generalresources/article17.htm

U. S. Department of Education. (1995). *Seventeenth annual report to Congress on the implementation of the Individuals with Disabilities Education Act.* Washington, DC: Author. Retrieved from http://www.ed.gov/about/reports/annual/osep/ 2002/index.html

U.S. Department of Education. (2005). *Twenty-seventh annual report to Congress on implementation of the Individuals with Disabilities Education Act.* Washington, DC: Author.

U.S. Department of Education. (2009). *Twenty-eighth annual report to Congress on implementation of the Individuals with Disabilities Education Act.* Washinton, DC: Author.

Walsh, J. M., & Jones, B. (2004). New models of cooperative teaching. *Teaching Exceptional Children, 36*(5), 14–20.

Warnock, M. (2005). *Special educational needs: A new look. Impact No. 11.* London: Philosophy of Education Society of Great Britain.

Wolfensberger, W. (1972). *The principle of normalization in human services.* Toronto: National Institute on Mental Retardation.

Yell, M. L. (2006). *The law and special education* (2nd ed.). Upper Saddle River, NJ: Pearson.

Yell, M., & Crockett, J. B. (2011). Free appropriate public educaiton. In J. M. Kauffman & D. P. Hallahan (Eds.), *Handbook of special education.* New York: Routledge.

Yell, M. L., & Drasgow, E. (2005). *No child left behind: A guide for professionals.* Upper Saddle River, NJ: Merrill/Pearson.

Zigmond, N. (2003). Where should students with disabilities receive special education services? Is one place better than another? *The Journal of Special Education, 37,* 193–199. doi:10.1177/00224669030370030901

Zigmond, N. (2007). Delivering special education is a two-person job: A call for unconventional thinking. In J. B. Crockett, M. M. Gerber, & T. J. Landrum (Eds.), *Achieving the radical reform of special education: Essays in honor of James M. Kauffman* (pp. 115–137). Mahwah, NJ: Erlbaum.

Zigmond, N., & Kloo, A. (2011). General and special education are (and should be) different. In J. M. Kauffman & D. P. Hallahan (Eds.), *Handbook of special education.* New York: Routledge.

CHAPTER 3

Abedi, J., Hofstetter, C., & Lord, C. (2004). Assessment accommodations for English language learners: Implications for policy-based empirical research. *Review of Educational Research, 74,* 1–28. doi:10.3102/00346543074001001

Ahlberg, M. (2004). Concept maps: Theory, methodology, technology. *Proceedings of the First International Conference on Concept Mapping.* Pamplona, Spain.

Albus, D., Thurlow, M., Liu, K., & Bielinski, J. (2005). Reading test performance of English-language learners using an English Dictionary. *The Journal of Educational Research, 98,* 245–254. doi:10.3200/JOER.98.4.245-256

Anastasiou, D., Gardner, R., & Michail, D. (2011). Ethnicity and exceptionality. In J. M. Kauffman & D. P. Hallahan (Eds.), *Handbook of special education.* New York: Routledge.

Armendariz, F., & Umbriet, J. (1999). Using active responding to reduce disruptive behavior in a general education classroom. *Journal of Positive Behavior Interventions, 1,* 152–158.

Artiles, A. J., Rueda, R., Salazar, J. J., & Higareda, I. (2005). Within-group diversity in minority disproportionate representation: English language learners in urban school districts. *Exceptional Children, 71,* 283–301.

Artiles, A. J., Trent, S. C., Hoffman-Kipp, P., & Lopez-Torres, L. (2000). From individual acquisition to cultural-historical practices in multicultural teacher education. *Remedial and Special Education, 21,* 79–89, 120. doi:10.1177/074193250002100203

Associated Press. (2004, April 18). Gay teens harassed at school: Persecution leads to law. *Charlottesville Daily Progress,* p. A11.

Banks, J. A. (2006). *Cultural diversity and education: Foundations, curriculum, and teaching* (5th ed.). Bosten: Allyn & Bacon/Pearson.

Banks, J. A., & Banks, C. A. (2007). *Multicultural education: Issues and perspectives* (6th ed.). Hoboken, NJ: Wiley.

Banks, J. A., & Banks, C. A. (2010). *Multicultural education: Issues and perspectives* (7th ed.). Hoboken, NJ: Wiley.

Bateman, B. D. (1994). Who, how, and where: Special education's issues in perpetuity. *The Journal of Special Education, 27,* 509–520. doi:10.1177/002246699402700410

Bell, K. (2004). GLSEN in tough times: Training educators about LGBT issues in a challenging political, economic, and educational climate. *Beyond Behavior, 13*(2), 29–30.

Bennett, L. (2000). Equality by design: Three charter schools try new approaches to integration. *Teaching Tolerance, 17,* 43–49.

Calhoon, M. B., Al Otaiba, S., Cihak, D., King A., & Avalos, A. (2007). Effects of a peer-mediated program on reading skill acquisition for two-way bilingual first-grade classroom. *Learning Disability Quarterly, 30,* 169–184.

Calhoon, M. B., Al Otaiba, S., Greenberg, D., King, A., & Avalos, A. (2006). Improving reading skills in predominantly Hispanic Title 1 first-grade classrooms: The promise of peer-assisted learning strategies. *Learning Disabilities Research & Practice, 21,* 261–272. doi:10.1111/j.1540-5826.2006.00222.x

Cartledge, G. (2004). Another look at the impact of changing demographics on public education for culturally diverse learners with behavior problems: Implications for teacher preparation. In L. M. Bullock & R. A. Gable (Eds.), *Quality personnel preparation in emotional/behavioral disorders: Current perspectives and future directions* (pp. 64–69). Denton, TX: Institute for Behavioral and Learning Differences at the University of North Texas.

Cartledge, G., & Kourea, L. (2008). Culturally responsive classrooms for culturally diverse students with and at risk for disabilities. *Exceptional Children, 74,* 351–371.

Cartledge, G., & Loe, S. A. (2001). Cultural diversity and social skill instruction. *Exceptionality, 9* 33–46. doi:10.1207/S15327035EX091&2_4

Cho, S., Singer, G. H. S., & Brenner, M. (2000). Adaptation and accommodation to young children with disabilities: A comparison of Korean and Korean American parents. *Topics in Early Childhood Special Education, 20,* 236–249. doi:10.1177/027112140002000404

Christle, C. A., & Schuster, J. W. (2003). The effects of using response cards on student participants, academic achievement, and on-task behavior during whole-class math instruction. *Journal of Behavior Education, 12,* 147–165.

Chularut, P., & DeBacker, T. (2003). The influence of concept mapping on achievement, self-regulation, and self-efficacy in students of English as a second language. *Contemporary Educational Psychology, 29,* 248–263. doi:10.1016/j.cedpsych.2003.09.001

Cloud, N. (2002). Culturally and linguistically responsive instructional planning. In A. J. Artiles and A. A. Ortiz (Eds.). *English language learners with special education needs: Identification, assessment and instruction.* McHenry, IL: Center for Applied Linguistics.

Collins, K. (2000). No place for bigotry: An anti-bias club changes the atmosphere at a suburban high school. *Teaching Tolerance, 17,* 26–27.

Colon, E. P., & Kranzler, J. H. (2007). Effects of instructions on curriculum-based measurement of reading. *Journal of Psychoeducational Assessment, 24,* 318–328. doi:10.1177/0734282906287830

Council for Exceptional Children. (2000). Improving results for culturally and linguistically diverse students. *Research Connections in Special Education, 7.*

Coutinho, M. J., & Oswald, D. P. (2000). Disproportionate representation in special education: A synthesis and recommendations. *Journal of Child and Family Studies, 9,* 135–156. doi:10.1023/A:1009462820157

Coutinho, M. J., & Oswald, D. P. (2011). Gender and exceptionality. In J. M. Kauffman & D. P.

Hallahan (Eds.), *Handbook of special education.* New York: Routledge.

Cushner, K., McClelland, A., & Safford, P. (2006). *Human diversity in education: An interactive approach* (5th ed.). Boston: McGraw-Hill.

Dadurka, D. (2004, April 22). Ruffner's life, work honored. *Charlottesville Daily Progress,* p. A2.

Daley, T. C., & Carlson, E. (2009). Predictors of change in eligibility status among preschoolers in special education. *Exceptional Children, 75,* 412–426.

De Melendez, W. R., & Beck, V. (2010). *Teaching young children in multicultural classrooms: Issues, concepts, and strategies* (2nd ed.). Clifton Park, NY: Thomson Delmar.

Denton, C. A., Anthony, J. L., Parker, R., & Hasbrouck, J. E. (2004). The effects of two tutoring programs on the English reading development of Spanish-English bilingual students. *Elementary School Journal, 104,* 289–305.

Elksnin, L. K., & Elksnin, N. (2000). Teaching parents to teach their children to be prosocial. *Intervention in School and Clinic, 36,* 27–35. doi:10.1177/105345120003600104

Elliot, B. (2000). Finding my stride: A gay student takes the bold step of being true to himself. *Teaching Tolerance, 17,* 40–41.

Everston, C. M., & Weinstein, C. S. (Eds.). (2006). *Handbook of classroom management: Research, practice, and contemporary issues.* Mahwah, NJ: Erlbaum.

Fuchs, D., Fuchs, L. S., & Compton, D. L. (2004). Identifying reading disabilities by responsiveness to instruction: Specifying measure and criteria. *Learning Disabilities Quarterly, 27,* 216–227. doi:10.2307/1593674.

Fujiura, G. T., & Yamaki, K. (2000). Trends in demography of childhood poverty and disability. *Exceptional Children, 66,* 187–199.

Fulk, B. M., & King, K. (2001). Classwide peer tutoring at work. *Teaching Exceptional Children, 34*(2), 49–53.

Gallucci, J. P. (2000). Signs of remembrance: A school for the deaf celebrates Dia de los Muertos. *Teaching Tolerance, 18,* 30–31.

Gelman, J. A., Pullen, P. L., & Kauffman, J. M. (2005). The meaning of highly qualified and a clear roadmap to accomplishment. *Exceptionality, 12,* 195–207. doi:10.1207/s15327035ex1204_2

George, C. C. & Vannest, K. J. (2009). The participation in high stakes assessment of students with emotional and behavioral disorders: Implications for teachers. *Beyond Behavior, 18,* 33–39.

Gersten, R., & Baker, S. (2000). What we know about effective instructional practices for English-language learners. *Exceptional Children, 66,* 454–470.

Gersten, R., Brengelman, S., & Jimenez, R. (1994). Effective instruction for culturally and linguistically diverse students: A reconceptualization. *Focus on Exceptional Children, 27*(1), 1–16.

Gollnick, D. M., & Chinn, P. C. (2006). *Multicultural education in a pluralistic society* (7th ed.). New York: Macmillan.

Good, R. H., & Kaminski, R. A. (Eds.). (2002). *Dynamic Indicators of Basic Early Literacy Skills* (6th ed.). Eugene, OR: Institute for the Development of Educational Achievement. Available: http://dibels.uoregon.edu

Good, T. L., & Nichols, S. L. (2001). Expectancy effects in the classroom: A special focus on improving the reading performance of minority students in first grade classrooms. *Educational Psychologist, 36,* 113–126.

Greenwood, C. R., Arrega-Mayer, C., Utley, C. A., Gavin, K. M, & Terry, B. J. (2001). Classwide peer tutoring learning management system: Applications with elementary-level English language learners. *Remedial and Special Education, 22,* 34–47. doi:10.1177/074193250102200105

Greenwood, C. R., Hart, B., Walker, D., & Risely, T. (1994). The opportunity to respond and academic performance revisited: A behavioral theory of developmental retardation and its prevention. In R. Gardner, D. M. Sainato, J. O. Cooper, T. E. Heron, W. L. Heward, J. Eshlemann, & T. A. Grossi (Eds.), *Behavior analysis in education: Focus on measurably superior instruction* (pp. 213–223). Pacific Grove, CA: Brooks/Cole.

Gunn, B., Smolkowski, K, Biglan, A., Black, C., & Blair, J. (2005). Fostering the development of reading skill through supplemental instruction: Results for Hispanic and non-Hispanic students. *The Journal of Special Education, 39,* 66–85. doi:10.1177/00224669050390020301

Hallahan, D. P., Lloyd, J. W., Kauffman, J. M., Weiss, M., & Martinez, E. (2005). *Introduction to learning disabilities* (3rd ed.). Boston: Allyn & Bacon.

Hammill, D. D. (2004). What we know about correlates of reading. *Exceptional Children, 70,* 453–468.

Heward, W. L. (2003). Ten faulty notions about teaching and learning that hinder the effectiveness of special education. *The Journal of Special Education, 36,* 186–205. doi:10.1177/002246690303600401

Hicks, M. A. (2005). Lessons from rental cars: The struggle to create seeing communities. Educational Studies, *38,* 120–126. doi:10.1207/s15326993es3802_4

Horwitz, S. (1998, April 5). Lessons in black and white; crossing color lines in room 406 with Miss Kay and her kids. *The Washington Post,* p. F1.

Hosp, J. L., & Reschly, D. J. (2004). Disproportionate representation of minority students in special education: Academic, demographic, and economic predictors. *Exceptional Children, 70,* 185–199.

Kauffman, J. M. (2001). *Characteristics of emotional and behavioral disorders of children and youths* (7th ed.). New York: Merrill/Pearson.

Kauffman, J. M. (2003). Appearances, stigma, and prevention. *Remedial and Special Education, 24,* 195–198. doi:10.1177/07419325030240040201

Kauffman, J. M., Conroy, M., Gardner, R., & Oswald, D. (2008). Cultural sensitivity in the application of behavior principles to education. *Education and Treatment of Children, 31,* 239–262.

Kauffman, J. M., & Hallahan, D. P. (2005). *Special education: What it is and why we need it.* Boston: Allyn & Bacon/Pearson.

Kauffman, J. M., & Konold, T. R. (2007). Making sense in education: Pretense (including NCLB) and realities in rhetoric and policy about schools and schooling. *Exceptionality, 15,* 75–96.

Kauffman, J. M., & Landrum, T. (2009). Politics, civil rights, and disproportional identification of students with emotional and behavioral disorders. *Exceptionality, 17,* 177–188. doi:10.1080/09362830903231903

Kauffman, J. M., McGee, K., & Brigham, M. (2004). Enabling or disabling? Observations on changes in special education. *Phi Delta Kappa, 85,* 613–620.

Kauffman, J. M., Mostert, M. P., Trent, S. C., & Pullen, P. L. (2006). *Managing classroom behavior: A reflective case-based approach* (4th ed.). Boston: Allyn & Bacon/Pearson.

Klingner, J. K., & Edwards, P. A. (2006). Cultural considerations with response to intervention models. *Reading Research Quarterly, 41,* 108–117. doi:10.1598/RRQ.41.1.6

Lewis, A. C. (2004). Desegregation and degeneration. *Phi Delta Kappan, 85,* 643–644.

Linan-Thompson, S., Vaughn, S., Hickman-Davis, P., & Kouzekanani, K. (2003). Effectiveness of supplemental reading instruction of English language learners with reading difficulties. *Elementary School Journal, 103,* 221–238. doi:10.1086/499724

Linan-Thompson, S., Vaughn, S., Prater, K., & Cirino, P. T. (2006). The response to intervention of English language learners at risk for reading problems. *Journal of Learning Disabilities, 39,* 390–398. doi:10.1177/00222194060390050201

Lustig, D. G., & Strauser, D. R. (2007). Causal relationships between poverty and disability. *Rehabilitation Counseling Bulletin, 50,* 194-202. doi: 10.1177/00343552070500040101

MacSwan, J., & Rolstad, K. (2006). How language proficiency tests mislead us about ability: Implications for English language learner placement in special education. *Teachers College Record, 108,* 2304–2328. doi:10.1111/j.1467-9620.2006.00783.x

McAfee, M. (2000). Welcome to Park Day School: A bay area teacher shares her independent school's commitment to community. *Teaching Tolerance, 18,* 24–29.

McCardle, P., & Leung, C. Y. Y. (2006). English language learners: Development and intervention. *Topics in Language Disorders, 26,* 302–304.

McCardle, P., McCarthy, J. M., & Leos, K. (2005). English language learners and learning disabilities: Research agenda and implications for practice. *Learning Disabilities Research & Practice, 20,* 68–78. doi:10.1111/j.1540-5826.2005.00122.x

McCourt, F. (1996). *Angela's ashes.* New York: Scribner.

McDonnell, L. M., McLaughlin, M. J., & Morison, P. (Eds.). (1997). *Educating one and all: Students with disabilities and standards-based reform.* Washington, DC: National Academy Press.

McIntyre, T. (2007). *Are behaviorist interventions inappropriate for culturally different youngsters with learning and behavior disorders?* Retrieved from http://maxweber.hunter.cuny.edu/pub/eres/EDSPC715_MCINTYRE/CBehModR.html

Mostert, M. P. (2002). Useless eaters: Disability as handicap in Nazi Germany. *The Journal of Special Education, 36,* 155–168. doi:10.1177/00224669020360030601

Mundy, L. (2002, March 31). A world of their own. *The Washington Post Magazine,* pp. 22–29, 38–43.

Nguyen, L., Huang, L. N., Areganza, G. F., & Liao, Q. (2007). The influence of race and ethnicity on psychiatric diagnoses and clinical characteristics of children and adolescents in children's services. *Cultural Diversity and Ethnic Minority Psychology, 13,* 18–25. doi:10.1037/1099-9809.13.1.18

Novak, J. D., & Gowin, D. B. (1984). *Learning how to learn.* New York: Cambridge University Press.

Osher, D., Cartledge, G., Oswald, D., Sutherland, K. S., Artiles, A. J., & Coutinho, M. (2004). Cultural and linguistic competency and disproportionate representation. In R. B. Rutherford, M. M. Quinn, & S. R. Mathur (Eds.), *Handbook of research in emotional and behavioral disorders* (pp. 54–77). New York: Guilford.

Oswald, D. P., & Coutinho, M. J. (2001). Trends in disproportionate representation: Implications for multicultural education. In C. A. Utley & F. E. Obiakor (Eds.), *Special education, multicultural education, and school reform: Components of quality education for learners with mild disabilities* (pp. 53–73). Springfield, IL: Charles C. Thomas.

Pavri, S. (2001). Loneliness in children with disabilities: How teachers can help. *Teaching Exceptional Children, 33*(6), 52–58.

Peck, A., & Scarpati, S. (2004). Literacy instruction and research. *Teaching Exceptional Children, 36*(6), 71.

Pierce, R. L., Adams, C. M., Speirs Neumeister, K. L., Cassady, J. C., Dixon, F. A., & Cross, T. L. (2007). Development of an identification procedure for a large urban school corporation: Identifying culturally divers and academically gifted elementary students. *Roeper Review, 29,* 113–118. doi:10.1080/02783190709554394

Pollard-Durodola, S. D., Mathes, P. G., Vaughn, S., Cardenas-Hagan, E., & Linan-Thompson, S. (2006). The role of oracy in developing comprehension in Spanish-speaking English language learners. *Topics in Language Disorders, 26,* 365–384.

Pullen, P. L. (2004). *Brighter beginnings for teachers.* Lanham, MD: Scarecrow Education.

Randolph, J. J. (2007). Meta-analysis of the research on response cards: Effects on test achievement, quiz achievement, participation, and off-task behavior. *Journal of Positive Behavior Interventions, 9*(2), 113–128.

Ravitch, D. (2003). *The language police: How pressure groups restrict what students learn.* New York: Knopf.

Reschly, D. J. (2001, July 13). *Overrepresentation, it's not what you think it is: Equal treatment studies.* Presentation at the Office of Special Education Programs Annual Research Project Directors' Conference, Washington, DC.

Reyna, V. F. (2004). Why scientific research? The importance of evidence in changing educational practice. In P. McCardle, & V. Chhabra (Eds.), *The voice of evidence in reading research* (pp. 47–58). Baltimore: Paul H. Brookes.

Ruzic, R., & O'Connell, K. (2001). *Concept maps.* National Center on Accessing the General Curriculum. Retrieved from http://udl.cast.org/ncac/ConceptMaps1669.cfm

Shealey, M. W., & Callins, T. (2007). Creating culturally responsive literacy programs in inclusive classrooms. *Intervention in School and Clinic, 42,* 195–197. doi:10.1177/10534512070420040101

Singh, N. N., Baker, J., Winton, A. S. W., & Lewis, D. K. (2000). Semantic equivalence of assessment instruments across cultures. *Journal of Child and Family Studies, 9,* 123–134. doi:10.1023/A:1009424003319

Sutphin, M. (2007, January). *Mapping concepts from the classroom to the computer: Instructors hope to combined concept maps and the Internet to test agriculture students.* Blacksburg, VA: Virginia Technical University College of Agriculture and Life Sciences. Retrieved from http://www.cals.vt.edu/news/pubs/innovations/jan2007/concepts.html

Takaki, R. (1994). Interview: Reflections from a different mirror. *Teaching Tolerance, 3*(1), 11–15.

Thurlow, M. L., Nelson, J. R., Teelucksingh, W., & Draper, I. L. (2001). Multiculturalism and disability in a results-based educational system: Hazards and hopes for today's schools. In C. A.

Utley & F. E. Obiakor (Eds.), *Special education, multicultural education, and school reform: Components of quality education for learners with mild disabilities* (pp. 155–172). Springfield, IL: Charles C. Thomas.

Tyler, N. C., Yzquierdo, Z., Lopez-Reyna, N., & Flippin, S. S. (2004). Cultural and linguistic diversity and the special education workforce: A critical overview. *The Journal of Special Education, 38,* 22–38. doi:10.1177/00224669040380010301

U.S. Department of Education. (2005). *Twenty-seventh annual report to Congress on the implementation of the Individuals with Disabilities Education Act.* Washington, DC: Author.

U.S. Department of Education. (2009). *Twenty-eighth annual report to Congress on the implementation of the Individuals with Disabilities Education Act.* Washington, DC: Author.

Utley, C. A., & Obiakor, F. E. (2001a). Learning problems or learning disabilities of multicultural learners: Contemporary perspectives. In C. A. Utley & F. E. Obiakor (Eds.), *Special education, multicultural education, and school reform: Components of quality education for learners with mild disabilities* (pp. 90–117). Springfield, IL: Charles C. Thomas.

Utley, C. A., & Obiakor, F. E. (2001b). Multicultural education and special education: Infusion for better schooling. In C. A. Utley & F. E. Obiakor (Eds.), *Special education, multicultural education, and school reform: Components of quality education for learners with mild disabilities* (pp. 3–29). Springfield, IL: Charles C. Thomas.

Utley, C. A., & Obiakor, F. E. (Eds.). (2001c). *Special education, multicultural education, and school reform: Components of quality education for learners with mild disabilities.* Springfield, IL: Charles C. Thomas.

Vaughn, S., Cirino, P. T., Linan-Thompson, S., Mathes, P. G., Carlson, C. D., Cardenas-Hagan, E., Pollard-Durodola, S. D., Fletcher, J. M., & Francis, D. J. (2006). Effectiveness of a Spanish intervention and an English intervention for English language learners at risk for reading problems. *American Educational Research Journal, 43,* 449–487. doi:10.3102/00028312043003449

Vaughn, S., Linan-Thompson, S., Mathes, P. G., Cirino, P. T., Carlson, C. D., Pollard-Durodola, S. D., et al. (2006). Effectiveness of a Spanish intervention for first-grade English language learners at risk for reading difficulties. *Journal of Learning Disabilities, 39,* 56–73. doi:10.1177/00222194060390010601

Vaughn, S., Mathes, P., Linan-Thompson, S., Cirino, P., Carlson, C. Pollard-Durodola, S., et al. (2006). Effectiveness of an English intervention for first-grade English language learners at risk for reading problems. *The Elementary School Journal, 107,* 153–180. doi:10.1086/510653

Vaughn, S., Mathes, P., Linan-Thompson, S., & Francis, D. (2005). Teaching English language learners at risk for reading difficulties to read in Spanish or English. *Learning Disabilities Research & Practice, 20*(1), 58–67. doi:10.1111/j.1540-5826.2005.00121.x

Villegas, A. M., & Lucas, T. (2007). The culturally responsive teacher. *Educational Leadership, 64*(6), 28–33.

Walker, T. (2000). Street smart: Sidewalk libraries open a world of learning for urban youth. *Teaching Tolerance, 17,* 22–25.

Welsh, P. (2004, June 20). When the street and the classroom collide. *The Washington Post,* pp. B1, B4.

Wiesel, E. (2004, July 4). The America I love. *Parade*, pp. 4–5.

Xu, Y., Gelfer, J. I., Sileo, N., Filler, J., & Perkins, P. (2008). Effects of peer tutoring on young children's social interactions. *Early Child Development and Care, 178*, 617–635. doi:10.1080/03004430600857485

CHAPTER 4

Anderson, L., Larson, S., Lakin, C., & Kwak, N. (2002). Children with disabilities: Social roles and family impacts in the NHIS-D. *DD Data Brief, 4*(1), 1–11.

Bailey, D. B., Raspa, M., Humphreys, B. P., & Sam, A. M. (2011). Promoting family outcomes in early intervention. In J. M. Kauffman & D. P. Hallahan (Eds.), *The handbook of special education*. New York: Routledge.

Bell, R. Q., & Harper, L. V. (1977). *Child effects on adults*. Hillsdale, NJ: Erlbaum.

Bellefontaine, S., Hastings, P., Parker, R., & Forman, D. (2006, June 19). Child compliance to mothers and fathers: Sequential analysis of a clean-up task. Paper presented at the annual meeting of the XVth Biennial International Conference on Infant Studies, Westin Miyako, Kyoto, Japan. Retrieved from http://www.allacademic.com/meta/p94058_index.html

Berry, J. O., & Hardman, M. L. (1998). *Lifespan perspectives on the family and disability*. Boston: Allyn & Bacon.

Blacher, J., & Baker, B. L. (2007). Positive impact of intellectual disability on families. *American Journal on Mental Retardation, 112*, 330–348. doi:10.1352/0895-8017(2007)112[0330:PIOIDO]2.0.CO;2

Brooks-Gunn, J., & Lewis, M. (1984). Maternal responsivity in interactions with handicapped infants. *Child Development, 55*, 858–868.

Clay, V. (2006). Lessons from my brother. *Exceptional Parent, 36*(12), 24–25.

Davis, N. O., & Carter, A. S. (2008). Parenting stress in mothers and fathers of toddlers with autism spectrum disorders: Associations with child characteristics. *Journal of Autism and Developmental Disorders, 38*, 1278–1291 doi:10.1007/s10803-007-0512-z

Drotar, D., Baskiewicz, A., Irvin, N., Kennell, J., & Klaus, M. (1975). The adaptation of parents to the birth of an infant with a congenital malformation: A hypothetical model. *Pediatrics, 56*, 710–717.

Esquivel, S. L., Ryan, C. S., & Bonner, M. (2008). Involved parents' perceptions of their experiences in school-based team meetings. *Journal of Educational and Psychological Consultation, 18*, 234–258. doi:10.1080/10474410802022589

Featherstone, H. (1980). *A difference in the family: Life with a disabled child*. New York: Basic Books.

Ferguson, P. M. (2002). A place in the family: An historical interpretation of research on parental reactions to having a child with a disability. *The Journal of Special Education, 36*, 124–130. doi:10.1177/00224669020360030201

Fiedler, C. R., Simpson, R. L., & Clark, D. M. (2007). *Parents and families of children with disabilities: Effective school-based support services*. Upper Saddle River, NJ: Merrill/Pearson.

Floyd, F. J., Purcell, S. E., Richardson, S. S., & Kupersmidt, J. B. (2009). Sibling relationship quality and social functioning of children and adolescents with intellectual disability. *American Journal of Intellectual and Developmental Disabilities, 114*, 110–127. doi:10.1352/2009.114.110-127

Fox, L., Vaughn, B. J., Wyatte, M. L., & Dunlap, G. (2002). "We can't expect other people to understand": Family perspectives on problem behavior. *Exceptional Children, 68*, 437–450.

Gallagher, P. A., Powell, T. H., & Rhodes, C. A. (2006). *Brothers & sisters: A special part of exceptional families* (3rd ed.). Baltimore: Brookes.

Gerlach, E. K. (1999). *Just this side of normal: Glimpses into life with autism*. Eugene, OR: Four Leaf Press.

Glidden, L. M., & Jobe, B. M. (2006). Brief research report: The longitudinal course of depression in adoptive and birth mothers of children with intellectual disabilities. *Journal of Policy and Practice in Intellectual Disabilities, 2*, 139–142. doi:10.1111/j.1741-1130.2006.00067.x

Groneberg, J. G. (2008). *Road map to Holland: How I found my way through my son's first two years with Down syndrome*. New York: New American Library.

Harry, B. (2002). Trends and issues in serving culturally diverse families of children with disabilities. *The Journal of Special Education, 36*, 131–138. doi:10.1177/00224669020360030301

Hastings, R. P., Daley, D., Burns, C., & Beck, A. (2006). Maternal distress and expressed emotion: Cross-sectional and longitudinal relationships with behavior problems of children with intellectual disabilities. *American Journal on Mental Retardation, 111*, 48–61. doi:10.1352/0895-8017(2006)111[48:MDAEEC]2.0.CO;2

Howell, A., Hauser-Cram, P., & Kersh, J. E. (2007). Setting the stage: Early child and family characteristics as predictors of later loneliness in children with developmental disabilities. *American Journal on Mental Retardation, 112*, 18–30. doi:10.1352/0895-8017(2007)112[18:STSECA]2.0.CO;2

Jurbergs, N., Palcic, J., & Kelley, M. L. (2007). School–home notes with and without response cost: Increasing attention and academic performance in low-income children with attention-deficit/hyperactivity disorder. *School Psychology Quarterly, 22*, 358–379. doi:10.1037/1045-3830.22.3.358

Kauffman, J. M., Mostert, M. P., Trent, S. C., & Pullen, P. L. (2011). *Managing classroom behavior: A reflective case-based approach*. Upper Saddle River, NJ: Pearson.

Kelley, M. L., (1990). *School–home notes: Promoting children's classroom success*. New York: Guilford Press.

Keogh, B. K., Garnier, H. E., Bernheimer, L. P., & Gallimore, R. (2000). Models of child–family interactions for children with developmental delays: Child-driven or transactional? *American Journal on Mental Retardation, 105*, 32–46.

Lambie, R. (2000). *Family systems within educational contexts: Understanding at-risk and special-needs students*. Denver, CO: Love.

Lehmann, J. P., & Baker, C. (1995). Mothers' expectations for their adolescent children: A comparison between families with disabled adolescents and those with non-labeled adolescents. *Education and Training in Mental Retardation and Developmental Disabilities, 30*, 27–40.

Lenhard, W., Breitenbach, E., Ebert, H., Schindelhauer-Deutscher, H. J., Zang, K. D., & Henn, W. (2007). *Intellectual and Developmental Disabilities, 45*, 98–102. doi:10.1352/1934-9556(2007)45[98:AOMTTC]2.0.CO;2

Lessenberry, B. M., & Rehfeldt, R. A. (2004). Evaluating stress levels of parents with disabilities. *Exceptional Children, 70*, 231–244.

Lucyshyn, J. M., Horner, R. H., Dunlap, G., Albin, R. W., & Ben, K. R. (2002). Positive behavior support with families. In J. M. Lucyshyn, G. Dunlap, & R. W. Albin (Eds.), *Families and positive behavior support: Addressing problem behavior in family contexts* (pp. 3–43). Baltimore: Brookes.

Magana, S., Schwartz, S. J., Rubert, M. P., & Szapocznik, J. (2006). Hispanic caregivers of adults with mental retardation: Importance of family functioning. *American Journal on Mental Retardation, 111*, 250–262. doi:10.1352/0895-8017(2006)111[250:HCOAWM]2.0.CO;2

Mahoney, G., & Robenalt, K. (1986). A comparison of conversational patterns between mothers and their Down syndrome and normal infants. *Journal of the Division for Early Childhood, 10*, 172–180.

Mangelsdorf, S. C., & Schoppe-Sullivan, S. J. (2007). Introduction: Emergent family systems. *Infant Behavior & Development, 30*, 60–62. doi:10.1016/j.infbeh.2006.11.006

Meadow-Orlans, K. P., Mertens, D. M., & Sass-Lehrer, M. A. (2003). *Parents and their deaf children: The early years*. Washington, DC: Gallaudet University Press.

Meyer, D. J., & Vadasy, P. F. (2008). *Sibshops: Workshops for siblings of children with special needs*. Baltimore: Brookes.

Mueller, T. G., Singer, G. H., & Draper, L. M. (2008). Reducing parental dissatisfaction with special education in two school districts: Implementing conflict prevention and alternative dispute resolution. *Journal of Educational and Psychological Consultation, 18*, 191–233. doi:10.1080/10474410701864339

Orsmond, G. I., & Seltzer, M. M. (2000). Brothers and sisters of adults with mental retardation: Gendered nature of the sibling relationship. *American Journal on Mental Retardation, 105*, 486–508.

Orsmond, G. I., Seltzer, M. M., Greenberg, J. S., & Krauss, M. W. (2006). Mother–child relationship quality among adolescents and adults with autism. *American Journal on Mental Retardation, 111*, 121–137. doi:10.1352/0895-8017(2006)111[121:MRQAAA]2.0.CO;2

O'Shea, D. J., & O'Shea, L. J. (2001). Why learn about students' families? In D. J. O'Shea, L. J. O'Shea, R. Algozzine, & D. J. Hammittee (Eds.), *Families and teachers of individuals with disabilities: Collaborative orientations and responsive practices* (pp. 5–24). Boston: Allyn & Bacon.

O'Shea, D. J., O'Shea, L. J., Algozzine, R., & Hammitte, D. J. (Eds.). (2001). *Families and teachers of individuals with disabilities: Collaborative orientations and responsive practices*. Boston: Allyn & Bacon.

Parette, H. P., & Petch-Hogan, B. (2000). Approaching families: Facilitating culturally/linguistically diverse family involvement. *Teaching Exceptional Children, 33*(2), 4–10.

Parish, S. L., Rose, R. A., Grinstein-Weiss, M., Richman, E. L., & Andrews, M. E. (2009). Material hardship in U.S. families raising children with disabilities. *Exceptional Children, 75*, 71–92.

Plant, K. M., & Sanders, M. R. (2007). Predictors of care-giver stress in families of preschool-aged children with developmental disabilities. *Journal of Intellectual Disability Research, 51, Part 2*, 109–124. doi:10.1111/j.1365-2788.2006.00829.x

Rossiter, L., & Sharpe, D. (2001). The siblings of individuals with mental retardation: A quantitative integration of the literature. *Journal of Child and Family Studies, 10*, 65–84. doi:10.1023/A:1016629500708

Scorgie, K., & Sobsey, D. (2000). Transformational outcomes associated with parenting children who have disabilities. *Mental Retardation, 38,* 195–206. doi:10.1352/0047-6765(2000)038 <0195:TOAWPC>2.0.CO;2

Silverman, A. (2005). No overalls for Sophie! KJZZ, The National Public Radio Affiliate in Phoenix, AZ.

Singer, G. H. S. (2002). Suggestion for a pragmatic program of research on families and disability. *The Journal of Special Education, 36,* 148–154. doi:10.1177/00224669020360030501

Singer, G. H. S. (2006). Meta-analysis of comparative studies of depression in mothers of children with and without developmental disabilities. *American Journal on Mental Retardation, 111,* 155–169. doi:10.1352/0895-8017(2006)111 [155:MOCSOD]2.0.CO;2

Singer, G. H. S., Goldberg-Hamblin, S. E., Peckham-Hardin, K. D., Barry, L., & Santarelli, G. E. (2002). Toward a synthesis of family support practices and positive behavior support. In J. M. Lucyshyn, G. Dunlap, & R. W. Albin (Eds.), *Families and positive behavior support: Addressing problem behavior in family contexts* (pp. 155–183). Baltimore: Brookes.

Skinner, D., Bailey, D. B., Correa, V., & Rodriguez, P. (1999). Narrating self and disability: Latino mothers' construction of identities vis-à-vis their child with special needs. *Exceptional Children, 65,* 481–495.

Slonims, V., & McConachie, H. (2006). Analysis of mother–infant interaction in infants with Down syndrome and typically developing infants. *American Journal on Mental Retardation, 111,* 273–289. doi:10.1352/0895-8017(2006)111 [273:AOMIII]2.0.CO;2

Smith, L. E., Greenberg, J. S., Seltzer, M. M., & Hong, J. (2008). Symptoms and behavior problems of adolescents and adults with autism: Effects of mother–child relationship quality, warmth, and praise. *American Journal on Mental Retardation, 113,* 387–402. doi: 10.1352/ 2008.113:387-402

Stoneman, Z., & Gavidia-Payne, S. (2006). Marital adjustment in families of young children with disabilities: Associations with daily hassles and problem-focused coping. *American Journal on Mental Retardation, 111,* 1–14. doi:10.1352/ 0895-8017(2006)111 [1:MAIFOY]2.0.CO;2

Taylor, N. E., Wall, S. M., Liebow, H., Sabatino, C. A., Timberlake, E. M., & Farber, M. Z. (2005). Mother and soldier: Raising a child with a disability in a low-income military family. *Exceptional Children, 72,* 83–99.

Technical Assistance Alliance for Parent Centers. (2009). About the Alliance. Retrieved from http://www.taalliance.org/about/index.asp

Turnbull, A., & Turnbull, R. (2006). Fostering family–professional partnerships. In M. E. Snell & F. Brown (Eds.), *Instruction of students with severe disabilities* (6th ed.). Upper Saddle River, NJ: Merrill/Pearson.

Turnbull, A., Turnbull, R., Erwin, E., & Soodak, L. (2006). *Families, professionals, and exceptionality: Positive outcomes through partnerships and trust.* Upper Saddle River, NJ: Merrill/Pearson.

Warger, C. (2003–2004). *Five homework strategies for teaching students with disabilities.* ERIC Clearinghouse on Disabilities and Gifted Education. Retrieved from http://www .ericdigests.org/2002-1/homework.html

Zuniga, M. E. (1992). Families with no roots. In E. W. Lynch & M. J. Hanson (Eds.), *Developing cross-cultural competence* (2nd ed., pp. 151–179). Baltimore: Brookes.

CHAPTER 5

AAMR Ad Hoc Committee on Terminology and Classification. (2010). *Mental retardation: Definition, classification, and systems of supports* (11th ed.). Washington, DC: American Association on Mental Retardation.

Abbeduto, L., Brady, N. & Kover, S. T. (2007). Language development and Fragile X syndrome: Profiles, syndrome-specificity, and within-syndrome differences. *Mental Retardation and Development Disabilities Research Reviews, 13,* 36–46. doi:10.1002/mrdd.20142

Abbeduto, L., Keller-Bell, Y., Richmond, E. K., & Murphy, M. M. (2006). Research on language development and mental retardation: History, theories, findings, and future directions. *International Review of Research in Mental Retardation, 32,* 1–39. doi:10.1016/S0074-7750(06)32001-0

Abbeduto, L., Murphy, M. M., Cawthon, S. W., Richmond, E. K., Weissman, M. D., Karadottir, S., et al. (2003). Receptive language skills of adolescents and young adults with Down or Fragile X syndrome. *American Journal on Mental Retardation, 108,* 149–160.

Abbeduto, L., Murphy, M. M., Richmond, E. K., Amman, A., Beth, P., Weissman, M. D., et al. (2006). Collaboration in referential communication: Comparison of youth with Down syndrome or Fragile X syndrome. *American Journal on Mental Retardation, 111,* 170–183. doi:10.1352/0895-8017(2006)111 [170:CIRCCO]2.0.CO:2

Ager, A. K. (1990). *The Life Experiences Checklist.* Windsor, Ontario, Canada: NFER-Nelson.

Agran, M., Fodor-Davis, J., Moore, S., & Deer, M. (1989). The application of a self-management program on instruction-following skills. *Journal of the Association for the Severely Handicapped, 14,* 147–154.

Alvarez, H. (2008, January 10). Alzheimer's disease in individuals with Down syndrome. *eMedicine,* Retrieved from http://emedicine.medscape.com/article/1136117-overview

Ashbaugh, J. W. (2002). Down the garden path of self-determination. *Mental Retardation, 40,* 416–417.

Atkins v. State of Virginia, 536 U.S. 304 (2002).

Bailey, D. B., Raspa, M., Holiday, D., Bishop, E., & Olmsted, M. (2009). Functional skills of individuals with Fragile X syndrome: A lifespan cross-sectional analysis. *American Journal of Intellectual and Developmental Disabilities, 114,* 289–303. doi:10.1352/1944-7558-114.4.289-303

Baumeister, A. A. (2006). Mental retardation: Confusing sentiment with science. In H. N. Switsky & S. Greenspan (Eds.), *What is mental retardation? Ideas for an evolving disability in the 21st Century* (rev. ed., pp. 95–126). Washington, DC: American Association on Mental Retardation.

Bebko, J. M., & Luhaorg, H. (1998). The development of strategy use and metacognitive processing in mental retardation: Some sources of difficulty. In J. A. Burack, R. M. Hodapp, & E. Zigler (Eds.), *Handbook of mental retardation and development* (pp. 382–407). New York: Cambridge University Press.

Beck, S., Wojdyla, D., Say, L., Betran, A. P., Merialdi, M., Requejo, J. H. & Van Look, P. F. A. (2010). The worldwide incidence of preterm birth: A systematic review of maternal mortality and morbidity. *Bulletin of the World Health Organization, 88,* 31–38. doi:10.2471/BLT.08 .062554

Beirne-Smith, M., Patton, J., & Kim, S. (2006). *Mental retardation: An introduction to intellectual disability* (7th ed.). Upper Saddle River, NJ: Merrill/Person.

Belser, R. C., & Sudhalter, V. (2001). Conversational characteristics of children with fragile X syndrome: Repetitive speech. *American Journal on Mental Retardation, 106,* 28–38.

Brown, R. I., & Brown, I. (2005). The application of quality of life. *Journal of Intellectual Disability Research, 49,* 718–727. doi:10.1111/i.1365-2788.2005.00740.x

Bush, A., & Beail, N. (2004). Risk factors for dementia in people with Down syndrome: Issues in assessment and diagnosis. *American Journal on Mental Retardation, 109,* 83–97.

Caballo, C., Crespo, M., Jenaro, C., Verdugo, M. A., & Martinez, J. L. (2005). Factor structure of the Schalock and Keith Quality of Life Questionnaire (QOL-Q): Validation on Mexican and Spanish samples. *Journal of Intellectual Disability Research, 49,* 773–776. doi:10.1111/j.1365-2788.2005.00750.x

Campbell, F. A., Ramey, C. T., Pungello, E., Sparling, J., & Miller-Johnson, S. (2002). Early childhood education: Young adult outcomes from the Abecedarian Project. *Applied Developmental Science, 6,* 42–57. doi:10.1207/S1532480 XADS0601_05

Carr, J. (1994). Annotation: Long term outcome for people with Down's syndrome. *Journal of Child Psychology and Psychiatry, 35,* 425–439. doi:10.1111/j.1469-7610.1994.tb01732.x

Carter, E. W., Hughes, C., Guth, C. B., & Copeland, S. R. (2005). Factors influencing social interaction among high school students with intellectual disabilities and their general education peers. *American Journal on Mental Retardation, 110,* 366–377. doi:10.1352/ 0895-8017(2005)110[366:FISIAH]2.0.CO;2

Chapman, D. A., Scott, K. G., & Mason, C. A. (2002). Early risk factors for mental retardation: Role of maternal age and maternal education. *American Journal on Mental Retardation, 107,* 46–59.

Collodi, C. (1930). *Pinocchio: The adventures of a puppet* (M. A. Murray, Trans.). New York: A. L. Burt Co. (Original work published 1883)

Conners, F. A. (2003). Phonological working memory difficulty and related interventions. In J. A. Rondal & S. Buckley (Eds.), *Speech and language intervention in Down syndrome* (pp. 31–48). London: Colin Whurr.

Council for Exceptional Children. (2003). *What every special educator must know: Ethics, standards, and guidelines for special educators* (5th ed.). Arlington, VA: Author.

Cummins, R. A. (2005a). Instruments for assessing quality of life. In J. Hogg & A. Langa (Eds.), *Assessing adults with intellectual disabilities: A service provider's guide* (pp. 119–137). Malden, MA: Blackwell.

Cummins, R. A. (2005b). Issues in the systematic assessment of quality of life. In J. Hogg & A. Langa (Eds.), *Assessing adults with intellectual disabilities: a service provider's guide* (pp. 9–22). Malden, MA: Blackwell.

Davis, P. K., & Cuvo, A. J. (1997). Environmental approaches to mental retardation. In D. M. Baer & E. M. Pinkerston (Eds.), *Environment and behavior* (pp. 231–242). Boulder, CO: Westview Press.

Davis, S. (1997). *The Human Genome Project: Examining the Arc's concerns regarding the Human Genome Project's ethical, legal, and social implications.* Presentation at the DOE Human Genome Program Contractor-Grantee Workshop VI. Retrieved from www.ornl.gov/hgmis/resource/arc.html

Delquadri, J. C., Greenwood, C. R., Stretton, K., & Hall, R. V. (1983). The peer tutoring spelling game: A classroom procedure for increasing opportunity to respond and spelling performance. *Education and Treatment of Children, 6*, 225–239.

Dienst, J. (2007, January 25). *Woman cleared of murder*. New York: WNBC.com

Dimitropoulos, A., Feurer, I. D., Butler, M. G., & Thompson, T. (2001). Emergence of compulsive behavior and tantrums in children with Prader-Willi syndrome. *American Journal on Mental Retardation, 106*, 39–51.

Drew, C. J., & Hardman, M. L. (2007). *Intellectual disabilities across the life span* (9th ed.). Upper Saddle River, NJ: Pearson.

Dykens, E. (2001). Introduction to special issue. *American Journal on Mental Retardation, 106*, 1–3.

Dykens, E. M., Hodapp, R. M., & Finucane, B. M. (2000). *Genetics and mental retardation syndromes: A new look at behavior and interventions*. Baltimore: Brookes.

Elliott, A. (Director.) (2005). *The collector of Bedford Street* [Documentary short]. New York: Welcome Change Productions. (Available from New Day Films, 190 Route 17M, P.O. Box 1084, Harriman, NY 10926; www.Newday.com).

Evenhuis, H. M. (1990). The natural history of dementia in Down's syndrome. *Archives of Neurology, 47*, 263–267.

Everson, J. M., & Trowbridge, M. H. (2011). Preparing students with low-incidence disabilities for community living opportunities. In J. M. Kauffman & D. P. Hallahan (Eds.). *The handbook of special education*. New York: Routledge.

Fidler, D. J., Hepburn, S. L., Most, D. E., Philofsky, A., & Rogers, S. J. (2007). Emotional responsivity in young children with Williams syndrome. *American Journal on Mental Retardation, 112*, 194–206. doi:10.1352/0895-8017(2007)112 [194:ERIYCW]2.0.CO;2

Fidler, D. J., Hodapp, R. M., & Dykens, E. M. (2002). Behavioral phenotypes and special education: Parent report of educational issues for children with Down syndrome, Prader-Willi syndrome, and Williams syndrome. *The Journal of Special Education, 36*, 80–88. doi:10.1177/00224669020360020301

Fraser, J., & Mitchell, A. (1876). Kalmuc idiocy: Report of a case with autopsy, with notes on sixty-two cases. *Journal of Mental Science, 22*, 161–179.

Glidden, L. M. (2006). An update on the label and definitional asynchrony: The missing *mental* and *retardation* in mental retardation. In H. N. Switsky & S. Greenspan (Eds.), *What is mental retardation? Ideas for an evolving disability in the 21st century* (rev. ed., pp. 39–49). Washington, DC: American Association on Mental Retardation.

Greenspan, S. (2004). Why Pinocchio was victimized: Factors contributing to social failure in people with mental retardation. *International Review of Research in Mental Retardation, 28*, 121–144. doi:10:10.1016/S0074-7750(04)28004-1

Greenspan, S. (2006a). Functional concepts in mental retardation: Finding the natural essence of an artificial category. *Exceptionality, 14*, 205–224. doi:10.1207/s1532703ex1404_3

Greenspan, S. (2006b). Mental retardation in the real world: Why the AAMR definition is not there yet. In H. N. Switsky & S. Greenspan (Eds.), *What is mental retardation? Ideas for an evolving disability in the 21st century* (rev. ed.,

pp. 165–183). Washington, DC: American Association on Mental Retardation.

Greenspan, S. (2009). Foolish action in adults with intellectual disabilities: The forgotten problem of risk-unawareness. In L. Glidden (Ed.), *International review of research in mental retardation* (Vol. 36, pp. 147–194). New York: Elsevier. doi:10.1016/s0074-7750(08)00005-0

Greenspan, S., Loughlin, G., & Black, R. S. (2001). Credulity and gullibility in people with developmental disorders: A framework for future research. *International Review of Research in Mental Retardation, 24*, 101–135. doi:10.1016/S0074-7750(01)80007-0

Greenspan, S., & Switsky, H. N. (2006). Lessons from the *Atkins* decision for the next AAMR manual. In H. N. Switsky & S. Greenspan (Eds.), *What is mental retardation? Ideas for an evolving disability in the 21st century* (rev. ed., pp. 283–302). Washington, DC: American Association on Mental Retardation.

Greenwood, C. R. (1991). Classwide peer tutoring: Longitudinal effects on the reading, language, and mathematics achievement of at-risk students. *Reading & Writing Quarterly, 7*, 105–123.

Hagerman, R. J. (2001). Fragile X syndrome. In S. B. Cassidy & J. E. Allanson (Eds.), *Management of genetic syndromes* (pp. 165–183). New York: Wiley-Liss.

Haldeman-Englert, C. (2008, February). Williams syndrome. *Medline Plus*, Retrieved from http://www.nlm.nih.gov/medlineplus/ency/article/001116.htm

Hardman, M. L., & Clark, C. (2006). Promoting friendship through Best Buddies: A national survey of college program participants. *Mental Retardation, 44*, 56–63. doi:10.1352/0047-6765(2006)44[56:PFTBBA]2.0CO;2

Harrison, P. L., & Boney, T. L. (2002). Best practices in the assessment of adaptive behavior. In A. Thomas & J. Grimes (Eds.), *Best practices in school psychology IV* (pp. 1167–1179). Washington, DC: National Association of School Psychologists.

Hatton, D. D., Wheeler, A. C., Skinner, M. L., Bailey, D. B., Sullivan, K. M., Roberts, J. E., et al. (2003). Adaptive behavior in children with Fragile X syndrome. *American Journal on Mental Retardation, 108*, 373–390.

Hodapp, R. M., & Dykens, E. M. (2007). Behavioral effects of genetic mental retardation disorders. In J. W. Jacobson, J. A. Mullick, & J. Rojahn (Eds.), *Handbook of intellectual and developmental disabilities* (pp. 115–131). New York: Springer.

Hodapp, R. M., & Fidler, D. J. (1999). Special education and genetics: Connections for the 21st century. *Journal of Special Education, 33*, 130–137. doi:10.1177/002246699903300301

Hof, P. R., Bouras, C., Perl, D. P., Sparks, L., Mehta, N., & Morrison, J. H. (1995). Age-related distribution of neuropathologic changes in the cerebral cortex of patients with Down's syndrome. *Archives of Neurology, 52*, 379–391.

Human Genome Project. (2008, September 16). *Human Genome Project Information: Ethical, legal, and social issues*. Retrieved from http://www.ornl.gov/sci/techresources/Human_Genome/elsi/elsi.shtml

Human Genome Project. (2009a, June 11). *Human Genome Project Information: Gene Therapy*. Retrieved from http://www.ornl.gov/sci/techresources/Human_Genome/medicine/genetherapy.shtml#3

Human Genome Project. (2009b, August 12). *Human Genome Project Information*. Retrieved from http://www.ornl.gov/sci/techresources/Human_Genome/home.shtml

Inge, K. J., & Moon, M. S. (2011). Preparing students with low incidence disabilities to work in the community. In J. M. Kauffman & D. P. Hallahan (Eds.). *The handbook of special education*. New York, Routledge.

Institute of Education Sciences, National Center for Special Education Research. (2009, July). *Facts from NLTS2: Secondary Experiences and Academic Performance of students with mental retardation*. Retrieved from http://nces.ed.gov/pubSearch/pubsinfo.asp?pubid=NCSER20093020

John, A. E., Rowe, M. L., & Mervis, C. B. (2009). Referential communication skills of children with Williams syndrome: Understanding when messages are not adequate. *American Journal of Intellectual and Developmental Disabilities, 114*, 85–99. doi:10.1352/2009.114.85-99

Kaiser, A. P., & Grim, J. C. (2006). Teaching functional communication skills. In M. E. Snell & F. Brown (Eds.), *Instruction of students with severe disabilities* (6th ed., pp. 447–488). Upper Saddle River, NJ: Pearson.

Kasari, C., Freeman, S. F. N., & Hughes, M. A. (2001). Emotion recognition by children with Down syndrome. *American Journal on Mental Retardation, 106*, 59–72.

Kaufman, S. Z. (1999). *Retarded isn't stupid, mom!* (rev. ed.). Baltimore: Brookes.

Kazdin, A. E. (n.d.). Helping parents with intellectual disabilities raise their children: A review of *The health and wellness program: A parenting curriculum for families at risk*. Retrieved from http://psycnet.apa.org/critiques/52/14/16.html

Kemp, C., & Carter, M. (2006). Active and passive task related behavior, direction following and the inclusion of children with disabilities. *Education and Training in Developmental Disabilities, 41*, 14–27.

Kresnak, J. (2001, February 27). Some question cops' methods when grilling youth. *Detroit Free Press*.

Kuna, J. (2001). The Human Genome Project and eugenics: Identifying the impact on individuals with mental retardation. *Mental Retardation, 39*, 158–160. doi:10.1352/0047-6765(2001)039<0158:THGPAE>2.0.CO;2

Lancioni, G. E., O'Reilly, M. F., Seedhouse, P., Furniss, F., & Cunha, B. (2000). Promoting independent task performance by persons with severe developmental disabilities through a new computer-aided system. *Behavior Modification, 24*, 700–718. doi:10.1177/0145445500245005

Lenhoff, H. M., Wang, P. P., Greenberg, F., & Bellugi, U. (1997). Williams syndrome and the brain. *Scientific American, 277*(6), 68–73. doi:10.1177/scientificamerican1297-68

MacMillan, D. L., Gresham, F. M., Bocian, K. M., & Lambros, K. M. (1998). Current plight of borderline students: Where do they belong? *Education and Training in Mental Retardation and Developmental Disabilities, 33*, 83–94.

Mank, D., Cioffi, A., & Yovanoff, P. (2003). Supported employment outcomes across a decade: Is there evidence of improvement in the quality of implementation? *Mental Retardation, 41*, 188–197.

Martin, J. E., Rusch, F. R., James, V. L., Decker, P. J., & Trtol, K. A. (1982). The use of picture cues to establish self-control in the preparation of complex meals by mentally retarded adults. *Applied Research in Mental Retardation, 3*, 105–119. doi:10.1016/0270-3092(82)90001-7

McDonnell, J. J. (2011). Instructional contexts for students with significant cognitive disabilities. In J. M. Kauffman & D. P. Hallahan (Eds.), *Handbook of special education*. New York: Routledge.

McDonnell, J. J., Hardman, M. L., & McDonnell, A. P. (2003). *An introduction to persons with moderate and severe disabilities* (2nd ed.). Boston: Allyn & Bacon.

Mechling, L. C., Gast, D. L., & Fields, E. A. (2008). Evaluation of a portable DVD player and system of least prompts to self-prompt cooking task completion by young adults with moderate intellectual disabilities. *The Journal of Special Education, 42*, 179–190. doi:10.1177/0022466907313348

Medline Plus. (2007, October 19). Inborn errors of metabolism. Retrieved from http://www.nlm.nih.gov/medlineplus/ency/article/002438.htm

Mervis, C. B., & Becerra, A. M. (2007). Language and communicative development in Williams syndrome. *Mental Retardation and Developmental Disabilities Research Reviews, 13*, 3–15. doi:10.1002/mrdd.20140

Mervis, C. B., Klein-Tasman, B. P., & Mastin, M. E. (2001). Adaptive behavior of 4- through 8-year-old children with Williams syndrome. *American Journal on Mental Retardation, 106*, 82–93.

Meyer, G. A., & Batshaw, M. L. (2002). Fragile X syndrome. In M. L. Batshaw (Ed.), *Children with disabilities* (5th ed.). Baltimore: Brookes.

Moldavsky, M., Lev, D., & Lerman-Sagie, T. (2001). Behavioral phenotypes of genetic syndromes: A reference guide for psychiatrists. *Journal of the American Academy of Child and Adolescent Psychiatry, 40*, 749–761. doi:10.1097/00004583-200107000-00009

Morse, T. E., & Schuster, J. W. (2000). Teaching elementary students with moderate intellectual disabilities how to shop for groceries. *Exceptional Children, 66*, 273–288.

Mortweet, S. L., Utley, C. A., Walker D., Dowson, H. L., Delquadri, J. C., Reddy, S. S., & Ledford, D. (1999). Classwide peer tutoring: Teaching students with mild mental retardation in inclusive classrooms. *Exceptional Children, 65*, 524–536.

MR/DD Data Brief. (2001, April). *Characteristics of service use by persons with MR/DD living in their own homes or with family members: NHIS-D analysis*. Minneapolis, MN: University of Minnesota Research and Training Center on Community Living, Institute on Community Integration.

National Institute of Neurological Disorders and Stroke. (2008, October 29). *NINDS Microcephaly Information Page*. Retrieved from http://www.ninds.nih.gov/disorders/microcephaly/microcephaly.htm

Patton, J. P., & Keyes, D. W. (2006). Death penalty issues following *Atkins. Exceptionality, 14*, 237–255. doi:10.1207/s15327035ex1404_5

Percy, M., Lewkis, S. Z., & Brown, I. (2007). Introduction to genetics and development. In I. Brown & M. Percy. (Eds.), *A comprehensive guide to intellectual disabilities* (pp. 87–108). Baltimore: Brookes.

Perske, R. (2008). False confessions from 53 persons with intellectual disabilities: The list keeps growing. *Intellectual and Developmental Disabilities, 46*, 468–479. doi:10.1352/2008.46:468-479

Polloway, E. A., Patton, J. R., & Nelson, M. A. (2011). Intellectual and developmental disabilities. In J. M. Kauffman & D. P. Hallahan (Eds.), *Handbook of special education*. New York: Routledge.

Polloway, E. A., Smith, J. D., & Antoine, K. (2010). Biological causes. In M. Beirne-Smith, J. R. Patton, & S. H. Kim (Eds.), *Intellectual disabilities* (8th ed.). Upper Saddle River, NJ: Pearson.

Ramey, C. T., & Campbell, F. A. (1984). Preventive education for high-risk children: Cognitive consequences of the Carolina Abecedarian Project. *American Journal of Mental Deficiency, 88*, 515–523.

Ramey, C. T., & Campbell, F. A. (1987). The Carolina Abecedarian Project: An educational experiment concerning human malleability. In J. J. Gallagher & C. T. Ramey (Eds.), *The malleability of children* (pp. 127–139). Baltimore: Brookes.

Roberts, J. E., Price, J., & Malkin, C. (2007). Language and communication development in Down syndrome. *Mental Retardation and Developmental Disabilities Research Reviews, 13*, 26–35. doi:10.1002/mrdd.20136

Romer, L. T., Richardson, M., Aigbe, E., & Porter, A. (2003). Down the garden path of self-determination: A response to Ashbaugh. *Mental Retardation, 41* 290–298. doi:10.1352/0047-6765(2003)41<292:DTGPOS>2.0.CO;2

Rueda, R., Monzo, L., Shapiro, J., Gomez, J., & Blacher, J. (2005). Cultural models of transition: Latina mothers of young adults with developmental disabilities. *Exceptional Children, 71*, 401–414.

Rusch, F. R. (2008). *Beyond high school: Preparing adolescents for tomorrow's challenges*. Upper Saddle River, NJ: Pearson.

Sands, D., & Wehmeyer, M. (2005). Teaching goal setting and decision making to students with developmental disabilities. In M. L. Wehmeyer, M. Agran, M. L. Wehmeyer, & M. Agran (Eds.), *Mental retardation and intellectual disabilities: Teaching students using innovative and research-based strategies* (pp. 273–296). Auckland, New Zealand: Pearson.

Schalock, R. L., Brown, I., Brown, R. I., Cummins, R., Felce, D., Matikka, L., et al. (2002). Quality of life: Its conceptualization, measurement, and application. A consensus document. *Mental Retardation, 40*, 457–470. doi:10.1352/0047-6765(2002)040<0457:CMAAOQ>2.0.CO;2

Schalock, R. L., & Keith, K. D. (1993). *Quality of life questionnaire*. Worthington, OH: IDA Publishing.

Schweinhart, L. J., Montie, J., Xiang, Z., Barnett, W. S., Belfield, C. R., & Nores, M. (2005). *Lifetime effects: The High/Scope Perry Preschool study through age 40.* (Monographs of the High/Scope Educational Research Foundation, 14). Ypsilanti, MI: High/Scope Press.

Scott, N., Lakin, C., & Larson, S. A. (2008). The 40th anniversary of deinstitutionalization in the United States: Decreasing state institutionalization populations, 1967–2007. *Intellectual and Developmental Disabilities, 46*, 402–405. doi:10.1352/2008.46:402-405

Sigafoos, J., O'Reilly, Cannella, H., Upadyaya, M., Edrisinha, C., Lancioni, G. E., & Young, D. (2005). Computer-presented video prompting for teaching microwave oven use to three adults with developmental disabilities. *Journal of Behavioral Education, 14*, 189–201. doi:10.1007/s10864-005-6297-2

Sitlington, P. L., Neubert, D. A., & Clark, G. M. (2010). *Transition education services for students with disabilities*. Upper Saddle River, NJ: Pearson.

Snell, M. E., Luckasson, R., et al. (2009). Characteristics and needs of people with intellectual disability who have higher IQs. *Intellectual and Developmental Disabilities, 47*, 220–233. doi:10.1352/1934-9556-47.3.220

Sparrow, S. S., Chicchetti, D. V., & Balla, D. A. (2005). *Vineland Adaptive Behavior scales* (2nd ed.). Circle Pines, MN: American Guidance Service.

Spinath, F. M., Harlaar, N., Ronald, A., & Plomin, R. (2004). Substantial genetic influence on mild mental impairment in early childhood. *American Journal on Mental Retardation, 109*, 34–43.

Spinelli, C. G. (2006). *Classroom assessment for students in special and general education* (2nd ed.). Upper Saddle River, NJ: Merrill/Pearson.

Stancliffe, R. J., Abery, B. H., & Smith, J. (2000). Personal control and the ecology of community living settings: Beyond living unit size and type. *American Journal on Mental Retardation, 105*, 431–454.

Switsky, H. N. (2006). The importance of cognitive-motivational variables in understanding the outcome performance of persons with mental retardation: A personal view from the early twenty-first century. *International Review of Research in Mental Retardation, 31*, 1–29. doi:10.1016/S0074-7750(05)31001-9

Tansley, G. H., Burgess, B. L., Bryan, M. T., Su, Y., Hirsch-Reinshagen, V., Pearce, J., et al. (2007). The cholesterol transporter ABCG1 modulates the subcellular distribution and proteolytic processing of β-amyloid precursor protein. *Journal of Lipid Research, 48*, 1022–1034. doi:10.1194/jlr.M600542-JLR200

Tarleton, B., & Ward, L. (2007). "Parenting with support": The views and experiences of parents with intellectual disabilities. *Journal of Policy and Practice in Intellectual Disabilities, 4*, 194–202. doi:10.1111/j.1741-1130.2007.00118.x

Taylor, H. G., Klein, N., Minich, N. M., & Hack, M. (2000). Middle-school-age outcomes in children with very low birthweight. *Child Development, 71*, 1495–1511. doi:10.1111/1467-8624.00242

Taylor, R. L., Richards, S. B., & Brady, M. P. (2005). *Mental retardation: Historical perspectives, current practices, and future directions*. Boston: Allyn & Bacon.

Thompson, J. R., Bradley, V. J., Buntinx, W. H. E., Schalock, R. L., Shogren, K. A., Snell, M. E., et al. (2009). Conceptualizing supports and the support needs of people with intellectual disability. *Intellectual and Developmental Disabilities, 47*, 135–146. doi:10.1352/1934-9556-47.2.135

Tymchuk, A. J. (2006). *The health and wellness program: A parenting curriculum for families at risk*. Baltimore: Brookes.

Urv, T. K., Zigman, W. B., & Silverman, W. (2008). Maladaptive behaviors related to dementia status in adults with Down syndrome. *American Journal of Mental Retardation, 113*, 73–86. doi:10.1352/0895-8017(2008)113[73:MBRTDS]2.0.CO;2

Van der Molen, M. J., Van Luit, J. E. H., Jongmans, M. J., & Van der Molen, M. W. (2007). Verbal working memory in children with mild intellectual disabilities. *Journal of Intellectual Disability Research, 51*, 162–169. doi:10.1111/j.1365-2788.2006.00863.x

Venn, J. J. (2007). *Assessing students with special needs*. Upper Saddle River, NJ: Prentice Hall.

Wade, C., Llewellyn, G., & Matthews, J. (2008). Review of parent training interventions for parents with intellectual disability. *Journal of Applied Research in Intellectual Disabilities, 21*, 351–366. doi:10.1111/j.1468-3148.2008.00449.x

Wechsler, D. (2003). *Wechsler intelligence scale for children* (4th ed.). San Antonio, TX: Psychological Corporation.

Wehman, P., Moon, M. S., Everson, J. M., Wood, W., & Barcus, J. M. (1988). *Transition from school to work: New challenges for youth with severe disabilities*. Baltimore: Brookes.

Wehmeyer, M. L., Garner, N., Yeager, D., Lawrence, M., & Davis, A. K. (2006). Infusing self-determination into 18–21 services for students with intellectual or developmental disabilities: A multi-stage, multiple component model. *Education and Training in Developmental Disabilities, 41,* 1–13.

Wehymeyer, M. L., & Mithaug, D. E. (2006). Self-determination, causal agency, and mental retardation. *International Review of Research in Mental Retardation, 31,* 31–71. doi:10.1016/S0074-7750(05)31002-0

Wehmeyer, M. L., Palmer, S. B., Agran, M., Mithaug, D. E., & Martin, J. E. (2000). Promoting causal agency: The self-determined learning model of instruction. *Exceptional Children, 66,* 439–453.

Whitaker, S. (2008). The stability of IQ in people with low intellectual ability: An analysis of the literature. *Intellectual and Developmental Disabilities, 46,* 120–128. doi:10.1352/0047-6765(2008)46[120:TSOIIP]2.0.CO;2

Winsor, J., & Butterworth, J. (2008). Participation in integrated employment and community-based nonwork services for individuals supported by state disability agencies. *Intellectual and Developmental Disabilities, 46,* 166–168. doi:10.1352/0047-6765(2008)46[166:PIIEAC]2.0.CO;2

Wolfensberger, W. (2002). Social role valorization and, or versus, "empowerment." *Mental Retardation 40,* 252–258.

Ysseldyke, J., & Olsen, K. (1999). Putting alternate assessments into practice: What to measure and possible sources of data. *Exceptional Children, 65,* 175–185.

CHAPTER 6

Aarnoudse-Moens, C. S. H., Weisglas-Kuperus, N., van Goudoever, J. B., & Oosterlaan, J. (2009). Meta-analysis of neurobehavioral outcomes in very preterm and/or very low birth weight children. *Pediatrics, 124,* 717–728. doi:10.1542/peds.2008-2816

Adams, G. L., & Engelmann, S. (1996). *Research on direct instruction: 25 years beyond DISTAR.* Seattle: Educational Achievement Systems.

Al-Yagon, M. (2007). Socioemotional and behavioral adjustment among school-age children with learning disabilities: The moderating role of maternal personal resources. *The Journal of Special Education, 40,* 205–217. doi:10.1177/00224669070400040201

Allsopp, D. H., Kyger, M. M., & Lovin, L. (2008). Mathematics dynamic assessment: Informal assessment that responds to the needs of struggling learners in mathematics. *Teaching Exceptional Children, 40,* 6–16.

Bear, G. G., Kortering, L. J., & Braziel, P. (2006). School completers and noncompleters with learning disabilities: Similarities in academic achievement and perceptions of self and teachers. *Remedial and Special Education, 27,* 293–300. doi:10.1177/0741932506070050401

Beichtman, J. H., Hood, J., & Inglis, A. (1992). Familial transmission of speech and language impairment: A preliminary investigation. *Canadian Journal of Psychiatry, 37,* 151–156.

Bender, W. N., Rosenkrans, C. B., & Crane, M. K. (1999). Stress, depression, and suicide among students with learning disabilities: Assessing the risk. *Learning Disability Quarterly, 22,* 143–156. doi:10.2307/1511272

Berkeley, S., Bender, W. N., Peaster, L. G., & Saunders, L. (2009). Implementation of response to intervention: A snapshot of progress. *Journal of Learning Disabilities, 42,* 85–95. doi:10.1177/0022219408326214

Blachman, B. (2001). Phonological awareness. In D. P. Pearson (Ed.), *Handbook of reading research* (pp. 483–502). Mahwah, NJ: Erlbaum.

Boada, R., & Pennington, B. F. (2006). Deficient implicit phonological representations in children with dyslexia. *Journal of Experimental Child Psychology, 95,* 153–193. doi:10.1016/j.jecp.2006.04.003

Bryan, T., Burstein, K., & Ergul, C. (2004). The social-emotional side of learning disabilities: A science-based presentation of the state of the art. *Learning Disability Quarterly, 27,* 45–51. doi:10.2307/1593631

Bryan, T. H., Donahue, M., Pearl, R., & Sturm, C. (1981). Learning disabled children's conversational skills—The "TV Talk Show." *Learning Disability Quarterly, 4,* 250–260. doi:10.2307/1510946

Bryan, T. H., & Sullivan-Burstein, K. (1998). Teacher-selected strategies for improving homework completion. *Remedial and Special Education, 19,* 263–275. doi:10.1177/074193259801900502

Butler, D. L. (1998). Metacognition and learning disabilities. In B. Y. L. Wong (Ed.), *Learning about learning disabilities* (2nd ed., pp. 277–307). San Diego, CA: Academic Press.

Case, L. P., Harris, K. R., & Graham, S. (1992). Improving the mathematical problem-solving skills of students with learning disabilities. *The Journal of Special Education, 26,* 1–19.

Clarizio, H. F., & Phillips, S. E. (1986). Sex bias in the diagnosis of learning disabled students. *Psychology in the Schools, 23,* 44–52. doi:10.1002/1520-6807(198601)23:1<44::AID-PITS2310230108>3.0.CO;2-L

Cobb, R. B., & Alwell, M. (2009). Transition planning/coordinating interventions for youth with disabilities: A systematic review. *Career Development for Exceptional Individuals, 32,* 70–81. doi:10.1177/0885728809336655

Cook, B. G., McDuffie, K. A., Oshita, L., & Cook, S. C. (2011). Co-teaching for students with disabilities: A critical analysis of the empirical literature. In J. M. Kauffman & D. P. Hallahan (Eds.), *Handbook of special education.* New York: NY: Routledge.

Cortiella, C. (2009). *The state of learning disabilities.* New York: National Center for Learning Disabilities. Retrieved from www.ld.org/stateofld

Council for Exceptional Children. (2003). *What every special educator must know: Ethics, standards, and guidelines for special educators* (5th ed.). Arlington, VA: Author.

Daniel, S. S., Walsh, A. K., Goldston, D. B., Arnold, E. M., Reboussin, B. A., & Wood, F. B. (2006). Suicidality, school dropout, and reading problems among adolescents. *Journal of Learning Disabilities, 39,* 507–514. doi:10.1177/00222194060390060301

DeFries, J. C., Gillis, J. J., & Wadsworth, S. J. (1993). Genes and genders: A twin study of reading disability. In A. M. Galaburda (Ed.), *Dyslexia and development: Neurobiological aspects of extra-ordinary brains* (pp. 187–294). Cambridge, MA: Harvard University Press.

Deno, S. L. (1985). Curriculum-based measurement: The emerging alternative. *Exceptional Children, 52,* 219–232.

Deshler, D. D., Schumaker, J. B., Lenz, B. K., Bulgren, J. A., Hock, M. F., Knight, J., et al. (2001). Ensuring content-area learning by secondary students with learning disabilities. *Learning Disabilities Research & Practice, 16,* 96–108. doi:10.1111/0938-8982.00011

DeThorne, L. S., Hart, S. A., Petrill, S. A., Deater-Deckard, K., Thompson, L. A., Schatschneider, C., et al. (2006). Children's history of speech-language difficulties: Genetic influences and associations with reading-related measures. *Journal of Speech, Language, and Hearing Research, 49,* 1280–1293. doi:10.1044/1092-4388(2006/092)

Ellis, A. (2001). *Research on educational innovations* (3rd ed.). Larchmont, NY: Eye On Education.

Ellis, A. K., & Fouts, J. T. (1997). *Research on educational interventions.* Larchmont, NY: Eye on Education.

Ellis, E. S., & Howard, P. W. (2007, Spring). Graphic organizers: Power tools for teaching students with learning disabilities. *Current Practice Alerts, 13.* Retrieved from http://www.teachingld.org/pdf/alert13.pdf

Engelmann, S., & Bruner, E. C. (1969). DISTAR reading I: An instructional system. Chicago: SRA.

Epstein, M. H., Munk, D. D., Bursuck, W. D., Polloway, E. A., & Jayanthi, M. (1998). Strategies for improving home–school communication about homework for students with disabilities. *Journal of Special Education, 33,* 166–176. doi:10.1177/002246699903300304

Fisher, S. E., & Francks, C. (2006). Genes, cognition and dyslexia: Learning to read the genome. *Trends in Cognitive Sciences, 10,* 250–257. doi:10.1016/j.tics.2006.04.003

Foegen, A., Jiban, C., & Deno, S. (2007). Progress monitoring measures in mathematics: A review of the literature. *The Journal of Special Education, 41,* 121–139. doi:10.1177/00224669070410020101

Forness, S. R., & Kavale, K. A. (2002). Impact of ADHD on school systems. In P. Jensen & J. R. Cooper (Eds.), *NIH consensus conference on ADHD.* Bethesda, MD: National Institutes of Health.

Frostig, M., & Horne, D. (1964). *The Frostig program for the development of visual perception: Teacher's guide.* Chicago: Follett.

Fuchs, D., & Fuchs, L. S. (2005). Peer-assisted learning strategies: Promoting word recognition, fluency, and reading comprehension in young children. *The Journal of Special Education, 39,* 34–44. doi:10.1177/00224669050390010401

Fuchs, D., Fuchs, L., & Burish, P. (2000). Peer-assisted learning strategies: An evidence-based practice to promote reading achievement. *Learning Disabilities Research & Practice, 15*(2), 85–91. doi:10.1207/SLDRP1502_4

Fuchs, D., Fuchs, L. S., McMaster, K. L., Yen, L., & Svenson, E. (2004). Nonresponders: How to find them? How to help them? What do they mean for special education? *Teaching Exceptional Children, 37,* 72–77.

Fuchs, D., Mock, D., Morgan, P. L., & Young, C. L. (2003). Responsiveness-to-intervention: Definitions, evidence, and implications for the learning disabilities construct. *Learning Disabilities Research & Practice, 18,* 157–171. doi:10.1111/1540-5826.00072

Fuchs, L. S. (2003). Assessing intervention responsiveness: Conceptual and technical issues. *Learning Disabilities Research & Practice, 18,* 172–186. doi:10.1111/1540-5826.00073

Fuchs, L. S., Deno, S. L., & Mirkin, P. K. (1984). The effects of frequent curriculum-based measurement and evaluation of pedagogy, student achievement and student awareness of learning. *American Educational Research Journal, 24,* 449–460.

Fuchs, L. S., Powell, S. R., Seethaler, P. M., Cirino, P. T., Fletcher, J. M., Fuchs, D., & Hamlett, C. L. (2011). The development of arithmetic and word-problem skill among students with mathematics disability. In J. M. Kauffman & D. P. Hallahan (Eds.), *Handbook of special education.* New York: Routledge.

Gabrieli, J. D. E. (2009). Dyslexia: A new synergy between education and neuroscience. *Science, 325,* 280–283. doi:10.1126/Science.1171999

Gajria, M., Jitendra, S., Sood, S., & Sacks, G. (2007). Improving comprehension of expository text in students with LD: A research synthesis. *Journal of Learning Disabilities, 40,* 210–225. doi:10.1177/00222194070400030301

Galaburda, A. M., LoTurco, J., Ramus, F., Fitch, R. H., & Rosen, G. D. (2006). *Nature Neuroscience, 9,* 1213–1217.

Gerber, P. J. (2009). Transition and adults with learning disabilities. In J. M. Taymans (Ed.), *Learning to achieve: A review of the research literature on serving adults with learning disabilities* (pp. 211–228). Washington, DC: National Institute for Literacy.

Gerber, P. J., Ginsberg, R., & Reiff, H. B. (1992). Identifying alterable patterns in employment success for highly successful adults with learning disabilities. *Journal of Learning Disabilities, 25,* 475–487. doi:10.1177/002221949202500802

Gersten, R., Chard, D. J., Jayanthi, M., Baker, S. K., Morphy, P., & Flojo, J. (2009). Mathematics instruction for students with learning disabilities: A meta-analysis of instructional components. *Review of Educational Research, 79,* 1202–1242. doi:10.3102/0034654309334431

Good, R. H., Simmons, D. C., & Kame'enui, E. J. (2001). The importance and decision-making utility of a continuum of fluency-based indicators of foundational reading skills for third-grade high-stakes outcomes. *Scientific Studies of Reading, 5,* 257–288. doi:10.1207/S1532799XSSR0503_4

Graham, S., & Harris, K. R. (2003). Students with learning disabilities and the process of writing: A meta-analysis of SRSD studies. In H. L. Swanson, K. R. Harris, & S. Graham (Eds.), *Handbook of learning disabilities* (pp. 323–344). New York: Guilford.

Graham, S., & Harris, K. R. (2011). Writing and students with disabilities. In J. M. Kauffman & D. P. Hallahan (Eds.), *Handbook of special education.* New York: Routledge.

Guttorm, T. K., Leppanen, P. H. T., Poikkeus, A.-M., Eklund, K. M., Lyytinen, P., & Lyytinen, H. (2005). Brain event-related potentials (ERPs) measured at birth predict later language development in children with and without risk for dyslexia. *Cortex, 41,* 291–303. doi:10.1016/S0010-9452(08)70267-3

Hallahan, D. P. (1975). Comparative research studies on the psychological characteristics of learning disabled children. In W. M. Cruickshank & D. P. Hallahan (Eds.), *Perceptual and learning disabilities in children. Vol. 1: Psychoeducational practices* (pp. 29–60). Syracuse, NY: Syracuse University Press.

Hallahan, D. P. (1992). Some thoughts on why the prevalence of learning disabilities has increased. *Journal of Learning Disabilities, 25,* 523–528. doi:10.1177/002221949202500806

Hallahan, D. P., & Cruickshank, W. M. (1973). *Psychoeducational foundations of learning disabilities.* Upper Saddle River, NJ: Pearson.

Hallahan, D. P., Kneedler, R. D., & Lloyd, J. W. (1983). Cognitive behavior modification techniques for learning disabled children: Self-instruction and self-monitoring. In J. D. McKinney & L. Feagans (Eds.), *Current topics in learning disabilities* (Vol. 1, pp. 207–244). New York: Ablex.

Hallahan, D. P., Lloyd, J. W., Kauffman, J. M., Weiss, M. P., & Martinez, E. A. (2005). *Learning disabilities: Foundations, characteristics, and effective teaching.* Boston: Allyn & Bacon.

Hallahan, D. P., & Mercer, C. D. (2002). Learning disabilities: Historical perspectives. In R. Bradley, L. Danielson, & D. P. Hallahan (Eds.), *Identification of learning disabilities: Research to practice* (pp. 1–67). Mahwah, NJ: Erlbaum.

Hallgren, B. (1950). Specific dyslexia (congenital word blindness: A clinical and genetic study). *Acta Psychiatrica et Neurologica, 65,* 1–279.

Hammill, D. D. (1990). On defining learning disabilities: An emerging consensus. *Journal of Learning Disabilities, 23,* 74–84. doi:10.1177/002221949002300201

Hammill, D. D., Leigh, J. E., McNutt, G., & Larsen, S. C. (1981). A new definition of learning disabilities. *Learning Disability Quarterly, 4,* 336–342.

Harris, K. R., Graham, S., & Mason, L. H. (2003). Self-regulated strategy development in the classroom: Part of a balanced approach to writing instruction for students with disabilities. *Focus on Exceptional Children, 35*(7), 1–16.

Hayworth, C. M. A., Kovas, Y., Harlaar, N., Hayiou-Thomas, M. E., Petrill, S. A., Dale, P. S., & Plomin, R. (2009). Generalist genes and learning disabilities: A multivariate genetic analysis of low performance in reading, mathematics, language and general cognitive ability in a sample of 8000 12-year-old twins. *The Journal of Child Psychology and Psychiatry, 50,* 1318–1325. doi:10.1111/j.1469-7610.2009.02114.x

Helmuth, L. (2001). Dyslexia: Same brains, different languages. *Science, 291,* 2064.

Hoeft, F., Ueno, T., Reiss, A. L., Meyler, A., Whitfield-Gabrieli, S., Glover, S., & Gabrieli, J. D. E. (2007). Prediction of children's reading skills using behavioral, functional, and structural neuroimaging measures. *Behavioral Neuroscience, 121,* 602–613. doi:10.1037/0735-7044.121.3.602

Hosp, M. K., Hosp, J. L., & Howell, K. W. (2007). *The abcs of CBM: A practical guide to curriculum-based measurement.* New York: Guilford.

Kauffman, J. M., & Hallahan, D. P. (2005). *Special education: What it is and why we need it.* Boston: Allyn & Bacon.

Kavale, K. A. (1988). The long-term consequences of learning disabilities. In M. C. Wang, M. C. Reynolds, & H. J. Walberg (Eds.), *Handbook of special education: Research and practice. Vol. 2: Mildly handicapped conditions.* New York: Pergamon Press.

Kephart, N. C. (1971). *The slow learner in the classroom* (2nd ed.). Columbus, OH: Merrill/Pearson.

Kirk, S. A. (1963). Behavioral diagnosis and remediation of learning disabilities. In *Proceedings of the Conference on Exploration into the Problems of the Perceptually Handicapped Child, First Annual Meeting, Vol. 1.* Chicago: April 6, 1963.

Kirk, S. A., & Kirk, W. D. (1971). *Psycholinguistic learning disabilities: Diagnosis and remediation.* Urbana: University of Illinois Press.

Kourea, L., Cartledge, G., & Musti-Rao, S. (2007). Improving the reading skills of urban elementary students through total class peer tutoring. *Remedial and Special Education, 28,* 95–107. doi:10.1177/07419325070280020801

Kunsch, C. A., Jitendra, A. K., & Sood, S. (2007). The effects of peer-mediated instruction in mathematics for students with learning problems: A research synthesis. *Learning*

Disabilities Research & Practice, 22, 1–12. doi:10.1111/j.1540-5826.2007.00226.x

Lasley II, T. J., Matczynski, T. J., & Rowley, J. B. (2002). *Instructional models: Strategies for teaching in a diverse society.* Belmont, CA: Wadsworth/Thomas Learning.

Leinhardt, G., Seewald, A., & Zigmond, N. (1982). Sex and race differences in learning disabilities classrooms. *Journal of Educational Psychology, 74,* 835–845. doi:10.1037/0022-0663.74.6.835

Levin, J. R. (1993). Mnemonic strategies and classroom learning: A twenty year report card. *Elementary School Journal, 27,* 301–321.

Lewis, B. A. (1992). Pedigree analysis of children with phonology disorders. *Journal of Learning Disabilities, 25,* 586–597. doi:10.1177/002221949202500908

Lewis, B. A., & Thompson, L. A. (1992). A study of development of speech and language disorders in twins. *Journal of Speech and Hearing Research, 35,* 1086–1094.

Lindstrom, L. E., & Benz, M. R. (2002). Phases of career development: Case studies of young women with learning disabilities. *Exceptional Children, 69,* 67–83.

Maag, J. W., & Reid, R. (2006). Depression among students with learning disabilities: Assessing the risk. *Journal of Learning Disabilities, 39,* 3–10. doi:10.1177/00222194060390010201

MacMillan, D. L., Gresham, F. M., & Bocian, K. M. (1998). Discrepancy between definitions of learning disabilities and school practices: An empirical investigation. *Journal of Learning Disabilities, 31,* 314–326. doi:10.1177/002221949803100401

MacMillan, D. L., & Siperstein, G. N. (2002). Learning disabilities as operationally defined by schools. In R. Bradley, L. Danielson, & D. P. Hallahan (Eds.), *Identification of learning disabilities: Research to practice* (pp. 287–333). Mahwah, NJ: Erlbaum.

Madaus, J. W., & Banerjee, M. (2011). Transition to postsecondary education. In J. M. Kauffman & D. P. Hallahan (Eds.), *Handbook of special education.* New York: NY: Routledge.

Maheady, L., Harper, G. F., & Mallette, B. (2003, Spring). Classwide peer tutoring. *Current Practice Alerts.* Retrieved from http://www.teachingld.org/pdf/PeerTutoring_rev1.pdf

Margalit, M. (2006). Loneliness, the salutogenic paradigm and learning disabilities: Current research, future directions, and interventional implications. *Thalamus, 24,* 38–48.

Mastropieri, M. A., & Scruggs, T. E. (1998). Constructing more meaningful relationships in the classroom: Mnemonic research into practice. *Learning Disabilities Research & Practice, 13,* 138–145.

Mastropieri, M. A., Scruggs, T. E., & Whedon, T. B. (1997). Using mnemonic strategies to teach information about U.S. Presidents: A classroom-based investigation. *Learning Disability Quarterly, 20,* 13–21. doi:10.2307/1511089

McGrady, H. J., Lerner, J. W., & Boscardin, M. L. (2001). The educational lives of students with learning disabilities. In P. Rodis, A. Garrod, & M. L. Boscardin (Eds.), *Learning disabilities and life stories* (pp. 177–193). Boston: Allyn & Bacon.

McGrath, L. M., Smith, S. D., & Pennington, B. F. (2006). Breakthroughs in the search for dyslexia candidate genes. *Trends in Molecular Medicine, 12,* 333–341. doi:10.1016/j.molmed.2006.05.007

McMaster, K., & Espin, C. (2007). Technical features of curriculum-based measurement in writing: A review of the literature. *The Journal of Special Education, 41,* 68–84. doi:10.1177/00224669070410020301

Mercer, C. D., Mercer, A. R., & Pullen, P. C. (2011). *Teaching students with learning problems.* Boston: Pearson.

Molfese, D. M. (2000). Predicting dyslexia at 8 years of age using neonatal brain responses. *Brain and Language, 72,* 238–245. doi:10.1006/brln.2000.2287

Morgan, P. L., & Fuchs, D. (2007). Is there a bidirectional relationship between children's reading skills and reading motivation? *Exceptional Children, 73,* 165–183.

Murawski, W. W., & Swanson, H. L. (2001). A meta-analysis of co-teaching research: Where are the data? *Remedial and Special Education, 22,* 258–267. doi:10.1177/074193250102200501

National Institute of Child Health and Human Development. (2000). *Report of the National Reading Panel: Teaching children to read: An evidence-based assessment of the scientific research literature on reading and its implications for instruction.* Washington, DC: National Institute of Child Health and Human Development. Retrieved from http://www.nichd.nih.gov/publications/nrp/upload/smallbook_pdf.pdf

National Joint Committee on Learning Disabilities. (1989, September 18). *Modifications to the NJCLD definition of learning disabilities.* Letter from NJCLD to member organizations. Washington, DC: Author.

National Joint Committee on Learning Disabilities. (2006). *Learning disabilities and young children: Identification and intervention.* Retrieved from http://www.ldonline.org/article/11511

O'Connor, R. E., & Sanchez, V. (2011). Responsiveness to intervention models for reducing reading difficulties and identifying learning disability. In J. M. Kauffman & D. P. Hallahan (Eds.), *Handbook of special education.* New York: Routledge.

Olson, R., Wise, B., Conners, F., Rack, J., & Fulker, D. (1989). Specific deficits in component reading and language skills: Genetic and environmental influences. *Journal of Learning Disabilities, 22,* 339–348. doi:10.1177/002221948902200604

Paulesu, E., Demonet, J. F., Fazio, F., McCrory, E., Chanonine, V., Brunswick, N., et al. (2001). Dyslexia: Cultural diversity and biological unity. *Science, 291,* 2165–2167. doi:10.1126/science.1057179

Pelkey, L. (2001). In the LD bubble. In P. Rodis, A. Garrod, & M. L. Boscardin (Eds.), *Learning disabilities and life stories* (pp. 17–28). Boston: Allyn & Bacon.

Pennington, B. F. (1990). Annotation: The genetics of dyslexia. *Journal of Child Psychology and Child Psychiatry, 31,* 193–201. doi:10.1111/j.1469-7610.1990.tb01561.x

Petrill, S. A., Deater-Deckard, K., Thompson, L. A., DeThorne, L. S., & Schatschneider, C. (2006). Reading skills in early readers: Genetic and shared environmental influences. *Journal of Learning Disabilities, 39,* 48–55. doi:10.1177/00222194060390010501

Plomin, R., & Kovas, Y. (2005). Generalist genes and learning disabilities. *Psychological Bulletin, 131,* 592–617. doi:10.1037/0033-2909.131.4.592

Pullen, P. C. (2002, October 1). Expert connection: Phonological awareness. *TeachingLD.org.* Retrieved from http://TeachingLD.org/expert_connection/phonological.html

Queen, O. (2001). Blake Academy and the Green Arrow. In P. Rodis, A. Garrod, & M. L. Boscardin (Eds.), *Learning disabilities and life stories* (pp. 3–16). Boston: Allyn & Bacon.

Raskind, M. H., Goldberg, R. J., Higgins, E. L., & Herman, K. L. (1999). Patterns of change and predictors of success in individuals with learning disabilities: Results from a twenty-year longitudinal study. *Learning Disabilities Research & Practice, 14,* 35–49. doi:10.1207/sldrp1401_4

Raskind, W. H. (2001). Current understanding of the genetic basis of reading and spelling disability. *Learning Disability Quarterly, 24,* 141–157. doi:10.2307/1511240

Reiff, H. B., Gerber, P. J., & Ginsberg, R. (1997). *Exceeding expectations: Successful adults with learning disabilities.* Austin, TX: Pro-Ed.

Reynolds, C. A., Hewitt, J. K., Erickson, M. T., Silberg, J. L., Rutter, M., Simonoff, E., et al. (1996). The genetics of children's oral reading performance. *Journal of Child Psychology and Psychiatry, 37,* 425–434. doi:10.1111/j.1469-7610.1996.tb01423.x

Rojewski, J. W., & Gregg, N. (2011). Career choice patterns of work-bound youth with high incidence disabilities. In J. M. Kauffman & D. P. Hallahan (Eds.), *Handbook of special education.* New York: Routledge.

Rooney, K. J. (1998). *Independent strategies for efficient study.* Richmond, VA: Educational Enterprises.

Rourke, B. P. (1995). *Syndrome of nonverbal learning disabilities: Neurodevelopmental manifestations.* New York: Guilford Press.

Rumsey, J. M., Horwitz, B., Donohue, B. C., Nace, K. L., Maisog, J. M., & Andreason, P. (1999). A functional lesion in developmental dyslexia: Left angular gyral blood flow predicts severity. *Brain and Language, 70,* 187–204. doi:10.1006/brln.1999.2158

Scanlon, D., Patton, J. R., & Raskind, M. (2011). Transition to daily living for persons with high incidence disabilities. In J. M. Kauffman & D. P. Hallahan (Eds.), *Handbook of special education.* New York: Routledge.

Schulte-Korne, G., Deimel, W., Muller, K., Gutenbrunner, C., & Remschmidt, H. (1996). Familial aggregation of spelling disability. *Journal of Child Psychology and Psychiatry, 37,* 817–822. doi:10.1111/j.1469-7610.1996.tb01477.x

Schulte-Korne, G., Ziegler, A., Deimel, W., Schumaker, J., Plume, E., Bachmann, C., et al. (2006). Interrelationship and familiality of dyslexia related quantitative measures. *Annals of Human Genetics, 71,* 160–175. doi:10.1111/j.1469-1809.2006.00312.x

Scruggs, T., Mastropieri, M., & Marshak, L. (2011). Science and social studies. In J. M. Kauffman & D. P. Hallahan (Eds.), *Handbook of special education.* New York: Routledge.

Semrud-Clikeman, M., Walkowiak, J., Wilkinson, A., & Minne, E. P. (2010). Direct and indirect measures of social perception, behavior, and emotional functioning in children with Asperger's disorder, nonverbal learning disability, or ADHD. *Journal of Abnormal Child Psychology, 38,* 509–519. doi:10.1007/s10802-009-9380-7

Sexton, M., Harris, K. R., & Graham, S. (1998). Self-regulated strategy development and the writing process: Effects on essay writing and attributions. *Exceptional Children, 64,* 295–311.

Shalev, R. S. (2004). Developmental dyscalculia. *Journal of Child Neurology, 19,* 765–771.

Shaywitz, S. E., Shaywitz, B. A., Fletcher, J. M., & Escobar, M. D. (1990). Prevalence of reading disability in boys and girls: Results of the Connecticut Longitudinal Study. *Journal of the American Medical Association, 264,* 998–1002.

Smith, S. D. (2007). Genes, language development, and language disorders. *Mental Retardation and Developmental Disabilities Research Reviews, 13,* 96–105. doi:10.1002/mrdd.20135

Spekman, N. J., Goldberg, R. J., & Herman, K. L. (1992). Learning disabled children grow up: A search for factors related to success in the young adult years. *Learning Disabilities Research & Practice, 7,* 161–170.

Swanson, H. L., & Jerman, O. (2006). Math disabilities: A selective meta-analysis of the literature. *Review of Educational Research, 76,* 249–274. doi:10.3102/00346543076002249

Swanson, H. L., Kehler, P, & Jerman, O. (2010). Working memory, strategy knowledge, and strategy instruction in children with reading disabilities. *Journal of Learning Disabilities, 43,* 24–47. doi:10.1177/0022219409338743

Swanson, H. L., Zheng, X., & Jerman, O. (2009). Working memory, short-term memory, and reading disabilities: A selective meta-analysis of the literature. *Journal of Learning Disabilities, 42,* 260–287. doi:10.1177/0022219409331958

Tarver, S. G. (1999, Summer). Direct instruction. *Current Practice Alerts, 2.* Retrieved from http://www.teachingld.org/pdf/Alert2.pdf

Troia, G. A. (2004, Summer). A focus on phonological awareness acquisition and intervention. *Current Practice Alerts, 10.* Retrieved from http://www.dldcec.org/pdf/alert10.pdf

Vaughn, S., & Fuchs, L. S. (2003). Redefining learning disabilities as inadequate response to instruction: The promise and potential problems. *Learning Disabilities Research & Practice, 18,* 137–146. doi:10.1111/1540-5826.00070

Willows, D. M. (1998). Visual processes in learning disabilities. In H. L. Swanson (Ed.), *Handbook of assessment of learning disabilities: Theory, research, and practice* (pp. 147–175). Austin, TX: Pro-Ed.

Worling, D. E., Humphries, T., & Tannock, R. (1999). Spatial and emotional aspects of language inferencing in nonverbal learning disabilities. *Brain and Language, 70,* 220–239. doi:10.1006/brln.1999.2156

Wright, V. R., Chau, M., & Aratani, Y. (2010). *Who are America's poor children: The official story.* The National Center for Children in Poverty. Retrieved from http://www.nccp.org/publications/pdf/text_912.pdf

Zigmond, N., & Kloo, A. (2011). General and special education are (and should be) different. In J. M. Kauffman & D. P. Hallahan (Eds.), *Handbook of special education.* New York: Routledge.

CHAPTER 7

Allsopp, D. H. (1999). Using modeling, manipulatives, and mnemonics with eighth-grade math students. *Teaching Exceptional Children, 32,* 74–81.

American Psychiatric Association. (2000). *Diagnostic and statistical manual of mental disorders* (4th ed., rev.). Washington, DC: Author.

American Psychiatric Association. (2010, May 20). American Psychiatric Association: DSM-V Development: 314.0x Attention Deficit/Hyperactivity Disorder: Proposed Revision. Retrieved from http://www.dsm5.org/ProposedRevisions/Pages/proposedrevision.aspx?rid=383#

Arnsten, A. F. T., Berridge, C. W., & McCracken, J. T. (2009). The neurological basis of attention-deficit/hyperactivity disorder. *Primary Psychiatry, 16,* 47–54.

Barbaresi, W. J., Katusic, S. K., Colligan, R. C., Weaver, A. L., Leibson, C. L., & Jacobsen, S. J. (2006). Long-term stimulant medication treatment of ADHD: Results from a population based study. *Journal of Developmental and Behavioral Pediatrics, 27,* 1–10. doi:10.1079/00004703-200602000-00001

Barkley, R. A. (1994). Impaired delayed responding: A unified theory of attention-deficit hyperactivity disorder. In D. K. Routh (ED.) *Disruptive behavior disorder in childhood* (pp.11–58). New York: Plenum Press.

Barkley, R. A. (1997). Behavioral inhibition, sustained attention, and executive functions: Constructing a unifying theory of ADHD. *Psychological Bulletin, 121,* 65–94. doi:10.1037/0033-2909.121 .1.65

Barkley, R. A. (2000a). *A new look at ADHD: Inhibition, time, and self-control* [video manual]. Baltimore: Guilford Press.

Barkley, R. A. (2000b). *Taking charge of ADHD: The complete, authoritative guide for parents* (rev. ed.). New York: Guilford Press.

Barkley, R. A. (2006a). Associated cognitive, developmental, and health problems. In R. A. Barkley (Ed.), *Attention-deficit hyperactivity disorder: A handbook for diagnosis and treatment* (3rd ed., pp. 122–183). New York: Guilford Press.

Barkley, R. A. (2006b). Etiologies. In R. A. Barkley (Ed.), *Attention-deficit hyperactivity disorder: A handbook for diagnosis and treatment* (3rd ed., pp. 219–247). New York: Guilford Press.

Barkley, R. A. (2006c). History. In R. A. Barkley (Ed.), *Attention-deficit hyperactivity disorder: A handbook for diagnosis and treatment* (3rd ed., pp. 3–75). New York: Guilford Press.

Barkley, R. A. (2006d). Primary symptoms, diagnostic criteria, prevalence, and gender differences. In R. A. Barkley (Ed.), *Attention-deficit hyperactivity disorder: A handbook for diagnosis and treatment* (3rd ed., pp. 76–121). New York: Guilford Press.

Barkley, R. A. (2006e). A theory of ADHD. In R. A. Barkley (Ed.), *Attention-deficit hyperactivity disorder: A handbook for diagnosis and treatment* (3rd ed., pp. 297–334). New York: Guilford Press.

Barkley, R. A. (2008). Commentary on excerpt of Chrichton's chapter, On attention and its diseases. *Journal of Attention Disorders, 12,* 205–206. doi:10.1177/1087054708320391

Barkley, R. A., & Edwards, G. (2006). Diagnostic interview, behavior rating scales, and medical examination. In R. A. Barkley (Ed.), *Attention-deficit hyperactivity disorder: A handbook for diagnosis and treatment* (3rd ed., pp. 337–368). New York: Guilford Press.

Barkley, R. A., & Murphy, K. R. (1998). *Attention-deficit hyperactivity disorder: A clinical workbook* (2nd ed.). New York: Guilford Press.

Barkley, R. A., & Murphy, K. R. (2007). Comorbid psychiatric disorders in adults with ADHD. *The ADHD Report, 15*(2), 1–7. doi: 10.1521/adhd .2007.15.2.1

Barkley, R. A. Murphy, K., & Kwanik, D. (1996). Psychological adjustment and adaptive impairments in young adults with ADHD. *Journal of Attention Disorders, 1,* 41–54. doi:10.1177/108705479600100104

Bateman, B., Warner, J. O., Hutchinson, E., Dean, T., Rowlandson, P., Gant, C., et al. (2004). The effects of a double blind, placebo controlled, artificial food colourings and benzoate preservative challenge on hyperactivity in a general population sample of preschool children. *Archives of Disease in Childhood, 89,* 506–511. doi: 10.1136/adc.2003.031435

Bauermeister, J. J., Canino, G., Polanczyk, G., & Rohde, L. A. (2010). ADHD across cultures: Is there evidence for a bidimensional organization of symptoms? *Journal of Clinical & Adolescent Psychology, 39,* 362–372. doi:10.1080/ 15374411003691743

Bender, S., Banaschewski, T., & Resch, F. (2010). Attention-deficit [hyperactivity] disorder. In R. A. Carlstedt (Ed.). *Handbook of integrative clinical psychology, psychiatry, and behavioral medicine* (pp. 379–410). New York: Springer.

Biederman, J., Faraone, S. V., Mick, E., Spencer, T., Wilens, T., Kiely, K., et al. (1995). High risk for attention deficit hyperactivity disorder among children of parents with childhood onset of the disorder: A pilot study. *American Journal of Psychiatry, 152,* 431–435.

Biederman, J., Petty, C. R., Monuteaux, M. C., Fried, R., Byrne, D., Mirto, T., & Faraone, S. V. (2010). Adult psychiatric outcomes of girls with attention deficit hyperactivity disorder: 11-year follow-up in a longitudinal case-control study. *American Journal of Psychiatry, 167,* 409–417. doi:10.1176/appi.ajp.2009.09050736

Birch, H. G. (1964). *Brain damage in children: The biological and social aspects.* Baltimore: Williams & Wilkins.

Campbell, S. B., & von Stauffenberg, C. (2009). Delay and inhibition as early predictors of ADHD symptoms in third grade. *Journal of Abnormal Child Psychology, 37,* 1–15. doi:10.1007/ s10802-008-9270-4

Castle, L., Aubert, R. E., Verbrugge, R. R., Khalid, M., & Epstein, R. S. (2007). Trends in medication treatment for ADHD. *Journal of Attention Disorders, 10,* 335–342. doi:10.1177/ 1087054707299597

Cepeda, N. J., Cepeda, M. L., & Kramer, A. F. (2000). Task switching and attention deficit hyperactivity disorder, *Journal of Abnormal Child Psychology, 28,* 213–226. doi:10.1023/A:1005143419092

Cherkasova, M. V., & Hechtman, L. (2009). Neuroimaging in attention-deficit hyperactivity disorder: Beyond the frontostriatal circuitry. *The Canadian Journal of Psychiatry, 54,* 651–664.

Chrichton, A. (1798). *An inquiry into the nature and origins of mental derangement* (Vols. I and II). London: Strand Publishers.

Christakis, D. A., Zimmerman, F. J., DiGiuseppe, D. L., & McCarty, C. A. (2004). Early television exposure and subsequent attentional problems in children. *Pediatrics, 113,* 708–713. doi:10.1542/peds.113.4.708

Cobb, B., Sample, P. L., Alwell, M., & Johns, N. R. (2006). Cognitive-behavioral interventions, dropout, and youth with disabilities. *Remedial and Special Education, 27,* 259–275. doi:10.1177/07419325060270050201

Conners, C. K. (2007). *Conners-3.* Boston: Pearson.

Conners, C. K., Erhardt, D., & Sparrow, E. (2000). *Conners' Adult ADHD Rating Scales.* North Tonawanda, NY: Multi-Health Systems.

Connor, D. F. (2006). Simulants. In R. A. Barkley (Ed.), *Attention-deficit hyperactivity disorder: A handbook for diagnosis and treatment* (3rd ed., pp. 608–647). New York: Guilford Press.

Cooper, P. (1999). ADHD and effective learning: Principles and practical approaches. In P. Cooper & K. Bilton (Eds.), *ADHD: Research, practice and opinion* (pp. 138–157). London: Whurr.

Corkum, P., Andreou, P., Schachar, R., Tannock, R., & Cunningham, C. (2007). The telephone interview probe: A novel measure of treatment response in children with attention deficit hyperactivity disorder. *Educational and Psychological Measurement, 67,* 169–185. doi:10.1177/0013164406292038

Cox, D. J., Merkel, R. L., Kovatchev, B., & Seward, R. (2000). Effect of stimulant medication on driving performance of young adults with attention-deficit hyperactivity disorder. *Journal of Nervous and Mental Disease, 188,* 230–234. doi:10.1097/ 00005053-200004000-00006

Cruickshank, W. M., Bentzen, F. A., Ratzeburg, F. H., & Tannhauser, M. T. (1961). *A teaching method of brain-injured and hyperactive children.* Syracuse, NY: Syracuse University Press.

Cruickshank, W. M., Bice, H. V., & Wallen, N. E. (1957). *Perception and cerebral palsy.* Syracuse, NY: Syracuse University Press.

Danckaerts, M., Sonuga-Barke, E. J. S., Banaschewski, T., Buitelaar, J., Dopfner, M., Hollis, C., & Coghill, D. (2010). The quality of life of children with attention deficit/ hyperactivity disorder: A systematic review. *European Child and Adolescent Psychiatry, 19,* 83–105. doi:10.1007/s00787-009-0046-3

Davies, S., & Witte, R. (2000). Self-management and peer-monitoring within a group contingency to decrease uncontrolled verbalizations of children with attention-deficit/hyperactivity disorder. *Psychology in the Schools, 37,* 135–147. doi:10.1002/(SICI)1520-6807(200003)37:2[lt]135: :AID-PITS5[gt]3.0.C0;2-U

DeRamirez, R. D., & Shapiro, E. S. (2005). Effects of student ethnicity on judgments of ADHD symptoms among Hispanic and White teachers. *School Psychology Quarterly, 20,* 268–287.

DuPaul, G. J., Arbolino, L. A., & Booster, G. D. (2009). Cognitive-behavioral interventions for attention-deficit/hyperactivity disorder. In M. J. Mayer, J. E. Lochman, & F. M. Gresham (Eds.), *Cognitive-behavioral interventions for emotional and behavioral disorders: School-based practices* (pp. 295–327). New York: Guilford Press.

DuPaul, G. J., Barkley, R. A., & Connor, D. F. (1998). Stimulants. In R. A. Barkley (Ed.), *Attention-deficit hyperactivity disorder: A handbook for diagnosis and treatment* (pp. 510–551). New York: Guilford Press.

DuPaul, G. J., & Eckert, T. L. (1997). The effects of school-based interventions for attention deficit hyperactivity disorder: A meta-analysis, *School Psychology Review, 26,* 5–27.

DuPaul, G. J., Eckert, T. L., & McGoey, K. E. (1997). Interventions for students with attention-deficit/hyperactivity disorder: One size does not fit all. *School Psychology Review, 26,* 369–381.

DuPaul, G. J., & Ervin, R. A. (1996). Functional assessment of behaviors related to attention-deficit hyperactivity disorder: Linking assessment to intervention design. *Behavior Therapy, 27,* 601–622. doi:10.1016/S0005-7894(96)80046-3

DuPaul, G. J., Power, D. T. J., Anastopolos, A. D., & Reid, R. (1998). *ADHD Rating Scale-IV: Checklists, norms, and clinical interpretations.* New York: Guilford Press.

Ervin, R. A., DuPaul, G. J., Kern, L., & Friman, P. C. (1998). Classroom-based functional and adjunctive assessments: Proactive approaches to intervention selection for adolescents with attention deficit hyperactivity disorder. *Journal of Applied Behavior Analysis, 31,* 65–78. doi:10.1901/jaba.1998.31-65

Evans, S. W., Pelham, W. E., Smith, B. H., Bukstein, O., Gnagy, E. M., Greiner, A. R., et al. (2001). Dose-response effects of methylphenidate on ecologically valid measures of academic performance and classroom behavior in adolescents with ADHD. *Experimental and Clinical Pharmacology, 9,* 163–175.

Fabiano, G. A., Pelham, W. E., Gnagy, E. M., Burrows-MacLean, L., Coles, E. K., Chacko. A., et al. (2007). The single and combined effects of multiple intensities of behavior modification and methylphenidate for children with attention deficit hyperactivity disorder in a classroom setting. *School Psychology Review, 36,* 195–216.

Faraone, S. V., & Doyle, A. E. (2001). The nature and heritability of attention-deficit/hyperactivity disorder. *Child and Adolescent Psychiatric Clinics of North America, 10,* 299–316.

Feingold, B. (1975). *Why your child is hyperactive.* New York: Random House.

Fischer, M., Barkley, R. A., Smallish, L., & Fletcher, K. (2007). Hyperactive children as young adults: Driving abilities, safe driving behavior, and adverse driving outcomes. *Accident Analysis and Prevention, 39,* 94–105. doi:10.1016/j.aap.2006.06.008

Floet, A. M. W., Scheiner, C., & Grossman, L. (2010). Attention-deficit/hyperactivity disorder. *Pediatrics in Review, 31,* 56–69. doi:10.1542/pir.31-2-56

Forness, S. R., & Kavale, K. A. (2002). Impact of ADHD on school systems. In P. Jensen & J. R. Cooper (Eds.), *Attention deficit hyperactivity disorder: State of the science; Best practices* (pp. 1–20). Kingston, NJ: Civic Research Institute.

Frazier, T. W., Youngstrom, E. A., Glutting, J. J., & Watkins, M. W. (2007). ADHD and achievement: Meta-analysis of the child, adolescent, and adult literatures and a concomitant study with college students. *Journal of Learning Disabilities, 40,* 49–65. doi:10.1177/00222194070400010401

Goldstein, K. (1936). The modification of behavior consequent to cerebral lesions. *Psychiatric Quarterly, 10,* 586–610.

Goldstein, K. (1939). *The organism.* New York: American Book Co.

Goldstein, S., & Kennemer, K. (2009). Neuropsychological aspects of attention-deficit hyperactivity disorder. In C. R. Reynolds & E. Fletcher-Janzen (Eds.). *Handbook of clinical child neuropsychology* (3rd ed., pp. 617–633). New York: Springer.

Hallahan, D. P., & Cottone, E. A. (1997). Attention deficit hyperactivity disorder. In T. E. Scruggs & M. A. Mastropieri (Eds.), *Advances in learning and behavioral disabilities, Vol. 11* (pp. 27–67). Greenwich, CT: JAI Press.

Hallowell, E. M., & Ratey, J. J. (2006). *Delivered from distraction: Getting the most out of life with attention deficit disorder.* New York: Ballentine Books.

Harris, K. R., Friedlander, B. D., Saddler, B., Frizzelle, R., & Graham, S. (2005). Self-monitoring of attention versus self-monitoring of academic performance: Effects among students with ADHD in the general education classroom. *The Journal of Special Education, 39,* 145–156. doi:10.1177/002246699703100108

Hoffmann, H. (1865). Die Geschichte vom Zappel-Philipp [The Story of Fidgety Philip]. In *Der Struuwelpeter* [Shaggy Peter]. Germany: Pestalozzi-Verlag.

Horner, R. H., & Carr, E. G. (1997). Behavioral support for students with severe disabilities: Functional assessment and comprehensive intervention. *The Journal of Special Education, 31,* 1–11.

Kameenui, E. J., & Carnine, D. W. (1998). *Effective teaching strategies that accommodate diverse learners.* Englewood Cliffs, NJ: Pearson.

Katusic, S. K., Barbaresi, W. J., Colligan, R. C., Weaver, A. L., Leibson, C. L., & Jacobsen, S. J. (2005). Psychostimulant treatment and risk for substance abuse among young adults with a history of attention-deficit/hyperactivity disorder: A population-based, birth cohort study. *Journal of Child and Adolescent Psychopharmacology, 15,* 764–776. doi:10.1089/cap.2005.15.764

Kavale, K. A., & Forness, S. R. (1983). Hyperactivity and diet treatment: A meta-analysis of the Feingold hypothesis. *Journal of Learning Disabilities, 16,* 324–330. doi:10.1177/002221948301600604

Kemp, L., Fister, S., & McLaughlin, P. J. (1995). Academic strategies for children with ADD. *Intervention in School and Clinic, 30,* 203–210.

Kohn, A. (1993). *Punished by rewards: The trouble with gold stars, incentive plans, A's, praise, and other bribes.* Boston: Houghton Mifflin.

Kucan, L., & Beck, I. L. (1997). Thinking aloud and reading comprehension research: Inquiry, instruction, and social interaction. *Review of Educational Research, 67,* 271–299.

Landau, S., Milich, R., & Diener, M. B. (1998). Peer relations of children with attention-deficit hyperactivity disorder. *Reading and Writing Quarterly: Overcoming Learning Difficulties, 14,* 83–105.

Lawrence, V., Houghton, S., Tannock, R., Douglas, G., Durkin, K., & Whiting, K. (2002). ADHD outside the laboratory: Boys' executive function performance on tasks in videogame play and on a visit to the zoo. *Journal of Abnormal Child Psychology, 30,* 447–462. doi:10.1023/A:1019812829706

Levy, F., Barr, C., & Sunohara, G. (1998). Directions of aetiologic research on attention deficit hyperactivity disorder. *Australian and New Zealand Journal of Psychiatry, 32,* 97–103. doi:10.3109/00048679809062715

Levy, F., & Hay, D. A. (2001). *Attention, genes, and attention-deficit hyperactivity disorder.* Philadelphia: Psychology Press.

Li, D., Sham, P. C., Owen, M. J., & He, L. (2006). Meta-analysis shows significant association between dopamine system genes and attention deficit hyperactivity disorder (ADHD). *Human Molecular Genetics, 15,* 2276–2284. doi:10.1093/hmg/ddl152

Lloyd, J. W., Hallahan, D. P., Kauffman, J. M., & Keller, C. E. (1998). Academic problems. In R. J. Morris & T. R. Kratochwill (Eds.), *The practice of child therapy* (pp. 167–198). Boston: Allyn & Bacon.

Majewicz-Hefley, A., & Carlson, J. S. (2007). A meta-analysis of combined treatments for children diagnosed with ADHD. *Journal of Attention Disorders, 10,* 239–250. doi:10.1177/1087054706289934

Marshall, R. M., Hynd, G. W., Handwerk, M. J., & Hall, J. (1997). Academic underachievement in ADHD subtypes. *Journal of Learning Disabilities, 30,* 635–642. doi:10.1177/002221949703000607

Meszaros, A., Czobor, P., Balint, S., Komlosi, S., Simon, V., & Bitter, I. (2009). Pharmacotherapy of adult attention deficit hyperactivity disorder (ADHD) a meta-analysis. *International Journal of Neuropsychopharmacology, 12,* 1137–1147.

Mikami, A., Jack, A., & Lerner, M. D. (2009). Attention-deficit/hyperactivity disorder. In J. L. Matson (Ed.), *Social behavior and skills in children* (pp. 159–185). New York: Springer.

Milberger, S., Biederman, J., Faraone, S. V., Guite, J., & Tsuang, M. T. (1997). Pregnancy, delivery and infancy complications and attention deficit hyperactivity disorder: Issues of gene–environment interaction. *Biological Psychiatry, 41,* 65–75. doi:10.1016/0006-3223(95)00653-2

Molina, B. S. G., Flory, K., Hinshaw, S. P., Greiner, A. R., Arnold, L. E., Swanson, J. M., et al. (2007). Delinquent behavior and emerging substance use in the MTA at 36 months: Prevalence, course, and treatment effects. *Journal of the American Academy of Child and Adolescent*

Psychiatry, 46, 1028–1040. doi:10.1097/chi.0b013e3180686d96

Molina, B. S. G., Hinshaw, S. P., Swanson, J. M., Arnold, L. E., Vitiello, B., Jensen, P. S., & MTA Cooperative Group. (2009). MTA at 8 years: Prospective follow-up of children treated for combined-type ADHD in a multisite study. *Journal of the Academy of Child and Adolescent Psychiatry, 48,* 484–500. doi:10.1097/chi.0b013e31819c23d0

MTA Cooperative Group. (1999). A 14-month randomized clinical trial of treatment strategies for attention-deficit/hyperactivity disorder. *Archives of General Psychiatry, 56,* 1073–1086.

National Institutes of Health. (1998). Diagnosis and Treatment of Attention Deficit Hyperactivity Disorder. NIH Consensus Statement Online 1998 Nov 16–18; *16*(2), 1–37. Retrieved September from http://consensus.nih.gov/1998/1998AttentionDeficitHyperactivityDisorder110html.htm

Neuman, R. J., Lobos, E., Reich, W., Henderson, C. A., Sun, L.-W., & Todd, R. D. (2007). Prenatal smoking exposure and dopaminergic genotypes interact to cause a severe ADHD subtype. *Biological Psychiatry, 61,* 1320–1328. doi:10.1016/j.biopsych.2006.08.049

Nigg, J. T. (2006). *What causes ADHD? Understanding what goes wrong and why.* New York: Guilford Press.

Nigg, J. T., Nikolas, M., Knottnerus, G. M., Cavanagh, K., & Friderici, K. (2010). Confirmation and extension of association of blood lead with attention-deficit/hyperactivity disorder (ADHD) and ADHD symptom domains at population-typical exposure levels. *The Journal of Child Psychology and Psychiatry, 51,* 58–65. doi:10.1111/j.1469-7610.2009.02135.x

Nikolas, M. A., & Burt, S. A. (2010). Genetic and environmental influences on ADHD symptom dimensions of inattention and hyperactivity: A meta-analysis. *Journal of Abnormal Psychology, 119,* 1–17. doi:10.1037/a0018010

Palmer, E. D., & Finger, S. (2001). An early description of ADHD (Inattentive Subtype): Dr. Alexander Chrichton and 'mental restlessness' (1798). *Child Psychology and Psychiatry Review, 6,* 66–73. doi:10.1017/S1360641701002507

Pasamanick, B., Lilienfeld, A. M., & Rogers, M. E. (1956). Pregnancy experience and the development of behavior disorders in children. *American Journal of Psychiatry, 112,* 613–617.

Pfiffner, L. J., Barkley, R. A., & DuPaul, G. J. (2006). Treatment of ADHD in school settings. In R. A. Barkley (Ed.), *Attention-deficit hyperactivity disorder: A handbook for diagnosis and treatment* (3rd ed., pp. 122–183). New York: Guilford Press.

Pinel, J. P. J. (2006). *Biopsychology* (5th ed.). Boston: Allyn & Bacon.

Polanczyk, G., Silva de Lima, M., Horta, B. L., Biederman, J., & Rhode, L. A. (2007). The worldwide prevalence of ADHD: A systematic review and metaregression analysis. *American Journal of Psychiatry, 164,* 942–948. doi:10.1176/appi.ajp.164.6.942

Posner, K., Pressman, A. W., & Greenhill, L. L. (2009). ADHD in preschool children. In T. E. Brown (Ed.), *ADHD comorbidities: Handbook for ADHD complications in children and adults* (pp. 37–53). Washington, DC: American Psychiatric Publishing.

Ramsay, J. R. (2010). *Nonmedication treatments for adult ADHD: Evaluating impact on daily functioning and well-being.* Washington, DC: American Psychological Association.

Reid, R., Casat, C. D., Norton, H. J., Anastopoulos, A. D., & Temple, E. P. (2001). Using behavior rating scales for ADHD across ethnic groups: The IOWA Conners. *Journal of Emotional & Behavioral Disorders, 9,* 210–218. doi:10.1177/106342660100900401

Reid, R., & Lienemann, R. O. (2006). Self-regulated strategy development for written expression with students with attention deficit/hyperactivity disorder. *Exceptional Children, 73,* 53–68.

Reid, R., Trout, A. L., & Schartz, M. (2005). Self-regulation interventions for children with attention deficit/hyperactivity disorder. *Exceptional Children, 71,* 361–377.

Richards, T. L., Deffenbacher, J. L., Rosen, L. A., Barkley, R. A., & Rodricks, T. (2007). Driving anger and driving behavior in adults with ADHD. *Journal of Attention Disorders, 10,* 54–64. doi:10.1177/1087054705284244

Rooney, K. J. (1995). Teaching students with attention disorders. *Intervention in School and Clinic, 30,* 221–225.

Rosenshine, B. (1995). Advances in research on instruction. *The Journal of Educational Research, 88,* 262–268.

Rowland, A. S., Umbach, D. M., Catoe, K. E., Stallone, L., Long, S., Rabiner, D., et al. (2001). Studying the epidemiology of attention-deficit hyperactivity disorder: Screening method and pilot results. *Canadian Journal of Psychiatry, 46,* 931–940.

Rucklidge, J., Brown, D., Crawford, S., & Kaplan, B. (2007). Attributional styles and psychosocial functioning of adults with ADHD: Practice issues and gender differences. *Journal of Attention Disorders, 10,* 288–298. doi:10.1177/1087054706289942

Schachar, R., Mota, V. L., Logan, G. D., Tannock, R., & Klim, P. (2000). Confirmation of an inhibitory control deficit in attention-deficit/hyperactivity disorder. *Journal of Abnormal Child Psychology, 28,* 227–235. doi:10.1023/A:1005140103162

Schatz, D. B., & Rostain, A. L. (2007). ADHD with comorbid anxiety: A review of the current literature. *Journal of Attention Disorders, 10,* 141–149. doi:10.1177/1087054706286698

Scheffler, R. M., Brown, T. T., Fulton, B. D., Hinshaw, S. P., Levine, P., & Stone, S. (2009). Positive association between attention-deficit/hyperactivity disorder medication use and academic achievement during elementary school. *Pediatrics, 123,* 1273–1279. doi:10.1542/peds.2008-1597

Semrud-Clikeman, M., Steingard, R. J., Filipek, P., Biederman, J., Bekken, K., & Renshaw, P. F. (2000). Using MRI to examine brain–behavior relationships in males with attention deficit disorder with hyperactivity. *Journal of the American Academy of Child and Adolescent Psychiatry, 39,* 477–484. doi:10.1097/00004583-200004000-00017

Shapiro, E. S., DuPaul, G. J., & Bradley-Klug, K. L. (1998). Self-management as a strategy to improve the classroom behavior of adolescents with ADHD. *Journal of Learning Disabilities, 31,* 545–555. doi:10.1177/002221949803100604

Shaw, P., & Rabin, C. (2009). New insights into attention-deficit/hyperactivity disorder using structural neuroimaging. *Current Psychiatry Reports, 11,* 393–398. doi:10.1007/s11920-009-0059-0

Solanto, M. V. (1998). Neuropsychopharmacological mechanisms of stimulant drug action in attention-deficit hyperactivity disorder: A review and integration. *Behavioural Brain Research, 94,* 127–152. doi:10.1016/S0166-4328(97)00175-7

Spencer, T. J., Biederman, J., & Wilens, T. E. (2010). Medications used for attention-deficit/hyperactivity disorder. In M. K. Dulcan (Ed.), *Dulcan's textbook of child and adolescent psychiatry* (published on-line) American Psychiatric Publishing. Retrieved from http://www.psychiatryonline.com/content.aspx?aid=468068

Still, G. F. (1902). Some abnormal psychical conditions in children. *The Lancet, 1,* 1008–1012, 1077–1082, 1153–1168.

Strauss, A. A., & Werner, H. (1942). Disorders of conceptual thinking in the brain-injured child. *Journal of Nervous and Mental Disease, 96,* 153–172.

Swanson, J., Arnold, L. E., Hechtman, L., Molina, B., Hinshaw, S., Vitiello, B., & MTA Cooperative Group. (2008). *Journal of Attention Disorders, 12,* 4–14. doi:10.1177/1087054708319345

Tankersley, M. (1995). A group-oriented contingency management program: A review of research on the good behavior game and implications for teachers. *Preventing School Failure, 40,* 59–72.

Tripp, G., & Alsop, B. (2001). Sensitivity to reward delay in children with attention deficit hyperactivity disorder (ADHD). *Journal of Child Psychology and Psychiatry, 42,* 691–698. doi:10.1111/1469-7610.00764

Tripp, G., & Wickens, J. R. (2009). Neurobiology of ADHD. *Neuropharmacology, 57,* 579–589. doi:10.1016/j.neuropharm.2009.07.026

Vaughn, S., Schumm, J. S., & Arguelles, M. E. (1997). The ABCDEs of Co-teaching. *Teaching Exceptional Children, 30*(2), 4–10.

Volkow, N. D., Wang, G.-J., Newcorn, J., Telang, F., Solanto, M. V., Fowler, J. S., et al. (2007). Depressed dopamine activity in caudate and preliminary evidence of limbic involvement in adults with attention-deficit/hyperactivity disorder. *Archives of General Psychiatry, 64,* 932–940. doi:10.1001/archpsyc.64.8.932

Walcott, C. M., Scheemaker, A., & Bielski, K. (2009). A longitudinal investigation of inattention and preliteracy development. *Journal of Attention Disorders, 14,* 79–85. doi: 10.1177/1087054709333330

Weiss, L. (1992). *Attention deficit disorder in adults.* Lanham, MD: Taylor Publishing.

Weiss, M., Hechtman, L., & Weiss, G. (2000). ADHD in parents. *Journal of the American Academy of Child and Adolescent Psychiatry, 39,* 1059–1061. doi:10.1097/00004583-200008000-00023

Werner, H., & Strauss, A. A. (1939). Types of visuo-motor activity in their relation to low and high performance ages. *Proceedings of the American Association on Mental Deficiency, 44,* 163–168.

Werner, H., & Strauss, A. A. (1941). Pathology of figure-background relation in the child. *Journal of Abnormal and Social Psychology, 36,* 236–248. doi:10.1037/h0058060

Weyandt, L. L. (2009a). Attention-deficit/hyperactivity disorder in adults. In M. C. Smith & N. DeFrates-Densch, N. (Eds.), *Handbook of research on adult learning and development* (pp. 670–692). New York: Routledge.

Weyandt, L. L. (2009b). Executive functions and attention deficit hyperactivity disorder. *The ADHD Report, 17*(6), 1–7. doi:10.1521/adhd.2009.17.6.1

Weyandt, L. L., & DuPaul, G. (2006). ADHD in college students. *Journal of Attention Disorders, 10,* 9–19. doi:10.1177/1087054705286061

Whalen, C. K., Henker, B., Ishikawa, S. S., Jamner, L. D., Floro, J. N., Johnston, J. A., et al. (2006). An electronic diary study of contextual triggers

and ADHD: Get ready, get set, get mad. *Journal of the American Academy of Child and Adolescent Psychiatry, 45,* 166–174. doi:10.1097/01.chi.0000189057.67902.10

Wilens, T. E., & Biederman, J. (1992). Pediatric psychopharmacology: The stimulants. *Pediatric Clinics of North America, 15*(1), 191–222.

Willcutt, E. G., Chhabildas, N., & Pennington, B. F. (2001). Validity of the DSM-IV subtypes of ADHD. *ADHD Report, 9*(1), 2–5. doi:10.1521/adhd.9.1.2.16970

Willcutt, E. G., Pennington, B. F., Boada, R., Ogline, J. S., Tunick, R. A., Chhabildas, N. A., et al. (2001). A comparison of the cognitive deficits in reading disability and attention-deficit/hyperactivity disorder. *Journal of Abnormal Psychology, 110,* 157–172. doi:10.1037/0021-843X.110.1.157

Wolraich, M. L., Wilson, D. B., & White, J. W. (1995). The effect of sugar on behavior or cognition in children: A meta-analysis. *Journal of the American Medical Association, 274,* 1617–1621.

Woodward, L. J., Fergusson, D. M., & Horwood, L. J. (2000). Driving outcomes for young people with attentional difficulties in adolescence. *Journal of the American Academy of Child and Adolescent Psychiatry, 39,* 627–634. doi:10.1097/00004583-200005000-00017

CHAPTER 8

Anastasiou, D., Gardner, R., & Michail, D. (2011). Ethnicity and exceptionality. In J. M. Kauffman & D. P. Hallahan (Eds.), *Handbook of special education.* New York: Routledge.

Bateman, B. D., & Linden, M. A. (2006). *Better IEPs: How to develop legally correct and educationally useful programs* (4th ed.). Verona, WI: Attainment.

Bower, E. M. (1982). Defining emotional disturbance: Public policy and research. *Psychology in the Schools, 19,* 55–60. doi:10.1002/1520-6807(19820108)19:1<55::AID-PITS2310190112>3.0.CO;2-2

Brigham, F. J., & Kauffman, J. M. (1998). Creating supportive environments for students with emotional or behavioral disorders. *Effective School Practices, 17*(2), 25–35.

Brolin, D. E., & Loyd, R. J. (2004). *Career development and transition services: A functional life-skills approach* (4th ed.) Upper Saddle River, NJ: Prentice Hall.

Cheney, D., & Bullis, M. (2004). The school-to-community transition of adolescents with emotional and behavioral disorders. In R. B. Rutherford, M. M. Quinn, & S. R. Mathur (Eds.). *Handbook of research in emotional and behavioral disorders* (pp. 369–384). New York: Guilford.

Chesapeake Institute. (1994, September). *National agenda for achieving better results for children and youth with serious emotional disturbance.* Washington, DC: Author.

Coleman, M., & Vaughn, S. (2000). Reading interventions for students with emotional/behavioral disorders. *Behavioral Disorders, 25,* 93–104.

Colvin, G. (2004). *Managing the cycle of acting-out behavior in the classroom.* Eugene, OR: Behavior Associates.

Cooper, P. (2005). Biology and behaviour: The educational relevance of a "biopsychosocial" perspective. In P. Clough, P. Garner, J. T. Pardeck, & F. K. O. Yuen (Eds.), *Handbook of emotional and behavioural difficulties in education* (pp. 91–105). London: Sage.

Costello, E. J., Egger, H., & Angold, A. (2005). 1-year research update review: The epidemiology of child and adolescent psychiatric disorders: I. Methods and public health burden. *Journal of the American Academy of Child and Adolescent Psychiatry, 44,* 972–986.

Costello, E. J., Foley, D., & Angold, A. (2006). 10-year research update review: The epidemiology of child and adolescent psychiatric disorders: II. Developmental epidemiology. *Journal of the American Academy of Child and Adolescent Psychiatry, 45,* 8–25.

Council for Exceptional Children. (2008). *What every special educator should know* (6th ed.). Reston, VA: Author.

Coutinho, M. J., & Oswald, D. P. (2011). Gender and exceptionality. In J. M. Kauffman & D. P. Hallahan (Eds.), *Handbook of special education.* New York: Routledge.

Cullinan, D. (2004). Classification and definition of emotional and behavioral disorders. In R. B. Rutherford, M. M. Quinn, & S. R. Mathur (Eds.), *Handbook of research in emotional and behavioral disorders* (pp. 32–53). New York: Guilford.

Cullinan, D. (2007). *Students with emotional and behavior disorders: An introduction for teachers and other helping professionals* (2nd ed.). Upper Saddle River, NJ: Merrill/Pearson.

DiPerna, J. C. (2006). Academic enablers and student achievement: Implications for assessment and intervention in the schools. *Psychology in the Schools, 43,* 7–17. doi:10.1002/pits.20125

DiPerna, J. C., & Elliott, S. N. (2000). *Academic competence evaluation scales.* San Antonio, TX: Psychological Corporation.

Dunlap, G., Strain, P. S., Fox, L., Carta, J. J., Conroy, M., Smith, B. J., et al. (2006). Prevention and intervention with young children's challenging behavior: Perspectives regarding current knowledge. *Behavioral Disorders, 32,* 29–45.

Epstein, M. H., & Sharma, J. (1997). *Behavioral and Emotional Rating Scale* (BERS): A strength-based approach to assessment. Austin, TX: Pro-Ed.

Evertson, C., & Weinstein, C. (Eds.). (2006). *Handbook of classroom management: Research, practice and contemporary issues.* Mahwah, NJ: Erlbaum.

Farmer, E. M. Z., & Farmer, T. W. (1999). The role of schools in outcomes for youth: Implications for children's mental health services research. *Journal of Child and Family Studies, 8,* 377–396. doi:10.1023/A:1021943518480

Farmer, T. W. (2000). Misconceptions of peer rejection and problem behavior: Understanding aggression in students with mild disabilities. *Remedial and Special Education, 21,* 194–208. doi:10.1177/074193250002100401

Farmer, T. W., Farmer, E. M. Z., & Gut, D. (1999). Implications of social development research for school based intervention for aggressive youth with emotional and behavioral disorders. *Journal of Emotional and Behavioral Disorders, 7,* 130–136. doi:10.1177/106342669900700301

Farmer, T. W., Quinn, M. M., Hussey, W., & Holahan, T. (2001). The development of disruptive behavioral disorders and correlated constraints: Implications for intervention. *Behavioral Disorders, 26,* 117–130.

Fenning, P. A., & Bohanon, H. (2006). Schoolwide discipline policies: An analysis of discipline codes of conduct. In C. Everston & C. Weinstein (Eds.), *Handbook of classroom management: Research, practice, and contemporary issues* (pp. 1021–1039). Mahwah, NJ: Erlbaum.

Forness, S. R., & Beard, K. Y. (2007). Strengthening the research base in special education: Evidence-based practice and interdisciplinary collaboration. In J. Crockett, M. Gerber, & T. Landrum (Eds.), *Achieving the radical reform of special education* (pp. 169–188). Mahwah, NJ: Erlbaum.

Forness, S. R., & Kavale, K. A. (2001). Ignoring the odds: Hazards of not adding the new medical model to special education decisions. *Behavioral Disorders, 26,* 269–281.

Forness, S. R., & Knitzer, J. (1992). A new proposed definition and terminology to replace "serious emotional disturbance" in Individuals with Disabilities Act. *School Psychology Review, 21,* 12–20.

Fox, J., & Davis, C. (2005). Functional behavior assessment in schools: Current research findings and future directions. *Journal of Behavioral Education, 14*(1), 1–4. doi:10.1007/s10864-005-0957-0

Fox, J. J., & Gable, R. A. (2004). Functional behavioral assessment. In R. B. Rutherford, M. M. Quinn, & S. R. Mathur (Eds.), Handbook of research in emotional and behavioral disorders (pp. 143–162). New York: Guilford.

Furlong, M. J., Morrison, G. M., & Fisher, E. S. (2005). The influences of the school contexts and processes on violence and disruption in American schools. In P. Clough, P. Garner, J. T. Pardeck, & F. K. O. Yuen (Eds.), *Handbook of emotional and behavioural difficulties in education* (pp. 106–120). London: Sage.

Furlong, M. J., Morrison, G. M., & Jimerson, S. (2004). Externalizing behaviors of aggression and violence and the school context. In R. B. Rutherford, M. M. Quinn, & S. R. Mathur (Eds.), *Handbook of research in emotional and behavioral disorders* (pp. 243–261). New York: Guilford.

Garrity, C., Jens, K., Porter, W. W., Sager, N., & Short-Camilli, C. (1997). Bullyproofing your school: Creating a positive climate. *Intervention in School and Clinic, 32,* 235–243.

Garrity, C., Jens, K., Porter, W. W., Sager, N., & Short-Camilli, C. (2000). *Bully proofing your school: A comprehensive approach for elementary schools* (2nd ed.) Longmont, CO: Sopris West.

Gresham, F. M., & Kern, L. (2004). Internalizing behavior problems in children and adolescents. In R. B. Rutherford, M. M. Quinn, & S. R. Mathur (Eds.), *Handbook of research in emotional and behavioral disorders* (pp. 262–281). New York: Guilford.

Hallenbeck, B. A., & Kauffman, J. M. (1995). How does observational learning affect the behavior of students with emotional or behavioral disorders? A review of research. *Journal of Special Education, 29,* 45–71. doi:10.1177/002246699502900103

Huefner, D. S. (2006). *Getting comfortable with special education law: A framework for working with children with disabilities* (2nd ed.). Norwood, MA: Christopher-Gordon.

Ishii-Jordan, S. R. (2000). Behavioral interventions used with diverse students. *Behavioral Disorders, 25,* 299–309.

Jolivette, K., Stichter, J. P., & McCormick, K. M. (2002). Making choices—improving behavior—engaging in learning. *Teaching Exceptional Children, 34*(3), 24–30.

Jones, V., Dohrn, E., & Dunn, C. (2004). *Creating effective programs for students with emotional and behavioral disorders.* Boston: Allyn & Bacon.

Kauffman, J. M. (1997). Conclusion: A little of everything, a lot of nothing is an agenda for failure. *Journal of Emotional and Behavioral Disorders, 5,* 76–81.

Kauffman, J. M. (1999). How we prevent the prevention of emotional and behavioral disorders. *Exceptional Children, 65,* 448–468.

Kauffman, J. M. (2005). How we prevent the prevention of emotional and behavioural difficulties in education. In P. Clough, P. Garner, J. T. Pardeck, & F. K. O. Yuen (Eds.), *Handbook of emotional and behavioural difficulties in education* (pp. 366–376). London: Sage.

Kauffman, J. M. (2010). The problem of early identification. In H. Ricking & G. C. Schulze (Eds.), *Förderbedarf in der emotionalen und sozialen Entwicklung: Prävention, Interdisziplinarität, und Professionalisierung.* (pp. 171–177) Bad Heilbrunn, Germany: Klinkhardt Verlag.

Kauffman, J. M., Bantz, J., & McCullough, J. (2002). Separate and better: A special public school class for students with emotional and behavioral disorders. *Exceptionality, 10,* 149–170.

Kauffman, J. M., & Brigham, F. J. (2009). *Working with troubled children.* Verona, WI: Attainment.

Kauffman, J. M., Conroy, M., Gardner, R., & Oswald, D. (2008). Cultural sensitivity in the application of behavior principles to education. *Education and Treatment of Children, 31,* 239–262. doi:10.1353/etc.0.0019

Kauffman, J. M., & Landrum, T. J. (2006). *Children and youth with emotional and behavioral disorders: A brief history of their education.* Austin, TX: Pro-Ed.

Kauffman, J. M., & Landrum, T. J. (2009a). *Cases in emotional and behavioral disorders of children and youth* (2nd ed.). Upper Saddle River, NJ: Merrill/Pearson.

Kauffman, J. M., & Landrum, T. J. (2009b). *Characteristics of emotional and behavioral disorders of children and youth* (9th ed.). Upper Saddle River, NJ: Merrill/Pearson.

Kauffman, J. M., & Landrum, T. J. (2009c). Politics, civil rights, and disproportional identification of students with emotional and behavioral disorders. *Exceptionality, 17,* 177–188. doi:10.1080/09362830903231903

Kauffman, J. M., Mock, D. R., & Simpson, R. L. (2007). Problems related to underservice of students with emotional or behavioral disorders. *Behavioral Disorders, 33,* 43–57.

Kauffman, J. M., Mock, D. R., Tankersley, M., & Landrum, T. J. (2008). Effective service delivery models. In R. J. Morris & N. Mather (Eds.), *Evidence-based interventions for students with learning and behavioral challenges* (pp. 359–378). Mahwah, NJ: Erlbaum.

Kauffman, J. M., Nelson, C. M., Simpson, R. L., & Mock, D. R. (2011). Contemporary issues. In J. M. Kauffman & D. P. Hallahan (Eds.), *Handbook of special education.* New York: Routledge.

Kauffman, J. M., Pullen, P. L., Mostert, M. P., & Trent, S. C. (2011). *Managing classroom behavior: A reflective case-based approach* (5th ed.). Upper Saddle River, NJ: Merrill/Pearson.

Kauffman, J. M., Simpson, R. L., & Mock, D. R. (2009). Problems related to underservice: A rejoinder. *Behavioral Disorders, 34,* 172–180.

Kazdin, A. E. (2008). *The Kazdin method for parenting the defiant child.* Boston: Houghton Mifflin.

Keogh, B. K. (2003). *Temperament in the classroom: Understanding individual differences.* Baltimore: Brookes.

Kerr, M. M., & Nelson, C. M. (2010). *Strategies for addressing behavior problems in the classroom* (6th ed.). Upper Saddle River, NJ: Merrill/Pearson.

Konopasek, D., & Forness, S. R. (2004). Psychopharmacology in the treatment of emotional and behavioral disorders. In R. B. Rutherford, M. M. Quinn, & S. R. Mathur (Eds.), *Handbook of research in emotional and behavioral disorders* (pp. 352–368). New York: Guilford.

Landrum, T. J. (2000). Assessment for eligibility: Issues in identifying students with emotional or behavioral disorders. *Assessment for Effective Intervention, 26*(1), 41–49.

Landrum, T. J. (2011). Emotional and behavioral disorders. In J. M. Kauffman & D. P. Hallahan (Eds.), *Handbook of special education.* New York: Routledge.

Landrum, T. J., & Kauffman, J. M. (2003). Emotionally disturbed, education of. In J. W. Guthrie (Ed.), *Encyclopedia of education* (2nd ed., pp. 726–728). New York: Macmillan Reference.

Landrum, T. J., Tankersley, M., & Kauffman, J. M. (2003). What's special about special education for students with emotional and behavioral disorders? *The Journal of Special Education, 37*, 148–156. doi:10.1177/00224669030370030401

Lane, K. L., Kalberg, J. R., & Menzies, H. M. (2009). *Developing schoolwide programs to prevent and manage problem behaviors: A step-by-step approach.* New York: Guilford.

Lane, K. L., & Menzies, H. M. (Eds.). (2010). Academic problems. *Behavioral Disorders* [special issue].

Lewis, T. (2000). Establishing and promoting disciplinary practices at the classroom and individual student level that ensure safe, effective, and nurturing learning environments. In L. M. Bullock & R. A. Gable (Eds.), *Positive academic and behavioral supports: Creating safe, effective, and nurturing schools for all students.* Reston, VA: Council for Exceptional Children.

Liaupsin, C. J., Jolivette, K., & Scott, T. M. (2004). School-wide systems of behavior support: Maximizing student success in schools. In R. B. Rutherford, M. M. Quinn, & S. R. Mathur (Eds.), *Handbook of research in emotional and behavioral disorders.* New York: Guilford.

Martella, R. C., Nelson, J. R., & Marchand-Martella, N. E. (2003). *Managing disruptive behaviors in the schools: A schoolwide, classroom, and individualized learning approach.* Boston: Allyn & Bacon.

Masia, C. L., Klein, R. G., Storch, E. A., & Corda, B. (2001). School-based behavioral treatment for social anxiety disorder in adolescents: Results of a pilot study. *Journal of the American Academy of Child and Adolescent Psychiatry, 40*, 780–786.

Mattison, R. E. (2004). Psychiatric and psychological assessment of emotional and behavioral disorders during school mental health consultation. In R. B. Rutherford, M. M. Quinn, & S. R. Mathur (Eds.), *Handbook of research in emotional and behavioral disorders* (pp. 163–180). New York: Guilford.

Mayer, M. J., & Cornell, D. G. (Eds.). (2010). New perspectives on school safety and violence prevention. *Educational Researcher* [special issue], 39(5). doi:10.3102/0013189X09356778

Merrell, K. W. (2002). *School social behavior scales* (2nd ed.). Eugene, OR: Assessment-Intervention Resources.

Mueller, M. M., Edwards, R. P., & Trahant, D. (2003). Translating multiple assessment techniques into an intervention selection model for classrooms.

Journal of Applied Behavior Analysis, 36, 563–573. doi:10.1901/jaba.2003.36-563

Nelson, C. M., & Kauffman, J. M. (1977). Educational programming for secondary school age delinquent and maladjusted pupils. *Behavioral Disorders, 2,* 102–113.

Nelson, C. M., Leone, P. E., & Rutherford, R. B., (2004). Youth delinquency: Prevention and intervention. In R. B. Rutherford, M. M. Quinn, & S. R. Mathur (Eds.), *Handbook of research in emotional and behavioral disorders* (pp. 282–301). New York: Guilford.

O'Mahony, P. (2005). Juvenile delinquency and emotional and behavioral difficulties in education. In P. Clough, P. Garner, J. T. Pardeck, & F. K. O. Yuen (Eds.), *Handbook of emotional and behavioural difficulties in education* (pp. 142–154). London: Sage.

Qi, C. H., & Kaiser, A. P. (2003). Behavior problems of preschool children from low-income families: Review of literature. *Topics in Early Childhood Special Education, 23,* 188–216. doi:10.1177/02711214030230040201

Rogers-Adkinson, D., & Griffith, P. (Eds.). (1999). *Communication disorders and children with psychiatric and behavioral disorders.* San Diego: Singular.

Sasso, G. M., Conroy, M. A., Stichter, J. P., & Fox, J. J. (2001). Slowing down the bandwagon: The misapplication of functional assessment for students with emotional and behavioral disorders. *Behavioral Disorders, 26,* 282–296.

Schaffner, L. (2006). *Girls in trouble with the law.* New Brunswick, NJ: Rutgers University Press.

Sitlington, P. L., & Clark, G. M. (2006). *Transition education and services for students with disabilities* (4th ed.). Boston: Allyn & Bacon.

Skiba, R. J., & Rausch, M. K. (2006). Zero tolerance, suspension, and expulsion: Questions of equity and effectiveness. In C. Evertson & C. Weinstein (Eds.), *Handbook of classroom management: Research, practice, and contemporary issues* (pp. 1063–1089). Mahwah, NJ: Erlbaum.

Sprague, J., & Walker, H. (2000). Early identification and intervention for youth with antisocial and violent behavior. *Exceptional Children, 66,* 367–379.

Sugai, G., & Horner, R. H. (Ed.). (1999–2000). Special issue: Functional behavioral assessment. *Exceptionality, 8*(3).

Thomas, J. M., & Guskin, K. A. (2001). Disruptive behavior in young children: What does it mean? *Journal of the American Academy of Child and Adolescent Psychiatry, 40,* 44–51.

U.S. Department of Education. (2008). *Thirtieth annual report to Congress on implementation of the Individuals with Disabilities Education Act.* Washington, DC: Author.

U.S. Department of Education, Office of Special Education Programs, Technical Assistance Center on Positive Behavioral Interventions and Supports. (2009). *Is school-wide positive behavior support an evidence-based practice?* Retrieved from http://www.pbis.org/research/default.aspx

U.S. Department of Health and Human Services. (2001). *Report of the Surgeon General's Conference on Children's Mental Health: A National Action Agenda.* Washington, DC: Author.

Van Acker, R., Boreson, L., Gable, R. A., & Patterson, T. (2005). Are we on the right course? Lessons learned about current FBA/BIP practices in schools. *Journal of Behavioral Education, 14*(1), 35–56. doi:10.1007/s10864-005-0960-5

Walker, H. M., Ramsey, E., & Gresham, F. M. (2003–2004a). Heading off disruption: How early

intervention can reduce defiant behavior—and win back teaching time. *American Educator, 27*(4), 6–21.

Walker, H. M., Ramsey, E., & Gresham, F. M. (2003–2004b). How disruptive students escalate hostility and disorder—and how teachers can avoid it. *American Educator, 27*(4), 22–27, 47.

Walker, H. M., Ramsey, E., & Gresham, F. M. (2004). *Antisocial behavior in school: Strategies and best practices* (2nd ed.). Pacific Grove, CA: Brooks/Cole.

Walker, H. M., & Sprague, J. R. (2007). Early, evidence-based intervention with school-based behavior disorders: Key issues, continuing challenges, and promising practices. In J. B. Crockett, M. M. Gerber, & T. J. Landrum (Eds.), *Achieving the radical reform of special education: Essays in honor of James M. Kauffman* (pp. 37–58). Mahwah, NJ: Erlbaum.

Weinstein, C. E., Palmer, D. R., & Schulte, A. C. (2002). *Learning and study strategies inventory* (2nd ed.). Clearwater, FL: H & H.

Wolf, M. M., Braukmann, C. J., & Ramp, K. A. (1987). Serious delinquent behavior as part of a significantly handicapping condition. *Journal of Applied Behavior Analysis, 20,* 347–359.

Yell, M. L. (2006). *The law and special education* (2nd ed.). Upper Saddle River, NJ: Pearson Education.

Yell, M. L., Katsiyannis, A., & Bradley, M. R. (2011). The Individuals with Disabilities Education Act: The evolution of special education law. In J. M. Kauffman & D. P. Hallahan (Eds.), *Handbook of special education.* New York: Routledge.

CHAPTER 9

Adamson, L. B., Bakeman, R., Deckner, D. F., & Romiski, M. (2009). Joint engagement and the emergence of language in children with autism and Down syndrome. *Journal of Autism and Developmental Disorders, 39,* 84–96. doi:10.1007/s10803-008-0601-7

Adreon, D., & Stella, J. (2001). Transition to middle and high school: Increasing the success of students with Asperger syndrome. *Intervention in School and Clinic, 36,* 266–271. doi:10.1177/10534512103600502

Ali, S., & Frederickson, N. (2006). Investigating the evidence base of social stories. *Educational Psychology in Practice, 22,* 355–377.

American Psychiatric Association: DSM-V Development. (2010). 299.00: Autism Spectrum Disorder: Proposed Revision. Retrieved from http://www.dsm5.org/ProposedRevisions/Pages/proposedrevision.aspx?rid=94

Asperger, H. (1991). The "Autistic Psychopathy" in childhood. In U. Frith (Ed. & Trans.), *Autism and Asperger syndrome* (pp. 37–92). Cambridge, UK: Cambridge University Press, 1991. (Original work published 1944)

Autism Genome Project Consortium. (2007). Mapping autism risk loci using genetic linkage and chromosomal rearrangements. *Nature Genetics, 39,* 319–328. doi:10.1038/ng1985

Auyeung, B., Baron-Cohen, S., Ashwin, E., Knickmeyer, R., Taylor, K., & Hackett, G. (2009). Fetal testosterone and autistic traits. *British Journal of Psychology, 100,* 1–22. doi:10.1348/000712608X311731

Barbeau, E. B., Mendrek, A., & Motton, L. (2009). Are autistic traits autistic? *British Journal of Psychology, 100,* 23–28. doi:10.1348/000712608X337788

Baron-Cohen, S. (2002). The extreme male brain theory of autism. *Trends in Cognitive Sciences, 6,* 248–254. doi:10.1016/S1364-6613(02)01904-6

Baron-Cohen, S. (2003). *The essential difference: Men, women and the extreme male brain*. London: Penguin.

Baron-Cohen, S., Auyeung, B., Ashwin, E., & Knickmeyer, R. (2009). Fetal testosterone and autistic traits: A response to three fascinating commentaries. *British Journal of Psychology, 100,* 39–47. doi:10.1348/000712608X394271

Baron-Cohen, S., Leslie, A. M., & Frith, U. (1985). Does the autistic child have a "theory of mind"? *Cognition, 21,* 37–46. doi:10.1016/0010-0277(85)90022-8

Bedford, H., Booy, R., Dunn, D., DiGuiseppi, C., Gibb, D., Gilbert, R., et al. (1998). Correspondence. *The Lancet, 351,* 907. doi:10.1016/S0140-6736(05)70320-2

Bell, R. Q., & Harper, L. V. (1977). *Child effects on adults*. Hillsdale, NJ: Erlbaum.

Bellini, S., & Hopf, A. (2007). The development of the autism social skills profile: A preliminary analysis of psychometric properties. *Focus on Autism and Other Developmental Disabilities, 22,* 80–87. doi:10.1177/10883576070220020801

Ben-Sasson, A., Hen, L., Fluss, R., Cermak, S. A., Engel-Yeger, B., & Gal, E. (2009). A meta-analysis of sensory modulation symptoms in individuals with autism spectrum disorders. *Journal of Autism and Developmental Disorders, 39,* 1–11. doi:10.1007/s10803-0593-3

Bettelheim, B. (1967). *The empty fortress*. New York: Free Press.

Bishop. D. V. M., Whitehouse, A. J. O., Watt, H. J., & Line, E. A. (2008). *Developmental Medicine & Child Neurology, 50,* 1–5.

Bleuler, E. (1951). *Textbook of psychiatry* (A. A. Brill, Trans.). New York: Dover. (Original work published 1916)

Cadigan, K., & Estrem, T. (Fall/Winter, 2006/2007). Identification and assessment of autism spectrum disorders. *Impact, 19*(3), 4–5.

Cannon, J. (2004, July 22). Youth uses Web to help others on "wrong planet." *Charlottesville Daily Progress.*

Causton-Theoharis, J., Ashby, C., & Cosier, M. (2009). Islands of loneliness: Exploring social interaction through the autobiographies of individuals with autism. *Intellectual and Developmental Disabilities, 47,* 84–96. doi:10.1352/1934-9556-47.2.84

Cederlund, M., Hagberg, B., Billstedt, E., Gillberg, I. C., & Gillberg, C. (2008). Asperger syndrome and autism: A comparative longitudinal follow-up study more than 5 years after original diagnosis. *Journal of Autism and Developmental Disorders, 38,* 72–85. doi:10.1007/s10803-007-0364-6

Centers for Disease Control and Prevention. (2008, October 20). *Update: Measles outbreaks continue in U.S.* Retrieved from http://cdc.gov/Features/MeaslesUpdate/

Centers for Disease Control and Prevention. (2009, December 18). Prevalence of autism spectrum disorders—Autism and Developmental Disabilities Monitoring Network, United States, 2006. *Morbidity and Mortality Weekly Report, 58,* SS-10; 1–20.

Chen, R. T., & DeStefano, F. (1998). Vaccine adverse events: Causal or coincidental? *The Lancet, 351,* 611–612. doi:10.1016/S0140-6736(05)78423-3

Clifford, S. M., & Dissanayake, C. (2008). The early development of joint attention in infants with autistic disorder using home video observations and parental interview. *Journal of Autism and Developmental Disorders, 38,* 791–805. doi:10.1007/s10803-007-0444-7

Cohen, I. L., Schmidt-Lackner, S., Romanczyk, R., & Sudhalter, V. (2003). The PDD behavior inventory: A rating scale for assessing response to intervention in children with pervasive developmental disorder. *Journal of Autism and Developmental Disabilities, 33,* 31–45. doi:10.1023/A:1022226403878

Cohen, I. L., & Sudhalter, V. (2005). *PDD Behavior Inventory (PDDBI)*. Lutz, FL: Psychological Assessment Resources.

Colle, L., Baron-Cohen, S., Wheelwright, S., & van der Lely, H. K. J. (2008). Narrative discourse in adults with high-functioning autism or Asperger syndrome. *Journal of Autism and Developmental Disorders, 38,* 28–40. doi:10.1007/s10803-007-0357-5

Conroy, M., Stichter, J. P., & Gage, N. (2011). Current issues and trends in the education of children and youth with autism spectrum disorders. In J. M. Kauffman & D. P. Hallahan (Eds.), *Handbook of special education*. New York: Routledge.

Constantino, J. N., & Gruber, C. P. (2005). *The social responsiveness scale (SRS)*. Los Angeles: Western Psychological Services.

Coo, H., Ouellette-Kuntz, H., Lloyd, J. E. V., Kasmara, L., Holden, J. J. A., & Lewis, M. E. S. (2008). Trends in autism prevalence: Diagnostic substitution revisited. *Journal of Autism and Developmental Disorders, 38,* 1036–1046. doi:10.1007/s10803-007-0478-x

Courchesne, E., Carper, R., & Akshoomoff, N. (2003). Evidence of brain overgrowth in the first year of life in autism. *Journal of the American Medical Association, 290,* 337–344.

Courchesne, E., Karns, C. M., Davis, H. R., Ziccardi, R., Carper, R. A., Tigue, B. S., et al. (2001). Unusual brain growth patterns in early life in patients with autistic disorder. *Neurology, 57,* 245–254.

Editors of *The Lancet*. (2010, February 2). Retraction—Ileal-lymphoid-nodular hyperplasia, non-specific colitis, and pervasive developmental disorder in children. *The Lancet*. Retrieved from http://www.thelancet.com/journals/lancet/article/PIIS0140-6736%2810% 2960175-4/fulltextdoi:10.1016/S0140-6736 (10)60175-4

Eisenberg, L., & Kanner, K. (1956). Early infantile autism, 1943–1955. *American Journal of Orthopsychiatry, 26,* 556–566.

Elder, L. M., Dawson, G., Toth, K., Fein, D., & Munson, J. (2008). Head circumference as an early predictor of autism symptoms in younger siblings of children with autism spectrum disorder. *Journal of Autism and Developmental Disorders, 38,* 1104–1111. doi:10.1007/s10803-007-04959

Eldevik, S., Hastings, R. P., Hughes, J. C., Jahr, E., Eikeseth, S., & Cross, S. (2009). Meta-analysis of Early Intensive Behavioral Intervention for children with autism. *Journal of Clinical Child & Adolescent Psychology, 38,* 439–450. doi:10.1080/15374410902851739

Falter, C. M., Plaisted, K. C., & Davis, G. (2008). Male brains, androgen, and the cognitive profile in autism: Convergent evidence from 2D:4D and congenital adrenal hyperplasia. *Journal of Autism and Developmental Disorders, 38,* 997–998. doi:10.1007/s10803-008-0552-z

Fenson, L. (2007). *MacArthur-Bates Communicative Development Inventories (CDIs)* (3rd ed.). Baltimore: Brookes.

Fenson, L., Marchman, V. A., Thal, D. J., Dale, P. S., Reznick, J. S., & Bates, E. (2003). *MacArthur-Bates Communicative Development Inventories (CDIs)* (2nd ed.). Baltimore: Brookes.

Fombonne, E. (2001). Is there an autism epidemic? *Pediatrics, 107,* 411–412. doi:10.1542/peds.107.2.411

Fombonne, E., Roge, B., Claverie, J., Courty, S., & Fremoile, J. (1999). Microcephaly and macrocephaly in autism. *Journal of Autism and Developmental Disorders, 29,* 113–119. doi:10.1023/A:1023036509476

Frith, U. (2003). *Autism: Explaining the enigma* (2nd ed.). Malden, MA: Blackwell.

Fukomoto, A., Hashimoto, T., Ito, H., Nishimura, M., Tsuda, Y., Miyazaki, M., & Kagami, S. (2008). Growth of head circumference in autistic infants during the first year of life. *Journal of Autism and Developmental Disorders, 38,* 411–418.

Gerhardt, P. F. (2003). Transition support for learners with Asperger syndrome: Toward a successful adulthood. In R. W. Du Charme & T. P. Gullotta (Eds.). *Asperger syndrome: A guide for professionals and families* (pp. 157–171). New York: Kluwer Academic/Plenum.

Gilliam, J. E. (1995). *Gilliam Autism Rating Scale*. Austin, TX: Pro Ed.

Glessner, J. T., Wang, K., Cai, G., Korvatska, O., Kim, C. E., Wood, S., & Hakonarson, H. (2009). Autism genome-wide copy number variation reveals ubiquitin and neuronal genes. *Nature, 459,* 569–573. doi:10.1038/nature07953

Graetz, J. E., Mastropieri, M. A., & Scruggs, T. E. (2009). Decreasing inappropriate behaviors for adolescents with autism spectrum disorders using modified social stories. *Education and Training in Developmental Disabilities, 44*(1), 91–104.

Grandin, T. (1995). *Thinking in pictures*. New York: Doubleday.

Grandin, T. (2002, May 6). First person: Myself. *Time,* 56.

Gray, C., & Garand, J. (1993). Social stories: Improving responses of students with autism with accurate social information. *Focus on Autistic Behavior, 8,* 1–10

Guber, P. (Producer), & Levinson, B. (Director). (1988). *Rain Main* [Motion picture]. United States: United Artists.

Hendricks, D., & Wehman, P. (2009). Transition from school to adulthood for youth with autism spectrum disorders: Review and recommendations. *Focus on Autism and Other Developmental Disorders, 24*(2), 77–88. doi:10.1177/1088357608329827

Hermelin, B. (1976). Coding and the sense modalities. In L. Wing (Ed.), *Early childhood autism*. London: Pergamon.

Herschkowitz, N. (2000). Neurological bases of behavioral development in infancy. *Brain Development, 22,* 411–416. doi:10.1016/S0387-7604(00)00185-6

Hertz-Picciotto, I., & Delwiche, L. (2009). The rise of autism and the role of age at diagnosis. *Epidemiology, 20,* 84–90. doi:10.1097/EDE.0b013e3181902d15

Hewetson, A. (2002). *The stolen child: Aspects of autism and Asperger syndrome*. Westport, CT: Bergin & Garvey.

Hoopman, K. (2000). *Blue bottle mystery*. London: Jessica Kingsley.

Hoopman, K. (2001). *Of mice and aliens*. London: Jessica Kingsley.

Hoopman, K. (2002). *Lisa and the lacemaker*. London: Jessica Kingsley.

Hoopman, K. (2003). *Haze*. London: Jessica Kingsley.

Hoopman, K. (2006). *All cats have Asperger syndrome*. London: Jessica Kingsley.

Horner, R. H., Albin, R. W., Sprague, J. R., & Todd, A. W. (2000). Positive behavior support. In M. E. Snell & F. Brown (Eds.), *Instruction of students with severe retardation* (5th ed., pp. 207–243). Upper Saddle River, NJ: Merrill/Pearson.

Howlin, P., Magiati, I., & Charman, T. (2009). Systematic review of Early Intensive Behavioral Interventions for children with autism. *American Journal on Intellectual and Developmental Disabilities, 114,* 23–41. doi:10.1352/2009.114:23–41

Individuals With Disabilities Education Improvement Act of 2004. (2004). 20 U.S.C. § 1400 *et seq.*

Institute of Medicine. (2004). *Immunization safety review: Vaccines and autism.* Washington, DC: National Academies Press.

Joint Attention. (n.d.). In *Wikipedia.* Retrieved from http://en.wikipedia.org/wiki/Joint_attention

Kaland, N., Callesen, K., Moller-Nielson, A., Mortensen, E. L., & Smith, L. (2008). Performance of children and adolescents with Asperger syndrome or high functioning autism on advanced theory of mind tasks. *Journal of Autism and Developmental Disorders, 38,* 1112–1123. doi:10.1007/s10803-007-0496-8

Kanner, L. (1973). *Childhood psychosis: Initial studies and new insights* (pp. 1–43). Washington, DC: V. H. Winston. (Reprinted from Autistic disturbances of affective contact. *Nervous Child, 2,* 217–250, by L. Kanner, 1943.)

Koegel, L. K., Koegel, R. L., Harrower, J. K., & Carter, C. M. (1999). Pivotal response intervention I: Overview of approach. *Journal of the Association for Persons with Severe Handicaps, 24,* 174–185. doi:10.2511/rpsd.24.3.174

Koegel, R. L., & Koegel, L. K. (Eds.). (2006). *Pivotal response treatments for autism: Communication, social, and academic development.* Baltimore, MD: Brookes.

Kogan, M. D., Blumberg, S. J., Schieve, L. A., Boyle, C. A., Perrin, J. M., Ghandour, R. M., & van Dyck, P. C. (2009). Prevalence of parent-reported diagnosis of autism spectrum disorder among children in the US, 2007. *Pediatrics, 124*(4), 1–9.

Kuusikko, S., Pollock-Wurman, R., Jussila, K., Carter, A. S., Mattila, M.-J., Ebeling, H., & Moilanen, I. (2008). Social anxiety in high-functioning children and adolescents with autism and Asperger syndrome. *Journal of Autism and Developmental Disorders, 38,* 1697–1709. doi:10.1007/s10803-008-0555-9

Lainhart, J. E. (2003). Increased rate of head growth during infancy in autism. *Journal of the American Medical Association, 290,* 393–394.

Landa, R. J., Holman, K. C., & Garrett-Mayer, E. (2007). Social and communication development in toddlers with early and later diagnosis of autism spectrum disorders. *Archives of General Psychiatry, 64,* 853–864. doi:10.1001/archpsyc.64.7.853

Le Couteur, A., Haden, G., Hammal, D., & McConachie, H. (2008). Diagnosing autism spectrum disorders in pre-school children using two standardised [sic] assessment instruments: The ADI-R and the ADOS. *Journal of Autism and Developmental Disorders, 38,* 362–372. doi:10.1007/s10803–007-0403–3

Lotter, V. (1966). Epidemiology of autistic conditions in young children: I. Prevalence. *Social Psychiatry, 1,* 124–137. doi:10.1007/BF00584048

Luna, B., Doll, S. K., Hegedus, S. J., Minshew, N. J., & Sweeney, J. A. (2007). Maturation of executive function in autism. *Biological Psychiatry, 61,* 474–481. doi:10.1016/j.biopsych.2006.02.030

Luyster, R., Lopez, K., & Lord, C. (2007). Characterizing communicative development in children referred for autism spectrum disorders using the MacArthur-Bates Communicative Development Inventory (CDI). *Journal of Child Language, 34,* 623–654. doi:10.1017/S0305000907008094

Luyster, R., Qiu, S., Lopez, K., & Lord, C. (2007). Predicting outcomes of children referred for autism using the MacArthur-Bates Communicative Development Inventory. *Journal of Speech, Language, and Hearing Research, 50,* 667–681. doi:10.1044/1092-4388(2007/047)

Mandell, D. S., Wiggins, L. D., Carpenter, L. A., Daniels, J., Diguiseppi, C., Durkin, M. S., . . . Kirby, R. S. (2009). Racial/ethnic disparities in the identification of children with autism spectrum disorders. *American Journal of Public Health, 99,* 493–498. doi:10.2105/AJPH.2007.131243

Mills, J. L., Hediger, M. L., Molloy, C. A., Chrousos, G. P., Manning-Courtney, P., Yu, K. F., et al. (2007). Elevated levels of growth-related hormones in autism and autism spectrum disorder. *Clinical Endocrinology, 67,* 230–237.

Minshew, N. J., Sweeney, J., & Luna, B. (2002). Autism as a selective disorder of complex information processing and underdevelopment of neocortical systems. *Molecular Psychiatry, 7*(Suppl. 2), S12–S15. doi:10.1038/sj.mp.4001166

Muller, R. A. (2007). The study of autism as a distributed disorder. *Mental Retardation and Developmental Disabilities Research Reviews, 13,* 85–95. doi:10.1002/mrdd.20141

Murch, S. H., Anthony, A., Casson, D. H., Malik, M., Berelowitz, M., Dhillon, A. P., et al. (2004). Retraction of an interpretation. *The Lancet, 363,* 750. doi:10.1016/S0140-6736(04)15715-2

Murray, D. S., Creaghead, N. A., Manning-Courtney, P., Shear, P. K., Bean, J., & Prendville, J. (2008). The relationship between joint attention and language in children with autism spectrum disorders. *Focus on Autism and Other Developmental Disabilities, 23,* 5–8. doi:10.1177/1088357607311443

Myles, B. S. (2003). Social skills instruction for children with Asperger syndrome. In R. W. Du Charme & T. P. Gullotta (Eds.). *Asperger syndrome: A guide for professionals and families* (pp. 21–42). New York: Kluwer Academic/Plenum.

Myles, B. S., & Simpson, R. L. (2001). Understanding the hidden curriculum: An essential social skill for children and youth with Asperger syndrome. *Intervention in School and Clinic, 36,* 279–286. doi:10.1177/10534512010360601504

Myles, B. S., & Simpson, R. L. (2003). *Asperger syndrome: A guide for parents and teachers.* Austin, TX: Pro-Ed.

Naess, P. (Director), & Bass, R. (2005). *Mozart and the Whale* [Motion picture]. United States: Millennium Films.

National Research Council. (2001). *Educating children with autism.* Washington, DC: National Academy Press.

Page, T. (2007, August 20). Parallel play: A lifetime of restless isolation explained. *The New Yorker,* pp. 36–41.

Piven, J., Arndt, S., Bailey, J., & Andreason, N. C. (1996). Regional brain enlargement in autism: a magnetic resonance imaging study. *Journal of the American Academy of Child and Adolescent Psychiatry, 35,* 530–536. doi:10.1097/00004583-199604000-00020

Piven, J., Arndt, S., Bailey, J., Havercamp, S., Andreason, N. C., & Palmer, P. (1995). An MRI study of brain size in autism. *American Journal of Psychiatry, 152,* 1145–1149.

Reichow, B., & Wolery, M. (2009). Comprehensive synthesis of Early Intensive Behavioral Interventions for young children with autism based on the UCLA Young Autism Project Model. *Journal of Autism and Developmental Disorders, 39,* 23–41. doi:10.1007/s10803-008-0596-0

Robison, J. E. (2007). *Look me in the eye: My life with Asperger's.* New York: Crown.

Rogers, S. J. (2000). Diagnosis of autism before the age of 3. *International Review of Mental Retardation, 23,* 1–31. doi:10.1016/S0074-7750(00)80004-X

Sacks, O. (1995). *An anthropologist on Mars.* New York: Knopf.

Sallows, G. O., & Graupner, T. D. (2005). Intensive behavioral treatment for children with autism: Four-year outcome and predictors. *American Journal on Mental Retardation, 110,* 417–438. doi:10.1352/0895-8017(2005)110[417:IBTFCW]2.0.CO;2

Sayers, B. (2010). Book Review: *All cats have Asperger's syndrome.* BellaOnline: The Voice of Women. Retrieved from http://www.bellaonline.org/articles/art49950.asp

Schechter, R., & Grether, J. K. (2008). Continuing increases in autism reported to California's developmental services system: Mercury in retrograde. *Archives of General Psychiatry, 65,* 19–24. doi:10.1001/archgenpsychiatry.2007.1

Scheuermann, B., & Webber, J. (2002). *Autism: Teaching does make a difference.* Stamford, CT: Wadsworth Group.

Schopler, E., Reichler, R. J., & Renner, B. (1988). *Childhood autism rating scale (CARS).* Los Angeles: Western Psychological Services.

Schuler, A. L. (1995). Thinking in autism: Differences in learning and development. In K. A. Quill (Ed.), *Teaching children with autism: Strategies to enhance communication and socialization* (pp. 11–32). New York: Delmar.

Scott, J. (Producer), & Hicks, S. (Writer/Director). (1996). *Shine* [Motion picture]. Australia: New Line Cinema.

Sebat, J., Lakshmi, B., Malhotra, D., Troge, J., Lese-Martin, C., Walsh, T., et al. (2007). Strong association of de novo copy number mutations with autism. *Science, 316,* 445–449. doi:10.1126/science.1138659

Semel, E., Wiig, E. H., Secord, W. A. (2004). Clinical evaluation of language fundamentals (4th ed.). Upper Saddle River, NJ: Pearson.

Shattuck, P. T. (2006). The contributions of diagnostic substitution to the growing administrative prevalence of autism in U.S. special education. *Pediatrics, 117,* 1028–1037. doi:10.1542/peds.2005-1516

Shore, S. (2003). My life with Asperger syndrome. In R. W. Du Charme & T. P. Gullotta (Eds.), *Asperger syndrome: A guide for professionals and families* (pp. 189–209). New York: Kluwer Academic/Plenum.

Simpson, R. L. (2004). Finding effective intervention and personnel preparation practices for students with autism spectrum disorders. *Exceptional Children, 70,* 135–144.

Simpson, R. L., de Boer-Ott, S. R., Griswold, D. E., Myles, B. S., Byrd, S. E., Ganz, J. B., et al. (2005). *Autism spectrum disorders: Interventions and treatments for children and youth.* Thousand Oaks, CA: Corwin Press.

Simpson, R. L., de Boer-Ott, S. R., & Smith-Myles, B. (2003). Inclusion of learners with autism spectrum disorders in general education settings. *Topics in Language Disorders, 23,* 116–133. doi:10.1097/00011363-200304000-00005

Skuse, D. H. (2009). Commentary: Is autism really a coherent syndrome in boys, or girls? *British Journal of Psychology, 100,* 33–37. doi:10.1348/000712608X369459

Stone, W. L., McMahon, C. R., Yoder, P. J., & Walden, T. A. (2007). Early social-communicative and cognitive development of younger siblings of children with autism spectrum disorders. *Archives of Pediatric and Adolescent Medicine, 161,* 384–390. doi:10.1001/ archpedi.161.4.384

Strock, M. (2004). *Autism spectrum disorders (pervasive developmental disorders).* Bethesda, MD: U.S. Department of Health and Human Services, National Institutes of Health, National Institute of Mental Health. Retrieved from www .nimh.nih.gov/publicat/autism.cfm

Sulzer-Azaroff, B., Hoffman, A. O., Horton, C. B., Bondy, A., & Frost, L. (2009). The Picture Exchange Communication System (PECS): What do the data say? *Focus on Autism and Other Developmental Disabilities, 24*(2), 89–103. doi:10.1177/1088357609332743

Sutcliffe, J. S. (2008). Genetics: Insights into the pathogenesis of autism. *Science, 321,* 208–209. doi:10.1126/science.1160555

Tager-Flusberg, H., Rogers, S., Cooper, J., Landa, R., Lord, C., Paul, R., . . . , & Yoder, P. (2009). Defining spoken language benchmarks and selecting measures of expressive language development for children with Autism Spectrum Disorders. *Journal of Speech, Language, and Hearing Research, 52,* 643–652. doi:10.1044/1092-4388(2009/08-0136)

Tammet, D. (2006). *Born on a blue day: A memoir of Asperger's and an extraordinary mind.* London: Hodder & Stoughton.

Travis, L. L., & Sigman, M. D. (2000). A developmental approach to autism. In A. J. Sameroff, M. Lewis, & S. M. Miller (Eds.), *Handbook of developmental psychopathology* (2nd ed., pp. 641–655). New York: Kluwer Academic/Plenum.

Treffert, D. A. (2006). *Extraordinary people: Understanding savant syndrome.* New York: Authors Guild Backprint Bookstore.

Volkmar, F. R., & Pauls, D. (2003). Autism. *The Lancet, 362,* 1133–1141. doi:10.1016/S0140-6736(03)14471-6

Wakefield, A. J., Murch, S. H., Anthony, A., Linnell, J., Casson, D. M., Malik, M., et al. (1998). Illeal-lymphoid-nodular hyperplasia, non-specific colitis, and pervasive developmental disorder in children. *The Lancet, 351,* 637–641. doi:10.1016/S0140-6736(97)11096-0

Wang, K., Zhang, H., Ma, D., Bucan, M., Glessner, J. T., Abrahams, B. S., & Hakonarson, H. (2009). Common genetic variants on 5p14.1 associate with autism spectrum disorders. *Nature, 459,* 528–533. doi:10.1038/nature07999

Werner, E., & Dawson, G. (2005). Validation of the phenomenon of autistic regression using home videotapes. *Archives of General Psychiatry, 62,* 889–895. doi:10.1001/archpsyc.62.8.889

Wing, L. (1981). Asperger syndrome: A clinical account. *Psychological Medicine, 11,* 115–129. doi:10.1017/S0033291700053332

Wing, L., & Potter, D. (2002). The epidemiology of autistic spectrum disorders: Is prevalence rising? *Mental Retardation & Developmental Disabilities Research Reviews, 8*(3), 151–161. doi:10.1002/mrdd.10029

CHAPTER 10

American Speech–Language–Hearing Association. (1993). Definitions of communication disorders and variations. *ASHA, 35*(Suppl. 10), 40–41.

Anderson, N. B., & Shames, G. H. (2006). *Human communication disorders* (7th ed.). Boston: Allyn & Bacon.

Audet, L. R., & Tankersley, M. (1999). Implications of communication and behavioral disorders for classroom management: Collaborative intervention techniques. In D. Rogers-Adkinson & P. Griffith (Eds.), *Communication disorders and children with psychiatric and behavioral disorders* (pp. 403–440). San Diego: Singular.

Bernthal, J. E., & Bankson, N. W. (1998). *Articulation and phonological disorders* (4th ed.). Boston: Allyn & Bacon.

Bernthal, J. E., & Bankson, N. W. (2004). *Articulation and phonological disorders* (5th ed.). Boston: Allyn & Bacon.

Calandrella, A. M., & Wilcox, M. J. (2000). Predicting language outcomes for young prelinguistic children with developmental delay. *Journal of Speech, Language and Hearing Research, 43,* 1061–1071. PMid:11063230

Campbell, S. L., Reich, A. R., Klockars, A. J., & McHenry, M. A. (1988). Factors associated with dysphonia in high school cheerleaders. *Journal of Speech and Hearing Disorders, 53,* 175–185. PMid:3361859

Cannito, M. P., Yorkston, K. M., & Beukelman, D. R. (Eds.). (1998). *Neuromotor speech disorders: Nature, assessment, and management.* Baltimore: Brookes.

Catts, H., Adlof, S., Hogan, T., & Ellis Weismer, S. (2005). Are specific language impairment and dyslexia distinct disorders? *Journal of Speech, Language, and Hearing Research, 48,* 1378–1396. doi:10.1044/1092-4388(2005/096)

Catts, H. W., Fey, M. E., Zhang, X., & Tomblin, J. (2001). Estimating the risk of future reading difficulties in kindergarten children: A research-based model and its clinical implications. *Language, Speech, and Hearing Services in Schools, 32,* 38–50. doi:10.1044/0161-1461(2001/004)

Choudhury, N., & Benasich, A. A. (2003). A family aggregation study: The influence of family history and other risk factors on language development. *Journal of Speech, Language, and Hearing Research, 46,* 261–272. doi:10.1044/1092-4388(2003/021)

Conti-Ramsden, G., Durkin, J., & Simkin, Z. (2010). Language and social factors in the use of cell phone technology by adolescents with and without specific language impairment (SLI). *Journal of Speech, Language, and Hearing Research, 53,* 196–208. doi:10.1044/0192-4388(2009/08/0241)

Conture, E. G. (2001). *Stuttering: Its nature, diagnosis, and treatment.* Boston: Allyn & Bacon.

DeThorne, L. S., Petrill, S. A., Schatschneider, C., & Cutting, L. (2010). Conversational language use as a predictor of early reading development: Language history as a modeling variable. *Journal of Speech, Language, and Hearing Research, 53,* 209–223. doi:10.1044/0192-4388(2009/08/0060).

Donahue, M. L., Hartas, D., & Cole, D. (1999). Research on interactions among oral language and emotional/behavioral disorders. In D. Rogers-Adkinson & P. Griffith (Eds.), *Communication disorders and children with psychiatric and behavioral disorders* (pp. 69–97). San Diego: Singular.

Fey, M. E., Catts, H. W., & Larrivee, L. S. (1995). Preparing preschoolers for academic and social challenges of school. In M. E. Fey, J. Windsor, & S. F. Warren (Eds.), *Language intervention: Preschool through the elementary years* (pp. 3–37). Baltimore: Brookes.

Foundas, A. L. (2001). The anatomical basis of language. *Topics in Language Disorders, 21*(3), 1–19.

Goldstein, B., & Iglesias, A. (2004). Language and dialectical variations. In J. E. Bernthal & N. W. Bankson (Eds.), *Articulation and phonological disorders* (5th ed., pp. 348–375). Boston: Allyn & Bacon.

Graham, S., Harris, K. R., MacArthur, C., & Schwartz, S. (1998). Writing instruction. In B. Y. L. Wong (Ed.), *Learning about learning disabilities* (2nd ed., pp. 391–424). San Diego: Academic Press.

Gustason, G., & Zawolkow, E. (1993). *Signing exact English dictionary.* Los Alamitos, CA: Modern Signs Press.

Hallahan, D. P., Lloyd, J. W., Kauffman, J. M., Weiss, M., & Martinez, E. (2005). *Introduction to learning disabilities* (3rd ed.). Boston: Allyn & Bacon.

Hammer, C. S., & Weiss, A. L. (2000). African American mothers' views of their infants' language development and language-learning environment. *American Journal of Speech-Language Pathology, 9,* 126–140.

Hart, B., & Risley, T. R. (1995). *Meaningful differences in the everyday experience of young American children.* Baltimore: Brookes.

Hulit, L. M., & Howard, M. R. (2010). *Born to talk: An introduction to speech and language development* (4th ed.). Boston: Allyn & Bacon.

Justice, L. M. (2006). *Communication sciences and disorders: An introduction.* Upper Saddle River, NJ: Pearson.

Justice, L. M., & Schuele, C. M. (2004). Phonological awareness: Description, assessment, and intervention. In J. E. Bernthal & N. W. Bankson (Eds.), *Articulation and phonological disorders* (5th ed., pp. 376–411). Boston: Allyn & Bacon.

Klein, H. B., & Moses, N. (1999). *Intervention planning for adults with communication problems: A guide for clinical practicum and professional practice.* Boston: Allyn & Bacon.

Kohnert, K., Windsor, J., & Yim, D. (2006). Do language-based processing tasks separate children with language impairment from typical bilinguals? *Learning Disabilities Research and Practice, 21,* 19–29. doi:10.1111/j.1540-5826.2006 .00204.x

Koury, L. N. (2007). Service delivery issues in early intervention. In R. Lubinski, L. A. C. Golper, & C. M. Frattali (Eds). *Professional issues in speech language pathology and audiology* (pp. 349–370). Clifton Park, NY: Thomson Delmar.

Lane, H. B., & Pullen, P. C. (2004). *Phonological awareness assessment and instruction: A sound beginning.* Boston: Allyn & Bacon.

McCabe, P. C., & Marshall, D. J. (2006). Measuring the social competence of preschool children with specific language impairment: Correspondence among informant ratings and behavioral observations. *Topics in Early Childhood Special Education, 26,* 234–246. doi:10.1177/0271121406026004004 01

McCormick, L., Loeb, D. F., & Schiefelbusch, R. L. (1997). *Supporting children with communication difficulties in inclusive settings: School-based language intervention.* Boston: Allyn & Bacon.

McGregor, K. K. (2000). The development and enhancement of narrative skills in a preschool classroom: Towards a solution to clinician–client mismatch. *American Journal of Speech-Language Pathology, 9,* 55–71.

Mercer, C. D., & Pullen, P. C. (2009). *Students with learning disabilities* (7th ed.). Upper Saddle River, NJ: Merrill/Pearson.

Mullen, R., & Schooling, T. (2010). The National Outcomes Measurement System for pediatric speech-language pathology. *Language, Speech, and Hearing Services in Schools, 41,* 44–60. doi:10.1044/0161-1461(2009/08-0051)

Muter, V., Hulme, C., Snowling, M. J., & Stevenson, J. (2004). Phonemes, rimes, vocabulary and grammatical skills as foundations of early reading development: Evidence from a longitudinal study. *Developmental Psychology, 40,* 665–681. doi:10.1037/0012-1649.40.5.665

Nelson, K. (1993). The psychological and social origins of autobiographical memories. *Psychological Science, 4,* 7–14. doi:10.1111/j.1467-9280.1993.tb00548.x

Onslow, M., Packman, A., & Payne P. A. (2007). Clinical identification of early stuttering: Methods, issues, and future directions. *Asia Pacific Journal of Speech Pathology and Audiology, 10,* 15–31.

Owens, R. E., Jr. (2004). *Language disorders: A functional approach to assessment and intervention* (4th ed.). Boston: Allyn & Bacon.

Owens, R. E., Jr., Evans, D. E., & Haas, B. A. (2000). *Introduction to communication disorders: A life span perspective.* Boston: Allyn & Bacon.

Owens, R. E., Metz, D. E., & Haas, A. (2007). *Introduction to communication disorders: A lifespan perspective.* Boston: Allyn & Bacon.

Owens, R. E., Metz, D. E., & Farinella, K. A. (2010). *Introduction to communication disorders: A lifespan evidence-based perspective.* Upper Saddle River, NJ: Pearson.

Peterson, R. L., Pennington, B. F., Shriberg, L. D., & Boada, R. (2009). What influences literacy outcome in children with speech sound disorder? *Journal of Speech, Language, and Hearing Research, 52,* 1175-1188. doi:10.1044/0192-4388(2009/08-0024)

Plante, E., & Beeson, P. M. (2004). *Communication and communication disorders: A clinical introduction* (2nd ed.). Boston: Allyn & Bacon.

Prizant, B. M. (1999). Early intervention: Young children with communication and emotional/behavioral problems. In D. Rogers-Adkinson & P. Griffith (Eds.), *Communication disorders and children with psychiatric and behavioral disorders* (pp. 295–342). San Diego: Singular.

Raspberry, W. (2001, August 21). Bi-English education: Low-income children might benefit from early immersion in standards. *Charlottesville Daily Progress,* p. A6.

Robinson, R. L., & Crowe, T. A. (2001). Fluency and voice. In D. M. Ruscello (Ed.), *Tests and measurements in speech-language pathology* (pp. 163–183). Boston: Butterworth-Heinemann.

Rogers-Adkinson, D., & Griffith, P. (Eds.). (1999). *Communication disorders and children with psychiatric and behavioral disorders.* San Diego: Singular.

Sawyer, D. J. (2006). Dyslexia: A generation of inquiry. *Topics in Language Disorders, 26,* 95–109.

Shields, D. (1990). *Dead languages.* St. Paul, MN: Greywolf Press.

Silliman, E. R., & Scott, C. M. (2006). Language impairment and reading disability: Connections and complexities. *Learning Disabilities Research and Practice, 21,* 1–7. doi:10.1111/j.1540-5826.2006.00202.x

Snowling, M. J., & Hayiou-Thomas, M. E. (2006). The dyslexia spectrum: Continuities between reading, speech, and language impairments. *Topics in Language Disorders, 26,* 110–126.

Soto, G., Solomon-Rice, P., & Caputo, M. (2009). Enhancing the personal narrative skills of elementary school-aged students who use AAC: The effectiveness of personal narrative intervention. *Journal of Communication*

Disorders, 42, 43–57. doi:10.1016/j.jcomdis.2008.08.001

Staskowski, M., & Nelson, N. W. (2007). Service delivery issues in educational settings. In R. Lubinski, L. A. C. Golper, & C. M. Frattali (Eds). *Professional issues in speech language pathology and audiology* (pp. 329–348). Clifton Park, NY: Thomson Delmar.

Stockman, I. J. (2010). A review of developmental and applied language research on African American children: From a deficit to difference perspective on dialect differences. *Language, Speech, and Hearing Services in Schools, 41,* 23–38. doi:10.1044/0161-1461(2009/08-0086)

Throneburg, R. N., Calvert, L. K., Sturm, J. J., Paramboukas, A. A., & Paul, P. J. (2000). A comparison of service delivery models: Effects on curricular vocabulary skills in the school setting. *American Journal of Speech-Language Pathology, 9,* 10–20.

Vellutino, F. R., Fletcher, J. M., Snowling, M. J., & Scanlon, D. M. (2004). Specific reading disability (dyslexia): What have we learned in the past four decades? *Journal of Child Psychology and Psychiatry, 45,* 2–40. doi:10.1046/j.0021-9630.2003.00305.x

Vinson, B. (2007). *Language disorders across the lifespan* (2nd ed.). New York: Thornson.

Warren, S. F., & Abbaduto, L. (1992). The relation of communication and language development to mental retardation. *American Journal on Mental Retardation, 97,* 125–130. PMid:1418929

Yairi, E., & Ambrose, N. (2004). Stuttering: Recent developments and future directions. *The AHSA Leader, 18,* 4–5, 14–15.

Yoder, P. J., & Warren, S. F. (2001). Relative treatment effects of two prelinguistic communication interventions on language development of toddlers with developmental delays vary by maternal characteristics. *Journal of Speech and Hearing Research, 44,* 224–237. doi:10.1044/1092-4388(2001/019)

CHAPTER 11

Adams, M. (1990). *Beginning to read: Thinking and learning about print.* Cambridge, MA: MIT Press.

Aldersley, S. (2002). Least restrictive environment and the courts. *Journal of Deaf Studies and Deaf Education, 7,* 189–199. doi:10.1093/deafed/7.3.189

Allinder, R. M., & Eccarius, M. A. (1999). Exploring the technical adequacy of curriculum-based measurement in reading for children who use manually coded English. *Exceptional Children, 65,* 271–288.

American Academy of Otolaryngology—Head and Neck Surgery. (2007). *Noise & Hearing Protection.* Retrieved from http://www.entnet.org/healthinfo/hearing/noise_hearing.cfm

Andrews, J. F., Leigh, I. W., & Weiner, M. T. (2004). *Deaf people: Evolving perspectives from psychology, education, and sociology.* Boston: Allyn & Bacon.

Andrews, J. F., Shaw, P. C., & Lomas, G. (2011). Deaf and hard of hearing students. In J. M. Kauffman & D. P. Hallahan (Eds.). *Handbook of special education.* New York: Routledge

Andrews, J. F., & Zmijewski, G. (1997). How parents support home literacy with deaf children. *Early Child Development and Care, 127,* 131–139. doi:10.1080/0300443971270111

Bornstein, M. H., Selmi, A. M., Haynes, O. M., Painter, K. M., & Marx, E. S. (1999). Representational abilities and the hearing status of child/mother dyads. *Child Development, 70,* 833–852. doi:10.1111/1467-8624.00060

Brashear, H., Henderson, V., Park, K-H., Hamilton, H., Lee, S., & Starner, T. (2006). American Sign Language recognition game development for deaf children. In *Proceedings of the 8th International ACM SIGACCESS Conference on Computers and Accessbility* (pp. 79–86). Portland, OR: ACM Press.

Brill, R. G., MacNeil, B., & Newman, L. R. (1986). Framework for appropriate programs for deaf children. *American Annals of the Deaf, 131,* 65–77.

Brown, A. S. (2009). Intervention, education, and therapy for children who are deaf and hard of hearing. In J. Katz, L. Medwetsky, R. Burkhard, & L. Hood (Eds.), *Handbook of clinical audiology* (6th ed., pp. 934–954). Philadelphia: Lippincott, Williams, & Wilkins.

Buchino, M. A. (1993). Perceptions of the oldest hearing child of deaf parents. *American Annals of the Deaf, 138,* 40–45.

Cambra, C. (1996). A comparative study of personality descriptors attributed to the deaf, the blind, and individuals with no sensory disability. *American Annals of the Deaf, 141,* 24–28.

Campbell, K. C. M., & Mullin, G. (2006, May 31). Otoacoustic emissions. *eMedicine.* Retrieved from http://www.emedicine.com/ent/topic372.htm

Campbell, R., & MacSweeney, M. (2004). Neuroimaging studies of crossmodal plasticity and language processing in deaf people. In G. A. Calvert, C. Spence, & B. E. Stein (Eds.), *The handbook of multisensory processing* (pp. 773–784). Cambridge, MA: MIT Press.

Cawthon, S. (2009). Professional development for teacher of students who are deaf or hard of hearing: Facing the assessment challenge. *American Annals of the Deaf, 154,* 50–61. doi:10.1353/aad.0.0073

Cawthon, S. W. (2010). Science and evidence of success: Two emerging issues in assessment accommodations for students who are deaf or hard of hearing. *Journal of Deaf Studies and Deaf Education, 15,* 185–203. doi: 10.1093/deafed/enq002

Charlson, E., Strong, M., & Gold, R. (1992). How successful deaf teenagers experience and cope with isolation. *American Annals of the Deaf, 137,* 261–270.

Cheng, S., & Rose, S. (2009). Investigating the technical adequacy of curriculum-based measurement in written expression for students who are deaf or hard of hearing. *Journal of Deaf Studies and Deaf Education, 14,* 503–515. doi:10.1093/deafed/enp013

Christiansen, J. B. (2009). The 2006 protest at Gallaudet University: Reflections and explanations. *Sign Language Studies, 10,* 69–89. doi:10.1353/sls.0.0033

Council for Exceptional Children. (2003). *What every special educator must know: Ethics, standards, and guidelines for special educators* (5th ed.). Arlington, VA: Author.

Emery, S. D., Middleton, A., & Turner, G. H. (2010). Whose deaf genes are they anyway? The Deaf community's challenge to legislation on embryo selection. *Sign Language Studies, 10,* 155–169. doi:10.1353/sls.0.0037

Emmorey, K. (2002). *Language, cognition, and the brain: Insights from sign language research.* Mahwah, NJ: Erlbaum.

Feldman, H. M., Dollaghan, C. A., Campbell, T. F., Colborn, D. K., Janosky, J., Kurs-Lasky, M., et al. (2003). Parent-reported language skills in relation to otitis media during the first 3 years of life. *Journal of Speech, Language, and Hearing*

Research, 46, 273–287. doi:10.1044/1092-4388(2003/022)

Gallaudet Research Institute. (2008, November). *Regional and National Summary Report of Data from the 2007–08 Annual Survey of Deaf and Hard of Hearing Children and Youth.* Washington, DC: GRI, Gallaudet University, Retrieved from http://gri.gallaudet.edu/Demographics/2008_National_Summary.pdf

Geers, A. E., Moog, J. S., Biedenstein, J., Brenner, C., & Hayes, H. (2009). Spoken language scores of children using cochlear implants compared to hearing age-mates at school entry. *Journal of Deaf Studies and Deaf Education, 14,* 371–385. doi:10.1093/deafed/enn046

Goldin-Meadow, S. (2003). *The resilience of language: What gesture creation in deaf children can tell us about how all children learn language.* New York: Psychology Press.

Individuals With Disabilities Data Accountability Center. (2010, April 12). Part B: Educational Environment, 2007. Retrieved from https://www.ideadata.org/PartBData.asp

Kegl J., Senghas A., & Coppola, M. (1999). Creation through contact: Sign language emergence and sign language change in Nicaragua. In M. DeGraff (Ed.), *Comparative grammatical change: The intersection of language acquisition, creole genesis, and diachronic syntax* (pp. 179–237). Cambridge, MA: MIT Press.

Kenneson A., & Cannon M. J. (2007). Review and meta-analysis of the epidemiology of congenital cytomegalovirus (CMV) infection. *Review of Medical Virology, 17,* 253–276. doi:10.1002/rmv.535

Kluwin, T. N., Stinson, M. S., & Colarossi, G. M. (2002). Social processes and outcomes of inschool contact between deaf and hearing peers. *Journal of Deaf Studies and Deaf Education, 7,* 200–213. doi:10.1093/deafed/7.3.200

Ladd, P. (2003). *Understanding Deaf culture: In search of Deafhood.* Clevedon, England: Multilingual Matters.

Lane, H. (1984). *When the mind hears: A history of the deaf.* New York: Random House.

Lane, H. (1992). *The mask of benevolence: Disabling the Deaf community.* New York: Knopf.

Lane, H., Hoffmeister, R., & Bahan, B. (1996). *A journey into the Deaf world.* San Diego, CA: Dawn Sign Press.

Lazarus, S. S., Thurlow, M. L., Lail, K. E., Eisenbraun, K. D., & Kato, K. (2006). *2005 state policies on assessment participation and accommodations for students with disabilities* (Synthesis Report 64). Minneapolis, MN: University of Minnesota, National Center on Educational Outcomes. Retrieved from http://education.umn.edu/NCEO/OnlinePubs/Synthesis64/

Lederberg, A. R., & Golbach, T. (2002). Parenting stress and social support in hearing mothers of deaf and hearing children: A longitudinal study. *Journal of Deaf Studies and Deaf Education, 7,* 330–345.

Lee, S., Henderson, V., & Brashear, H. (2005, June). CopyCat: An ASL game for deaf children. Paper presented at the meeting of the Rehabilitation Engineering & Assistive Technology Society of North America Student Design Competition, Atlanta, GA.

Marschark, M. (2002). *Language development in children who are deaf: A research synthesis.* Alexandria, VA: National Association of State Directors of Special Education (NASDE).

Marschark, M., Pelz, J. B., Convertino, C., Sapare, P., Arndt, M. E., & Seewagen, R. (2005). Classroom interpreting and visual information processing in mainstream education for deaf students: Live or Memorex®? *American Educational Research Journal, 42,* 727–761. doi:10.3102/00028312042004727

Marschark, M., Sapare, P., Convertino, C., & Seewagen, R. (2005). Access to postsecondary education through sign language interpreting. *Journal of Deaf Studies and Deaf Education, 10,* 38–50. doi:10.1093/deafed/eni002

Marschark, M., Sapare, P., Convertino, C., Seewagen, R., & Maltzen, H. (2004). Comprehension of sign language interpreting: Deciphering a complex task situation. *Sign Language Studies, 4,* 345–368. doi:10.1353/sls.2004.0018

Mason, T. C. (2005). Cross-cultural instrument translation: Assessment, translation, and statistical applications. *American Annals of the Deaf, 150,* 67–72. doi:10.1353/aad.2005.0020

Meadow-Orlans, K. P. (1987). An analysis of the effectiveness of early intervention programs for hearing-impaired children. In M. J. Guralnick & F. C. Bennett (Eds.), *The effectiveness of early intervention for at-risk and handicapped children* (pp. 325–362). New York: Academic Press.

Meadow-Orlans, K. P. (1990). Research on developmental aspects of deafness. In D. F. Moores & K. P. Meadow-Orlans (Eds.), *Educational and developmental aspects of deafness* (pp. 283–298). Washington, DC: Gallaudet University Press.

Mehra, S., Eavey, R. D., & Keamy, D. G. (2009). The epidemiology of hearing impairment in the United States: Newborns, children, and adolescents. *Otolaryngology—Head and Neck Surgery, 140,* 461–472. doi:10.1016/j.otohns.2008.12.022

Menchel, R. S. (1988). Personal experience with speechreading. *Volta Review, 90*(5), 3–15.

Middleton, A., Emery, S. D., & Turner, S. D. (2010). Views, knowledge, and beliefs about genetics and genetic counseling among deaf people. *Sign Language Studies, 10,* 170–196. doi:10.1353/sls.0.0038

Mitchell, R. E., & Karchmer, M. A. (2004). Chasing the mythical ten percent: Parental hearing status of deaf and hard of hearing students in the United States. *Sign Language Studies, 4,* 138–163. doi:10.1353/sls.2004.0005

Mitchell, R. E., & Karchmer, M. A. (2005). Parental hearing status and signing among deaf and hard of hearing children. *Sign Language Studies, 5,* 231–244. doi:10.1353/sls.2005.0004

Moeller, M. P., & Luetke-Stahlman, B. (1990). Parents' use of signing exact English: A descriptive analysis. *Journal of Speech and Hearing Disorders, 55,* 327–338.

Mueller, V., & Hurtig, R. (2010). Technology-enhanced shared reading with deaf and hard-of-hearing children: The role of a fluent signing narrator. *Journal of Deaf Studies and Deaf Education, 15,* 72–101. doi:10.1093/deafed/enp023

Mundy, L. (2002, March 31). A world of their own. *The Washington Post Magazine,* pp. 22–31.

Narr, R. A. F. (2006). Teaching phonological awareness with deaf and hard-of-hearing students. *Teaching Exceptional Children, 38*(4), 53–58.

National Institute on Deafness and Other Communication Disorders. (2008, August 4). Quick statistics. Retrieved from NIDC website: http://www.nidcd.nih.gov/health/statistics/quick.htm

National Institute on Deafness and Other Communication Disorders. (2009, August). Cochlear implants. Retrieved from http://www.nidcd.nih.gov/health/hearing/coch.htm#c

Nicaraguan sign language. (2010, March 15). Wikipedia. Retrieved from http://en.wikipedia.org/wiki/Nicaraguan_Sign_Language

Oliva, G. A. (2004). *Alone in the mainstream: A deaf woman remembers public school.* Washington, DC: Gallaudet University Press.

Padden, C., & Humphries, T. (1988). *Deaf in America: Voices from a culture.* Cambridge, MA: Harvard University Press.

Padden, C., & Humphries, T. (2005). *Inside deaf culture.* Cambridge, MA: Harvard University Press.

Padden, C. A. (1996). Early bilingual lives of Deaf children. In I. Parasnis (Ed.), *Cultural and language diversity and the Deaf experience* (pp. 99–116). Cambridge, England: Cambridge University Press.

Paul, P. (1998). *Literacy and deafness: The development of reading, writing, and literate thought.* Boston: Allyn & Bacon.

Powers, S. (2003). Influences of student and family factors on academic outcomes of mainstream secondary school deaf students. *Journal of Deaf Studies and Deaf Education, 8,* 57–78. doi:10.1093/deafed/8.1.57

Prinz, P. M., Strong, M., Kuntze, M., Vincent, M., Friedman, J., Moyers, P., et al. (1996). A path to literacy through ASL and English for Deaf children. In C. E. Johnson & J. H. V. Gilbert (Eds.), *Children's language* (Vol. 9, pp. 235–251). Mahwah, NJ: Erlbaum.

Punch, R., Creed, P. A., & Hyde, M. B. (2006). Career barriers perceived by hard-of-hearing adolescents: Implications for practice from a mixed-methods study. *Journal of Deaf Studies and Deaf Education, 11,* 225–237.

Punch, R., Hyde, M., & Creed, P. A. (2004). Issues in the school-to-work transition of hard of hearing adolescents. *American Annals of the Deaf, 149,* 28–38. doi:10.1353/aad.2004.0015

Quigley, S., Jenne, W., & Phillips, S. (1968). *Deaf students in colleges and universities.* Washington, DC: Alexander Graham Bell Association for the Deaf.

Reagan, T. (1990). Cultural considerations in the education of deaf children. In D. F. Moores & K. P. Meadow-Orlans (Eds.), *Educational and developmental aspects of deafness* (pp. 73–84). Washington, DC: Gallaudet University Press.

Renaissance Learning. (2006). *STAR early literacy assessment.* Wisconsin Rapids, WI: Author.

Sanghavi, D. M., (2006, December 5). Wanting babies like themselves, some parents choose genetic defects. *The New York Times.* Retrieved from www.nytimes.com/2006/12/05/health/05essa.html?ex=1322974800&en=9fbb1b0e738b55d1&ei=5088partner=rssnyt&emc=rss

Schick, B., Williams, K., & Kupermintz, H. (2006). Look who's being left behind: Educational interpreters and access to education for deaf and hard-of-hearing students. *Journal of Deaf Studies and Deaf Education, 11,* 3–20. doi:10.1093/deafed/enj007

Schirmer, B. R. (2001). *Psychological, social, and educational dimensions of deafness.* Boston: Allyn & Bacon.

Schroedel, J. G., & Geyer, P. D. (2000). Long-term career attainments of deaf and hard of hearing college graduates: Results from a 15-year follow-up survey. *American Annals of the Deaf, 145,* 303–314.

Seal, B. C. (2004). *Best practices in educational interpreting* (2nd ed.). Boston: Allyn & Bacon.

Senghas, A. (2003). Intergenerational influence and ontogenetic development in the emergence of spatial grammar in Nicaraguan Sign Language. *Cognitive Development, 18,* 511–531. doi:10 .1016/j.cogdev.2003.09.006

Sheridan, M. (2001). *Inner lives of deaf children: Interviews and analysis.* Washington, DC: Gallaudet University Press.

Siegel, L. (2000). The educational and communication needs of deaf and hard of hearing children: A statement of principle on fundamental educational change. *American Annals of the Deaf, 145,* 64–77.

Simms, L., Andrews, J., & Smith, A. (2005). A balanced approach to literacy instruction for deaf signing students, *Balanced Reading Instruction, 12,* 39–54.

Snow, C., Burns, N., & Griffin, P. (1998). *Preventing reading difficulties in young children.* Washington, D.C.: National Academy of the Sciences.

Stinson, M. S., & Whitmire, K. (1992). Students' views of their social relationships. In T. N. Kluwin, D. F. Moores, & M. G. Gaustad (Eds.), *Toward effective public school programs for deaf students: Context, process, and outcomes* (pp. 149–174). New York: Teachers College Press.

Stokoe, W. C. (1960). *Sign language structure.* Silver Spring, MD: Linstok Press.

Stokoe, W. C., Casterline, D. C., & Croneberg, C. G. (1976). *A dictionary of American Sign Language on linguistic principles* (2nd ed.). Silver Spring, MD: Linstok Press.

Takruri, L. (2006, October 30). Gallaudet exposes debate over deafness. *The Washington Post.* Retrieved from http://www.washingtonpost .com/wp-dyn/content/article/2006/10/30/ AR2006103000087.html

Tapper, J., & Sandell, C. (2006, May 10). *Is deaf university president not 'deaf enough'?* ABC News Internet Ventures. Retrieved from http:// www.abcnews.go.com/WNT/story?id=1947073

Thompson, S. J., Johnstone, C. J., Thurlow, M. L., & Altman, J. R. (2005). *2005 State special education outcomes: Steps forward in a decade of change.* Minneapolis, MN: University of Minnesota, National Center on Educational Outcomes. Retrieved from http://education.umn .edu/NCEO/OnlinePubs/2005StateReport.htm/

Thrasher, R. D. (2009, October 26). Middle ear, otitis media with effusion. *eMedicine,* Retrieved from http://emedicine.medscape.com/article/ 858990-overview

Trezek, B., Wang, Y., & Paul, P. (2010). *Reading and deafness: theory, research, and practice.* Clifton Park, NY: Delmar.

U.S. Department of Education, National Center on Student Progress Monitoring. (2006). *Review of progress monitoring tools.* Retrieved from http:// www.studentprogress.org/chart/chart.asp

Walker, L. A. (1986). *A loss for words: The story of deafness in a family.* New York: Harper & Row.

Waters, D., Campbell, R., Capek, C. M., Woll, B., David, A. S., McGuire, P. K., et al. (2007). Fingerspelling, signed language, text and picture processing in deaf native signers: The role of the mid-fusiform gyrus. *NeuroImage, 35,* 832–840. doi:10.1016/j.neuroimage.2007.01.025

CHAPTER 12

Barlow, J. M., Bentzen, B. L., & Bond, T. (2005). Blind pedestrians and the changing technology and geometry of signalized intersections: Safety, orientation, and independence. *Journal of Visual Impairment and Blindness, 99,* 587–598.

Barlow-Brown, F., & Connelly, V. (2002). The role of letter knowledge and phonological awareness in

young Braille readers. *Journal of Research in Reading, 25,* 259–270. doi:10.1111/1467-9817 .00174

Berk, L. E. (2005). *Infants and children: Infants through middle childhood* (5th ed.). Boston: Allyn & Bacon.

Bishop, V. E. (2004). *Teaching visually impaired children* (3rd ed.). Springfield, IL: Charles C. Thomas.

Bogart, D. (2009). Unifying the English Braille codes. *Journal of Visual Impairment and Blindness, 103,* 581–583.

Cameto, R., & Nagle, K. (2007). Orientation and mobility skills of secondary school students with visual impairments. Facts from NLTS2. NCSER 2008-3007. Retrieved from http://ies.ed.gov/ ncser/pdf/20083007.pdf

Capella-McDonnall, M. E. (2005). Predictors of competitive employment for blind and visually impaired consumers of vocational services. *Journal of Visual Impairment and Blindness, 99,* 303–315.

Castellano, C. (2005). *Making it work: Educating the Blind/VI student in the regular school.* Greenwich CT: Information Age Publishing.

Celeste, M. (2002). A survey of motor development for infants and young children with visual impairments. *Journal of Visual Impairment and Blindness, 96,* 169–174.

Celeste, M. (2006). Play behaviors and social interactions of a child who is blind: In theory and practice. *Journal of Visual Impairment and Blindness, 100,* 75–90.

Chong, C. (2004). Appropriate use of the electronic notetaker in school. *Braille Monitor, 47,* 29–31.

Corn, A. L., & Koenig, A. J. (2002). Literacy for students with low vision: A framework for delivering instruction. *Journal of Visual Impairment and Blindness, 96,* 305–321.

Council for Exceptional Children. (2003). *What every special educator must know: Ethics, standards, and guidelines for special educators* (5th ed.). Arlington, VA: Author.

D'Allura, T. (2002). Enhancing the social interaction skills of preschoolers with visual impairments. *Journal of Visual Impairment and Blindness, 96,* 576–584.

Emerson, R. W., Holbrook, M. C., & D'Andrea, F. M. (2009). Acquisition of literacy skills by young children who are blind: Results from the ABC Braille Study. *Journal of Visual Impairment and Blindness, 103,* 610–624.

Erin, J. N. (2006). Teaching social skills to elementary and middle school students with visual impairments. In S. Z. Sacks & K. E. Wolffe (Eds.), *Teaching social skills to students with visual impairments: From theory to practice* (pp. 364–404). New York: American Foundation for the Blind.

Fichten, C. S., Judd, D., Tagalakis, V., Amsel, R., & Robillard, K. (1991). Communication cues used by people with and without visual impairments in daily conversations and dating. *Journal of Visual Impairment and Blindness, 85,* 371–378.

Gal, E., & Dyck, M. J. (2009). Stereotyped movements among children who are visually impaired. *Journal of Visual Impairment and Blindness, 103,* 754–765.

Gillon, G. T., & Young, A. A. (2002). The phonological-awareness skills of children who are blind. *Journal of Visual Impairment and Blindness, 96,* 38–49.

Glaucoma Research Foundation. (2008, September 4). *What is glaucoma?* Retrieved from http://www .glaucoma.org/learn/what_is_glaucom.php

Grice, N. (2002). *Touch the universe.* Washington DC: Joseph Henry Press, National Academies press.

Harris, T. (2010, May 9). Howstuffworks: How guide dogs work. Retrieved from http://animals .howstuffworks.com/animal-facts/guide-dog.htm

Hatlen, P. (1998). Goal 8: Educational and developmental goals, including instruction, will reflect the assessed needs of each student in all areas of academic and disability-specific core curricular. In A. L. Corn & K. M. Huebner (Eds.), *A report to the nation: The national agenda for the education of children and youths with visual impairments, including those with multiple disabilities* (pp. 50–52). New York: AFP Press.

Hill, J., & Black, J. (2003). The Miniguide: A new electronic travel device. *Journal of Visual Impairment and Blindness, 97,* 655–656.

Houtenville, A. J. (2003). A comparison of the economic status of working-age persons with visual impairments and those of other groups. *Journal of Visual Impairment and Blindness, 97,* 133–148.

Huebner, K. M., & Wiener, W. (2005). Guest editorial. *Journal of Visual Impairment and Blindness, 99,* 579–583.

Hull, J. M. (1997). *On sight and insight: A journey into the world of blindness.* Oxford, England: Oneworld Publications.

Jernigan, K. (1992, June). Equality, disability, and empowerment. *Braille Monitor, 35,* 292–298.

Jindal-Snape, D. (2005). Self-evaluation and recruitment of feedback for enhanced social interaction by a student with visual impairment. *Journal of Visual Impairment and Blindness, 99,* 486–498.

Kirchner, C., & Smith, B. (2005). Transition to what? Education and employment outcomes for visually impaired youths after high school. *Journal of Visual Impairment and Blindness, 99,* 499–504.

Kleege, G. (1999). *Sight unseen.* New Haven, CT: Yale University Press.

Knott, N. I. (2002). *Teaching orientation and mobility in the schools: An instructor's companion.* New York: American Foundation for the Blind Press.

Koenig, A. J., & Holbrook, M. C. (2000). Ensuring high-quality instruction for students in braille literacy programs. *Journal of Visual Impairment and Blindness, 94,* 677–694.

Koenig, A. J., Sanspree, M. J., & Holbrook, M. C. (n.d.). Determining the reading medium for students with visual impairments. *D.V.I. Quarterly.* Retrieved from http://www.ed .arizona.edu/dvi/Postion%20Papers/ determining_ Read_med.htm

Kurson, R. (2005, June). Into the light. *Esquire.* Retrieved from http://www.esquire.com/ print-this/ESQ0605BLIND_114.2

Kurson, R. (2007). *Crashing through: A true story of risk, adventure, and the man who dared to see.* New York: Random House.

Kuusisto, S. (2004, June). Elegy for Ray Charles.

Kuusisto, S. (2006). *Eavesdropping.* New York: W. W. Norton. *Ragged Edge.*

Lansaw, J. (2000, December). Citizenship and the irony at the top of the world. *Braille Monitor, 43,* 963–965.

Lazarus, S. S., Thurlow, M. L., Lail, K. E., Eisenbraun, K. D., & Kato, K. (2006). *2005 state policies on assessment participation and accommodations for students with disabilities* (Synthesis Report 64). Minneapolis, MN: University of Minnesota, National Center on Educational Outcomes.

Lewis, S., & Iselin, S. A. (2002). A comparison of the independent living skills of primary students with visual impairments and their sighted peers:

A pilot study. *Journal of Visual Impairment and Blindness, 96,* 335–344.

Lewis, V., & Klauber, J. (2002). [Image] [Image] [Image] [Link] [Link] [Link]: Inaccessible Web design from the perspective of a blind librarian. *Library Hi Tech, 20,* 137–140. doi:10.1108/07378830210432499

Lussenhop, K., & Corn, A. L. (2003). Comparative studies of the reading performance of students with low vision. *RE:view, 34,* 57–69.

Maurer, M. (2000, April). Blindness, quotas, and the disadvantages of civil rights. *Braille Monitor, 43,* 287–296.

Maurer, M. (2003). The Federation is attacked for seeking to enhance mobility and safety. *Braille Monitor, 46,* 1–5.

McDonnall, M. C., & Crudden, A. (2009). Factors affecting the successful employment of transition-age youths with visual impairments. *Journal of Visual Impairment and Blindness, 103,* 329–341.

McHugh, E., & Lieberman, L. (2003). The impact of developmental factors on stereotypic rocking of children with visual impairments. *Journal of Visual Impairment and Blindness, 97,* 453–473.

Miura, R., Muraoka, T., & Ifukube, T. (2010). Comparison of obstacle sense ability between the blind and the sighted: A basic psychophysical study of designs of acoustic assistive devices. *Acoustical Science and Technology, 31,* 137–147. doi: 10.1250/ast.31.137

Morgan, S. K., & Bradley-Johnson, S. (1995). Technical adequacy of curriculum-based measurement for Braille readers. *School Psychology Review, 24,* 94–103.

National Cooperative Highway Research Program. (n.d.) Accessible pedestrian signals: A guide to best practices. Retrieved from http://www.apsguide.org/index.cfm

National Eye Institute. (2010, May). Facts about retinopathy of prematurity (ROP). Retrieved from http://www.nei.nih.gov/health/rop/rop.asp#5

National Federation of the Blind. (2006). NFB-NEWSLINE® Retrieved from http://www.nfb.org/nfb/Newspapers_by_Phone.asp?SnID=389319

Pare, J. G. (2005, June). Am I blind? *Braille Monitor, 48,* 412–414.

Perez-Pereira, M., & Conti-Ramsden, G. (1999). *Language development and social interaction in blind children.* East Sussex, England: Psychology Press, Ltd.

Prevent Blindness America. (2005). *Signs of possible eye trouble.* Retrieved from http://www.prevent blindness.org/children/trouble_signs.html

Raeder, W. N. (2010, May). The case for Braille. National Braille Press. Retrieved from http://www.nbp.org/ic/nbp/braille/case_for_braille.html

Rapp, D. W., & Rapp, A. J. (1992). A survey of the current status of visually impaired students in secondary mathematics. *Journal of Visual Impairment and Blindness, 86,* 115–117.

Rex, E. J., Koenig, A. J., Wormsley, D., & Baker, R. (1994). *Foundations of braille literacy.* New York: American Foundation for the Blind.

Rodgers, M. D., & Emerson, R. W. (2005, October). Human factor analysis of long cane design: Weight and length. *Journal of Visual Impairment and Blindness, 99,* 622–632.

Rosel, J., Caballer, A., Jara, P., & Oliver, J. C. (2005). Verbalism in the narrative language of children who are blind and sighted. *Journal of Visual Impairment and Blindness, 99,* 413–425.

Rumrill, P. D., Roessler, R. T., Battersby-Longden, J. C., & Schuyler, B. R. (1998). Situational assessment of the accommodation needs of employees who are visually impaired. *Journal of Visual Impairment and Blindness, 92,* 42–54.

Rumrill, P. D., Schuyler, B. R., & Longden, J. C. (1997). Profiles of on-the-job accommodations needed by professional employees who are blind. *Journal of Visual Impairment and Blindness, 91,* 66–76.

Ryles, R. (2000). Braille as a predictor of success. In *Braille into the next millennium.* Washington, DC: National Library Service for the Blind and Physically Handicapped and Friends of Libraries for Blind and Physically Handicapped Individuals in North America.

Ryles, R. N. (1997). The relationship of reading skills on employment, income, education, and reading habits. *Journal of Visual Impairment & Blindness, 83,* 306–313.

Sacks, O. (1996). *An anthropologist on Mars: Seven paradoxical tales.* New York: Vintage Books.

Sacks, S. Z. (2006). The development of social skills: A personal perspective. In S. Z. Sacks & K. E. Wolffe (Eds.), *Teaching social skills to students with visual impairments: From theory to practice* (pp. 3–19). New York: American Foundation for the Blind.

Sauerburger, D. (2005). Street crossings: Analyzing risks, developing strategies, and making decisions. *Journal of Visual Impairment and Blindness, 99,* 659–663.

Schroeder, F. K. (2002). Research and future opportunities for the blind. *Braille Monitor, 45,* 581–586.

Spungin, S. J. (2003). Cannibalism is alive and well in the blindness field. *Journal of Visual Impairment and Blindness, 97,* 69–71.

Thompson, S., & Thurlow, M. T. (2003). *2003 state special education outcomes: Marching on.* Minneapolis, MN: University of Minnesota, National Center on Educational Outcomes, University of Minnesota.

Thompson, S. J., Johnstone, C. J., Thurlow, M. L., & Altman, J. R. (2005). *2005 state special education outcomes: Steps forward in a decade of change.* Minneapolis, MN: University of Minnesota, National Center on Educational Outcomes.

Thurber, R. S., Shinn, M. R., & Smolkowski, K. (2002). What is measured in mathematics tests? Construct validity of curriculum-based mathematics measures. *School Psychology Review, 31,* 498–513.

Ulrey, P. (1994). When you meet a guide dog. *RE:view, 26,* 143–144.

Visual Prosthesis. (2010, May 10). In *Wikipedia.* Retrieved from http://en.wikipedia.org/wiki/Visual_prosthesis#cite_note-Ings-0

Warren, D. H. (1994). *Blindness and children: An individual differences approach.* New York: Cambridge University Press.

Webster, A., & Roe, J. (1998). *Children with visual impairments: Social interaction, language, and learning.* London: Routledge.

Weihenmayer, E. (2001). Touch the top of the world: A blind man's journey to climb farther than the eye can see. New York: Dutton.

Wolffe, K. E., Sacks, S. Z., Corn, A. L., Erin, J. N., Huebner, K. M., & Lewis, S. (2002). Teachers of students with visual impairments: What are they teaching? *Journal of Visual Impairment and Blindness, 96,* 293–303.

Wright, T., Wormsley, D. P., & Kamei-Hannan, C. (2009). Hand movements and Braille reading efficiency: Data from the Alphabetic Braille and Contracted Braille Study. *Journal of Visual Impairment and Blindness, 103,* 649–661.

Wunder, G. (1993, March). Mobility: Whose responsibility is it? *Braille Monitor, 36,* 567–572.

Zebehazy, K., Hartmann, E., & Durando, J. (2006). High-stakes testing and implications for students with visual impairments and other disabilities. *Journal of Visual Impairment and Blindness, 100,* 598–601.

Zimmerman, G. J., (2011). Blindness and low vision. In J. M. Kauffman & D. P. Hallahan (Eds.), *Handbook of special education.* New York: Routledge.

Zimmerman, G. J., Zebehazy, K. T., & Moon, M. L. (2010). Optics and low vision devices. In A. L. Corn & J. N. Erin (Eds.), *Foundations of low vision: Clinical and functional perspectives* (2nd ed., pp. 192–237). New York: AFB Press.

CHAPTER 13

Aitken, S. (2000). Understanding deafblindness. In S. Aitken, M. Buultjens, C. Clark, J. T. Eyre, & L. Pease (Eds.), *Teaching children who are deafblind: Contact, communication, and learning* (pp. 1–34). London: David Fulton.

Ashley, M. J. (Ed.). (2004). *Traumatic brain injury: Rehabilitative treatment and case management* (2nd ed.). Boca Raton, FL: CRC Press.

Best, S. J., Heller, K. W., & Bigge, J. L. (2010). *Teaching individuals with physical or multiple disabilities* (6th ed.). Upper Saddle River, NJ: Pearson.

Beukelman, D. R., Yorkston, K. M., & Reichle, J. (Eds.). (2000). *Augmentative and alternative communication for adults with acquired neurologic disorders.* Baltimore: Brookes.

Bodfish, J. W. (2007). Stereotypy, self-injury, and related abnormal repetitive behaviors. In J. W. Jacobson, J. A. Mulick, & J. Rojahn (Eds.), *Handbook of intellectual and developmental disabilities* (pp. 481–505). New York: Springer.

Cardona, G. W. (2000). Spaghetti talk. In M. Oken-Fried & H. A. Bersani (Eds.), *Speaking up and spelling it out: Personal essays on augmentative and alternative communication* (pp. 237–244). Baltimore: Brookes.

Chen, D., Alsop, L., & Minor, L. (2000). Lessons from Project PLAI in California and Utah: Implications for early intervention services to infants who are deaf-blind and their families. *Deaf-Blind Perspectives, 7*(3), 1–8.

Chen, D., Downing, J., & Rodriguez-Gil, G. (2000/2001). Tactile learning strategies for children who are deaf-blind: Concerns and considerations from Project SALUTE. *Deaf-Blind Perspectives, 8*(2), 1–6.

Council for Exceptional Children. (2001). Traumatic brain injury: The silent epidemic. *CEC Today, 7*(7), 1, 5, 15.

Crimmins, C. (2000). *Where is the mango princess?* New York: Knopf.

Cullen, C., & Mudford, O. C. (2005). Gentle teaching. In J. W. Jacobson, R. M. Foxx, & J. A. Mulick (Eds.), *Controversial therapies for developmental disabilities: Fad, fashion, and science in professional practice* (pp. 423–432). Mahwah, NJ: Erlbaum.

Dell Orto, A. E., & Power, P. W. (2000). *Brain injury and the family: A life and living perspective* (2nd ed.). Washington, DC: CRC Press.

DePompei, R., & Tyler, J. (2004). Children and adolescents: Practical strategies for school participation. In M. J. Ashley (Ed.), *Traumatic brain injury: Rehabilitative treatment and case management* (2nd ed., pp. 559–580). Boca Raton, FL: CRC Press.

Dunst, C. J. (2011). Advances in theory, assessment and intervention with infants and toddlers with disabilities. In J. M. Kauffman & D. P. Hallahan (Eds.), *Handbook of special education.* New York: Routledge.

Dykens, E. M., Hodapp, R. M., & Finucaine, B. M. (2000). *Genetics and mental retardation syndromes: A new look at behavior and interventions*. Baltimore, MD: Brookes.

Everson, J. M., & Trowbridge, M. H. (2011). Preparing students with low-incidence disabilities for community living opportunities. In J. M. Kauffman & D. P. Hallahan (Eds.), *Handbook of special education*. New York: Routledge.

Fagbemi, M. (2009). Internet social networking sites: Building community one friend at a time. *Deaf-Blind Perspectives, 17*, 8–9.

Franklin, P., & Bourquin, E. (2000). Picture this: A pilot study for improving street crossings for deaf-blind travelers. *RE:view, 31*, 173–179.

Freeberg, E. (2001). *The education of Laura Bridgman: First deaf and blind person to learn language*. Cambridge, MA: Harvard University Press.

Gardner, W. I. (2007). Aggression in persons with intellectual disabilities and mental disorders. In J. W. Jacobson, J. A. Mulick, & J. Rojahn (Eds.), *Handbook of intellectual and developmental disabilities* (pp. 541–562). New York: Springer.

Gense, D. J., & Gense, M. (2004). *The importance of orientation and mobility skills for students who are deaf-blind*. Retrieved from http://dblink.org/lib/o&m.htm

Gerenser, J., & Forman, B. (2007). Speech and language deficits in children with developmental disabilities. In J. W. Jacobson, J. A. Mulick, & J. Rojahn (Eds.), *Handbook of intellectual and physical disabilities* (pp. 563–579). NY: Springer.

Grandinette, S., & Best, D. J. (2009). Traumatic brain injury. In K. W. Heller, P. E. Forney, P. A. Alberto, S. J. Best, & M. N. Schwartzman, *Understanding physical, health, and multiple disabilities* (2nd ed., pp. 118–138). Upper Saddle River, NJ: Pearson.

Green, P. M. (Producer), & Penn, A. (Director). (1962). *The Miracle Worker*. United States: Paramount Pictures.

Hall, B. D. (1979). Choanal atresia and associated multiple anomalies. *Journal of Pediatrics, 95*, 395–398. doi:10.1016/S0022-3476(79)80513-2

Heller, K. W., & Bigge, J. L. (2010). Augmentative and alternative communication. In S. J. Best, K. W. Heller, J. L. Bigge, *Teaching individuals with physical or multiple disabilities* (6th ed., pp. 221–254). Upper Saddle River, NJ: Pearson.

Heller, K. W., Forney, P. E., Alberto, P. A., Best, S. J., & Schwartzman, M. N. (2009). *Understanding physical, health, and multiple disabilities* (2nd ed.). Upper Saddle River, NJ: Pearson.

Hodges, L. (2000). Effective teaching and learning. In S. Aitken, M. Buultjens, C. Clark, J. T. Eyre, & L. Pease (Eds.), *Teaching children who are deafblind: Contact, communication, and learning* (pp. 167–199). London: David Fulton Publishers.

Horner, R. H., Vaughn, B., Day, H. M. & Ard, B. (1996) The relationship between setting events and problem behavior. In L. K. Koegel, R. L. Koegel, & G. Dunlap (Eds.), *Positive behavioral support: Including people with difficult behavior in the community* (pp. 381–402). Baltimore: Brookes.

Individuals With Disabilities Education Improvement Act of 2004. (2004). 20 U.S.C. § 1400 *et seq.*

Inge, K. J., & Moon, M. S. (2011). Preparing students with low incidence disabilities to work in the community. In J. M. Kauffman & D. P. Hallahan (Eds.), *Handbook of special education*. New York: Routledge.

Janssen, M. J., Riksen-Walraven, J. M., & van Dijk, J. P. M. (2004). Enhancing the interactive competence of deafblind children: Do intervention effects endure? *Journal of Developmental and Physical Disabilities, 16*, 73–94. doi:10.1023/B:JODD.0000010040.54094.0f

Kauffman, J. M. (2002). *Education deform: Bright people sometimes say stupid things about education*. Lanham, MD: Scarecrow Education.

Kauffman, J. M. (2008). Special education. In T. L. Good (Ed.), *21st century education: A reference handbook* (pp. 405–413). Thousand Oaks, CA: Sage.

Kauffman, J. M., Conroy, M., Gardner, R., & Oswald, D. (2008). Cultural sensitivity in the application of behavior principles to education. *Education and Treatment of Children, 31*, 239–262. doi:10.1353/etc.0.0019

Kauffman, J. M., & Hallahan, D. P. (2005). *Special education: What it is and why we need it*. Boston: Allyn & Bacon.

Kauffman, J. M., & Landrum, T. J. (2009). *Characteristics of emotional and behavioral disorders of children and youth* (9th ed.). Upper Saddle River, NJ: Merrill/Pearson.

Kauffman, J. M., Pullen, P. L., Mostert, M. P., & Trent, S. C. (2011). *Managing classroom behavior: A reflective case-based approach* (5th ed.). Upper Saddle River, NJ: Pearson.

Keller, H. (1905). *The story of my life*. New York: Grosset & Dunlap.

Klein, M. D., Chen, D., & Haney, C. M. (2000). *Promoting learning through active interation: A guide to early communication with young children who have multiple disabilities*. Baltimore: Brookes.

Kleopfer, H. W., Laguaite, J. K., & McLaurin, J. W. (1966). The hereditary syndrome of congenital deafness and retinitis pigmentosa (Usher's syndrome). *Laryngoscope, 76*, 850–862.

Koegel, L. K., Koegel, R. L., & Dunlap, G. (Eds.). (1996). *Positive behavioral support: Including people with difficult behavior in the community*. Baltimore: Brookes.

Lajiness-O'Neill, R., & Erdodi, L. A. (2011). Traumatic brain injury. In J. M. Kauffman & D. P. Hallahan (Eds.), *Handbook of special education*. New York: Routledge.

Melancon, F. (2000). A group of students with Usher syndrome in south Louisiana. *Deaf Blind Perspectives, 8*(1), 1–3.

Miles, B. (1998). *Overview of deaf-blindness*. Monmouth, OR: DB-LINK. Retrieved from www.tr.wou.edu/dblink/Overview2.htm

Miles, B. (1999, March 9). *Talking the language of the hands*. Retrieved June 1, 2001, from www.tr.wou.edu/dblink/hands2.htm

Miner, I., & Cioffi, J. (1999, October 25). *Usher syndrome in the school setting*. Retrieved May 15, 2001, from www.tr.wou.edu/dblink/usherfulltext.htm

Morris, R. J., & Mather, N. (Eds.). (2008). *Evidence-based interventions for students with learning and behavioral challenges*. London: Taylor & Francis.

Moss, K., & Hagood, L. (1995). *Teaching strategies and content modifications for the child with deaf blindness*. Austin, TX: Texas School for the Blind and Visually Impaired.

Mostert, M. P. (1998). *Interprofessional collaboration in schools*. Boston: Allyn & Bacon.

Mulick, J. A., & Butter, E. M. (2005). Positive behavior support: A paternalistic utopian delusion. In J. W. Jacobson, R. M. Foxx, & J. A. Mulick (Eds.), *Controversial therapies for developmental*

disabilities: Fad, fashion, and science in professional practice (pp. 385–404). Mahwah, NJ: Erlbaum.

National Data Accountability Center. (2010, June). Individuals with Disabilities Education Act (IDEA) Data. Retrieved from https://www.ideadata.org/default.asp

National Institute on Deafness and Other Communication Disorders. (2010, June 7). Usher syndrome. Retrieved from http://www.nidcd.nih.gov/health/hearing/usher.asp

Newsom, C., & Kroeger, K. A. (2005). Nonaversive treatment. In J. W. Jacobson, R. M. Foxx, & J. A. Mulick (Eds.), *Controversial therapies for developmental disabilities: Fad, fashion, and science in professional practice* (pp. 405–422). Mahwah, NJ: Erlbaum.

Noonan, M. J., & McCormick, L. (2006). *Young children with disabilities in natural environments*. Baltimore: Brookes.

Oken-Fried, M., & Bersani, H. A. (Eds.). (2000). *Speaking up and spelling it out: Personal essays on augmentative and alternative communication*. Baltimore: Brookes.

Oley, C. A. (2001). CHARGE association. In S. B. Cassidy & J. E. Allanson (Eds.), *Management of genetic syndromes* (pp. 71–84). New York: Wiley-Liss.

Osborne, J. G. (2005). Person-centered planning: A *faux fixe* in the service of humanism? In J. W. Jacobson, R. M. Foxx, & J. A. Mulick (Eds.), *Controversial therapies for developmental disabilities: Fad, fashion, and science in professional practice* (pp. 313–329). Mahwah, NJ: Erlbaum.

Pease, L. (2000). Creating a communicating environment. In S. Aitken, M. Buultjens, C. Clark, J. T. Eyre, & L. Pease (Eds.), *Teaching children who are deafblind: Contact, communication, and learning* (pp. 35–82). London: David Fulton Publishers.

Persel, C. S., & Persel, C. H. (2004). The use of applied behavior analysis: Traumatic brain injury rehabilitation. In M. J. Ashley (Ed.), *Traumatic brain injury: Rehabilitative treatment and case management* (2nd ed., pp. 403–453). Boca Raton, FL: CRC Press.

Smith, K. G., Smith, I. M., & Blake, K. (2010). CHARGE syndrome: An educator's primer. *Education and Treatment of Children, 33*, 289–314.

Snell, M. E., & Brown, F. (2006). *Instruction of students with severe disabilities* (6th ed.). Upper Saddle River, NJ: Pearson.

Stichter, J. P., Conroy, M. A., & Kauffman, J. M. (2008). *An introduction to students with high-incidence disabilities*. Upper Saddle River, NJ: Merrill-Prentice Hall.

Thompson, R. H., & Iwata, B. A. (2001). A descriptive analaysis of social consequences following problem behavior. *Journal of Applied Behavior Analysis, 34*, 169–178. doi:10.1901/jaba.2001.34-169

Walther-Thomas, C., Korinek, L., McLaughlin, V. L., & Williams, B. T. (2000). *Collaboration for inclusive education: Developing successful programs*. Boston: Allyn & Bacon.

Westling, D. L., & Fox, L. (2000). *Teaching students with severe disabilities* (2nd ed.). Upper Saddle River, NJ: Merrill.

Wrong Diagnosis. (2010, June 26). Prevalence and incidence of Usher syndrome. Retrieved from http://www.wrongdiagnosis.com/u/usher_syndrome/prevalence.htm

Yoder, D. E. (2001). Having my say. *Augmentative and Alternative Communication, 17*, 2–10.

Zentner, G. E., Layman, W. S., Martin, D. M., & Scacheri, P. C. (2010). Molecular and phenotypic aspects of CHD7 mutation in CHARGE syndrome. *American Journal of Medical Genetics Part A, 152A*, 674–686.

CHAPTER 14

Arzimanoglou, A., Guerrini, R., & Aicardi, J. (2004). *Aicardi's epilepsy in children* (3rd ed.). Philadelphia: Lippincott Williams & Wilkins.

Auxter, D., Pyfer, J., & Huettig, C. (2005). *Principles and methods of adapted physical education and recreation* (10th ed.). New York: McGraw-Hill.

Barkovich, A. J. (2005). *Pediatric neuroimaging* (4th ed.). Philadelphia: Lippincott Williams & Wilkins.

Batshaw, M. L. (Ed.). (2002). *Children with disabilities* (5th ed.). Baltimore: Brookes.

Batshaw, M. L., & Tuchman, M. (2002). PKU and other inborn errors of metabolism. In M. L. Batshaw (Ed.), *Children with disabilities* (5th ed., pp. 333–345). Baltimore: Brookes.

Bax, M. (2001). Editorial: What's in a name? *Developmental Medicine and Child Neurology, 43*, 75.

Best, S. J., & Bigge, J. L. (2010). Cerebral palsy. In S. J. Best, K. W. Heller, & J. L. Bigge, *Teaching individuals with physical or multiple disabilities* (6th ed.). Upper Saddle River, NJ: Merrill/Pearson.

Best, S. J., Heller, K. W., & Bigge, J. L. (2010). *Teaching individuals with physical or multiple disabilities* (6th ed.). Upper Saddle River, NJ: Merrill/Pearson.

Bottos, M., Feliciangeli, A., Sciuto, L., Gericke, C., & Vianello, A. (2001). Functional status of adults with cerebral palsy and implications for treatment of children. *Developmental Medicine and Child Neurology, 43*, 516–528. doi:10.1017/S0012162201000950

Cascio, J. (2007, June 13). *The accidental cyborg.* Retrieved from http://ieet.org/index.php/IEET/more/cascio20070613/

DeFord, S. (1998, July 26). High tech for the disabled. *The Washington Post Education Review, 4*, 30.

Dunst, C. J. (2011). Advances in theory, assessment and intervention with infants and toddlers with disabilities. In J. M. Kauffman & D. P. Hallahan (Eds.), *Handbook of special education.* New York: Routledge.

Earley, T. (2000). *Jim the boy.* Boston: Little, Brown.

Goodman, E. (2007, May 29). Wheels competing with feet. *Charlottesville Daily Progress*, A8.

Heller, K. W., Alberto, P. A., Forney, P. E., & Schwartzman, M. N. (2009). *Understanding physical, sensory, and health impairments: Characteristics and educational implications* (2nd ed.). Upper Saddle River, NJ: Pearson.

Holmes, M. S. (2004). *Fictions of affliction: Physical disability in Victorian culture.* Ann Arbor, MI: University of Michigan Press.

Howe, M. (n.d.) *Born to run.* Retrieved from www.spectrum.ieee.org/print/2189

Kelly, L. E., & Block, M. E. (2011). Physical education. In J. M. Kauffman & D. P. Hallahan (Eds.), *Handbook of special education.* New York: Routledge.

Lajiness-O'Neill, R., & Erdodi, L. A. (2011). Traumatic brain injury. In J. M. Kauffman & D. P. Hallahan (Eds.), *Handbook of special education.* New York: Routledge.

Levy, S. E., & O'Rourke, M. (2002). Technological assistance: Innovations for independence. In M. L. Batshaw (Ed.), *Children with disabilities* (5th ed., pp. 629–645). Baltimore: Brookes.

Lindsey, J. E. (Ed.). (2000). *Technology and exceptional individuals* (3rd ed.). Austin, TX: Pro-Ed.

Liptak, G. (2002). Neural tube defects. In M. L. Batshaw (Ed.), *Children with disabilities* (5th ed., pp. 467–492). Baltimore: Brookes.

Longman, J. (2007, May 15). An amputee sprinter: Is he disabled or too-abled? *The New York Times.* Retrieved from http://www.nytimes.com/2007/05/15/sports/othersports/15runner.html?ex=1183176000&en=1a1cac2e919125c0&ei=5070

Martin, S. (2006). *Teaching motor skills to children with cerebral palsy and similar movement disorders: A guide for parents and professionals.* Bethesda, MD: Woodbine House.

McGrath, B. (2007, July 30). Muscle memory: The next generation of bionic prostheses. *The New Yorker*, pp.40–45.

Metzler, I. (2006). *Disability in medieval Europe: Thinking about physical impairment during the Middle Ages, c. 1100–1400.* New York: Routledge.

Moon, M. S. (Ed.). (2011). Section X. Transition of adults with low incidence disabilities. In J. M. Kauffman & D. P. Hallahan (Eds.), *Handbook of special education.* New York: Routledge.

Nabors, L. A., & Lehmkuhl, H. D. (2004). Children with chronic medical conditions: Recommendations for school mental health clinicians. *Journal of Developmental and Physical Disabilities, 16*, 1–19. doi:10.1023/B:JODD.0000010036.72472.55

Navarro, M. (2007, May 13). "This is who I am. If you have a problem with it, that's your problem." *The New York Times*, Section 9, 1, 8–9.

Olrick, J. T., Pianta, R. C., & Marvin, R. S. (2002). Mother's and father's responses to signals of children with cerebral palsy during feeding. *Journal of Developmental and Physical Disabilities, 14*, 1–17. doi:10.1023/A:1013537528167

Perrin, J. M., Bloom, S. R., & Gortmaker, S. L. (2007). The increase of childhood chronic conditions in the United States. *Journal of the American Medical Association, 297*, 2755–2759.

Robertson, C. M. T., Watt, M., & Yasui, Y. (2007). Changes in the prevalence of cerebral palsy for children born very prematurely within a population-based program over 30 years. *Journal of the American Medical Association, 297*, 2733–2740.

Saslow, E. (2007, April 12). In Maryland, a fight to the finish line: Wheelchair racer's quest for inclusion spurs debate. *The Washington Post*, A1, A16.

Scanlon, D. J. (Ed.). (2011). Section IX. Transition of adults with high incidence disabilities. In J. M. Kauffman & D. P. Hallahan (Eds.), *Handbook of special education.* New York: Routledge.

Sherman, E. M. S., Slick, D. J., & Eyrl, K. L. (2006). Executive dysfunction is a significant predictor of poor quality of live in children with epilepsy. *Epilepsia, 47*, 1936–1942. doi:10.1111/j.1528-1167.2006.00816.x

Singh, D. K. (2003). Families of children with spina bifida: A review. *Journal of Developmental and Physical Disabilities, 15*, 37–55. doi:10.1023/A:1021452220291

Specter, S. (2009). *Denialism: How irrational thinking hinders scientific progress, harms the planet, and threreatens our lives.* New York: Penguin.

Torpy, J. M. (2010). Chronic diseases of children. *Journal of the American Medical Association, 303*(7), 682. doi:10.001/jama.303.7.682

Vig, S., & Kaminer, R. (2002). Maltreatment and developmental disabilities in children. *Journal of Developmental and Physical Disabilities, 14*, 371–386. doi:10.1023/A:1020334903216

Weinstein, S. (2002). Epilepsy. In M. L. Batshaw (Ed.), *Children with disabilities* (5th ed., pp. 493–523). Baltimore: Brookes.

Welch, E. M., Barton, E. R., Zhuo, J., Tomizawa, Y., Friesen, W. J., Trifillis, P., et al. (2007, May 3). PTC124 targets genetic disorders caused by nonsense mutations. *Nature, 447*, 87–91. Retrieved from www.nature.com/nature/journal/vaop/ncurrent/abs/nature05756.html

White, P. H., Schuyler, V., Edelman, A., Hayes, A., & Batshaw, M. L. (2002). Future expectations: Transition from adolescence to adulthood. In M. L. Batshaw (Ed.), *Children with disabilities* (5th ed., pp. 693–705). Baltimore: Brookes.

Willen, E. J. (2006). Neurocognitive outcomes in pediatric HIV. *Mental Retardation and Developmental Disabilities Research Reviews, 12*, 223–228. doi:10.1002/mrdd.20112

Zylke, J. W., & DeAngelis, C. D. (2007). Pediatric chronic diseases—stealing childhood. *Journal of the American Medical Association, 297*, 2765–2766.

CHAPTER 15

Ambrose, D. (Ed.). (2010). STEM high schools. *Roeper Review, 32*(1), special issue.

Assouline, S. G., & Colangelo, N. (2006). Social-emotional development of gifted adolescents. In F. A. Dixon & S. M. Moon (Eds.), *The handbook of secondary gifted education* (pp. 65–86). Waco, TX: Prufrock Press.

Assouline, S. G., & Lupkowski-Shoplik, A. (2003). *Developing mathematical talent: A guide for challenging and educating gifted students.* Waco, TX: Prufrock Press.

Assouline, S. G., Nicpon, M. F., & Doobay, A. (2009). Profoundly gifted girls and autism spectrum disorder. *Gifted Child Quarterly, 53*, 89–105. doi: 10.1177/0016986208330565

Assouline, S. G., Nicpon, M. F., & Whiteman, C. (2010). Cognitive and psychosocial characteristics of gifted students with written language disability. *Gifted Child Quarterly, 54*, 102–115. doi: 10.1177/0016986209355974

Borland, J. H. (1989). *Planning and implementing programs for the gifted.* New York: Teachers College Press.

Borland, J. H. (1997). The construct of giftedness. *Peabody Journal of Education, 72*(3&4), 6–20.

Borland, J. H. (2004). *Issues and practices in the identification and education of gifted students from under-represented groups.* Storrs, CT: National Research Center on the Gifted and Talented.

Brighton, C. M., & Jarvis, J. M. (2011). Early identification and intervention in gifted education: Developing talent in diverse learners. In J. M. Kauffman & D. P. Hallahan (Eds.), *Handbook of special education.* New York: Routledge.

Brody, L. E., & Stanley, J. C. (2005). Youths who reason exceptionally well mathematically and/or verbally. In R. J. Sternberg & J. E. Davidson (Eds.), *Conceptions of giftedness* (2nd ed., pp. 20–37). New York: Cambridge University Press.

Callahan, C. M. (2000). Evaluation as a critical component of program development and implementation. In K. A. Heller, F. J. Monks, R. J. Sternberg, & R. F. Subotnik (Eds.), *International handbook of giftedness and talent* (2nd ed., pp. 537–548). New York: Pergamon.

Callahan, C. M. (2001). Evaluating learner and program outcomes in gifted education. In F. A.

Karnes & S. M. Bean (Eds.), *Methods and materials for teaching the gifted* (pp. 253–298). Waco, TX: Prufrock Press.

Callahan, C. M. (2003). *Advanced placement and international baccalaureate programs for talented students in American high schools: A focus on science and mathematics.* Storrs, CT: National Research Center on the Gifted and Talented.

Callahan, C. M. (2011). Special gifts and talents. In J. M. Kauffman & D. P. Hallahan (Eds.), *Handbook of special education.* New York: Routledge.

Chan, D. W. (2006). Perceived multiple intelligences among male and female Chinese gifted students in Hon Kong: The structure of the Student Multiple Intelligences Profile. *Gifted Child Quarterly, 50,* 325–338.

Cline, S., & Hegeman, K. (2001). Gifted children with disabilities. *Gifted Child Today, 24*(3), 16–24.

Colangelo, N., & Assouline, S. G. (2000). Counseling gifted students. In K. A. Heller, F. J. Monks, R. J. Sternberg, & R. F. Subotnik (Eds.), *International handbook of giftedness and talent* (2nd ed., pp. 595–608). New York: Pergamon.

Colangelo, N., Assouline, S. G., & Gross, M. U. M. (2004a). *A nation deceived: How schools hold back America's brightest students. Vol. I.* Iowa City, IA: Connie Belin & Jacqueline N. Blank International Center for Gifted Education and Talent Development.

Colangelo, N., Assouline, S. G., & Gross, M. U. M. (Eds.). (2004b). *A nation deceived: How schools hold back America's brightest students. Vol. II.* Iowa City, IA: Connie Belin & Jacqueline N. Blank International Center for Gifted Education and Talent Development.Council for Exceptional Children. (2001). *Performance-based standards.* Retrieved from www.cec.sped.org/ps/perf_based_stds/index.html

Dale, E. J. (2000). Technology for individuals with gifts and talents. In J. E. Lindsey (Ed.), *Technology and exceptional individuals* (3rd ed., pp. 375–407). Austin, TX: Pro-Ed.

Davis, G. A., & Rimm S. B. (2004) *Education of the gifted and talented* (5th ed.). Boston: Allyn & Bacon.

De Hahn, E. L. H. (2000). Cross-cultural studies in gifted education. In K. A. Heller, F. J. Monks, R. J. Sternberg, & R. F. Subotnik (Eds.), *International handbook of giftedness and talent* (2nd ed., pp. 549–561). New York: Pergamon.

DiGennaro, J. (2007, February 10). Gifted minds we need to nurture. *The Washington Post,* A17.

Dixon, F. A., & Moon, S. M. (Eds.). (2006). *The handbook of secondary gifted education.* Waco. TX: Prufrock Press.

Ford, D. Y., & Moore, J. L. (2006). Being gifted and adolescent: Issues and needs of students of color. In F. A. Dixon & S. M. Moon (Eds.), *The handbook of Secondary gifted education* (pp. 113–136). Waco, TX: Prufrock Press.

Freeman, J. (2000). Families: The essential context for gifts and talents. In K. A. Heller, F. J. Monks, R. J. Sternberg, & R. F. Subotnik (Eds.), *International handbook of giftedness and talent* (2nd ed., pp. 573–586). New York: Pergamon.

Freeman, J. (2005). Permission to be gifted: How conceptions of giftedness can change lives. In R. J. Sternberg & J. E. Davidson (Eds.), *Conceptions of giftedness* (2nd ed., pp. 80–97). New York: Cambridge University Press.

Gallagher, J. J. (1998). Accountability for gifted students. *Phi Delta Kappan, 79,* 739–742.

Gallagher, J. J. (2000a). Changing paradigms for gifted education in the United States. In K. A. Heller, F. J. Monks, R. J. Sternberg, & R. F. Subotnik (Eds.), *International handbook of giftedness and talent* (2nd ed., pp. 681–693). New York: Pergamon.

Gallagher, J. J. (2000b). Unthinkable thoughts: Education of gifted students. *Gifted Child Quarterly, 44,* 5–12. doi: 10.1177/001698620004400102

Gallagher, J. J. (2002). Society's role in educating gifted students: The role of public policy. Storrs, CT: National Research Center on the Gifted and Talented.

Gallagher, J. J. (2004). Public policy and acceleration of gifted students. In N. Colangelo, S. G. Assouline, & M. U. M. Gross (Eds.), *A nation deceived: How schools hold back America's brightest students. Vol. II* (pp. 39–45). Iowa City, IA: Connie Belin & Jacqueline N. Blank International Center for Gifted Education and Talent Development.

Gallagher, J. J. (2006). According to Jim: Best and worst of gifted education. *Roeper Review, 29,* 10.

Gardner, H., & Hatch, T. (1989). Multiple intelligences go to school: Educational implications of the theory of multiple intelligences. *Educational Researcher, 18*(8), 4–9.

Gentry, M. (2006). No Child Left Behind: Neglecting excellence. *Roeper Review, 29,* 24–27.

Goldsmith, B. (2005). *Obsessive genius:The inner world of Marie Curie.* New York: Norton.

Goodkin, S. (2005, December 27). Leave no gifted child behind. *The Washington Post,* A 25.

Gould, S. J. (1996). *The mismeasure of man* (Rev. ed.). New York: Norton.

Gross, M. U. M. (2000). Issues in the cognitive development of exceptionally and profoundly gifted individuals. In K. A. Heller, F. J. Monks, R. J. Sternberg, & R. F. Subotnik (Eds.), *International handbook of giftedness and talent* (2nd ed., pp. 179–192). New York: Pergamon.

Gross, M. U. M. (2002). Social and emotional issues for exceptionally intellectually gifted students. In M. Neihart, S. M. Reis, N. M. Robinson, & S. M. Moon (Eds.), *The social and emotional development of gifted children. What do we know?* (pp. 19–29). Waco, TX: Prufrock Press.

Heller, K. A., Monks, F. J., Sternberg, R. J., & Subotnik, R. F. (Eds.). (2000). *International handbook of giftedness and talent* (2nd ed.). New York: Pergamon.

Herbert, T. P., & Kelly, K. R. (2006). Identity and career development in gifted students. In F. A. Dixon & S. M. Moon (Eds.), *The handbook of secondary gifted education* (pp. 35–64). Waco, TX: Prufrock Press.

Huefner, D. S. (2006). *Getting comfortable with special education law: A framework for working with children with disabilities* (2nd ed.). Norwood, MA: Christopher-Gordon.

Hunsaker, S. L., & Callahan, C. M. (1995). Creativity and giftedness: Published instrument uses and abuses. *Gifted Child Quarterly, 39,* 110–114. doi:10.1177/001698629503900207

Karnes, M. B., & Bean, S. M. (Eds.). (2001). *Methods and materials for teaching the gifted.* Waco, TX: Prufrock Press.

Kauffman, J. M., & Hallahan, D. P. (2005). *Special education: What it is and why we need it.* Boston: Allyn & Bacon.

Kauffman, J. M., & Konold, T. R. (2007). Making sense in education: Pretense (including NCLB) and realities in rhetoric and policy about schools and schooling. *Exceptionality, 15,* 75–96.

Kerr, B. (2000). Guiding gifted girls and young women. In K. A. Heller, F. J. Monks, R. J. Sternberg, & R. F. Subotnik (Eds.), *International handbook of giftedness and talent* (2nd ed., pp. 649–658). New York: Pergamon.

Kohler, P. D., & Field, S. (2006). Transition-focused education: Foundation for the future. In B. G. Cook & B. R. Schirmer (Eds.), *What is special about special education? Examining the role of evidence-based practices* (pp. 86–99). Austin, Tx: Pro-Ed.

Landrum, M. S., Callahan, C. M., & Shaklee, B. D. (Eds.). (2001). *Aiming for excellence: Gifted program standards.* Waco, TX: Prufrock Press.

Lloyd, J. W., & Hallahan, D. P. (2007). Advocacy and reform of special education. In J. B. Crockett, M. M. Gerber, & T. J. Landrum (Eds.), *Achieving the radical reform of special education: Essays in honor of James M. Kauffman* (pp. 245–263). Mahwah, NJ: Lawrence Erlbaum Associates.

Lohman, D. F. (2005, September). *Identifying academically talented minority students* (RM05216). Storrs, CT: University of Connecticut, National Research Center on the Gifted and Talented.

Lohman, D. F. (2006). Exploring perceptions and awareness of high ability. *Roeper Review, 29,* 32–40.

Lubinski, D., Benbow, C. P., & Morelock, M. J. (2000). Gender differences in engineering and the physical sciences among the gifted: An inorganic–organic distinction. In K. A. Heller, F. J. Monks, R. J. Sternberg, & R. F. Subotnik (Eds.), *International handbook of giftedness and talent* (2nd ed., pp. 633–648). New York: Pergamon.

Manstetten, R. (2000). Promotion of the gifted in vocational training. In K. A. Heller, F. J. Monks, R. J. Sternberg, & R. F. Subotnik (Eds.), *International handbook of giftedness and talent* (2nd ed., pp. 439–446). New York: Pergamon.

Martin, L. T. Burns, R. M., & Schonlou, M. (2010). Mental disorders among gifted and nongifted youth: A selected review of the epidemiological literature. *Gifted Child Quarterly, 54,* 31–41. doi:10.1177/0016986209352684

McCluskey, K. W., Baker, P. A., & McCluskey, A. L. A. (2005). Creative problem solving with marginalized populations: Reclaiming lost prizes through in-the-trenches interventions. *Gifted Child Quarterly, 49,* 330–341.

Mendoza, C. (2006). Inside today's classrooms: Teacher voices on No Child Left Behind and the education of gifted children. *Roeper Review, 29,* 28–31.

Monks, F. J., & Katzko, M. W. (2005). Giftedness and gifted education. In R. J. Sternberg & J. E. Davidson (Eds.), *Conceptions of giftedness* (2nd ed., pp. 187–200). New York: Cambridge University Press.

Moore, J. L., Ford, D. Y., & Milner, H. R. (2005). Recruitment is not enough: Retaining African American students in gifted education. *Gifted Child Quarterly, 49,* 51–67.

Mueller, C. E. (2009). Protective factors as barriers to depression in gifted and nongifted adolescents. *Gifted Child Quarterly, 53,* 3–14. doi:10.1177/0016986208326552

Muratori, M. C., Stanley, J. C., Gross, M. U. M., Ng., L., Tao, T., Ng., J., et al. (2006). Insights from SMPY's greatest former child prodigies: Drs. Terence ("Terry") Tao and Lenhard ("Lenny") Ng reflect on their talent development. *Gifted Child Quarterly, 50,* 307–324.

Murray, S. (2005, July 19). Grants for gifted children face major threat from budget ax. *The Washington Post,* A19.

Neihart, M., Reis, S. M., Robinson, N. M., & Moon, S. M. (Eds.). (2002). *The social and emotional development of gifted children. What do we know?* Waco, TX: Prufrock Press.

Odom, S. L., & Wolery, M. (2006). A unified theory of practice in early intervention/early childhood special education. In B. G. Cook & B. R. Schirmer (Eds.), *What is special about special education? Examining the role of evidence-based practices* (pp. 72–85). Austin, TX: Pro-Ed.

Peterson, J., Duncan, N., & Canady, K. (2009). A longitudinal study of negative life events, stress, and school experiences of gifted youth. *Gifted Child Quarterly, 53,* 34–49. doi:10.1177/0016 986208326553

Peterson, J. S., & Ray, K. E. (2006). Bullying among the gifted: The subjective experience. *Gifted Child Quarterly, 50,* 252–269

Plucker, J. A., & Stocking, V. B. (2001). Looking outside and inside: Self-concept development of gifted adolescents. *Exceptional Children, 67,* 535–548.

Porter, L. (2005). *Gifted young children: A guide for teachers and parents* (2nd ed.). Berkshire, England: Open University Press.

Reis, S. M., & Renzulli, J. S. (2009). Myth 1: The gifted and talented constitute one single homogeneous group and giftedness is a way of being that stays in the person over time and experiences. *Gifted Child Quarterly, 53,* 233–235. doi: 10.1177/ 0016986209346824

Renzulli, J. S., & Park. S. (2002). *Giftedness and high school dropouts: Personal, family, and school-related factors.* Storrs, CT: National Research Center on the Gifted and Talented.

Robinson, A., Shore, B. M., & Enersen, D. L. (2007). *Best practices in gifted education: An evidence-based guide.* Waco, TX: Prufrock Press.

Robinson, N. M. (2005). In defense of a psychometric approach to the definition of academic giftedness: A conservative view from a die-hard liberal. In R. J. Sternberg & J. E. Davidson (Eds.), *Conceptions of giftedness* (2nd ed., pp. 280–294). New York: Cambridge University Press.

Ruf, D. L. (2005). *Losing our minds: Gifted children left behind.* Scottsdale, AZ: Great Potential Press.

Smutny, J. F. (2001). Creative strategies for teaching language arts to gifted students (K–8). (ERIC Digest No. E612). Retrieved from www.ericec .org

Sternberg, R. J. (1997). A triarchic view of giftedness: Theory and practice. In N. Colangelo & G. A. Davis (Eds.), *Handbook of gifted education* (2nd ed., pp. 43–53). Boston: Allyn & Bacon.

Sternberg, R. J. (1998). Abilities are forms of developing expertise. *Educational Researcher, 27*(3), 11–20.

Sternberg, R. J. (2000). Giftedness as developing expertise. In K. A. Heller, F. J. Monks, R. J. Sternberg, & R. F. Subotnik (Eds.), *International handbook of giftedness and talent* (2nd ed., pp. 23–54). New York: Pergamon.

Sternberg, R. J. (2001). What is the common thread of creativity? Its dialectical relation to intelligence and wisdom. *American Psychologist, 56,* 360–362.

Tannenbaum, A. J. (1993). History of giftedness and "gifted education" in world perspective. In K. A. Heller, F. J. Monks, & A. H. Passow (Eds.), *International handbook of research and development of giftedness and talent* (pp. 3–27). New York: Pergamon.

Tannenbaum, A. J. (2000a). A history of giftedness in school and society. In K. A. Heller, F. J. Monks, R. J. Sternberg, & R. F. Subotnik (Eds.), *International handbook of giftedness and talent* (2nd ed., pp. 23–54). New York: Pergamon.

Tannenbaum, A. J. (2000b). Giftedness: The ultimate instrument for good and evil. In K. A. Heller, F. J. Monks, R. J. Sternberg, & R. F. Subotnik (Eds.), *International handbook of giftedness and talent* (2nd ed., pp. 447–466). New York: Pergamon.

Tomlinson, C. (1995). *Differentiating instruction for advanced learners in the mixed-ability middle school classroom.* (ERIC Digest No. E536). Retrieved from www.ericec.org

Tomlinson, C. A., Ford, D. Y., Reis, S. M., Briggs, C. J., & Strickland, C. A. (Eds.). (2004). *In search of the dream: Designing schools and classrooms that work for high potential students from diverse cultural backgrounds.* Washington, DC: National Association for Gifted Children.

Tomlinson, C. A., Kaplan, S. N., Renzulli, J. S., Purcell, J., Leppien, J., & Burns, D. (2002). *The parallel curriculum: A design to develop high potential and challenge high-ability learners.* Thousand Oaks, CA: Corwin.

Van Tassel-Baska, J. (2000). Theory and research on curriculum development for the gifted. In K. A. Heller, F. J. Monks, R. J. Sternberg, & R. F. Subotnik (Eds.), *International handbook of giftedness and talent* (2nd ed., pp. 345–365). New York: Pergamon.

Van Tassel-Baska, J. (2006). A content analysis of evaluation findings across 20 gifted programs: A clarion call for enhanced gifted program development. *Gifted Child Quarterly, 50,* 199–215.

Van Tassel-Baska, J., & Stambaugh, T. (2006). *Comprehensive curriculum for gifted learners* (3rd ed.). Boston: Allyn & Bacon.

Von Karolyi, C., & Winner, E. (2005). Extreme giftedness. In R. J. Sternberg & J. E. Davidson (Eds.). *Conceptions of giftedness* (2nd ed., pp. 377–394). New York: Cambridge University Press.

Willard-Holt, C. (1999). *Dual exceptionalities.* (ERIC Digest No. E574.) Alexandria, VA: ERIC Clearinghouse on Disabilities and Gifted Education.

Willingham, D. T. (2009). *Why don't students like school? A cognitive scientist answers questions about how the mind works and what it means for your classroom.* San Francisco: Jossey-Bass.

Yoon, S. Y., & Gentry, M. (2009). Racial and ethnic representation in gifted programs. *Gifted Child Quarterly, 53,* 121–136. doi: 10.1177/00169862 08330564

Zirkel, P. A. (2003). *The law and gifted education.* Storrs, CT: National Research Center on the Gifted and Talented.

SUBJECT INDEX